Pascal Reference Chart (cont.)

Program Composition (Page in Text)	Example
Variable section (51, 79)	

Variable section (51, 79)
   (predefined types)
    integer
    real
    character
    boolean
    text file
   (user-defined types)

```
var
    Count, I, Number : integer;
    Hours, Rate, Wages : real;
    DeptCode, FirstInit, SecondInit : char;
    OverTime : boolean;
    OutFile : text;
    Dept : DepartmentName;
    EmpCode : Digit;
    Product, Item : List;
    ProductName : String;
    EmpRec : InfoRecord;
    Letters : CapLetterSet;
    InFile : EmployeeFile;
    FirstPtr, TempPtr : ListPointer;
```

Subprogram section (133)
   Procedure definition (133)

```
procedure ReadCodes (var Department,
                              Employee : char);
(* Read department & employee codes *)
begin (* ReadCodes *)
    write ('Enter dept. & employee codes: ');
    readln (Department, Employee)
end (* ReadCodes *);
```

   Function definition (195)

```
function RoundCents(Amount : real) : real;
(* Round Amount to nearest cent *)
begin (* RoundCents *)
    RoundCents := round(100 * Amount) / 100
end (* RoundCents *);
```

Statement part (48, 79)

```
begin (* main program *)
    statement-1;
        .
        .
        .
    statement-n
end (* main program *).
```

PASCAL
**Programming and
Problem Solving**

SANFORD LEESTMA
LARRY NYHOFF
Department of Mathematics and Computer Science
Calvin College

PASCAL
Programming and Problem Solving

THIRD EDITION

Macmillan Publishing Company
NEW YORK

Collier Macmillan Publishers
LONDON

Acquisition Editor: Ed Moura
Production Supervisor: Ron Harris
Production Manager: Sandra E. Moore
Cover Designer: Tyrone Randall
Cover photograph: M. D. Ippolito

This book was set in 10½ × 12 Times Roman by Waldman Graphics, Inc., printed and bound by
Von Hoffman Press, Inc. The cover was printed by Von Hoffman Press, Inc.

Macmillan Publishing Company
866 Third Avenue, New York, New York 10022

Collier Macmillan Canada, Inc.

Library of Congress Cataloging-in-Publication Data

Leestma, Sanford.
    PASCAL : programming and problem solving/Sanford Leestma, Larry Nyhoff.—3rd ed.
p.   cm.
    Includes index.
    ISBN 0-02-369685-0
    1. Pascal (Computer program language)   I. Nyhoff,
Larry R.   II. Title.
QA76.73.P2L44 1990   005.13′3—dc20   89-31964
                                                                                  CIP

Printing: 1 2 3 4 5 6 7 8   Year: 9 0 1 2 3 4 5 6 7 8

PREFACE

Pascal was developed in the late 1960s and early 1970s by Niklaus Wirth, a Swiss computer scientist at the Eidgenössische Technishe Hochshule (ETH) in Zurich, Switzerland. His primary goal was to develop a language that makes it possible "to teach programming as a systematic discipline based on certain fundamental concepts clearly and naturally reflected by the language." *The Pascal User Manual and Report,* written by Wirth and K. Jensen and published in 1974, serves as the basic definition of the Pascal language. As the use of Pascal grew, some differences appeared in various implementations. To ensure that Pascal programs written on one system can be executed on another, national and international standards for the language have been formulated. A recent standard is *An American National Standard IEEE Standard Pascal Computer Programming Language,* which was published in 1983 by the Institute of Electrical and Electronics Engineers (IEEE). This standard was approved by the IEEE Standards Board and the American National Standards Institute (ANSI) and serves as the basis for this text. Differences between this standard and other popular versions of Pascal are described in brief sections at the ends of appropriate chapters and in Appendix G.

This text is a complete introduction to the Pascal programming language and is designed to meet the objectives of the course CS1: *Introduction to Programming Methodology* as described in the Curriculum '84 recommendations of the Association of Computing Machinery (ACM). The course objectives as described in this curriculum guideline are (cf. "Recommended Curriculum for CS1, 1984," *Communications of the ACM,* October, 1984):

- to introduce a disciplined approach to problem-solving methods and algorithm development;
- to introduce procedural and data abstraction;
- to teach program design, coding, debugging, testing, and documentation using good programming style;
- to teach a block-structured high-level programming language;
- to provide a familiarity with the evolution of computer hardware and software technology;
- to provide a foundation for further studies in computer science.

To meet these objectives, this text emphasizes problem solving using structured algorithm and program design throughout and illustrates these with a large number of complete examples and applications, many of which include algo-

rithms given in pseudocode and/or structure diagrams, complete Pascal programs implementing the algorithms, and sample runs. Each of the examples is
intended to demonstrate good algorithm design and programming style. At the
end of each chapter a Programming Pointers section summarizes the main points
regarding structure and style as well as language features presented and some
problems that beginning programmers may experience. In addition to presenting
the basic features of Pascal, the text introduces such topics as data representation, machine language, and compilers, and the last two chapters introduce
some elementary data structures, such as stacks, queues, linked lists, and trees.

Like the earlier editions, this text is intended for an introductory computer
programming course using Pascal. Thus, the level is the same as that of the
first two editions, with the intended audience being freshman and/or sophomore
college students whose mathematical background includes high school algebra.
The first edition was written for the course CS1 as described in the Curriculum
'78 guidelines of the ACM. A new course description appeared in 1984, however, and the second and third editions have been carefully revised to implement
these recommendations. We have also benefited from constructive comments
of instructors and students who used the earlier editions and we have incorporated many of these suggestions in this third edition. Specifically, the changes
in the new edition include the following:

- The topics in Chapters 4 and 5 have been rearranged so that concepts
  of structured programming and modular design (including procedures)
  are introduced earlier.
- There are more ''stand-alone'' chapters or parts of chapters to satisfy a
  variety of teaching styles in beginning programming courses.
- The chapter on control structures has been split so that one selection
  structure (the **if** statement) and one repetition structure (the **while** statement) can be introduced early and the others studied later.
- The chapter on procedures and functions has been split so that procedures
  can be introduced early and reconsidered together with functions in a
  later chapter.
- A separate chapter on strings has been added.
- More examples and exercises from nonmathematical applications such
  as calculating depreciation, using finite automata in lexical analysis, and
  using sets to check course requirements have been added.
- Examples have been expanded so that they illustrate better how algorithms and programs are developed.
- The treatment of user-defined data structures and abstract data types such
  as stacks and queues has been expanded.

SUPPLEMENTARY MATERIALS

A number of supplementary materials are available from the publisher. These include the following:

- An instructor's manual containing lecture notes, a test bank, and transparency masters.
- A solutions manual.
- Data disks containing all the sample programs and data files used in the text.

ACKNOWLEDGMENTS

We express our appreciation to our erudite editors David Johnstone and Ed Moura, whose professional competence has kept us on course and whose friendship has made this an enjoyable experience; to our punctilious production supervisor Ronald Harris, whose attention to details and deadlines has compensated for our lack thereof; to the following reviewers: Randy Baker (Fairmont State College), Ed Banos (University of Texas at Arlington), Ruth Barton (Michigan State University), David Berman (University of North Carolina), Charles Burchard (Pennsylvania State University at Behrend), Sandra DeLoach (Norfolk State University), Jeanne Douglas (University of Vermont), Larre Egbert (Utah State University), Linda Elliot (Lasalle University), Jimmy Hatlemer (Southern Illinois University), D. Hearn (University of Illinois at Urbana-Champaign), Sandy Huerter (East Texas State University), Thomas O'Loughlin (State University of New York at Cortland), Jackie Palmer (Wright State University), Richard Rinwalt (Texas Christian University), Robert Riser (East Tennessee State University), Leon Robbins (Villanova University), Ned Rosen (Boston College), Paul Sand (University of New Hampshire), Ann Smith (Michigan Technological University), David Valentine (State University of New York at Potsdam), James Williams (University of Maryland), whose comments were constructive and encouraging; to our wives Marge and Shar, whose love, patience, and understanding have stayed with us and kept us going; to our kids, Michelle, Sandy, Michael, Jeff, Dawn, Jim, Julie, and Joan, whose needs and wants were too often slighted in our busyness; and above all, to God, for giving us the opportunity, ability, and stamina to prepare this new edition of the text.

S.C.L.
L.R.N.

CONTENTS

1

Introduction
and History

I wish these calculations had been executed by steam.

CHARLES BABBAGE

For, contrary to the unreasoned opinion of the ignorant, the choice of a system of numeration is a mere matter of convention.

BLAISE PASCAL

The modern electronic computer is one of the most important products of the twentieth century. It is an essential tool in many areas, including business, industry, government, science, and education; indeed, it has touched nearly every aspect of our lives. The impact of this twentieth-century information revolution brought about by the development of high-speed computing systems has been nearly as widespread as the impact of the nineteenth-century industrial revolution. This chapter gives a summary of the history of computer systems and briefly describes their components.

1.1 History of Computing Systems

There are two important concepts in the history of computation: the **mechanization of arithmetic** and the concept of a **stored program** for the automatic control of computations. We shall focus our attention on some of the devices that have implemented these concepts.

A variety of computational devices were used in ancient civilizations. One of the earliest, which might be considered a forerunner of the modern computer, is the **abacus** (Figure 1.1), which has movable beads strung on rods to count and make computations. Although its exact origin is unknown, the abacus was used by the Chinese perhaps three to four thousand years ago and is still used today.

1

Figure 1.1.
Abacus.

The ancient British stone monument **Stonehenge** (Figure 1.2a), located in southern England, was built between 1900 and 1600 B.C. and evidently was an astronomical calculator used to predict the changes of the seasons. Five hundred years ago, the Inca Indians of South America used a system of knotted cords called **quipus** (Figure 1.2b) to count and record divisions of land among the various tribal groups. In Western Europe, **Napier's bones** (Figure 1.2c) and tables of **logarithms** were designed by the Scottish mathematician John Napier (1550–1617) to simplify calculations. These led to the subsequent invention of the **slide rule** (Figure 1.2d).

In 1642, the young French mathematician **Blaise Pascal** (1623–1662) invented one of the first mechanical adding machines (Figure 1.3). This device used a system of gears and wheels similar to that used in odometers and other modern counting devices. **Pascal's adder** could both add and subtract, and was invented to calculate taxes. Pascal's announcement of his invention reveals the labor-saving motivation for its development:

Dear reader, this notice will serve to inform you that I submit to the public a small machine of my invention, by means of which you alone may, without any effort, perform all the operations of arithmetic, and may be relieved of the work which has often times fatigued your spirit, when you have worked with the counters or with the pen. As for simplicity of movement of the operations, I have so devised it that, although the operations of arithmetic are in a way opposed the one to the other—as addition to subtraction, and multiplication to division—nevertheless they are all performed on this ma-

Figure 1.2. (a) Stonehenge. (b) Quipus. (Courtesy of the American Museum of Natural History.) (c) Napier's bones. (Courtesy of the Smithsonian Institution.) (d) Slide rule.

3

Figure 1.3.   Pascal's adder. (Courtesy of IBM.)

chine by a single movement. The facility of this movement of operation is very evident since it is just as easy to move one thousand or ten thousand dials, all at one time, if one desires to make a single dial move, although all accomplish the movement perfectly. The most ignorant find as many advantages as the most experienced. The instrument makes up for ignorance and for lack of practice, and even without any effort of the operator, it makes possible shortcuts by itself, whenever the numbers are set down.

Although Pascal built more than fifty of his adding machines, his commercial venture failed because the devices could not be built with sufficient precision for practical use.

In the 1670s, the German mathematician *Gottfried Wilhelm von Leibniz* (1646–1716) produced a machine that was similar in design to Pascal's, but somewhat more reliable and accurate (Figure 1.4). Leibniz's calculator could

Figure 1.4.   Leibniz's calculator. (Courtesy of IBM.)

perform all four of the basic arithmetic operations: addition, subtraction, multiplication, and division.

A number of other mechanical calculators followed that further refined the designs of Pascal and Leibniz. By the end of the nineteenth century, these calculators had become important tools in science, business, and commerce.

As noted earlier, the second idea to emerge in the history of computing was the concept of a stored program to control the calculations. One early example of an automatically controlled device is the weaving loom (Figure 1.5) invented by the Frenchman *Joseph Marie Jacquard* (1752–1834). This automatic loom, introduced at a Paris exhibition in 1801, used metal cards punched with holes to position threads for the weaving process. A collection of these cards made up a program that directed the loom. Within a decade, 11,000 of these machines were in use in French textile plants, resulting in what may have been the first incidence of unemployment caused by automation. Unemployed workers rioted and destroyed several of the new looms and cards. Jacquard wrote: ''The iron was sold for iron, the wood for wood, and I its inventor delivered up to public ignominy.'' The *Jacquard loom* is still used today, although modern versions are controlled by magnetic tape rather than punched cards.

These two concepts, mechanized calculation and stored program control, were combined by the English mathematician *Charles Babbage* (1792–1871),

Figure 1.5.
Jacquard loom. (Courtesy of IBM.)

who began work in 1822 on a machine that he called the ***Difference Engine*** (Figure 1.6a). This machine was designed to compute polynomials for the preparation of mathematical tables. Babbage continued his work until 1833 with support from the British government, which was interested in possible military applications of the Difference Engine. But Babbage later abandoned this project, since the metal-working technology of that time was not sufficiently advanced to manufacture the required precision gears and linkages. Babbage was not discouraged, however, but designed a more sophisticated machine that he called his ***Analytical Engine*** (Figure 1.6b). This machine had several special-purpose components that were intended to work together. The "mill" was supposed to carry out the arithmetic computations; the "store" was the machine's memory for storing data and intermediate results; and other components were designed for the input and output of information and for the transfer of information between components. The operation of this machine was to be fully automatic, controlled by punched cards, an idea based on Jacquard's earlier work. In fact, Babbage himself said, "The analogy of the Analytical Engine with this well-known process is nearly perfect." ***Ada Augusta***, Lord George Byron's daughter and the Countess of Lovelace, understood how the device was to work and supported Babbage. Considered by some to be the first programmer, Lady Lovelace described the similarity of Jacquard's and Babbage's inventions: "The Analytical Engine weaves algebraic patterns just as the Jacquard loom weaves flowers and leaves." Although Babbage's machine was not built during his lifetime, it is nevertheless part of the history of computing because many of the concepts of its design are used in modern computers.

A related development in the United States was the Census Bureau's use of punched-card systems to help compile the 1890 census (Figure 1.7). These systems, designed by ***Herman Hollerith***, a young mathematician employed by the bureau, used electrical sensors to interpret the information stored on the punched cards. In 1896, Hollerith left the Census Bureau and formed his own tabulating company, which in 1924 became the International Business Machines Corporation (IBM).

The development of computing devices continued at a rapid pace in the United States. Some of the pioneers in this effort were Howard Aiken, J. P. Eckert, J. W. Mauchly, and John von Neumann. Repeating much of Babbage's work, Aiken designed a system consisting of several mechanical calculators working together. This work, which was supported by IBM, led to the invention in 1944 of the electromechanical ***Mark I*** computer (Figure 1.8). This machine is the best-known computer built before 1945 and may be regarded as the first realization of Babbage's Analytical Engine.

The first fully electronic computer was developed by ***John Atanasoff*** at Iowa State University. With the help of his assistant, ***Clifford Berry***, he built a prototype in 1939 and completed the first working model in 1942 (Figure 1.9a). The best known of the early fully electronic computers was the ***ENIAC*** (Electronic Numerical Integrator and Computer), constructed in 1946 by J. P. Eckert and J. W. Mauchly at the Moore School of Electrical Engineering of the University of Pennsylvania (Figure 1.9b). This extremely large machine contained over 18,000 vacuum tubes and 1,500 relays and nearly filled a room 20 feet by 40 feet in size. It could multiply numbers approximately 1,000 times

(a)

(b)

Figure 1.6. (a) Babbage's Difference Engine. (b) Babbage's Analytical Engine. (Courtesy of IBM.)

Figure 1.7. Hollerith equipment. (Courtesy of IBM.)

Figure 1.8. Mark I. (Courtesy of IBM.)

(a)

(b)

Figure 1.9. (a) Atanasoff–Berry computer. (Courtesy of Iowa State University.) (b) ENIAC. (Courtesy of Unisys Corporation.)

faster than the Mark I could, though it was quite limited in its applications and was used primarily by the Army Ordnance Department to calculate firing tables and trajectories for various types of shells. Eckert and Mauchly later left the University of Pennsylvania to form the Eckert–Mauchly Computer Corporation, which built the *UNIVAC* (Universal Automatic Computer), the first commercially available computer designed for both scientific and business applications. The first UNIVAC was sold to the Census Bureau in 1951.

The instructions, or program, that controlled the ENIAC's operation were entered into the machine by rewiring some parts of the computer's circuits. This complicated process was very time-consuming, sometimes taking several persons several days, and during this time the computer was idle. In other early computers, the instructions were stored outside the machine on punched cards or some other medium and were transferred into the machine one at a time for interpretation and execution. A new scheme, developed by Princeton mathematician John von Neumann and others, used internally stored commands. The advantages of this stored program concept are that internally stored instructions can be processed more rapidly and, more important, can be modified by the computer itself while computations are taking place. The stored program concept makes possible the general-purpose computers so common today.

The actual physical components used in constructing a computer system are its *hardware*. Several generations of computers can be identified by the type of hardware used. The ENIAC and UNIVAC are examples of *first-generation* computers, which are characterized by their extensive use of vacuum tubes. Advances in electronics brought changes in computing systems, and in 1958 IBM introduced the first of the *second-generation* computers, the IBM 7090. These computers were built between 1959 and 1965 and used transistors in place of vacuum tubes. Consequently, these computers were smaller and less expensive, required less power, generated far less heat, and were more reliable than their predecessors. The *third-generation* computers that followed used integrated circuits and introduced new techniques for better system utilization, such as multiprogramming and time-sharing. The IBM System/360 introduced in 1964 is commonly accepted as the first of this generation of computers. Computers of the 1980s, commonly called *fourth-generation* computers, used very-large-scale integrated (VLSI) circuits on silicon chips and other microelectronic advances to shrink their size and cost still more while enlarging their capability. A typical memory chip is equivalent to many thousands of transistors, is smaller than a baby's fingernail, weighs a small fraction of an ounce, requires only a trickle of power, and costs but a few dollars. Such miniaturization made possible the development of the personal computers so popular today (Figure 1.10). One of the pioneers in the development of microcomputers, Robert Noyce, contrasted them with the ENIAC as follows:

> An individual integrated circuit on a chip perhaps a quarter of an inch square now can embrace more electronic elements than the most complex piece of electronic equipment that could be built in 1950. Today's microcomputer, at a cost of perhaps $300, has more computing capacity than the first electronic computer, ENIAC. It is twenty times faster, has a larger memory, consumes the power of a light bulb rather than that of a locomotive, occupies 1/30,000 the volume and costs 1/10,000 as much. It is available by mail order or at your local hobby shop.

The stored program concept was a significant improvement over manual programming methods, but early computers were still difficult to use because of the complex coding schemes required for the representation of programs and

Figure 1.10.   A modern personal computer. (Courtesy of IBM.)

data. Consequently, in addition to improved hardware, computer manufacturers began to develop collections of programs known as *system software*, which makes computers easier to use. One of the more important advances in this area was the development of *high-level languages*, which allow users to write programs in a language similar to natural language. A program written in a high-level language is known as a *source program*. For most high-level languages, the instructions that make up a source program must be translated into *machine language*, that is, the language used directly by a particular computer in all its calculations and processing. This machine language program is called an *object program*. The programs that translate source programs into object programs are called *compilers*. Another part of the system software, the *operating system*, controls the translation of the source program, allocates storage for the program and data, and carries out many other supervisory functions.

One of the first high-level languages to gain widespread acceptance was FORTRAN (FORmula TRANslation). It was developed for the IBM 704 computer by John Backus and a team of thirteen other programmers at IBM over a three-year period (1954–1957). Since that time many other high-level languages have been developed, including ALGOL, BASIC, COBOL, Pascal, C, Ada, and Modula-2. In this text we shall discuss the Pascal programming language.

Pascal, named in honor of the French mathematician Blaise Pascal, was designed by Niklaus Wirth at the Eidgenössische Technishe Hochshule (ETH) in Zurich, Switzerland. The first Pascal compiler appeared in 1970, and the first report on the language was published in 1971.[1] A revised user manual and report was published in 1974.[2] The first two paragraphs of the introduction to this report describe Wirth's reasons for developing Pascal:

> The development of the language Pascal is based on two principal aims. The first is to make available a language suitable to teach programming as a systematic discipline based on certain fundamental concepts clearly and naturally reflected by the language. The second is to develop implementations of this language which are both reliable and efficient on presently available computers.
>
> The desire for a new language for the purpose of teaching programming is due to my dissatisfaction with the presently used major languages whose features and constructs too often cannot be explained logically and convincingly and which too often defy systematic reasoning. Along with this dissatisfaction goes my conviction that the language in which the student is taught to express his ideas profoundly influences his habits of thought and invention, and that the disorder governing these languages directly imposes itself onto the programming style of the students.

For Pascal, Wirth used much of the framework of ALGOL. Pascal itself has served as the basis for more recent programming languages such as Ada (named after Ada Augusta) and Modula-2 (also developed by Wirth).

In summary, the history of computation and computational aids began several thousands of years ago, and in some cases, the theory underlying such devices developed much more rapidly than did the technical skills required to produce working models. Although the modern electronic computer, with its mechanized calculation and automatic program control has its roots in the mid-nineteenth-century work of Charles Babbage, the electronic computer is a fairly recent development. The rapid changes that have marked its progression since its inception in 1945 can be expected to continue into the future.

1.2 Computing Systems

In our discussion of the history of computing, we noted that Babbage designed his Analytical Engine as a system of several separate components, each with its own particular function. This general scheme was incorporated in many later computers and is, in fact, a common feature of most modern computers. In this section we briefly describe the major components of a modern computing system.

---

[1] N. Wirth, "The Programming Language Pascal," *Acta-Informatica* 1 (1971):35–63.
[2] K. Jensen and N. Wirth, *Pascal User Manual and Report* (Heidelberg: Springer-Verlag, 1974).

The heart of any computing system is its ***central processing unit***, or ***CPU***. The CPU controls the operation of the entire system, performs the arithmetic and logic operations, and stores and retrieves instructions and data. The instructions and data are stored in a high-speed ***memory unit***, and the ***control unit*** fetches these instructions from memory, decodes them, and directs the system to execute the operations indicated by the instructions. Those operations that are arithmetic or logical are carried out using special registers and circuits of the ***arithmetic-logic unit (ALU)*** of the CPU.

The memory unit is called the ***internal*** or ***main*** or ***primary memory*** of the computer system. It is used to store the instructions and data of programs being executed. Most computing systems also contain components that serve as ***external*** or ***auxiliary*** or ***secondary memory***. Common forms of this type of memory are magnetic disks and magnetic tapes. These ***peripheral devices*** provide long-term storage for large collections of information. The rate of transfer of information to and from them is considerably slower than that of internal memory.

Other peripherals are used to transmit instructions, data, and computed results between the user and the CPU. These are the ***input/output devices*** and may take a variety of forms, such as card readers, remote terminals, optical scanners, voice input devices, and high-speed printers. Their function is to convert information from an external form understandable to the user to a form that can be processed by the computer system, and vice versa.

Figure 1.11 shows the relationship between these components in a computer system. The arrows indicate how information flows through the system.

Figure 1.11. Major components of a computing system.

1.3 Internal Representation

The devices that comprise the memory unit of a computer are two-state devices. If one of the states is interpreted as 0 and the other as 1, then it is natural to use a *binary scheme*, using only the two binary digits (*bits*) 0 and 1 for representing information within a computer. These two-state devices are organized into groups called *bytes*, each of which contains a fixed number of these devices, usually eight, and thus can store a fixed number of bits. Memory is commonly measured in bytes, and a block of $2^{10} = 1024$ bytes is called *1K* of memory. Thus, a 512K memory usually refers to a memory that consists of $512 \times 2^{10} = 2^9 \times 2^{10} = 2^{19} = 524,288$ bytes, or, equivalently, $2^{19} \times 2^3 = 2^{22} = 4,194,304$ bits (1 byte = 8 bits).

A larger grouping of bits and bytes is into *words*. Word sizes vary with computers, but common sizes are 16 bits (= 2 bytes) and 32 bits (= 4 bytes). Each word is identified by an *address* and can be directly accessed using this address. This makes it possible to store information in a specific memory word and then retrieve it later. To understand how this is done, we must first examine the binary number system.

The number system that we are accustomed to using is a *decimal* or *base-10* number system, which uses the digits 0, 1, 2, 3, 4, 5, 6, 7, 8, and 9. The significance of these digits in a numeral depends on the positions that they occupy in that numeral. For example, in the numeral

$$485$$

the digit 4 is interpreted as

$$4 \text{ hundreds}$$

and the digit 8 as

$$8 \text{ tens}$$

and the digit 5 as

$$5 \text{ ones}$$

Thus, the numeral 485 represents the number four-hundred eighty-five and can be written in *expanded form* as

$$(4 \times 100) + (8 \times 10) + (5 \times 1)$$

or

$$(4 \times 10^2) + (8 \times 10^1) + (5 \times 10^0)$$

The digits that appear in the various positions of a decimal (base-10) numeral thus represent coefficients of powers of 10.

Similar positional number systems can be devised using numbers other than 10 as a base. The *binary* number system uses 2 as the base and has only two digits, 0 and 1. As in a decimal system, the significance of the bits in a binary numeral is determined by their positions in that numeral. For example, the binary numeral

101

can be written in expanded form (using decimal notation) as

$$(1 \times 2^2) + (0 \times 2^1) + (1 \times 2^0)$$

that is, the binary numeral 101 has the decimal value

$$4 + 0 + 1 = 5$$

Similarly, the binary numeral 111010 has the decimal value

$$(1 \times 2^5) + (1 \times 2^4) + (1 \times 2^3) + (0 \times 2^2) + (1 \times 2^1) + (0 \times 2^0)$$
$$= 32 + 16 + 8 + 2$$
$$= 58$$

When necessary, to avoid confusion about which base is being used, it is customary to write the base as a subscript for nondecimal numerals. Using this convention, we could indicate that 5 and 58 have the binary representations just given by writing

$$5 = 101_2$$

and

$$58 = 111010_2$$

When an integer value such as 5 or 58 must be stored in the computer's memory, the binary representation of that value is typically stored in one memory word. To illustrate, consider a computer whose word length is sixteen, and suppose that the integer value 58 is to be stored. A memory word is selected, and a sequence of sixteen bits formed from the binary representation 111010 of 58 is stored there:

Memory

Negative integers must also be stored in a binary form in which the sign of the integer is part of the representation. There are several ways this can be done, but one of the most common is the *two's complement* representation. In this scheme, nonnegative integers are represented in binary form as just described, with the leftmost bit set to 0 to indicate that the value is not negative. The representation of a negative integer $-n$ is obtained by first finding the binary representation of n, complementing it, that is, changing each 0 to 1 and each 1 to 0, and then adding 1 to the result. For example, the two's complement representation of -58 using a string of sixteen bits is obtained as follows:

1. Represent 58 by a 16-bit binary numeral:

$$0000000000111010$$

2. Complement this bit string:

$$1111111111000101$$

3. Add 1:

$$1111111111000110$$

Note that the leftmost bit in this two's complement representation of a negative integer will always be 1, indicating that the number is negative.

The fixed word size limits the range of the integers that can be stored internally. For example, the largest positive integer that can be stored in a 16-bit word is

$$0111111111111111_2 = 2^{15} - 1 = 32767$$

and the smallest negative integer is

$$1000000000000000_2 = -2^{15} = -32768$$

The range of integers that can be represented using a 32-bit word is

$$10000000000000000000000000000000_2 = -2^{31} = -2147483648$$

through

$$01111111111111111111111111111111_2 = 2^{31} - 1 = 2147483647$$

Representation of an integer outside the allowed range would require more bits than can be stored in a single word, a phenomenon known as ***overflow***. This limitation may be partially overcome by using more than one word to store an integer. Although this technique enlarges the range of integers that can be stored exactly, it does not resolve the problem of overflow; the range of representable integers is still finite.

Numbers that contain decimal points are called ***real numbers*** or ***floating point numbers***. In the decimal representation of such numbers, each digit is the coefficient of some power of 10. Digits to the left of the decimal point are coefficients of nonnegative powers of 10, while those to the right are coefficients of negative powers of 10. For example, the decimal numeral 56.317 can be written in expanded form as

$$(5 \times 10^1) + (6 \times 10^0) + (3 \times 10^{-1}) + (1 \times 10^{-2}) + (7 \times 10^{-3})$$

or, equivalently, as

$$(5 \times 10) + (6 \times 1) + \left(3 \times \frac{1}{10}\right) + \left(1 \times \frac{1}{100}\right) + \left(7 \times \frac{1}{1000}\right)$$

Digits in the binary representation of a real number are coefficients of powers of two. Those to the left of the ***binary point*** are coefficients of nonnegative powers of two, and those to the right are coefficients of negative powers of two. For example, the expanded form of 110.101 is

$$(1 \times 2^2) + (1 \times 2^1) + (0 \times 2^0) + (1 \times 2^{-1}) + (0 \times 2^{-2}) + (1 \times 2^{-3})$$

and thus has the decimal value

$$4 + 2 + 0 + \frac{1}{2} + 0 + \frac{1}{8} = 6.625$$

There is some variation in the schemes used for storing real numbers in computer memory, but one common method is illustrated by the following. The binary representation

$$110.101_2$$

of the real number 6.625 can be written equivalently as

$$0.110101_2 \times 2^3$$

Typically, one part of a memory word (or words) is used to store a fixed number of bits of the **mantissa** or **fractional part** 0.110101_2, and another part to store the **exponent** $3 = 11_2$. For example, if the leftmost eleven bits in a 16-bit word are used for the mantissa and the remaining five bits for the exponent, 6.625 could be stored as

in which the first bit in each part is reserved for the sign.

Since the binary representation of the exponent may require more than the available number of bits, we see that the overflow problem discussed in connection with integer representation may also occur in storing a real number. Also, there obviously are some real numbers whose mantissas have more than the allotted number of bits; consequently, some of these bits will be lost in storing such numbers. In fact, most real numbers do not have finite binary representations and thus cannot be stored exactly in any computer. For example, the binary representation of the real number 0.7 is

$$(0.10110011001100110 \ldots)_2$$

where the block 0110 is repeated indefinitely. If only the first eleven bits are stored and all remaining bits are truncated, the stored representation of 0.7 will be

$$0.1011001100_2$$

which has the decimal value 0.69921875. If the binary representation is rounded to eleven bits, then the stored representation for 0.7 is

$$0.1011001101_2$$

which has the decimal value 0.700195312. In either case, the stored value is not exactly 0.7. This error, called **roundoff error**, can be reduced, but not eliminated, by using a larger number of bits to store the binary representation of real numbers.

Computers store and process not only numeric data but also boolean or logical data (false or true), character data, and other types of nonnumeric

TABLE 1.1 Character codes

Character	ASCII		EBCDIC	
	Decimal	Binary	Decimal	Binary
A	65	01000001	193	11000001
B	66	01000010	194	11000010
C	67	01000011	195	11000011
D	68	01000100	196	11000100
E	69	01000101	197	11000101
F	70	01000110	198	11000110
G	71	01000111	199	11000111
H	72	01001000	200	11001000
I	73	01001001	201	11001001
J	74	01001010	209	11010001
K	75	01001011	210	11010010
L	76	01001100	211	11010011
M	77	01001101	212	11010100
N	78	01001110	213	11010101
O	79	01001111	214	11010110
P	80	01010000	215	11010111
Q	81	01010001	216	11011000
R	82	01010010	217	11011001
S	83	01010011	226	11100010
T	84	01010100	227	11100011
U	85	01010101	228	11100100
V	86	01010110	229	11100101
W	87	01010111	230	11100110
X	88	01011000	231	11100111
Y	89	01011001	232	11101000
Z	90	01011010	233	11101001

information. Storing boolean values is easy; false can be encoded as 0, true as 1, and these bits stored. The schemes used for the internal representation of character data are based on the assignment of a numeric code to each of the characters in the character set. Several standard coding schemes have been developed, such as *ASCII* (American Standard Code for Information Interchange) and *EBCDIC* (Extended Binary Coded Decimal Interchange Code). Table 1.1 shows these codes for uppercase letters. A complete table of ASCII and EBCDIC codes for all characters is given in Appendix A.

Characters are represented internally using these binary codes. A byte consisting of eight bits can thus store the binary representation of one character, and a 16-bit word consisting of two bytes can store two characters. For example, the character string HI can be stored in a single 16-bit word, with the code for H in the left byte and the code for I in the right byte; with ASCII code, the result would be as follows:

Memory words of length 32 (bits) are usually divided into four bytes and thus can store four characters. Character strings of a length greater than the number of bytes in a word are usually stored in two or more consecutive memory words.

We have now seen how various types of data can be stored in a computer's memory. Program instructions for processing data must also be stored in memory. As an example, suppose three values $8 = 1000_2$, $24 = 11000_2$, and $58 = 111010_2$ have been stored in memory locations with addresses 4, 5, and 6, and we want to multiply the first two values, add the third, and store the result in memory word 7.

```
    Address          Memory
       0        ┌───────────────────┐
       1        ├───────────────────┤
       2        ├───────────────────┤
       3        ├───────────────────┤
       4        │ 0000000000001000  │◄─── 8
       5        │ 0000000000011000  │◄─── 24
       6        │ 0000000000111010  │◄─── 58
       7        │                   │◄─── Result
                └───────────────────┘
                         ⋮
```

To perform this computation, the following instructions must be executed:

1. Fetch the contents of memory word 4 and load it into the accumulator register of the ALU.
2. Fetch the contents of memory word 5 and compute the product of this value with the value in the accumulator.
3. Fetch the contents of memory word 6 and add this value to the value in the accumulator.
4. Store the contents of the accumulator in memory word 7.

In order to store these instructions in computer memory, they must be represented in binary form. The addresses of the data present no problem, since they can easily be converted to binary addresses:

$$4 = 100_2$$
$$5 = 101_2$$
$$6 = 110_2$$
$$7 = 111_2$$

The operations load, multiply, add, store, and other basic machine instructions are represented by numeric codes, called *opcodes*; for example,

$$\text{LOAD} = 16 = 10000_2$$
$$\text{STORE} = 17 = 10001_2$$
$$\text{ADD} = 35 = 100011_2$$
$$\text{MULTIPLY} = 36 = 100100_2$$

Using part of a word to store the opcode and another part for the address of the *operand*, we could represent our sequence of instructions in *machine lan-*

guage as

1. 0001000000000100
2. 0010010000000101
3. 0010001100000110
4. 0001000100000111

opcode   operand

These instructions can then be stored in four (consecutive) memory words. When the program is executed, the control unit will fetch each of these instructions, decode it to determine the operation and the address of the operand, fetch the operand, and then perform the required operation, using the ALU if necessary.

Programs for early computers had to be written in machine language. Later it became possible to write programs in *assembly language*, which uses mnemonics (names) in place of numeric opcodes and variable names in place of numeric addresses. For example, the preceding sequence of instructions might be written in assembly language as

1. LOAD *A*
2. MULT *B*
3. ADD *C*
4. STORE *X*

An *assembler*, part of the system software, translates such assembly language instructions into machine language.

Today most programs are written in a high-level language such as Pascal, and a *compiler* translates each statement in this program into a sequence of basic machine (or assembly) language instructions.

Source Program
(high-level language)

Compiler

Object Program
(machine language)

For example, for the preceding problem, the programmer could write the Pascal statement

$$X := A * B + C$$

which instructs the computer to multiply the values of A and B, add the value of C, and assign the value to X. The compiler would then translate this statement into the sequence of four machine (or assembly) language instructions considered earlier.

As the preceding diagram indicates, a compiler translates the entire source program into an equivalent object program consisting of machine language instructions. After this translation is complete, this object program is executed by the computer. Some languages are processed using an *interpreter* rather than a compiler. An interpreter also examines a source program statement by statement. However, after each statement is translated, the resulting machine language instructions are immediately executed before the next statement is examined; no object program is actually produced. Still another approach is to compile the source program into a simple machine-independent language called *intermediate code*. The resulting program might be either interpreted or compiled. In any case, the original source program in a high-level language must be translated into strings of 0s and 1s that represent machine instructions.

Exercises

1. Describe the importance of each of the following persons to the history of computing:

   (a) Charles Babbage   (b) Blaise Pascal
   (c) John von Neumann   (d) Herman Hollerith
   (e) Joseph Jacquard   (f) Gottfried Wilhelm von Leibniz
   (g) John Atanasoff

2. Describe the importance of each of the following devices to the history of computing:

   (a) ENIAC   (b) Analytical Engine
   (c) Jacquard loom   (d) UNIVAC
   (e) Mark I

3. Distinguish the four different generations of computers.

4. Briefly define each of the following terms:

   (a) stored program concept   (b) FORTRAN
   (c) hardware   (d) CPU
   (e) ALU   (f) peripheral devices
   (g) bit   (h) byte
   (i) word   (j) overflow
   (k) roundoff error   (l) ASCII
   (m) EBCDIC   (n) source program
   (o) object program   (p) compiler
   (q) assembler   (r) assembly language
   (s) machine language

5. Convert each of the following unsigned binary numerals into base 10:

   (a) 1001   (b) 110010
   (c) 1000000   (d) 111111111111111 (fifteen 1s)
   (e) 1.1   (f) 1010.10101

6. An *octal* numeration system uses a base of 8 and the digits 0, 1, 2, 3, 4, 5, 6, and 7. In an octal numeral such as 1703_8, the digits represent coefficients of powers of 8, and so this numeral is an abbreviation for the expanded form

$$(1 \times 8^3) + (7 \times 8^2) + (0 \times 8^1) + (3 \times 8^0)$$

and hence has the decimal value

$$512 + 448 + 0 + 3 = 963$$

Convert each of the following octal numerals to base 10:

(a) 123   (b) 2705   (c) 10000
(d) 77777   (e) 7.2   (f) 123.45

7. A *hexadecimal* numeration system uses a base of 16 and the digits 0, 1, 2, 3, 4, 5, 6, 7, 8, 9, A (ten), B (eleven), C (twelve), D (thirteen), E (fourteen), and F (fifteen). The hexadecimal numeral $5E4_{16}$ has the expanded form

$$(5 \times 16^2) + (14 \times 16^1) + (4 \times 16^0)$$

which has the decimal value

$$1280 + 224 + 4 = 1508$$

Convert each of the following hexadecimal numerals to base 10:

(a) 12   (b) 1AB   (c) ABC
(d) FFF   (e) 8.C   (f) AB.CD

8. Conversion from octal representation (see Exercise 6) to binary representation is easy, as we need only replace each octal digit with its three-bit binary equivalent. For example, to convert 617_8 to binary, replace 6 with 110, 1 with 001, and 7 with 111, to obtain 110001111_2. Convert each of the octal numerals in Exercise 6 to binary numerals.

9. Imitating the conversion scheme in Exercise 8, convert each of the hexadecimal numerals in Exercise 7 to binary numerals.

10. To convert a binary numeral to octal, place the digits in groups of three, starting from the binary point, or from the right end if there is no binary point, and replace each group with the corresponding octal digit. For example, $10101111_2 = 010\ 101\ 111_2 = 257_8$. Convert each of the binary numerals in Exercise 5 to octal numerals.

11. Imitating the conversion scheme in Exercise 10, convert each of the binary numerals in Exercise 5 to hexadecimal numerals.

12. One method for finding the *base-b* representation of a whole number given in base-10 notation is to divide the number repeatedly by b until a quotient of zero results. The successive remainders are the digits, from right to left, of the base-b representation. For example, the binary representation of 26 is 11010_2, as the following computation shows:

$$
\begin{array}{r}
0\ \text{R}\ 1 \\
2\overline{)1}\ \text{R}\ 1 \\
2\overline{)3}\ \text{R}\ 0 \\
2\overline{)6}\ \text{R}\ 1 \\
2\overline{)13}\ \text{R}\ 0 \\
2\overline{)26}
\end{array}
$$

Convert each of the following base-10 numerals to (i) binary, (ii) octal, (iii) hexadecimal:

(a) 27   (b) 99   (c) 314   (d) 5280

13. To convert a decimal fraction to its base-b equivalent, repeatedly multiply the fractional part of the number by b. The integer parts are the digits from left to right of the base-b representation. For example, the decimal numeral 0.6875 corresponds to the binary numeral 0.1011_2, as the following computation shows:

$$
\begin{array}{r|l}
 & .6875 \\
 & \underline{\times 2} \\
1 & .375 \\
 & \underline{\times 2} \\
0 & .75 \\
 & \underline{\times 2} \\
1 & .5 \\
 & \underline{\times 2} \\
1 & .0
\end{array}
$$

Convert the following base-10 numerals to (i) binary, (ii) octal, (iii) hexadecimal:

(a) 0.5   (b) 0.25   (c) 0.625
(d) 16.0625   (e) 8.828125

14. Even though the base-10 representation of a fraction may terminate, its representation in some other base need not terminate. For example, the following computation shows that the binary representation of 0.7 is $(0.1011001100110011001100110\ldots)_2$, where the block of bits 0110 is repeated indefinitely. This representation is commonly written as $0.1\overline{0110}_2$.

$$
\begin{array}{r|l}
 & .7 \\
 & \underline{\times 2} \\
1 & .4 \leftarrow \\
 & \underline{\times 2} \\
0 & .8 \\
 & \underline{\times 2} \\
1 & .6 \\
 & \underline{\times 2} \\
1 & .2 \\
 & \underline{\times 2} \\
0 & .4\ —
\end{array}
$$

Convert the following base-10 numerals to (i) binary, (ii) octal, (iii) hexadecimal:

(a) 0.3   **(b)** 0.6   **(c)** 0.05   **(d)** $0.\overline{3} = 0.33333 \cdots = 1/3$

15. Find the decimal value of each of the following 16-bit integers, assuming a two's complement representation:

(a) 0000000001000000   **(b)** 1111111111111110
(c) 1111111110111111   **(d)** 0000000011111111
(e) 1111111100000000   **(f)** 1000000000000001

16. Find the 16-bit two's complement representation for each of the following integers:

(a) 255   **(b)** 1K
(c) −255   **(d)** −256
(e) -34567_8 **(f)** $-3ABC_{16}$

17. Assuming two's complement representation, what range of integers can be represented in 8-bit words?

18. Assuming an 11-bit mantissa and a 5-bit exponent as described in the text, and assuming that two's complement representation is used for each, indicate how each of the following real numbers would be stored in a 16-bit word if extra bits in the mantissa are (i) truncated or (ii) rounded:

(a) 0.375   **(b)** 37.375
(c) 0.03125   **(d)** 63.84375
(e) 0.1   **(f)** 0.01

19. Using the tables for ASCII and EBCDIC in Appendix A, indicate how each of the following character strings would be stored in 2-byte words using (i) ASCII and (ii) EBCDIC:

(a) TO   **(b)** FOUR   **(c)** AMOUNT
(d) ETC.   **(e)** J. DOE   **(f)** A#∗4−C

20. Using the instruction mnemonics and opcodes given in the text, write a sequence of (a) assembly language and (b) machine language instructions equivalent to the Pascal statement

$$X := (A + B) * C$$

For the machine language instructions, assume that the values of A, B, and C are stored in memory words 15, 16, and 17, respectively, and the value of X is to be stored in memory word 23.

21. Repeat Exercise 20 for the Pascal statement

$$X := (A + B) * (C + D)$$

assuming that the value of D is stored in memory word 18.

2

Program Development

People always get what they ask for; the only trouble is that they never know, until they get it, what it actually is that they have asked for.

ALDOUS HUXLEY

The main reason that people learn programming languages is to use the computer as a problem-solving tool. At least four steps can be identified in the computer-aided problem-solving process:

1. Problem analysis and specification.
2. Algorithm development.
3. Program coding.
4. Program execution and testing.

In this chapter we describe and illustrate each of these steps. In the last section, we discuss one additional step that is particularly important in the *life cycle* of programs developed in real-world applications:

5. Program maintenance.

2.1 Problem Analysis and Specification

Because the initial description of a problem may be somewhat vague and imprecise, the first step in the problem-solving process is to review the problem carefully in order to determine its *input*—what information is given and which items are important in solving the problem—and its *output*—what information must be produced to solve the problem. Input and output are the two major parts of the problem's *specification*, and for a problem that appears in a programming text, they are usually not too difficult to identify. In a real-world problem encountered by a professional programmer, however, the specification of the problem often includes other items, as described in Section 2.5, and

25

considerable effort may be required to formulate it completely. In this section we illustrate this first step of the problem-solving process with three simple examples.

PROBLEM 1: Calculating Revenue.   Sam Shyster installs coaxial cable for the Cawker City Cable Company. For each installation, there is a basic service charge of $25.00 and an additional charge of $2.00 for each foot of cable. During the month of January, Sam installed 263 yards of cable at 27 different locations. What was the total revenue that Sam generated for the month?

Identifying the input and output in this textbook problem is easy:

Input	Output
Basic service charge: $25.00 Unit cable cost: $2.00 Number of installations: 27 Yards of cable: 263	Revenue generated

The other items of information—the employee's name, his job, the name of the company, and the month—are not relevant (at least not for this problem) and can be ignored.

The revenue that Sam Shyster generated can be easily calculated by hand, or still more easily by using a calculator, and does not warrant the development of a computer program for its solution. A program written to solve this particular problem would probably be used just once; if Sam installs cables at 42 locations in February using 455 yards of cable or if the basic service charge or the unit cost of cable changes, we would have a new problem requiring the development of a new program. This is obviously a waste of effort, since it is clear that each such problem is a special case of the more general problem of finding the revenue generated for any number of installations, any amount of cable, any basic service charge, and any unit cost of cable. A program that solves the general problem can be used in a variety of situations and is consequently more useful than one designed to solve only the original special problem.

One important aspect of problem analysis, therefore, is *generalization*. The effort involved in later phases of the problem-solving process demands that the program eventually developed be sufficiently flexible, that it solve not only the given specific problem but also any related problem of the same kind with little, if any, modification required. In this example, the specification of the problem could thus better be formulated in general terms:

Input	Output
Basic service charge Unit cable cost Number of installations Yards of cable	Revenue generated

Obviously, we could generalize still more—allow several employees, other kinds of charges, different kinds of cable, and so on—but the line must be drawn somewhere or we could go on generalizing forever. In this elementary introduction to the problem-solving process, we wish to keep our examples quite simple.

PROBLEM 2: Pollution Indices. The level of air pollution in the city of Dogpatch is measured by a pollution index. Readings are made at 12:00 P.M. at three locations: the Abner Coal Plant, downtown at the corner of Daisy Avenue and 5th Street, and at a randomly selected location in a residential area. The average of these three readings is the pollution index, and values of 50 or greater for this index indicate a hazardous condition, whereas values of less than 50 indicate a safe condition. Since this calculation must be done daily, the Dogpatch Environmental Statistician would like a program that calculates the pollution index and then determines the appropriate condition, safe or hazardous.

The relevant given information consists of the three pollution readings and the cutoff value used to distinguish between safe and hazardous conditions. A solution to the problem consists of the pollution index and a message indicating the condition. Generalizing so that any cutoff value, not just 50, can be used, we could specify the problem as follows:

Input	Output
Three pollution readings	Pollution index = the average of the pollution readings
Cutoff value to distinguish between safe and hazardous conditions	Condition—safe or hazardous

PROBLEM 3: Summation. When the famous mathematician Carl Friedrich Gauss was a young student, his teacher instructed him to add the first 100 positive integers, 1, 2, 3, . . . , 100. (Perhaps this was a form of punishment comparable to "writing lines" today.) What is the value of this sum,

$$1 + 2 + 3 + \cdots + 100 = ?$$

Here the problem analysis is straightforward. Generalizing to find the sum

$$1 + 2 + 3 + \cdots + \textit{LastNumber}$$

for any positive integer *LastNumber*, we can specify the problem by

Input	Output
LastNumber	Value of $1 + 2 + \cdots + \textit{LastNumber}$

2.2 Algorithm Development

Once a problem has been specified, a procedure to produce the required output from the given input must be designed. Since the computer is a machine possessing no inherent problem-solving capabilities, this procedure must be formulated as a detailed sequence of simple steps. Such a procedure is called an *algorithm*.

The steps that comprise an algorithm must be organized in a logical, clear manner so that the program that implements this algorithm is similarly well structured. *Structured algorithms* and *programs* are designed using three basic methods of control:

1. *Sequential:* Steps are performed in a strictly sequential manner, each step being executed exactly once.
2. *Selection*: One of several alternative actions is selected and executed.
3. *Repetition:* One or more steps is performed repeatedly.

These three structures appear to be very simple, but in fact they are sufficiently powerful that any algorithm can be constructed using them.

Programs to implement algorithms must be written in a language that the computer can understand. It is natural, therefore, to describe algorithms in a language that resembles the language used to write computer programs, that is, in a "pseudoprogramming language," or as it is more commonly called, *pseudocode*.

Unlike the definitions of high-level programming languages such as Pascal, there is no set of rules that defines precisely what is and what is not pseudocode. It varies from one programmer to another. Pseudocode is a mixture of natural language and symbols, terms, and other features commonly used in one or more high-level languages. Typically one finds the following features in the various pseudocodes that appear in textbooks:

1. The usual computer symbols are used for arithmetic operations: + for addition, − for subtraction, * for multiplication, and / for division.
2. Symbolic names (identifiers) are used to represent the quantities being processed by the algorithm.
3. Some provision is made for including comments. This is usually done by enclosing each comment between a pair of special symbols such as (* and *).
4. Certain key words that are common in high-level languages may be used: for example, *read* or *enter* to indicate an input operation; *display*, *print*, or *write* for output operations.
5. Indentation is used to indicate certain key blocks of instructions.

The structure of an algorithm can also be displayed in a *structure diagram* that shows the various tasks that must be performed and their relation to one another. These diagrams are especially useful in describing algorithms for more complex problems and will be described in more detail in Section 2.5. In this section we restrict our attention to the three simple examples introduced in the preceding section. Using these examples, we illustrate the three basic control structures—sequential, selection, and repetition—and how to present algorithms in pseudocode.

PROBLEM 1: Revenue Calculation—Sequential Structure. As we noted in the preceding section, the input for this problem consists of the basic service charge, unit cable cost, number of installations, and yards of cable used; the output to be produced is the amount of revenue generated.

The first step in an algorithm for solving this problem is to obtain the values for the input items—basic service charge, unit cable cost, number of installations, and yards of cable. The next step is to determine the number of feet of cable used by multiplying the number of yards of cable by 3. The revenue generated can then be obtained by multiplying the number of locations by the basic service charge, multiplying the unit cable cost by the number of feet of cable, and adding these two products. Finally, the output value—revenue generated—must be displayed.

This algorithm can be expressed in pseudocode as follows:

ALGORITHM FOR REVENUE CALCULATION

(* This algorithm calculates *Revenue* generated by the installation of a certain number of yards of cable (*YardsOfCable*) at a given number (*Locations*) of locations. For each installation there is a fixed basic service charge (*ServiceCharge*) and an additional charge of *UnitCost* dollars for each foot of cable. *)

1. Enter *ServiceCharge, UnitCost, Locations,* and *YardsOfCable.*
2. Calculate *FeetOfCable* = 3 * *YardsOfCable.*
3. Calculate

   Revenue = *Locations* * *ServiceCharge* + *UnitCost* * *FeetOfCable*

4. Display *Revenue.*

This algorithm uses only sequential control; the steps are executed in order, from beginning to end, with each step being performed exactly once. For other problems, however, the solution may require that some of the steps be performed in some situations and bypassed in others. This is illustrated by our second example.

PROBLEM 2: Pollution Index—Selection Structure.   Recall that for this problem, the input consists of three pollution readings and a cutoff value that distinguishes between safe and hazardous conditions. The output to be produced consists of the pollution index, which is the average of the three readings, and a message indicating the appropriate condition.

Once again, the first step in an algorithm to solve this problem is to obtain values for the input items—the three pollution readings and the cutoff value. The next step is to calculate the pollution index by averaging the three readings. Now, one of two possible actions must be selected; either a message indicating a safe condition must be displayed, or a message indicating a hazardous condition must be displayed. The appropriate action is selected by comparing the pollution index with the cutoff value. In the pseudocode description of this algorithm that follows, this selection is indicated by

    If *Index* < *Cutoff* then
        Display 'Safe condition'
    Else
        Display 'Hazardous condition'

ALGORITHM FOR THE POLLUTION INDEX PROBLEM

(* This algorithm reads three pollution levels, *Level1*, *Level2*, and
Level3, and a *Cutoff* value. It then calculates the pollution *Index*.
If the value of *Index* is less than *Cutoff*, a message indicating a safe
condition is displayed; otherwise, a message indicating a hazardous
condition is displayed. *)

1. Enter *Level1*, *Level2*, *Level3*, and *Cutoff*.
2. Calculate

$$Index = \frac{Level1 + Level2 + Level3}{3}$$

3. If *Index* < *Cutoff* then
   Display 'Safe condition'
   Else
   Display 'Hazardous condition'

In addition to the sequential processing and selection illustrated in the
preceding two examples, the solution of other problems may require that a step
or a collection of steps be repeated. This is illustrated in our third example.

PROBLEM 3: Summation—Repetition Structure. For this problem, the
input consists simply of some positive integer *LastNumber*, and the output is
the value of the sum $1 + 2 + \cdots + LastNumber$. To solve this problem in
a "brute force" manner (and not using the clever technique discovered by
Gauss), we might begin as follows:

$$
\begin{array}{r}
0 \\
+\ 1 \\
\hline
1 \\
+\ 2 \\
\hline
3 \\
+\ 3 \\
\hline
6 \\
+\ 4 \\
\hline
10 \\
+\ 5 \\
\hline
15 \\
\cdot \\
\cdot \\
\cdot
\end{array}
$$

(Although we might not actually write down the first two lines, but rather
only "think" them, they are included here for completeness.) We see that the
procedure involves two quantities:

1. A counter that ranges over consecutive integers 1, 2, 3, ...
2. The cumulative sum of these integers.

$$
\begin{array}{r}
0 \longrightarrow \text{sum} \\
+ \ 1 \longrightarrow \text{counter} \\
\hline
1 \longrightarrow \text{sum} \\
+ \ 2 \longrightarrow \text{counter} \\
\hline
3 \longrightarrow \text{sum} \\
+ \ 3 \longrightarrow \text{counter} \\
\hline
6 \longrightarrow \text{sum} \\
+ \ 4 \longrightarrow \text{counter} \\
\hline
10 \longrightarrow \text{sum} \\
\cdot \\
\cdot \\
\cdot
\end{array}
$$

The procedure begins with 1 as the value of the counter and with 0 as the initial value of the sum. At each stage, the value of the counter is added to the sum, producing a new sum, and the value of the counter is increased by 1. These steps are repeated until eventually we reach

$$
\begin{array}{r}
\cdot \\
\cdot \\
\cdot \\
+ \quad LastNumber \longrightarrow \text{counter} \\
\hline
?????????? \longrightarrow \text{sum} \\
LastNumber + 1 \longrightarrow \text{counter} \quad \text{Stop!}
\end{array}
$$

When the value of the counter exceeds *LastNumber*, the value of the sum is the desired answer, and the computation stops.

In the pseudocode description of this algorithm that follows, the repetition is indicated by

> While *Counter* ≤ *LastNumber* do the following:
> a. Add *Counter* to *Sum*.
> b. Increment *Counter* by 1.

This instruction specifies that Statements a and b are to be repeated as long as the condition *Counter* ≤ *LastNumber* remains true. Thus, when the value of *Counter* exceeds that of *LastNumber*, this repetition is terminated, and Statement 5 is executed.

ALGORITHM FOR THE SUMMATION PROBLEM

(∗ This algorithm calculates the value of the sum

$$ 1 + 2 + \cdots + LastNumber $$

for some positive integer *LastNumber*. It uses the variable *Counter* as a counter and the variable *Sum* for this sum. ∗)

1. Enter *LastNumber*.
2. Set *Counter* to 1.
3. Set *Sum* to 0.

4. While *Counter* ≤ *LastNumber* do the following:
    a. Add *Counter* to *Sum*.
    b. Increment *Counter* by 1.
5. Display *Sum*.

The three control structures in these examples, ***sequential, selection***, and ***repetition***, are used throughout this text in designing algorithms to solve problems. The implementation of each of them in the Pascal language is considered in detail in later chapters.

2.3 Program Coding

The third step in using the computer to solve a problem is to express the algorithm in a programming language. In the second step, the algorithm may be described in a natural language or pseudocode, but the program that implements that algorithm must be written in the vocabulary of a programming language and must conform to the ***syntax***, or grammatical rules, of that language. The major portion of this text is concerned with the vocabulary and syntax of the programming language Pascal. In this section, we introduce some elementary features of this language and give an example of a simple Pascal program. These features will be discussed in detail in subsequent chapters.

In the three examples in the preceding section, we used names to identify various quantities. These names are called ***variables***. In the first example, the variables *ServiceCharge, UnitCost, Installations*, and *YardsOfCable* represented the basic service charge, the cost per foot of cable, the number of installations, and the yards of cable used, respectively. The output in this example was the revenue generated and was represented by the variable *Revenue*. In the second example, the variables *Level1, Level2, Level3, Cutoff*, and *Index* were used, and in the third example, the variables were *LastNumber, Counter*, and *Sum*.

In Pascal, variable names must begin with a letter, which may be followed by any number of letters and digits. This allows us to choose names that suggest what the variable represents, for example, *ServiceCharge, UnitCost, Installations, YardsOfCable, Revenue, Level1, LastNumber*, and *Sum. Meaningful variable names should always be used because they make a program easier to read and understand.*

In the examples we have been considering, two types of numbers are used. The values of *YardsOfCable, FeetOfCable*, and *Installations* in the first example, *Level1, Level2, Level3, Cutoff*, and *Index* in the second example, and *LastNumber, Counter*, and *Sum* in the third example are integers, whereas the values of *ServiceCharge, UnitCost*, and *Revenue* in the first example are real; that is, they have fractional parts. Pascal distinguishes between several types of numeric data, and the types of the values that each variable may have must be specified. This is done by placing variable declarations of the form

    var
      list1 : *integer*;
      list2 : *real*;

at the beginning of the program, where *list1* is a list of the variable names of integer type and *list2* is a list of variable names of real type. Thus, the types of the Pascal variables in the first example can be specified by

var
      YardsOfCable, FeetOfCable, Installations : *integer*;
      ServiceCharge, UnitCost, Revenue : *real*;

and those in the third example by

var
      Counter, Sum : *integer*;

Notice that **var** is shown here in boldface. In this text, the words printed in boldface are ***reserved words*** in Pascal. They may not be used for any purpose other than those designated by the rules of the language. For example, reserved words may not be used as variable names.

Addition and subtraction are denoted in Pascal by the usual $+$ and $-$ symbols. Multiplication is denoted by $*$ and division by $/$. The assignment operation is denoted by $:=$ in Pascal programs. For example, the statement

    FeetOfCable $:=$ 3 $*$ *YardsOfCable*;

calculates the value of the product

    3 $*$ *YardsOfCable*

and assigns this value to the variable *FeetOfCable*.

In the pseudocode description of an algorithm in the preceding section, we used the words "enter" and "read" for input operations and "display," "print," and "write" for output operations. One Pascal statement that may be used for input is the *readln* statement. A simple form of this statement is

    readln (*list*)

where *list* is a list of variables for which values are to be read. For example, the statement

    readln (*ServiceCharge, UnitCost, Installations, YardsOfCable*);

reads values for the variables *ServiceCharge, UnitCost, Installations,* and *YardsOfCable* entered by the user from some input device.

A simple output statement in Pascal is the *writeln* statement of the form

    writeln (*list*)

where *list* is a list of items to be displayed. For example, the statement

    writeln ('Revenue generated $=$ \$', *Revenue*)

displays the label

  Revenue generated = $

followed by the value of the variable *Revenue*.

  Comments can also be incorporated into Pascal programs. They are indicated by enclosing them within (* and *)

  (comment *)*

or within braces

  { comment }

Figure 2.1 shows a Pascal program for the algorithm to solve the revenue calculation problem considered earlier in this chapter. The program begins with the **program heading**

  program *CalculateRevenue (input, output)*;

where *CalculateRevenue* is the name assigned to the program by the programmer, and *input* and *output* indicate that information will be input to the program from an external source and that the program will also produce some output.

This is followed by documentation in the form of a comment that describes the program. The next part of the program consists of the variable declarations that specify the types of all the variables used in the program.

The first step in the algorithm is an input instruction to enter values for the variables *ServiceCharge, UnitCost, Installations,* and *YardsOfCable*:

  1. Enter *ServiceCharge, UnitCost, Installations,* and *YardsOfCable*.

This is translated into the following statements in the program:

  writeln ('Enter service charge, cost of one foot of cable,');
  writeln ('number of installations, and yards of cable used:');
  readln (*ServiceCharge, UnitCost, Installations, YardsOfCable*);

The two *writeln* statements are used to prompt the user that values are to be entered. The *readln* statement actually assigns the four values entered by the user to the four variables *ServiceCharge, UnitCost, Installations,* and *YardsOfCable*. Thus, in the sample run shown, when the user enters

  25.00 2.00 27 263

the value 25.00 is assigned to *ServiceCharge*, 2.00 to *UnitCost*, 27 to *Installations*, and 263 to *YardsOfCable*.

The next two steps in the algorithm

  2. Calculate *FeetOfCable* = 3 * *YardsOfCable*.

3. Calculate
   Revenue = ServiceCharge * Installations + UnitCost * FeetOfCable.

translate into the Pascal assignment statements

   FeetOfCable := 3 * *YardsOfCable*;
   Revenue := *ServiceCharge* * *Installations* + *UnitCost* * *FeetOfCable*;

The output instruction

4. Display *Revenue*.

is translated into the Pascal statement

   writeln ('Revenue generated = $', *Revenue*:7:2);

```
PROGRAM CalculateRevenue (input, output);

(**************************************************************

    Program to calculate the revenue generated by an employee
    installing coaxial cable.  A basic service charge, cost per
    foot of cable, number of installations, and yards of cable
    used are input to the program.

    **********************************************************)

VAR
    Installations,              (* number of installations *)
    YardsOfCable,               (* yards of cable used *)
    FeetOfCable : integer;      (* equivalent feet of cable *)
    ServiceCharge,              (* basic service charge *)
    UnitCost,                   (* cost per foot of cable *)
    Revenue : real;             (* revenue generated *)

BEGIN
    writeln ('Enter service charge, cost of one foot of cable,');
    writeln ('number of installations, and yards of cable used:');
    readln (ServiceCharge, UnitCost, Installations, YardsOfCable);
    FeetOfCable := 3 * YardsOfCable;
    Revenue := ServiceCharge * Installations + UnitCost * FeetOfCable;
    writeln;
    writeln ('Revenue generated = $', Revenue:7:2)
END.
```

Sample run:

```
Enter service charge, cost of one foot of cable,
number of installations, and yards of cable used:
25.00 2.00 27 263

Revenue generated = $2253.00
```

Figure 2.1.

As the sample run shows, this statement produces one line of output that consists of the label Revenue generated = $ followed by the value of *Revenue*, rounded to two decimal places, in a seven-space zone:

```
Revenue generated = $2253.00
```

The end of the program is indicated by the Pascal reserved word **end** followed by a period. Note that the statements in the program are separated by semicolons.

2.4 Program Execution and Testing

The fourth step in using the computer to solve a problem is to execute and test the program. The procedure for submitting a program to a computer varies from one system to another; the details regarding your particular system can be obtained from your instructor, computer center personnel, or user manuals supplied by the manufacturer.

Access to the computer system must first be obtained. In the case of a personal computer, this may require turning the machine on and inserting the appropriate diskette in the disk drive. For a larger system, some *login* procedure may be required to establish contact between a remote terminal and the computer. Once access has been gained, the program must be entered, often using an *editor* provided in the system's software.

Once the program has been entered, it is compiled and executed by giving appropriate system commands. If no errors are detected during compilation, the resulting object program can be executed, and output like the following will appear on the screen:

```
Enter service charge, cost of one foot of cable,
number of installations, and yards of cable used.
25.00 2.00 27 263

Revenue generated = $2253.00
```

A message prompting the user for four input values was displayed by the program, and after these values were entered, the desired output value was calculated and displayed.

In this example, we have illustrated the *interactive mode* of processing, in which the user enters data values 25.00, 2.00, 27, and 263 during program execution (from the keyboard), and the output produced by the program is displayed directly to the user (usually on a video screen). Another mode of operation is *batch processing*. In this mode, a file containing the program, the data, and certain command lines must be prepared by the user. This file is then submitted to the system, and execution proceeds without any user interaction.

In this example, the program was entered, compiled, and executed without error. Usually, however, the beginning programmer will make some errors in designing the program or in attempting to enter and execute it. Errors may be detected at various stages of program processing and may cause the processing to be terminated ("aborted"). For example, an incorrect system command will be detected early in the processing and will usually prevent compilation and execution of the program. Errors in the program's syntax, such as incorrect punctuation or misspelled key words, will be detected during compilation. (In some systems, syntax errors may be detected while the program is being entered.) Such errors are called **syntax errors** or **compile-time errors** and usually make it impossible to complete the compilation and execution of the program. For example, if the first *writeln* statement that prompts the user to enter values was mistakenly entered as

   writeln ('Enter service charge, cost of one foot of cable,';

with the right parenthesis missing, an attempt to compile the program might result in a message like the following, signaling a "fatal" error:

```
        writeln ('Enter service charge, cost of one foot
of cable,';
*****        ↑
***** Symbol expected was ")"

1 error reported
```

Less severe errors may generate "warning" messages, but the compilation will continue and execution of the resulting object program will be attempted.

Other errors, such as an attempt to divide by zero in an arithmetic expression, may not be detected until the execution of the program has begun. Such errors are called **run-time errors**. The error messages displayed by your particular system can be found in the user manuals supplied by the manufacturer. In any case, the errors must be corrected by replacing the erroneous statements with correct ones, and the modified program must be recompiled and then reexecuted.

Errors that are detected by the computer system are relatively easy to identify and correct. There are, however, other errors that are more subtle and difficult to identify. These are **logical errors** that arise in the design of the algorithm or in the coding of the program that implements the algorithm. For example, if the statement

   FeetOfCable := 3 * *YardsOfCable*;

in the program of Figure 2.1 were mistakenly entered as

   FeetOfCable := 3 + *YardsOfCable*;

with the multiplication symbol (*) replaced by the symbol for addition (+), the program would still be syntactically correct. No error would occur during the compilation or execution of the program. But the output produced by the program would be incorrect because an incorrect formula would have been used in calculating *FeetOfCable*. Thus, if the values 25.00, 2.00, 27, and 263 were entered for the variables *ServiceCharge*, *UnitCost*, *Installations*, and *Yards-OfCable*, respectively, the output produced by the program would be

```
Revenue generated = $1207.00
```

instead of the correct output

```
Revenue generated = $2253.00
```

as shown in the sample run in Figure 2.1.

Since it may not be obvious whether the results produced by a program are correct, *it is important that the user run a program several times with input data for which the correct results are known in advance.* For the preceding example, it is easy to calculate by hand the correct answer for values such as 1, 1, 1, and 1 for *ServiceCharge, UnitCost, Installations,* and *YardsOfCable,* respectively, to check the output produced by the program. This process of **program validation** is extremely important, as a *program cannot be considered to be correct if it has not been validated with several sets of test data.* The test data should be carefully selected so that each part of the program is checked.

2.5 Software Engineering

Programming and problem solving is an art in that it requires a good deal of imagination, ingenuity, and creativity. But it is also a science in that certain techniques and methodologies are commonly used. The term **software engineering** has come to be applied to the study and use of these techniques.

As we noted in the introduction to this chapter, the **life cycle** of software, that is, programs, consists of five basic phases:

1. Problem analysis and specification.
2. Algorithm development.
3. Program coding.
4. Program execution and testing.
5. Program maintenance.

In the preceding sections we have described the first four phases and illustrated them with some examples. It must be emphasized, however, that these examples were deliberately kept simple so that the main ideas could be emphasized without getting lost in a maze of details. In real-world applications and in later problems in this text, these phases may be considerably more complex. In this section we reexamine each of these phases and describe some of the additional questions and complications that face professional programmers, together with some of the software engineering techniques used in dealing with them.

Problem Analysis and Specification.   Like exercises and problems in most programming texts, the examples we have considered thus far were quite simple and, we hope, clearly stated. Analysis of these problems to identify the input and output was, therefore, quite easy. This is not the case, however, in most real-world problems. These problems are often stated vaguely and imprecisely, because the person posing the problem often does not fully understand it. For example, a problem might be presented to a programmer as a request to ''computerize the payroll system for the Celestial Cookie Company.''

In these situations, there are many questions that must be answered in order to complete the problem's specification. Some of these answers are required to describe the problem's input and output more completely. What information is available for each employee? How is the program to access this data? Has this information been validated, or must the program provide error checking? In what format should the output be displayed? Are paychecks being printed? Must additional reports be generated for company executives and/or government agencies?

Other questions deal more directly with the processing that is required. Are employees paid on an hourly or a salaried basis, or are there some of each? What premium, if any, is paid for overtime? What items must be withheld— for federal, state, and city income taxes, retirement plans, insurance, etc.— and how are they to be computed?

Many other questions must be answered before the specification of the problem is complete and before design of the algorithms and programs can begin. Will the users of the program be technically sophisticated, or must the program be made very user friendly to accommodate novice users? How often will the program be used? What are the response time requirements? What is the expected life of the program; that is, how long will it be used and what changes can be expected in the future? What hardware and software are available?

Although this list is by no means exhaustive, it does indicate the wide range of information that must be obtained in analyzing and specifying the problem. In some situations this is done by a *systems analyst*, whereas in others it is part of the programmer's responsibility.

Algorithm Design.   The solution of a complex problem may require so many steps in the final algorithm that they cannot all be anticipated at the outset. To attack such problems, a *top-down* approach is commonly used. We begin by identifying the major tasks to be performed to solve the problem and arranging them in the order in which they are to be carried out. These tasks and their relation to one another can be displayed in a one-level *structure diagram*. For example, a first structure diagram for processing a payroll might have the form

Usually one or more of these first-level tasks are still quite complex and must be divided into subtasks. For example, in the payroll system, some of the input data, such as the employee's name, social security number, and number of dependents, are permanent information and may be stored in a system file, whereas other information, such as hours worked, will be entered during program execution. Consequently, the task "Obtain input data" can be subdivided into two subtasks:

1. Obtain permanent employee information.
2. Obtain current information.

Similarly, the task "Perform calculations" may be split into three subtasks:

1. Calculate gross pay.
2. Calculate withholding.
3. Calculate net pay.

Finally, the third task, "Display results," might be subdivided into

1. Print paychecks.
2. Print summary reports.

In a structure diagram, these subtasks are placed on a second level below the corresponding main task, as pictured in the first diagram in Figure 2.2.

These subtasks may require further division into still smaller subtasks, resulting in additional levels, as illustrated in the second diagram in Figure 2.2. This *successive refinement* continues until each subtask is sufficiently simple that design of an algorithm for that subtask is straightforward.

This *divide-and-conquer* approach can thus be used to divide a complex problem into a number of simpler subproblems. This allows the programmer to design and test an algorithm and a corresponding program *module* for each subproblem independently of the others. For very large projects, a team approach might be used in which the low-level subtasks are assigned to different programmers. The individual program modules developed by them are eventually combined into one complete program that solves the original problem.

Program Coding.   The first decision that must be made in translating an algorithm into a program is what programming language to use. This obviously depends on the languages available to the programmer, but other factors also influence the decision. There may be characteristics of the problem that make one language more appropriate than another. For example, if the problem involves scientific computations requiring extended precision and/or complex arithmetic, FORTRAN may be the most suitable language. Business-oriented problems that involve a large amount of file input/output and report generation can perhaps best be handled in COBOL. Structured algorithms, especially those developed in a top-down manner, can be implemented most easily in a structured language like Pascal.

Regardless of which language is used, certain programming practices contribute to the development of *correct, readable, and understandable programs.* One principle is that *programs should be well structured.* Two helpful guidelines in this regard are

- *Use a top-down approach when developing a program for a complex problem.* Divide the problem into simpler and simpler subproblems, and develop individual procedures and modules to solve these subproblems.
- *Strive for simplicity and clarity.* Clever programming tricks intended only to demonstrate the programmer's ingenuity or to produce code that executes only slightly more efficiently should be avoided.

A second principle is that *each program unit should be documented.* In particular:

- *Each program unit should include opening documentation.* Comments should be included at the beginning of each program (procedure, func-

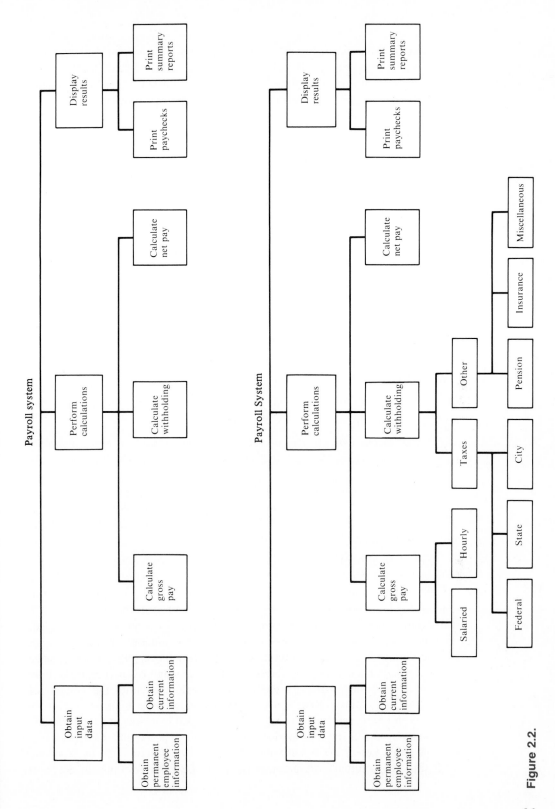

Figure 2.2.

41

tion) to explain what it does, how it works, any special algorithms it uses, and so on, and may also include such items of information as the name of the programmer, the date the program was written and when it was last modified, and references to books and manuals that give additional information about the program. In addition, it is a good practice to explain the variables that are being used in the program.

- *Comments should also be used to explain key program segments and/or segments whose purpose or design is not obvious.* However, too many or too detailed or unnecessary comments clutter the program and make it more difficult to read and understand, instead of easier.
- *Meaningful identifiers should be used.* For example, the statement

  $Distance := Rate * Time;$

  is more meaningful than

  $D := R * T;$

  or

  $X7 := R * Zeke;$

  Don't use "skimpy" abbreviations just to save a few keystrokes. Also, avoid "cute" identifiers, as in

  $HowFar := GoGo * HowLongBaby;$

A third principle has to do with a program's appearance. *A program should be formatted in a style that enhances its readability.* In particular, the following are some guidelines for good program style:

- *Use spaces between the items in a statement to make it more readable,* for example, before and after each operator ($+$, $-$, $<$, $:=$, etc.).
- *Insert a blank line between sections of a program and wherever appropriate in a sequence of statements to set off blocks of statements.*
- *Adhere rigorously to alignment and indentation guidelines to emphasize the relationship between various parts of the program.* For example, indent statements that make up the body of a loop.

It is often difficult for beginning programmers to appreciate the importance of practicing good programming habits that lead to the design of programs that are readable and understandable. The reason for this is that programs developed in an academic environment are often quite different from those developed in real-world situations, in which program style and form are critical. Student programs are usually quite small (more than a few hundred lines of code are uncommon); are executed and modified only a few times (almost never, once they have been handed in); are rarely examined in detail by anyone other than the student and the instructor; and are not developed within the context of severe budget restraints. Real-world programs, on the other hand, may be very large (several thousand lines of code); are developed by teams of programmers; are commonly used for long periods of time and thus require maintenance if they are to be kept current and correct; and are often maintained by someone other than the original programmer. As hardware costs continue to decrease and programmer costs increase, it becomes increasingly important that programs be written that can be easily read and understood by others.

As we discuss features of the Pascal language in the chapters that follow, additional principles for program design will be given. It is important for the beginning programmer to follow these guidelines, even in early simple programs, so that good habits are established and carried on into the design of more complex programs.

Program Execution and Testing. Obviously, the most important characteristic of any program is that it be *correct*. No matter how well structured, how well documented, or how nice the program looks, if it does not produce correct results, it is worthless. As we have seen, the fact that a program executes with no error messages is no guarantee that it is correct. The results produced may be erroneous due to logical errors that the computer system cannot detect. It is the responsibility of the programmer to test each program in order to ensure that it is correct. (See Section 4.5 for more about program testing.)

Program Maintenance. The life cycle of a program written by a student programmer normally ends with the fourth phase; that is, once the program has been written, executed, and tested, the assignment is complete. Programs in real-world applications, however, will likely be used for a number of years and will probably require some modification as time passes. Especially in large programs developed for complex projects, there will usually be obscure bugs that do not become apparent until after the program has been placed in use. Correction of these flaws is obviously one aspect of program maintenance. It may also be necessary or desirable to modify the program in order to improve its performance, add new features, and so on. Other modifications may be required because of changes in the computer hardware and/or the system software such as the operating system. External factors may also force program modification; for example, changes in the tax laws may require revision of part of a payroll program.

Software maintenance is, in fact, a major component of the life cycle of a program and may account for as much as 80 percent of its total cost. This fact, combined with the fact that most program maintenance is done by someone not involved in the original design, makes it mandatory that the programmer do his or her utmost to design a program that is readable, documented, and well structured so that it is easy to understand and modify.

Exercises

For each of the problems described in Exercises 1 through 10, identify the information that must be produced to solve the problem and the given information that will be useful in obtaining the solution. Then design an algorithm to solve the problem.

1. Calculate and display the perimeter and area of a square with a given side.

2. Two common temperature scales are the Fahrenheit and Celsius scales. The boiling point of water is 212° on the Fahrenheit scale and 100° on the Celsius scale. The freezing point of water is 32° on the Fahrenheit scale and 0° on the Celsius scale. Assuming a linear relationship ($F = a \cdot C + b$) between these two temperature scales, convert a temperature on the Celsius scale to the corresponding Fahrenheit temperature.

3. Calculate and display the largest and smallest of three given test scores.

4. Calculate and display the largest, the smallest, and the range (largest minus smallest) of any given set of test scores.

5. The business manager of a certain company wants a program to calculate the wages for the company's employees. This program should accept an employee number, base pay rate per hour, and the number of hours worked. All hours above 40 are to be paid at the overtime rate of 1.5 times the base rate. For each employee, the program should print the employee number, total number of hours worked, base pay rate, and total wages, and it should also print the total of all wages paid by the company.

6. A certain city classifies a pollution index of less than 35 as "pleasant," 35 through 60 as "unpleasant," and above 60 as "hazardous." The city pollution control office wants a program that will accept several values of the pollution index and will produce the appropriate classification for each.

7. Suppose that a professor gave a quiz to her class and compiled a list of scores ranging from 50 through 100. She intends to use only three grades: A if the score is 90 or greater, B if it is below 90 but above or equal to 75, and C if it is below 75. She would like a program to assign the appropriate letter grades to the numeric scores.

8. The "divide and average" algorithm for approximating the square root of any positive number A is as follows: Take any initial approximation X that is positive, and then find a new approximation by calculating the average of X and A/X, that is, $(X + A/X)/2$. Repeat this procedure with X replaced by this new approximation, stopping when X and A/X differ in absolute value by some specified error allowance, such as 0.00001.

9. The quadratic equation $Ax^2 + Bx + C = 0$ has no real roots if the discriminant $B^2 - 4AC$ is negative; it has one real root, $-B/2A$, if the discriminant is zero; and it has two real roots given by the quadratic formula

$$\frac{-B \pm \sqrt{B^2 - 4AC}}{2A}$$

if the discriminant is positive. A program is to be developed to solve several different quadratic equations or to indicate that there are no real solutions.

10. The Rinky Dooflingy Company currently sells 200 dooflingies per month at a profit of $300 per dooflingy. The company now spends $2,000 per month on advertising and has a fixed operating cost of $10,000 per month that does not depend on the volume of sales. If the company doubles the amount spent on advertising, its sales will increase by 20 percent. The company president would like to know, beginning with the company's current status and successively doubling the amount spent on advertising, at what point the net profit will "go over the hump," that is, begin to decline.

11. Enter and execute the following short Pascal program on your computer system:

> **program** *Exercise11* (*input, output*);
> (* Program to perform various arithmetic
>   operations on two numbers *X* and *Y*. *)
>
> **var**
>   *X, Y, Sum* : *integer*;
>
> **begin**
>   *X* := 214;
>   *Y* := 2057;
>   *Sum* := *X* + *Y*;
>   *writeln* ('Sum of', *X, Y*, ' is', *Sum*)
> **end**.

12. Make the following changes in the program in Exercise 11 and execute the modified program:

(a) Change 214 to 1723 in the statement assigning a value to *X*.
(b) Change the variable names *X* and *Y* to *Alpha* and *Beta* throughout.
(c) Insert the comment

> (* Calculate the sum *)

before the statement

> *Sum* := *Alpha* + *Beta*;

(d) Insert the following comment and statement before the *writeln* statement:

> (* Now calculate the difference *)
> *Difference* := *Alpha* − *Beta*;

change the variable declaration to

> **var**
>   *Alpha, Beta, Sum, Difference* : *integer*;

and add the following statement after the *writeln* statement:

writeln ('Difference of', *Alpha, Beta*, ' is', *Difference*)

Note: For the modified program to work correctly, you must also insert a semicolon at an appropriate location.

13. Using the program in Figure 2.1 as a guide, write a Pascal program for the algorithm in Exercise 1.

14. Using the program in Figure 2.1 as a guide, write a Pascal program for the algorithm in Exercise 2.

3

Basic Pascal

Kindly enter them in your note-book.
And, in order to refer to them
conveniently, let's call them A, B, and Z.

THE TORTOISE IN LEWIS CARROLL'S
What the Tortoise Said to Achilles

In language, clarity is everything.

CONFUCIUS

One important phase in using the computer to solve a problem is the implementation of the algorithm for solving that problem as a program. Whereas algorithms can be described somewhat informally in a pseudoprogramming language, the corresponding program must be written in strict compliance with the rules of some programming language. In this chapter we begin a detailed study of the language Pascal.

As we noted in Chapter 1, Pascal was developed in the late 1960s and early 1970s by the Swiss computer scientist Niklaus Wirth. Different versions of Pascal have appeared since its introduction, and for several years the *Pascal User Manual and Report* written by Wirth and Kathleen Jensen and published in 1974 served as the de facto standard. In 1983 an official standard was prepared by committees of the American National Standards Institute (ANSI) and the Institute of Electrical and Electronic Engineers (IEEE) and was published as the *American National Standard Pascal Computer Programming Language*. This ANSI/IEEE standard is the basis for this text. However, a number of other versions of Pascal that provide useful variations of and extensions to the standard have become popular. Some of these features are summarized in the Variations and Extensions sections at the chapters' ends, and Appendix G gives additional details.

3.1 From Algorithms to Programs

An algorithm for the solution of a problem is a sequence of steps that must be performed in order to obtain the solution of the problem from the information given in the problem's specification. Thus, a computer program that implements such an algorithm must accept and store the given information, perform the sequence of steps required to solve the problem (which may also require calculating and storing some intermediate results), and, finally, display the results. This general structure is reflected in the organization of a Pascal program.

The first statement of a Pascal program is the ***program heading***. This statement gives the program a name and, more importantly, indicates the kinds of input/output operations that will be performed. The heading is normally followed by some ***opening documentation*** in the form of one or more comments about the nature and purpose of the program and other relevant information such as the date the program was written and the name of the programmer. The next part of the program is the ***declaration part***, in which the variables (among other things) that will be used to store input and output values as well as intermediate results are listed. The last part of a Pascal program is the ***statement part***. It is this part that contains the statements that actually carry out the steps of the algorithm.

A Pascal program thus has the general form

program heading
declaration part
statement part.

(Note the required period that follows the statement part.) Each of these parts is described in detail in the following sections.

3.2 Data Types

Computer programs, regardless of the language in which they are written, are designed to manipulate some kind of data. Thus we begin by considering the types of data that can be processed in a Pascal program.

Pascal provides four standard types of data:

integer
real
char
boolean

The first two are numeric types and are used to process different kinds of numbers. The type *char* is used to process character data. The type *boolean* is used to process boolean or logical data; such data may have either the value true or the value false.

Constants. *Constants* are quantities whose values do not change during program execution. They may be of numeric, character, or boolean type (or one of the other types considered later). An ***integer*** constant is a string of digits that does not include commas or a decimal point; negative integer constants must be preceded by a negative sign, but a plus sign is optional for nonnegative integers. Thus

$$0$$
$$137$$
$$-2516$$
$$+17745$$

are valid integer constants, whereas the following are invalid for the reasons indicated:

5,280	(Commas are not allowed in integer constants.)
16.0	(Integer constants may not contain decimal points.)
$--5$	(Only one algebraic sign is allowed.)
$7-$	(The algebraic sign must precede the string of digits.)

Another type of numeric data is the **real** type. Constants of this type may be represented as ordinary decimal numbers or in scientific notation. The **decimal** representation of real constants must include exactly one decimal point, but the constant may not begin or end with a decimal point. As in the case of integer constants, no commas are allowed. Negative real constants must be preceded by a minus sign, but a plus sign is optional for nonnegative reals. Thus

$$1.234$$
$$-0.1536$$
$$+56473.0$$

are valid real constants, whereas the following are invalid for the reasons indicated:

1,752.63	(Commas are not allowed in real constants.)
82	(Real constants in decimal form must contain a decimal point.)
.01	(Real constants may not begin with a decimal point.)
24.	(Real constants may not end with a decimal point.)

The **exponential** or **floating point** representation of a real constant consists of an integer or real constant in decimal form followed by the letter E (or e) followed by an integer constant that is interpreted as an exponent on the base 10. For example, the real constant 337.456 may also be written as

$$3.37456E2$$

which means

$$3.37456 \times 10^2$$

or it may be written in a variety of other forms, such as

$$0.337456E3$$
$$337.456E0$$
$$33745.6E-2$$
$$337456E-3$$

A **character** is one of the symbols in the Pascal character set. Although this character set may vary from one Pascal implementation to another, it usually includes digits 0 through 9; uppercase letters A through Z; lowercase letters a through z; usual punctuation symbols such as the semicolon (;), comma (,), and period (.); and special symbols such as $+$, $=$, $>$, and $\uparrow$. In fact, many Pascal implementations allow a character to be any symbol from the character set for that machine. (See Appendix A for two commonly used character sets, ASCII and EBCDIC.)

A *character constant* consists of a character enclosed within single quotes (apostrophes); for example,

'A', '+', '3', ':'

If a character constant is to consist of an apostrophe, it must appear as a pair of apostrophes enclosed within single quotes (apostrophes):

''''

A sequence of characters is commonly called a *string*, and a *string constant* consists of a string enclosed within single quotes. Thus

'John Q. Doe'

and

'PDQ123−A'

are valid string constants. Again, if an apostrophe is one of the characters in a string constant, it must appear as a pair of apostrophes; for example,

'Don''t'

The type *boolean* is named after the nineteenth-century mathematician George Boole, who originated the logical calculus. There are only two *boolean constants*,

true

and

false

These constants are called *logical* constants in some programming languages.

Identifiers. *Identifiers* are names given to programs, constants, variables, and other entities in a program. Identifiers must begin with a letter, which may be followed by any number of letters or digits. *This allows one to choose meaningful identifiers that suggest what they represent.*

Pascal *reserved words* such as **var**, **begin**, and **end** may not be used as identifiers, since they have a special meaning in Pascal. A complete list of reserved words is given in Appendix B. Pascal also contains certain **standard identifiers**, such as *integer, real, true, false, read, readln, write*, and *writeln. These identifiers have predefined meanings, but they are not reserved words. Consequently, they may be redefined by the programmer, but it is not good practice to do so.* A complete list of standard identifiers is given in Appendix B.

Since *Pascal makes no distinction between uppercase and lowercase* (except in character and string constants), one may use uppercase and lowercase letters in any way that will improve the program's readability. A common practice—and one that we use in the sample programs in this text—is to write all reserved words in uppercase and all identifiers in lowercase, usually capitalizing the first letter if they are user defined. If an identifier is made up of several words, we usually capitalize the first letter of each. For example, *HourlyRate* is a valid identifier and will not be distinguished from *HOURLYRATE, hourlyrate*, or *HoURlyRaTE*, even if one form is used in one place in the program and another is used somewhere else.

Variables. In mathematics, a symbolic name is often used to refer to a quantity. For example, the formula

$$A = l \cdot w$$

is used to calculate the area (denoted by A) of a rectangle with a given length (denoted by l) and a given width (denoted by w). These symbolic names, A, l, and w, are called **variables**. If specific values are assigned to l and w, this formula can be used to calculate the value of A, which then represents the area of a particular rectangle.

Variables were also used in Chapter 2 in the discussion of algorithms and programs. When a variable is used in a Pascal program, the compiler associates it with a particular memory location. The value of a variable at any time is the value stored in the associated memory location at that time. Variable names are identifiers and thus must follow the rules for forming valid identifiers.

The type of a Pascal variable must be one of the four data types described earlier (or one of the other data types discussed later), and the type of each variable determines the type of value that may be stored in that variable. It is therefore necessary to specify the type of each variable in a Pascal program. This is done in the **variable section** of the declaration part of the program. This section begins with the reserved word **var** and has the form

```
var
    variable-list-1 : type-1;
    variable-list-2 : type-2;
            ⋮
    variable-list-m : type-m;
```

where each *variable-list-i* is a single variable or a list of variables separated by commas, and each *type-i* is one of the Pascal data types *integer, real, char,* or *boolean* (or one of the other types discussed later). For example, the variable declaration section

> **var**
>> *EmpNumber* : *integer*;
>> *DeptCode* : *char*;
>> *CityResident* : *boolean*;
>> *Hours* : *real*;
>> *Rate* : *real*;
>> *Wages* : *real*;

or equivalently,

> **var**
>> *EmpNumber* : *integer*;
>> *DeptCode* : *char*;
>> *CityResident* : *boolean*;
>> *Hours, Rate, Wages* : *real*;

declares that only the six variables *EmpNumber, DeptCode, CityResident, Hours, Rate*, and *Wages* are used in the program and that *EmpNumber* is of type *integer*; *DeptCode* is of type *char*; *CityResident* is of type *boolean*; and *Hours, Rate*, and *Wages* are of type *real*.

It is good programming practice to use meaningful variable names that suggest what they represent, since this makes the program more readable and easier to understand. It is also good practice to include brief comments that indicate how the variable is to be used. These comments may be included in the variable declaration section. The following illustrates:

> **var**
>> *EmpNumber* : *integer*;   (* employee number *)
>> *DeptCode* : *char*;   (* department code *)
>> *CityResident* : *boolean*;   (* indicates if a city resident *)
>> *Hours*,   (* hours worked *)
>> *Rate*,   (* hourly pay rate *)
>> *Wages* : *real*;   (* total wages *)

Named Constants.   Certain constants occur so frequently that they are given names. For example, the name "pi" is commonly given to the constant 3.14159 . . . and "e" to the base 2.71828 . . . of natural logarithms. Pascal allows the programmer to assign identifiers to certain constants in the *constant section* of the program's declaration part. This section, if included, must precede the variable section and must begin with the reserved word **const**; it has the form

> **const**
>> *identifier-1* = *constant-1*;
>> *identifier-2* = *constant-2*;
>>> ⋮
>> *identifier-k* = *constant-k*;

For example, the constant section

> **const**
> Pi = 3.14159;
> $NegPi$ = $-Pi$;
> $MyName$ = 'John Doe';
> $CurrentYear$ = 1990;

associates the names Pi and $NegPi$ with the real constants 3.14159 and -3.14159, respectively, $MyName$ with the string constant 'John Doe', and $CurrentYear$ with the integer 1990. These names can then be used anywhere in the program that the corresponding constant value can be used.

One reason for using named constants is to make the program easier to read and to modify. Programmers should not use "magic numbers" that suddenly appear without explanation, as in

> $PopChange := (0.1758 - 0.1257) * Population$;

If these numbers must be changed, someone must search through the program to determine what they represent and which are the appropriate ones to change, and to locate all the places where they appear. It is thus better to use named constants, as in

> **const**
> $BirthRate$ = 0.1758;
> $DeathRate$ = 0.1257;

and to rewrite the preceding statement as

> $PopChange := (BirthRate - DeathRate) * Population$;

Readability is improved and the flexibility of the program is increased, because if these constants must be changed, one need only change the definitions of $BirthRate$ and $DeathRate$ in the constant section at the beginning of the program.

Pascal also includes three predefined constant identifiers: the boolean constant identifiers *true* and *false* and the integer constant identifier *maxint*. The value of *maxint* is the largest integer that can be represented in the particular computer being used. Typical values are 32767 ($2^{15} - 1$) or 2147483647 ($2^{31} - 1$).

Exercises

1. Which of the following are legal Pascal identifiers?

(a) *XRay*	**(b)** *X-Ray*	**(c)** *Jeremiah*	**(d)** R2D2
(e) 3M	**(f)** *PDQ*123	**(g)** *PS*.175	**(h)** *x*
(i) 4	**(j)** *N*/4	**(k)** $M	**(l)** ZZZZZZ
(m) *night*	**(n)** *ngiht*	**(o)** *nite*	**(p)** *to day*

2. Classify each of the following as an integer constant, real constant, or neither:

(a) 12   **(b)** 12.   **(c)** 12.0   **(d)** '12'
(e) 8+4   **(f)** −3.7   **(g)** 3.7−   **(h)** 1,024
(i) +1   **(j)** $3.98   **(k)** 0.357E4   **(l)** 24E0
(m) E3   **(n)** five   **(o)** 3E.5   **(p)** .000001
(q) 1.2×10 **(r)** −(−1)   **(s)** 0E0   **(t)** 1/2

3. Which of the following are legal string constants?

(a) 'X'   **(b)** '123'   **(c)** IS'   **(d)** 'too yet'
(e) 'DO''ESNT'   **(f)** 'isn''t'   **(g)** 'constant'   **(h)** '$1.98'
(i) 'DON'T'   **(j)** '12 + 34'   **(k)** '''twas'   **(l)** 'A''B''C'

4. Write variable sections to declare:

(a) *Item, Number*, and *Job* to be of type *real*.
(b) *ShoeSize* to be of type *integer*.
(c) *Mileage* to be of type *real* and *Cost* and *Distance* to be of type *integer*.
(d) *Alpha* and *Beta* to be of type *integer, Code* to be of type *char, Root* to be of type *real*, and *RootExists* to be of type *boolean*.

5. For each of the following, write constant sections to name each given constant with the specified name:

(a) 1.25 with the name *Rate*.
(b) 40.0 with the name *RegHours* and 1.5 with the name *Overtime-Factor*.
(c) 1776 with the name *Year*, 'F' with *Female*, and a blank character with *Blank*.
(d) *true* with the name *Exists*, 0 with *Zero*, ∗ with *Asterisk*, an apostrophe with *Apostrophe*, and the string CPSC151A with *Course*.

3.3 Arithmetic Operations and Functions

In the preceding section we considered variables and constants of various types. These variables and constants can be processed by using operations and functions appropriate to their types. In this section we discuss the arithmetic operations and functions that are used with numeric data.

In Pascal, addition and subtraction are denoted by the usual plus (+) and minus (−) signs. Multiplication is denoted by an asterisk (∗). This symbol must be used to denote every multiplication; thus to multiply *n* by 2, we must use 2 ∗ *n* or *n* ∗ 2, not 2*n*. There are three other arithmetic operations in Pascal: a real division operation denoted by a slash (/); an integer division operation denoted by the reserved word **div**; and an integer operation denoted by the reserved word **mod** that reduces one integer modulo another. The following table summarizes these arithmetic operations:

Operator	Operation
+	addition
−	subtraction, unary minus
*	multiplication
/	real division
div	integer division
mod	modulo

For the operators $+$, $-$, and $*$, the operands may be of either integer or real type. If both are integer, the result is integer; but if either is of real type, the result is real. For example,

$$2 + 3 = 5$$

$$2 + 3.0 = 5.0$$

$$2.0 + 3 = 5.0$$

$$2.0 + 3.0 = 5.0$$

The division operator $/$ produces a real result, regardless of the type of the operands; for example,

$$7 / 2 = 3.5$$

$$7.0 / 2 = 3.5$$

$$7 / 2.0 = 3.5$$

$$7.0 / 2.0 = 3.5$$

For the operators **div** and **mod**, both the operands must be of integer type, and the result is also of integer type. If i and j are of integer type, then i **div** j produces the integer quotient obtained when i is divided by j. The value of i **mod** j is the value obtained when i is reduced modulo j; when j is positive, this value is the positive remainder that results when i is divided by j.[1] For example,

7 **div** 2 =	3	7 **mod** 2 = 1
12 **div** 3 =	4	12 **mod** 3 = 0
0 **div** 5 =	0	0 **mod** 5 = 0
4 **div** 5 =	0	4 **mod** 5 = 4
-8 **div** 3 =	-2	-8 **mod** 3 = 1

The expression i **div** j is defined for all nonzero integers j, but i **mod** j is defined only for positive values of j.

There are two *priority levels* for these arithmetic operators: high and low. The high-priority operators are $*$, $/$, **div**, and **mod**, and the low-priority operators are $+$ and $-$. When an expression containing several of these operators is evaluated, first all high-priority operations are performed in the order in

---

[1] In some versions of Pascal, i **mod** j produces the remainder (possibly negative) that results when i is divided by j. For example, -8 **mod** $3 = -2$.

which they occur, from left to right, and then all low-priority operations are carried out in the order in which they occur, from left to right.

To illustrate, consider the expression

$$7 * 10 - 5 \textbf{ mod } 3 * 4 + 9$$

The leftmost multiplication is performed first, giving the intermediate result

$$70 - 5 \textbf{ mod } 3 * 4 + 9$$

The next high-priority operator encountered is **mod**, which gives

$$70 - 2 * 4 + 9$$

The second multiplication is the final operation of high priority; when it is performed, it yields

$$70 - 8 + 9$$

Next, the low-priority operations are performed in the order in which they occur, from left to right. The subtraction is thus performed first, giving

$$62 + 9$$

and then the addition is carried out, giving the final result

$$71$$

The standard order of evaluation can be modified by using parentheses to enclose subexpressions within an expression. These subexpressions are first evaluated in the standard manner, and the results are then combined to evaluate the complete expression. If the parentheses are "nested," that is, if one set of parentheses is contained within another, the computations in the innermost parentheses are performed first.

For example, consider the expression

$$(7 * (10 - 5) \textbf{ mod } 3) * 4 + 9$$

The subexpression $10 - 5$ is evaluated first, producing

$$\underline{(7 * 5 \textbf{ mod } 3)} * 4 + 9$$

Next the subexpression $7 * 5 \textbf{ mod } 3$ is evaluated in the standard order, giving

$$2 * 4 + 9$$

Now the multiplication is performed, giving

$$8 + 9$$

and the addition produces the final result

17

Care must be taken in writing expressions containing two or more operations to ensure that they are evaluated in the order intended. Even though parentheses may not be required, they should be used freely to clarify the intended order of evaluation and to write complicated expressions in terms of simpler subexpressions. One must make sure, however, that the parentheses balance, that is, that they occur in pairs, since an unpaired parenthesis results in an error.

The symbols $+$ and $-$ can also be used as **unary operators**; for example, $-x$ and $+(a + b)$ are allowed. But unary operators must be used carefully, since Pascal does not allow two operators to follow in succession. For example, the expression $n * -2$ is not allowed; rather, it must be written $n * (-2)$. These unary operations have low priority, as do the corresponding binary operations.

In summary, the following rules govern the evaluation of arithmetic expressions:

1. The high-priority operators $*$, $/$, **div**, and **mod** are performed first. The low-priority operators $+$ and $-$ (both binary and unary) are performed last. Operators having the same priority are evaluated from left to right.
2. If an expression contains subexpressions enclosed within parentheses, these are evaluated first, using the standard order specified in Rule 1. If there are nested parentheses, the innermost subexpressions are evaluated first.

There are also a number of predefined arithmetic functions in the Pascal language, as given in Table 3.1. To use any of these functions, we simply give the function name followed by its parameter—the constant, variable, or expression to which the function is to be applied—enclosed within parentheses. Thus, to calculate the square root of 5, we write

$$sqrt(5)$$

and to calculate $\sqrt{b^2 - 4ac}$, we could use

$$sqrt(sqr(b) - 4 * a * c)$$

TABLE 3.1 Predefined Arithmetic Functions

Function	Description	Type of Parameter	Type of Value
$abs(x)$	Absolute value of x	Integer or real	Same as argument
$arctan(x)$	Inverse tangent of x (value in radians)	Integer or real	Real
$cos(x)$	Cosine of x (in radians)	Integer or real	Real
$exp(x)$	Exponential function e^x	Integer or real	Real
$ln(x)$	Natural logarithm of x	Integer or real	Real
$round(x)$	x rounded to nearest integer	Real	Integer
$sin(x)$	Sine of x (in radians)	Integer or real	Real
$sqr(x)$	x^2	Integer or real	Same as argument
$sqrt(x)$	Square root of x	Integer or real	Real
$trunc(x)$	x truncated to its integer part	Real	Integer

If the value of the expression $sqr(b) - 4 * a * c$ is negative, an error results because the square root of a negative number is not defined.

Exercises

1. Find the value of each of the following expressions or explain why it is not a valid expression:

   (a) 9 − 5 − 3
   (b) 2 **div** 3 + 3 / 5
   (c) 9 **div** 2 / 5
   (d) 9 / 2 **div** 5
   (e) 2.0 / 4
   (f) (2 + 3) **mod** 2
   (g) 7 **mod** 5 **mod** 3
   (h) (7 **mod** 5) **mod** 3
   (i) 7 **mod** (5 **mod** 3)
   (j) (7 **mod** 5 **mod** 3)
   (k) 25 ∗ 1 / 2
   (l) 25 ∗ 1 **div** 2
   (m) 25 ∗ (1 **div** 2)
   (n) −3.0 ∗ 5.0
   (o) 5.0 ∗ −3.0
   (p) 12 / 2 ∗ 3
   (q) ((12 + 3) **div** 2) / (8 − (5 + 1))
   (r) ((12 + 3) **div** 2) / (8 − 5 + 1)
   (s) (12 + 3 **div** 2) / (8 − 5 + 1)
   (t) $sqrt(sqr(4))$
   (u) $sqrt(sqr(-4))$
   (v) $sqr(sqrt(4))$
   (w) $sqr(sqrt(-4))$
   (x) $trunc(8 / 5) + round(8 / 5)$

2. If $R1$ and $R2$ are of type *real*, $I1, I2, I3$ are of type *integer*, and $R1 = 2.0$, $R2 = 3.0$, $I1 = 4$, $I2 = 5$, and $I3 = 8$, find the value of each of the following:

   (a) $R1 + R2 + R2$
   (b) $I3$ **div** 3
   (c) $I3$ / 3
   (d) $(R2 + R1) * I1$
   (e) $I3$ **div** $I2 * 5.1$
   (f) $sqr(I1) / sqr(R1)$
   (g) $sqr(I2) / sqr(R1)$
   (h) $sqrt(R1 + R2 + I1)$

3. Write Pascal expressions to compute the following:

   (a) $10 + 5B - 4AC$.
   (b) Three times the difference $4 - n$ divided by twice the quantity $m^2 + n^2$.

(c) The square root of $a + 3b^2$.

(d) The square root of the average of m and n.

(e) $|A/(m + n)|$ ($|x|$ denotes the absolute value of x.)

(f) The real quantity *Amount* rounded to the nearest hundredth.

3.4 The Assignment Statement

The ***assignment statement*** is used to assign values to variables and has the form

   variable $:=$ *expression*

where *expression* may be a constant, another variable to which a value has previously been assigned, or a formula to be evaluated. For example, suppose that *xCoord* and *yCoord* are real variables, *Number* and *Position* are integer variables, *Code* is a character variable, and *Found* is a boolean variable as declared by the following variable section:

  var
   xCoord, yCoord : *real*;
   Number, Position : *integer*;
   Code : *char*;
   Found : *boolean*;

These declarations associate memory locations with the six variables. This might be pictured as follows, with the question marks indicating that these variables are initially undefined:

xCoord	?
yCoord	?
Number	?
Position	?
Code	?
Found	?

Now consider the following assignment statements:

  xCoord $:=$ 5.23;
  yCoord $:=$ *sqrt*(25.0);
  Number $:=$ 17;
  Code $:=$ 'M';
  Found $:=$ *false*;

Note that the boolean constant *false* is not enclosed in quotes; 'false' is a string constant, not a boolean constant. Also note that the value of a variable of type *char* is a single character and not a string of characters.

The first assignment statement assigns the real constant 5.23 to the real variable *xCoord*, and the second assigns the real constant 5.0 to the real variable *yCoord*. The next three assignment statements assign the integer constant 17 to the integer variable *Number*, the character M to the character variable *Code*, and the boolean value *false* to the boolean variable *Found*. When these assignment statements are executed, the values 5.23, 5.0, 17, M, and *false* are stored in the memory locations associated with the variables *xCoord*, *yCoord*, *Number*, *Code*, and *Found*, respectively. The variable *Position* is still undefined, and the content of the memory location associated with it is uncertain.

xCoord	5.23
yCoord	5.0
Number	17
Position	?
Code	M
Found	*false*

These values are substituted for the variables in any subsequent expression containing these variables. Thus, in the assignment statement

$$Position := Number \textbf{ div } 3 + 2;$$

the value 17 is substituted for the variable *Number*; the expression *Number* **div** 3 + 2 is evaluated yielding 7, and this value is then assigned to the integer variable *Position*; and the value of *Number* is unchanged.

xCoord	5.23
yCoord	5.0
Number	17
Position	7
Code	M
Found	*false*

In the assignment statement

$$xCoord := 2.0 * xCoord;$$

the variable *xCoord* appears on both sides of the assignment operator $(:=)$. In this case, the current value 5.23 for *xCoord* is used in evaluating the expression $2.0 * xCoord$, yielding the value 10.46; this value is then assigned to *xCoord*. The old value 5.23 is lost because it has been replaced with the new value 10.46.

xCoord	10.46
yCoord	5.0
Number	17
Position	7
Code	**M**
Found	*false*

In every assignment statement, the variable to be assigned a value must appear on the left of the assignment operator $(:=)$, and a legal expression must appear on the right. Furthermore, both the variable and the expression must be of the same type. However, *it is legal to assign an integer value to a real variable;* the integer value will be converted to the corresponding real value. *One may not, however, assign a real value to an integer variable.*

The following are examples of invalid Pascal assignment statements. A reason is given for each to explain why it is not valid. The variables in these statements are assumed to have the types specified earlier.

Statement	Error
$5 := Number$	Variable must appear on the left of the assignment operator.
$xCoord + 3.5 := 2.7$	Arithmetic expressions may not appear on the left of the assignment operator.
$Code := 5$	Numeric value may not be assigned to a character variable.
$Code := 'ABC'$	Value of a *char* variable is a single character.
$Number := '5'$	Character constant may not be assigned to a numeric variable.
$Number := 3.4$	Real value may not be assigned to an integer variable.
$Number := '2' + '3'$	'2' + '3' is not a legal expression.
$Position := Number := 1$	*Number* := 1 is not a legal expression.
$Found := 'false'$	'false' is not a boolean expression.

It is important to remember that *the assignment statement is a replacement statement.* Some beginning programmers forget this and write an assignment statement like

$$A := B$$

when the statement

$$B := A$$

is intended. These two statements produce very different results: The first assigns the value of *B* to *A*, leaving *B* unchanged, and the second assigns the value of *A* to *B*, leaving *A* unchanged.

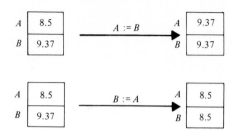

To illustrate further that an assignment statement is a replacement statement, suppose that *Alpha* and *Beta* are integer variables with values 357 and 59, respectively. The following statements interchange the values of *Alpha* and *Beta*, using the auxiliary integer variable *Temp*:

Temp := *Alpha*;
Alpha := *Beta*;
Beta := *Temp*;

As another example, consider the statement

Sum := *Sum* + *Counter*

Such a statement, in which the same variable appears on both sides of the assignment operator, often confuses beginning programmers. Execution of this statement causes the values of *Sum* and *Counter* to be substituted for these variables to evaluate the expression *Sum* + *Counter*, and the resulting value is then assigned to *Sum*. The following diagram illustrates this for the case in which the integer variables *Sum* and *Counter* have the values 120 and 16, respectively.

Note that the old value of the variable *Sum* is lost because it was replaced with a new value.

Another statement in which the same variable appears on both sides of the assignment operator is

Counter := *Counter* + 1

This statement implements the operation "increment *Counter* by 1." When it is executed, the current value of *Counter* is substituted for this variable to evaluate the expression *Counter* + 1, and this new value is then assigned to *Counter*. For example, if *Counter* has the value 16, the value of *Counter* + 1 is 16 + 1 = 17, which is then assigned as the new value for *Counter*:

Note once again that the old value of the variable has been lost because it was replaced with a new value.

In a Pascal program, *variables are undefined until their values have been explicitly specified* by an assignment statement or by one of the other statements discussed later. The results of attempting to use undefined variables are unpredictable and depend on the particular Pascal compiler being used.

Exercises

1. Assuming that *Number* is of integer type, *xValue* and *yValue* are of real type, *Grade* is of character type, and *Found* is of boolean type, determine which of the following are valid Pascal assignment statements. If they are not valid, explain why they are not.

   (a) *xValue* := 2.71828
   (b) 3 := *Number*
   (c) *Grade* := 'B+'
   (d) *Number* := *Number* + 1
   (e) *xValue* := 1
   (f) *Grade* := A
   (g) *Number* + 1 := *Number*
   (h) *xValue* := '1'
   (i) *Found* := *Grade*
   (j) *yValue* := *yValue*
   (k) *xValue* := A
   (l) *Grade* := *Grade* + 10
   (m) *Found* := 'true'
   (n) *xValue* := *Number*
   (o) *Number* := *yValue*

2. Given that *R1*, *R2*, *R3*, and *xCoord* are real variables with *R1* = 2.0, *R2* = 3.0, and *R3* = 4.0; *I1*, *I2*, and *I3* are integer variables with *I1* = 8 and *I2* = 5; and *Numeral* and *Symbol* are character variables with *Numeral* = '2', find the value assigned to the given variable by each of the following, or indicate why the statement is not valid:

   (a) *xCoord* := (*R1* + *R2*) * *R2*
   (b) *xCoord* := (*R2* + *R1* / *R3*) * 2
   (c) *xCoord* := *I1* / *I2* + 5
   (d) *I3* := *I1* **div** *I2* + 5
   (e) *xCoord* := sqr(*I2*) / sqr(*I1*)
   (f) *I3* := sqr(*I2*) / sqr(*I1*)
   (g) *Symbol* := 4
   (h) *Symbol* := *Numeral*
   (i) *Symbol* := '4'
   (j) *Symbol* := *R3*
   (k) *R1* := 2

(l) $R1 := \text{'2'}$
(m) $R1 := Numeral$
(n) $I1 := I1 + 2$
(o) $I3 := 1 + Numeral$
(p) $I3 := round(sqr(I1 \textbf{ mod } I2) / R3)$

3. For each of the following, write an assignment statement that changes the value of the integer variable *Number* by the specified amount.

   (a) Increment *Number* by 77.
   (b) Decrement *Number* by 3.
   (c) Increment *Number* by twice its value.
   (d) Add the rightmost digit of *Number* to *Number*.
   (e) Decrement *Number* by the integer part of the real value *X*.

4. Write a Pascal assignment statement for each of the following that calculates the given expression and assigns the result to the specified variable. Assume that all variables are of type *real*, except where otherwise noted.

   (a) *Rate* times *Time* to *Distance*.
   (b) *X* incremented by an amount *DeltaX* to *X*.
   (c) $\dfrac{1}{\dfrac{1}{R1} + \dfrac{1}{R2} + \dfrac{1}{R3}}$ to *Resistance*.
   (d) Area of a triangle of base *b* and height *h* (one-half base times height) to *Area*.
   (e) The last three digits of the integer *StockNumber* with a decimal point before the last two digits to *Price* (e.g., if *StockNumber* is 1758316, *Price* is assigned the value of 3.16).
   (f) *Tax* rounded to the nearest dollar to *Tax*.

5. For each of the following, give values for the integer variables *a*, *b*, and *c* for which the two given expressions have different values:

   (a) $a * (b \textbf{ div } c)$ and $a * b \textbf{ div } c$
   (b) $a \textbf{ div } b$ and $a * (1 / b)$
   (c) $(a + b) \textbf{ div } c$ and $a \textbf{ div } c + b \textbf{ div } c$

3.5 Input/Output

In the preceding section we considered the assignment statement, which enables us to calculate the values of expressions and store the results of these computations by assigning them to variables. An assignment statement does not, however, display these results on some output device, nor does it allow the user to enter new values during execution. For example, a program to calculate the wages earned by John Doe, employee #31564, for 38.5 hours of work at an hourly rate of $8.75 could contain the variable section

var
    EmpNumber : *integer*;   (∗ employee number ∗)
    Hours,   (∗ hours worked ∗)
    Rate,   (∗ hourly pay rate ∗)
    Wages : *real*;   (∗ total wages ∗)

and the statement part

begin
    EmpNumber : = 31564;
    Hours : = 38.5;
    Rate : = 8.75;
    Wages : = *Hours* ∗ *Rate*
end.

The value of *Wages* is calculated as desired but is stored only internally in the memory location associated with *Wages* and is not displayed to the user. Moreover, if the same wage calculation is to be done for Mary Smith, employee #31565, who worked 37.5 hours at an hourly rate of $9.25, the statement part of the program must be almost completely rewritten, as follows:

begin
    EmpNumber : = 31565;
    Hours : = 37.5;
    Rate : = 9.25;
    Wages : = *Hours* ∗ *Rate*
end.

The output statement that we consider in this section provides a method for easily displaying information. We also consider an input statement that provides a convenient method of assigning values from an external source to variables during execution of the program.

Program Heading. Any collection of data to be input to a program or output from a program is called a ***file***. Some programs do not require any input from a file, since all values to be processed are assigned within the program. This is true, for example, in the preceding program segments. All useful programs, however, do produce some output, because the results obtained would not otherwise be displayed to the user.

The program heading in a Pascal program has the form

    program *name* (*file-list*);

where *name* is a valid Pascal identifier used to name the program and *file-list* is a list of files used in the program. Two standard files provided by the Pascal language are *input* and *output*. The file *input* refers to a system input device such as a terminal, and the file *output* refers to a system output device such as a terminal or a printer. An appropriate program heading for a Pascal program that does not require input could have the form

    program *name* (*output*);

A program that requires input and produces output could have a program heading of the form

    program *name* (*input, output*);

Output. There are two output statements in Pascal, the *write* and the *writeln* (read "write-line") statements. A simple form of the *writeln* statement is

    writeln (*output-list*)

where *output-list* is a single expression or a list of expressions separated by commas. Each of these expressions may be a constant, a variable, or a formula. Execution of a *writeln* statement displays the values of the items in the output list on the current line and then advances to the next line so that subsequent output will appear on a new line. For example, the statements

    writeln (*Alpha, Beta*);
    writeln (*Gamma, Delta*);

display the values of *Alpha* and *Beta* on one line and the values of *Gamma* and *Delta* on the next line. Subsequent output would begin on yet another line.

The values of the expressions in the output list of a *writeln* statement are displayed in **fields**, which are zones of consecutive positions in the output line. To illustrate, suppose that *Counter, RealNum, Code,* and *BooleVar* are variables declared by

    var
        Counter : *integer*;
        RealNum : *real*;
        Code : *char*;
        BooleVar : *boolean*;

and consider the following statements:

    Counter := 16;
    RealNum := 123.456;
    Code := 'A';
    BooleVar := *true*;
    writeln ('Counter');
    writeln (*Counter*);
    writeln (*Counter*, ' is even', *Counter* + 1, ' is odd');
    writeln (*RealNum, RealNum* / 70000);
    writeln (*Code*, 'B', 'C', '***');
    writeln (*BooleVar, false*);

These statements produce output similar to the following:

```
Counter_____
_____16_____
_____16 is even_____17 is odd_
_1.234560000E+02 1.763657143E-03
ABC***_____
TRUE FALSE_____
```

The format of the output will vary from one system to another, since the field widths used for integer, real, and boolean values are compiler dependent. For a character or a string value, however, the field width is the number of characters in that value. Note that numeric values are **right-justified** in their fields— that is, they are placed so that the last digit is in the rightmost position of the field—and that real values are displayed in floating point notation.

The *write* statement has the form

    write (output-list)

where the output list has the same form as for *writeln*. When this statement is executed, the values are displayed on the current line, but *there is no advance to a new line.*[2] Consequently, any subsequent output will be displayed on this same line. For example, the statements

    write ('A');
    write ('B');
    write ('C');
    writeln ('DEF');
    writeln ('GHI')

produce as output

```
ABCDEF
GHI___
```

The *writeln* statement, but not *write*, may also be used with no output list to advance to a new line. In this case, the parentheses used to enclose the output list are also omitted, and so the statement has the form

    writeln

Execution of this statement produces a blank line unless the last preceding output statement was a *write* statement, in which case output to the current line

---

[2]In some implementations of Pascal, *write* may not produce immediate output but, rather, "buffer" it (store it temporarily) for output at a later time. In fact, this may also be true for *writeln*. In this text, however, we assume that both *write* and *writeln* produce immediate output.

is terminated and subsequent output begins on a new line. For example, consider the statements

Counter := 16;
write (*Counter*, ' is even');
write (*Counter* + 1, ' is odd');
writeln;
writeln ('**********');
writeln ('*   *');
writeln ('**********');
writeln;
writeln (2 * *Counter*, ' is even');

These statements produce output similar to the following:

```
_____16 is even_____17 is odd
**********_____
*_____*_____
**********_____
_____
_____32 is even_____
```

In an earlier example in this section we considered the problem of calculating wages for an employee. To display some of the relevant information from this example, we might add several *writeln* statements, as shown in the program in Figure 3.1.

```
PROGRAM WageCalculation (output);

(*******************************************************************

   This program calculates wages as hours * rate for a given number
   of hours worked and a given hourly rate for some employee
   identified by his/her employee number.

*******************************************************************)

VAR
   EmpNumber : integer;    (* employee number *)
   Hours,                  (* hours worked *)
   Rate,                   (* hourly rate *)
   Wages : real;           (* gross wages earned *)

BEGIN
   EmpNumber := 31564;
   Hours := 38.5;
   Rate := 8.75;
   Wages := Hours * Rate;
   writeln ('Employee #', EmpNumber);
   writeln ('Hours worked:  ', Hours);
   writeln ('Hourly rate:  $', Rate);
   writeln ('Total Wages:  $', Wages)
END.
```

Figure 3.1

Figure 3.1 (cont.)

<u>Sample run:</u>

```
Employee #   31564
Hours worked:   3.850000000E+01
Hourly rate:  $ 8.750000000E+00
Total Wages:  $ 3.368750000E+02
```

The output produced by this program is not really satisfactory, for two reasons. First, too many spaces are used to display the values, and second, the real values are displayed in an exponential form that is not appropriate for monetary values. These deficiencies can be remedied by specifying the format of the output, by appending **_format descriptors_** to the items in the output list.

A format descriptor can have one of two forms

:*w*

or

:*w*:*d*

In both forms, *w* is a positive integer expression that specifies the field width to be used in displaying the corresponding value. For example, in the statement

writeln (*Counter*:2, ' is even', *Counter* + 1 : 5, ' is odd')

the format descriptor :2 specifies that the value of *Counter* is to be displayed in a field of width 2, and the format descriptor :5 specifies that the value of *Counter* + 1 is to be displayed in a field of width 5. If *Counter* has the value 16, the output produced by this statement will be

<u>16 is even   17 is odd</u>

If *Zone* is an integer variable with value 2, the statement

writeln (*Counter*:*Zone*, ' is even', *Counter* + 1 : *Zone* + 3, ' is odd')

will produce this same output. The statement

writeln (*Counter*:1, ' is even', *Counter* + 1 : 1, ' is odd')

produces

<u>16 is even17 is odd</u>

As this last example demonstrates, if a numeric value is too large for the specified field, then the field is automatically enlarged to accommodate it. Thus, because the value 16 of *Counter* has two digits, the field of size 1 specified for it by *Counter*:1 is enlarged so that both digits are displayed. But if a field is too small for a character, string, or boolean value, it is not enlarged, and only the leftmost *w* characters are displayed where *w* is the specified field width. Consequently, the output produced by the statement

>   *writeln* (*Counter*:1, ' is even':7, *Counter* + 1 : 1,' is odd':5)

is

```
16 is eve17 is o
```

If the field width is larger than necessary, the value is *right-justified* in the field. Thus, the output produced by the statement

>   *writeln* (*Counter*:5, 'is even':8, *Counter* + 1 : 10, 'is odd':8)

is

```
      16 is even          17   is odd
```

If a real value is output using the format descriptor :*w*, it is displayed in exponential form. If the usual decimal form for a real value is desired, a format descriptor of the form :*w*:*d* must be used. In this descriptor, *d* is an integer expression specifying the number of digits to be displayed to the right of the decimal point. To illustrate, suppose that *Alpha* and *Beta* are real variables with the values 3.51 and − 123.47168, respectively. The statements

>   *write* (*Alpha*:4:2);
>   *write* (*Beta*:12:5);
>   *writeln*;

produce the output

```
3.51  -123.47168
```

Note that the values are right-justified in the specified fields.

If *d* is larger than the number of digits to the right of the decimal point in the value being displayed, zeros are added as necessary. For example, the statement

>   *writeln* (*Alpha*:8:4, *Beta*:12:6);

produces the output

```
  3.5100 -123.471680
```

If the value of *d* is too small, the value to be displayed is *rounded* to *d* decimal places. Thus the output produced by the statements

> *writeln* (*Alpha*:8:2, *Beta*:12:3);
> *writeln* (*Alpha*:8:1, *Beta*:12:1);

is

```
     3.51      -123.472
      3.5         -123.5
```

If *w* is too small, the field is enlarged as necessary. For example, the statement

> *writeln* (*Alpha*:3:1, *Beta*:3:1);

produces the output

```
3.5-123.5
```

Either *w* or *d* in a descriptor of the form :*w*:*d* may be an expression. To illustrate, suppose that *Zone* and *NumDigits* are integer variables with the values 8 and 2, respectively. The statements

> *writeln* (*Alpha* + 3 : *Zone* : *NumDigits*);
> *writeln* (*Beta* + 1 : *Zone* + 1 : *NumDigits* + 1);

produce the output

```
     6.51
 -122.472
```

We remarked earlier that the output produced by the program in Figure 3.1 is not really satisfactory. The program in Figure 3.2 is a modification that uses format descriptors to display the results in a more acceptable format.

```
PROGRAM WageCalculation (output);

(*****************************************************************

    This program calculates wages as hours * rate for a given number
    of hours worked and a given hourly rate for some employee
    identified by his/her employee number.

    *************************************************************)

VAR
    EmpNumber : integer;    (* employee number *)
    Hours,                  (* hours worked *)
    Rate,                   (* hourly rate *)
    Wages : real;           (* gross wages earned *)
```

Figure 3.2

Figure 3.2   (cont.)

```
BEGIN
    EmpNumber := 31564;
    Hours := 38.5;
    Rate := 8.75;
    Wages := Hours * Rate;
    writeln ('Employee # ', EmpNumber:1);
    writeln ('Hours worked:  ', Hours:7:2);
    writeln ('Hourly rate:  $', Rate:7:2);
    writeln ('Total wages:  $', Wages:7:2)
END.
```

Sample run:

```
Employee # 31564
Hours worked:    38.50
Hourly rate: $    8.75
Total wages: $ 336.88
```

Input.   There are two input statements in Pascal, the *read* and the *readln* (read "read line") statements. A simple form of the *readln* statement is

>   *readln* (*input-list*)

where *input-list* consists of a single variable or a list of variables separated by commas. A *readln* statement reads values from the standard file *input* and assigns them to the variables in the input list. Recall that the standard file *input* refers to a system input device such as a terminal. Most of the examples in this text assume interactive input, so that data values are entered by the user during program execution rather than from some file prepared before execution begins.

To illustrate, consider the statement

>   *readln* (*EmpNumber, Hours, Rate*)

where *EmpNumber* is an integer variable and *Hours* and *Rate* are real variables. If the data values

>   31564 38.5 8.75

are entered, the value 31564 is assigned to the variable *EmpNumber*, 38.5 to *Hours*, and 8.75 to *Rate*. Thus this single *readln* statement can replace the three assignment statements

>   *EmpNumber* := 31564;
>   *Hours* := 38.5;
>   *Rate* := 8.75;

used in the programs of Figures 3.1 and 3.2. The modified program is shown in Figure 3.3. Note that because the program involves both input and output, the program heading includes both of the standard files *input* and *output*.

```
PROGRAM WageCalculation (input, output);

(****************************************************************

   This program calculates wages as hours * rate for an employee
   identified by his/her employee number.  The employee number,
   hours worked, and hourly rate are read during execution.

****************************************************************)

VAR
   EmpNumber : integer;    (* employee number *)
   Hours,                  (* hours worked *)
   Rate,                   (* hourly rate *)
   Wages : real;           (* gross wages earned *)

BEGIN
   readln (EmpNumber, Hours, Rate);
   Wages := Hours * Rate;
   writeln ('Employee # ', EmpNumber:1);
   writeln ('Hours worked:   ', Hours:7:2);
   writeln ('Hourly rate:  $', Rate:7:2);
   writeln ('Total wages:  $', Wages:7:2)
END.


Sample run:

31564 38.5 8.75
Employee # 31564
Hours worked:     38.50
Hourly rate:  $    8.75
Total wages:  $ 336.88
```

Figure 3.3

Data values entered for the variables in the input list of a *readln* statement must be constants, and consecutive numbers should be separated by one or more blanks. They must be arranged so that the type of each value agrees with that of the variable to which it is to be assigned. Assignment of a real value to an integer variable is not allowed, although an integer value may be read and assigned to a real variable.

After values have been read for all of the variables in the input list, a *readln* statement causes an advance to a new input line from which subsequent values will be read. Consequently, if there are more values in the current input line than there are variables in the input list, the first data values are read, but all remaining values are ignored.

If there are fewer entries in a line of input data than variables in the input list, successive lines of input data are processed until values for all variables in the input list have been obtained. Thus for the statement

readln (EmpNumber, Hours, Rate)

the values for *EmpNumber, Hours,* and *Rate* can all be entered on the same line:

31564 38.5 8.75

or on three separate lines:

31564
38.5
8.75

or with the value for *EmpNumber* on the first line and the values for *Hours* and *Rate* on the next line:

31564
38.5 8.75

and so on.

In a batch mode of operation, these lines of input data are obtained from some previously prepared data file. When a *readln* statement is encountered, the values from this file are retrieved automatically and assigned to the variables in the input list.

In an interactive mode of operation, the values assigned to variables in an input list are entered by the user. In this case, when a *readln* statement is encountered, program execution is suspended until the user enters values for all variables in the input list. Program execution then automatically resumes. Because execution is interrupted and because the correct number and types of values must be entered before execution can resume, *it is good practice to provide some message to prompt the user when it is necessary to enter data values.* This is accomplished by preceding input statements with output statements that display appropriate prompts. The program in Figure 3.4 illustrates this by prompting the user when values for *EmpNumber, Hours,* and *Rate* are to be entered; it is a modification of the program in Figure 3.3.

```
PROGRAM WageCalculation (input, output);

(****************************************************************

   This program calculates wages as hours * rate for an employee
   identified by his/her employee number.  The employee number,
   hours worked, and hourly rate are read during execution.

****************************************************************)
```

Figure 3.4

Figure 3.4   (cont.)

```
VAR
   EmpNumber : integer;    (* employee number *)
   Hours,                  (* hours worked *)
   Rate,                   (* hourly rate *)
   Wages : real;           (* gross wages earned *)


BEGIN
   write ('Enter employee number:  ');
   readln (EmpNumber);
   write ('Enter hours worked and hourly rate:  ');
   readln (Hours, Rate);
   Wages := Hours * Rate;
   writeln ('Employee # ', EmpNumber:1);
   writeln ('Hours worked:  ', Hours:7:2);
   writeln ('Hourly rate:  $', Rate:7:2);
   writeln ('Total wages:  $', Wages:7:2)
END.
```

Sample run:

```
Enter employee number:  31564
Enter hours worked and hourly rate:  38.5 8.75
Employee # 31564
Hours worked:    38.50
Hourly rate:  $    8.75
Total wages:  $ 336.88
```

Another input statement is a *read* statement of the form

>   read *(input-list)*

where *input-list* has the same form as for *readln*. This statement is similar to the *readln* statement except that it does *not* advance to a new input line after values have been read for the variables in the input list. To illustrate, consider the statement

>   read *(EmpNumber, Hours, Rate)*

and suppose that the data values are entered as follows:

>   31564 38.5 8.75 31523
>   40.0   8.25

As in the case of the earlier *readln* statement, the values read for *EmpNumber*, *Hours*, and *Rate* are 31564, 38.5, and 8.75, respectively. However, if this statement is executed again, the value 31523 will be read for *EmpNumber*, 40.0 for *Hours* (ends of lines are ignored for numeric input), and 8.25 for *Rate*.

Another distinction between the *read* and *readln* statements is that *readln*, but not *read*, may be used with no input list:

readln

Note that in this case the parentheses are also omitted. Execution of this statement terminates input from the current line, so that subsequent input begins with a new line. It may thus be used to skip a line of input or to skip over values that remain in the current line.

Exercises

1. Assuming that *Alpha* and *Beta* are real variables with values -567.392 and 0.0004, respectively, and that *Rho* is an integer variable with a value 436, show precisely the output that each of the following sets of statements produces, or explain why an error occurs:

   (a) *writeln (Rho);*
        writeln (Rho + 1);
        writeln (Rho + 2);

   (b) *write (Rho);*
        write (Rho + 1);
        writeln (Rho + 2);

   (c) *write ('Alpha = ');*
        write (Alpha:9:3);
        write ('Beta =':7);
        writeln (Beta:7:4);

   (d) *write (Rho:5, 2 * Rho:5);*
        writeln;
        writeln (Beta:10:5);

   (e) *writeln (Alpha:8:1, Rho:5);*
        writeln ('Tolerance:', Beta:8:5);

   (f) *writeln ('Alpha =', Alpha:12:5);*
        writeln ('Beta =', Beta:6:2, ' ':4, 'Rho =', Rho:6);
        writeln (Alpha + 4.0 + Rho:15:3);

   (g) *write ('Tolerance =' :8);*
        writeln (Beta:5:3);
        writeln;
        writeln;
        writeln (Rho:2, Alpha:4:2);

   (h) *writeln (10 * Alpha:8:1, trunc(10 * Alpha):8, round(10 * Alpha):8);*
        *writeln (sqr(Rho **div** 100):5, sqrt(Rho **div** 100):5);*

   (i) *writeln ('Rho =':7, Rho:8:2);*
        *writeln ('*****');*

   (j) *write (Alpha:10);*
        write;
        writeln (Beta:10);

2. Assuming that *I* and *J* are integer variables with $I = 15$ and $J = 8$, that *C* and *D* are character variables with $C =$ 'C' and $D =$ ' $-$ ', and

that *X* and *Y* are real variables with *X* = 2559.50 and *Y* = 8.015, show precisely the output that each of the following sets of statements produce:

(a) *writeln* ('New balance =':*I*, *X*:*J*:2);
   writeln (*C*:*I* **mod** 10, *Y*:*J*:*J* − 6);
(b) *write* ('I =' :*I*);
   write (*I*:*I*);
   writeln ('J =' :*J*, *J*:*J*);
   writeln;
   writeln (*I*:*J*, *J*:*I*);
   writeln (*trunc*(*X* / *J*):*J*, *J* − *Y*:*I*:*J*, *D*:*J* **div** 7)

3. Assume that *N1* and *N2* are integer variables with values 39 and −5117, respectively; that *R1* and *R2* are real variables with values 56.7173 and −0.00247, respectively; and that *C* is a character variable with value F. For each of the following, write a set of output statements that use these variables to produce the given output:

(a) __56.7173___F___39
   −5117PDQ−0.00247__

(b) __56.717_____−0.0025***39__F
   ____56.72__39−5117_____

(c) ROOTS_ARE__56.717_AND_−0.00247

(d) APPROXIMATE_ANGLES:__56.7_AND_−0.0
   MAGNITUDES_ARE_____39_AND__5117___

4. Assuming that *A*, *B*, and *C* are integer variables and *X*, *Y*, and *Z* are real variables, tell what value, if any, will be assigned to each of these variables, or explain why an error occurs, when each of the following sets of statements is executed with the given input data:

(a) *readln* (*A*, *B*, *C*, *X*, *Y*, *Z*);   Input: 1 2 3
                      4 5.5 6.6

(b) *readln* (*A*, *B*, *C*);   Input: 1
   readln (*X*, *Y*, *Z*);   2
                 3
                 4
                 5
                 6

(c) *read* (*A*, *X*);   Input: 1 2.2
   read (*B*, *Y*);   3 4.4
   read (*C*, *Z*);   5 6.6

(d) *read* (*A*, *B*, *C*);   Input: 1 2.2
   readln (*X*, *Y*, *Z*);   3 4.4
                   5 6.6

    (e) *read (A);*   Input: 1   2   3
         readln (B, C);   4 5.5 6.6
         read (X, Y);
         readln (Z);

    (f) *readln (A);*   Input: 1   2   3
         read (B, C);   4 5.5 6.6
         readln (X, Y);
         read (Z);

    (g) *read (A, B);*   Input: 1   2   3
         readln;   4 5.5 6.6
         read (C);   7 8.8 9.9
         read (X);   10 11.11 12.12
         readln;   13 14.14 15.15
         readln (Y);
         readln;
         readln (Z);

3.6 Program Composition

As noted in Section 3.1, a Pascal program consists of three parts:

    program heading
    declaration part
    statement part.

These three parts *must* appear in the order shown. The **_program heading_** is a single statement of the form

    program *name* (*file-list*);

as described in the preceding section. The name assigned to the program must be a legal Pascal identifier, distinct from any other identifier used in the program. The program heading should normally be followed by **_opening documentation_** in the form of comments that describe the nature and purpose of the program and other information, such as the author of the program, when it was written, when it was last modified, and so on.

    The **_declaration part_** of a Pascal program may contain up to five sections that define various entities used in the program. These sections in the order in which they must appear are

    label section
    constant section
    type section
    variable section
    subprogram section

The **_constant section_** has the form

const
 identifier-1 = *constant-1*;
 identifier-2 = *constant-2*;
   ⋮
 identifier-k = *constant-k*;

and is used to assign names to constants, as described in Section 3.2. The
variable section has the form

var
 variable-list-1 : *type-1*;
 variable-list-2 : *type-2*;
   ⋮
 variable-list-m : *type-m*;

and is used to declare *all* the variables used in the program, that is, to specify
their names and types. This also was discussed in Section 3.2. The other
sections of the declaration part will be discussed later.

 The *statement part* of the program has the form

begin
 statement-1;
 statement-2;
   ⋮
 statement-n
end

This part of the program contains the statements that implement the steps of
an algorithm. It may include such statements as assignment statements, in-
put/output statements, and other statements considered in subsequent chapters
of this book.

 Correct punctuation is critical in a Pascal program, and each of the sections
must be punctuated exactly as indicated. In particular, the program heading,
each constant definition, and each variable declaration must end with a semicolon. In the statement part, the statements are *separated* by semicolons, but
there need be no semicolon following the last statement. Finally, note that a
period must follow the reserved word **end** that closes the statement part of the
program.

 We have seen that comments are indicated in a Pascal program by enclosing them between (∗ and ∗):

 (∗ *comment* ∗)

or within braces:

 { *comment* }

These comments are not program statements and may be placed anywhere in
the program, except, of course, in the middle of a reserved word, an identifier,

a constant, and so on. As discussed in Section 2.5, comments should be used to explain the use of variables, to explain the purpose of the program or a program segment, and to provide other pertinent information about the program. Such documentation is intended to clarify the purpose and structure of the program. It is invaluable if revisions and modifications are made to the program in the future, especially if such maintenance is done by persons other than the original programmer.

3.7   Example: Truck Fleet Accounting

Suppose that a manufacturing company maintains a fleet of trucks to deliver its products. On each trip, the driver records the distance traveled in miles, the number of gallons of fuel used, the cost of the fuel, and the other costs of operating the truck. As part of the accounting process, the comptroller needs to calculate and record for each truck and for each trip the miles per gallon, the total cost of that trip, and the cost per mile. A simple program is to be designed to carry out these calculations.

The input to the program is the miles traveled, gallons of fuel used, fuel cost, and other operating costs, and the output must include the miles per gallon, the total cost of the trip, and the cost per mile. The calculations required to solve this program are quite simple. The miles per gallon is obtained by dividing the number of miles traveled by the number of gallons of fuel used. The total cost is obtained by adding the cost of fuel to the other operating costs. This sum is divided by the number of miles traveled to yield the cost per mile.

Expressing this algorithm in pseudocode is quite straightforward once we select the appropriate variable names to represent the quantities involved. Selecting names that are self-documenting, we use the following:

Miles	Total miles traveled
Fuel	Total gallons of fuel used
FuelCost	Total cost of fuel
OperCost	Total of other operating costs
Mpg	Miles per gallon
TotalCost	Total cost of the trip
CostPerMile	Cost per mile

A pseudocode description of the algorithm is the following:

ALGORITHM TO CALCULATE TRUCK COSTS

(∗ This algorithm calculates miles per gallon (*Mpg*), total cost of the trip (*TotalCost*), and cost per mile (*CostPerMile*), given the number of miles traveled (*Miles*), gallons of fuel used (*Fuel*), cost of the fuel (*FuelCost*) and other operating costs (*OperCost*). ∗)

1. Enter *Miles, Fuel, FuelCost*, and *OperCost*.
2. Calculate *Mpg = Miles / Fuel*.
3. Calculate *TotalCost = FuelCost + OperCost*.

  4. Calculate *CostPerMile = TotalCost / Miles*.
  5. Display *Mpg, TotalCost*, and *CostPerMile*.

A Pascal program implementing this algorithm with two sample runs using test data to verify its correctness are shown in Figure 3.5.

```
PROGRAM TruckCosts (input, output);

(*********************************************************************

   This program calculates the miles per gallon, total cost, and cost
   per mile for the operation of a vehicle based on the miles traveled,
   fuel consumed, cost of fuel, and other operating costs.

*********************************************************************)

VAR
    Miles : integer;       (* total miles traveled *)
    Fuel,                  (* total gallons of fuel used *)
    FuelCost,              (* total cost of fuel *)
    OperCost,              (* total of other operating costs *)
    Mpg,                   (* miles per gallon *)
    TotalCost,             (* total cost of the trip *)
    CostPerMile : real;    (* cost per mile *)

BEGIN
    writeln ('Enter miles traveled, gallons of fuel used,');
    writeln ('total cost of fuel, and total of other costs:');
    readln (Miles, Fuel, FuelCost, OperCost);
    Mpg := Miles / Fuel;
    TotalCost := FuelCost + OperCost;
    CostPerMile := TotalCost / Miles;
    writeln ('Miles per gallon:', Mpg:7:2);
    writeln ('Total cost:      $', TotalCost:7:2);
    writeln ('Cost per mile:   $', CostPerMile:7:2)
END.
```

Sample runs:

```
Enter miles traveled, gallons of fuel used,
total cost of fuel, and total of other costs:
10 1 1.50 3.50
Miles per gallon:   10.00
Total cost:      $    5.00
Cost per mile:   $    0.50


Enter miles traveled, gallons of fuel used,
total cost of fuel, and total of other costs:
100 10 15 10
Miles per gallon:   10.00
Total cost:      $   25.00
Cost per mile:   $    0.25
```

Figure 3.5

3.8 Syntax and Semantics

In this chapter we introduced enough of the basic features of the Pascal language that we can write simple Pascal programs like that in the preceding section. We have described the general structure of a program as well as some of the declarations, operations, statements, and other items that make up a program. In each case we described the general form of these items and what they are intended to accomplish. The rules that specify the precise form of a program and of each of its components are called the ***syntax rules*** of the language, and the interpretation or meaning of these items is called the ***semantics*** of the language.

A ***syntax diagram*** is one convenient method for presenting syntax rules. For example, in Section 3.2 we specified the syntax of a Pascal identifier by stating that it must begin with a letter, which may be followed by any number of letters or digits. This syntax rule can also be given by the following syntax diagram:

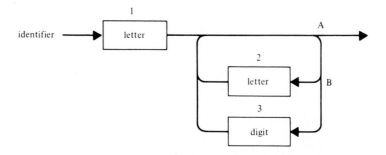

To use this diagram as a syntax rule for forming identifiers, we begin on the left and proceed to the right. Each time we pass through one of the boxes, we record a character of the specified type. At a junction in the diagram, any one of the paths may be followed. When we exit from the right, we will have formed a legal identifier. For example, the identifier *x14a* can be formed as follows: Beginning on the left and passing through the first box, we record the letter *x*. Moving to the right, at Junction A we loop back, passing through Box 3, and record the digit *1*. When we return to Junction A, we loop back again and record the digit *4* when we pass through Box 3. At Junction A we loop back one final time, but this time at Junction B we take the path through Box 2 and record the letter *a*. Finally, at Junction A we proceed to the right and exit, having formed the identifier *x14a*. (We labeled the boxes and junctions of the syntax diagram to facilitate our discussion, though normally such labels are not used.)

A syntax diagram may also be used to specify the syntax of a Pascal statement. For example, a syntax diagram specifying the correct form of an assignment statement is the following:

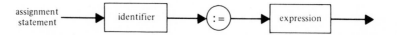

In a syntax diagram such as this one, the rectangular boxes indicate a language construct for which syntax rules must be specified, perhaps using syntax diagrams like that for an identifier. The circles or oval figures indicate symbols or reserved words in Pascal that must appear exactly as shown. For example, : = is a symbol that must be used to represent the assignment operator in an assignment statement.

It must be noted that such a diagram displays only the syntax of this statement but not its semantics. Additional information must be given to describe the meaning of this statement, namely, that the expression is evaluated and this value is then assigned to a variable of appropriate type; that is, it is stored in the memory location associated with the variable.

A syntax diagram may also be used to specify the form of a Pascal program:

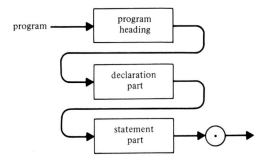

Each of the three parts of a program can also be described by a syntax diagram. For example,

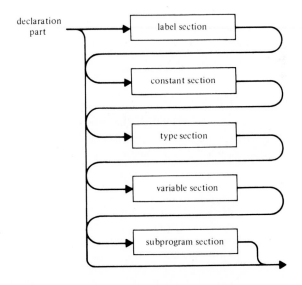

specifies the structure of the declaration part and

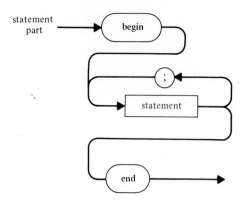

specifies the syntax of the statement part.

Syntax diagrams provide a convenient mechanism for precisely defining the syntax rules for Pascal, and in subsequent chapters, we will use them to summarize the syntax of each new Pascal feature. A complete set of syntax diagrams for the various components of a Pascal program is given in Appendix C.

Exercises

1. A "thing" is defined by the following syntax diagrams:

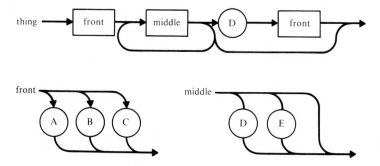

Determine which of the following are valid things:

(a) ADDDDDDA **(b)** ADDA **(c)** ADA **(d)** ABC **(e)** ADC **(f)** A

2. A widget is defined by the following syntax rules:

(a) A widget is a jabber followed by a wocky followed by a slash (/).
(b) A jabber is a thunk or a thunk followed by * or a thunk followed by a wocky.
(c) A thunk is the letter T followed by one of the digits 1, 2, or 3.
(d) A wocky is a thunk or a list of thunks separated by commas.

Give a complete set of syntax diagrams for widgets.

3. Write a program heading for a program named *Sample*, which will involve both input and output, a constant section to name 1900 with the name *Year* and the string Nat'l Science with *FieldOfStudy*, and a variable section that declares *Number* and *Prime* to be of integer type and *Initial* to be of character type.

4. **(a)** Verify that the expression *round*(100.0 ∗ *Cost*)/100 converts the real value *Cost* to dollars, rounding to the nearest cent, using the following values of *Cost*: (i) 12.342   (ii) 12.348   (iii) 12.345   (iv) 12.340   (v) 13.0.

   (b) Write an expression similar to that in part (a) that will round a real amount *X* to the nearest tenth.

   (c) Write an expression similar to that in part (a) that will round a real amount *X* to the nearest thousandth.

5. Describe the syntax errors in the following program:

```
(*  1 *)   PROGRAM Eror (output; input)
(*  2 *)      (* 'Example BEGIN END' *)
(*  3 *)   VAR
(*  4 *)      Alpha, Beta, Rho
(*  5 *)      : real;
(*  6 *)      Add, Sub, Mult, Div : integer
(*  7 *)   CONST Year := 1776;
(*  8 *)   BEGIN
(*  9 *)      Mult := 3.14;
(* 10 *)      readln (Div);
(* 11 *)      ALPha := 3;
(* 12 *)      Beta = Alpha + 1;
(* 13 *)      Rho := Beta MOD 3;
(* 14 *)      writeln ('Value is, Alpha:3:1);
(* 15 *)      writeln ('Gamma isn''t' negative');
(* 16 *)      writeln (Mult:3:1);
(* 17 *)      Year := Year + 1
(* 18 *)   END
```

6. Write a program that reads two three-digit integers and then calculates and prints their product and the quotient and the remainder that result when the first is divided by the second. The output should be formatted to appear as follows:

```
      739                   61 R    7
   x  12                   -----
   -----            12 ) 739
    8868
```

7. Write a program to read the lengths of the two legs of a right triangle, and calculate and print the area of the triangle (one half of the product of the legs) and the length of the hypotenuse (square root of the sum of the squares of the legs).

8. Write a program to read values for the coefficients *A*, *B*, and *C* of the quadratic equation $Ax^2 + Bx + C = 0$ and then find the two roots

of this equation by using the quadratic formula

$$\frac{-B \pm \sqrt{B^2 - 4AC}}{2A}$$

Execute the program with several values of A, B, and C for which the quantity $B^2 - 4AC$ is nonnegative, including $A = 4$, $B = 0$, $C = -36$; $A = 1$, $B = 5$, $C = -36$; $A = 2$, $B = 7.5$, $C = 6.25$.

9. Write a program to convert a measurement given in feet to the equivalent number of (a) yards, (b) inches, (c) centimeters, and (d) meters. (1 ft = 12 in., 1 yd = 3 ft, 1 in. = 2.54 cm, 1 m = 100 cm.) Read the number of feet, and print, with the appropriate labels, the number of yards, number of feet, number of inches, number of centimeters, and number of meters.

10. Write a program to read a student's number, his or her old GPA (grade point average), and old number of course credits (e.g., 31479, 3.25, 66) and to then print these with appropriate labels. Next, read the course credit and grade for each of four courses; for example, *Course1* = 5.0, *Grade1* = 3.7, *Course2* = 3.0, *Grade2* = 4.0, and so on. Calculate:

old # of honor points = (old # of course credits) ∗ (old GPA)

new # of honor points = *Course1* ∗ *Grade1* +
                                 Course2 ∗ *Grade2* + ⋯
total # of new course credits = *Course1* + *Course2* + ⋯

current GPA $= \dfrac{\text{\# of new honor points}}{\text{\# of new course credits}}$

Print the current GPA with appropriate label. Finally, calculate

cumulative GPA =

$$\frac{(\text{\# of old honor points}) + (\text{\# of new honor points})}{(\text{\# of old course credits}) + (\text{\# of new course credits})}$$

and print this with a label.

11. The shipping clerk at the Rinky Dooflingy Company (Exercise 10 of Section 2.5) is faced with the following problem: Dooflingies are very delicate and must be shipped in special containers. These containers are available in four sizes, huge, large, medium, and small, which can hold 50, 20, 5, and 1 dooflingy, respectively. Write a program that reads the number of dooflingies to be shipped and prints the number of huge, large, medium, and small containers needed to send the shipment in the minimum number of containers and with the minimum amount of wasted space. Use constant definitions for the number of dooflingies each type of container can hold. The output should be similar to the following:

```
Container   Number
=========   ======
  Huge        21
  Large        2
  Medium       1
  Small        3
```

Execute the program for 3, 18, 48, 78, and 10,598 dooflingies.

12. Write a program that reads the amount of a purchase and the amount received in payment (both amounts in cents) and then computes the change in dollars, half-dollars, quarters, dimes, nickels, and pennies.

13. Angles are often measured in degrees (°), minutes ('), and seconds ("). There are 360 degrees in a circle, 60 minutes in one degree, and 60 seconds in one minute. Write a program that reads two angular measurements given in degrees, minutes, and seconds and then calculates and prints their sum. Use the program to verify each of the following:

$$74°29'13'' + 105°8'16'' = 179°37'29''$$
$$7°14'55'' + 5°24'55'' = 12°39'50''$$
$$20°31'19'' + 0°31'30'' = 21°2'49''$$
$$122°17'48'' + 237°42'12'' = 0°0'0''$$

14. Write a program that reads two three-digit integers and then prints their product in the following format:

```
          749
   x      381
      --------
          749
         5992
         2247
      --------
        285369
```

Execute the program with the following values: 749 and 381; −749 and 381; 749 and −381; −749 and −381; 999 and 999.

Programming Pointers

In this section we consider some aspects of program design and suggest guidelines for good programming style. We also point out some errors that may occur in writing Pascal programs.

Program Design

1. *Programs cannot be considered correct if they have not been validated using test data.* Test all programs with data for which the results are known or can be checked by hand calculations.

2. *Programs should be readable and understandable.*

   ● *Use meaningful identifiers.*

   For example,

   Wages := *Hours* ∗ *Rate*

   is more meaningful than

   W := *H* ∗ *R*

   or

   Z7 := *Alpha* ∗ *X*

   Also, avoid "cute" identifiers, as in

   BaconBroughtHome := *HoursWasted* ∗ *Pittance*

   ● *Use comments to describe the purpose of a program or other key program segments.* However, don't clutter the program with needless comments; for example, the comment in the statement

   Counter := *Counter* + 1 (∗ add 1 to counter ∗)

   is not helpful and should not be used.

   ● *Label all output produced by a program.* For example,

   writeln ('Employee #', *EmpNumber*:5, ' Wages = $', *Wages*:8:2)

   produces more informative output than does

   writeln (*EmpNumber*:5, *Wages*:8:2)

3. *Programs should be general and flexible.* They should solve a class of problems rather than one specific problem. It should be relatively easy to modify a program to solve a related problem without changing much of the program. Using named constants instead of "magic numbers," as described in Section 3.2, is helpful in this regard.

Potential Problems

1. *Real constants must have at least one digit before and at least one digit after the decimal point.* Thus, 2. and .1 are not valid real constants.

2. *String constants must be enclosed within single quotes.* If either the beginning or ending quote is missing, an error will result. An apostrophe is represented in a character constant or a string constant as a pair of apostrophes, for example, 'isn''t'.

3. *Single characters, not strings of several characters, are assigned to variables of type* char.

4. *The boolean constants* true *and* false *are not the same as the string constants* 'true' *and* 'false'.

5. *Parentheses within expressions must be paired.* That is, for each left parenthesis there must be exactly one matching right parenthesis.

6. *Real division is denoted by* /, *integer division by* **div**. Thus 8 / 5 = 1.6, 8 **div** 5 = 1, 8.0 / 4.0 = 2.0, but 8.0 **div** 4.0 is not a valid expression.

7. *All multiplications must be indicated by* *. For example, 2 * *n* is valid, but 2*n* is not.

8. *A semicolon must appear*

   - *at the end of the program heading.*
   - *at the end of each constant declaration.*
   - *at the end of each variable declaration.*
   - *between statements.*

   No semicolon is necessary after the last statement of a program. However, it is not an error if one is used; for example,

   begin
     ⋮
     writeln ('Hourly rate: $', *Rate*);
     writeln ('Total Wages: $', *Wages*);
   end.

   The semicolon at the end of the last *writeln* statement produces an ***empty statement*** between this statement and the reserved word **end**.

9. *Comments are enclosed within* (* *and* *) *or* { *and* }. Each beginning delimiter (* must have a matching end delimiter *). Failure to use these in pairs can produce strange results. For example, in the statement part

   begin
     (* Read employee data)
     readln (*EmpNumber*, *Hours*, *Rate*);
     (* Calculate wages *)
     Wages := *Hours* * *Rate*
   end.

   everything from "Read employee data . . . " through "Calculate wages," including the *readln* statement, is a single comment. No values are read for *EmpNumber*, *Hours*, and *Rate*, and so *Hours* and *Rate* are undefined when the statement *Wages* := *Hours* * *Rate* is executed.

10. *There must be a period after the reserved word* **end** *at the end of the program.* Failure to include it is an error.

11. *All identifiers must be declared.* Failure to declare an identifier used in a program is an error.

12. *Pascal does not distinguish between uppercase and lowercase letters except in string constants.* For example, *Sum*, *sum*, and *SUM* all represent the same identifier. Thus, variable declarations such as

    var
       Sum : *integer*;
       SUM : *real*;

    produce an error, since the same identifier is declared more than once.

13. *All variables are initially undefined.* Although some compilers may initialize variables to specific values (e.g., 0 for numeric variables), it should be assumed that all variables are initially undefined. For example, the statement $y := x + 1$ usually produces a ''garbage'' value for y if x has not previously been assigned a value.

14. *The type of a variable and the type of its value must be the same.* Thus, entering the value 2.7 for the integer variable *Counter* in the statement

    readln (*Counter*)

    may generate an error message such as

    ```
    *** I/O error while reading input from the
    terminal.
    '.' found where '+', '-', or digit expected.
    ```

    Similarly, the assignment statement

    Counter := 2.7

    is also incorrect. An integer value may, however, be assigned to a real variable and is automatically converted to real type.

15. *Reserved words, identifiers, and constants, as well as the assignment operator, may not be broken at the end of a line, nor may they contain blanks (except, of course, a string constant may contain blanks).* Thus, the statements

    EmpNumber := 12345;
    writeln ('Employee number is ',
          EmpNumber:5)

    are valid, whereas the statements

    Emp Number := 12 345;
    writeln ('Employee number
          is ', *EmpNumber*:5)

    are not valid.

16. *An equal sign* (=) *is used in constant declarations to associate an identifier with a constant. The assignment operator* (:=) *is used in assignment statements to assign a value to a variable.* These two operators are not interchangeable; do not confuse them. Also, note that : = is a single operator; : and = may not be separated by a blank.

Program Style

In the examples in this text, we adopt certain stylistic guidelines for Pascal programs, and you should write your program in a similar style. In this text the following standards are used; others are described in the Programming Pointers of subsequent chapters.

1. *Put each statement of the program on a separate line.*

2. *Use uppercase and lowercase letters in a way that contributes to program readability;* for example, put reserved words in uppercase and identifiers in lowercase, capitalizing the first letter if it is user defined.

3. *Put the program heading and the reserved words* **begin, end, const,** *and* **var** *on separate lines.*

4. *When a statement is continued from one line to another, indent the continuation line(s).*

5. *Each* **begin** *and its corresponding* **end** *should be aligned. The statements enclosed by* **begin** *and* **end** *are indented.*

> **begin**
>   *statement-1;*
>   ⋮
>   *statement-n*
> **end**

6. *Indent each constant declaration and each variable declaration;* for example,

> **const**
>   *TaxRate* = 0.1963;
>   *InterestRate* = 0.185;
>
> **var**
>   *EmpNumber* : *integer;*
>   *Hours, Rate, Wages* : *real;*

7. *Insert a blank line before the* **const** *section, the* **var** *section, the beginning of the statement part of the program, and wherever appropriate in a sequence of statements to set off blocks of statements.*

8. *Use spaces between the items in a statement to make it more readable.*

Variations and Extensions

Variations and extensions of the features described in this chapter are provided in many versions of Pascal (see Appendix G for details). Some of these are

- Additional data types such as *shortint, longint, byte, word, single, double, extended, comp,* and *string*.

- Alternative representations of numbers (hexadecimal).

- Specified values for predefined constants (*maxint* = 32767) and/or additional predefined functions such as *pi*.

- Additional reserved words (**shl, shr, otherwise**).

- Other characters (underscore) allowed in identifiers and/or limits on the number of characters.

- Additional arithmetic operators (**shl, shr, not, and, or, xor**) and functions (*frac, int, log, pwroften*).

- Optional and/or modified forms of the program heading.

- Alternative forms of the declaration part.

- Variables may be initialized in the declaration part of a program.

- A program may include an import part which makes available to the program items defined externally.

4

Structured Programming and Modular Design

A journey of a thousand miles begins with a single step.

ANCIENT PROVERB

Then Logic would take you by the throat, and force you to do it!

ACHILLES IN LEWIS CARROLL'S
What the Tortoise Said to Achilles

But what has been said once can always be repeated.

ZENO OF ELEA

Great things can be reduced to small things, and small things can be reduced to nothing.

CHINESE PROVERB

In Chapter 2 we described several software engineering techniques that assist in the design of programs that are easy to understand and whose logical flow is easy to follow. Such programs are more likely to be correct when first written than are poorly structured programs; and if they are not correct, the errors are easier to find and correct. Such programs are also easier to modify, which is especially important, since such modifications may be required long after the program was originally written and are often made by someone other than the original programmer.

In this chapter we continue our study of basic software engineering principles and describe some of the features of the Pascal language that facilitate the development of well-structured programs. In a *structured program,* the logical flow is governed by the three basic control structures, *sequential, selection,* and *repetition.* Pascal provides several constructs that implement these control structures, and we now consider three of them: compound statements,

93

the **if** statement, and the **while** statement. Other Pascal control structures are described in the next chapter.

We also noted in Chapter 2 that complex problems can best be solved in a *top-down* manner that uses a *divide-and-conquer* approach of subdividing the problem into a number of simpler subproblems. In this chapter we introduce *procedures*, one of the features of Pascal that support this *modular* approach to programming.

4.1 Sequential Structure: Compound Statements; *begin* and *end*

Sequential structure, as illustrated in the following diagram, refers to the execution of a sequence of statements in the order in which they appear so that each statement is executed exactly once. The arrows in this diagram, called *flow lines,* indicate the order in which the statements are executed. In the case of a sequential structure, they clearly illustrate the ''straight-line'' pattern of execution. All the sample programs in Chapter 3 are straight-line programs in which the only control used is sequential.

In a Pascal program, a sequential structure is implemented by a *compound statement* whose syntax diagram is

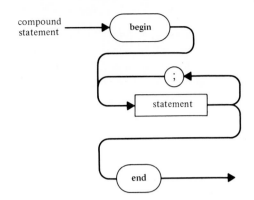

A compound statement thus consists of the reserved word **begin,** followed by a sequence of statements, followed by the reserved word **end,** and so has the form

> **begin**
>   *statement*-1;
>   *statement*-2;
>   ⋮
>   *statement*-n
> **end**

Note that semicolons are used to separate the statements that make up a compound statement.

Execution of the statements in a compound statement proceeds sequentially. For example, the compound statement

> **begin**
>   *write* ('Enter two numbers: ');
>   *readln (Number1, Number2)*;
>   *Sum* := *Number1* + *Number2*;
>   *writeln* ('Sum =', *Sum*)
> **end**

first displays a prompt to the user and then reads two numbers; next, it calculates their sum; and finally, it displays the result.

4.2   The Boolean Data Type

Several of the most useful Pascal statements that implement selection and repetition structures involve boolean expressions. Consequently, before we can describe these statements, we must examine in more detail the ***boolean*** data type.

Recall that there are two boolean constants, *true* and *false,* and that boolean variables may have only these values. The standard type identifier *boolean* is used to specify the type of a boolean variable; for example,

    var

      Male, Graduate, OnDeansList, OddValue : boolean;

declares that *Male, Graduate, OnDeansList,* and *OddValue* are boolean variables.

    Three predefined boolean-valued functions are provided in Pascal. One is the function *odd,* which returns the value *true* or *false* according to whether its integer parameter is an odd or even number. For example, if the integer variable *Number* has the value 17, then the value of the boolean expression

    odd(Number)

is *true*. The other two predefined boolean-valued functions, *eoln* and *eof,* are used in connection with file processing and are described in Chapter 7.

    Boolean values may be displayed with *write* or *writeln* statements, as described in Section 3.5, but values for boolean variables cannot be read (except from certain types of files, as described in Chapter 14). A boolean variable may, however, be assigned a value with an assignment statement of the form

    boolean-variable := *boolean-expression*

For example,

    Male := *true*;

assigns the boolean constant *true* to the boolean variable *Male,* and

    OddValue := *odd*(5 * *Number* + 1);

assigns *false* to *OddValue* if the integer variable *Number* has the value 3.

    Boolean expressions may be either **simple** or **compound.** Boolean constants and variables, as well as references to boolean-valued functions, are simple boolean expressions, as are expressions of the form

    expression-1 relational-operator expression-2

where *expression-1* and *expression-2* are of the same type and the **relational operator** may be any of the following:

Relational Operator	Definition
<	is less than (or precedes)
>	is greater than (or follows)
=	is equal to
<=	is less than or equal to
>=	is greater than or equal to
<>	is not equal to

These relational operators may be used with any of the four standard data types: integer, real, boolean, and character (as well as other ordinal types considered in Chapter 8). The following are examples of boolean expressions formed using these relational operators:

$x < 5.2$
$sqr(b) >= 4*a*c$
$Number = 500$
$Initial <> 'Q'$

For character data, a **collating sequence** is used to establish an ordering for the character set. This sequence varies from one machine to another, but in all cases, the letters are in alphabetical order, and the digits are in numerical order. Thus

$'A' < 'F'$
$'6' > '4'$

are true boolean expressions. Comparison of characters and strings is discussed in more detail in Chapter 8.

For boolean values, the constant *false* is less than the constant *true*. Thus,

$false < true$
$true > false$

are true boolean expressions.

For numeric data, the relational operators are the standard ones used to compare numbers. Thus, if x has the value 4.5, the expression $x < 5.2$ is true. If *Number* has the value 400, the expression $Number = 500$ is false.

When using the relational operators $=$ and $<>$ to compare numeric quantities, it is important to remember that *many real values cannot be stored exactly* (see Section 1.3). *Consequently, boolean expressions formed by comparing real quantities with $=$ may be evaluated as false, even though these quantities are algebraically equal.* The program in Figure 4.1 demonstrates this by showing that for most real values X, the value of Y computed by

$Y := X * (1.0 / X);$

is not 1. In this program, the assignment statement

$EqualsOne := (Y = 1.0);$

calculates the value of the boolean expression $Y = 1.0$ and assigns this value to the boolean variable *EqualsOne*. The value of this expression is the boolean constant *true* if the value of Y is equal to 1.0 and is *false* otherwise.

```
PROGRAM RoundoffError (input, output);

(*******************************************************************

        Program to show inexact representation of reals.

*******************************************************************)

VAR
    X,                       (* real number entered *)
    Y : real;                (* Y = X * (1 / X) *)
    EqualsOne : boolean; (* indicates if value of Y is 1 *)

BEGIN
    write ('Enter real # :  ');
    readln (X);
    Y := X * (1.0 / X);
    writeln ('X = ', X:7:5, '   Y = X*(1/X) = ', Y:7:5,
           '  1.0 - Y = ', 1.0 - Y:12);
    EqualsOne := (Y = 1.0);    (* Assigns true to EqualsOne if Y
                                  is equal to one; false otherwise *)
    writeln ('Y equals 1?   ', EqualsOne)
END.
```

Sample runs:

```
Enter real # :  0.5
X = 0.50000    Y = X*(1/X) = 1.00000    1.0 - Y =  0.00000E+00
Y equals 1?    TRUE


Enter real # :  0.1
X = 0.10000    Y = X*(1/X) = 1.00000    1.0 - Y =  7.10543E-15
Y equals 1?    FALSE


Enter real # :  0.2
X = 0.20000    Y = X*(1/X) = 1.00000    1.0 - Y =  7.10543E-15
Y equals 1?    FALSE


Enter real # :  6.39631
X = 6.39631    Y = X*(1/X) = 1.00000    1.0 - Y =  7.10543E-15
Y equals 1?    FALSE
```

Figure 4.1

Compound boolean expressions are formed by combining boolean expressions using the ***boolean operators***

> **not**
> **and**
> **or**

These operators are defined as follows:

Boolean Operator	Boolean Expression	Definition
not	not *p*	*negation* of *p*: **not** *p* is false if *p* is true; **not** *p* is true if *p* is false.
and	*p* and *q*	*conjunction* of *p* and *q*: *p* **and** *q* is true if both *p* and *q* are true; it is false otherwise.
or	*p* or *q*	*disjunction* of *p* and *q*: *p* **or** *q* is true if either *p* or *q* or both are true; it is false otherwise.

These definitions are summarized by the following ***truth tables,*** which display all possible values for *p* and *q* and the corresponding values of the boolean expression:

p	not *p*
true	false
false	true

p	*q*	*p* or *q*
true	true	true
true	false	true
false	true	true
false	false	false

p	*q*	*p* and *q*
true	true	true
true	false	false
false	true	false
false	false	false

In a boolean expression containing several of these operators, the operations are performed in the order **not, and, or.** Parentheses may be used to indicate subexpressions that should be evaluated first. For example, given the boolean variables *Male, OnDeansList,* and *Graduate,* we can form boolean expressions such as

> *Male* **and** *OnDeansList*
> **not** *Male* **and** *Graduate*
> *Male* **and** (*OnDeansList* **or** *Graduate*)

The first expression, *Male* **and** *OnDeansList,* is true only in the case that both *Male* and *OnDeansList* are true. In the second example, the subexpression **not** *Male* is evaluated first, and this result is then combined with the value of *Graduate,* using the operator **and.** The entire expression is therefore true only in the case that *Male* is false and *Graduate* is true. In the last example, the subexpression *OnDeansList* **or** *Graduate* is evaluated first; the possible values it may have are displayed in the following truth table:

Male	*OnDeansList*	*Graduate*	*Male* **and** (*OnDeansList* **or** *Graduate*)
true	true	true	true
true	true	false	true
true	false	true	true
true	false	false	false
false	true	true	true
false	true	false	true
false	false	true	true
false	false	false	false

This value is then combined with the value of *Male* using the operator **and:**

Male	OnDeansList	Graduate	Male **and** (OnDeansList **or** Graduate)	
true	true	true	true	true
true	true	false	true	true
true	false	true	true	true
true	false	false	false	false
false	true	true	false	true
false	true	false	false	true
false	false	true	false	true
false	false	false	false	false

As this truth table indicates, the entire expression is true only in the case that *Male* is true and either *OnDeansList* or *Graduate* (or both) is true.

The evaluation of a boolean expression that contains an assortment of arithmetic operators, boolean operators, and relational operators is carried out using the following *priority levels*:

Operator	Priority	
not	1	highest (performed first)
/, *, div, mod, and	2	
+, −, or	3	
<, >, =, <=, >=, <>	4	lowest (performed last)

As an example, consider the expression

$$(N <> 0) \textbf{ and } (X < 1/N)$$

Had the parentheses not been used to enclose the two simple boolean expressions, the resulting expression

$$N <> 0 \textbf{ and } X < 1/N$$

would be equivalent to the expression

$$N <> (0 \textbf{ and } X) < 1/N$$

since the highest priority operator **and** is evaluated first. This is clearly not a valid expression because the boolean operator **and** cannot be applied to numeric operands.

As an application of boolean expressions, consider the following logical circuit, called a ***binary half-adder***, which can be used to add two binary digits:

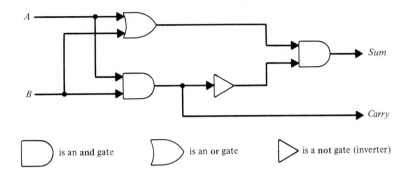

This circuit is designed to accept two inputs, *A* and *B*, and produce two outputs, *Sum* and *Carry*. It contains four basic electronic components called ***gates,*** two **and** gates, one **or** gate, and one **not** gate (also called an *inverter*). The inputs to these gates are pulses of current applied to the lines leading into the gates, and the outputs are pulses of current on the lines emanating from the gates. In the case of an **and** gate, an output pulse is produced only if there are pulses on both input lines. An **or** gate produces an output only if there is an input pulse on at least one of the input lines. A **not** gate is designed to produce an output pulse only when there is no incoming pulse. If we associate the boolean expression ''a pulse is present'' with each line, that is, if we interpret *true* as the presence of a pulse and *false* as the absence of a pulse, then the boolean operators **and, or,** and **not** can be used to model **and, or,** and **not** gates, respectively.

Boolean expressions can thus be used to model logical circuits. For example, the output *Sum* in the circuit for a binary half-adder can be represented by the boolean expression

(*A* **or** *B*) **and not** (*A* **and** *B*)

and the output *Carry* by

A **and** *B*

The values of these boolean expressions are displayed in the following truth table:

A	*B*	*Carry*	*Sum*
true	true	true	false
true	false	false	true
false	true	false	true
false	false	false	false

If we now take the value *false* to represent the binary digit 0 and *true* to represent the binary digit 1, then the preceding truth table can be written as

A	B	Carry	Sum
1	1	1	0
1	0	0	1
0	1	0	1
0	0	0	0

If we interpret *Sum* and *Carry* as the sum and carry bits produced when two binary digits are added as specified by the addition table

+	0	1
0	0	1
1	1	10

then we see that the circuit does in fact carry out this addition correctly.

The program in Figure 4.2 reads binary values (0 or 1) for *ANum* and *BNum* and converts them to boolean values for *A* and *B* with

$$0 \leftrightarrow false$$
$$1 \leftrightarrow true$$

by means of the assignment statements

$$A := (ANum = 1);$$
$$B := (BNum = 1);$$

The values of the two boolean expressions representing the sum and carry outputs are then assigned to boolean variables *Sum* and *Carry*, respectively, and are displayed.

```
PROGRAM HalfAdder (input, output);

(*****************************************************************

   Program to calculate the outputs from a logical circuit that
   represents a binary half-adder.

   *****************************************************************)
VAR
    ANum, BNum : integer;      (* the two binary inputs to the circuit *)
    A, B,                      (* their boolean equivalents *)
    Sum, Carry : boolean;      (* the outputs of the circuit *)
```

Figure 4.2

Figure 4.2 (cont.)

```
BEGIN
   write ('Enter two binary inputs: ');
   readln (ANum, BNum);

   (* Find boolean equivalents of ANum and BNum,
          0 <-> FALSE, 1 <-> TRUE
      and calculate Sum and Carry outputs *)

   A := (ANum = 1);
   B := (BNum = 1);
   Sum := (A OR B) AND NOT (A AND B);
   Carry := A AND B;

   (* Display boolean equivalents of binary outputs *)

   write ('Carry = ', Carry, '  Sum = ',Sum);
   writeln ('  (FALSE = 0, TRUE = 1)');
END.
```

Sample runs:

```
Enter two binary inputs: 0 0
Carry = FALSE   Sum = FALSE   (FALSE = 0, TRUE = 1)

Enter two binary inputs: 0 1
Carry = FALSE   Sum = TRUE    (FALSE = 0, TRUE = 1)

Enter two binary inputs: 1 0
Carry = FALSE   Sum = TRUE    (FALSE = 0, TRUE = 1)

Enter two binary inputs: 1 1
Carry = TRUE    Sum = FALSE   (FALSE = 0, TRUE = 1)
```

Exercises

1. Assuming that a, b, and c are boolean variables, use truth tables to display the values of the following boolean expressions for all possible values of a, b, and c:

   (a) a **or not** b (b) **not**(a **and** b)
   (c) **not** a **or not** b (d) a **and** *true* **or** $(1 + 2 = 4)$
   (e) a **and** (b **or** c)   (f) (a **and** b) **or** (a **and** c)

2. Write boolean expressions to express the following conditions:

   (a) x is greater than 3.
   (b) y is strictly between 2 and 5.
   (c) r is negative and z is positive.
   (d) Both *Alpha* and *Beta* are positive.
   (e) *Alpha* and *Beta* have the same sign (both are negative or both are positive).
   (f) $-5 < x < 5$.

(g) *a* is less than 6 or is greater than 10.
(h) $p = q = r$.
(i) *x* is less than 3, or *y* is less than 3, but not both.

3. Given the boolean variables *a*, *b*, and *c*, write a boolean expression that is

(a) true if and only if *a* and *b* are true and *c* is false.
(b) true if and only if *a* is true and at least one of *b* or *c* is true.
(c) true if and only if exactly one of *a* and *b* is true.

4. The Cawker City Credit Company approves a loan application if the applicant's income is at least \$25,000 or the value of his assets is at least \$100,000; in addition, his total liabilities must be less than \$50,000. Write a program that accepts three numbers representing income, assets, and liabilities, assigns the value *true* or *false* to the boolean variable *CreditOK* according to these criteria, and displays this value.

5. A **binary full-adder** has three inputs: the two bits *A* and *B* being added and a "carry-in" bit *CIn* (representing the carry bit that results from adding the bits to the right of *A* and *B* in two binary numbers). It can be constructed from two binary half-adders and an **or** gate:

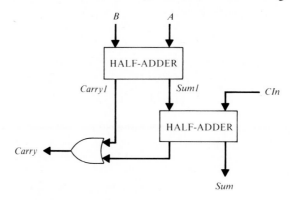

(a) Write boolean expressions for
(i) *Sum1* and *Carry1* in terms of *A* and *B*.
(ii) *Sum* and *Carry* in terms of *CIn*, *Sum1*, and *Carry1*.
(b) Write a program to implement this binary full-adder, and use it to verify the results shown in the following table:

A	B	CIn	Sum	Carry
0	0	0	0	0
0	0	1	1	0
0	1	0	1	0
0	1	1	0	1
1	0	0	1	0
1	0	1	0	1
1	1	0	0	1
1	1	1	1	1

6. An ***adder*** to calculate binary sums of two-bit numbers

$$\begin{array}{r} A2\ A1 \\ +\ B2\ B1 \\ \hline COut\ S2\ S1 \end{array}$$

where *S1* and *S2* are the sum bits and *COut* is the carry-out bit, can be constructed from a binary half-adder and a binary full-adder:

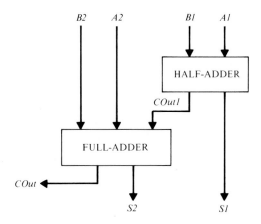

(a) Write boolean expressions for
   (i) *S1* and *COut1* in terms of *A1* and *B1*.
   (ii) *S2* and *COut* in terms of *A2*, *B2*, and *COut1*.

(b) Write a program to implement this adder and use it to demonstrate that $00 + 00 = 000$, $01 + 00 = 001$, $01 + 01 = 010$, $10 + 01 = 011$, $10 + 10 = 100$, $11 + 10 = 101$, and $11 + 11 = 110$.

7. Write a program that reads three real numbers and assigns the appropriate value *true* or *false* to the following boolean variables:

Triangle:	*true* if the three real numbers can represent lengths of the sides of a triangle, and *false* otherwise. (The sum of any two of the numbers must be greater than the third.)
Equilateral:	*true* if *Triangle* is *true* and the triangle is equilateral (three sides are equal).
Isosceles:	*true* if *Triangle* is *true* and the triangle is isosceles (at least two sides are equal).
Scalene:	*true* if *Triangle* is *true* and the triangle is scalene (no two sides are equal).

4.3 Selection Structure: The *if* Statement

A ***selection structure*** makes possible the selection and execution of one of a number of alternative actions. This enables the programmer to introduce decision points in a program, that is, points at which a decision is made *during program execution* to follow one of several courses of action.

In the simplest selection structure, a sequence of statements is executed or bypassed depending on whether a given boolean expression is true or false. This is illustrated in the following diagram, where a diamond indicates the evaluation of a boolean expression, and the two possible execution parts are indicated using arrows.

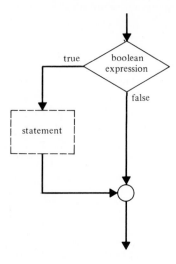

This selection structure can be implemented in Pascal using an **if** *statement* of the form

> **if** *boolean-expression* **then**
>   *statement*

If the boolean expression is true, the specified statement is executed; otherwise, it is bypassed, and execution continues with the next statement in the program. For example, in the statement

> **if** *Score* $<=$ 60 **then**
>   *writeln* ('F');

the boolean expression *Score* $<=$ 60 is evaluated, and if it is true, the letter F is displayed. Otherwise, the *writeln* statement is bypassed. In either case, execution continues with the statement following this **if** statement. The statement that appears in an **if** statement may be a compound statement, for example,

> **if** *Hours* $>$ 40 **then**
>   **begin**
>   *Overtime* := *Hours* $-$ 40;
>   *OvertimePay* := 1.5 $*$ *Overtime* $*$ *Rate*
>   **end** ($*$ **if** $*$);

Here the values of *Overtime* and *OvertimePay* are calculated only in the case that the boolean expression *Hours* > 40 is true. Similarly, for the **if** statement

> **if** (1 < X) **and** (X < 3) **then**
>   **begin**
>   Y := X * X;
>   W := sqrt(X)
>   **end** (* **if** *);

Y is set equal to the square of X and W is set equal to the square root of X only in the case that X is strictly between 1 and 3; otherwise, these assignment statements are not executed and the values of Y and W are unchanged.

In these examples of an **if** statement, we have attached a comment (* **if** *) to the reserved word **end** that marks the end of the compound statement in these **if** statements. As we shall see, such compound statements may be used in several other Pascal constructs, and attaching such comments to each of its occurrences clearly indicates the structure in which it is contained.

In the preceding selection structure, the selection is between (1) executing a given statement and (2) bypassing this statement. In the two-way selection pictured in the following diagram, the selection is between (1) executing one statement and (2) executing another statement.

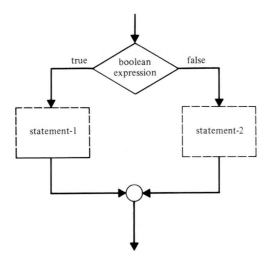

This selection structure is implemented in Pascal by an **if** statement that allows the programmer not only to specify the statement selected for execution when the boolean expression is true but also to indicate an alternative statement for execution when it is false. This **if** statement (together with the earlier form) is specified by the following syntax diagram.

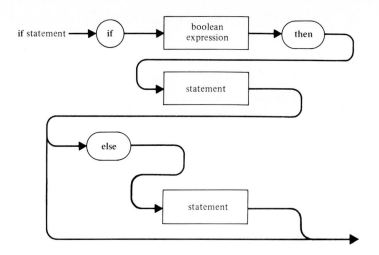

Its form thus is

> **if** *boolean-expression* **then**
>   *statement-1*
> **else**
>   *statement-2*

If the boolean expression is true, *statement-1* is executed and *statement-2* is bypassed. Otherwise, *statement-1* is bypassed and *statement-2* is executed. In either case, execution continues with the statement following the **if** statement.

A problem that requires this type of selection structure is the pollution index problem considered in Chapter 2. In this problem, a pollution index is to be calculated, and if this index is less than some cutoff value, a message indicating a safe condition must be displayed; if not, a message indicating a hazardous condition must be displayed. This selection was indicated in the algorithm for solving this problem (see Section 2.2) by

> If *Index* < *Cutoff* then
>   Display 'Safe condition'
> Else
>   Display 'Hazardous condition'

and is implemented in the Pascal program in Figure 4.3 by the following Pascal statement:

> **if** *Index* < *Cutoff* **then**
>   *writeln* ('Safe condition')
> **else**
>   *writeln* ('Hazardous condition')

```
PROGRAM PollutionIndex (input, output);

(****************************************************************

   Program that reads 3 pollution levels, calculates a pollution
   index as their average, and then displays a "safe condition"
   message if this index is less than some cutoff value, otherwise
   displays a "hazardous condition" message.

****************************************************************)

CONST
   Cutoff = 50;              (* bottom line for a safe condition *)

VAR
   Level1, Level2, Level3,   (* three pollution readings *)
   Index : integer;          (* pollution index *)
BEGIN
   write ('Enter 3 pollution readings:   ');
   readln (Level1, Level2, Level3);
   Index := (Level1 + Level2 + Level3) DIV 3;
   IF Index < Cutoff THEN
      writeln ('Safe condition')
   ELSE
      writeln ('Hazardous condition')
END.


Sample runs:


Enter 3 pollution readings:   55 39 48
Safe condition


Enter 3 pollution readings:   68 49 57
Hazardous condition
```

Figure 4.3

As another illustration of using an **if** statement to implement a two-alternative selection structure, suppose that students in a computer programming class will receive a passing grade if their final course average is 60 or above and will fail otherwise. The final average is computed as a weighted average of the homework average, the average on tests, and the exam score:

$$Average = 0.2 * Homework + 0.5 * Tests + 0.3 * Exam$$

A program is to be written to determine the pass/fail grade for a given student in this class. An algorithm for calculating grades is as follows:

GRADE ASSIGNMENT ALGORITHM—VERSION 1

(∗ Algorithm to determine the pass/fail grade for a student using a weighted average of the student's *Homework* average, average on *Tests*, and *Exam* score. ∗)

1. Read *Homework, Tests,* and *Exam.*
2. Calculate
   $$Average = 0.2 * Homework + 0.5 * Tests + 0.3 * Exam.$$
3. If *Average* ≥ 60 then
   Set *Grade* = 'P'
   Else
   Set *Grade* = 'F'.
4. Display *Average* and *Grade.*

A Pascal program to implement this algorithm is given in Figure 4.4. An **if** statement is used to implement the selection structure that selects the appropriate grade assignment, depending on the boolean expression *Average* >= 60. Note the use of the four constant identifiers *HWWeight, TestWeight, ExamWeight,* and *PassFailLine* in place of the constants 0.2, 0.5, 0.3, and 60. These identifiers are defined in the constant section and then used throughout the program. If the program has to be modified to assign grades when weighting factors are different or the pass/fail line changes, we need change only the definitions of these constant identifiers; the statement part of the program need not be modified.

```
PROGRAM GradeAssignment1 (input, output);

(*************************************************************************

    Program to compute a final course average using three inputs:
    homework average, average on tests, and an exam score;  a pass or
    fail grade is then assigned.

    *************************************************************************)
CONST
    HWWeight = 0.2;          (* weight factors for homework, *)
    TestWeight = 0.5;        (*      tests, *)
    ExamWeight = 0.3;        (*      and the exam *)
    PassFailLine = 60.0;     (* pass/fail line *)

VAR
    Homework, Tests, Exam,   (* homework, test, and exam averages *)
    Average : real;          (* final course average *)
    Grade : char;            (* grade assigned (P or F) *)
```

Figure 4.4

Figure 4.4 (cont.)

```
BEGIN
   write ('Enter homework, test and exam scores: ');
   readln (Homework, Tests, Exam);
   Average := HWWeight * Homework + TestWeight * Tests
            + ExamWeight * Exam;
   IF Average >= PassFailLine THEN
      Grade := 'P'
   ELSE
      Grade := 'F';
   writeln ('Average = ', Average:5:1, '  Grade = ', Grade);
   writeln
END.
```

Sample runs:

```
Enter homework, test and exam scores: 60 60 60
Average =  60.0  Grade = F

Enter homework, test and exam scores: 60 70 80
Average =  71.0  Grade = P

Enter homework, test and exam scores: 55.2 50.7 45.5
Average =  50.0  Grade = F

Enter homework, test and exam scores: 99.5 58.3 75
Average =  71.5  Grade = P
```

The statement sequences in an **if** statement may themselves contain other **if** statements. In this case, one **if** statement is said to be ***nested*** within the other **if** statement. To illustrate, suppose that in the preceding example, students who pass are awarded special honors if their average is 80 or above. The following algorithm solves this problem:

GRADE ASSIGNMENT ALGORITHM—VERSION 2

(* Algorithm to determine the pass/fail grade for a student using a weighted average of the student's *Homework* average, average on *Tests,* and *Exam* score. Passing students are awarded *Honors* if their average is sufficiently high. *)

1. Read *Homework, Tests,* and *Exam.*
2. Calculate
   Average = 0.2 * *Homework* + 0.5 * *Tests* + 0.3 * *Exam.*
3. Set *Honors* equal to a blank.
4. If *Average* ≥ 60 then do the following:
   a. Set *Grade* = 'P'.
   b. If *Average* ≥ 80 then
         Set *Honors* equal to 'H'.
   Else
         Set *Grade* = 'F'.
5. Display *Average, Honors,* and *Grade.*

The pseudocode description of the algorithm clearly shows the selection structure for determining honors designation based on the condition *Average* ≥ 80 nested within the larger selection structure based on the condition *Average* ≥ 60. This nested selection structure is implemented in the Pascal program in Figure 4.5 by nested **if** statements.

```
PROGRAM GradeAssignment2 (input, output);

(***********************************************************************

    Program to compute a final course average using three inputs:
    homework average, average on tests, and an exam score;  a pass or
    fail grade is then assigned.  Passing students receive an honors
    grade if their averages are sufficiently high.

    **********************************************************************)

CONST
    HWWeight = 0.2;          (* weight factors for homework, *)
    TestWeight = 0.5;        (*     tests, *)
    ExamWeight = 0.3;        (*     and the exam *)
    PassFailLine = 60.0;     (* pass/fail line *)
    HonorsLine = 80.0;       (* honors/no honors line *)

VAR
    Homework, Tests, Exam,   (* homework, test, and exam averages *)
    Average : real;          (* final course average *)
    Grade,                   (* grade assigned (P or F) *)
    Honors : char;           (* honors designation (H or blank) *)

BEGIN
    write ('Enter homework, test and exam scores: ');
    readln (Homework, Tests, Exam);
    Average := HWWeight * Homework + TestWeight * Tests
            + ExamWeight * Exam;
    Honors := ' ';
    IF Average >= PassFailLine THEN
        BEGIN
            Grade := 'P';
            IF Average >= HonorsLine THEN
                Honors := 'H'
        END (* IF *)
    ELSE
        Grade := 'F';
    writeln ('Average = ', Average:5:1, '  Grade = ', Honors, Grade);
    writeln
END.
```

Sample runs:

```
Enter homework, test and exam scores: 60 60 60
Average =  60.0  Grade =  F
```

Figure 4.5

Figure 4.5 (cont.)

```
Enter homework, test and exam scores: 60 70 80
Average =  71.0  Grade =  P


Enter homework, test and exam scores: 55.2 50.7 45.5
Average =  50.0  Grade =  F


Enter homework, test and exam scores: 99 98 97
Average =  97.9  Grade = HP
```

In a nested **if** *statement, each* **else** *clause is matched with the nearest preceding unmatched* **if.** For example, in the statement

> **if** $x > 0$ **then**
>   **if** $y > 0$ **then**
> $z := sqrt(x) + sqrt(y)$
>   **else**
> $readln\ (z)$;

the **else** clause is associated with the **if** statement containing the boolean expression $y > 0$. Consequently, the *readln* statement is executed only in the case that x is positive and y is nonpositive. If we wish to associate this **else** clause with the outer **if** statement, we can write

> **if** $x > 0$ **then**
>   **begin**
>   **if** $y > 0$ **then**
> $z := sqrt(x) + sqrt(y)$
>   **end** (∗ **if** x ∗)
> **else**
> $readln\ (z)$;

Here the *readln* statement is executed whenever x is nonpositive.

In these examples, note that each **else** clause is aligned with the corresponding **if.** This alignment emphasizes the relationship between each **if** and its associated **else.**

The selection structures considered thus far involve selecting one of two alternatives. It is also possible to use the **if** statement to design selection structures that contain more than two alternatives. These ***multialternative selection structures*** can be constructed using nested **if** statements, but such compound **if** statements may become quite complex, and the correspondence between **if**s and **else**s may not be clear if indentation is not used properly. A better format is

> **if** *boolean-expression-1* **then**
>   *statement-1*
> **else if** *boolean-expression-2* **then**
>   *statement-2*
>   ⋮
> **else**
>   *statement-n*

This format clarifies the correspondence between **if**s and **else**s and also emphasizes that the statement implements an *n*-way selection structure in which exactly one of *statement-1, statement-2, . . . , statement-n* is executed.

When an **if–else if** *construct* is executed, the boolean expressions are evaluated to determine the first expression that is true. The associated statement is executed, and execution then continues with the statement following the construct. If none of the boolean expressions is true, the statement associated with the **else** clause is executed, and execution then continues with the statement following the construct; if the **else** part is omitted, execution "falls through" to the next statement of the program. This **if–else if** construct therefore implements an *n*-way selection structure in which exactly one of *statement-1, statement-2, . . . , statement-n* is executed.

As an illustration of multialternative selection, suppose that the grade assignment program in Figure 4.4 is to be modified so that letter grades are assigned as indicated in the following table:

Average	Letter Grade
Average ≥ 90	A
80 ≤ average < 90	B
70 ≤ average < 80	C
60 ≤ average < 70	D
Average < 60	F

The algorithm for solving this problem is an easy modification of that given earlier:

GRADE ASSIGNMENT ALGORITHM—VERSION 3

(∗ Algorithm to determine a letter grade for a student using a weighted average of the student's *Homework* average, average on *Tests,* and *Exam* score. ∗)

1. Read *Homework, Tests,* and *Exam.*
2. Calculate
      Average = 0.2 ∗ *Homework* + 0.5 ∗ *Tests* + 0.3 ∗ *Exam.*
3. If *Average* ≥ 90 then
      Set *Grade* = 'A'
   Else if *Average* ≥ 80 then
      Set *Grade* = 'B'
   Else if *Average* ≥ 70 then
      Set *Grade* = 'C'

Else if *Average* ≥ 60 then
   Set *Grade* = 'D'
Else
   Set *Grade* = 'F'.
4. Display *Average* and *Grade*.

The program in Figure 4.6 implements this algorithm, using the following **if** statement to implement the five-way selection structure in Step 3:

if *Average* >= *ABLine* **then**
   Grade := 'A'
else if *Average* >= *BCLine* **then**
   Grade := 'B'
else if *Average* >= *CDLine* **then**
   Grade := 'C'
else if *Average* >= *DFLine* **then**
   Grade := 'D'
else
   Grade := 'F';

```
PROGRAM GradeAssignment3 (input, output);

(********************************************************************

   Program to compute a final course average using three inputs:
   homework average, average on tests, and an exam score;  a letter
   grade is then assigned.

   ********************************************************************)

CONST
    HWWeight = 0.2;          (* weight factors for homework, *)
    TestWeight = 0.5;        (*     tests, *)
    ExamWeight = 0.3;        (*     and the exam *)
    ABLine = 90.0;           (* A/B line *)
    BCLine = 80.0;           (* B/C line *)
    CDLine = 70.0;           (* C/D line *)
    DFLine = 60.0;           (* D/F line *)

VAR
    Homework, Tests, Exam,   (* homework, test, and exam averages *)
    Average : real;          (* final course average *)
    Grade : char;            (* grade assigned (A, B, C, D or F) *)

BEGIN
    write ('Enter homework, test and exam scores: ');
    readln (Homework, Tests, Exam);
    Average := HWWeight * Homework + TestWeight * Tests
              + ExamWeight * Exam;
```

Figure 4.6

Figure 4.6 (cont.)

```
   IF Average >= ABLine THEN
      Grade := 'A'
   ELSE IF Average >= BCLine THEN
      Grade := 'B'
   ELSE IF Average >= CDLine THEN
      Grade := 'C'
   ELSE IF Average >= DFLine THEN
      Grade := 'D'
   ELSE
      Grade := 'F';
   writeln ('Average = ', Average:5:1, '  Grade = ', Grade);
   writeln
END.
```

Sample runs:

```
Enter homework, test and exam scores: 100 100 100
Average = 100.0  Grade = A

Enter homework, test and exam scores: 30 40 50
Average =  41.0  Grade = F

Enter homework, test and exam scores: 68.2 62.7 66.5
Average =  64.9  Grade = D

Enter homework, test and exam scores: 87.5 91.3 80
Average =  87.1  Grade = B
```

Exercises

1. Write a Pascal statement for each of the following:

   (a) If *TaxCode* is 'T', increase *Price* by adding *TaxRate* percentage of *Price* to it.
   (b) If *Code* has the value 1, read values for *x* and *y* and calculate and print the sum of *x* and *y*.
   (c) If *A* is strictly between 0 and 5, set *B* equal to $1/A^2$; otherwise set *B* equal to A^2.
   (d) Assign *true* to the boolean variable *LeapYear* if the integer variable *Year* is the number of a leap year. (A leap year is a multiple of 4, and if it is a multiple of 100, it must also be a multiple of 400.)
   (e) Assign the value to *Cost* corresponding to the value of *Distance* given in the following table:

Distance	Cost
0 through 100	5.00
More than 100 but not more than 500	8.00
More than 500 but less than 1000	10.00
1000 or more	12.00

(f) Display the number of days in the month corresponding to the value of *Month* (1, 2, . . . , 12). Use part (d) to determine the number of days if the value of *Month* is 2, assuming that a value has been assigned to *Year*.

2. Describe the output produced by the following poorly indented program segment:

   Number := 4;
   Alpha := −1.0;
   if *Number* > 0 **then**
       if *Alpha* > 0 **then**
           writeln ('First writeln')
   else
       writeln ('Second writeln');
   writeln ('Third writeln');

3. A student used the following **if** statement in a program:

   if *Honors* = *true* **then**
       if *Awards* = *true* **then**
           GoodStudent := *true*
       else
           GoodStudent := *false*
   else if *Honors* = *false* **then**
       GoodStudent := *false*;

   (a) Write a simpler **if** statement that is equivalent to this one.
   (b) Write a single assignment statement that is equivalent to this **if** statement.

4. Write a program to check a quadratic equation of the form $Ax^2 + Bx + C = 0$ to see if it has real roots, and if so, find these roots. If there are no real roots, print an appropriate message. (See Exercise 9 of Section 2.5.)

5. A certain city classifies a pollution index less than 35 as "pleasant," 35 through 60 as "unpleasant," and above 60 as "hazardous." Write a program that reads a real number representing a pollution index and displays the appropriate classification for it.

6. Write a program that reads an employee's number, hours worked, and hourly rate and calculates his or her wages. All hours over 40 are paid at 1.5 times the regular hourly rate.

7. Write a wage calculation program like that in Exercise 6, but with the following modification: If an employee's number is greater than or equal to 1000, the program should read an annual salary and calculate the employee's weekly pay as this salary divided by 52. If the employee's number is less than 1000, wages are calculated on an hourly basis, as described in Exercise 6.

4.4   Repetition Structure: The *while* Statement

The third basic control structure is a ***repetition structure*** or ***loop*** that makes possible repeated execution of one or more statements. Pascal provides three statements that implement repetition structures: the **while** statement, the **repeat-until** statement, and the **for** statement. In this chapter we consider the first of these statements, the **while** statement. (The **repeat-until** and **for** statements are described in Chapter 5.) This statement can be used to implement a repetition structure called a ***while loop*** in which repetition is controlled by a boolean expression and continues while this expression remains true, terminating when it becomes false.

The syntax diagram for a ***while statement*** is

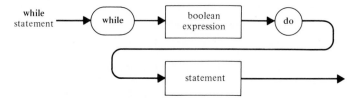

Thus a **while** statement has the form

    while *boolean-expression* **do**
        statement

When a **while** statement is executed, the boolean expression is evaluated, and if it is true, the specified statement, called the ***body*** of the loop, is executed. The boolean expression is then reevaluated, and if it is still true, this statement is executed again. As the following diagram indicates, this process of evaluating the boolean expression and executing the specified statement is repeated as long as the boolean expression is true. When it becomes false, repetition is terminated. Note that this means that repeated execution of the body of the loop

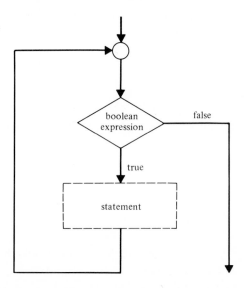

must eventually cause the value of the boolean expression to become false, since otherwise repetition would continue *ad infinitum*.

To demonstrate the use of the **while** statement, consider the following problem:

> For a given value of *Limit,* what is the smallest positive integer *Number* for which the sum
>
> $$1 + 2 + \cdots + Number$$
>
> is greater than *Limit,* and what is the value of this sum?

To solve this problem we will use three variables:

Number:	A positive integer added to the sum.
Sum:	$1 + 2 + \cdots + Number$.
Limit:	The specified limit for the sum.

We begin with *Number* and *Sum* initialized to 0. If this value of *Sum* exceeds the value of *Limit,* the problem is solved. Otherwise we increment *Number* by 1, add it to *Sum,* and then check to see if this value of *Sum* exceeds *Limit.* Once again, if it does, the problem is solved; and if not, *Number* must again be incremented and added to *Sum.* This process is continued as long as the value of *Sum* is less than or equal to *Limit.* Eventually the value of *Sum* will exceed *Limit* and the problem is solved. This leads to the following algorithm:

ALGORITHM FOR SUMMATION PROBLEM

(∗ Algorithm to find the smallest positive integer *Number* for which the sum $1 + 2 + \cdots + Number$ is greater than *Limit.* ∗)

1. Enter *Limit*.
2. Set *Number* equal to 0.
3. Set *Sum* equal to 0.
4. While *Sum* ≤ *Limit* do the following:
   a. Increment *Number* by 1.
   b. Add *Number* to *Sum*.
5. Display *Number* and *Sum*.

In this algorithm, the body of the while loop in Step 4 consists of two statements, but in Pascal, a **while** statement may only contain one statement. Consequently, we must combine the two statements into one compound statement:

```
while Sum <= Limit do
   begin
      Number := Number + 1;
      Sum := Sum + Number
   end (* while *);
```

The program in Figure 4.7 uses this **while** statement in implementing this algorithm.

```
PROGRAM Summation (input, output);

(*******************************************************************

   Program to find the smallest positive integer Number for which
   the sum
                        1 + 2 + ... + Number
   is greater than the value of a specified number Limit.  It also
   displays the value of this sum.

********************************************************************)

VAR
   Number,              (* positive integer added to the sum *)
   Sum,                 (* 1 + 2 + ... + Number *)
   Limit : integer;     (* limit for sum *)
BEGIN
   write ('Enter value that 1 + 2 + ... + ? is to exceed:   ');
   readln (Limit);
   Number := 0;
   Sum := 0;
   WHILE Sum <= Limit DO
      BEGIN
         Number := Number + 1;
         Sum := Sum + Number
      END (* WHILE *);
   writeln ('1 + ... + ', Number:1, ' = ', Sum:1, ' > ', Limit:1)
END.


Sample runs:

Enter value that 1 + 2 + ... + ? is to exceed:   10
1 + ... + 5 = 15 > 10


Enter value that 1 + 2 + ... + ? is to exceed:   10000
1 + ... + 141 = 10011 > 10000


Enter value that 1 + 2 + ... + ? is to exceed:   -1
1 + ... + 0 = 0 > -1
```

Figure 4.7

In the first sample run of Figure 4.7 in which the value 10 is entered for
Limit, the body of the while loop is executed five times, as indicated in the
following table, which traces its execution:

Number	Sum	Sum <= Limit	Action
0	0	true	Execute body of while loop
1	1	true	Execute body of while loop
2	3	true	Execute body of while loop
3	6	true	Execute body of while loop
4	10	true	Execute body of while loop
5	15	false	Terminate repetition

A similar trace table for the second sample run would show that the loop body is executed 141 times. The third sample run demonstrates that the boolean expression in a **while** statement is evaluated before repetition begins. When the value -1 is entered for *Limit,* the **while** statement causes an immediate transfer of control to the *writeln* statement that displays the value 0 for both *Number* and *Sum.*

As another example of a repetition structure, we develop a program to calculate the mean of a set of test scores. The program is to be used with sets of scores from various classes. Since the number of students in each class is not known in advance, the program should count the scores being averaged.

In this problem, the input is a set of real scores, one for each student in the class. The output is the number of students in the class and the mean score. An algorithm for solving the problem consists of repeatedly reading a new score, counting it, and adding it to the sum of scores previously read. After all of the scores have been read, the mean score must be calculated and displayed.

Since the number of scores is not known in advance, we must devise some way of determining that all of the data values have been read. One common scheme is to append to the data an artificial value called an ***end-of-data flag,*** which is distinct from any possible data item. As each data item is read, it is checked to determine whether it is this end-of-data flag. If it is not, the value is processed. When the end-of-data flag is read, it must not be processed as a regular data value but, rather, should serve only to terminate repetition.

This scheme can be implemented by using a while loop:

1. Read first data value.
2. While the data value is not the end-of-data flag do the following:
   a. Process the data value.
   b. Read the next data value.

Note that the first data value must be read before the while loop so that the boolean expression that controls repetition can be evaluated. If this data value is not the end-of-data flag, the body of the while loop is entered and the value is processed. The next data value must then be read and checked to determine whether it is the end-of-data flag. If it is not, it also is processed and the next data value is read. When the end-of-data flag is eventually read, the while loop will be exited without processing this artificial data value.

This standard technique for reading and processing is used in the following algorithm for solving the previous problem:

ALGORITHM TO FIND MEAN SCORE

(∗ Algorithm to read a list of scores, count them, and find the mean score (*MeanScore*); *Score* represents the current score read, *NumScores* is the number of scores, and *Sum* is the sum of the scores. Scores are read until the end-of-data flag is encountered. ∗)

1. Set *Sum* equal to 0.
2. Set *NumScores* equal to 0.
3. Read first *Score*.

4. While *Score* is not the end-of-data flag, do the following:
   a. Add 1 to *NumScores*.
   b. Add *Score* to *Sum*.
   c. Read next *Score*.
5. Calculate *MeanScore* = *Sum* / *NumScores*.
6. Display *MeanScore* and *NumScores*.

In the Pascal program in Figure 4.8 that implements this algorithm, a negative score is used as an end-of-data flag, and the repetition structure in Step 4 is implemented as a **while** statement controlled by the boolean expression *Score* >= 0.

```
PROGRAM CalculateMeanScore (input, output);

(*********************************************************************

   This program reads a list of scores, counts them, and
   calculates the mean score.  Any negative number serves
   as an end-of-data flag.

*********************************************************************)

VAR
    NumScores : integer;    (* number of scores *)
    Sum,                    (* sum of the scores *)
    Score,                  (* current score being processed *)
    MeanScore : real;       (* mean of the scores *)

BEGIN
    writeln ('*** Enter a negative score to signal the end of input.');
    writeln;
    Sum := 0;
    NumScores := 0;
    write ('Score:   ');
    readln (Score);
    WHILE Score >= 0 DO
        BEGIN
            NumScores := NumScores +1;
            Sum := Sum + Score;
            write ('Score:   ');
            readln (Score)
        END;
    MeanScore := Sum / NumScores;
    writeln;
    writeln (NumScores:1, ' scores with mean = ', MeanScore:5:2)
END.
```

Figure 4.8

Figure 4.8   (cont.)

Sample runs:

*** Enter a negative score to signal the end of input.

Score: 60
Score: 70
Score: 80
Score: -1

3 scores with mean = 70.00

*** Enter a negative score to signal the end of input.

Score: 55
Score: 86.5
Score: 79.5
Score: 86
Score: 84
Score: 55
Score: 97.5
Score: 100
Score: 57
Score: 83.5
Score: 72
Score: -1

11 scores with mean = 77.82

4.5   Program Testing and Debugging Techniques: An Example

In Section 2.4 we noted that three types of errors may occur in developing a program to solve a problem: syntax or compile-time errors, run-time errors, and logical errors. *Syntax errors* such as incorrect punctuation, unbalanced parentheses, and misspelled reserved words will be detected during compilation of the program, and an appropriate error message will usually be displayed. *Run-time errors* such as division by zero and integer overflow are detected during execution of the program, and again, a suitable error message will often be displayed. These two types of errors are, for the most part, relatively easy to correct, since the system error messages displayed will often indicate the type of error and where it occurred. *Logical errors,* on the other hand, are usually more difficult to detect, since they arise in the design of the algorithm or in coding the algorithm as a program, and in most cases, no error messages are displayed to assist the programmer in identifying such errors.

In this text, the Programming Pointers at the end of each chapter include warnings about some of the more common errors. As programs become increasingly complex, however, logical errors that occur will be more subtle and consequently more difficult to identify and correct. In this section we consider an example of a program that contains logical errors and describe techniques that are useful in detecting them.

Suppose that, as a programming exercise, students were asked to write a program to read a list of positive integers representing employee salaries in thousands of dollars and determine the salary range, that is, the difference between the largest salary and the smallest. The following program heading and declaration part were given, and the students were asked to write the statement part of the program:

```
PROGRAM SalaryRange (input, output);

(*******************************************************************

   Program to read a list of salaries in thousands of dollars and
   determine the range of salaries.  A zero value for the salary
   is used to signal the end of data.

   ******************************************************************)

VAR
   Salary,                    (* the current salary being processed *)
   MaxSalary,                 (* largest salary read so far *)
   MinSalary : integer;       (* smallest  "      "   "  "   *)
```

One attempted solution was the following (where the lines have been numbered for easy reference):

```
(1)   BEGIN
(2)      writeln ('Enter salaries in thousands of dollars (0 to stop).');
(3)      MaxSalary := 0;         (* initialize maximum salary very small *)
(4)      MinSalary := maxint;    (* and minimum salary very large *)
(5)      WHILE Salary <> 0 DO
(6)         BEGIN
(7)            write ('Enter salary:  ');
(8)            readln (Salary);
(9)            IF Salary > MaxSalary THEN
(10)              MaxSalary := Salary
(11)           ELSE IF Salary < MinSalary THEN
(12)              MinSalary := Salary
(13)        END (* WHILE *);
(14)     writeln;
(15)     writeln ('Salary Range = ', MaxSalary - MinSalary : 1, 'thousand')
(16) END.
```

Execution of the program produced

```
Enter salaries in thousands of dollars (0 to stop).
Salary range = 32767 thousand
```

Since the user was not allowed to enter any data, it is clear that the body of the while loop was not entered. This suggests that the boolean expression

Salary <> 0 that controls repetition was initially false, thus causing immediate termination.

This is in fact what happened. Since the student did not ensure that *Salary* had been assigned a value before the **while** statement in Line 5 was encountered, *Salary* had an undefined value when the boolean expression *Salary* <> 0 was evaluated. (The student did not heed the warning in Potential Problem 11 in the Programming Pointers of Chapter 3!) The particular system in which the program was executed used a value of 0 for *Salary,* making this boolean expression true and causing the while loop to terminate immediately.

To remedy the problem, the student inserted the statement *Salary* := 1 ahead of the **while** statement to force an entrance into the while loop:

```
(1)   BEGIN
(2)      writeln ('Enter salaries in thousands of dollars (0 to stop).');
(3)      MaxSalary := 0;        (* initialize maximum salary very small *)
(4)      MinSalary := maxint;   (* and minimum salary very large *)
(5)      Salary := 1;
(6)      WHILE Salary <> 0 DO
(7)         BEGIN
(8)            write ('Enter salary:  ');
(9)            readln (Salary);
(10)           IF Salary > MaxSalary THEN
(11)              MaxSalary := Salary
(12)           ELSE IF Salary < MinSalary THEN
(13)              MinSalary := Salary
(14)        END (* WHILE *);
(15)     writeln;
(16)     writeln ('Salary Range = ', MaxSalary - MinSalary : 1, 'thousand')
(17) END.
```

This "quick and dirty patch" fixed the problem of premature termination of the while loop, and execution of this revised program produced

```
Enter salaries in thousands of dollars (0 to stop).
Enter salary:   10
Enter salary:   7
Enter salary:   15
Enter salary:   0
Salary range = 15 thousand
```

Data values were read and processed, terminating when the end-of-data flag 0 was read. The correct salary range for this set of data is $8000, however, and not $15000 as computed by the program.

One common technique used to locate logical errors is to construct manually a *trace table* of the segment of the program that is suspect. This technique is also known as *walking through the code* or *desk checking,* and consists of recording in a table the values of all or certain key variables in the program segment, step by step. In this example, the following trace table for the while loop might be obtained:

Statements	Salary	MaxSalary	MinSalary	
	1	0	32767	← Initial values
6	1	0	32767	⎫
7–9	10	0	32767	⎬ First pass through the loop
10–11	10	10	32767	⎭
6	10	10	32767	⎫
7–9	7	10	32767	⎬ Second pass through the loop
12–13	7	10	7	⎭
6	7	10	7	⎫
7–9	15	15	7	⎬ Third pass through the loop
10–11	15	15	7	⎭
6	15	15	7	⎫
7–9	0	15	7	⎬ Fourth pass through the loop
12–13	0	15	0	⎭

The last line in this trace table shows why the salary range was incorrect; the value of *MinSalary* became 0 on the last pass through the loop, and this occurred because the value 0 used to signal the end of data was read and processed as a salary.

The execution of a program segment can also be traced automatically by inserting temporary output statements or by using special system-debugging software to display the values of key variables at selected stages of program execution. For example, we might insert the statement

> *writeln* ('Salary ', *Salary*);

after the *readln* statement to echo the data values as they are entered, and the statement

> *writeln* ('Max ', *MaxSalary*, ' Min ', *MinSalary*)

at the bottom of the loop to display the values of these variables at the end of each pass through the loop. (Note that a semicolon must also be appended to the statement preceding this last *writeln* statement.) The resulting output then is

```
Enter salaries in thousands of dollars (0 to stop).
Enter salary:  10
Salary        10
Max        10 Min      32767
Enter salary:  7
Salary         7
Max        10 Min          7
Enter salary: 15
Salary        15
Max        15 Min          7
Enter salary:  0
Salary         0
Max        15 Min          0
Salary range = 15 thousand
```

This technique must not be used indiscriminately, however, since incorrect placement of such temporary debugging statements may display output that is not helpful in locating the source of the error. Also, if too many such statements are used, so much output may be produced that it is difficult to isolate the error.

Either manual or automatic tracing of this program reveals that the source of difficulty is that the value 0 used to signal the end of data is processed as an actual salary. A first reaction might be to fix this error by using a nested **if** statement:

> **if** *Salary* > 0 **then**
> 　**if** *Salary* $>$ *MaxSalary* **then**
> 　　*MaxSalary* $:=$ *Salary*
> 　**else if** *Salary* $<$ *MinSalary* **then**
> 　　*MinSalary* $:=$ *Salary*

Patches like this one and the one used earlier are not recommended, however, because they often fail to address the real source of the problem and make the program unnecessarily complicated and messy.

The real source of difficulty in the preceding example is that the student did not use the correct technique for reading and processing data. As we noted in the preceding section, when an end-of-data flag is used to signal the end of data, the correct approach is to read the first data value before the while loop is entered to ensure that the boolean expression controlling repetition is evaluated correctly the first time. This would solve the problem in the student's first version of the program. Also, as we noted, subsequent data values should be read at the "bottom" of the while loop so that they are compared with the end-of-data flag *before* they are processed in the next pass through the loop.

Using this standard technique for reading and processing data, the student rewrote his program as follows:

```
(1)   BEGIN
(2)      writeln ('Enter salaries in thousands of dollars (0 to stop).');
(3)      MaxSalary := 0;        (* initialize max. salary very small *)
(4)      MinSalary := maxint;   (* and min. salary very large *)
(5)      write ('Enter salary:  ');
(6)      readln (Salary);
(7)      WHILE Salary <> 0 DO
(8)         BEGIN
(9)            IF Salary > MaxSalary THEN
(10)              MaxSalary := Salary
(11)           ELSE IF Salary < MinSalary THEN
(12)              MinSalary := Salary;
(13)           write ('Enter salary:  ');
(14)           readln (Salary)
(15)        END (* WHILE *);
(16)     write;
(17)     writeln ('Salary range = ', MaxSalary - MinSalary:1, ' thousand')
(18)  END.
```

A sample run using the same data values now produces the correct output:

```
Enter salaries in thousands of dollars (0 to stop).
Enter salary:  10
Enter salary:  7
Enter salary:  15
Enter salary:  0
Salary range = 8 thousand
```

The student may now be tempted to conclude that the program is correct. However, to establish one's confidence in the correctness of a program, it is necessary to test it with several sets of data. For example, the following sample run reveals that the program still contains a logical error:

```
Enter salaries in thousands of dollars (0 to stop).
Enter salary:  7
Enter salary:  10
Enter salary:  15
Enter salary:  0
Salary range = -32752 thousand
```

Tracing the execution of the while loop produces the following:

Statements	Salary	MaxSalary	MinSalary	
	7	0	32767	← Initial values
7–8	7	7	32767	⎫
9–10	7	7	32767	⎬ First pass through the loop
13–14	10	7	32767	⎭
7–8	10	7	32767	⎫
9–10	10	10	32767	⎬ Second pass through the loop
13–14	15	10	32767	⎭
7–8	15	10	32767	⎫
9–10	15	15	32767	⎬ Third pass through the loop
13–14	0	15	32767	⎭

This trace table reveals that the value of *MinSalary* never changes, suggesting that the statement

> *MinSalary* := *Salary*

is never executed. This is because the boolean expression *Salary* > *MaxSalary* is true for each data value, since these values are entered in increasing order; consequently, the **else if** part of the **if** statement is never executed. This error can be corrected by using two **if** statements:

> **if** *Salary* > *MaxSalary* **then**
>   *MaxSalary* := *Salary*;
> **if** *Salary* < *MinSalary* **then**
>   *MinSalary* := *Salary*;

The resulting program is then correct, but is not as efficient as it could be, since the boolean expressions in both of these **if** statements must be evaluated on each pass through the loop. A more efficient alternative is described in Exercise 9 at the end of this section.

In summary, logical errors may be very difficult to detect, especially as programs become more complex, and it is very important that test data be carefully selected so that each part of the program is thoroughly tested. The program should be executed with data values entered in several different orders, with large data sets and with small data sets, with extreme values, and with ''bad'' data. For example, entering the salaries in increasing order revealed the existence of a logical error in the program considered earlier. Also, even though the last version of the program produces correct output if legitimate data values are read, the output

```
Salary range = -32767 thousand
```

would be produced if the value 0 were entered immediately. Although it may not be necessary to guard against invalid data input in student programs, those written for the public domain, especially programs used by computer novices, should be as *robust* as possible and should not ''crash'' or produce ''garbage'' results when unexpected data values are read.

When a logical error is detected, a trace table is an effective tool for locating the source of the error. Once it has been found, the program must be corrected and then tested again. It may be necessary to repeat this cycle of testing, tracing, and correcting many times before the program produces correct results for a wide range of test data, allowing us to be reasonably confident of its correctness. It is not possible, however, to check a program with every possible set of data, and thus obscure bugs may still remain. In some applications, this may not be critical, but in others, for example, in programs used to guide a space shuttle, errors cannot be tolerated. Certain formal techniques have been developed for proving that a program is correct and will always execute correctly (assuming no system malfunction), but a study of these techniques is beyond the scope of this introductory text.

Exercises

1. Assuming that I, J, and K are integer variables, describe the output produced by each of the following program segments:

   (a) $K := 5;$
       $I := -2;$
       while $I <= K$ **do**
         begin
            $I := I + 2;$
            $K := K - 1;$
            writeln $(I + K:2)$
         end (* **while** *);

(b) *Number* : = 4;
 while *Number* >= 0 **do**
  begin
   Number : = *Number* − 1;
   writeln (Number:1);
   writeln
  end (∗ **while** ∗);
 writeln ('∗∗∗∗∗');

2. Write a Pascal statement to

 (a) Print the value of x and decrease x by 0.5 as long as x is positive.
 (b) Read values for a, b, and c and print their sum, repeating this as long as none of a, b, or c is negative.
 (c) Print the squares of the first 100 positive integers in increasing order.
 (d) Print the cubes of the first 50 positive integers in decreasing order.
 (e) Print the square roots of the first 25 odd positive integers.
 (f) Calculate and print the squares of consecutive positive integers until the difference between a square and the preceding one is greater than 50.
 (g) Print a list of points (x, y) on the graph of $y = x^3 − 3x + 1$ for x ranging from $−2$ to 2 in steps of 0.1.

3. Describe the output produced by the following poorly indented program segment:

 Number : = 4;
 while *Number* > 0 **do**
  Number : = *Number* − 1;
  writeln (Number:1);
  writeln;
 writeln ('∗∗∗∗∗');

4. Write a program to read data values as shown in the following table, calculate the miles per gallon in each case, and print the values with appropriate labels:

Miles Traveled	Gallons of Gasoline Used
231	14.8
248	15.1
302	12.8
147	9.25
88	7
265	13.3

5. Write a program to read several values representing miles, convert miles to kilometers (1 mile = 1.60935 kilometers), and print all values with appropriate labels.

6. A certain product is to sell for *UnitPrice* dollars. Write a program that reads values for *UnitPrice* and *TotalNumber* and then produces a table showing the total price of from 1 through *TotalNumber* units. The table should have a format like the following:

```
Number of Units    Total Price
================    ===========
       1              $ 1.50
       2              $ 3.00
       3              $ 4.50
       4              $ 6.00
       5              $ 7.50
```

Design the program so that after a table is printed, it calls for the input of new values for *UnitPrice* and *TotalNumber* and generates a new table. Execute the program using the following pairs of values for *UnitPrice* and *TotalNumber*: 1.20, 5; 15.49, 8; 4.99, 15; 177.89, 10.

7. Write a program that reads the exchange rate for converting English currency to U.S. currency and then reads several values for *Pounds, Shillings,* and *Pence* and converts the amount of currency represented into the equivalent amount of U.S. dollars and cents. Display all amounts with appropriate labels.

8. Proceed as in Exercise 7, but convert several values from U.S. currency to English currency.

9. (a) Write a program that solves the salary range problem discussed in Section 4.5 but is more efficient than those described in the text. (*Hint:* Initialize *MaxSalary* and *MinSalary* to the first data value.)
   (b) For each of the following data sets, construct a trace table for the repetition structure used in your program and determine the salary range that will be computed by your program:

   (i) 7, 15, 10, -1 **(ii)** 7, 10, 15, -1 **(iii)** 15, 10, 7, -1
   (iv) 7, -1 **(v)** -1

10. Write a program to read a set of numbers, count them, and calculate and display the mean, variance, and standard deviation of the set of numbers. The **mean** and **variance** of numbers $x_1, x_2, \ldots, x_n$ can be calculated using the formulas

$$\text{mean} = \frac{1}{n} \sum_{i=1}^{n} x_i, \quad \text{variance} = \frac{1}{n} \sum_{i=1}^{n} x_i^2 - \frac{1}{n^2} \left(\sum_{i=1}^{n} x_i \right)^2$$

The **standard deviation** is the square root of the variance.

11. Write a program that implements the "divide and average" algorithm for approximating square roots (see Exercise 8 of Section 2.5). It should accept positive real values for the variables *PosReal, Approx,* and *Epsilon,* and approximate the square root of *PosReal* by repeatedly replacing *Approx* by the average of *Approx* and *PosReal / Approx,* until *Approx* and *PosReal / Approx* differ in absolute value by less than *Epsilon,* when the value of *Epsilon* is small. Have the program display each of the successive values of *Approx.*

12. The sequence of *Fibonacci numbers* begins with the integers

$$1, 1, 2, 3, 5, 8, 13, 21, \ldots$$

where each number after the first two is the sum of the two preceding numbers. In this sequence, the ratios of consecutive Fibonacci numbers $(1/1, 1/2, 2/3, 3/5, \ldots)$ approach the "golden ratio"

$$\frac{\sqrt{5} - 1}{2}$$

Write a program to calculate all the Fibonacci numbers smaller than 5000 and the decimal values of the ratios of consecutive Fibonacci numbers.

13. The Rinky Dooflingy Company (Exercise 10 of Section 2.5) currently sells 200 dooflingies per month at a profit of $300 per dooflingy. The company now spends $2000 per month on advertising and has fixed operating costs of $1000 per month that do not depend on the volume of sales. If the company doubles the amount spent on advertising, sales will increase by 20 percent. Write a program that prints under appropriate headings the amount spent on advertising, the number of sales made, and the net profit. Begin with the company's current status and successively double the amount spent on advertising until the net profit "goes over the hump," that is, begins to decline. The output should include the amounts up through the first time that the net profit begins to decline.

14. Write a program that accepts a positive integer and gives its prime factorization, that is, expresses the integer as a product of primes or indicates that it is a prime.

4.6 Introduction to Procedures[1]

The problems we have considered thus far have been simple enough that the algorithms for their complete solution were quite straightforward. As we noted in Chapter 2, more complex problems are best solved using a *top-down* approach that uses a *divide-and-conquer* strategy to divide a problem into a

[1] In the preceding section we considered three of Pascal's control structures, compound statements, **if** statements, and **while** statements. Pascal also provides one additional selection structure, the **case** statement, and two additional repetition structures, the **for** and the **repeat–until** statements. These are considered in the next chapter. Those who prefer to complete the study of these basic control structures before undertaking the study of procedures should go on to Sections 5.1, 5.2, and 5.3 now and then return to this section.

number of simpler subproblems. Each of these subproblems is then considered individually, and in some cases it may be necessary to divide them further until the resulting subproblems are simple enough that algorithms for their solution can be easily designed. The complete algorithm for the original problem is then described in terms of these subalgorithms. **Subprograms** or **modules** can be written to implement each of these subalgorithms, and these subprograms combined to give a complete program that solves the original problem. In Pascal, these subprograms are **procedures** and **functions** whose execution is controlled by some other program unit, either the **main program** or some other subprogram.

Because the program units in this modular style of programming are independent of one another, the programmer can write each module and test it without worrying about the details of other modules. This makes it considerably easier to locate an error when it arises, since it often occurs in the module most recently written and added to the program and since the effects of these modules are easily isolated. Programs developed in this manner are also usually easier to understand because the structure of each program unit can be studied independently of that of the other program units.

In a Pascal program, procedures are defined in the **subprogram section** of the declaration part of a program (see the syntax diagram in Section 3.8). Once defined they may be referenced in other parts of the program unit, with information passed to and from these procedures by means of special variables called **parameters.**

A procedure definition has a syntax similar to that of a Pascal program in that it consists of a heading, a declaration part, and a statement part. Its syntax diagram is

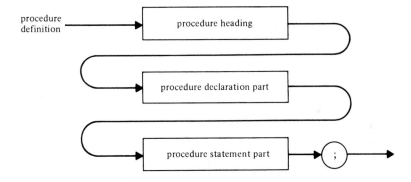

The syntax diagram for the procedure heading is

From this diagram we see that a procedure heading may have the form

procedure *name*;

or

   procedure *name* (*formal-parameter-list*);

Here *name* is the name of the procedure and may be any legal Pascal identifier. The first form of the procedure heading is appropriate when it is not necessary to pass information to or from the procedure (e.g., procedure *DisplayMenu* in Figure 4.12). The second form is more common, and in it the *formal-parameter-list* specifies the formal parameters of the procedure. These parameters are used to pass information to the procedure and/or to return information from it to the program unit that references it. This formal parameter list has the form

   ind-1 list-1 : type-1; ind-2 list-2 : type-2; . . . ; ind-k list-k : type-k

where each *list-i* is a single identifier or a list of identifiers separated by commas, and *type-i* specifies their types; *ind-i* indicates how the identifiers in *list-i* are to be used. If this indicator is the reserved word **var,** then the identifiers in the list are ***variable parameters,*** sometimes called ***in-out parameters,*** which may be used *both* to transfer information to the procedure from the program unit that references it *and* to return information from the procedure. If this indicator is omitted, then the identifiers in the list may be used *only* to pass information to this procedure and not to return information; such parameters are called ***value parameters*** or ***in parameters.*** The following syntax diagram displays this form for the formal parameter list. (A more general form is given in Appendix C.)

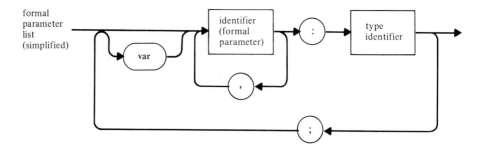

       The statement part of a procedure definition has the same form as the statement part of a Pascal program. However, a semicolon rather than a period follows the reserved word **end** marking the end of the procedure definition.
       To illustrate, suppose we wish to develop a procedure that accepts from the main program a month number, a day number, and a year number, and displays them in the form

   mm/dd/yy

For example, the values 8, 14, 1941 are to be displayed as

   8/14/41

and the values 9, 3, 1905 as

9/3/05

This procedure must have three formal parameters, each of integer type, representing the number of the month, day, and year, respectively. Since these parameters are used only to pass values to the procedure, they need not be designated as variable parameters. Thus, an appropriate procedure heading is

procedure *DisplayDate* (*Month, Day, Year* : *integer*);

Only the last two digits of the year are to be displayed, and these can be obtained using the statement

Year := *Year* **mod** 100;

For example, if the value passed to *Year* is 1941, this statement assigns the value 41 to *Year,* which can then be displayed. If, however, the value passed to *Year* is 1905, this statement assigns the value 5 to *Year;* displaying this value produces 5 rather than 05. Thus, we must calculate and display each digit individually. An appropriate output statement is therefore

writeln (*Month*:1, '/', *Day*:1, '/', *Year* **div** 10 : 1, *Year* **mod** 10 : 1)

Using these two statements in the statement part of the procedure *DisplayDate,* we obtain the following complete procedure:

procedure *DisplayDate* (*Month, Day, Year* : *integer*);
   (∗ Procedure to accept a *Month* number, a *Day* number, and
      a *Year* number and display the date in the form *mm/dd/yy.*∗)

begin (∗ *DisplayDate* ∗)
   Year := *Year* **mod** 100;
   writeln (*Month*:1, '/', *Day*:1 '/', *Year* **div** 10 : 1,
         Year **mod** 10 : 1)
end (∗ *DisplayDate* ∗);

Note that a comment is included to describe the procedure. It is good practice to include such documentation to describe briefly what the procedure does, what its parameters represent, and other information that explains the procedure definition.

A procedure definition is placed after the variable section in the declaration part of a Pascal program. This procedure can then be called with a ***procedure reference statement*** of the form

name (*actual-parameter-list*)

where *name* is the name of the procedure and *actual-parameter-list* is a list of ***actual parameters*** that are to be associated with the parameters in the formal parameter list of the procedure heading. For example, the procedure *DisplayDate* is called by the statement

      DisplayDate (TheMonth, TheDay, TheYear)

in the program of Figure 4.9. This statement causes the values of the actual parameters *TheMonth, TheDay,* and *TheYear* to be assigned to the formal parameters *Month, Day,* and *Year,* respectively, of the procedure *DisplayDate,* and initiates execution of the procedure. When the end of the procedure is reached, execution resumes with the statement following this procedure reference statement in the main program.

```
PROGRAM Date (input, output);

(******************************************************************

   Program demonstrating use of  a procedure to display a given date
   in the form:        mm/dd/yy

*******************************************************************)

VAR
    TheMonth, TheDay, TheYear : integer;    (* month, day, year *)

PROCEDURE DisplayDate (Month, Day, Year : integer);

   (***************************************************************

          Displays a date in the form mm/dd/yy.

   ***************************************************************)

   BEGIN (* DisplayDate *)
      Year := Year MOD 100;
      writeln (Month:1, '/', Day:1, '/', Year DIV 10 : 1, Year MOD 10 : 1);
   END (* DisplayDate *);

BEGIN (* main program *)
   write ('Enter month, day, and year:  ');
   readln (TheMonth, TheDay, TheYear);
   writeln;
   DisplayDate (TheMonth, TheDay, TheYear)
END (* main program *).


Sample runs:

Enter month, day, and year:  8 14 1941

8/14/41


Enter month, day, and year:  9 3 1905

9/3/05
```

Figure 4.9

In this example, the procedure *DisplayDate* does not return any values to the main program; it only displays information that is passed to it. Thus, its formal parameters *Month, Day,* and *Year* are value parameters. Before a procedure is referenced, its value parameters are undefined. At the time of reference, memory locations are associated with them, and the values of the corresponding actual parameters are copied into these locations. Thus, for the procedure *DisplayDate*, the formal parameters *Month, Day,* and *Year* are undefined until the procedure reference statement

DisplayDate (TheMonth, TheDay, TheYear)

is encountered. The values of the actual parameters *TheMonth, TheDay,* and *TheYear* are then copied to *Month, Day,* and *Year,* respectively.

After execution of the procedure, these value parameters once again become undefined, so that any values they had during execution of the procedure or function are lost.

We noted earlier that variable parameters may be used to return values from a procedure. A variable formal parameter and the corresponding actual parameter are associated with the same memory location, and thus a variable formal parameter is merely a temporary **alias** or **synonym** for the actual parameter it represents. Consequently, any modification of a variable formal parameter in a procedure changes the value of the corresponding actual parameter. The actual parameter must therefore be a variable; constants and expressions are not allowed. Also, actual parameters must be of the same type as the corresponding formal parameters.

As a simple example of variable parameters, consider the problem of determining which of two real numbers is the larger and which is the smaller. The following procedure solves this problem:

```
procedure FindMaxAndMin (Num1, Num2 : real;
                         var Max, Min : real);

   (* Procedure to find and return the Maximum and the
      Minimum of two real numbers Num1 and Num2.*)

begin (* FindMaxAndMin *)
   if Num1 > Num2 then
      begin
         Max := Num1;
         Min := Num2
      end (* if *)
```

                 else
                   begin
                     Max := *Num2*;
                     Min := *Num1*
                  end (* **else** *)
             end (* *FindMaxAndMin* *);

Because the values of *Max* and *Min* are to be returned by the procedure, they must be declared to be variable parameters. Figure 4.10 shows a complete program that reads a pair of real numbers, calls procedure *FindMaxAndMin* to find the largest and the smallest number in the pair, and displays these numbers with appropriate labels.

```
PROGRAM MaxMin (input, output);

(************************************************************

   Program demonstrating use of a procedure to find the
   maximum and the minimum of two real numbers.

************************************************************)

VAR
   X, Y,                        (* two real numbers *)
   Largest, Smallest : real;  (* largest and smallest of the numbers *)

PROCEDURE FindMaxAndMin (Num1, Num2 : real; VAR Max, Min : real);

   (*********************************************************

      Procedure to find and return the Maximum and the
      Minimum of two real numbers Num1 and Num2.

   *********************************************************)

   BEGIN (* FindMaxAndMin *)
      IF Num1 > Num2 THEN
         BEGIN
            Max := Num1;
            Min := Num2
         END (* IF *)
      ELSE
         BEGIN
            Max := Num2;
            Min := Num1
         END (* ELSE *)
   END (* FindMaxAndMin *);

BEGIN (* main program *)
   write ('Enter two numbers:  ');
   readln (X, Y);
   FindMaxAndMin (X, Y, Largest, Smallest);
   writeln ('Largest is ', Largest:4:1, ' and smallest is ', Smallest:4:1)
END (* main *).
```

Figure 4.10

Figure 4.10 (cont.)

Sample runs:

Enter two numbers: 2.0 1.1
Largest is   2.0 and smallest is   1.1

Enter two numbers: -33.6 25.5
Largest is 25.5 and smallest is -33.6

In this program, the variable declarations

var
    X, Y,   (* two real numbers *)
    Largest, Smallest : *real*;   (* largest and smallest of the numbers *)

associate memory locations with the four variables *X, Y, Largest*, and *Smallest*.

$$X ----\boxed{}$$

$$Y ----\boxed{}$$

$$Largest ----\boxed{}$$

$$Smallest ----\boxed{}$$

When the statement

    FindMaxAndMin (*X, Y, Largest, Smallest*);

is executed, new memory locations are associated with the value parameters *Num1* and *Num2*, and the values of *X* and *Y* are copied into these locations. No new memory locations are obtained for the variable parameters *Max* and *Min*; instead these formal parameters are associated with the existing memory locations of the corresponding actual parameters *Largest* and *Smallest*.

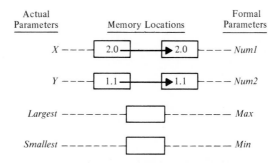

When the procedure *FindMaxAndMin* is executed, values are determined for *Max* and *Min*, and because *Max* and *Min* are associated with the same memory locations as *Largest* and *Smallest,* these values are also the values of *Largest* and *Smallest.*

Because the memory locations associated with *Num1* and *Num2* are distinct from those for *X* and *Y,* changes to *Num1* and *Num2* in procedure *FindMaxAndMin* could not change the values of *X* and *Y.* When execution of the procedure is completed, the association of memory locations with *Num1, Num2, Max,* and *Min* is terminated, and these formal parameters become undefined.

When a procedure is referenced, the number of actual parameters must be the same as the number of formal parameters, and the type of each actual parameter must be the same as the type of the corresponding formal parameter. One exception is that an actual parameter of integer type may be associated with a value parameter of real type. Thus, in a program in which variables *N1* and *N2* have been declared to be of integer type and *R1* and *R2* of real type, the procedure *FindMaxAndMin* could be called with either of the statements

FindMaxAndMin (N1, N2, R1, R2);

FindMaxAndMin (N1 / 4, 7.5, R1, R2);

The following would not be valid, however, for the reasons indicated:

FindMaxAndMin (R1, R2);   (The number of actual parameters does not agree with the number of formal parameters.)

FindMaxAndMin (N1, R1, 5.1, R2);   (The constant 5.1 may not be associated with the variable parameter *Max.*)

FindMaxAndMin (N1, R1, N2, R2);   (The integer actual parameter *N2* may not be associated with the real variable parameter *Max.*)

The following rules summarize the relation between actual and formal parameters:

Rules for Parameter Association

1. There must be the same number of formal parameters as there are actual parameters.
2. The types of associated formal and actual parameters must agree; however, an actual parameter of integer type may be associated with a formal value parameter of real type.
3. An actual parameter associated with a variable formal parameter must be a variable; it may not be a constant or an expression.

Some procedure definitions may require the use of constants and/or variables in addition to the formal parameters. These are usually defined and declared within the procedure itself, in the constant and variable sections of the procedure's declaration part, which has the same form as the declaration part of a Pascal program. For example, suppose we wish to develop a program that reads the amount of a purchase and the amount tendered in payment, calls a procedure to determine the change in dollars, half-dollars, quarters, dimes, nickels, and pennies, and then displays these values.

A procedure *MakeChange* to calculate the required change will have two value parameters, *Purchase* and *Payment,* of real type, whose values will be passed from the main program. It will also have variable parameters *Dollars, Halves, Quarters, Dimes, Nickels,* and *Pennies* of integer type, whose values must be returned to the main program. An appropriate procedure heading is therefore

> **procedure** *MakeChange (Purchase, Payment : real*;
> **var** *Dollars, Halves, Quarters, Dimes,*
> *Nickels, Pennies : integer*);

In addition, an auxiliary variable *Change* is needed to store intermediate results; this variable is declared in the declaration part of this procedure:

> **var**
> *Change : integer*;

In the statement part of procedure *MakeChange, Change* is initially calculated by

> *Change* := *round*(100 ∗ (*Payment* − *Purchase*));

(The function *round* is used because the real values *Payment* and *Purchase* may not be stored exactly.) In subsequent calculations, *Change* represents the change yet to be dispensed. The program in Figure 4.11 shows the complete procedure.

```
PROGRAM ChangeMaker (input, output);

(*******************************************************************

    Program to read a given purchase and payment, and call the
    procedure MakeChange to determine change to be tendered.

*******************************************************************)

VAR
    AmountPurchased,              (* purchase made *)
    AmountPaid : real;            (* payment received; assumed >= AmountPurchased *)
    NumberOfDollars,              (* number of bills *)
    NumberOfHalves,               (*   and *)
    NumberOfQuarters,             (*    :   *)
    NumberOfDimes,                (* coins *)
    NumberOfNickels,              (*    :   *)
    NumberOfPennies : integer;    (* to be returned in change *)

PROCEDURE MakeChange (Purchase, Payment : real;
                      VAR Dollars, Halves, Quarters, Dimes,
                          Nickels, Pennies : integer);

    (*******************************************************************

        Procedure to determine various denominations of change to be
        tendered for a given Purchase and Payment.

    *******************************************************************)

    VAR
        Change : integer;   (* amount of change to be tendered *)

    BEGIN (* MakeChange *)
        Change := round (100 * (Payment - Purchase));
        Dollars := Change DIV 100;
        Change := Change MOD 100;
        Halves := Change DIV 50;
        Change := Change MOD 50;
        Quarters := Change DIV 25;
        Change := Change MOD 25;
        Dimes := Change DIV 10;
        Change := Change MOD 10;
        Nickels := Change DIV 5;
        Pennies := Change MOD 5
    END (* MakeChange *);

BEGIN (* main program *)
    write ('Amount purchased and amount paid?  ');
    readln (AmountPurchased, AmountPaid);
    MakeChange (AmountPurchased, AmountPaid, NumberOfDollars, NumberOfHalves,
                NumberOfQuarters, NumberOfDimes, NumberOfNickels,
                NumberOfPennies);
    writeln ('Change tendered:');
    writeln (NumberOfDollars:1, ' Dollars');
    writeln (NumberOfHalves:1, ' Halves');
    writeln (NumberOfQuarters:1, ' Quarters');
    writeln (NumberOfDimes:1, ' Dimes');
    writeln (NumberOfNickels:1, ' Nickels');
    writeln (NumberOfPennies:1, ' Pennies')
END (* main program *).
```

Figure 4.11

Figure 4.11   (cont.)

Sample runs:

```
Amount purchased and amount paid?   1.01 5.00
Change tendered:
3 Dollars
1 Halves
1 Quarters
2 Dimes
0 Nickels
4 Pennies


Amount purchased and amount paid?   1.99 2.00
Change tendered:
0 Dollars
0 Halves
0 Quarters
0 Dimes
0 Nickels
1 Pennies
```

In this example, the variables *Purchase, Payment, Dollars, Halves, Quarters, Dimes, Nickels, Pennies,* and *Change* have values only when the procedure *MakeChange* is referenced, and these values are accessible only within this procedure. These variables are therefore said to be ***local*** to the procedure. The portion of a program in which a variable is accessible is called the ***scope*** of that variable. Thus the scope of these variables is the procedure *MakeChange*.

One consequence of this scope rule for local variables is that the same identifier can be used without conflict in two different program units. For example, both the procedure *MakeChange* and some other procedure can be used in the same program, even though both procedures use the variable name *Payment*. When these procedures are referenced, the variable *Payment* in procedure *MakeChange* is associated with a different memory location than is the variable *Payment* in the other procedure. Thus, changing the value of one does not change the value of the other. Similarly, any of the other local variables in procedure *MakeChange* may be used without conflict elsewhere in the program.

4.7   Example of Modular Programming: Menu-Driven Checkbook-Balancing Program

In the introduction to this chapter, we claimed that one of the advantages of procedures is that they enable a programmer to develop programs in a ***modular*** fashion. This means that the major tasks to be performed by the program can be identified and individual procedures for these tasks can then be designed and tested. Programs written in this manner are not only easier to develop and test and easier to understand, but also easier to modify, since individual modules can be added, deleted, or altered. In this section we illustrate this technique of modular programming by developing a simple checkbook-balancing program.

Suppose we wish to develop a program that allows the user to reconcile his checkbook with a monthly statement received from the bank. There are three main tasks that must be performed:

1. Deposits must be added to the current balance.
2. The amount of each check written and a check-processing charge must be subtracted from the current balance.
3. A summary of the month's activity must be printed. This summary should include the initial balance, number of checks, total amount of checks, number of deposits, total deposits, total service charges, and the final balance.

One procedure of the program will be an initialization module that obtains a value for *InitialBalance* and initializes the variable *Balance* to *InitialBalance*, the variables *TotalDeposits, TotalChecks, TotalServiceCharges, NumberOf-Checks,* and *NumberOfDeposits* to 0, and a boolean variable *DoneProcessing* to false. A second procedure will be designed to process deposits and a third to process checks. There will also be another procedure to print the monthly summary. The main program will first reference the procedure *Initialize* and then repeatedly call four other procedures, *DisplayMenu, ProcessDeposit, ProcessCheck,* and *PrintSummary,* as necessary. The following **structure diagram** summarizes the structure of the program:

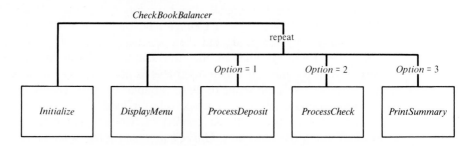

The user will select an option from a **menu,** and the appropriate procedure will be called. The statement part of the main program will thus have the form

```
begin (* main program *)
    Initialize (InitialBalance, Balance, TotalDeposits, TotalChecks,
            TotalServiceCharges, NumberOfDeposits,
            NumberOfChecks, DoneProcessing);
    while not DoneProcessing do
        begin
            DisplayMenu;
            write ('Enter Option:  ');
            readln (Option);
            if Option = 0 then
                DoneProcessing := true
            else if Option = 1 then
                ProcessDeposit (Balance, TotalDeposits,
                        NumberOfDeposits)
```

> **else if** *Option* = 2 **then**
>   *ProcessCheck* (*Balance, TotalChecks,*
>   *TotalServiceCharges,*
>   *NumberOfChecks*)
> **else if** *Option* = 3 **then**
>   *PrintSummary* (*InitialBalance, Balance, TotalDeposits,*
>   *TotalChecks, TotalServiceCharges,*
>   *NumberOfDeposits, NumberOfChecks*)
> **else**
>   *writeln* ('*** Invalid Option ***')
> **end** (* while *)
> **end** (* main program *).

For the procedure *Initialize,* all of the parameters must be variable parameters, since each of the values must be returned. An appropriate procedure heading is therefore

> **procedure** *Initialize* (**var** *InitialBalance, Balance, TotalDeposits,*
>   *TotalChecks, TotalServiceCharges : real*;
>   **var** *NumberOfChecks, NumberOfDeposits : integer*;
>   **var** *DoneProcessing : boolean*);

Note that although in previous examples we used different names for the actual parameters and the corresponding formal parameters, this is not necessary, as this example illustrates.

The procedure *DisplayMenu* simply displays the menu of options available to the user; no information is passed to or from it. Its heading thus requires no formal parameter list:

> **procedure** *DisplayMenu*;

The parameters for procedure *ProcessDeposit* must be in-out parameters, that is, variable parameters, because the current values for *Balance, TotalDeposits,* and *NumberOfDeposits* will be passed to the procedure, which must then update them and return those new values. Similarly, each of the parameters for procedure *ProcessCheck* must be variable parameters. Appropriate headings for these procedures are therefore

> **procedure** *ProcessDeposit* (**var** *Balance, TotalDeposits : real*;
>   **var** *NumberOfDeposits : integer*);

and

> **procedure** *ProcessCheck* (**var** *Balance, TotalChecks,*
>   *TotalServiceCharges : real*;
>   **var** *NumberOfChecks : integer*);

The procedure *PrintSummary* simply displays information that is passed to it. Its formal parameters are thus in parameters, that is, value parameters, so that its heading is

procedure *PrintSummary (InitialBalance, Balance, TotalDeposits,*
TotalChecks, TotalServiceCharges : real;
NumberOfDeposits, NumberOfChecks : integer);

Figure 4.12 shows the complete ***menu-driven program*** with complete procedures. Although the final program is given here, it could well have been developed in a piecewise manner by writing and testing only some of the procedures before writing the others. In this case, undeveloped procedures could simply have empty statement parts:

begin (* *ProcessCheck* *)
end (* *ProcessCheck* *);

Usually, however, they would be ***program stubs*** that at least signal execution of these procedures:

begin (* *ProcessCheck* *)
    writeln ('Executing ProcessCheck')
end (* *ProcessCheck* *);

and they might also produce temporary printouts to assist in checking other procedures.

```
PROGRAM CheckbookBalancer (input, output);

(***************************************************************

   Menu-driven program for reconciling a checkbook with a monthly
   statement.

 ***************************************************************)
CONST
   NumberOfOptions = 3;        (* # of options in menu *)

VAR
   InitialBalance,             (* beginning balance in checking account *)
   Balance,                    (* current balance *)
   TotalDeposits,              (* sum of all deposits for the month *)
   TotalChecks,                (* sum of all checks processed *)
   TotalServiceCharges : real; (* total check-processing charges *)
   NumberOfDeposits,           (* total number of deposits made *)
   NumberOfChecks,             (*                and checks written *)
   Option : integer;           (* option selected by user *)
   DoneProcessing : boolean;   (* indicates if processing completed *)
```

Figure 4.12

Figure 4.12   (cont.)

```pascal
PROCEDURE Initialize (VAR InitialBalance, Balance, TotalDeposits,
                          TotalChecks, TotalServiceCharges : real;
                      VAR NumberOfDeposits, NumberOfChecks : integer;
                      VAR DoneProcessing : boolean);

   (*************************************************************

       Procedure to get initial balance from user and
       initialize variables.

    *************************************************************)

   BEGIN (* Initialize *)
      write ('Enter beginning balance:  $');
      readln (InitialBalance);
      Balance := InitialBalance;
      TotalDeposits := 0;
      TotalChecks := 0;
      TotalServiceCharges := 0;
      NumberOfDeposits := 0;
      NumberOfChecks := 0;
      DoneProcessing := false;
   END (* Initialize *);

PROCEDURE DisplayMenu;

   (*************************************************************

          Procedure to display the menu of options.

    *************************************************************)

   BEGIN (* DisplayMenu *)
      writeln;
      writeln ('Options available are:');
      writeln ('0.  Quit processing');
      writeln ('1.  Process a deposit.');
      writeln ('2.  Process a check.');
      writeln ('3.  Print summary of month''s activities');
   END (* DisplayMenu *);

PROCEDURE ProcessDeposit (VAR Balance, TotalDeposits : real;
                          VAR NumberOfDeposits : integer);

   (*************************************************************

       Procedure to process a deposit.  Returns updated values of
       Balance, TotalDeposits, and NumberOfDeposits.

    *************************************************************)

   VAR
      Deposit : real;             (* amount of deposit *)

   BEGIN (* ProcessDeposit *)
      write ('Enter deposit:  $');
      readln (Deposit);
      Balance := Balance + Deposit;
      TotalDeposits := TotalDeposits + Deposit;
      NumberOfDeposits := NumberOfDeposits + 1
   END (* ProcessDeposit *);
```

Figure 4.12   (cont.)

```
PROCEDURE ProcessCheck (VAR Balance, TotalChecks, TotalServiceCharges : real;
                        VAR NumberOfChecks : integer);

    (*****************************************************************

        Procedure to process a check.  Returns updated values of
        Balance, TotalChecks, and NumberOfChecks.

    *****************************************************************)

    CONST
        CheckCharge = 0.20;     (* per check processing charge *)

    VAR
        Check : real;           (* amount of check *)

    BEGIN (* ProcessCheck *)
        write ('Enter check:  $');
        readln (Check);
        Balance := Balance - Check - CheckCharge;
        TotalChecks := TotalChecks + Check;
        TotalServiceCharges := TotalServiceCharges + CheckCharge;
        NumberOfChecks := NumberOfChecks + 1
    END (* ProcessCheck *);

PROCEDURE PrintSummary (InitialBalance, Balance, TotalDeposits,
                        TotalChecks, TotalServiceCharges : real;
                        NumberOfDeposits, NumberOfChecks : integer);

    (*****************************************************************

        Procedure to print summary of month's transactions.

    *****************************************************************)

    BEGIN (* PrintSummary *)
        writeln;
        writeln ('Initial Balance  . . . . . . . . $', InitialBalance:8:2);
        writeln ('Total Deposits . . . . . . . . . $', TotalDeposits:8:2);
        writeln ('Total Checks . . . . . . . . . . $', TotalChecks:8:2);
        writeln ('Total Service Charges  . . . . . $', TotalServiceCharges:8:2);
        writeln ('Final Balance  . . . . . . . . . $', Balance:8:2);
        writeln ('Number of Deposits:  ', NumberOfDeposits:1);
        writeln ('Number of Checks:    ', NumberOfChecks:1)
    END (* PrintSummary *);

BEGIN (* main program *)
    Initialize (InitialBalance, Balance, TotalDeposits, TotalChecks,
                TotalServiceCharges, NumberOfDeposits, NumberOfChecks,
                DoneProcessing);
    WHILE NOT DoneProcessing DO
        BEGIN
            DisplayMenu;
            write ('Enter Option:  ');
            readln (Option);
            IF Option = 0 THEN
                DoneProcessing := TRUE
            ELSE IF Option = 1 THEN
                ProcessDeposit (Balance, TotalDeposits, NumberOfDeposits)
```

Figure 4.12   (cont.)

```
        ELSE IF Option = 2 THEN
            ProcessCheck (Balance, TotalChecks, TotalServiceCharges,
                          NumberOfChecks)
        ELSE IF Option = 3 THEN
            PrintSummary (InitialBalance, Balance, TotalDeposits,
                          TotalChecks, TotalServiceCharges,
                          NumberOfDeposits, NumberOfChecks)
        ELSE
            writeln ('*** Invalid Option ***')
    END (* WHILE *)
END (* main program *).
```

Sample run:

```
Enter beginning balance:  $357.40

Options available are:
0.  Quit processing
1.  Process a deposit.
2.  Process a check.
3.  Print summary of month's activities
Enter Option:  1
Enter deposit:  $250.00

Options available are:
0.  Quit processing
1.  Process a deposit.
2.  Process a check.
3.  Print summary of month's activities
Enter Option:  2
Enter check:  $35.00

Options available are:
0.  Quit processing
1.  Process a deposit.
2.  Process a check.
3.  Print summary of month's activities
Enter Option:  2
Enter check:  $14.00

Options available are:
0.  Quit processing
1.  Process a deposit.
2.  Process a check.
3.  Print summary of month's activities
Enter Option:  3

Initial Balance  . . . . . . . . $  357.40
Total Deposits . . . . . . . . . $  250.00
Total Checks . . . . . . . . . . $   49.00
Total Service Charges  . . . . . $    0.40
Final Balance  . . . . . . . . . $  558.00
Number of Deposits:  1
Number of Checks:    2
```

Figure 4.12   (cont.)

```
Options available are:
0.  Quit processing
1.  Process a deposit.
2.  Process a check.
3.  Print summary of month's activities
Enter Option:  0
```

A major advantage of the modular design of a program such as this is that it is relatively easy to modify when necessary. For example, if the bank changes the amount charged for processing checks, we know immediately that procedure *ProcessCheck* is the one to modify; we simply change the value of *CheckCharge* to the new value. Similarly, if a charge is to be made for processing deposits, procedure *ProcessDeposit* is the one requiring modification. Some changes may require modification of more than one procedure, but the task is still considerably easier than in a nonmodular program, since one can usually determine which procedures require change and which ones must be added or deleted. For example, suppose we wish to modify the program to handle cash withdrawals as well, such as those from an automatic teller machine for which no processing charge is made. We could design a new procedure *ProcessATM* with variable parameters *Balance, TotalATMs,* and *NumberOfATMs.* To incorporate this procedure into the program, we need only do the following:

1. Change *NumberOfOptions* to 4.
2. Add a call to procedure *ProcessATM* in the **if-else if** construct with a new option number 4 (or perhaps renumber *PrintSummary* with 4 and use 3 for *ProcessATM*).
3. Add another *writeln* statement to procedure *DisplayMenu* to display this new option.
4. Modify the heading of and the reference to procedure *Initialize* to include *TotalATMs* and *NumberOfATMs* as variable parameters and add statements in *Initialize* to set these to 0.
5. Modify the heading of and the reference to procedure *PrintSummary* to include *TotalATMs* and *NumberOfATMs* as parameters and add statements in *PrintSummary* to display their values.

Exercises

1. Consider the following program skeleton:

program *Demo* (*input, output*);

const
   pi = 3.14159;
   two = 2;

var
   Month, Day, Year, p, q : *integer*;
   Hours, Rate, Amount, u, v : *real*;
   Code, Class : *char*;

procedure *Calculate* (*a* : *real*; **var** *b* : *real*;
        m : *integer*; **var** *k, n* : *integer*;
        var *c* : *char*);
        ⋮

Determine whether each of the following statements can be used in
the statement part of the program. If it cannot be used, explain why.

(a) *Calculate* (*u, v, two, p, q, Code*);
(b) *Calculate* (*pi, u, two, p, v, Class*);
(c) *Calculate* (*Hours, pi, two, Day, Year, Class*);
(d) **while** *u* > 0 **do**
         Calculate (*Rate, u, Day* + 2, *p, q,* 'M');
(e) *Calculate* (0, *Hours,* (*p* + 1)/2, *Day, Year, Code*);
(f) **while** *Amount* > 0 **do**
         Calculate (*two, Amount, Day, p* + *q, Day, Class*)

2. Write a procedure *CalculateWages* that calculates and returns the wages
   for a given number of hours worked and a given hourly pay rate.
   Hours over 40 should be paid at 1.5 times the regular hourly rate.

3. Write a procedure *DisplayMonth* that displays the name of a month
   whose number is passed to it.

4. Write a procedure *Switch* that interchanges the values of two variables. For example, if *a* has the value 3 and *b* has the value 4, then
   the reference *Switch* (*a, b*) causes *a* to have the value 4 and *b* the
   value 3.

5. With ***polar coordinates*** (*r, θ*) of a point *P*, the first polar coordinate
   r is the distance from the origin to *P*, and the second polar coordinate
   θ is the angle from the positive *x* axis to the ray joining the origin
   with *P*.

The formulas that relate polar coordinates of a point to ***rectangular
coordinates*** are

$$x = r \cos \theta$$
$$y = r \sin \theta$$

Write a procedure *Convert* that converts polar coordinates to rectangular coordinates. Use it in a program that reads the polar coordinates
for several points, calls *Convert* to find the rectangular coordinates
for each point, and then displays both pairs of coordinates.

6. Write a procedure that calculates the amount of city income tax and
   the amount of federal income tax to be withheld from an employee's

pay for one pay period. Assume that city income tax withheld is computed by taking 1.15 percent of gross pay on the first $15,000 earned per year and that federal income tax withheld is computed by taking the gross pay less $15 for each dependent claimed and multiplying by 20 percent.

Use this procedure in a program that for each of several employees reads his or her employee number, number of dependents, hourly pay rate, city income tax withheld to date, federal income tax withheld to date, and hours worked for this pay period, and then calculates and prints the employee number, gross pay and net pay for this pay period, the amount of city income tax and amount of federal income tax withheld for this pay period, and the total amounts withheld through this pay period.

7. The **greatest common divisor** of two integers a and b, GCD(a, b), not both of which are zero, is the largest positive integer that divides both a and b. The **Euclidean algorithm** for finding this greatest common divisor of a and b is as follows: Divide a by b to obtain the integer quotient q and remainder r, so that $a = bq + r$. (If $b = 0$, GCD(a, b) = a.) Then GCD(a, b) = GCD(b, r). Replace a with b and b with r and repeat this procedure. Since the remainders are decreasing, eventually a remainder of 0 results. The last nonzero remainder is GCD(a, b). For example,

$$
\begin{aligned}
1260 &= 198 \cdot 6 + 72 & \text{GCD}(1260, 198) &= \text{GCD}(198, 72) \\
198 &= 72 \cdot 2 + 54 & &= \text{GCD}(72, 54) \\
72 &= 54 \cdot 1 + 18 & &= \text{GCD}(54, 18) \\
54 &= 18 \cdot 3 + 0 & &= 18
\end{aligned}
$$

(*Note*: If either a or b is negative, we replace them with their absolute values.) The **least common multiple** of a and b, LCM(a, b), is the smallest nonnegative integer that is a multiple of both a and b and can be calculated using

$$
\text{LCM}(a, b) = \frac{|a \cdot b|}{\text{GCD}(a, b)}
$$

Write a program that reads two integers, calls a procedure that calculates and returns their greatest common divisor and least common multiple, and then displays these two values.

8. Write a program that reads two positive integers n and b and then calls a procedure *ChangeBase* to calculate and display the base-b representation of n. Assume that b is not greater than 10 (see Exercise 12 of Section 1.3 for one method for converting from base 10 to another base).

9. Write a program that reads a positive integer n and then calls a procedure *Hexadecimal* to display the base-16 representation of n. The symbols A, B, C, D, E, and F should be displayed for 10, 11, 12,

13, 14, and 15, respectively (see Exercises 7 and 12 of Section 1.3 and the preceding exercise).

10. Write a menu-driven program that allows the user to convert measurements from either minutes to hours or feet to meters (1 foot = 0.3048 meter), or from degrees Fahrenheit to degrees Celsius ($C = \frac{5}{9}(F - 32)$). Use procedures to implement the various options. A sample run of the program should proceed somewhat as follows:

```
Available options are
0. Display this menu.
1. Convert minutes to hours.
2. Convert feet to meters.
3. Convert degrees Fahrenheit to degrees Celsius.
4. Quit.

Enter an option (0 to see menu): 3
Enter degrees Fahrenheit: 212
This is equivalent to 100.0 degrees Celsius

Enter an option (0 to see menu): 5
*** 5 is not a valid option ***

Enter an option (0 to see menu): 0
Available options are
0. Display this menu.
1. Convert minutes to hours.
2. Convert feet to meters.
3. Convert degrees Fahrenheit to degrees Celsius.
4. Quit.

Enter an option (0 to see menu): 1
Enter minutes: 3600
This is equivalent to 60.0 hours

Enter an option (0 to see menu): 2
Enter number of feet: 1
This is equivalent to 0.3048 meters

Enter an option (0 to see menu): 4
```

11. Modify the checkbook-balancing program in Figure 4.12 to process ATM transactions as described in the text. While there is no charge for making a deposit using an ATM, there is a 20¢ charge for each withdrawal.

Programming Pointers

Program Design

1. All programs can be written using the three control structures considered in this chapter: sequence, selection, and repetition.

2. *Use constant identifiers in place of specific constants for values that may need to be changed when revising a program.* For example, the statements

   $Tax := 0.1963 * Wages;$

   and

   $NewBalance := OldBalance + 0.185 * OldBalance;$

   are better expressed without the magic numbers 0.1963 and 0.185 as

   $Tax := TaxRate * Wages;$

   and

   $NewBalance := OldBalance + InterestRate * OldBalance;$

   where *TaxRate* and *InterestRate* are constants defined by

   const
       $TaxRate = 0.1963;$
       $InterestRate = 0.185;$

3. *Multialternative selection structures can be implemented more efficiently with an **if-else if** construct than with a sequence of **if** statements.* For example, using the statements

   if *Score* < 60 **then**
       $Grade := 'F';$
   if (*Score* $>= 60$) **and** (*Score* < 70) **then**
       $Grade := 'D';$
   if (*Score* $>= 70$) **and** (*Score* < 80) **then**
       $Grade := 'C';$
   if (*Score* $>= 80$) **and** (*Score* < 90) **then**
       $Grade := 'B';$
   if *Score* $>= 90$ **then**
       $Grade := 'A';$

   is less efficient than

   if *Score* < 60 **then**
       $Grade := 'F'$
   else if *Score* < 70 **then**
       $Grade := 'D'$
   else if *Score* < 80 **then**
       $Grade := 'C'$
   else if *Score* < 90 **then**
       $Grade := 'B'$
   else
       $Grade := 'A';$

   In the first case, all of the **if** statements are executed for each score processed, and three of the boolean expressions are compound expressions. In the second case, each boolean expression is simple, and not all of them are evaluated for each score; for example, for a score of 65, only the boolean expressions *Score* < 60 and *Score* < 70 are evaluated.

4. *Programs for solving complex problems should be designed in a modular fashion. A problem should be divided into simpler subproblems so that a procedure can be written to solve each of these subproblems.*

Potential Problems

1. *Semicolons must be used to separate the statements in a compound statement.* For many compilers, a missing semicolon at the end of a line will not be detected until the next line. For example, compiling the erroneous compound statement

> **begin**
>   *Number* := *Number* + 1
>   *Sum* := *Sum* + *Number*
> **end**

may produce the error message

```
Sum := Sum + Number
↑
*** Unexpected symbol
```

Since a statement may be continued from one line to the next, the absence of a semicolon at the end of the statement

> *Number* := *Number* + 1

is not detected until the next line is examined, and "S" is not a symbol that can legally follow this statement.

2. *Each* **begin** *must have a matching* **end.** A missing **end** may be rather difficult to detect. The compiler may even search to the end of the program for an **end** to match an earlier **begin** and produce an error message such as

```
END.
    ↑
*** Unexpected symbol
*** End of source file—missing "." or unclosed comment?
```

3. *Parentheses must be used within boolean expressions to indicate those subexpressions that are to be evaluated first.* The precedence of operators that may appear in boolean expressions is

not	1 highest priority (performed first)
*, /, **div, mod, and**	2
+, −, **or**	3
<, >, =, <=, >=, <>	4 lowest priority (performed last)

To illustrate, consider the statement

if $1 < x$ and $x < 10$ then
 writeln (x)

where x is of real type. The first operation performed in evaluating the boolean expression is the **and** operation. However, the subexpression x **and** x is not a valid boolean expression, because boolean operators cannot be applied to numeric quantities; thus an error message such as the following results:

 *** Illegal types of operand(s). Types of operands
  conflict.

4. *When real quantities that are algebraically equal are compared with* $=$, *the result may be a false boolean expression, because most real values are not stored exactly.* For example, even though the two real expressions $x * (1/x)$ and 1.0 are algebraically equal, the boolean expression $x * (1/x) = 1.0$ is false for most real values x.

5. *In an* if *statement containing an* else *clause, there is no semicolon immediately before the* else. A statement such as

if $x > 0$ then
 writeln (x);
else
 writeln $(2 * x)$

results in an error. A semicolon immediately following **then** or **else** as in

if $x > 0$ then;
 writeln (x);
or
if $x > 0$ then
 $x := abs (x)$
else;
 writeln (x);

is syntactically correct, but it is almost surely a mistake, since it indicates an empty statement. In both of these examples, the statement *writeln* (x) is executed, regardless of whether or not x is positive.

6. *In a nested* if *statement, each* else *clause is matched with the nearest preceding unmatched* if. For example, consider the following statements, which are given without indentation:

if $x > 0$ then
if $y > 0$ then
$z := x + y$
else
$z := x + abs (y)$;
$w := x * y * z$;

With which **if** is the **else** associated? According to the rule just stated, these statements are executed as

```
if x > 0 then
   if y > 0 then
      z := x + y
   else
      z := x + abs (y);
w := x * y * z;
```

where the **else** clause matches the **if** statement containing the boolean expression $y > 0$.

7. *It should be assumed that all subexpressions are evaluated in determining the value of a compound boolean expression.* Suppose, for example, we write the statement

```
if (x >= 0) and (sqrt(x) < 5.0) then
   writeln ('Square root is less than 5')
```

where the subexpression $x >= 0$ is intended to prevent an attempt to calculate the square root of a negative number when x is negative. Some Pascal compilers may evaluate the subexpression $x >= 0$ and if it is false, will not evaluate the second subexpression $sqrt(x) < 5.0$. Other compilers evaluate both parts, and thus an error results when x is negative. This error can be avoided by rewriting the statement as

```
if x >= 0 then
   if sqrt(x) < 5.0 then
      writeln ('Square root is less than 5')
```

8. *The statement within a* **while** *statement must eventually cause the boolean expression controlling repetition to become false.* An ***infinite loop*** is the result otherwise. For example, if x is a real variable, the statements

```
x := 0;
while x <> 1.0 do
   begin
      writeln (x:4:1);
      x := x + 0.3
   end (* while *);
```

produce an infinite loop.

Output:
0.0
0.3
0.6
0.9
1.2
1.5
1.8
⋮

Since the value of x is never equal to 1.0, repetition is not terminated. In view of Potential Problem 4, the statements

```
x := 0;
while x <> 1.0 do
  begin
     writeln (x:4:1);
     x := x + 0.2
  end (* while *);
```

may also produce an infinite loop.

Output:
0.0
0.2
0.4
0.6
0.8
1.0
1.2
1.4
1.6
$\vdots$

Since x is initialized to 0 and 0.2 is added to x five times, x should have the value 1.0. But the boolean expression $x <> 1.0$ remains true, because most real values are not stored exactly.

9. *In a* **while** *statement, the boolean expression is evaluated before execution of the statement within the* **while** *statement.* Thus, the statement within a **while** statement is not executed if the boolean expression is false,

10. *The* **while** *statement controls repetition of only one statement.* For example, the statements

```
Count := 1;
while Count <= 10 do
  begin
     writeln (Count:2, sqr(Count):5);
     Count := Count + 1
  end (* while *)
```

display a list of the integers from 1 through 10 and their squares. The statements

```
Count := 1;
while Count <= 10 do
  writeln (Count:2, sqr(Count):5);
  Count := Count + 1
```

produce an infinite loop.

Output:
```
1      1
1      1
1      1
⋮      ⋮
```

11. *When a procedure is referenced, the number of actual parameters must be the same as the number of formal parameters in the procedure heading, and the type of each actual parameter must be compatible with the type of the corresponding formal parameter.* For example, consider the function with the heading

> **procedure** *PrintData* (*Number1*, *Number2* : *integer*) : *integer*;

The statements

> *PrintData* (*k*, *m*, *n*);

and

> *PrintData* (*Number*, 3.75);

are incorrect. In the first case, the number of actual parameters does not agree with the number of formal parameters, and in the second, the real value 3.75 cannot be assigned to the integer parameter *Number2*.

12. *Parameters that are to return values from a procedure must be declared as variable parameters using the indicator* **var**. *The corresponding actual parameters must be variables; they may not be constants or expressions.* For example, the procedure whose heading is

> **procedure** *Taxes* (*Income* : *real*; **var** *NetIncome*, *Tax* : *real*);

can return only values of *NetIncome* and *Tax* to the calling program unit, and it cannot be called by the statement

> *Taxes* (*Salary*, 3525.67, *IncomeTax*)

because the constant 3525.67 cannot be associated with the variable parameter *NetIncome*.

13. *Formal parameters in procedures are defined only during execution of that procedure; they are undefined both before and after execution.* Any attempt to use these parameters outside the procedure is an error.

14. *The scope of any identifier is the program unit in which it is declared.* For example, for the procedure

> **procedure** *Calculate* (*x* : *integer*; *y* : *real*);
>
> > **var**
> > *a*, *b* : *integer*;
> > ⋮

the local variables *x*, *y*, *a*, and *b* cannot be accessed outside the procedure *Calculate*.

Program Style

In this text, we use the following conventions for formatting the statements considered in this chapter.

1. *In a compound statement,* **begin** *and* **end** *are aligned, and the statements they enclose are indented.*

    begin
        statement-1;
            ⋮
        statement-n
    end

2. *For an* **if** *statement,* **if . . . then** *is on one line, with its statement indented on the next line. If there is an* **else** *clause,* **else** *is on a separate line, aligned with* **if,** *and its statement is indented on the next line.*

    if . . . then
        statement-1
    else
        statement-2

    if . . . then
        begin
            statement-1;
                ⋮
            statement-k
        end (∗ **if** ∗)
    else
        begin
            statement-k + 1;
                ⋮
            statement-n
        end(∗ **else** ∗)

    An exception is made when an **if** − **else if** *construct is used to implement a multialternative selection structure. In this case the format used is*

    if . . . then
        statement-1
    else if . . . then
        statement-2
    else if . . . then
        statement-3
            ⋮
    else
        statement-n

3. *In a* **while** *statement,* **while . . . do** *is on one line, with the body of the loop indented on the next line(s).*

> **while . . . do**
>   *statement*

> **while . . . do**
>   **begin**
>   *statement-1*;
>   ⋮
>   *statement-n*
>   **end** (∗ **while** ∗)

4. *A comment of the form* (∗ **if** ∗) *or* (∗ **while** ∗) *is attached to the reserved word* **end** *which marks the end of a compound statement that serves as one of the alternatives in an* **if** *statement or as the body of a while loop, respectively.*

5. *Procedures should be documented in the same way that programs are.* The documentation should include a brief description of the processing carried out by the procedure, the values passed to it, and the values returned by it.

6. *Procedures are separate program units, and the program format should reflect this.* In this text we

   (a) Insert a blank line before and after each procedure definition to separate it from other program units.
   (b) Indent the declarations and statements within each procedure.
   (c) Follow the stylistic standards for programs described in earlier chapters when writing procedures.

Variations and Extensions

The standard Pascal control structures described in this chapter are provided in nearly every version of Pascal. In some versions, however,

- It may not be possible to display boolean values. (UCSD)
- Boolean operators/functions may be applied (bitwise) to integer values. (Macintosh, Turbo) Additional operators and functions may be provided, for example, **xor** (exclusive or). (Turbo)

Also,

- Other program constructs may be provided to facilitate modular programming, for example, *units* or *modules*, which are collections of constant and type definitions, variable declarations, and procedure and function definitions that can be imported into programs as needed. (Turbo)

See Appendix G for details.

5

More About
Control Structures

We are all special cases.

ALBERT CAMUS

Progress might be a circle, rather than a straight line.

EBERHARD ZEIDLER

The basic control structures used in writing programs are *sequence, selection,* and *repetition.* In Chapter 4 we described compound statements in Pascal for implementing sequential structures. We also introduced the **if** statement to implement selection structures and the **while** statement to implement repetition structures. In this chapter we consider the **case** statement that can also be used to implement certain selection structures, and the **repeat-until** and **for** statements for implementing repetition structures.

5.1 Multialternative Selection Structure:
The *case* Statement

Recall from Chapter 4 that an **if** statement can be used to implement a selection structure in which exactly one of several alternative actions is selected and performed. In this statement, a selection is made by evaluating one or more boolean expressions, and because selection criteria can usually be formulated as boolean expressions, an **if-else if** construct can be used to implement almost any multialternative selection structure. In this section we describe the **case** statement, which, although it is not as general as the **if** statement, is useful for implementing some selection structures. The syntax diagram for a **case** *statement* is

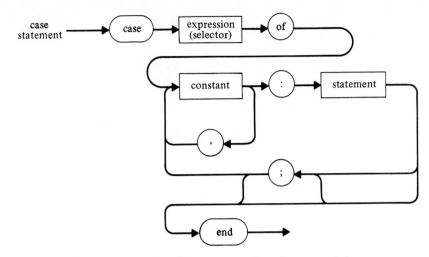

From this diagram we see that this statement has the general form

> **case** *selector* **of**
>   *label-list-1* : *statement-1*;
>   *label-list-2* : *statement-2*;
>   ⋮
>   *label-list-n* : *statement-n*
> **end**

where *selector* is an expression of integer, boolean, or character type (or of enumerated or subrange type, as defined in Chapter 8). Note that the selector may not be of real type. Each *label-list-i* is a list of one or more possible values of the selector. When a **case** statement is executed, the selector is evaluated; if this value is in *label-list-i*, then *statement-i* is executed, and execution continues with the statement following the reserved word **end** that marks the end of the **case** statement. It is an error if the selector's value is not in any of the label lists.[1]

As an application of the **case** statement, consider the problem of converting an integer class code to a class name. If the value of the variable *Class* is 1, 2, 3, or 4, the following **case** statement is appropriate:

> **case** *Class* **of**
>   1: *writeln* ('Freshman');
>   2: *writeln* ('Sophomore');
>   3: *writeln* ('Junior');
>   4: *writeln* ('Senior')
> **end** (∗ **case** ∗);

[1] Many implementations of Pascal allow execution of a **case** statement to "fall through" if the value of the selector is not in any of the label lists; that is, execution continues with the statement following the **case** statement. Many implementations also allow an **else** or **otherwise** clause that is executed if the value of the selector does not appear in any of the label lists.

> **case** *selector* **of**
>   *label-list-1* : *statement-1*;
>   ⋮
>   *label-list-n* : *statement-n*
>   **else** (∗ **otherwise** in some versions ∗)
>   *statement*
> **end** (∗ **case** ∗);

To ensure that the value of the selector *Class* is in the range from 1 through 4, an **if** statement should be used:[2]

if (*Class* < 1) **or** (*Class* > 4) **then**
   writeln ('Illegal class code')
else
  case *Class* **of**
    1: *writeln* ('Freshman');
    2: *writeln* ('Sophomore');
    3: *writeln* ('Junior');
    4: *writeln* ('Senior')
  end (* **case** *);

Occasionally, no action is required for certain values of the selector in a **case** statement. In such situations, these values may be placed in a label list for which the corresponding statement is empty. For example, a program to count aces and face cards might use the **case** statement

case *Card* **of**
             'A': *ace* := *ace* + 1;
       'J', 'Q', 'K': *face* := *face* + 1;
'2', '3', '4', '5', '6',
    '7', '8', '9', 'T': (* no action required *)
end (* **case** *);

The program in Figure 4.6 used an **if** statement to implement the multialternative selection structure required to assign a letter grade to a student's average as specified in the following table:

Average	Letter Grade
Average ≥ 90	A
80 ≤ average < 90	B
70 ≤ average < 80	C
60 ≤ average < 70	D
Average < 60	F

If we assume that the value of *Average* does not exceed 100, we can use a **case** statement to implement this five-way selection structure:

[2] If an **otherwise** or **else** clause as described in the previous footnote is available, it can be used to check that the selector is in range; for example,

case *Class* **of**
  1: *writeln* ('Freshman');
  2: *writeln* ('Sophomore');
  3: *writeln* ('Junior');
  4: *writeln* ('Senior')
  else (* or **otherwise** *)
    writeln ('Illegal class code')
end (* **case** *);

```
case round(Average) div 10 of
        9, 10 : Grade := 'A';
            8 : Grade := 'B';
            7 : Grade := 'C';
            6 : Grade := 'D';
0, 1, 2, 3, 4, 5 : Grade := 'F'
end (* case *);
```

Note that the real quantity *Average* is converted to integer type by using the *round* function so that it can be used as a selector in a **case** statement. Also, we have divided this integer average by 10 so that the label lists are shortened. Had we used *round(Average)* as the selector, then all of the values it could have would have to be listed; for example, the last label list would have to contain all of the numbers 0, 1, 2, 3, 4, . . . , 50.

The program in Figure 5.1 is the modification of that in Figure 4.6 that results when the **if** statement is replaced by this **case** statement.

```
PROGRAM GradeAssignment4 (input, output);

(**********************************************************************

   Program to compute a final course average using three inputs:
   homework average, average on tests, and an exam score;  a letter
   grade is then assigned.

   *********************************************************************)

CONST
     HWWeight = 0.2;          (* weight factors for homework, *)
     TestWeight = 0.5;        (*      tests, *)
     ExamWeight = 0.3;        (*      and the exam *)
     ABLine = 90.0;           (* A/B line *)
     BCLine = 80.0;           (* B/C line *)
     CDLine = 70.0;           (* C/D line *)
     DFLine = 60.0;           (* D/F line *)

VAR
     Homework, Tests, Exam,   (* homework, test, and exam averages *)
     Average : real;          (* final course average *)
     Grade : char;            (* grade assigned (A, B, C, D or F) *)

BEGIN
     write ('Enter homework, test and exam scores: ');
     readln (Homework, Tests, Exam);
     Average := HWWeight * Homework + TestWeight * Tests
               + ExamWeight * Exam;
```

Figure 5.1

Figure 5.1 (cont.)

```
CASE round(Average) DIV 10 OF
        9, 10 : Grade := 'A';
            8 : Grade := 'B';
            7 : Grade := 'C';
            6 : Grade := 'D';
  0,1,2,3,4,5 : Grade := 'F';
END (* CASE *);
writeln ('Average = ', Average:5:1, ' Grade = ', Grade);
writeln
END.
```

Exercises

1. Write a **case** statement for each of the following:

   (a) If the value of the character variable *TransCode* is 'D', increase *Balance* by adding *Amount* to it; if *TransCode* is 'W', decrease *Balance* by subtracting *Amount* from it; if *TransCode* is 'P', display the value of *Balance*.

   (b) Display the name of a month or an error message for a given value of the integer variable *Month*. Use an **if** statement to display an error message if the value of *Month* is less than 1 or greater than 12.

   (c) Assign the value to *Cost* corresponding to the value of the integer variable *Distance* given in the following table:

Distance	Cost
0 through 99	5.00
At least 100 but less than 300	8.00
At least 300 but less than 600	10.00
At least 600 but less than 1000	12.00

   (d) Display the number of days in a month. (See Exercise 1(d) of Section 4.3 regarding the determination of leap years.)

2. Rewrite the while loop in the statement part of the checkbook-balancing program of Figure 4.12, using a **case** statement to process the various options.

3. Write the menu-driven program for converting measurements as described in Exercise 10 of Section 4.7, but use a **case** statement to process the various options.

4. Write a program that reads numbers representing TV channels and then uses a **case** statement to determine the call letters of the station that corresponds to each number or some message indicating that the channel is not used. Use the following channel numbers and call letters:

2:   WCBS
4:   WNBC
5:   WNEW
7:   WABC
9:   WOR
11:   WPIX
13:   WNET

5. A wholesale office supply company discounts the price of each of its products depending on the number of units bought and the price per unit. The discount increases as the numbers of units bought and/or the unit price increases. These discounts are given in the following table:

Number Bought	Unit Price (dollars)		
	0–10.00	10.01–100.00	100.01–
1–9	0%	2%	5%
10–99	5%	7%	9%
100–499	9%	15%	21%
500–999	14%	23%	32%
1000–	21%	32%	43%

Write a program that reads the number of units bought and the unit price, and then calculates and prints the total full cost, the total amount of the discount, and the total discounted cost.

6. Locating avenues' addresses in mid-Manhattan is not easy; for example, the nearest cross street to 866 3rd Avenue is 53rd Street, whereas the nearest cross street to 866 2nd Avenue is 46th Street. To locate approximately the nearest numbered cross street for a given avenue address, the following algorithm can be used:
Cancel the last digit of the address, divide by 2, and add or subtract the number given in the following (abbreviated) table:

1st Ave.	Add 3
2nd Ave.	Add 3
3rd Ave.	Add 10
4th Ave.	Add 8
5th Ave. up to 200	Add 13
5th Ave. up to 400	Add 16
6th Ave. (Ave. of the Americas)	Subtract 12
7th Ave.	Add 12
8th Ave.	Add 10
10th Ave.	Add 14

Write a program that reads an avenue address and then uses a **case** statement to determine the number of the nearest cross street according to the preceding algorithm.

7. An airline vice-president in charge of operations needs to determine whether or not the current estimates of flight times are accurate. Since

there is a larger possibility of variations due to weather and air traffic in the longer flights, he allows a larger error in the time estimates for them. He compares an actual flight time with the estimated flight time and considers the estimate to be too large, acceptable, or too small, depending on the following table of acceptable error margins:

Estimated Flight Time in Minutes	Acceptable Error Margin in Minutes
0–29	1
30–59	2
60–89	3
90–119	4
120–179	6
180–239	8
240–359	13
360–	17

For example, if an estimated flight time is 106 minutes, the acceptable error margin is 4 minutes. Thus, the estimated flight time is too large if the actual flight time is less than 102 minutes, or the estimated flight time is too small if the actual flight time is greater than 110 minutes; otherwise, the estimate is acceptable. Write a program that reads an estimated flight time and an actual flight time, uses a **case** statement to determine the acceptable error according to this table, and then prints whether the estimated time is too large, acceptable, or too small. If the estimated flight time is either too large or too small, the program should also print the amount of the overestimate or underestimate.

5.2 Repetition Structure: The *for* Statement

In Chapter 4 we described the **while** statement that can be used to implement repetition structures called while loops. In such loops the body of the loop is executed repeatedly while some boolean expression remains true. Another repetition structure is a ***for loop*** in which the body of the loop is executed for certain values in some specified range of values. This kind of loop can be implemented in Pascal using a **for** statement.

The syntax diagram for a **for** *statement* is

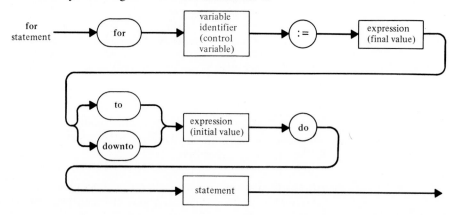

From this diagram we see that this statement has two forms:

> **for** *control-variable* : = *initial-value* **to** *final-value* **do**
>> *statement*

or

> **for** *control-variable* : = *initial-value* **downto** *final-value* **do**
>> *statement*

In these forms, the control variable, the initial value, and the final value all must be of the same type, which may be integer, character, or boolean (or of enumerated or subrange types, as described in Chapter 8). In the examples in this chapter, they are always of integer type. The initial and final values may be any valid Pascal expressions.

A **for** statement of the form

> **for** *control-variable* : = *initial-value* **to** *final-value* **do**
>> *statement*

implements the following repetition structure:

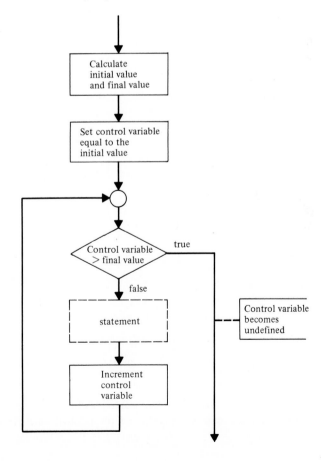

As this diagram shows, when a **for** statement of this form is executed, the control variable is assigned the initial value, and the specified statement is executed unless the initial value is greater than the limit. The control variable is then incremented by 1, and if this new value does not exceed the limit, the body of the loop is executed again. Execution of the **for** statement terminates when the value of the control variable exceeds the limit.

To illustrate, consider the statement

> **for** *Number* : = 1 **to** 10 **do**
>   *writeln (Number*:2, *sqr(Number)*:5);

where *Number* is of integer type. In this statement, *Number* is the control variable, the initial value is 1, and the final value is 10. When this statement is executed, the initial value 1 is assigned to *Number,* and the *writeln* statement is executed. The value of *Number* is then incremented by 1, and because this new value 2 is less than the final value 10, the *writeln* statement is executed again. This repetition continues as long as the value of the control variable *Number* is less than or equal to the final value 10. Thus, the output produced by this statement is

```
 1    1
 2    4
 3    9
 4   16
 5   25
 6   36
 7   49
 8   64
 9   81
10  100
```

To repeat more than one statement using a for loop, we combine them into a single compound statement. For example, to double space the preceding output, we might use

> **for** *Number* : = 1 **to** 10 **do**
>   **begin**
>   *writeln (Number*:2, *sqr(Number)*:5);
>   *writeln*
>   **end** (∗ **for** ∗);

In the second form of the **for** statement,

> **for** *control-variable* : = *initial-value* **downto** *final-value* **do**
>   *statement*

the control variable is decremented rather than incremented, and repetition continues as long as the value of the control variable is greater than or equal to the final value. This is illustrated in the following diagram:

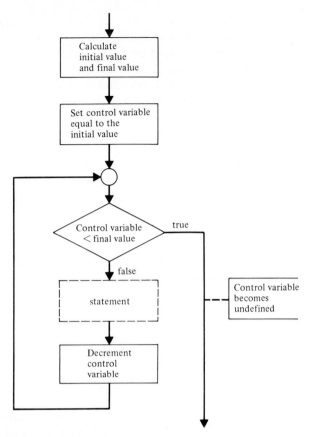

For example, consider the statement

for *Number* := 10 **downto** 1 **do**
   writeln (*Number*:2, *sqr*(*Number*):5);

The control variable *Number* is assigned the initial value 10, and because this value is greater than the final value 1, the *writeln* statement is executed. The value of *Number* is then decreased to 9, and because this new value is greater than the final value, the *writeln* statement is executed again. This process continues as long as the value of *Number* is greater than or equal to the final value 1. Thus, the output produced is

```
10   100
 9    81
 8    64
 7    49
 6    36
 5    25
 4    16
 3     9
 2     4
 1     1
```

Note that in this form of the **for** statement, **downto** is a single word.

As the diagrams illustrate, the value of the control variable is compared with the final value *before* the specified statement is executed. Thus, in the first form of the **for** statement, if the initial value is greater than the final value, the specified statement is never executed. This is also the case in the second form if the initial value is less than the final value.

The initial and/or final values in a **for** statement may be variables or expressions. To illustrate, consider the statements

> *write* ('Enter table size: ');
> *readln* (*TableSize*);
> **for** *Number* := 1 **to** *TableSize* **do**
>   *writeln* (*Number*:4, *sqr*(*Number*):8);

The value entered for *TableSize* is the final value in this **for** statement. These statements are used in the program of Figure 5.2 to print a table of squares whose size is read during program execution.

```
PROGRAM TableOfSquares (input, output);

(******************************************************************

    This program prints a table of integers and their squares.
    The size of the table is entered during execution.

******************************************************************)

VAR
    TableSize,          (* number of rows in table *)
    Number : integer;   (* number whose square is calculated *)

BEGIN
    write ('Enter table size:   ');
    readln (TableSize);
    writeln;
    writeln ('Number  Square');
    writeln ('------  ------');
    FOR Number := 1 TO TableSize DO
        writeln (Number:4, sqr(Number):8)
END.


Sample run:

Enter table size:   10
```

Figure 5.2

Figure 5.2 (cont.)

```
Number   Square
------   ------
     1        1
     2        4
     3        9
     4       16
     5       25
     6       36
     7       49
     8       64
     9       81
    10      100
```

The initial and final values of the control variable are determined before repetition begins and cannot be changed during execution of the **for** *statement.* Within the body of the for loop, values of variables that specify these initial and final values may change, but this does not affect the number of repetitions. Also, the statement within a **for** statement may use the value of the control variable, though *it must not modify the value of the control variable.* (See Potential Problem 2 in the Programming Pointers at the end of this chapter.) *When execution of the* **for** *statement is completed, the control variable becomes undefined.* Using this variable before assigning it a value yields unpredictable results.

The statement that appears within a **for** statement may itself be a **for** statement, that is, one **for** statement may be nested within another **for** statement. As an example, consider the program in Figure 5.3 that calculates and displays products of the form $X * Y$ for X ranging from 1 through *LastX* and Y ranging from 1 through *LastY* for integers *LastX* and *LastY*. The table of products is generated by the **for** statement

> **for** $X := 1$ **to** *LastX* **do**
>   **for** $Y := 1$ **to** *LastY* **do**
>   **begin**
>   *Product* $:= X * Y$;
>   *writeln* (X:2, '*', Y:2, ' = ', *Product*:3)
>   **end** (* **for** *);

In the sample run, both *LastX* and *LastY* are assigned the value 4. The control variable X is assigned its initial value 1, and the statement

> **for** $Y := 1$ **to** *LastY* **do**
>   **begin**
>   *Product* $:= X * Y$;
>   *writeln* (X:2, '*', Y:2, ' = ', *Product*:3)
>   **end** (* **for** *);

is executed. This calculates and displays the first four products $1 * 1$, $1 * 2$, $1 * 3$, and $1 * 4$. The value of X is then incremented by 1, and the preceding

for statement is executed again. This calculates and displays the next four products, $2 * 1$, $2 * 2$, $2 * 3$, and $2 * 4$. The control variable X is then incremented to 3, producing the next four products, $3 * 1$, $3 * 2$, $3 * 3$, and $3 * 4$, and finally X is incremented to 4, giving the last four products, $4 * 1$, $4 * 2$, $4 * 3$, and $4 * 4$.

```
PROGRAM Products (input, output);

(***************************************************************

   This program calculates and displays a list of products
   of two numbers.

****************************************************************)

VAR
  X, Y,                    (* two numbers being multiplied *)
  LastX, LastY,            (* last values of X and Y, respectively *)
  Product : integer;       (* product of X and Y *)

BEGIN
   write ('Enter upper limits for factors of product:  ');
   readln (LastX, LastY);
   writeln;
   FOR X := 1 TO LastX DO
      FOR Y := 1 TO LastY DO
         BEGIN
            Product := X * Y;
            writeln (X:2, ' *', Y:2, ' =', Product:3)
         END (* FOR *)
END.
```

Sample run:

```
Enter upper limits for factors of product:  4 4

1 * 1 =  1
1 * 2 =  2
1 * 3 =  3
1 * 4 =  4
2 * 1 =  2
2 * 2 =  4
2 * 3 =  6
2 * 4 =  8
3 * 1 =  3
3 * 2 =  6
3 * 3 =  9
3 * 4 = 12
4 * 1 =  4
4 * 2 =  8
4 * 3 = 12
4 * 4 = 16
```

Figure 5.3

5.3   Repetition Structure: The *repeat-until* Statement

Recall that a while loop is a pretest or "test-at-the-top" loop in which the boolean expression that controls repetition is evaluated *before* the body of the loop is executed. Sometimes, however, it is appropriate to use a ***posttest loop*** or "test-at-the-bottom" loop like that pictured in the following diagram, in which the termination test is made *after* the body of the loop is executed:

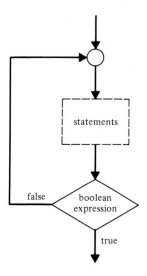

Such a posttest loop is also called a ***repeat-until loop*** and can be implemented in Pascal by using a **repeat-until** statement.

The syntax diagram for a **repeat-until** *statement* is

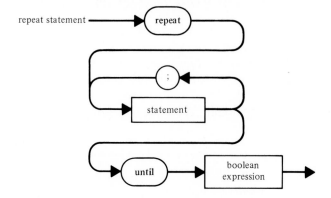

A **repeat-until** statement thus has the form

> **repeat**
>> *statement-1*;
>> *statement-2*;
>> ⋮
>> *statement-n*
> **until** *boolean expression*

When a **repeat-until** statement is executed, the specified statements *statement-1, statement-2, . . . , statement-n* are executed, and the *boolean expression* is evaluated. If its value is true, execution continues with the next statement in the program; otherwise, the specified statements are executed again. This repetition continues until the boolean expression becomes true.

To illustrate use of the **repeat-until** statement, we consider once again the problem of calculating the mean of a set of test scores as described in Section 4.4. Since the number of scores is not known in advance, a program to solve this problem must read and count the data values before the mean can be calculated. The program in Figure 4.8 used the standard technique of signaling the end of data with an end-of-data flag. An alternative approach is to ask the user repeatedly if there are more data items, terminating when the response is "no." And because there ordinarily will be at least one data item, it seems natural to check this termination condition at the bottom of the loop, that is, to use a repeat-until loop to read the data values.

This leads to the following modified algorithm:

MODIFIED ALGORITHM TO FIND MEAN SCORE

(* Algorithm to read a list of scores, count them, and find the mean
   score (*MeanScore*); *Score* represents the current score read, *NumScores*
   is the number of scores, and *Sum* is the sum of the scores. Scores
   are read until the user enters a value of 'N' or 'n' for *Response*. *)

1. Set *Sum* equal to 0.
2. Set *NumScores* equal to 0.
3. Repeat the following:
   a. Read first *Score*.
   b. Increment *NumScores* by 1.
   c. Add *Score* to *Sum*.
   d. Ask the user if there is more data and read *Response*.
   Until *Response* is 'N' or 'n'.
4. Calculate *MeanScore* = *Sum* / *NumScores*.
5. Display *MeanScore* and *NumScores*.

For this algorithm, the repetition structure in Step 3 can be implemented in Pascal by

```
repeat
    write ('Score:   ');
    readln (Score);
    NumScores := NumScores + 1;
    Sum := Sum + Score;
    write ('More scores (Y or N)? ');
    readln (Response)
until (Response = 'N') or (Response = 'n');
```

This **repeat-until** statement is used in the program in Figure 5.4 that implements the preceding algorithm.

```
PROGRAM CalculateMeanScore (input, output);

(*****************************************************************

   This program reads a list of scores, counts them, and
   calculates the mean score.  Scores are read and processed until
   the user responds with 'N' (or 'n') to the question 'More data?'.

*****************************************************************)

VAR
   NumScores : integer;    (* number of scores *)
   Sum,                    (* sum of the scores *)
   Score,                  (* current score being processed *)
   MeanScore : real;       (* mean of the scores *)
   Response  : char;       (* user's response to 'More data?' question *)

BEGIN
   Sum := 0;
   NumScores := 0;
   REPEAT
      write ('Score:   ');
      readln (Score);
      NumScores := NumScores + 1;
      Sum := Sum + Score;
      write ('More scores (Y or N)? ');
      readln (Response)
   UNTIL (Response = 'N') OR (Response = 'n');
   MeanScore := Sum / NumScores;
   writeln;
   writeln (NumScores:1, ' scores with mean = ', MeanScore:5:2)
END.
```

Sample runs:

```
Score:   60
More scores (Y or N)? Y
Score:   70
More scores (Y or N)? Y
Score:   80
More scores (Y or N)? N

3 scores with mean = 70.00
```

Figure 5.4

5.4   Example: Depreciation Tables

We have now considered all the statements provided in Pascal for implementing the basic control structures:

Control Structure	Pascal Implementation
Sequential	Compound statement
Selection	**if**
	case
Repetition	**while**
	for
	repeat-until

We have also introduced procedures that play an important role in the modular design of software. In this section we consider the problem of developing a program to calculate and display depreciation tables. This program will be designed in a modular fashion, using procedures to carry out the main processing tasks and will illustrate several of the Pascal control statements.

Depreciation is a decrease in the value over time of some asset due to wear and tear, decay, declining price, and so on. For example, suppose that a company purchases a new computer system for $200,000 that will serve its needs for a five-year period. After that time it can be sold at an estimated price of $50,000. Thus, the value of the computing equipment will have depreciated by $150,000 over a five-year period.

The calculation of depreciation tables that display the value lost in each of several years is an important accounting problem, and there are several ways of calculating depreciation. One of the simplest methods is the *straight-line method* in which the amount to be depreciated is divided evenly over the specified number of years. For example, straight-line depreciation of $150,000 over a five-year period would give an annual depreciation of $150,000/5 = $30,000. An algorithm for calculating depreciation using this method is simple:

ALGORITHM FOR STRAIGHT-LINE DEPRECIATION

(∗ Algorithm to depreciate *Amount* over *NumYears* years using the straight-line method of calculating depreciation. ∗)

1. Calculate *Depreciation* = *Amount* / *NumYears*.
2. For *Year* ranging from 1 through *NumYears* do the following:
        Display *Year* and *Depreciation*.

Another common method of calculating depreciation is the *sum-of-the-years-digits method.* To illustrate it, consider again depreciating $150,000 over a five-year period. We first calculate the "sum of the years" $1 + 2 + 3 + 4 + 5 = 15$. In the first year, 5/15 of $150,000 ($50,000) is depreciated, in the second year, 4/15 of $150,000 ($40,000) is depreciated, and so on, giving the following depreciation table:

Year	Depreciation
1	$50,000
2	$40,000
3	$30,000
4	$20,000
5	$10,000

An algorithm for calculating depreciation using this method is

ALGORITHM FOR SUM-OF-THE-YEARS-DIGITS DEPRECIATION

(* Algorithm to depreciate *Amount* over *NumYears* years using the sum-of-the-years-digits method of calculating depreciation. *)

1. Calculate *Sum* = 1 + 2 + · · · + *NumYears*.
2. For *Year* ranging from 1 through *NumYears* do the following:
   a. Calculate
      $$Depreciation = (NumYears - Year + 1) * Amount / Sum.$$
   b. Display *Year* and *Depreciation*.

A third method of calculating depreciation is the **double-declining balance method.** In this method, if an amount is to be depreciated over n years, $2/n$ times the undepreciated balance is depreciated annually. For example, in the depreciation of $150,000 over a five-year period using the double-declining balance method, 2/5 of $150,000 ($60,000) would be depreciated the first year, leaving an undepreciated balance of $90,000. In the second year, 2/5 of $90,000 ($36,000) would be depreciated, leaving an undepreciated balance of $54,000. Since in each year only a fraction of the remaining balance is depreciated, the entire amount would never be depreciated. Consequently, it is permissible to switch to the straight-line method at any time. Developing an algorithm for this method of depreciation is left as an exercise.

The program in Figure 5.5 is a menu-driven program for calculating depreciation tables and has the structure shown in the following diagram:

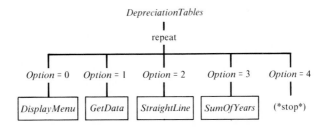

The user selects options from the menu, and an **if** statement containing a **case** statement is used to process these options:

> **if** (*Option* < 0) **or** (*Option* > 4) **then**
>   *writeln* ('Illegal option')
> **else**
>   **case** *Option* **of**
>   0 : *DisplayMenu*;
>   1 : *GetData* (*Amount, NumYears*);
>   2 : *StraightLine* (*Amount, NumYears*);
>   3 : *SumOfYears* (*Amount, NumYears*);
>   4 : (∗ stop ∗)
>   **end** (∗ **case** ∗)

Here *DisplayMenu, GetData, StraightLine,* and *SumOfYears* are procedures that carry out the operations specified by the user. A **repeat-until** statement is used to implement the repetition structure indicated in the structure diagram.

```
PROGRAM DepreciationTables (input, output);

(***********************************************************************

   Menu-driven program to calculate and display depreciation tables
   using various methods of depreciation.

 ***********************************************************************)

CONST
   MaxOption = 4;            (* maximum option number *)

VAR
   Option,                   (* option selected by the user *)
   NumYears : integer;       (* number of years over which to depreciate *)
   Amount : real;            (* amount to be depreciated *)

PROCEDURE DisplayMenu;

   (*******************************************************************

             Procedure to display the menu of options

    *******************************************************************)

   BEGIN
      writeln;
      writeln ('The following options are available:');
      writeln ('0:  Display this menu');
      writeln ('1:  Enter new amount and number of years');
      writeln ('2:  Print depreciation table using straight-line method');
      writeln ('3:  Print depreciation table using sum-of-years-digits method');
      writeln ('4:  Stop');
   END (* DisplayMenu *);
```

Figure 5.5

Figure 5.5 (cont.)

```
PROCEDURE GetData (VAR Amount : real;  VAR NumYears : integer);

   (*****************************************************************

      Procedure to read an Amount to be depreciated and the number
      of years over which to depreciate it.

   *****************************************************************)

   BEGIN
      write ('Enter amount to be depreciated:  ');
      readln (Amount);
      write ('Enter number of years:  ');
      readln (NumYears)
   END (* GetData *);

PROCEDURE StraightLine (Amount : real; NumYears : integer);

   (*****************************************************************

      Procedure to calculate and display a depreciation table for
      Amount over NumYears years using the straight-line method
      of depreciation.

   *****************************************************************)

   VAR
      Depreciation : real;              (* annual depreciation *)
      Year : integer;                   (* index -- year number *)

   BEGIN
      Depreciation := Amount / NumYears;
      writeln;
      writeln ('Year Depreciation');
      writeln ('-----------------');
      FOR Year := 1 TO NumYears DO
         writeln (Year : 3, Depreciation : 12:2)
   END (* StraightLine *);

PROCEDURE SumOfYears (Amount : real; NumYears : integer);

   (*****************************************************************

      Procedure to calculate and display a depreciation table for
      Amount over NumYears years using the sum-of-years-digits method
      of depreciation.

   *****************************************************************)

   VAR
      Depreciation : real;        (* annual depreciation *)
      Sum,                        (* 1 + 2 + ... + NumYears *)
      Year : integer;             (* index -- year number *)
```

Figure 5.5   (cont.)

```
   BEGIN
      Sum := 0;
      FOR Year := 1 TO NumYears DO
         Sum := Sum + Year;

      writeln;
      writeln ('Year Depreciation');
      writeln ('-----------------');
      FOR Year := 1 TO NumYears DO
         BEGIN
            Depreciation := (NumYears - Year + 1) * Amount / Sum;
            writeln (Year : 3, Depreciation : 12:2)
         END (* FOR *)
   END (* SumOfYears *);

   BEGIN (* main program *)
      writeln ('The following program allows you to print depreciation tables');
      writeln ('using various methods of depreciation.');
      DisplayMenu;
      REPEAT
         writeln;
         write ('Option? ');
         readln (Option);
         IF (Option < 0) OR (Option > MaxOption) THEN
            writeln ('Illegal option')
         ELSE
            CASE Option OF
               0 : DisplayMenu;
               1 : GetData (Amount, NumYears);
               2 : StraightLine (Amount, NumYears);
               3 : SumOfYears (Amount, NumYears);
               4 : (* quit *)
            END (* CASE *)
      UNTIL Option = 4
   END (* main program *).
```

Sample run:
_____

```
The following program allows you to print depreciation tables
using various methods of depreciation.

The following options are available:
0:  Display this menu
1:  Enter new amount and number of years
2:  Print depreciation table using straight-line method
3:  Print depreciation table using sum-of-years-digits method
4:  Stop

Option? 0

The following options are available:
0:  Display this menu
1:  Enter new amount and number of years
2:  Print depreciation table using straight-line method
3:  Print depreciation table using sum-of-years-digits method
4:  Stop
```

Figure 5.5   (cont.)

```
Option? 1
Enter amount to be depreciated:   1500.00
Enter number of years:   5

Option? 2

Year Depreciation
-----------------
   1        300.00
   2        300.00
   3        300.00
   4        300.00
   5        300.00

Option? 3

Year Depreciation
-----------------
   1        500.00
   2        400.00
   3        300.00
   4        200.00
   5        100.00

Option? 6
Illegal option

Option? 1
Enter amount to be depreciated:   1000.00
Enter number of years:   2

Option? 2

Year Depreciation
-----------------
   1        500.00
   2        500.00

Option? 4
```

Exercises

1. Describe the output produced by each of the following program segments:

(a) **for** $I := -2$ **to** 3 **do**
 writeln (I:1, ' squared $= $ ', $sqr(I)$:1);

(b) **for** $I := 1$ **to** 5 **do**
 begin
  write (I:1);
  for $J := I$ **downto** 1 **do**
   writeln (J:1)
 end;

(c) $K := 5;$
  for $I := -2$ **to** 3 **do**
    begin
      $writeln(I + K : 2);$
      $K := 1$
    end (* **for** *);

(d) for $I := 1$ **to** 3 **do**
    for $J := 1$ **to** 3 **do**
      for $K := I$ **to** J **do**
        $writeln\ (I{:}1,\ J{:}1,\ K{:}1);$

(e) for $I := 1$ **to** 3 **do**
    for $J := 1$ **to** 3 **do**
      begin
        for $K := I$ **to** J **do**
          $write\ (I{:}1,\ J{:}1,\ K{:}1);$
        $writeln$
      end;

(f) $I := 0;$
  repeat
    $K := I * I * I - 3 * I + 1;$
    $writeln\ (I{:}3,\ K{:}3)$
  until $I > 2;$

(g) $I := 0;$
  repeat
    $J := I * I * I;$
    $write\ (I{:}3);$
    repeat
      $K := I + 2 * J;$
      $write\ (J{:}3,\ K{:}3)$
      $J := J + 2$
    until $K > 10;$
    $writeln;$
    $I := I + 1$
  until $J > 5;$

2. Write a program that uses a for loop to generate the table of prices described in Exercise 6 of Section 4.5. Use a repeat loop to process the given data sets.

3. Write a program that reads a positive integer n and then uses a for loop to generate the first n Fibonacci numbers (see Exercise 12 of Section 4.5).

4. Suppose that at a given time, genotypes AA, AB, and BB appear in the proportions x, y, and z, respectively, where $x = 0.25$, $y = 0.5$, and $z = 0.25$. If individuals of type AA cannot reproduce, the probability that one parent will donate gene A to an offspring is

$$p = \frac{1}{2}\left(\frac{y}{y + z}\right)$$

since $y/(y + z)$ is the probability that the parent is of type AB and $1/2$ is the probability that such a parent will donate gene A. Then the proportions x', y', and z' of AA, AB, and BB, respectively, in the succeeding generation are given by

$$x' = p^2, \quad y' = 2p(1 - p), \quad z' = (1 - p)^2$$

and the new probability is given by

$$p' = \frac{1}{2}\left(\frac{y'}{y' + z'}\right)$$

Write a program to calculate and print the generation number and the proportions of AA, AB, and BB under appropriate headings for 30 generations. (Note that the proportions of AA and AB should approach 0, since gene A will gradually disappear.)

5. For a positive integer n, **n factorial** is denoted by $n!$ and is defined to be the product of the integers from 1 through n; $0!$ is defined as 1. Write a program that reads a nonnegative integer n and then uses a for loop to calculate $n!$

6. In an **infinite series,** the nth **partial sum** is the sum of the first n terms. The infinite series

$$\sum_{k=0}^{\infty} \frac{1}{k!}$$

converges to the number e. Write a program to calculate and display the first 10 partial sums of this series. (See Exercise 5 for a definition of $k!$.)

7. Write a program to calculate and print the first 20 partial sums of the **continued fraction**

$$1 + \cfrac{1}{1 + \cfrac{1}{1 + \cfrac{1}{1 + \cfrac{1}{1 +}}}}$$

$$\ddots$$

If S_k is the kth partial sum, then $S_1 = 1$, $S_2 = 1 + \dfrac{1}{1}$,

$S_3 = 1 + \cfrac{1}{1 + \cfrac{1}{1}}$, and so on. (*Hint*: Find a relationship between S_{k+1}

and S_k.)

8. Write a program that uses nested for loops to print the following multiplication table:

	1	2	3	4	5	6	7	8	9
1	1								
2	2	4							
3	3	6	9						
4	4	8	12	16					
5	5	10	15	20	25				
6	6	12	18	24	30	36			
7	7	14	21	28	35	42	49		
8	8	16	24	32	40	48	56	64	
9	9	18	27	36	45	54	63	72	81

9. Review the algorithm given in Section 4.4 for the summation problem of finding the smallest positive integer *Number* for which the sum $1 + 2 + \cdots + Number$ is greater than *Limit*. Suppose the while loop in this algorithm were replaced by a repeat-until loop so that the statements in the program of Figure 4.7 that implements this algorithm were replaced by

```
write ('Enter value that 1 + 2 + . . . + ? is to exceed:  ');
readln (Limit);
Number := 0;
Sum := 0;
REPEAT
   Number := Number + 1;
   Sum := Sum + Number;
UNTIL Sum > Limit;
writeln ('1 + . . . + ', Number:1, ' = ',
         Sum:1, ' > ', Limit:1)
```

Will the resulting program produce the same results as those in Figure 4.7 in all cases?

10. (a) Design an algorithm that uses a posttest loop to count the digits in a given positive integer.
    (b) Write Pascal statements to implement the algorithm in part (a).
    (c) Design an algorithm that uses a pretest loop to count the digits in a given positive integer.
    (d) Write Pascal statements to implement the algorithm in part (c).

11. Write a program that reads an amount of a loan, an annual interest rate, and a monthly payment and then displays under appropriate headings the payment number, the interest for that month, and the balance remaining after that payment. The monthly interest is $R/12$ percent of the unpaid balance after the payment is subtracted, where R is the annual interest rate. Also, keep a running total of the interest and display this after the last payment with an appropriate label. Design the program so that it will automatically construct such tables for several different loan amounts, interest rates, and monthly payments;

in particular, execute it with the following triples of values: $100, 18 percent, $10 and $500, 12 percent, $25. (*Note*: In general, the last payment will not be the same as the monthly payment; design the program so that it will display the exact amount of the last payment due.)

12. Proceed as in Exercise 11, but with the following modifications: During program execution, have the user enter a payment amount and the day of the month from 1 through 30. The monthly interest is to be calculated on the *average daily balance* for that month. (Assume that each month has 30 days and that the billing date is the first of the month.) For example, if the balance on June 1 is $500 and a payment of $20 is received on June 12, the interest is computed on $(500 * 11 + 480 * 19)/30$ dollars, which represents the average daily balance for that month.

13. Suppose that on January 1, April 1, July 1, and October 1 of each year, some fixed *Amount* is invested and earns interest at some annual interest rate R compounded quarterly (that is, $R/4$ percent is added at the end of each quarter). Write a program to calculate and display for a specified number of years, the year, the yearly dividend (total interest earned for that year), and the total savings accumulated through that year.

    A possible modification/addition to your program: Instead of investing *Amount* dollars each quarter, invest *Amount*/3 dollars on the first of each month. Then in each quarter, the first payment earns interest for three months ($R/4$ percent), the second for two months ($R/6$ percent), and the third for one month ($R/12$ percent).

14. The proper divisors of an integer n are the positive divisors less than n. A positive integer is said to be a **deficient, perfect,** or **abundant** number if the sum of its proper divisors is less than, equal to, or greater than the number, respectively. For example, 8 is deficient because its proper divisors are 1, 2, and 4, and $1 + 2 + 4 < 8$; 6 is perfect, because $1 + 2 + 3 = 6$; and 12 is abundant, because $1 + 2 + 3 + 4 + 6 > 12$. Write a program that classifies n as being deficient, perfect, or abundant for $n = 20$ to 30, then for $n = 490$ to 500, and finally for $n = 8120$ to 8130. Extra: Find the smallest odd abundant number.

15. **(a)** Develop an algorithm for the third method of calculating depreciation (double-declining balance combined with straight-line) described in Section 5.4.
    (b) Modify the program in Figure 5.5 so that it includes this third method of calculating depreciation as one of the options. Also, modify the output so that the year numbers in all of the depreciation tables begin with the current year rather than with year number 1.

Programming Pointers

Program Design

1. *All programs can be written using the three basic control structures: sequence, selection, and repetition.*

2. *Multialternative selection structures in which the selection is based on the value of some integer or character variable are sometimes better implemented with a* **case** *statement than with an* **if** *statement.* The **case** implementation may be more readable than the **if** implementation. For example, classifying the value of a character variable *Ch* as an arithmetic operator $(+, -, *, /)$, a relational operator $(<, >, =)$, or a punctuation symbol (semicolon, colon, comma, or period) by using the **case** statement

   case *Ch* **of**
       '+', '−', '*', '/' : *writeln* ('Arithmetic operator');
           '<', '>', '=' : *writeln* ('Relational operator');
         ';', ':', ',', '.' : *writeln* ('Punctuation')
   end (* **case** *);

   looks cleaner than does an implementation using an **if** statement:

   if $(Ch = '+')$ **or** $(Ch = '-')$
     or $(Ch = '*')$ **or** $(Ch = '/')$ **then**
       writeln ('Arithmetic operator')
   else if $(Ch = '<')$ **or** $(Ch = '>')$ **or** $(Ch = '=')$ **then**
       writeln ('Relational operator')
   else if $(Ch = ';')$ **or** $(Ch = ':')$
     or $(Ch = ',')$ **or** $(Ch = '.')$ **then**
       writeln ('Punctuation');

3. *Repetition structures can be implemented in Pascal using the* **while,** **for,** *and* **repeat-until** *statements, and it is important to select the one that best implements the repetition required in a given problem.* Some guidelines for selecting the appropriate statement are

   - *The* **while** *statement is usually the best choice for implementing repetition structures that are controlled by boolean expressions.* Since the boolean expression appears at the top of the loop, one can see immediately what the termination test is. This also ensures that the body of the loop is not entered inadvertently if the boolean expression is false initially.
   - *The* **for** *statement is appropriate for implementing repetition structures in which the number of repetitions can be determined before the loop is entered.*
   - *The* **repeat-until** *statement is appropriate for implementing repetition structures in which the body of the loop must be executed at least once.*

Potential Problems

1. *Each* **case** *statement must be terminated with the reserved word* **end.**
   As we noted in Potential Problem 2 of the Programming Pointers of
   Chapter 4, a missing **end** may be difficult to detect. The compiler may
   even search to the end of the program for an **end** to match an earlier
   begin or **case.**

2. *The control variable, initial value, and final value of a* **for** *statement
   cannot be modified within the body of the for loop.* Values of variables
   that specify these initial and/or final values may change within the loop
   body, but this does not change the number of repetitions. For example,
   the statements

   > $k := 5$;
   > **for** $i := 1$ **to** k **do**
   >   **begin**
   >   *writeln* (k);
   > $k := k - 1$
   >   **end** (∗ **for** ∗);

   produce the output

   > 5
   > 4
   > 3
   > 2
   > 1

   The statement

   > **for** $i := 1$ **to** 5 **do**
   >   **begin**
   >   *writeln* (i);
   > $i := i - 1$
   >   **end** (∗ **for** ∗);

   is an error and produces a message such as

   > ∗∗∗A control variable must not be altered in its
   > "FOR" loop.

   Similarly, the statement

   > **for** $i := 1$ **to** 5 **do**
   >   **begin**
   >   *writeln* (i);
   >   *readln* (i)
   >   **end** (∗ **for** ∗);

   is not allowed, since it has the potential to change the value of i.

3. *The* **repeat-until** *statement controls repetition of all statements between*
   repeat *and* **until,** *but* **for** *and* **while** *statements control repetition of
   only one statement.* For example, the statements

```
for I := 1 to 10 do
   J := sqr(I);
   writeln (J)
```

produce only one line of output:

   100

The body of the for loop contains only the assignment statement and not the output statement (even though the indentation suggests that it does). If both statements are to be included within the **for** statement, they must be combined into a single compound statement:

```
for I := 1 to 10 do
   begin
      J := sqr(I);
      writeln (J)
   end (* for *);
```

4. *The statements within a* **repeat-until** *statement must eventually cause the boolean expression in the* **until** *clause to become true.* An infinite loop is the result otherwise. For example, if x is a real variable, the statements

```
x := 0;
repeat
   writeln (x:4:1);
   x := x + 0.3
until x = 1.0
```

produce an infinite loop.

   Output:
   0.0
   0.3
   0.6
   0.9
   1.2
   1.5
   1.8
   ⋮

Since the value of x is never equal to 1.0, repetition is not terminated. Also, since comparisons of two algebraically equal real values with = may not be evaluated as true, the statements

```
x := 0;
repeat
   writeln (x:4:1);
   x := x + 0.2
until x = 1.0
```

may also produce an infinite loop:

Output:
0.0
0.2
0.4
0.6
0.8
1.0
1.2
1.4
1.6
⋮

Since x is initialized to 0 and 0.2 is added to x five times, x should have the value 1.0. But the boolean expression $x = 1.0$ may be false, because most real values are not stored exactly.

5. *In a while loop, the boolean expression that controls repetition is evaluated before execution of the body of the loop. In a repeat-until loop, the boolean expression that controls repetition is evaluated after execution of the body of the loop.* Thus, the body of a while loop is not executed if the boolean expression is false, but the statements within a repeat-until loop are always executed at least once.

6. *In a while loop, repetition continues as long as the boolean expression that controls repetition is true. In a repeat-until loop, repetition continues as long as the boolean expression is false.*

Program Style

In this text, we use the following conventions for formatting the control statements considered in this chapter:

1. *In* **case** *statements,* **case** *is aligned with its corresponding* **end,** *and the lines within the* **case** *statement are indented and the colons or the label lists are aligned.*

```
case selector of
    label-list-1 : statement-1;
            ⋮
    label-list-n : statement-n
end (* case *)
```

2. *In a* **repeat-until** *statement,* **repeat** *is aligned with the corresponding* **until** *and the body of the loop is indented.*

```
repeat
    statement-1;
        ⋮
    statement-n
until . . .
```

3. *In a* **for** *statement,* **for** . . . **do** *is on one line, with the body of the loop indented on the next line(s):*

> **for** . . . **do**
>   *statement*
>
> **for** . . . **do**
>   **begin**
>   *statement-1*;
>   ⋮
>   *statement-n*
>   **end** (* **for** *)

4. *A comment of the form* (* **case** *), (* **if** *), (* **while** *), (* **for** *), *and so on, is attached to the reserved word* **end**, *which marks the end of a* **case** *statement or the end of a compound statement that serves as one of the alternatives in an* **if** *statement, the body of a while loop, or the body of a for loop, respectively.*

Variations and Extensions

The standard Pascal control structures described in this chapter are provided in nearly every version of Pascal. In some versions, however,

- Execution may fall through a **case** statement to the next statement if the value of the selector is not in any of the label lists. (Turbo, UCSD)
- The **case** statement may have an **otherwise** (Macintosh) or **else** (Turbo) clause.
- Ranges of values of the form *first-value* .. *last-value* may be allowed in the label lists of a **case** statement. (Turbo).
- The value of the control variable in a for loop may retain its last value rather than become undefined when repetition terminates. (Turbo)

See Appendix G for details.

6

Procedures
and Functions

From a little distance one can perceive an order in what at the time seemed confusion.

F. SCOTT FITZGERALD

All the best work is done the way ants do things—by tiny but untiring and regular additions.

LAFCADIO HEARN

In Chapter 4 we introduced the basic software engineering technique known as *top-down design* and showed how subprograms (procedures and functions) are the basic building blocks from which modular programs are constructed. In the introduction to procedures given there, however, we emphasized only their most basic properties, and so in this chapter we consider procedures in more detail. After reviewing what we already know about procedures, we examine subprograms that are functions and illustrate them with several important examples. We also look at the various scope rules that govern the accessibility of items defined within procedures and functions. Top-down design is illustrated in some detail, by using this technique to develop a program for the rather complex problem of checking eligibility requirements for student athletes. We introduce recursion and give several examples of this powerful programming technique. Finally, we show how functions and procedures can be used as parameters of other functions and procedures.

6.1 Review of Procedures

The subprograms we have considered thus far are called ***procedures,*** as distinct from ***functions,*** which are considered in the next section. There are a number of predefined procedures included in Pascal itself. Those that we have already considered are *write, writeln, read,* and *readln*; others will be described later. (See Appendix D.)

Pascal also allows user-defined procedures, which were introduced in Section 4.6. There we saw that the form of such user-defined procedures is similar to that of Pascal programs:

> procedure heading
> procedure declaration part
> procedure statement part;

where the declaration part and the statement part are the same as those of a program.

The heading of a procedure has the form

> **procedure** *name*;

or

> **procedure** *name* (*formal-parameter-list*);

The second form is more common and is used when information must be passed to the procedure and/or returned from it to the program unit that calls the procedure. The formal parameter list has the form

> *ind-1 list-1 : type-1*; *ind-2 list-2 : type-2*; . . . ; *ind-k list-k : type-k*

where each *list-i* is an identifier or a list of identifiers separated by commas, and *type-i* specifies the type of these parameters; *ind-i* is either the reserved word **var** or it is omitted according to whether the parameters in *list-i* are variable parameters or value parameters. Recall that value parameters are used only to pass information into the procedure and not to return information; only variable parameters may be used both to transfer information to the procedure and to return information from it.

A procedure may be called from a program or another subprogram (or, as we shall see in Section 6.6, it may call itself) by using a ***procedure reference statement*** of the form

> *name*;

if the procedure heading has the first form, or

> *name* (*actual-parameter-list*)

if the heading has the second form. When a procedure reference statement is executed, the actual parameters (if any) are associated with the corresponding formal parameters. In the case of value parameters, the values of the actual parameters are actually copied into the memory locations associated with the corresponding formal parameters. For a variable parameter, its name and the name of the corresponding actual parameter (which must be a variable) are identified with the same memory location; thus, changing the value of a formal variable parameter within the procedure also changes the value of the corresponding actual parameter. This association of actual and formal parameters was described in more detail in Section 4.6.

Once this parameter association has been established, control is passed to the procedure, and the statements in its statement part are executed. When the **end** of the procedure is encountered, execution is terminated, and control returns to the statement immediately following the procedure reference statement in the program unit that called the procedure.

6.2 Functions

As we have seen, Pascal provides several **_predefined functions_** such as *sqr, round,* and *odd.* Recall that to use any of these functions to calculate some value in an expression, one need only give its name followed by the actual parameter to which it is to be applied, enclosed in parentheses. For example, the statements

> *writeln (sqr(x));*
>
> *Alpha := round(100 * Beta) / 100;*
>
> **if** *odd(Number)* **then**
>   *writeln (Number);*

display the square of *x,* assign to *Alpha* the value of *Beta* rounded to the nearest hundredth, and display the value of *Number* provided it is an odd integer.

In some programs it may be convenient for the user to define additional functions. Such **_user-defined functions_** are possible in Pascal, and once defined, they are used in the same way as the predefined functions.

Like procedures, functions are defined in the subprogram section of a program and consist of a heading, a declaration part, and a statement part. The syntax diagram for a function definition is

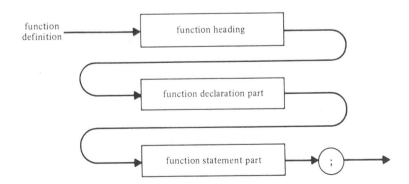

The function heading has the form

function *name* (*formal-parameter-list*) : *result-type*;

where *name* is the name of the function and may be any legal Pascal identifier. The type of the function value, *result-type*, may be any of the standard Pascal data types considered thus far (or certain other data types considered later). The *formal-parameter-list* has the same form as for a procedure heading. The syntax diagram for a function heading is

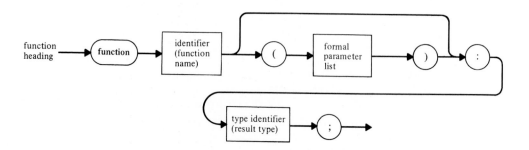

The declaration and statement parts of a function definition have the same forms as for procedures, with the additional stipulation that at least one of the statements in the statement part must assign a value to the identifier that names the function.

To illustrate, suppose that we wish to supplement the predefined function *sqr* by defining a function that computes the cube of a real number, that is, one that computes

$$f(x) = x^3$$

This function will have a single formal parameter of real type and the result type will also be real. Thus an appropriate function heading is

function *cube*(*x* : *real*) : *real*;

and the complete function definition is

function *cube*(*x* : *real*) : *real*;

    (* Function *cube* returns the cube (third power) of *x*. *)

begin (* *cube* *)
    cube := *x* * *sqr*(*x*)
end (* *cube* *);

If this function definition is placed in a subprogram section of the declaration part of a program, the function *cube* can then be referenced in the statement part of the program (or in later functions and procedures) in the same manner as are the predefined Pascal functions. The simple program in Figure 6.1 provides an illustration.

```
PROGRAM TableOfCubes (input, output);

(******************************************************************

    Program to print a table of cubes of a number entered by the user.

    ****************************************************************)

VAR
    Lower, Upper,    (* bounds on range of values *)
    Step,            (* increment *)
    Number : real;   (* actual argument *)

FUNCTION cube(x : real) : real;

    (*************************************************************

        Function cube returns the cube (third power) of x.

        *********************************************************)

    BEGIN (* cube *)
        cube := x * sqr(x)
    END (* cube *);

BEGIN (* main program *)
    write ('Enter range of values and step size: ');
    readln (Lower, Upper, Step);
    writeln;
    writeln ('number    its cube');
    writeln ('======    ========');
    Number := Lower;
    WHILE Number <= Upper DO
        BEGIN
            writeln (Number:5:2, cube(Number):12:4);
            Number := Number + Step
        END (* WHILE *)
END (* main program *).
```

Sample run:

Enter range of values and step size: 1 4 0.5

```
number    its cube
======    ========
 1.00       1.0000
 1.50       3.3750
 2.00       8.0000
 2.50      15.6250
 3.00      27.0000
 3.50      42.8750
 4.00      64.0000
```

Figure 6.1

Several of the sample programs and exercises in the preceding chapters calculated wages. In these examples, and in most programs involving monetary calculations, the amounts should be rounded to the nearest cent. A function to do this is the following:

function *RoundCents(Amount : real) : real*;

    (* Function to round *Amount* to the nearest cent. *)

    begin (* *RoundCents* *)
      RoundCents := *round*(100 * *Amount*) / 100
    end (* *RoundCents* *);

A statement such as

GrossPay := *RoundCents(Wages)*;

can then be used to reference this function.

As another example, consider a function to find the maximum of two integers. If we name the function *Maximum* and its formal parameters *Number1* and *Number2*, then the function definition is

function *Maximum(Number1, Number2 : integer) : integer*;

(* Function returns the maximum of two
   integers *Number1* and *Number2*. *)

begin (* *Maximum* *)
  if *Number1* >= *Number2* **then**
    Maximum := *Number1*
  else
    Maximum := *Number2*
end (* *Maximum* *);

In the preceding examples, the type of the function was the same as the type of its parameters, real for *Cube* and for *RoundCents* and integer for *Maximum*. This need not be the case, however. To illustrate, consider a function to assign a pass (P) or fail (F) grade according to whether a student's average is above or below some pass-fail line. If we name the function *PFGrade*, and its formal parameters *Average* and *PFLine*, the function definition is given by

function *PFGrade(Average, PFLine : real) : char*;

    (* Function returns a pass-fail grade of 'P' if
      Average ≥ *PFLine*, 'F' if *Average* < *PFLine*. *)

    begin
      if *Average* >= *PFLine* **then**
        PFGrade := 'P'
      else
        PFGrade := 'F'
    end (* *PFGrade* *);

Note that this function has real parameters but that its value is of character type. The program in Figure 6.2 reads several students' averages and for each calls this function to determine whether the student passed or failed.

```
PROGRAM PassFailChecker (input, output);

(**********************************************************************

   Program to determine which students have passed or failed.

**********************************************************************)

VAR
   Average,                 (* student's average *)
   PFLine : real;           (* pass/fail line *)
   Grade : char;            (* P/F grade assigned *)

FUNCTION PFGrade(Average, PFLine : real) : char;

   (*********************************************************************

      Function returns a pass-fail grade of 'P' if Average >= PFLine,
      'F' if Average < PFLine.

   *********************************************************************)

   BEGIN
      IF Average >= PFLine THEN
         PFGrade := 'P'
      ELSE
         PFGrade := 'F'
   END (* PFGrade *);

BEGIN (* main program *)
   write ('Enter pass-fail line:  ');
   readln (PFLine);
   writeln ('Enter a negative average to stop the program');
   writeln;
   write ('Student''s average? ');
   readln (Average);
   WHILE Average >= 0 DO
      BEGIN
         Grade := PFGrade(Average, PFLine);
         writeln ('          Grade is ', Grade);
         write ('Student''s average? ');
         readln (Average)
      END (* WHILE *)
END (* main program *).
```

Sample run:

```
Enter pass-fail line:  60
Enter a negative average to stop the program
```

Figure 6.2

Figure 6.2 (cont.)

```
Student's average? 90
         Grade is  P
Student's average? 60
         Grade is  P
Student's average? 59.5
         Grade is  F
Student's average? 40
         Grade is  F
Student's average? -1
```

Some function definitions may require the use of local variables other than the formal parameters to calculate the function value. For example, consider the operation of exponentiation, which, unfortunately, is not a standard operation in Pascal. The following function can be used to calculate x^n for a real variable x and an integer variable n:

function *Power*(*x* : *real*; *n* : *integer*) : *real*;

(∗ Function returns the *n*th power of *x* for any real value *x* and any integer value *n* (positive, zero, or negative). ∗)

var
   i : *integer*;
   Prod : *real*;

begin (∗ *Power* ∗)
  if *x* = 0 **then**
    Power := 0
  else
    begin
      Prod := 1;
      for *i* := 1 **to** *abs*(*n*) **do**
        Prod := *Prod* ∗ *x*;
      if *n* >= 0 **then**
        Power := *Prod*
      else
        Power := 1 / *Prod*
    end (∗ **else** ∗)
  end (∗ *Power* ∗);

Functions and procedures have many similarities, the following in particular:

1. The definition of each appears in the subprogram section of the declaration part of a program and in each case consists of a heading, a declaration part, and a statement part, followed by a semicolon.
2. Each of them is an independent program unit. Parameters, constants, and variables declared within a function or procedure are local to that function or procedure; they are accessible only within that subprogram.

3. When a function or procedure is referenced, the number of actual parameters must be the same as the number of formal parameters, and the types of actual parameters must agree with the types of the corresponding formal parameters, with one exception: An actual parameter of integer type may be associated with a value parameter of real type.

There are also a number of differences between functions and procedures:

1. Whereas a procedure is referenced by a procedure reference statement, a function is referenced by using its name in an expression.
2. Since a value must be associated with a function name, a type must also be associated with it. Thus, the heading of a function must include a type identifier that specifies the type of the result. No value is associated with the name of a procedure, however, and hence, no type is associated with it.
3. Functions usually return a single value to the program unit that references them. Procedures often return more than one value, or they may return no value at all but simply perform some task such as an output operation.
4. Values are returned from procedures by using variable parameters, but the value of a function is returned by assigning it to the function name within the statement part of the function definition. (Functions may also return values via parameters, but this is usually not done.)

6.3 Examples: Compound Interest, Simulation, Approximate Areas

EXAMPLE 1: Compound Interest.   Suppose that an amount is deposited in a savings account that earns interest compounded several times per year. We wish to determine the amount that will have accumulated in this account after a specified number of years, assuming that no additional deposits or withdrawals are made.

In developing a program to solve this problem, we use the following variables:

Amount:	Amount of initial deposit.
Rate:	Annual interest rate in decimal form.
NumTimes:	Number of times per year that interest is compounded.
Years:	Number of years interest is accumulated.

Because the interest rate for each interest period is *Rate/NumTimes,* the interest earned during the first interest period is

$$Amount * (Rate \, / \, NumTimes)$$

so that the accumulated value after this first period is

$$Amount \, + \, Amount * (Rate \, / \, NumTimes)$$

which can also be written as

$$Amount * (1 \, + \, Rate \, / \, NumTimes)$$

The interest earned on this amount during the second interest period is

$$[Amount * (1 + Rate / NumTimes)] * (Rate / NumTimes)$$

so the accumulated value at the end of this period will be

$$[Amount * (1 + Rate / NumTimes)]$$
$$+ [Amount * (1 + Rate / NumTimes)] * (Rate / NumTimes)$$

which can also be written as

$$[Amount * (1 + Rate / NumTimes)] * (1 + Rate / NumTimes)$$

or simply

$$Amount * (1 + Rate / NumTimes)^2$$

In general, after k interest periods, the accumulated value will be

$$Amount * (1 + Rate / NumTimes)^k$$

Since in this problem there are *Years* * *NumTimes* interest periods, the final accumulated value will be

$$Amount * (1 + Rate / NumTimes)^{Years * NumTimes}$$

The program in Figure 6.3 uses the function *AccumulatedValue* to evaluate this formula. It uses the function *Power* given in the preceding section to carry out the necessary exponentiation.

```
PROGRAM CompoundInterest (input, output);

(************************************************************************

   Program to calculate compound interest for various amounts,
   interest rates, number of years, and number of times interest
   is compounded.

 ************************************************************************)

VAR
   Amount,              (* amount of initial deposit *)
   Rate,                (* annual interest rate in decimal form *)
   AccumValue : real;   (* accumulated value *)
   NumTimes,            (* number of times per year interest is compounded *)
   Years : integer;     (* number of years interest is accumulated *)
   Response : char;     (* user's response to 'More Data (Y or N)?' *)

FUNCTION Power(x : real; n : integer) : real;

   (*********************************************************************

      Function returns the n-th power of x for any real value x and any
      integer value n (positive, zero, or negative).

    *********************************************************************)
```

Figure 6.3

Figure 6.3 (cont.)

```
   VAR
      i : integer;        (* index *)
      Product : real;   (* product of n x's *)

   BEGIN
      IF x = 0 THEN
         Power := 0
      ELSE
         BEGIN
            Product := 1;
            FOR i := 1 to abs (n) DO
               Product := Product * x;
            IF n >= 0 THEN
               Power := Product
            ELSE
               Power := 1.0 / Product
         END (* ELSE *)
   END (* Power *);

FUNCTION AccumulatedValue(Amount, Rate : real;
                          NumTimes, Years : integer) : real;

   (****************************************************************

      Function returns the value accumulated if a given Amount earns
      interest at annual interest Rate if interest is compounded NumTimes
      per year for a given number of Years.  It uses the function Power.

      ****************************************************************)

   BEGIN
      AccumulatedValue :=
                  Amount * Power(1 + Rate / NumTimes, Years * NumTimes);
   END (* AccumulatedValue *);

BEGIN (* main program *)
   REPEAT
      write ('Enter amount deposited: $');
      readln (Amount);
      write ('Enter annual interest rate (in decimal form): ');
      readln (Rate);
      write ('Enter number of times per year interest is compounded: ');
      readln (NumTimes);
      write ('Enter number of years interest is to be accumulated: ');
      readln (Years);
      AccumValue := AccumulatedValue(Amount, Rate, NumTimes, Years);
      writeln ('Accumulated value is: $', AccumValue:8:2);
      writeln;
      write ('More data (Y or N)? ');
      readln (Response)
   UNTIL (Response = 'N') OR (Response = 'n')
END (* main program *).
```

Figure 6.3   (cont.)

```
Sample run:

Enter amount deposited: $100.00
Enter annual interest rate (in decimal form): 0.04
Enter number of times per year interest is compounded: 1
Enter number of years interest is to be accumulated: 1
Accumulated value is: $  104.00

More data (Y or N)? Y
Enter amount deposited: $100.00
Enter annual interest rate (in decimal form): 0.04
Enter number of times per year interest is compounded: 4
Enter number of years interest is to be accumulated: 1
Accumulated value is: $  104.06

More data (Y or N)? Y
Enter amount deposited: $100.00
Enter annual interest rate (in decimal form): 0.09
Enter number of times per year interest is compounded: 12
Enter number of years interest is to be accumulated: 5
Accumulated value is: $  156.57

More data (Y or N)? N
```

EXAMPLE 2: Simulation.   The term *simulation* refers to modeling a dynamic process and using this model to study the behavior of the process. The behavior of some *deterministic* processes can be modeled with an equation or a set of equations. For example, processes that involve exponential growth or decay are commonly modeled with an equation of the form

$$A(t) = A_0 e^{kt}$$

where $A(t)$ is the amount of some substance A present at time t, A_0 is the initial amount of the substance, and k is a rate constant.

In many problems, however, the process being studied involves *randomness*, for example, Brownian motion, arrival of airplanes at an airport, number of defective parts manufactured by a machine, and so on. Computer programs that simulate such processes use a *random number generator*, which is a procedure that produces a number selected from some fixed range in such a way that a sequence of these numbers tends to be uniformly distributed over the given range. Although it is not possible to develop an algorithm that produces truly random numbers, there are some methods that produce sequences of *pseudorandom numbers* that are adequate for most purposes.

Many computer systems provide a random number generator that produces random real numbers uniformly distributed over the range 0 to 1. The numbers produced by such a generator can be used to generate random real numbers in other ranges or to generate random integers. To demonstrate the way in which this is done, suppose that the random number generator is implemented as a function *Random* having no arguments. The expression

$$a + (b - a) * Random$$

can be used to generate random real numbers in the range a to b, and the expression

$$m + trunc(n * Random)$$

can be used to generate random integers in the range m through $m + n - 1$.

To illustrate, suppose we wish to model the random process of tossing a pair of dice. Using the preceding expression for generating random integers, we might define the following function:

function *RandomInteger(m, n : integer) : integer*;

(∗ Function returns an integer randomly selected
from $m, m + 1, \ldots, m + n - 1$. It uses the
function *Random* that generates a random
real number in the interval from 0 to 1. ∗)

begin (∗ *RandomInteger* ∗)
RandomInteger := $m + trunc(n * Random)$
end (∗ *RandomInteger* ∗);

and then use the statements

Die1 := *RandomInteger*(1, 6);
Die2 := *RandomInteger*(1, 6);
Pair := *Die1* + *Die2*;

to simulate one roll of two dice; the value of *Pair* is the total number of dots showing.

If the random number generator is suitably constructed, the relative frequency of each value from 2 through 12 for *Pair* should correspond to the probability of that number occurring on one throw of a pair of dice. These probabilities (rounded to three decimal places) are given in the following table:

Outcome	Probability
2	0.028
3	0.056
4	0.083
5	0.111
6	0.139
7	0.167
8	0.139
9	0.111
10	0.083
11	0.056
12	0.028

The program in Figure 6.4 reads an integer indicating a possible outcome of a roll of two dice and an integer indicating the number of times the dice are to be tossed, and displays the relative frequency of this outcome. It assumes that a system function *Random* for generating random real numbers in the range

0 to 1 and a system procedure *Randomize* to initialize the random number generator are available. (If your system does not provide a random number generator, you might use the random number function described in Appendix F.)

```
PROGRAM DiceRoll (input, output);

(*******************************************************************

   Program that uses a random number generator to simulate
   rolling a pair of dice, counting the number of times a
   specified number of spots occurs.

*******************************************************************)

VAR
   Spots,          (* # of spots to be counted *)
   Count,          (* number of times Spots occurred *)
   Rolls,          (* # of rolls of dice *)
   Die1, Die2,     (* # of spots on die #1, #2, respectively *)
   Pair,           (* sum of Die1 and Die2 = total # of spots on the dice *)
   i : integer;    (* index variable *)

FUNCTION RandomInteger(m, n : integer) : integer;

   (****************************************************************

      Function to generate random integers in the range m through
      m + n - 1.  It uses the system random number generator Random.

   ****************************************************************)

   BEGIN (* RandomInteger *)
      RandomInteger := m + trunc(n * Random)
   END (* RandomInteger *);

BEGIN (* main program *)
   write ('# of spots to count: ');
   readln (Spots);
   write('# of times to roll the dice: ');
   readln (Rolls);
   Randomize;
   Count := 0;
   FOR i := 1 TO Rolls DO
      BEGIN
         Die1 := RandomInteger(1, 6);
         Die2 := RandomInteger(1, 6);
         Pair := Die1 + Die2;
         IF Pair = Spots THEN
            Count := Count + 1
      END (* FOR *);
   writeln;
   writeln ('Relative frequency of ', Spots:1, ' was ', Count / Rolls:5:3)
END (* main program *).
```

Figure 6.4

Figure 6.4   (cont.)

Sample run:

```
# of spots to count: 6
# of times to roll the dice: 500

Relative frequency of 6 was 0.138
```

EXAMPLE 3: Approximate Areas.   One problem in which numerical methods are often used is that of approximating the area under the graph of a nonnegative function $y = f(x)$ from $x = a$ to $x = b$, thus obtaining an approximate value of the integral

$$\int_a^b f(x)\ dx$$

One simple method is to divide the interval $[a, b]$ into n subintervals each of length $\Delta x = (b - a)/n$ and then to form rectangles having these subintervals as bases and with altitudes given by the values of the function at the midpoints (or left or right endpoints) $x_1, x_2, \ldots, x_n$ of the subintervals. This is illustrated in Figure 6.5. The sum of the areas of these rectangles

$$f(x_1)\ \Delta x + f(x_2)\ \Delta x + \cdots + f(x_n)\ \Delta x$$

which is the same as

$$[f(x_1) + f(x_2) + \cdots + f(x_n)]\ \Delta x$$

or, written more concisely using Σ (sigma) notation,

$$\left[\sum_{i=1}^{n} f(x_i)\right] \Delta x$$

is then an approximation to the area under the curve.

Figure 6.5 illustrates this method for a curve lying above the x axis. It may also be used to approximate the integral of a function whose graph falls below the x axis. In this case, the integral does not give the total area between the curve and the axis, but rather gives the area of the region(s) above the axis minus the area of the region(s) below the axis.

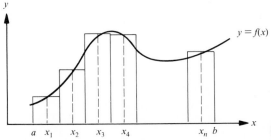

Figure 6.5

The program in Figure 6.6 uses this rectangle method to approximate the area under the graph of $y = x^2 + 1$ from $x = a$ to $x = b$. The endpoints a and b of the interval of integration and the number n of subintervals are read during execution.

```
PROGRAM FindArea (input, output);

(******************************************************************

    Program to approximate the area under the graph of a function f
    from x = a to x = b using the rectangle method with altitudes
    chosen at the midpoints of the subintervals.

******************************************************************)

VAR
    a, b,                  (* endpoints of interval *)
    x,                     (* the midpoint of one of the subintervals *)
    Deltax,                (* the length of the subintervals *)
    Sum : real;            (* the approximating sum *)
    n,                     (* number of subintervals used *)
    i : integer;           (* counter *)

FUNCTION f(x : real) : real;

    (***************************************************************

            The function for which area is being approximated.

    ***************************************************************)

    BEGIN (* f *)
        f := sqr(x) + 1
    END (* f *);

BEGIN (* main program *)
    write ('Enter interval endpoints and # of subintervals: ');
    readln (a, b, n);
    Deltax := (b - a) / n;
    Sum := 0;
    x := a + Deltax / 2;
    FOR i := 1 TO n DO
        BEGIN
            Sum := Sum + f(x);
            x := x + Deltax
        END (* FOR *);
    Sum := Deltax * Sum;
    writeln ('Approximate area using ', n:1, ' subintervals is ', Sum:8:4)
END (* main program *).


Sample runs:

Enter interval endpoints and # of subintervals: 0 1 10
Approximate area using 10 subintervals is   1.3325
```

Figure 6.6

Figure 6.6   (cont.)

```
Enter interval endpoints and # of subintervals: 0 1 20
Approximate area using 20 subintervals is    1.3331


Enter interval endpoints and # of subintervals: 0 1 100
Approximate area using 100 subintervals is    1.3333
```

Exercises

1. Consider the following program skeleton:

> **program** *Demo* (*input*, *output*);
>
> **const**
> > *pi* = 3.14159;
> > *two* = 2;
>
> **var**
> > *Month*, *Day*, *Year*, *p*, *q* : *integer*;
> > *Hours*, *Rate*, *Amount*, *u*, *v* : *real*;
> > *Code*, *Class* : *char*;
>
> **function** *f*(*x*, *y* : *real*; *d* : *integer*) : *real*;
> > ⋮
>
> **procedure** *Calculate* (*a* : *real*; **var** *b* : *real*; *m* : *integer*;
> > **var** *k*, *n* : *integer*; **var** *c* : *char*);
> > ⋮

Determine whether each of the following statements can be used in the statement part of the program. If it cannot be used, explain why.

(a) *Amount* := *f*(*pi*, *Rate*, *Month*);
(b) *Rate* := *f*(*Hours*, *Day*, *two*);
(c) *writeln* (*f*(0, 0, 0));
(d) *f*(*Hours*, *Rate*, *Month*);
(e) *Calculate* (*u*, *v*, *p*, *two*, *Day*, *Code*);
(f) *Hours* := *two* ∗ *f*(*pi*, *Amount*) / (2.71828 ∗ *Rate*);
(g) *Amount* := *f*(*pi* ∗ *Hours*, (2.71828 + *Day*) / *Rate*, *two*);
(h) **if** *Month* = *two* **then**
> > *Year* := *f*(*Hours*, *f*(*Rate*, *pi*, *two*), *Day*);
(i) **if** *u* > 0 **then**
> > *Amount* := *Calculate* (*u*, *v*, *two*, *p*, *q*, *Code*);
(j) **if** *Calculate* (0, *u*, 1, *p*, *Year*, *Class*) > 0 **then**
> > *writeln* ('Okay');
(k) **while** *f*(*Amount*, 0, 0) < *pi* **do**
> > *Amount* := *f*(*Amount*, *pi*, 1);
(l) **repeat**
> > *Amount* := *f*(*Amount*, 0, *Code*)
> > **until** *Amount* > 0;

(m) *Calculate* ($f(u, v, Day)$, *Rate*, 7, *p*, *q*, *Code*);
(n) *Amount* := $f(a, b, Day)$;

2. Write a function *Range* that calculates the range between two integers, that is, the larger integer minus the smaller integer.

3. Write a function that converts a temperature given in degrees Celsius to degrees Fahrenheit. (The conversion formula is $F = \frac{9}{5}C + 32$.)

4. Write a boolean-valued function *IsADigit* that determines whether a character is one of the digits 0 through 9.

5. Write a function *Binary* that converts a boolean value into its binary equivalent (false $\leftrightarrow$ 0, true $\leftrightarrow$ 1).

6. Write a function *RoundOff* that accepts a real value *Amount* and an integer value *NumPlaces* and returns the value of *Amount* rounded to the specified number of places. For example, the function references *RoundOff*(10.536, 0), *RoundOff*(10.536, 1), and *RoundOff*(10.536, 2) should give the values 11.0, 10.5, and 10.54, respectively.

7. Write a function *GPA* that accepts a letter grade and returns the corresponding numeric value (A = 4.0, B = 3.0, C = 2.0, D = 1.0, F = 0.0).

8. The number of bacteria in a culture can be estimated by

$$N \cdot e^{k \cdot t}$$

where N is the initial population, k is a rate constant, and t is time. Write a function to calculate the number of bacteria present at time t for given values of k and N; use it in a program that reads values for the initial population, the rate constant, and the time (e.g., 1000, 0.15, 100) and displays the number of bacteria at that time.

9. Write a program that uses the function *Power* given in the text to calculate a monthly loan payment given by

$$\frac{r \cdot A/n}{1 - \left(1 + \dfrac{r}{n}\right)^{-n \cdot y}}$$

where A is the amount borrowed, r is the interest rate (expressed as a decimal), y is the number of years, and n is the number of payments per year. Design the program to read values for the amount borrowed, the interest rate, the number of years, and the number of payments per year, and display the corresponding monthly payment.

10. Write a character-valued function *LetterGrade* that assigns a letter grade to an integer score using the following grading scale:

90–100: A
80–89: B
70–79: C
60–69: D
Below 60: F

Use the function in a program that reads several scores and displays the corresponding letter grades.

11. Write two boolean-valued functions that have formal parameters p and q of boolean type and that compute the logical expressions

$$\sim p \wedge \sim q \quad (\text{not } p \text{ and not } q)$$

and

$$\sim(p \vee q) \quad (\text{not } (p \text{ or } q))$$

Write a program that uses these functions to print truth tables for these expressions.

12. A *prime number* is an integer $n > 1$ whose only positive divisors are 1 and n itself. Write a boolean-valued function that determines whether n is a prime number. Use it in a program that reads several integers, uses the function to determine whether each is prime, and displays each number with the appropriate label "is prime" or "is not prime."

13. It is often necessary to find a *zero* of a function f, that is, a value c where $f(c) = 0$. Geometrically, we are looking for a point c on the x axis at which the graph of $y = f(x)$ crosses the x axis. If f is a continuous function between $x = a$ and $x = b$, that is, if there is no break in the graph of $y = f(x)$ between these two values, and $f(a)$ and $f(b)$ are of opposite signs, then f must have at least one zero between $x = a$ and $x = b$. One method for finding such a zero, or at least an approximation to it, is the *bisection method*. For this, bisect the interval $[a, b]$ and determine in which half f changes sign; then f must have a zero in that half of the interval. Now bisect this subinterval and determine in which half f changes sign. Repeating this process gives a sequence of smaller and smaller subintervals, each of which contains a zero of the function (see Figure 6.7). The process

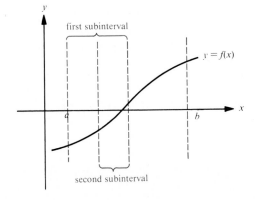

Figure 6.7

can be terminated when a small subinterval, say of length less than 0.0001, is obtained or f has the value 0 at one of the endpoints.

Define a Pascal function to compute $x - \cos x$, and then write a program to find a zero of this function in the interval $\left[0, \dfrac{\pi}{2} \right]$.

14. Another method used to locate a zero of a function f is **Newton's method**. This method consists of taking an initial approximation x_1 and constructing a tangent line to the graph of f at that point. The point x_2 where this tangent line crosses the x axis is taken as the second approximation to the zero. Then another tangent line is constructed at x_2, and the point x_3 where this tangent line crosses the x axis is the next approximation. Figure 6.8 shows this process.

If x is an approximation to the zero of f, then the formula for obtaining the next approximation by Newton's method is

$$\text{new approximation} = x - \frac{f(x)}{f'(x)}$$

where f' is the derivative of f. Using Pascal functions to define a function f and its derivative f', write a program to locate a zero of f, using Newton's method. The process should terminate when a value of $f(x)$ is sufficiently small in absolute value or when the number of iterations exceeds some upper limit. Display the sequence of successive approximations.

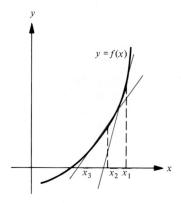

Figure 6.8

15. In Example 3, we considered approximation of areas using rectangles. As Figure 6.9 indicates, a better approximation can usually be obtained using trapezoids rather than rectangles. The sum of the areas of these trapezoids is given by

$$\sum_{i=1}^{n} [f(x_{i-1}) + f(x_i)] \frac{\Delta x}{2}$$

which can also be written

$$\frac{\Delta x}{2} [f(x_0) + 2f(x_1) + 2f(x_2) + \cdots + 2f(x_{n-1}) + f(x_n)]$$

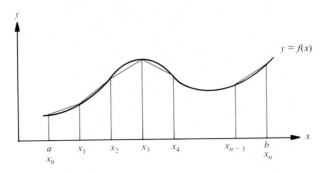

Figure 6.9

or

$$\Delta x \left[\frac{f(a) + f(b)}{2} + \sum_{i=1}^{n-1} f(x_i) \right]$$

Write a program to approximate an integral using this *trapezoidal method*.

16. Another method of numerical integration that in general produces better approximations than the rectangle method described in Example 3 or the trapezoidal method described in Exercise 15 is based on the use of parabolas and is known as **Simpson's Rule**. In this method, the interval [a, b] is divided into an even number n of subintervals, each of length Δx, and the sum

$$\frac{\Delta x}{3} [f(x_0) + 4f(x_1) + 2f(x_2) + 4f(x_3)$$
$$+ 2f(x_4) + \cdots + 2f(x_{n-2}) + 4f(x_{n-1}) + f(x_n)]$$

is used to approximate the integral of f over the interval [a, b]. Write a program to approximate an integral using Simpson's Rule.

Simulation Exercises

17. A coin is tossed repeatedly, and a payoff of 2^n dollars is made, where n is the number of the toss on which the first head appears. For example, TTH pays $8, TH pays $4, and H pays $2. Write a program to simulate playing this game 100 times, and print the average payoff for these games.

18. Suppose that a gambler places a wager of $5 on the following game: A pair of dice is tossed, and if the result is odd, the gambler loses his wager. If the result is even, a card is drawn from a standard deck of fifty-two playing cards. If the card drawn is an ace, 3, 5, 7, or 9, the gambler wins the value of the card; otherwise, he loses. What will be the average winnings for this game? Write a program to simulate the game.

19. Johann VanDerDoe, centerfielder for the Klavin Klodhoppers, has the following lifetime hitting percentages:

Out	63.4%
Walk	10.3%
Single	19.0%
Double	4.9%
Triple	1.1%
Home run	1.3%

Write a program to simulate 1000 times at bat for Johann, counting the number of outs, walks, singles, and so on, and calculating his batting average ((# of hits)/(1000 − # of walks)).

20. The classic *drunkard's walk problem* is as follows: Over an 8-block line, the home of an intoxicated chap is at block 8, and a pub is at block 1. Our poor friend starts at block n, $1 < n < 8$, and wanders at random, one block at a time, either toward or away from home. At any intersection, he moves toward the pub with a certain probability, say 2/3, and toward home with a certain probability, say 1/3. Having gotten either home or to the pub, he remains there. Write a program to simulate 500 trips in which he starts at block 2, another 500 in which he starts at block 3, and so forth up to block 7. For each starting point, calculate and print the percentage of the time he ends up at home and the average number of blocks he walked on each trip.

21. The famous *Buffon Needle Problem* is as follows: A board is ruled with equidistant parallel lines, and a needle of length equal to the distance between these lines is dropped at random on the board. Write a program to simulate this experiment and estimate the probability p that the needle crosses one of these lines. Display the values of p and $2/p$. (The value of $2/p$ should be approximately equal to a well-known constant. What constant is it?)

22. An unusual method for approximating the area under a curve is the following *Monte Carlo technique*. As illustrated in Figure 6.10, consider a rectangle with base $[a, b]$ and height m, where $f(x) \le m$ for all x in $[a, b]$. Imagine throwing q darts at rectangle $ABCD$ and

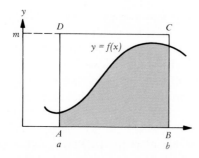

Figure 6.10

counting the total number p that hit the shaded region. For a large number of throws, we would expect

$$\frac{p}{q} \simeq \frac{\text{area of shaded region}}{\text{area of rectangle } ABCD}$$

Write a program to calculate areas using this Monte Carlo method. To simulate throwing a dart, generate two random numbers, X from $[a, b]$ and Y from $[0, m]$, and consider the point (X, Y) to be the point where the dart hits.

23. Figure 6.11 shows a cross section of the lead-shielding wall of a nuclear reactor. A neutron enters the wall at a point E and then follows a random path by moving forward, backward, right, or left, in jumps of one unit. A change of direction is interpreted as a collision with an atom of lead. Suppose that after 10 such collisions the neutron's energy is dissipated and that it dies within the lead shielding, provided that it has not already passed back inside the reactor or outside the shielding (by moving forward a net distance of 4 units). Write a program to simulate 100 neutrons entering this shield, and calculate how many reach the outside of the reactor.

Outside

Inside of reactor

Figure 6.11

6.4 Scope Rules

In a program that contains procedures and/or functions, there may be several points at which identifiers are declared—in the declaration part of the main program, in formal parameter lists of procedure and function headings, or in declaration parts within procedures and functions. The portion of the program in which any one of these identifiers is *visible*, that is, where it is accessible and can be used, is called its *scope*. In this section, we state several rules that govern the scopes of identifiers in programs.

There is one general principle that describes the scope of an identifier:

Fundamental Scope Principle

The scope of an identifier is the program unit in which it is declared.

One scope rule that follows from this principle applies to identifiers declared within a procedure or function, that is, to the formal parameters that appear in its heading and to the constants, variables, procedure names, and function names in its declaration part (and type identifiers, described in Chapter 8):

> **Scope Rule 1**
>
> An identifier declared within a procedure or function is not accessible outside that procedure or function.

To illustrate, we consider the problem of calculating depreciation that was introduced in Section 5.4. One of the methods of calculating depreciation described there is the *sum-of-the-years-digits* method. In this method, if a given *Amount* is to be depreciated over *NumYears* years, then the amount depreciated in the *k*th year is given by

$$\frac{(NumYears - k + 1) * Amount}{1 + 2 + \cdots + NumYears}$$

The program in Figure 6.12 reads values for *Amount*, *NumYears*, and *k*, uses the function *Sum* to calculate $1 + 2 + \cdots + NumYears$, and then calculates and displays the amount that can be depreciated in the *k*th year, repeating this until the user terminates execution.

```
PROGRAM Depreciation1 (input, output);

(*********************************************************************

   Program to calculate the amount that can be depreciated in a given
   year for a given amount and a given number of years, using the
   sum-of-the-years-digits method of depreciation.

*********************************************************************)

VAR
   Amount : real;       (* amount to be depreciated *)
   NumYears,            (* number of years over which to depreciate it *)
   k : integer;         (* year for which depreciation to be calculated *)
   Response : char;     (* user response *)

FUNCTION Sum(n : integer) : integer;

   (****************************************************

         Function to calculate 1 + 2 + ... + n

   ****************************************************)

   VAR
      TempSum,          (* used to accumulate the sum *)
      k : integer;      (* index running from 1 through n *)
```

Figure 6.12

Figure 6.12 (cont.)

```
   BEGIN (* Sum *)
      TempSum := 0;
      FOR k := 1 TO n DO
         TempSum := TempSum + k;
      Sum := TempSum
   END (* Sum *);

BEGIN (* main program *)
   REPEAT
      writeln ('Enter amount to be depreciated, number of years,');
      write ('and year in which to calculate depreciation:  ');
      readln (Amount, NumYears, k);
      writeln ('Amount depreciated in year ', k:1, ' is $',
                        (NumYears - k + 1) * Amount / Sum(NumYears) : 6:2);
      writeln;
      write ('More data (Y or N)? ');
      readln (Response)
   UNTIL (Response <> 'Y') AND (Response <> 'y')
END (* main program *).
```

The scope of the formal parameter *n* and the variables *TempSum* and *k* declared within the function *Sum* is the function *Sum*; by Scope Rule 1, they are not accessible outside this function. Such identifiers are said to be **local** to the function, and any attempt to use them outside the function results in an error.

An identifier declared in the declaration part of the main program is called a **global identifier**, because it is accessible throughout the entire program, except within program units in which the same identifier is declared locally.

Scope Rule 2

A global identifier is accessible in any program unit in which the same identifier is not declared locally.

For example, in the program in Figure 6.12, the variables *Amount*, *NumYears*, *k*, and *Response* as well as the function name *Sum* are global identifiers. All of them are accessible to the main program, and all but *k* are accessible to the function *Sum*. The global variable *k* is not accessible in *Sum* because *k* is declared locally within *Sum*; in fact, this is necessary because *control variables for* **for** *statements within a procedure or function must be local variables*. Reference to the variable *k* within the function *Sum* yields the value of the local variable *k*, whereas a reference to *k* outside the function gives the value of the global variable *k*. Thus these *k*'s represent two different variables that are associated with two different memory locations.

Although global variables can be used to share data between program units, it is usually unwise to do so, since this practice reduces the independence of the various program units and thus makes modular programming more difficult. Changing the value of a global variable in one program unit has the **side effect** of changing the value of that variable in all of the other program units. Consequently, it is difficult to determine the value of that variable at any particular point in the program.

Scope Rule 2 applies to identifiers in a main program and their accessibility in a subprogram. Recall that functions and procedures have declaration parts in which other functions and/or procedures may be defined. Scope Rule 3 applies to such nested functions and procedures.

Scope Rule 3

An identifier declared in a procedure can be accessed by any subprogram defined within it, provided that the same identifier is not declared locally in the internal subprogram.

To illustrate this scope rule, we extend the program in Figure 6.12 to print complete depreciation tables rather than simply display the amount depreciated in a specific year. The program in Figure 6.13 calls procedure *GetData* to obtain values for *Amount* and *NumYears* and then calls procedure *PrintDepreciationTable*, which displays a table showing the amount to be depreciated in the kth year for k ranging from 1 through *NumYears*. The relationship among these program units is indicated by the diagram in Figure 6.14, which shows clearly the nesting of the function *Sum* within procedure *PrintDepreciationTable* and *PrintDepreciationTable* within the main program.

```
PROGRAM Depreciation2 (input, output);

(*******************************************************************

   Program to calculate and display depreciation tables, using the
   sum-of-the-years-digits method of depreciation.

   *****************************************************************)

VAR
   Amount : real;      (* amount to be depreciated *)
   NumYears: integer;  (* number of years over which to depreciate it *)
   Response : char;    (* user response *)

PROCEDURE GetData (VAR Amount : real; VAR NumYears : integer);

   (**************************************************************

      Procedure to read and return the Amount to be depreciated
      and the number of years (NumYears) over which the
      depreciation is to be carried out.

      ************************************************************)

   VAR
      Response : char;           (* user response *)
```

Figure 6.13

Figure 6.13 (cont.)

```
    BEGIN (* GetData *)
        REPEAT
            write ('Enter amount to be depreciated, and the number',
                   ' of years: ');
            readln (Amount, NumYears);
            write ('Is the data okay (Y or N)? ');
            readln (Response)
        UNTIL (Response = 'Y') OR (Response = 'y')
    END (* GetData *);

PROCEDURE PrintDepreciationTable (Amount : real; NumYears : integer);

    (****************************************************************

        Procedure to calculate and display a depreciation table
        for a specified Amount over the given number of years
        (NumYears) using the sum-of-the-years-digits method.

    ****************************************************************)

    VAR
        SumOfYears,             (* 1 + 2 + ... + NumYears *)
        k : integer;            (* index -- year number *)
        Depreciation : real;    (* amount to depreciate in k-th year *)

        FUNCTION Sum(n : integer) : integer;

            (*********************************************************

                Function to calculate 1 + 2 + ... + n

            *********************************************************)

            VAR
                TempSum,        (* used to accumulate the sum *)
                k : integer;    (* index running from 1 through n *)

            BEGIN (* Sum *)
                TempSum := 0;
                FOR k := 1 TO n DO
                    TempSum := TempSum + k;
                Sum := TempSum
            END (* Sum *);

    BEGIN (* PrintDepreciationTable *)
        SumOfYears := Sum(NumYears);
        writeln ('Year Depreciation');
        writeln ('==== ============');
        FOR k := 1 TO NumYears DO
            BEGIN
                Depreciation := (NumYears - k + 1) * Amount / SumOfYears;
                writeln (k:3, Depreciation:12:2)
            END (* FOR *)
    END (* PrintDepreciationTable *);

BEGIN (* main program *)
    REPEAT
        GetData (Amount, NumYears);
        PrintDepreciationTable (Amount, NumYears);
        writeln;
        write ('More data (Y or N)? ');
        readln (Response)
    UNTIL (Response <> 'Y') AND (Response <> 'y')
END (* main program *).
```

program *Depreciation*

parameters: *input, output*
var *Amount, NumYears, Response*
procedure *GetData*

> parameters: *Amount, NumYears*
> **var** *Response*
> **begin** (* *GetData* *)
>   ⋮
> **end** (* *GetData* *);

procedure *PrintDepreciationTable*

> parameters: *Amount, NumYears*
> **var** *SumOfYears, k, Depreciation*
> **function** *Sum*
>
> > parameters: *n*
> > **var** *TempSum, k*
> > **begin** (* *Sum* *)
> >   ⋮
> > **end** (* *Sum* *);
>
> **begin** (* *PrintDepreciationTable* *)
>   ⋮
>   *SumOfYears* := *Sum(NumYears)*;
>   ⋮
>   *Depreciation* := (*NumYears* − *k* + 1) * *Amount/SumOfYears*;
>   ⋮
> **end** (* *PrintDepreciationTable* *);

begin (* main program *)
   ⋮
   GetData (*Amount, NumYears*);
   PrintDepreciationTable (*Amount, NumYears*);
   ⋮
end (* main program *).

Figure 6.14

Scope Rule 3 states that an identifier declared in a subprogram can be accessed in a subprogram contained in it, provided that the same identifier is not declared locally in the internal subprogram (and is not used as a control variable in a for loop). Thus, in this example, the local variables *Amount*, *NumYears*, *SumOfYears*, and *Depreciation* of the function *PrintDepreciationTable* are accessible within it as well as within the function *Sum*. The local variable *k* in *PrintDepreciationTable*, however, is not accessible to the function *Sum*, because *k* is declared as a local variable within *Sum*.

According to Scope Rule 2, the global variable *Response* (as well as the files *input* and *output*) is accessible to the procedure *PrintDepreciationTable* and thus also to the function *Sum*. On the other hand, *Response* is not accessible to the procedure *GetData*, since *Response* is a local variable within *GetData*. Similarly, the global variables *Amount* and *NumYears* are not accessible to either *GetData* or *PrintDepreciationTable*. (Their values, of course, are made available to these procedures through their formal parameter lists.)

It should be noted in this example that the function *Sum* is not accessible to the main program or to the procedure *GetData*, since it is defined within the procedure *PrintDepreciationTable*. This is undesirable if sums need to be calculated in the main program, because the function *Sum* is not available. In this case it would make sense to define all of the subprograms *GetData*, *Sum*, and *PrintDepreciationTable* in the main program so that the program has the structure shown in Figure 6.15.

program *Depreciation*

```
parameters: input, output
var Amount, NumYears, Response
procedure GetData

    parameters: Amount, NumYears
    var Response
    begin (* GetData *)
        ⋮
    end (* GetData *);

function Sum

    parameters: n
    var TempSum, k
    begin (* Sum *)
        ⋮
    end (* Sum *);

procedure PrintDepreciationTable

    parameters: Amount, NumYears
    var SumOfYears, k, Depreciation
    begin (* PrintDepreciationTable *)
        ⋮
        SumOfYears := Sum(NumYears);
        ⋮
        Depreciation := (NumYears − k + 1) * Amount/SumOfYears;
        ⋮
    end (* PrintDepreciationTable *);

begin (* main program *)
    ⋮
    GetData (Amount, NumYears);
    PrintDepreciationTable (Amount, NumYears);
    ⋮
end (* main program *).
```

Figure 6.15

Since the function *Sum* is referenced by the procedure *PrintDepreciation-Table*, it must be defined before *PrintDepreciationTable* is. In general, a function or procedure must be defined before it can be referenced by another function or procedure at the same level.

Scope Rule 4

If *SubA* and *SubB* are subprograms defined in the same program unit and if *SubA* is referenced by *SubB*, then *SubA* must be defined before *SubB*.

According to this scope rule, the program structure in Figure 6.15 is an acceptable alternative to that in Figure 6.14, because the subprograms are arranged in the order *GetData*, *Sum*, *PrintDepreciationTable*. Other acceptable orderings of these procedures and functions are *Sum*, *GetData*, *PrintDepreciationTable*, and *Sum*, *PrintDepreciationTable*, *GetData*. However, the ordering *PrintDepreciationTable*, *Sum*, *GetData* would not be valid, since *PrintDepreciationTable* references *Sum*, thus violating Scope Rule 4.

Exercises

1. Consider the following program skeleton:

```
program ScopeRules (input, output);

   var
       a, b : integer;

   function F(x : real) : real;

       var b, c : integer;
       begin (* F *)
          ⋮
       end (* F *);

   procedure P1(d : real);

       var e, f : integer;
       procedure P2(a : real);

          var e, g : integer;
          begin (* P2 *)
             ⋮
          end (* P2 *);

       begin (* P1 *)
          ⋮
       end (* P1 *);

begin (* main program *)
   ⋮
end (* main program *).
```

Answer the following true or false:

(a) The variable *a* declared in the main program is a global variable.
(b) The variable *a* declared in the main program is accessible within function *F*.
(c) The variable *a* declared in the main program is accessible within procedure *P2*.
(d) The function *F* is accessible within procedure *P2*.
(e) *g* is accessible only within procedure *P2*.
(f) The statement *b* := *c* within the statement part of *F* would assign the value of *c* to the global variable *b*.
(g) The statement *writeln* (*F*(*f*)) may be used in the statement part of *P1*.
(h) The statement *P2*(3) may be used in the statement part of *P1*.
(i) *f* is accessible within *P2*.
(j) The statement *P2*(*b*) may be used in the statement part of the main program.
(k) The statement *P1*(*F*(*a*)) may be used in the statement part of the main program.

2. Describe the output produced by the following program, or explain why an error occurs:

```
program Exercise2 (output);

function Product(x : integer) : integer;

   begin (* Product *)
      Product := 3 * x
   end (* Product *);

function Sum(x : integer) : integer;

   function Product(a : integer) : integer;

      begin (* Product *)
         Product := 4 * a
      end (* Product *);

   begin (* Sum *)
      Sum := 5 + Product(a)
   end (* Sum *);

begin (* main program *)
   writeln (Product(2):5, Sum(2):5);
   writeln (Sum(Product(3)):5, Product(Sum(3)):5)
end (* main program *).
```

3. Describe the output produced by the following program, or explain why an error occurs:

```
program Exercise3 (output);

var
   Num, i : integer;
```

```
procedure P(var Num : integer);

   begin (* P *)
      i := i + 1;
      Num := 2 * Num
   end (* P *);

begin (* main program *)
   i := 1;
   Num := 3;
   while i < = 4 do
      begin
         writeln (i:3, Num:3);
         P(Num);
         writeln (i:3, Num:3);
         i := i + 1
      end (* while *)
end (* main program *).
```

4. Describe the output produced by the following program, or explain why an error occurs:

```
program Exercise4 (output);

var
   Num, HalfNum : integer;

procedure Double(var Num : integer);

   begin (* Double *)
      Num := 2 * Num
   end (* Double *);

begin (* main program *)
   Num := 4;
   HalfNum := 2;
   writeln (HalfNum:3);
   writeln (Num:3);
   Double (HalfNum);
   writeln (HalfNum:3);
   writeln (Num:3)
end (* main program *).
```

6.5 Top-Down Design

At several places in this text we have indicated that large and complex problems can best be solved using *top-down design*. In this approach, a divide-and-conquer strategy is used in which the original problem is divided into a number of simpler subproblems. Each of these subproblems can then be solved independently, perhaps using this same divide-and-conquer strategy to divide them into still simpler subproblems. This refinement process continues until subproblems are obtained that are simple enough that algorithms can be easily developed to solve them. Procedures are then written to implement these algorithms, and these procedures are combined in a program that solves the original problem. Because this software engineering technique is so important and because we have now considered procedures in detail, it is appropriate to illustrate the use of this technique to solve a relatively complex problem.

Suppose that the athletic department at a certain university wants a program for its secretarial staff that can be used to determine the academic eligibility of its athletes for the next academic year. This eligibility check is made at the end of each of the first three years of the student's academic career. Eligibility is determined by two criteria: the number of hours that the student has successfully completed and his or her cumulative grade point average (GPA). To maintain eligibility, the student must have completed at least 25 hours with a minimum GPA of 1.7 by the end of the first year. At the end of the second year, 50 hours must have been completed with a cumulative GPA of 1.85 or higher, and at the end of the third year, 85 hours must have been completed with a minimum cumulative GPA of 1.95.

The program should display the student's number, class, cumulative hours, GPA for the current year, and cumulative GPA, as well as an indication of his or her eligibility. At the end of this report, the program should also display the total number of students processed, the number who are eligible, and the average current GPA for all students. The information to be supplied to the program is the student's number, class level, hours accumulated, cumulative GPA, and hours and grades for courses taken during the current year.

Since this program will be used by personnel who are generally not regular users of a computer system, some instructions should be displayed each time the program is used. The first procedure in the program will be designed to carry out this task. The second task is to accept the given information for each student, calculate the relevant statistics, and determine eligibility. The final task is to generate and display the desired summary statistics after all the student information has been processed. The following outline, along with the structure diagram, summarizes this analysis:

INPUT DATA

Student's number.
Class level (1, 2, or 3).
Cumulative hours.
Cumulative GPA.
Hours and grade for each course completed in the current year.

OUTPUT DATA

Student's number.
Current GPA.
Updated cumulative hours and cumulative GPA.
Indication of eligibility.
Number of students processed.
Number of students eligible.
Average of all current GPAs.

LEVEL 1 ALGORITHM FOR ELIGIBILITY PROBLEM

(* Algorithm to determine eligibility for student athletes based on hours of course work completed and cumulative grade point average. *)

1. Provide instructions to the user.
2. Repeat the following until there is no more data:
   Read the given information for a student, calculate statistics, determine eligibility, and display report.
3. Calculate and display summary statistics.

The three tasks we have identified can be implemented as three procedures: *Instruct*, *CheckStudent*, and *Summary*. Since the procedure *Instruct* simply displays instructions to the user, it requires no information from other program units. The procedure *PrintSummary* requires the total number of students processed (*StudentCount*), the total number who are eligible to participate in athletics (*EligibleCount*), and the sum of all the current GPAs (*SumOfGpas*). These values must be calculated by the procedure *CheckStudent* and shared with *PrintSummary*. Thus, the entire program has the form

```
program Eligibility (input, output);

var
    StudentCount, EligibleCount : integer;
    SumOfGpas : real;
    Response : char;

procedure Instruct;
        ⋮
procedure CheckStudent (var StudentCount, EligibleCount : integer;
                        var SumOfGpas : real);
        ⋮
procedure PrintSummary (StudentCount, EligibleCount : integer;
                        SumOfGpas : real);
        ⋮
begin (* main program *)
    Instruct;
    StudentCount := 0;
    EligibleCount := 0;
    SumOfGpas := 0;
```

```
    repeat
        CheckStudent (StudentCount, EligibleCount, SumOfGpas);
        writeln;
        write ('More (Y or N)? ');
        readln (Response)
    until Response <> 'Y';
    PrintSummary (StudentCount, EligibleCount, SumOfGpas)
end (* main program *).
```

Since *CheckStudent* is central to the entire program, we begin with its development. We can identify three main subtasks in *CheckStudent*. The first is to read the information for a student and calculate the relevant statistics. The second subtask is to use these statistics to determine whether the student is eligible for athletics. The third subtask is to generate a report displaying some of these statistics and an indication of eligibility. Using the second-level procedures *ReadAndCalculate*, *CheckEligibility*, and *Report* to carry out these subtasks within the procedure *CheckStudent*, we obtain the following structure diagram:

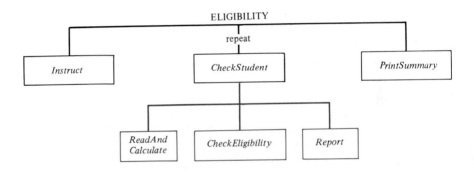

The development of procedure *ReadAndCalculate* is relatively straightforward, and an algorithm for it follows:

LEVEL 2 ALGORITHM FOR *ReadAndCalculate*

(* Algorithm to read a student's number (*Snumb*), class level (*Class*), cumulative hours (*CumHours*), and cumulative GPA (*CumGpa*), and then calculate the student's current GPA (*CurrGpa*), and update student's cumulative hours (*CumHours*) and *CumGpa*, *StudentCount*, and the sum of all GPAs (*SumOfGpas*). *)

1. Read *Snumb*, *Class*, *CumHours*, and *CumGpa* for student.
2. Calculate the number of honor points the student already has earned:

    $OldHonorPoints = CumHours * CumGpa$

3. Initialize *NewHours* and *NewHonorPoints* to 0.
4. Read *Hours* of credit and numeric *Grade* for first course taken by student.

5. While the end-of-data flag has not been read do the following:
   a. Add *Hours* to *NewHours*.
   b. Add *Hours* ∗ *Grade* to *NewHonorPoints*.
   c. Read *Hours* of credit and numeric *Grade* for next course.

6. Calculate student's current GPA (*CurrGpa*): 0 if student took no new courses; else

   $$CurrGpa = NewHonorPoints / NewHours$$

7. Update cumulative hours for student by adding *NewHours* to *CumHours*.

8. Calculate student's cumulative GPA:

   $$CumGpa = \frac{OldHonorPoints + NewHonorPoints}{CumHours}$$

9. Increment *StudentCount* by 1 and add *CurrGpa* to *SumOfGpas*.

The procedure *ReadAndCalculate* is now easy to write. Note that because the values of *Snumb*, *Class*, *CumHours*, *CumGpa*, *CurrGpa*, *StudentCount*, and *SumOfGpas* must be shared with other program units, they must be variable parameters for this procedure.

Once the procedure *ReadAndCalculate* has been written, it can be incorporated into the program and tested before the other procedures are developed, as shown in Figure 6.16. We simply insert output statements in the statement parts of the undeveloped procedures to signal when they are called. In this program, the procedures *Instruct, PrintSummary,* and *CheckEligibility* contain such **program stubs** to signal their execution, and *Report* produces a temporary printout to enable us to verify the correctness of *ReadAndCalculate*. The procedure *ReadAndCalculate* is in its final form, as is the statement part of the main program.

```
PROGRAM Eligibility (input, output);

(***********************************************************************

   Program to determine academic eligibility of athletes according to
   two criteria:  cumulative hours and cumulative gpa.  It also
   counts the total # of students checked, the # found to be eligible
   and calculates the average current gpa for all students.

***********************************************************************)

VAR
    StudentCount,              (* count of all students processed *)
    EligibleCount : integer;   (* count of the # found to be eligible *)
    SumOfGpas : real;          (* sum of current gpas of all students *)
    Response : char;           (* user response *)
```

Figure 6.16

Figure 6.16 (cont.)

```
PROCEDURE Instruct;

    BEGIN (* Instruct *)
        writeln ('********** Instruct called **********')
    END (* Instruct *);

PROCEDURE CheckStudent (VAR StudentCount, EligibleCount : integer;
                        VAR SumOfGpas : real);

    (*************************************************************

        Accepts student information, determines eligibility,
        and maintains counts of # processed and # eligible,
        and a sum of the current gpa's.

    *************************************************************)


    VAR
        Snumb,                 (* student number *)
        Class : integer;       (* student's class level -- 1, 2, or 3 *)
        CumHours,              (* cumulative hours *)
        CumGpa,                (* cumulative grade point average *)
        CurrGpa : real;        (* current grade point average *)
        Eligible : boolean;    (* true if student eligible, else false *)

    PROCEDURE ReadAndCalculate ( VAR Snumb, Class, StudentCount : integer;
                        VAR CumHours, CumGpa, CurrGpa, SumOfGpas : real);

        (*********************************************************

            Procedure to read a student's number, class, cumulative
            hours and cumulative gpa; then read hours and grades
            for courses taken during the current year, and calculate
            current gpa, update cumulative hours, cumulative gpa,
            and count of students processed.  Hours = 0 and grade = 0
            are used to signal the end of data for a student.

        *********************************************************)

        VAR
            Hours,                 (* hours of credit for a course *)
            Grade,                 (* numeric grade for that course *)
            NewHours,              (* total hours earned during current year *)
            NewHonorPts,           (* honor points earned in current year *)
            OldHonorPts : real;    (* honor points earned in past years *)

        BEGIN (* ReadAndCalculate *)
            writeln ('Enter student number, class, cum. hours, cum. gpa:');
            readln (Snumb, Class, CumHours, CumGpa);
            OldHonorPts := CumHours * CumGpa;
            NewHours := 0;
            NewHonorPts := 0;
            write ('Hours and grade? ');
            readln (Hours, Grade);
            WHILE Hours > 0 DO
                BEGIN
                    NewHours := NewHours + Hours;
                    NewHonorPts := NewHonorPts + Hours * Grade;
                    write ('Hours and grade? ');
                    readln (Hours, Grade);
                END (* WHILE *);
```

Figure 6.16 (cont.)

```
            IF NewHours = 0 THEN
               CurrGpa := 0
            ELSE
               CurrGpa := NewHonorPts / NewHours;
            SumOfGpas := SumOfGpas + CurrGpa;
            CumHours := CumHours + NewHours;
            CumGpa := (OldHonorPts + NewHonorPts) / CumHours;
            StudentCount := StudentCount + 1
         END (* ReadAndCalculate *);

   PROCEDURE CheckEligibility;

      BEGIN (* CheckEligibility *)
         writeln ('********** CheckEligibility called **********')
      END (* CheckEligibility *);

   PROCEDURE Report (Snumb, class : integer;
                     CumHours, CurrGpa, CumGpa : real);

      BEGIN (* Report *)
         writeln ('********** Report called **********');
         (***** Temporary printout *****)
         writeln ('Snumb:  ', Snumb:1);
         writeln ('Class:  ', Class:1);
         writeln ('Cum. hours:  ', CumHours:4:2);
         writeln ('Curr. gpa:  ', CurrGpa:4:2);
         writeln ('Cum. gpa:  ', CumGpa:4:2)
      END (* Report *);

   BEGIN (* CheckStudent *)
      ReadAndCalculate (Snumb, Class, StudentCount, CumHours, CumGpa,
                        CurrGpa, SumOfGpas);
      CheckEligibility;
      Report (Snumb, Class, CumHours, CurrGpa, CumGpa)
   END (* CheckStudent *);

PROCEDURE PrintSummary (StudentCount, EligibleCount : integer;
                        SumOfGpas : real);

   BEGIN (* PrintSummary *)
      writeln ('********** PrintSummary called **********')
   END (* PrintSummary *);

BEGIN (* main program *)
   Instruct;
   StudentCount := 0;
   EligibleCount := 0;
   SumOfGpas := 0;
   REPEAT
      Checkstudent (StudentCount, EligibleCount, SumOfGpas);
      writeln;
      write ('More (Y or N)? ');
      readln (Response)
   UNTIL Response <> 'Y';
   PrintSummary (StudentCount, EligibleCount, SumOfGpas)
END (* main program *).
```

Figure 6.16 (cont.)

Sample run:

```
********** Instruct called **********
Enter student number, class, cum. hours, cum. gpa:
1234 1 0 0
Hours and grade? 5 3.0
Hours and grade? 4 3.0
Hours and grade? 3.5 3.0
Hours and grade? 4 3.0
Hours and grade? 3 3.0
Hours and grade? 2 3.0
Hours and grade? 0 0
********** CheckEligibility called **********
********** Report called **********
Snumb:  1234
Class:  1
Cum. hours:  21.50
Curr. gpa:   3.00
Cum. gpa:    3.00

More (Y or N)? N
********** PrintSummary called **********
```

The sample run of this program indicates that the procedure *ReadAnd-Calculate* is correct. Therefore, we may now turn to developing the other procedures. A further analysis of the subtask of determining the student's eligibility reveals that there are two criteria used: an hours condition and a GPA condition. The two corresponding subtasks are shown in the following refined structure diagram. These can be conveniently implemented as boolean-valued functions *HoursCheck* and *GpaCheck* that return the value *true* or *false*, depending on whether the student satisfies the corresponding eligibility criteria. Replacing the temporary version of *CheckEligibility* and the reference to it in the statement part of procedure *CheckStudent* in the preceding program produces the refined program in Figure 6.17. Note that we have also modified the temporary version of *Report* and the reference to it in order to display the value of *Eligible*.

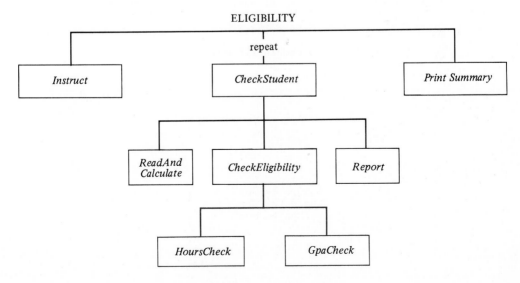

ELIGIBILITY

```
PROGRAM Eligibility (input, output);

                .
                .
                .

   PROCEDURE CheckEligibility (Class: integer; CumHours, CumGpa : real;
                               VAR Eligible : boolean;
                               VAR EligibleCount : integer);

      (****************************************************************

         Procedure to check eligibility.  Two criteria are used:
         cumulative hours, and cumulative gpa.  Functions HoursCheck
         GpaCheck implement these.

      ****************************************************************)

      FUNCTION HoursCheck(Class : integer; CumHours : real) : boolean;

         (****************************************************************

                Check student's cumulative hours.

         ****************************************************************)

         CONST
            Freshman = 25;
            Sophomore = 50;
            Junior = 85;

         BEGIN (* HoursCheck *)
            CASE Class OF
               1 : HoursCheck := CumHours >= Freshman;
               2 : HoursCheck := CumHours >= Sophomore;
               3 : HoursCheck := CumHours >= Junior
            END (* CASE *)
         END (* HoursCheck *);

      FUNCTION GpaCheck(Class : integer; CumGpa : real) : boolean;

         (****************************************************************

                Check student's cumulative gpa.

         ****************************************************************)

         CONST
            Gpa1 = 1.7;
            Gpa2 = 1.85;
            Gpa3 = 1.95;

         BEGIN (* GpaCheck *)
            CASE Class OF
               1 : GpaCheck := CumGpa >= Gpa1;
               2 : GpaCheck := CumGpa >= Gpa2;
               3 : GpaCheck := CumGpa >= Gpa3
            END (* CASE *)
         END (* GpaCheck *);
```

Figure 6.17

Figure 6.17 (cont.)

```
   BEGIN (* CheckEligibility *)
       IF (Class < 1) OR (Class > 3) THEN
           BEGIN
               writeln ('*** Illegal class code ***');
               Eligible := false
           END (* IF *)
       ELSE
           Eligible := HoursCheck(Class, CumHours)
                       AND GpaCheck(Class, CumGpa);
       IF Eligible THEN
           EligibleCount := EligibleCount + 1
   END (* CheckEligibility *);

  PROCEDURE Report (Snumb, Class : integer;
                    CumHours, CurrGpa, CumGpa : real;
                    Eligible : boolean);
                 .
                 .
                 .
       writeln ('Eligible:  ', Eligible)
   END (* Report *);
                 .
                 .
                 .
END (* main program *).
```

Sample run:

```
********** Instruct called **********
Enter student number, class, cum. hours, cum. gpa:
1234 1 0 0
Hours and grade? 5 3.0
Hours and grade? 4 3.0
Hours and grade? 3.5 3.0
Hours and grade? 4 3.0
Hours and grade? 3 3.0
Hours and grade? 2 3.0
Hours and grade? 0 0
********** Report called **********
Snumb:  1234
Class:  1
Cum. hours:  21.50
Curr. gpa:   3.00
Cum. gpa:    3.00
Eligible:  FALSE

More (Y or N)? Y
Enter student number, class, cum. hours, cumgpa:
5555 5 0 0
Hours and grade? 3 3.0
Hours and grade? 0 0
********** Illegal class code **********
********** Report called **********
Snumb:  5555
Class:  5
Cum. hours:  3.00
Curr. gpa:   3.00
Cum. gpa:    3.00
Eligible:  FALSE

More (Y or N)? N
********** PrintSummary called **********
```

Because the newly added procedure appears to be correct, we proceed to develop the remaining procedures *Report*, *Instruct*, and *PrintSummary*. The final version of the complete program is shown in Figure 6.18.

```
PROGRAM Eligibility (input, output);

(*******************************************************************

   Program to determine academic eligibility of athletes according to
   two criteria:  cumulative hours and cumulative gpa.  It also
   counts the total # of students checked, the # found to be eligible
   and calculates the average current gpa for all students.

*******************************************************************)

VAR
   StudentCount,                (* count of all students processed *)
   EligibleCount : integer;     (* count of the # found to be eligible *)
   SumOfGpas : real;            (* sum of current gpas of all students *)
   Response : char;             (* user response *)

PROCEDURE Instruct;

   (*****************************************************************

            Print instructions to the user.

   *****************************************************************)

   BEGIN (* Instruct *)
      writeln ('You will first be asked to enter the student''s');
      writeln ('number, class, cumulative hours, and cumulative gpa.');
      writeln ('Enter these with at least one space separating them.');
      writeln;
      writeln ('You will then be asked to enter the number of hours and');
      writeln ('the numeric grade earned for each of the courses the');
      writeln ('student took during the current year.  Separate the');
      writeln ('number of hours from the grade by at least one space.');
      writeln ('Enter 0 for hours and 0 for grades when you are finished');
      writeln ('entering the information for each student.');
      writeln;
      writeln;
      writeln;
      writeln
   END (* Instruct *);


PROCEDURE CheckStudent (VAR StudentCount, EligibleCount : integer;
                        VAR SumOfGpas : real);

   (*****************************************************************

      Accepts student information, determines eligibility,
      and maintains counts of # processed and # eligible,
      and a sum of the current gpa's.

   *****************************************************************)
```

Figure 6.18

Figure 6.18   (cont.)

```
VAR
    Snumb,                  (* student number *)
    Class : integer;        (* student's class level -- 1, 2, or 3 *)
    CumHours,               (* cumulative hours *)
    CumGpa,                 (* cumulative grade point average *)
    CurrGpa : real;         (* current grade point average *)
    Eligible : boolean;     (* true if student eligible, else false *)

PROCEDURE ReadAndCalculate (VAR Snumb, Class, StudentCount : integer;
                            VAR CumHours, CumGpa,
                                CurrGpa, SumOfGpas : real);

(***************************************************************

    Procedure to read a student's number, class, cumulative
    hours and cumulative gpa; then read hours and grades
    for courses taken during the current year, and calculate
    current gpa, update cumulative hours, cumulative gpa,
    and count of students processed.  Hours = 0 and grade = 0
    are used to signal the end of data for a student.

***************************************************************)

    VAR
        Hours,                  (* hours of credit for a course *)
        Grade,                  (* numeric grade for that course *)
        NewHours,               (* total hours earned during current year *)
        NewHonorPts,            (* honor points earned in current year *)
        OldHonorPts : real;     (* honor points earned in past years *)

    BEGIN (* ReadAndCalculate *)
        writeln ('Enter student number, class, cum. hours, cum. gpa:');
        readln (Snumb, Class, CumHours, CumGpa);
        OldHonorPts := CumHours * CumGpa;
        NewHours := 0;
        NewHonorPts := 0;
        write ('Hours and grade? ');
        readln (Hours, Grade);
        WHILE Hours > 0 DO
            BEGIN
                NewHours := NewHours + Hours;
                NewHonorPts := NewHonorPts + Hours * Grade;
                write ('Hours and grade? ');
                readln (Hours, Grade)
            END (* WHILE *);
        IF NewHours = 0 THEN
            CurrGpa := 0
        ELSE
            CurrGpa := NewHonorPts / NewHours;
        SumOfGpas := SumOfGpas + CurrGpa;
        CumHours := CumHours + NewHours;
        CumGpa := (OldHonorPts + NewHonorPts) / CumHours;
        StudentCount := StudentCount + 1
    END (* ReadAndCalculate *);
```

Figure 6.18 (cont.)

```
PROCEDURE CheckEligibility (Class: integer; CumHours, CumGpa : real;
                            VAR Eligible : boolean;
                            VAR EligibleCount : integer);

   (***************************************************************

      Procedure to check eligibility.  Two criteria are used:
      cumulative hours, and cumulative gpa.  Functions HoursCheck
      GpaCheck implement these.

   ***************************************************************)
FUNCTION HoursCheck(Class : integer; CumHours : real) : boolean;

   (*************************************************************

         Check student's cumulative hours.

   *************************************************************)

   CONST
      Freshman = 25;
      Sophomore = 50;
      Junior = 85;

   BEGIN (* HoursCheck *)
      CASE Class OF
         1 : HoursCheck := CumHours >= Freshman;
         2 : HoursCheck := CumHours >= Sophomore;
         3 : HoursCheck := CumHours >= Junior
      END (* CASE *)
   END (* HoursCheck *);

FUNCTION GpaCheck(Class : integer; CumGpa : real) : boolean;

   (*************************************************************

         Check student's cumulative gpa.

   *************************************************************)

   CONST
      Gpa1 = 1.7;
      Gpa2 = 1.85;
      Gpa3 = 1.95;

   BEGIN (* GpaCheck *)
      CASE Class OF
         1 : GpaCheck := CumGpa >= Gpa1;
         2 : GpaCheck := CumGpa >= Gpa2;
         3 : GpaCheck := CumGpa >= Gpa3
      END (* CASE *)
   END (* GpaCheck *);
```

Figure 6.18   (cont.)

```
    BEGIN (* CheckEligibility *)
        IF (Class < 1) OR (Class > 3) THEN
            BEGIN
                writeln ('*** Illegal class code ***');
                Eligible := false
            END (* IF *)
        ELSE
            Eligible := HoursCheck(Class, CumHours)
                        AND GpaCheck(Class, CumGpa);
        IF Eligible THEN
            EligibleCount := EligibleCount + 1
    END (* CheckEligibility *);

  PROCEDURE Report (Snumb, Class : integer;
                    CumHours, CurrGpa, CumGpa : real;
                    Eligible : boolean);

    (****************************************************************

        Display the statistics for a given student.

    ****************************************************************)

    BEGIN (* Report *)
        writeln;
        writeln ('***** Report for student ', Snumb:1, '  *****');
        writeln ('Class:              ', Class:1);
        writeln ('Cumulative hours: ', CumHours:4:2);
        writeln ('Current gpa:      ', CurrGpa:4:2);
        writeln ('Cumulative gpa:   ', CumGpa:4:2);
        IF Eligible THEN
            writeln ('ELIGIBLE')
        ELSE
            writeln ('*** NOT ELIGIBLE ***');
        writeln ('***********************************');
        writeln
    END (* Report *);

  BEGIN (* CheckStudent *)
      ReadAndCalculate (Snumb, Class, StudentCount, CumHours, CumGpa,
              CurrGpa, SumOfGpas);
      CheckEligibility (Class, CumHours, CumGpa, Eligible, EligibleCount);
      Report (Snumb, Class, CumHours, CurrGpa, CumGpa, Eligible)
  END (* CheckStudent *);

PROCEDURE PrintSummary (StudentCount, EligibleCount : integer;
                        SumOfGpas : real);

  (****************************************************************

            Print summary statistics.

  ****************************************************************)
```

Figure 6.18   (cont.)

```
    BEGIN (* PrintSummary *)
        writeln;
        writeln;
        writeln ('****************************************************');
        writeln ('*                  SUMMARY STATISTICS               *');
        writeln ('****************************************************');
        writeln;
        writeln ('NUMBER OF STUDENTS PROCESSED:     ', StudentCount:1);
        writeln ('AVERAGE CURRENT GPA OF STUDENTS:  ',
                    SumOfGpas / StudentCount : 4:2);
        writeln ('NUMBER FOUND TO BE ELIGIBLE:      ', EligibleCount:1)
    END (* PrintSummary *);

BEGIN (* main program *)
    Instruct;
    StudentCount := 0;
    EligibleCount := 0;
    SumOfGpas := 0;
    REPEAT
        Checkstudent (StudentCount, EligibleCount, SumOfGpas);
        writeln;
        write ('More (Y or N)? ');
        readln (Response)
    UNTIL Response <> 'Y';
    PrintSummary (StudentCount, EligibleCount, SumOfGpas)
END (* main program *).
```

Sample run:

You will first be asked to enter the student's
number, class, cumulative hours, and cumulative gpa.
Enter these with at least one space separating them.

You will then be asked to enter the number of hours and
the numeric grade earned for each of the courses the
student took during the current year. Separate the
number of hours from the grade by at least one space.
Enter 0 for hours and 0 for grades when you are finished
entering the information for each student.


```
Enter student number, class, cum. hours, cum. gpa:
1234 1 0 0
Hours and grade? 5 3.0
Hours and grade? 4 3.0
Hours and grade? 3.5 3.0
Hours and grade? 4 3.0
Hours and grade? 3 3.0
Hours and grade? 2 3.0
Hours and grade? 0 0

***** Report for student 1234  *****
Class:              1
Cumulative hours:   21.50
Current gpa:        3.00
Cumulative gpa:     3.00
*** NOT ELIGIBLE ***
*************************************
```

Figure 6.18   (cont.)

```
More (Y or N)? Y
Enter student number, class, cum. hours, cum. gpa:
3333 2 30 3.3
Hours and grade? 5 3.3
Hours and grade? 5 4.0
Hours and grade? 5 2.7
Hours and grade? 5 3.0
Hours and grade? 3 3.7
Hours and grade? 0 0

***** Report for student 3333   *****
Class:              2
Cumulative hours:   53.00
Current gpa:        3.31
Cumulative gpa:     3.30
ELIGIBLE
**************************************


More (Y or N)? Y
Enter student number, class, cum. hours, cum. gpa:
4444 3 60 2.0
Hours and grade? 5 1.0
Hours and grade? 5 1.3
Hours and grade? 4 0.7
Hours and grade? 3 0.7
Hours and grade? 5 1.0
Hours and grade? 0 0

***** Report for student 4444   *****
Class:              3
Cumulative hours:   82.00
Current gpa:        0.97
Cumulative gpa:     1.72
*** NOT ELIGIBLE ***
**************************************


More (Y or N)? N


******************************************************
*                SUMMARY STATISTICS                  *
******************************************************

NUMBER OF STUDENTS PROCESSED:     3
AVERAGE CURRENT GPA OF STUDENTS:  2.43
NUMBER FOUND TO BE ELIGIBLE:      1
```

Exercises

1. Use a top-down design strategy to develop a menu-driven program that
    computes any one of the following five quantities, given values for the
    other four:

Amount: Original amount (in dollars) deposited in a savings
              account or the original amount borrowed.
Balance: The final amount (in dollars)
Payment: Periodic payment made some specified number of times
              per year.
IntRate: Annual interest rate (percent).
Years: Number of years.

In each case, the user also enters the number of times per year payments are made and indicates whether these payments are loan payments or deposits into a savings account.

2. A ***complex number*** is a number of the form $a + bi$, where a and b are real numbers and $i^2 = -1$. Using a top-down approach, develop a menu-driven program that reads two complex numbers (where $a + bi$ is entered simply as the pair of real numbers a and b) and allows the user to select one of the operations of addition, subtraction, multiplication, or division to be performed. The program should then call an appropriate procedure to perform the specified arithmetic operation and display the result in the form $a + bi$. The four operations are defined as follows:

$$(a + bi) + (c + di) = (a + c) + (b + d)i$$

$$(a + bi) - (c + di) = (a - c) + (b - d)i$$

$$(a + bi) * (c + di) = (ac - bd) + (ad + bc)i$$

$$(a + bi)/(c + di) = \left(\frac{ac + bd}{c^2 + d^2}\right) + \left(\frac{bc - ad}{c^2 + d^2}\right)i$$

provided that c and d are not both zero in the case of division.

3. Many everyday situations involve ***queues*** (waiting lines): at supermarket checkout lanes, ticket counters, bank windows, gas stations, and so on. Consider the following example: An airport has one runway. Each airplane takes 3 minutes to land and 2 minutes to take off. On the average, 8 planes land and 8 take off in 1 hour. Assume that the planes arrive at random instants of time. (Delays make the assumption of randomness quite reasonable.) There are two types of queues: airplanes waiting to land and airplanes waiting to take off. Because it is more expensive to keep a plane airborne than to have one waiting on the ground, we assume that an airplane waiting to land has priority over one waiting to take off.

   Write a computer simulation of this airport's operation. To simulate landing arrivals, generate a random number corresponding to a 1-minute interval: if it is less than 8/60, then a "landing arrival" occurs and joins the queue of planes waiting to land. Generate another random number to determine whether a "take-off arrival" occurs; if so, it joins the take-off queue. Next, check to determine whether the runway is free. If so, first check the landing queue, and if planes are waiting, allow the first airplane in the landing queue to land; otherwise, consider the queue of planes waiting to take off. Have the program calculate the average queue lengths and the average time an airplane spends in a queue. For this, you might simulate a 24-hour day. You might also investigate the effect of varying arrival and departure rates to simulate prime and slack times of day, or what happens if the amount of time it takes to land or take off is increased or decreased.

6.6 Introduction to Recursion

We have seen in previous sections that a function or procedure may reference other functions and/or procedures. A function or procedure may even reference itself, a phenomenon known as *recursion*.

A function or procedure that references itself is said to be *recursive*. Recursion may be *direct*; that is, the function or procedure references itself directly, or it may be *indirect*; that is, the function or procedure references other functions and/or procedures that eventually reference this function or procedure again.

The definition of a recursive function (or procedure) consists of two parts: (1) an *anchor* in which one or more values of the function (or parameters being returned) are given and (2) an *inductive step* in which other values of the function (or parameters) are defined in terms of previously defined values. The classic example is the factorial function that is defined by

$$n! = \begin{cases} 1 \text{ if } n = 0 \\ 1 \times 2 \times \cdots \times n \text{ if } n > 0 \end{cases}$$

but that can also be defined recursively by

$$0! = 1$$
$$\text{If } n > 0, n! = n \times (n - 1)!$$

Here the first statement is the anchor and defines the value of the factorial function for 0. The second statement is the inductive step; it defines $n!$ for $n > 0$ in terms of n and the factorial of $n - 1$.

To calculate 5! using this definition, we must first calculate 4! since the definition specifies that 5! is the product of 5 and 4!. Similarly, to calculate 4!, we must first calculate 3! since 4! is defined as $4 \times 3!$. We continue applying the inductive step of the definition until the anchor case is reached:

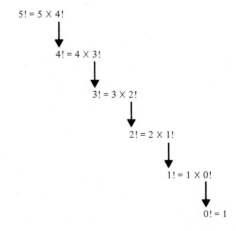

Since the value of 0! is given, we can *backtrack* to find the value of 1!:

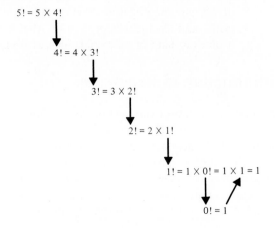

This value can then be used to find the value of 2!:

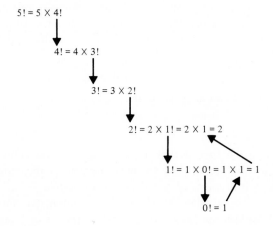

Backtracking continues until we finally obtain the value 120 for 5!:

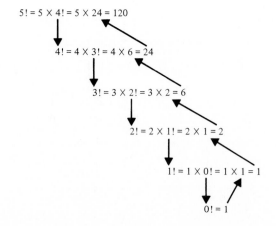

This recursive definition of the factorial function can be implemented as a recursive function in Pascal:

function *Factorial*(*n* : *integer*) : *integer*;

    (∗ Recursive function to calculate the factorial *n*! ∗)

  begin (∗ *Factorial* ∗)
    if *n* = 0 **then**
      Factorial := 1
    else
      Factorial := *n* ∗ *Factorial*(*n* − 1)
  end (∗ *Factorial* ∗);

When this function is referenced, the inductive step

  else
    Factorial := *n* ∗ *Factorial*(*n* − 1)

causes the function to reference itself repeatedly, each time with a smaller parameter, until the anchor case

  if *n* = 0 **then**
    Factorial := 1

is reached.

For example, the function reference *Factorial*(5) generates a function reference with parameter 5 − 1 = 4, which we might picture as follows:

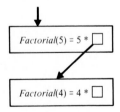

This second function reference, *Factorial*(4), then generates another reference with parameter 4 − 1 = 3, and so on until a reference with 0 is produced:

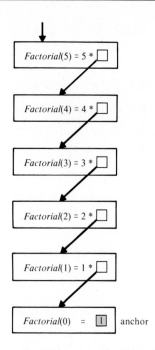

Since the anchor condition is now satisfied, no additional function references are generated. The value 1 is returned for the function reference *Factorial*(0), which is then used to calculate the value of *Factorial*(1), and so on until the value 120 is eventually returned as the value of the original function reference *Factorial*(5):

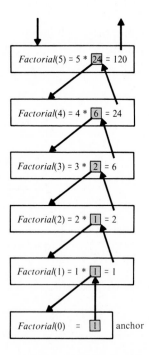

As a second example of a recursive function, consider the operation of exponentiation that can be defined recursively by

$x^0 = 1$ (anchor)

If $n > 0$, $x^n = x * x^{n-1}$ (inductive step)

Like the factorial definition, this definition leads naturally to a recursive Pascal function:

function *Power*(*x* : *real*; *n* : *integer*) : *real*;

    (* Recursive function to calculate
    *n*th power of *x* (*n* $>=$ 0). *)

    begin (* *Power* *)
      if *n* = 0 **then**
        Power := 1
      else
        Power := *x* * *Power*(*x*, *n* − 1)
    end (* *Power* *);

The following diagram pictures the five levels of function references generated by the initial reference *Power*(2, 4):

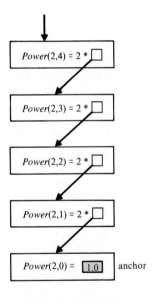

In the function reference with actual parameters 2 and 0, the value 1.0 is assigned to *Power*. This fifth function reference is thus completed, and control returns to the preceding reference in which the actual parameters are 2 and 1. This fourth reference is completed by calculating the expression 2 * *Power*(2, 0) = 2 * 1.0 = 2.0, and this value is returned to the previous function reference. Eventually the expression 2 * *Power*(2, 3) = 2 * 8.0 = 16.0 is calculated in the first function reference, and 16.0 is returned as the value for the initial function reference *Power*(2, 4). The following diagram summarizes:

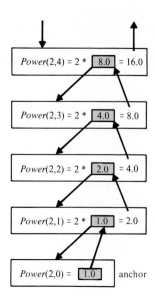

Procedures may also be recursive. To illustrate, consider the problem of printing the digits of a nonnegative integer in order from right to left. Although this problem can easily be solved without recursion (as the exercises ask you to do), it can also be solved by a recursive procedure.

procedure *Reverse* (*Number* : *integer*);

    (∗ Recursive procedure to display the digits of
      Number in order (from right to left). ∗)

var
    LeftDigits : *integer*;   (∗ the leftmost digits of *Number* ∗)

begin (∗ *Reverse* ∗)
    write (*Number* **mod** 10);
    LeftDigits := *Number* **div** 10;
    if *LeftDigits* = 0 **then**
      writeln   (∗ reversal complete ∗)
    else
      Reverse (*LeftDigits*)
end (∗ *Reverse* ∗);

The following diagram illustrates the procedure references generated by the initial call *Reverse* (6285):

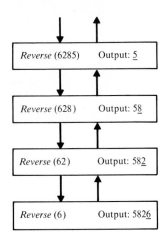

A classic example of a problem that can be solved quite easily by using recursion, but for which a nonrecursive solution is quite difficult, is the ***Towers of Hanoi*** problem. This problem involves solving the puzzle shown in Figure 6.19, in which one must move the disks from the left peg to the right peg according to the following rules:

1. When a disk is moved, it must be placed on one of the three pegs.
2. Only one disk may be moved at a time, and it must be the top disk on one of the pegs.
3. A larger disk may never be placed on top of a smaller one.

Legend has it that the priests in the Temple of Bramah were given a puzzle consisting of a golden platform with 3 golden needles on which were placed 64 golden disks. The world was to end when they had successfully finished moving the disks to another needle, following the rules just given. (*Query*: If the priests moved 1 disk per second and began their work in the year 0, when would the world come to an end?)

The Towers of Hanoi puzzle with only one disk is easy to solve: simply move the disk from peg A to peg C. This obviously does not violate any of the three rules. A solution for the problem of moving $n > 1$ disks can easily be described recursively:

1. Move the topmost $n - 1$ disks from peg A to peg B, using C as an auxiliary peg.
2. Move the large disk remaining on peg A to peg C.

Figure 6.19

3. Move the $n - 1$ disks from peg B to peg C, using peg A as an auxiliary peg.

This recursive scheme is implemented by the procedure *Move* in the program of Figure 6.20, which solves the Towers of Hanoi problem.

```
PROGRAM TowersOfHanoi (input, output);

(*******************************************************************

    Program using the recursive procedure Move to solve the
    Towers Of Hanoi puzzle.

*******************************************************************)

CONST
    Peg1 = 'A';
    Peg2 = 'B';
    Peg3 = 'C';

VAR
    NumDisks : integer;        (* number of disks *)

PROCEDURE Move (n : integer; StartPeg, AuxPeg, EndPeg : char);

    (*************************************************************

         Procedure to move n disks from StartPeg to EndPeg using
         AuxPeg as an auxiliary peg.

    *************************************************************)

    BEGIN (* Move *)
       IF n = 1 THEN
          writeln ('Move disk from ', StartPeg, ' to ', EndPeg)
       ELSE
          BEGIN
             (* Move n-1 disks from StartPeg to AuxPeg using EndPeg *)

             Move (n - 1, StartPeg, EndPeg, AuxPeg);

             (* Move disk from StartPeg to EndPeg *)

             Move (1, StartPeg, ' ', EndPeg);

             (* Move n-1 disks from AuxPeg to EndPeg using StartPeg *)

             Move (n - 1, AuxPeg, StartPeg, EndPeg)
          END (* ELSE *)
    END (* Move *);

BEGIN (* main program *)
   write ('# of disks:  ');
   readln (NumDisks);
   writeln;
   Move (NumDisks, Peg1, Peg2, Peg3)
END (* main program *).
```

Figure 6.20

Figure 6.20 (cont.)

Sample run:

```
# of disks:   4

Move disk from A to B
Move disk from A to C
Move disk from B to C
Move disk from A to B
Move disk from C to A
Move disk from C to B
Move disk from A to B
Move disk from A to C
Move disk from B to C
Move disk from B to A
Move disk from C to A
Move disk from B to C
Move disk from A to B
Move disk from A to C
Move disk from B to C
```

Many problems can be solved with equal ease using either a recursive or a nonrecursive algorithm. For example, the exponentiation operation was implemented in this section as a recursive function and in Section 6.2 as a nonrecursive one. Nonrecursive functions and procedures may execute more rapidly and utilize memory more efficiently than do corresponding recursive subprograms. Thus, if an algorithm can be described either recursively or nonrecursively with little difference in effort, it is usually appropriate to use the nonrecursive formulation.

For some problems, such as the Towers of Hanoi problem, recursion is the most natural and straightforward technique. For these problems, nonrecursive algorithms may not be obvious, may be more difficult to develop, and may be less readable than recursive ones are. For such problems, the simplicity of the recursive algorithms compensates for any inefficiency. Unless the programs are to be executed many times, the extra effort required to develop nonrecursive solutions is not warranted. Recursion is also appropriate when the problem's data are organized in a data structure that is defined recursively. Such data structures are considered in Chapter 16.

The examples of recursion in this section have illustrated direct recursion, in which a function or procedure references itself directly. Indirect recursion occurs when a subprogram references other subprograms, and some chain of subprogram references eventually results in a reference to the first subprogram again. For example, function A may reference function B, which calls procedure C, which references A again. The implementation of such indirect recursion in Pascal is discussed in Appendix F.

Exercises

1. Write a nonrecursive version of the recursive procedure *Reverse* in the text.

2. The ***Euclidean Algorithm*** for calculating the greatest common divisor GCD(a, b) of two integers a and b is described in Exercise 7 of Section 4.7. Write a recursive function or procedure to calculate GCD(a, b). Also, draw a diagram like those in the text to show the references generated by the initial reference GCD(1260, 198).

3. The sequence of ***Fibonacci numbers*** 1, 1, 2, 3, 5, 8, 13, 21, . . . (see Exercise 12 of Section 4.5) can be defined recursively by

$$\left. \begin{array}{l} f_1 = 1 \\ f_2 = 1 \end{array} \right\} \text{(anchor)}$$

   For $n > 2$, $f_n = f_{n-1} + f_{n-2}$ (inductive step)

where f_k denotes the kth Fibonacci number.

   (a) Write a recursive function procedure *Fib* to calculate the kth Fibonacci number for a positive integer k.
   (b) Draw a diagram like those in the text showing the function references generated by the initial reference *Fib*(5). Since there will be two function references at each stage after the first reference, the diagram will have a treelike structure.
   (c) Write a nonrecursive function to calculate the kth Fibonacci number.
   (d) Which of the two subprograms in (a) and (c) is more efficient?

4. A ***palindrome*** is a numeral that has the same value whether it is read from left to right or from right to left. For example, 121, 356653, and 1 are palindromes. Write a recursive function or procedure to determine whether a given number is a palindrome. Write a program to read an integer, call the subprogram to determine whether it is a palindrome, and display an appropriate message.

5. ***Binomial coefficients*** can be defined recursively as follows:

$$\left. \begin{array}{l} \dbinom{n}{0} = 1 \\[2mm] \dbinom{n}{n} = 1 \end{array} \right\} \text{(anchor)}$$

   For $0 < k < n$, $\dbinom{n}{k} = \dbinom{n-1}{k-1} + \dbinom{n-1}{k}$ (inductive step)

   (a) Write a recursive function or procedure to calculate binomial coefficients.
   (b) Draw a treelike diagram like that in Exercise 3, showing the subprogram references and returns involved in calculating the binomial coefficient $\dbinom{4}{2}$.
   (c) Use your recursive subprogram in a program that reads values for n and k and displays the value of $\dbinom{n}{k}$, using the subprogram to obtain this value.

*6.7 Functions and Procedures as Parameters

Subprograms considered thus far have involved two kinds of formal parameters, value parameters and variable parameters. In addition to these kinds of parameters, Pascal also allows functions and procedures as parameters.

To illustrate the use of *function parameters,* consider a function *ApproxArea* to approximate the area of the region under the graph of a function $f(x)$ for $a \leq x \leq b$, by subdividing this region into n rectangles and summing the areas of these rectangles, as described in Section 6.5. This subprogram *ApproxArea* must have the formal parameters a, b, and n, which are ordinary value parameters, and a function parameter f. When *ApproxArea* is referenced, actual parameters of real type are associated with the formal parameters a and b, an actual parameter of integer type is associated with the formal parameter n, and an actual function will be associated with the formal parameter f.

Function parameters are designated as such by a function heading (without the closing semicolon) within the formal parameter list. Thus an appropriate heading for *ApproxArea* is

> **function** *ApproxArea* (**function** $f(x : real) : real$;
> $a, b : real$; $n : integer) : real$;

Here **function** $f(x : real) : real$ specifies that f is a function parameter denoting a function whose formal parameter and value are of real type. The corresponding actual function parameter must be a real-valued function having a real formal parameter. For example, if *Poly* is a real-valued function with a real parameter,

> *Area* := *ApproxArea*(*Poly*, 0, 1.5, 20)

is a valid function reference. Note that only the name of the actual function parameter is given; it is not accompanied by its own actual parameters.

Figure 6.21 shows a program that uses the function *ApproxArea* to approximate the area under the graph of the function *Poly* defined by $Poly(x) = x^2 + 1$ for $0 \leq x \leq 1$.

```
PROGRAM FindArea2 (input, output);

(***************************************************************

   Program that uses the function ApproxArea to find the approximate
   area under the graph of the function y = Poly(x).

***************************************************************)

VAR
   a, b : real;                  (* endpoints of interval *)
   NumSubintervals : integer;    (* number of subintervals to use *)
```

Figure 6.21

Figure 6.21 (cont.)

```
FUNCTION Poly(x : real) : real;

    (****************************************************************

            The function for which area is being approximated.

    ****************************************************************)

    BEGIN (* Poly *)
        Poly := sqr(x) + 1.0
    END (* Poly *);

FUNCTION ApproxArea (FUNCTION f(x : real): real;
                     a, b : real; n : integer) : real;

    (****************************************************************

        Returns the approximate area under the graph of function f
        from x = a to x = b using the rectangle method with altitudes
        chosen at the midpoints of the n subintervals.

    ****************************************************************)

    VAR
        x,              (* the midpoint of one of the subintervals *)
        Deltax,         (* the length of the subintervals *)
        Sum : real;     (* the approximating sum *)
        i : integer;    (* counter *)

    BEGIN (* ApproxArea *)
        Deltax := (b - a) / n;
        Sum := 0;
        x := a + Deltax / 2;
        FOR i := 1 TO n DO
            BEGIN
                Sum := Sum + f(x);
                x := x + Deltax
            END (* FOR *);
        ApproxArea := Sum * Deltax
    END (* ApproxArea *);

BEGIN (* main program *)
    write ('Enter interval endpoints and # of subintervals: ');
    readln (a, b, NumSubintervals);
    writeln ('Approximate area using ',
             NumSubintervals:1, ' subintervals is ',
             ApproxArea(Poly, a, b, NumSubintervals):8:4)
END (* main program *).
```

Procedures may also be used as parameters in subprograms. In this case, a formal parameter is designated as a ***procedure parameter*** by including a procedure heading (without the closing semicolon) in the formal parameter list.

If *F* is a formal function or procedure parameter and *A* is the corresponding actual parameter, then the following rules apply:

1. *A* must be defined within the program; it may not be a predefined function or procedure.

2. If *F* denotes a function whose value is of type *T*, then *A* must also denote a function whose value is of type *T*.

3. If

   Flist-1 : *type-1*; *Flist-2* : *type-2*: . . . ; *Flist-n* : *type-n*

is the formal parameter list of *F*, then the formal parameter list of *A* must have the form

   Alist-1 : *type-1*; *Alist-2* : *type-2*; . . . ; *Alist-n* : *type-n*

where each *Flist-i* and *Alist-i* contain the same number of parameters, and all of these parameters are value parameters, all are variable parameters, all are function parameters, or all are procedure parameters. (In the case of function or procedure parameters, they must also satisfy these same rules.)

To illustrate Rule 2, consider the following procedure heading:

procedure *Demo* (**procedure** *F*(*x, y* : *integer*; **var** *V* : *real*));

The heading of the procedure defining the actual procedure *A* corresponding to *F* could be

procedure *A* (*Num1, Num2* : *integer*; **var** *Alpha* : *real*);

but it could not be any of the following:

procedure *A* (*Num1* , *Num2* : *integer*; **var** *Num3* : *integer*);
procedure *A* (*Num1* : *integer*; **var** *Alpha* : *real*);
procedure *A* (*Num1* , *Num2* : *integer*; *Alpha* : *real*);
procedure *A* (*Num1* : *integer*; *Num2* : *integer*; **var** *Alpha* : *real*);

Programming Pointers

Program Design

1. (From Wirth) *"We recommend to choose function identifiers which are nouns. The noun then denotes the function's result. Boolean functions are appropriately labeled by an adjective. In contrast, regular procedures should be designated by a verb describing their action."*

2. *Programs for solving complex problems should be designed in a modular fashion.*

   • *A problem should be divided into simpler subproblems so that a function or procedure can be written to solve each of these subproblems.*
   • *Local identifiers should be used whenever possible to avoid conflict with identifiers in other program units and to make the program as modular as possible.*

- *Formal parameters in subprograms should be declared as value parameters whenever possible so that subprograms cannot unexpectedly change the values of the actual parameters.*

3. *Recursive functions and procedures may be used when the problem's data is organized in a data structure that is defined recursively. They may also be used for problems for which a simple recursive algorithm can be given. If a nonrecursive algorithm can be given that is no more complex than the recursive one, it is usually best to use the nonrecursive version.*

Potential Problems

1. *When a procedure or function is referenced, the number of actual parameters must be the same as the number of formal parameters in the procedure or function heading, and the type of each actual parameter must be compatible with the type of the corresponding formal parameter.* For example, consider the function with the heading

    function *Maximum* (*Number1*, *Number2* : *integer*) : *integer*;

    The statements

    Larger1 := *Maximum*(*k*, *m*, *n*);

    and

    Larger2 := *Maximum*(*Number*, 3.75);

    are incorrect. In the first case, the number of actual parameters does not agree with the number of formal parameters, and in the second, the real value 3.75 cannot be assigned to the integer parameter *Number2*.

2. *Parameters that are to return values from a procedure must be declared as variable parameters using the indicator* **var**. *The actual parameters that correspond to variable formal parameters must be variables; they may not be constants or expressions.* For example, the procedure whose heading is

    procedure *FindTaxes* (*Income* : *real*; **var** *NetIncome*, *Tax* : *real*);

    can return only values of *NetIncome* and *Tax* to the calling program unit, and it cannot be called by the statement

    FindTaxes (*Salary*, 3525.67, *IncomeTax*)

    because the constant 3525.67 cannot be associated with the variable parameter *NetIncome*.

3. *Formal parameters in procedures and functions are defined only during execution of that procedure or function; they are undefined both before and after execution.* Any attempt to use these parameters outside the function or procedure is an error.

4. *The scope of a local identifier is the program unit in which it is declared.* For example, for the procedure

> **procedure** *Calculate* (*x* : *integer*; *y* : *real*);
>
> > **var**
> > *a, b* : *integer*;
> > ⋮

the local variables *x*, *y*, *a*, and *b* cannot be accessed outside the procedure *Calculate*.

5. *A control variable for a **for** statement must be declared within the program unit in which it is used.* A global variable or any variable declared in some larger program unit may not be used for this purpose.

6. *Using global variables to share information between different program units should usually be avoided, since changing the value of such a variable in one program unit changes its value in all program units.* This may make it difficult to determine the value of such a variable at any point in the program because its value may have been changed by any of the program units.

7. *A procedure or function must be defined before it is referenced.* For example, if the procedure *FindTaxes* references the procedure *Calculate*, then *Calculate* must be defined before *FindTaxes*.

> **procedure** *Calculate* . . . ;
> > ⋮
> **procedure** *FindTaxes* . . . ;
> > ⋮

8. *Procedures and functions that have formal parameters cannot be referenced without corresponding actual parameters.* An error commonly made by beginning programmers is illustrated by the following attempt to define the function *Sum* (which calculates the sum $1 + 2 + \cdots + n$):

> **function** *Sum*(*n* : *integer*) : *integer*;
>
> > **var**
> > *k* : *integer*;
>
> > **begin** (∗ *Sum* ∗)
> > *Sum* := 0;
> > > **for** *k* := 1 **to** *n* **do**
> > > *Sum* := *Sum* + *k*
> > **end** (∗ *Sum* ∗);

In this example, the statement

> *Sum* := *Sum* + *k*

is not valid because the right side of this assignment statement contains a reference to the function *Sum* with no actual parameter. Instead a local variable within *Sum* should be initialized

$TempSum := 0;$

and used in the for loop:

for $k := 1$ **to** n **do**
    $TempSum := TempSum + k;$

The final value of *TempSum* is then assigned to the function:

$Sum := TempSum$

See the program in Figure 6.12 for the complete function.

Program Style

1. *Procedures and functions should be documented in the same way that programs are.* The documentation should include a brief description of the processing carried out by the function or procedure, the values passed to it, and the values returned by it.

2. *Procedures and functions are separate program units, and the program format should reflect this.* In this text we

   (a) Insert a blank line before and after each procedure and function definition to separate it from other program units.
   (b) Indent the declarations and statements within each subprogram.
   (c) Follow the stylistic standards for programs described in earlier chapters when writing subprograms.

Variations and Extensions

An assortment of additional predefined procedures and functions is usually provided in the various versions of Pascal. Typically included are

- Additional arithmetic functions (e.g., *KeyPressed*, *BitShift*, *Log*, *PwrOfTen*).
- Random number generators.
- String functions and procedures (see the Variations and Extensions section of Chapter 10).
- Special graphics subprograms.

Such extended features are included in Macintosh, Turbo, and UCSD Pascal; see Appendix G for details. Also,

- Units may be provided to facilitate modular programming. (Turbo)
- Function and procedure parameters may not be allowed (UCSD) or their declarations may differ from standard Pascal. (Turbo)

7

Input/Output

When I read some of the rules for speaking and writing the English
language correctly . . . I think
    Any fool can make a rule
    And every fool will mind it.

HENRY THOREAU

All useful programs involve the input and output of information, and therefore, these operations deserve special consideration. Up to now we have restricted our attention primarily to numeric input/output and merely noted in Chapter 4 that the boolean-valued functions *eof* and *eoln* may be used in conjunction with input. In this chapter we discuss these functions in more detail, and we also consider the input and output of nonnumeric data.

In our introduction to input/output in Chapter 3, we observed that these operations are carried out using *files.* We have thus far used only the standard system files *input* and *output* that are associated with the standard system input and output devices. In this chapter we introduce text files because interactive input is cumbersome for large data sets and may be quite difficult with some Pascal compilers.

7.1 Input/Output Procedures

Up to now we have used *read, readln, write,* and *writeln* statements to perform input/output. These statements are in fact procedure reference statements that call the predefined Pascal procedures *read, readln, write,* and *writeln,* respectively. The input/output lists are in fact the parameter lists for these predefined procedures. These procedures have the special property that references to them may include any number of parameters.

The *writeln* procedure is called with a statement of the form

writeln (output-list)

where *output-list* is an expression or a list of expressions separated by commas. Execution of such a statement displays the values of the expressions on a single line and then advances to a new line. For example, if the value of the integer variable *Number* is 27, the statements

writeln ('Square of ', *Number*, ' is ', *sqr(Number)*);
writeln ('and its square root is ', *sqrt(Number)*)

produce output like the following:

```
Square of      27 is      729
and its square root is  5.196152423E+00
```

The actual spacing within each line and the form in which real values are displayed are system dependent and may not be exactly as shown.

Recall that the format of the output can be specified by appending a format descriptor of the form :*w* or :*w:d* to the items in the output list. For example, the statements

writeln ('Square of ', *Number*:2, ' is ', *sqr(Number)*:4);
writeln ('and its square root is ', *sqrt(Number)*:8:3)

produce as output

```
Square of 27 is  729
and its square root is    5.196
```

The *writeln* procedure may also be called with no output list:

writeln

and in this case the parentheses are also omitted. This statement serves simply to advance to the next line.

The *write* procedure is called with a statement of the form

write (output-list)

where the output list has the same form as for the *writeln* statement; format descriptors may be used as just described. When this statement is executed, the values are displayed on the current line, but there is no advance to a new line. Consequently, any subsequent output will be displayed on this same line.

For example, the statements

```
write ('The first 5 squares are:');
for i := 1 to 5 do
    write (sqr(i):3);
writeln (' *****');
writeln ('*****')
```

produce as output

```
The first 5 squares are:  1  4  9 16 25 *****
*****--------------------------------------------
```

The *readln* procedure is called with a statement of the form

readln (input-list)

where *input-list* is a variable or a list of variables of integer, real, or character type, separated by commas. When this statement is executed, values are read from the standard system file *input* and assigned to the variables in the input list. In a batch mode of operation, these values are typically obtained from a data file that accompanies the program. In an interactive mode, execution of the program is suspended while the user enters values for the variables. In this text the examples illustrate interactive input.

For example, when the statements

```
writeln ('Enter employee number, hours worked, and hourly rate:');
readln (EmpNumber, Hours, Rate)
```

are executed, the prompt

```
Enter employee number, hours worked, and hourly rate:
```

is displayed, and execution of the program is interrupted. The user must enter values for the three variables before execution of the program can resume. To assign the values 3123, 38.5, and 7.50 to *EmpNumber*, *Hours*, and *Rate*, respectively, where *EmpNumber* is of integer type and *Hours* and *Rate* are of real type, the appropriate input is

```
3123 38.5 7.50
```

The values that are read are actually obtained from the standard system file *input*. Values are copied into this file sequentially as they are entered, and each time a line of input is terminated by depressing the RETURN key, an **end-of-line mark** is placed in the file. Thus, if the user enters

```
3123 38.5 7.50
3164 40.0 8.75
```

the contents of the file *input* are

where we have used ● to indicate an end-of-line mark.

As values are read from this file by a *readln* statement, a data pointer, which is initially positioned at the beginning of the file, advances through the file. If we indicate the data pointer by ↑, then the initial status of the file *input* is

When a value for the integer variable *EmpNumber* is read from this file, the longest sequence of characters that forms an integer is read, *with leading blanks ignored*. This sequence of characters is then converted to an integer value and assigned to *EmpNumber,* and the data pointer advances to the first character that is not a digit. Thus, for the statement

> readln (*EmpNumber, Hours, Rate*)

the value read for *EmpNumber* is 3123, and the data pointer is advanced to the blank that follows the last digit of this number.

A value must now be read for the real variable *Hours*. The longest sequence of characters that represents a real value (in either decimal or exponential form) is read, *with leading blanks ignored*. This sequence of characters is converted to a real value and assigned to the appropriate real variable. Thus the value read for *Hours* is 38.5, and the data pointer advances to the blank following the last digit of this number.

Similarly, the value 7.50 is read for *Rate,* and the data pointer is advanced to the end-of-line mark.

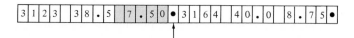

The *readln* procedure then advances the data pointer past this end-of-line mark so that the values read for variables in subsequent *readln* statements begin at this point.

For the statement

readln (EmpNumber, Hours, Rate)

the values might be entered one per line:

<u>3123</u>
<u>38.5</u>
<u>7.50</u>
<u>3164</u>
<u>40.0</u>
<u>8.75</u>

In this case, the contents of the file *input* are

The value read for *EmpNumber* is 3123, and the data pointer advances to the end-of-line mark following the last digit of this number.

Next, a value must be read for *Hours*; the end-of-line mark is interpreted as a blank and is thus ignored, so that the value 38.5 is read and assigned to *Hours* and the data pointer is advanced.

Similarly, the value 7.50 is read and assigned to *Rate,* and the data pointer is advanced.

Because values have been read and assigned to each variable in the input list, the *readln* procedure now advances the data pointer past this end-of-line mark.

Suppose that the preceding data values are entered as

<u>3123 38.5 7.50 3164</u>
<u>40.0 8.75</u>

so that the contents of the file *input* are

When the statement

    readln (EmpNumber, Hours, Rate)

is executed, the values 3123, 38.5, and 7.50 are read and assigned to *Emp-Number, Hours,* and *Rate,* respectively, as before. Because values have been read for each of the variables in the input list, the *readln* procedure now causes the data pointer to advance past the next end-of-line mark

so that the value 3164 is not read. Subsequent input continues from this point. If the statement

    readln (EmpNumber, Hours, Rate)

is executed again, the value read for *EmpNumber* is 40, since this is the longest sequence of characters that represents an integer; the data pointer advances to the decimal point following this integer.

Next, a value must be read for the real variable *Hours.* An error occurs and execution terminates, however, since a real number may not begin with a decimal point. The error message displayed might be

```
*** I/O ERROR at character 3 of line 2;
    '.' found where '+', '-', or digit expected.
```

Real values may also be entered in exponential form. For example, if the first real values in the preceding example are entered as 0.385E2 and 75E-1, the same values can be read and assigned as before:

The *read* procedure can also be used for input. It is called with a statement of the form

    read (input-list)

where *input-list* is a variable or a list of variables separated by commas. The *read* procedure is similar to the *readln* procedure except that the *read* procedure does *not* advance the data pointer past an end-of-line mark after values have been read for the variables in the input list. To illustrate, consider the statement

   read (EmpNumber, Hours, Rate)

and suppose that the data are entered as described previously:

   <u>3123 38.5 7.50 3164</u>
   <u>40.0   8.75</u>

As in the case of the *readln* statement, the values read for *EmpNumber, Hours,* and *Rate* are 3123, 38.5, and 7.50, respectively. For the *read* statement, however, the data pointer is not advanced past the end-of-line mark.

Thus if the statement

   read (EmpNumber, Hours, Rate)

is executed again, the value 3164 is read for *EmpNumber,* 40.0 for *Hours* (the end-of-line mark preceding this number is ignored), and 8.75 for *Rate,* and the data pointer is advanced to the end-of-line mark following this last value.

A second distinction between the *read* and *readln* procedures is that *readln,* but not *read,* may be called with no input list:

   readln

Note that in this case the parentheses are also omitted. Execution of this statement advances the data pointer past the next end-of-line mark so that subsequent input begins with a new line. It may thus be used to skip a line of input or to skip over values that remain in the current line.

When a value is read for a numeric variable, the longest sequence of characters that can be interpreted as a value for that variable is read, and the data pointer is advanced to the nondigit character that follows that value. The value of a character variable, however, is only a single character. Thus, when a value is read for a character variable, the next character is read and assigned to the variable, and the data pointer is advanced one position. Since blanks are legitimate characters, they are not ignored but, rather, are read and assigned as values for character variables. Similarly, end-of-line marks are not ignored but are read and interpreted as blanks when reading values for character variables.

To illustrate, consider the statement

read (Ch1, Ch2, Ch3, Ch4)

where *Ch1, Ch2, Ch3,* and *Ch4* are of character type. Suppose that the following data are entered:

AB_CD

so that the file *input* has the contents

When this statement is executed, the characters A and B are read and assigned to *Ch1* and *Ch2*, respectively; a blank is read and assigned to *Ch3*; C is read and assigned to *Ch4*; and the data pointer is advanced to the next character.

If characters are entered one per line

A
B
C
D

the contents of the file *input* are

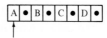

When the preceding *read* statement is executed, the value read for *Ch1* is A. The next character read is an end-of-line mark; it is interpreted as a blank and assigned to *Ch2*. Similarly, the letter B is read and assigned to *Ch3*; an end-of-line mark is read, interpreted as a blank, and assigned to *Ch4*; and the data pointer is advanced to the next character.

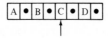

If we wish to assign A, B, C, and D to the character variables *Ch1, Ch2, Ch3,* and *Ch4*, respectively, by using the statement

read (Ch1, Ch2, Ch3, Ch4)

the data should be entered on a single line with no intervening blanks:

ABCD

When this statement is executed, the data pointer advances to the end-of-line mark following the D.

Subsequent reading of values begins at this point. Thus, if a value is read for a character variable, this end-of-line mark is read, and a blank is assigned to this variable.

It is important to remember how numeric and character values are read when variables of different types appear in the same input list. Suppose that *Num1* and *Num2* are integer variables and that *Ch1* and *Ch2* are character variables, and consider the statement

   readln (Num1, Ch1, Num2, Ch2)

If the following data are entered on a single line

23A45B

then the values read and assigned are

   Num1 ← 23
   Ch1 ← A
   Num2 ← 45
   Ch2 ← B

If we enter the values on separate lines, however,

23
A
45
B

then the value 23 is read and assigned to *Num1* and an end-of-line mark is read and a blank is assigned to *Ch1*. But an error now occurs in reading a value for the integer variable *Num2* because the next character, A, is not a digit. The same error occurs if the data are entered as

23 A 45 B

with blanks separating the values.

If the data is entered as

23A_45B

then the values read and assigned are

$Num1 \leftarrow 23$
$Ch1 \leftarrow A$
$Num2 \leftarrow 45$
$Ch2 \leftarrow B$

No error occurs, since the blank separating A and 45 is ignored when reading a value for *Num2*. These same values are read and assigned if they are entered as

23A
45B

since in this case the end-of-line mark separating A and 45 is ignored when reading a value for *Num2*.

Exercises

1. Suppose that *Num1*, *Num2*, *Num3*, and *Num4* are integer variables and that for each of the following *read* and *readln* statements, the following data is entered:

   1___−2_3
   4−5_6
   7_____−8_____9

   What values will be assigned to these variables when each of the following statements is executed?

   (a) *read (Num1, Num2, Num3, Num4);*

   (b) *readln (Num1, Num2, Num3, Num4);*

   (c) *read (Num1, Num2);*
       read (Num3);
       read (Num4);

   (d) *readln (Num1, Num2);*
       readln (Num3, Num4);

   (e) *readln;*
       readln (Num1, Num2, Num3, Num4);

2. Assume the following declarations:

    var
        N1, N2, N3 : *integer*;
        R1, R2, R3 : *real*;
        C1, C2, C3 : *char*;

and that for each of the following *read* and *readln* statements, the following data is entered:

<u>123   45.6</u>
<u>X78 −909.8 7</u>
<u>−65$ 432.10</u>

List the values that are assigned to each of the variables in the input list, or explain why an error occurs:

(a) *readln (N1, R1)*;
    read (C1, N2);
    readln (R2);
    read (C2, N3, C3);

(b) *readln (N1)*;
    read (C1, C2, R1, R2);
    read (N2, N3, C3);
    read (R3);

(c) *read (N1, R1)*;
    readln (C1, C2, R2, N2, C3, R3);
    readln (N3);

(d) *readln*;
    read (C1, N1, C2, R1, R2);
    read (N2, C3, R3);

(e) *read (N1, R1, C1)*;
    read (C2, N2, R2);
    readln (N3, C3, R3);

(f) *readln(N1, R1, C1, C2, N2, R2, N3, R3, C3)*;

(g) *read (N1, R1)*;
    readln (C1, N2, R2, N3);
    readln (R3, C3);

(h) *readln (N1, R1)*;
    readln (C1, N2, N3, R2);
    readln (R3, C3);

3. Assume the following declarations:

    var
        N1, N2, N3 : *integer*;
        R1, R2, R3 : *real*;
        C1, C2, C3 : *char*;

and that the contents of the file *input* are

List the values that are assigned to each of the variables in the input list for each of the following statements, or explain why an error occurs. Also, show the position of the data pointer after each of the sequences of statements is executed:

(a) *read (N1, N2, C1, C2, R1, C3, N3);*

(b) *read (N1, R1, R2, C1, C2, C3, N2);*

(c) *readln (N1, N2);*
    readln (C1, R1, C2, R2);

(d) *read (N1);*
    read (N2);
    read (C1);
    read (C2);
    read (R1);
    read (C3);
    read (N3);

(e) *readln (N1);*
    readln (N2);
    readln (N3);

(f) *read (C1, C2, C3, N1);*
    readln;
    readln (N2);

(g) *readln (R1, R2);*
    readln (C1, N1, C2, N2, C3, N3);

(h) *read (R1, C1, N1, C2);*
    readln (N2, C3, R2);

7.2 Introduction to Text Files; the *eof* and *eoln* Functions

Up to this point, we have assumed that the data for the sample programs were entered by the user during program execution. In this interactive mode, the data values are copied into the standard system file *input,* and values are obtained from this file by the *read* or *readln* procedures. In general, any collection of data items that are input to or output by a program is called a **file.** It is possible to create a file before a program is executed and then to read values from this file during execution. There are several reasons that this may be desirable. It may be inconvenient for the user to enter the data each time the program is executed, especially if the volume of data is large, and as we have noted, interactive input may be somewhat difficult with some systems. These problems can be avoided by preparing a data file in advance and designing the program to read the values from this file. In this section we introduce a simple kind of file called a **text file** and describe how input and output using such files are carried out.

Files are usually stored on magnetic tape or magnetic disk or some other form of external (secondary) memory. Magnetic tape is coated with a substance that can be magnetized and stores information for computer processing in somewhat the same way that an audio tape stores sound information. Information can be written to or read from a tape using a device called a **tape drive.** A magnetic disk is also coated with a substance that can be magnetized. Information is stored on such disks in tracks arranged in concentric circles and is written to or read from a disk using a **disk drive.** This device transfers information by means of a read/write head that is positioned over one of the tracks of the rotating disks.

To illustrate how text files are declared and accessed in Pascal programs, we consider the problem of processing employee wage information. Some employee information, such as the employee number and hourly pay rate, remains unchanged for long periods of time, and it is preferable to avoid entering this information each time that programs for processing it are executed. Consequently, a file containing data such as the following might be created to store this permanent employee information:

```
3123   7.50
3164   8.75
3185   9.35
3202  10.50
3559   6.35
        .
        .
        .
4813  11.60
```

This file might be created using a text editor and stored in secondary memory, or it might be produced by some other program. Here the information for each employee appears on a separate line, and one or more blanks separate the items in that line. A text file, like the standard system file *input,* is a sequence of characters, and thus this file should be viewed as having the form

where ● denotes an end-of-line mark and ▼ denotes an **end-of-file mark.** The manner in which the end-of-file mark is actually placed at the end of a file is system dependent. If the file is prepared by using a text editor or is an output file produced by some program, this mark is usually placed at the end of the file automatically, after the last data line has been entered. In an interactive mode, that is, when the file is *input,* the user must usually enter some special control character (e.g., control-z) from the keyboard to mark the end of the file.

In Pascal, text files are accessed using **file variables** of type *text.* The type identifier *text* is quite different from those considered up to now. The data types *integer, real, boolean,* and *char* are called **simple** data types because a datum of one of these types consists of a single item that cannot be subdivided. The type *text,* however, is a **structured** data type in which a datum is a collection of items. For example, to process the text file containing the permanent employee information, we might use the file variable *EmpFile* declared by

var
    EmpFile : text;

Files that exist before and/or after execution of a program are called **permanent** (or **external**) files. Names of all permanent files used in a program, including the standard files *input* and *output,* must appear in the file list of the program heading. In our example, *EmpFile* is a permanent file and must, therefore, be listed in the program heading:

program *Payroll* (*input, output, EmpFile*);

Before the contents of a file can be read, the file must be *opened for input*; that is, a data pointer must be positioned at the beginning of the file. This is done by using the predefined Pascal procedure *reset.* This procedure is called with a statement of the form

reset (file-variable)

Thus, for our example, the statement

reset (EmpFile);

opens the employee information file for input, positioning the data pointer at the beginning of the file.[1]

The data pointer is advanced sequentially through the file as the items are read, in the same manner as described for the file *input* in the preceding section.

The values in a text file are read by using the standard input procedures *readln* and *read.* In this case, the input statements have the form

readln (file-variable, input-list)

or

read (file-variable, input-list)

---

[1] In some implementations of Pascal, the procedure *reset* is also used to associate the file name used in the program with the name of the actual data file stored in secondary memory, by allowing a second parameter:

reset (file-variable, file-name)

In others, a separate procedure (e.g., *assign*) must be used to make this association. (See Appendix G for additional details.)

where *file-variable* denotes the text file from which the values are to be read. If *file-variable* is omitted, the standard file *input* is assumed; thus the statements

   readln (input-list)   and   *read (input-list)*

are equivalent to

   readln (input, input-list)   and   *read (input, input-list)*

respectively.

   When an input statement is executed, sequences of characters are read from the specified file and, if necessary, are converted to a value of the same type as that of the variable for which a value is being read. These values are then assigned to the variables in the input list. After each value is read, the data pointer is advanced in the same manner as described earlier for the standard file *input*. Thus, for the employee information file *EmpFile*, the statement

   readln (EmpFile, EmpNumber, Rate);

reads values for the integer variable *EmpNumber* and the real variable *Rate* from *EmpFile*. The data pointer is then advanced so that it is positioned after the next end-of-line mark. The first execution of this statement therefore assigns the value 3123 to *EmpNumber* and the value 7.50 to *Rate,* and then advances the data pointer past the first end-of-line mark.

   The end of a file can be detected by using the boolean-valued function *eof*. This function is referenced by an expression of the form

   eof(file-variable)

and has the value true if the data pointer is positioned at the end-of-file mark; otherwise, it has the value false.

   If the file name and the parentheses are omitted, the standard system file *input* is assumed. Thus

   eof

is equivalent to

   eof (input)

   The *eof* function can be used in a boolean expression to control repetition of an input loop, for example,

```
while not eof(EmpFile) do
   begin
      readln (EmpFile, EmpNumber, HourlyRate);
         ⋮
   end (* while *);
```

The program in Figure 7.1 uses this construction to read the contents of *EmpFile* and calculate the average hourly rate of all employees. After the last values 4813 and 11.60 are read from the file and assigned to *EmpNumber* and *HourlyRate,* respectively, the *readln* procedure advances the data pointer past the last end-of-line mark so that it is positioned at the end-of-file mark. The *eof* function now returns the value true, and execution of the while loop is terminated.

```
PROGRAM AverageHourlyRate (input, output, EmpFile);

(*******************************************************************

    Program to determine the average hourly rate for employees whose
    employee numbers and hourly rates are stored in the file EmpFile.

********************************************************************)

VAR
    EmpFile : text;          (* the permanent employee file *)
    EmpNumber,               (* employee number *)
    Count : integer;         (* counts number of employees *)
    HourlyRate,              (* hourly pay rate *)
    Sum : real;              (* sum of hourly pay rates *)

BEGIN
    reset (EmpFile);
    Count := 0;
    Sum := 0;
    WHILE NOT eof(EmpFile) DO
        BEGIN
            readln (EmpFile, EmpNumber, HourlyRate);
            Count := Count + 1;
            Sum := Sum + HourlyRate
        END (* WHILE *);
    IF Count > 0 THEN
        writeln ('Average hourly rate is $', Sum / Count :4:2)
    ELSE
        writeln ('No employees listed in the file')
END.
```

Listing of EmpFile:

```
3123   7.50
3164   8.75
3185   9.35
3202  10.50
3559   6.35
3600  10.85
4013   7.15
4409   9.15
4723   8.75
4813  11.60
```

Figure 7.1

Figure 7.1 (cont.)

Sample run:

Average hourly rate is $8.99

Care must be taken to avoid attempting to read beyond the end of the file. To illustrate, if the *readln* statement in this program is replaced with

   read (*EmpFile, EmpNumber, HourlyRate*);

an error results. After the last data values 4813 and 11.60 are read, the data pointer is positioned at the end-of-line mark following these values.

Since *eof(EmpFile)* has the value false, the *read* statement is executed again. Attempting to read a value for *EmpNumber* results in an attempt to read beyond the end of the file. Execution of the program is terminated and an error message such as the following is displayed:

```
***I/O ERROR while reading EMPFILE,
     trying to read past end of file.
```

It is also possible to write to a user-defined text file so that the output can be stored for later processing. For example, suppose that all the employees listed in *EmpFile* are granted a 5 percent raise and that we wish to generate a new employee file *NewEmpFile* with the new hourly rates. In this case, the file variable *NewEmpFile* must also be listed in the program heading and declared to be of type *text*:

   program *Payroll* (*input, output, EmpFile, NewEmpFile*);
       ⋮
   var
      EmpFile,
      NewEmpFile : *text*;

Before data can be written to a text file, the file must be opened for output by using the predefined procedure *rewrite*. A reference to this procedure has the form

   rewrite (*file-variable*)

This statement creates an empty file with the specified name, destroying any previous contents of the file.[2] In our example, we would thus include in the

---

[2] As in the case of the procedure *reset*, some implementations of Pascal also use the procedure *rewrite* to associate the file name used in the program with the name of the actual data file to be stored in secondary memory, by allowing a second parameter,

   rewrite (*file-variable, file-name*)

and others use a separate procedure. (See Appendix G for details.)

program the statement

     rewrite (NewEmpFile);

Output may be directed to a text file by using statements of the form

     writeln (file-variable, output-list)

or

     write (file-variable, output-list)

If *file-name* is omitted, the output is directed to the system file *output* and thus is displayed using the standard system output device. The statements

     writeln (output-list)   and   *write (output-list)*

are thus equivalent to

     writeln (output, output-list)   and   *write (output, output-list)*

respectively. In our example, the statement

     writeln (NewEmpFile, EmpNumber:5, NewHourlyRate:6:2)

is used in the program in Figure 7.2 to write the values of *EmpNumber* and *NewHourlyRate*, followed by an end-of-line mark to the text file *NewEmpFile*.

```
PROGRAM IncreaseHourlyRates (input, output, EmpFile, NewEmpFile);

(********************************************************************

   Program to read employee numbers and hourly rates from Empfile
   and generate NewEmpFile in which all hourly rates are increased
   by a specified percentage.

********************************************************************)

CONST
   Increase = 0.05;          (* percentage increase in decimal form *)

VAR
   EmpFile,                  (* the original permanent employee file *)
   NewEmpFile : text;        (* the new permanent file to be produced *)
   EmpNumber :integer;       (* employee number *)
   HourlyRate,               (* hourly pay rate *)
   NewHourlyRate : real;     (* new hourly rate *)
```

Figure 7.2

Figure 7.2   (cont.)

```
BEGIN
   reset (EmpFile);
   rewrite (NewEmpFile);
   WHILE NOT eof(EmpFile) DO
      BEGIN
         readln (EmpFile, EmpNumber, HourlyRate);
         NewHourlyRate := (1 + Increase) * HourlyRate;
         writeln (NewEmpFile, EmpNumber:5, NewHourlyRate:6:2)
      END (* WHILE *)
END.
```

Listing of EmpFile:

```
3123   7.50
3164   8.75
3185   9.35
3202  10.50
3559   6.35
3600  10.85
4013   7.15
4409   9.15
4723   8.75
4813  11.60
```

Listing of NewEmpFile:

```
3123   7.87
3164   9.19
3185   9.82
3202  11.02
3559   6.67
3600  11.39
4013   7.51
4409   9.61
4723   9.19
4813  12.18
```

A *writeln* statement of the form

writeln (file-variable)

in which the output list is omitted produces an advance to a new line in the specified text file. Such a statement can thus be used to write blank lines to this file. (The predefined procedure *page* can be used with text files to advance to a new page; it is described in Appendix F.)

File variables, like simple variables, may also be used as parameters in user-defined procedures and functions. In this case, they *must be variable parameters,* since allowing them to be value parameters would require assigning the value of one file variable to another file variable, and this is not allowed in Pascal.

To illustrate the use of file variables as parameters, consider the following problem: Wages are to be calculated for employees whose employee number and hourly rate are contained in the file *EmpFile* described earlier. For each of these employees, this information is to be read from the file, but the hours worked are to be entered by the user during program execution, since this value is usually not the same for all pay periods. The total of all employees' wages is also to be calculated and displayed. The program in Figure 7.3 solves this problem. The procedure *GetEmployeeInfo* reads an employee number and hourly rate from a file denoted by the formal parameter *InFile*, a file variable of type *text*. Since the corresponding actual parameter in the statement that calls this procedure in the main program is the file variable *EmpFile*, *GetEmployeeInfo* actually reads this information from the file *EmpFile*. It then prompts the user to enter the hours worked for this employee and returns this value, together with the employee's number and hourly rate, to the main program, which then calls procedure *CalculateWages* to determine the wages for this employee. When the end-of-file mark in *EmpFile* is encountered, the *eof* function causes repetition to terminate, and the main program then displays the total wages for all employees.

```
PROGRAM Payroll (input, output, EmpFile);

(**********************************************************************

   Program to calculate wages for several employees whose employee
   numbers and hourly rates are read from the file EmpFile and
   whose hours are entered by the user during execution.  Total
   wages for this payroll are also calculated.

**********************************************************************)

VAR
     EmpFile : text;          (* the permanent employee file *)
     EmpNumber : integer;     (* employee number *)
     Hours,                   (* hours worked *)
     HourlyRate,              (* hourly pay rate *)
     Wages,                   (* total wages for employee *)
     TotalPayroll : real;     (* total wages for this payroll *)

PROCEDURE GetEmployeeInfo (VAR InFile : Text; VAR EmpNumber : integer;
                           VAR HourlyRate, Hours : real);

   (***********************************************************

      Procedure to read and return the employee number EmpNumber
      and HourlyRate from a text file InFile; the Hours worked is
      entered by the user and is also returned.

   ***********************************************************)
```

Figure 7.3

Figure 7.3 (cont.)

```
    BEGIN (* GetEmployeeInfo *)
        readln (InFile, EmpNumber, HourlyRate);
        write ('Hours worked for ', EmpNumber:1,': ');
        readln (Hours)
    END (* GetEmployeeInfo *);

PROCEDURE CalculateWages (Hours, HourlyRate : real;
                          VAR Wages, TotalPayroll : real);

    (***********************************************************

        Procedure to calculate and return Wages for employee who has
        worked the given number of Hours at the given HourlyRate.
        Hours above HoursLimit are paid at OvertimeFactor times
        the hourly rate.  Total wages for this payroll are also
        accumulated and returned.  The function RoundCents is used
        to round wages to the nearest cent.

    ***********************************************************)

    CONST
        OvertimeFactor = 1.5; (* overtime multiplication factor *)
        HoursLimit = 40.0;    (* overtime hours limit *)

    VAR
        RegWages,               (* regular wages *)
        OverWages : real;       (* overtime pay *)

    FUNCTION RoundCents (Amount : real) : real;

        (***********************************************************

                Returns Amount rounded to the nearest cent.

        ***********************************************************)

        BEGIN (* RoundCents *)
            RoundCents := round(100 * Amount) / 100
        END (* RoundCents *);

    BEGIN (* CalculateWages *)
        IF Hours > HoursLimit THEN
            BEGIN (* Overtime *)
                RegWages := RoundCents(HourlyRate * HoursLimit);
                OverWages :=
                    RoundCents(OvertimeFactor * HourlyRate * (Hours - HoursLimit))
            END (* Overtime *)
        ELSE
            BEGIN (* No overtime *)
                RegWages := RoundCents(HourlyRate * Hours);
                OverWages := 0
            END (* No overtime *);
        Wages := RegWages + OverWages;
        TotalPayroll := TotalPayroll + Wages
    END (* CalculateWages *);
```

Figure 7.3   (cont.)

```
BEGIN (* main program *)
   reset (EmpFile);
   TotalPayroll := 0;
   WHILE NOT eof (EmpFile) DO
      BEGIN
         GetEmployeeInfo (EmpFile, EmpNumber, HourlyRate, Hours);
         writeln ('Hourly rate:    $', HourlyRate:4:2);
         CalculateWages (Hours, HourlyRate, Wages, TotalPayroll);
         writeln ('Wages:   $', Wages:4:2);
         writeln;
      END (* WHILE *);
   writeln;
   writeln ('Total wages = $', TotalPayroll:4:2)
END (* main program *).
```

Listing of EmpFile:

```
3123   7.50
3164   8.75
3185   9.35
3202 10.50
3559   6.35
3600 10.85
```

Sample run:

```
Hours worked for 3123:   40
Hourly rate:    $7.50
Wages:  $300.00

Hours worked for 3164:   35.5
Hourly rate:    $8.75
Wages:  $310.63

Hours worked for 3185:   43.5
Hourly rate:    $9.35
Wages:  $423.09

Hours worked for 3202:   45
Hourly rate:    $10.50
Wages:  $498.75

Hours worked for 3559:   29.5
Hourly rate:    $6.35
Wages:  $187.32

Hours worked for 3600:   39
Hourly rate:    $10.85
Wages:  $423.15


Total wages = $2142.94
```

The preceding examples used the boolean-valued function *eof* to detect the end-of-file mark. End-of-line marks can be detected by using the boolean-valued function *eoln*. This function is referenced by an expression of the form

eoln(file-name)

and has the value true if the data pointer is positioned at an end-of-line mark; otherwise, it has the value false. As with the *eof* function, if the file name and the parentheses are omitted, the standard system file *input* is assumed; thus

eoln

is equivalent to

eoln(input)

To illustrate the use of the *eoln* function, consider the problem of reading a text file and replacing multiple blanks with a single blank. Each line of the input file *InFile* is read, character by character, and copied to the output file *OutFile,* except that multiple blanks are not written.

To read each character in a line of *InFile,* we use an input loop whose repetition is controlled by the boolean expression **not** *eoln(Infile)*:

```
while not eoln(InFile) do
   begin
      read (InFile, Character);
            ⋮
   end (* while not eoln *);
```

A character is written to *OutFile* if it is not a blank or if the preceding character is not a blank; otherwise, it is not written. The following statements, in which *PreviousNotBlank* and *CurrentNotBlank* are boolean variables, accomplish this:

```
PreviousNotBlank := false;
while not eoln(InFile) do
   begin
      read (InFile, Character);
      CurrentNotBlank := Character <> Blank;
      if CurrentNotBlank or PreviousNotBlank then
         write (OutFile, Character);
      PreviousNotBlank := CurrentNotBlank
   end (* while not eoln *);
writeln (OutFile);
readln (InFile)
```

When an end-of-line mark is reached, the function *eoln* returns the value true, and no more characters are read from that line. The data pointer in *InFile* must be advanced past this end-of-line mark by using a *readln* statement with no input list:

readln (InFile)

An end-of-line mark must be written to *OutFile* by using the statement

writeln (OutFile)

containing no output list.

This processing can be repeated for each line of *InFile* by placing these statements within a **while** statement controlled by the boolean expression **not** *eof(InFile)*. The complete program together with listings of *InFile* and *OutFile* are shown in Figure 7.4.

```
PROGRAM BlankStripper (InFile, OutFile);

(*********************************************************************

   Program to read the file InFile character by character and
   copy each line to OutFile but with multiple blanks replaced
   by single blanks.

*********************************************************************)

CONST
   Blank = ' ';

VAR
   InFile,                      (* the input file *)
   OutFile : text;              (* the output file *)
   Character : char;            (* character read from InFile *)
   PreviousNotBlank,            (* previous character was not a blank *)
   CurrentNotBlank : boolean;   (* current character is not a blank *)

BEGIN
   reset (InFile);
   rewrite (OutFile);
   WHILE NOT eof (InFile) DO
      BEGIN
         PreviousNotBlank := false;
         WHILE NOT eoln(InFile) DO
            BEGIN
               read (InFile, Character);
               CurrentNotBlank := Character <> Blank;
               IF CurrentNotBlank OR PreviousNotBlank THEN
                  write (OutFile, Character);
               PreviousNotBlank := CurrentNotBlank
            END (* WHILE NOT eoln *);
         writeln (OutFile);
         readln (InFile)
      END (* WHILE NOT eof *)
END.
```

Figure 7.4

Figure 7.4 (cont.)

<u>Listing of InFile</u>:

```
Fourscore and     seven   years ago,
our   fathers   brought ´
      forth
on               this continent    a      new         nation
conceived         in                                  liberty
   and dedicated to the proposition
that
all           men
              are         created           equal.
```

<u>Listing of OutFile</u>:

```
Fourscore and seven years ago,
our fathers brought
forth
on this continent a new nation
conceived in liberty
and dedicated to the proposition
that
all men
are created equal.
```

Exercises

For descriptions of the files *UserFile, InventoryFile,* and *LeastSquares-File,* see Appendix E.

1. Suppose that *InFile* contains the following:

```
I think that I shall never see
A poem lovely as a tree
                                   —JOYCE KILMER (1914)
```

and that a program begins with

program *Echo* (*InFile, output*);

var
　　Character : *char*;
　　InFile : *text*;

What output will be produced by each of the following statement parts?

(a) begin
    reset (InFile);
    while not *eof(InFile)* **do**
      begin
        while not *eoln(InFile)* **do**
          begin
            read (InFile, Character);
            write (Character)
          end (* **while not** *eoln* *);
        readln (InFile);
        writeln
      end (* **while not** *eof* *)
end.

(b) begin
    reset (InFile);
    while not *eof(InFile)* **do**
      begin
        while not *eoln(InFile)* **do**
          begin
            read (InFile, Character);
            write (Character)
          end (* **while not** *eoln* *);
        readln (InFile)
      end (* **while not** *eof* *)
end.

(c) begin
    reset (InFile);
    while not *eof(InFile)* **do**
      begin
        while not *eoln(InFile)* **do**
          begin
            read (InFile, Character);
            write (Character)
          end (* **while not** *eoln* *);
        writeln
      end (* **while not** *eof* *)
end.

2. Write a program to read a text file and copy it into another text file in which the lines are numbered 1, 2, 3, . . . with a number at the left of each line.

3. Write a program that reads a text file and counts the vowels in the file.

4. Write a program that reads a text file and counts the occurrences in the file of specified characters entered during execution of the program.

5. People from three different income levels A, B, and C rated each of two different products with a number from 0 through 10. Construct a text file in which each line contains the income level and product rankings for one respondent. Then write a program that reads this information and calculates

   (a) For each income bracket, the average rating for Product 1.
   (b) The number of persons in Income Bracket B who rated both products with a score of 5 or higher.
   (c) The average rating for Product 2 by persons who rated Product 1 lower than 3.

   Label all output and design the program so that it automatically counts the number of respondents.

6. Write a program to search *UsersFile* to find and display the resources used to date for specified users whose identification numbers are entered during execution of the program.

7. Write a program to search *InventoryFile* to find an item with a specified item number. If a match is found, display the item number and the number currently in stock; otherwise, display a message indicating that it was not found.

8. At the end of each month, a report is produced that shows the status of each user's account in *UsersFile*. Write a program to accept the current date and produce a report of the following form:

USER ACCOUNTS—09/30/89

USER-ID	RESOURCE LIMIT	RESOURCES USED
10101	$750	$381
10102	$650	$599***
⋮	⋮	⋮

   where the three asterisks (***) indicate that the user has already used 90 percent or more of the resources available to him or her.

9. Suppose that a collection of data indicates that the relation between two quantities x and y is roughly linear; that is, if we plot the points (x, y), they will tend to fall along a straight line. In this case, one may ask for the linear equation

$$y = mx + b$$

   that "best fits" these observed points. This ***regression equation*** could then be used to predict the value of y by evaluating the equation for a given value of x. A standard method for finding the ***regression coefficients*** m and b is the ***method of least squares,*** so named because it produces the line $y = mx + b$, for which the sum of the squares of the deviations of the observed y values from the predicted y values (using the equation) is as small as possible. This least squares line has the equation $y = mx + b$, where

$$\text{slope} = m = \frac{(\Sigma xy) - (\Sigma x)\bar{y}}{(\Sigma x^2) - (\Sigma x)\bar{x}}$$

$$y \text{ intercept} = b = \bar{y} - m\bar{x}$$

where

Σx is the sum of the x values.
Σx^2 is the sum of the squares of the x values.
Σxy is the sum of the products xy of corresponding x and y values.
$\bar{x}$ and $\bar{y}$ are the means of the x and y values, respectively.

Write a program to calculate the regression coefficients m and b for your own test data and then use the data in *LeastSquaresFile*. Design the program to count the number of values so that it can be used for any collection of data.

10. Related to Exercise 9 is the problem of determining whether there is a linear relationship between the two quantities x and y. One statistical measure used for this purpose is the ***correlation coefficient***. It is equal to 1 if there is a perfect positive linear relationship between x and y, that is, if y increases linearly as x increases. If there is a perfect negative linear relationship between x and y, that is, if y decreases linearly as x increases, then the correlation coefficient has the value -1. A value of zero for the correlation coefficient indicates that there is no linear relationship between x and y, and nonzero values between -1 and 1 indicate a partial linear relationship between the two quantities. The correlation coefficient for a set of n pairs of x and y values is calculated by

$$\frac{n(\Sigma xy) - (\Sigma x)(\Sigma y)}{\sqrt{(n\Sigma x^2 - (\Sigma x)^2)(n\Sigma y^2 - (\Sigma y)^2)}}$$

where

Σx is the sum of the x values.
Σy is the sum of the y values.
Σx^2 is the sum of the squares of the x values.
Σy^2 is the sum of the squares of the y values.
Σxy is the sum of the products of corresponding x and y values.

Write a program to calculate the correlation coefficient for the x and y values in *LeastSquaresFile*.

11. Write a program that reads a text file and counts the number of characters in each line. The program should display the line number and the length of the shortest and longest lines in the file, as well as the average number of characters per line.

12. Write a program that reads a text file and writes it to another text file, but with leading blanks and blank lines removed. Run this program using the last two Pascal programs you have written as input files, and comment on whether you think indenting Pascal programs makes them more readable.

13. Write a file pagination program that reads a text file and prints it in blocks of 20 lines. If after printing a block of lines there still are lines in the file, then the program should allow the user to indicate whether more output is desired; if so, the next block should be printed; otherwise, execution of the program should terminate.

14. Write a program that reads a text file; counts the nonblank characters, the nonblank lines, the words, and the sentences; and calculates the average number of characters per word and the average number of words per sentence. You may assume the following: The file contains only letters, blanks, commas, periods, semicolons, and colons; a word is any sequence of letters that begins a line or is preceded by one or more blanks and that is terminated by a blank, comma, semicolon, colon, period, or the end of a line; and a sentence is terminated by a period.

Programming Pointers

In this chapter we described the input/output operations in Pascal programs and noted several features and rules that must be remembered. The major points are the following:

1. *After values have been read for each variable in the input list, the* readln *procedure advances the data pointer past the next end-of-line mark.* Thus, if there are more values in a line of input data than there are variables in the input list, some data values will not be read. For example, suppose that *Number* is an integer variable, *xCoord* is a real variable, and the file *input* from which values are to be read contains

Then the statement

   readln (*Number, xCoord*)

reads the value 137 for *Number* and 8.24 for *xCoord* and advances the data pointer past the end-of-line mark.

Consequently, the value 145 is skipped. Moreover, if this statement is executed again, the value 13 is read for *Number*, but an error then occurs, since a real value cannot begin with a decimal point.

2. *After values have been obtained for each variable in the input list, the* read *procedure advances the data pointer so that it is positioned immediately after the last character read.* Thus, if the preceding *readln* statement is replaced with

   read (Number, xCoord)

   the value 137 will be read for *Number*, 8.24 for *xCoord*, and the data pointer positioned at the blank following the character 4.

If the statement is executed again, the value 145 is read and assigned to *Number*, the end-of-line mark is ignored, and the value 13.75 is read for *xCoord*. The data pointer is then positioned at the blank following the character 5.

A potential problem in using the *read* statement is that an attempt to read beyond the end of the file may be made. For example, consider the following input loop:

```
while not eof(input) do
  begin
    read (Number, xCoord);
       ⋮
  end (* while *);
```

where the file *input* contains

The values read and assigned to *Number* and *xCoord* are

Number	xCoord
137	8.24
145	13.75
167	15.95

After the last pair of values is obtained, the data pointer is positioned at the last end-of-line mark.

Because the data pointer is not positioned at the end-of-file mark, *eof(input)* is false, and so the *read* statement is executed again. This results in an attempt to read past the end of the file, which is an error. Note that the error does not occur if a *readln* statement is used, since after the last values 167 and 15.95 are read, the data pointer is advanced past the last end-of-line mark to the end-of-file mark. The boolean expression *eof(input)* is then true, and so execution of the while loop is terminated.

The way that the end-of-file mark is actually placed at the end of the file is system dependent. Usually in a batch mode of operation, it is automatically placed at the end of the file after the last data line has been entered. In an interactive mode, the user must usually enter some special control character from the keyboard to signal the end of the file.

3. *Leading blanks and leading end-of-line marks are ignored when reading numeric values but not when reading values for character variables.* One consequence of this is that consecutive numeric values may be entered on separate lines. For example, if the data

    <u>123</u>
    <u>456</u>

is entered, the file *input* contains

The statement

    readln (Num1, Num2)

where *Num1* and *Num2* are integer variables, reads the value 123 for *Num1*, and advances the data pointer to the first end-of-line mark. This end-of-line mark is ignored when reading a value for *Num2* so that the value 456 is read. The *readln* procedure then advances the data pointer past the next end-of-line mark.

In contrast, if *Ch1* and *Ch2* are character variables and the data

    <u>A</u>
    <u>B</u>

is entered so that the file *input* contains

the statement

    readln (Ch1, Ch2)

reads and assigns the letter A to *Ch1* and advances the data pointer to the first end-of-line mark. This end-of-line mark is then read, and a blank is assigned to *Ch2*. The data pointer is then advanced past the next end-of-line mark, and thus the character B is not read.

4. *The data pointer in an input file always points to the next character to be read.* This "look-ahead" property of the data pointer is a common source of difficulty for beginning programmers. This is especially true for interactive input. To illustrate, consider the following statements:

```
Sum := 0;
while not eof(input) do
    begin
        writeln ('Enter number:');
        readln (Number);
        Sum := Sum + Number
    end (* while *);
```

On most systems, when the **while** statement is encountered, the boolean expression *eof(input)* cannot be evaluated, since the system file *input* is empty because no values have yet been copied into it from the keyboard. Before execution can proceed, the user must enter some value. As soon as the first character is entered, *eof(input)* can be evaluated and the statements within the loop executed. For example, if the user attempts to enter 123 as the first value for *Number*, the following may occur: As soon as the first character 1 is entered, the boolean expression *eof(input)* becomes false (since the data pointer is pointing at 1), and the *writeln* statement is executed:

```
1Enter number:
```

The remaining digits can then be entered and the return key depressed:

```
1Enter number:
23
```

The value 123 is then read for *Number* by the *readln* statement, the data pointer is advanced past the end-of-line mark, and the value 123 is added to *Sum*.

Since there is no character following this end-of-line mark, once again the boolean expression *eof(input)* cannot be evaluated, and the process is repeated. Thus, entering 456 as the second value for *Number* may result in

```
4Enter number:
56
```

One way to avoid this difficulty is to enter a blank as the first character to be read for *Number* so that the expression *eof(input)* can be evaluated and execution can proceed; this leading blank will be ignored in reading the value for *Number*:

```
ḇEnter number:
123
```

Of course, if a value for a character variable were being read, this leading blank would be read and assigned.

In summary, interactive input can be rather difficult with some systems, especially when the next character in the file *input* must be known so that some expression such as *eof(input)* can be evaluated. In the preceding example, perhaps the best solution is to use a data flag

> *Sum* := 0;
> *writeln* ('Enter number (− 999 to stop):');
> *readln* (*Number*);
> **while** *Number* <> − 999 **do**
>   **begin**
>   *Sum* := *Sum* + *Number*;
>   *writeln* ('Enter number:');
>   *readln* (*Number*)
>   **end** (∗ **while** ∗);

or to ask whether there are more data values:

> *Sum* := 0;
> **repeat**
>   *writeln* ('Enter number:');
>   *readln* (*Number*);
>   *Sum* := *Sum* + *Number*;
>   *write* ('More (Y or N)? ');
>   *readln* (*Response*)
> **until** *Response* <> 'Y';

5. *Each file variable that names a permanent text file must appear in the file list of the program heading and must be declared in the variable section of the program to be of type* text.

6. *Before any data can be read from a user-defined text file, that file must be opened for input by using the procedure* reset. *Similarly, before any data can be written to a user-defined text file, it must be opened for output by using the procedure* rewrite. Remember the following, however:

   ● Each call to *reset* positions the data pointer at the beginning of the file.
   ● Each call to *rewrite* creates an empty file and any previous contents of the file are destroyed.

7. *File variables used as parameters must be variable parameters.*

Variations and Extensions

Input/output is one area in which some versions of Pascal may vary considerably from the standard. One finds such variations and extensions as the following:

- Output of boolean values to text files may not be allowed. (UCSD)
- Values entered from the keyboard for variables in a *read* or *readln* statement (or in a modified form of reference to these procedures) may not be echoed on the screen. (UCSD)
- Modified forms of the program heading may be allowed or required (Macintosh, UCSD, Turbo).
- The file *input* may not be a text file but, rather, a special file type (e.g., *interactive*). In particular, the difficulty caused by the look-ahead property of the data pointer described in Programming Pointer 4 may not arise. (UCSD)
- As described in the footnotes on pages 270 and 273, modified references to procedures *reset* and *rewrite*,

  reset (file-variable, file-name)

  and

  rewrite (file-variable, file-name)

  may be required to open a file (Macintosh, UCSD), or it may be necessary to first call another procedure as in (Turbo)

  assign (file-variable, file-name);
  reset (file-variable)

  or

  assign (file-variable, file-name);
  rewrite (file-variable)

- It may be necessary to invoke a special *close* procedure to close a file before program execution is completed. (Macintosh, Turbo, UCSD)

See Appendix G for specific details.

8

Ordinal Data Types: Enumerated and Subrange

God created the integers; all the rest is the work of man.

LEOPOLD KRONECKER

The old order changeth, yielding place to new.

ALFRED, LORD TENNYSON

In Chapter 3 we introduced the four predefined Pascal data types:

> *integer*
> *boolean*
> *char*
> *real*

These are called **simple** because a datum of one of these types is atomic; that is, it consists of a single item that cannot be subdivided. In addition to these simple data types, Pascal provides **structured** data types such as *text* in which a datum is a collection of items, and a **pointer** type used for data that are memory addresses. Figure 8.1 shows the various Pascal data types. The structured data types and pointers are discussed further in later chapters.

A simple data type is said to be an **ordinal** type if the values of that type are ordered so that each one except the first has an immediate predecessor and each one except the last has an immediate successor. The type *integer* is an ordinal type, since integer values are ordered by the natural ordering $-maxint, \ldots, -2, -1, 0, 1, 2, \ldots, maxint$. The type *boolean* is an ordinal type with the ordering *false, true*. The type *char* is also an ordinal type in which the ordering is that established by the collating sequence for the Pascal character set (see Section 4.2). The type *real* is not an ordinal type, however, because a given real number does not have an immediate predecessor or an immediate successor.

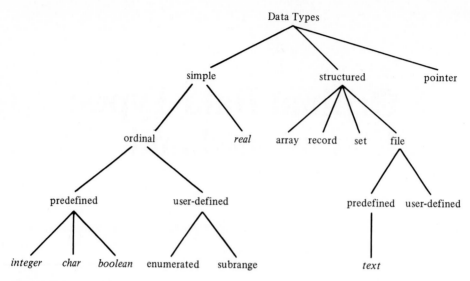

Figure 8.1

In addition to the predefined data types, Pascal allows user-defined data types. In this chapter we consider user-defined ordinal types.

8.1 The Type Section

The declaration part of a program consists of five sections arranged in the following order:

    label section
    constant section
    type section
    variable section
    subprogram section

We previously described the constant, variable, and subprogram sections, and we now consider the type section. (The label section is described in Appendix F.)

The type section is used to declare new data types or to rename previously defined types. It has the form

    type
        name-1 = *type-1*;
        name-2 = *type-2*;
                 ⋮
        name-n = *type-n*;

where each *name-i* is a legal identifier that names the data type given by *type-i*. Each *type-i* is a predefined Pascal data type or a user-defined type.

For example, the type section

```
type
    Symbol = char;
    Logical = boolean;
```

declares *Symbol* and *Logical* to be synonyms for *char* and *boolean*, respectively. In the variable section we can then declare variables to be of type *Symbol* or *Logical*:

```
var
    Code, Class : Symbol;
    p, q, r : Logical;
```

Of course, the standard identifiers *char* and *boolean* may still be used in place of, or in addition to, the names *Symbol* and *Logical*, respectively.

Because the names of user-defined data types are Pascal identifiers, the scope rules for identifiers given in Section 6.4 apply to type identifiers as well. Recall that Scope Rule 1 states that an identifier declared in a program unit is not accessible outside that unit. Thus, the data type *FloatingPoint* declared in the function *Power* by

```
function Power(x : real; n : integer) : real;
    type
        FloatingPoint = real;
    var
        Prod : FloatingPoint;
        ⋮
```

may be used only to declare the types of local variables such as *Prod* within the function *Power*. It is not accessible outside this function and thus cannot be used to declare the type of *Power* itself or any identifiers outside this function.

Scope Rule 2 states that a global identifier is accessible within any subprogram in which that identifier is not declared locally. Thus any type declared in the type section of the main program is accessible within any subprogram that does not declare that identifier locally. This is one instance in which the use of global identifiers is often necessary, since type identifiers may not be used as parameters for subprograms. For example, suppose that the type section

```
type
    Symbol = char;
    Logical = boolean;
```

appears in the declaration part of the main program, and consider the following procedure skeleton:

procedure *Gamma* (*x, y* : *Logical*; **var** *c* : *Symbol*);

  const
    Symbol = 'A';

  type
    Bit = *Logical*;
      ⋮

Since the global identifier *Logical* is not declared locally within procedure *Gamma*, it is accessible within *Gamma*. Thus parameters *x* and *y* may be declared of type *Logical*, and *Bit* may be declared as a synonym for *Logical* (and hence also *boolean*). The identifier *Symbol* is declared locally as the name of a constant in procedure *Gamma*; hence the global type identifier *Symbol* cannot be used in the declaration part of *Gamma*. Note, however, that it may be used to declare the type of parameter *c,* because this declaration occurs before the local identifier *Symbol* is defined within *Gamma*.

Scope Rule 3 asserts that identifiers declared in a subprogram can be accessed by any subprogram contained in it, provided that the identifier is not declared locally in the internal subprogram. Like the other scope rules, this rule also applies to type identifiers.

8.2 Enumerated Data Types

User-defined ordinal types can be divided into two classes: ***enumerated*** and ***subrange.*** Enumerated data types are considered in this section and subrange types in the next.

Enumerated data types are defined simply by listing the values of that data type, separated by commas and enclosed in parentheses. These values must be legal identifiers, and no identifier may be listed in two different enumerated type definitions. For example,

  (*Sunday, Monday, Tuesday, Wednesday, Thursday, Friday, Saturday*)

defines an enumerated data type whose values are the identifiers *Sunday, Monday, Tuesday, Wednesday, Thursday, Friday,* and *Saturday.*

The values of an enumerated data type are ordered by the listing of the values in the definition of that type. Thus, in this example, the predecessor of *Wednesday* is *Tuesday,* and *Thursday* is the successor of *Wednesday*; *Sunday* has no predecessor, and *Saturday* has no successor.

The listing of values that defines an enumerated type can be associated with a type identifier in the type section; for example,

  type
    DaysOfWeek = (*Sunday, Monday, Tuesday, Wednesday, Thursday, Friday, Saturday*);

This type identifier can then be used to specify the types of variables, formal parameters, and function values:

> **var**
>   *Day* : *DaysOfWeek*;
>   ⋮
> **function** *Convert*(*x*, *y* : *integer*) : *DaysOfWeek*;
>   ⋮
> **procedure** *Schedule* (*Day* : *DaysOfWeek*; **var** *NumberOfDay* : *integer*);
>   ⋮

It is also possible to use the listing of values that define an enumerated type in the variable section to specify the type of a variable, for example,

> **var**
>   *Day* : (*Sunday, Monday, Tuesday, Wednesday, Thursday,*
>   *Friday, Saturday*);

Such listings cannot be used, however, to declare the types of formal parameters or function values in function and procedure headings. Instead, a type identifier must be used; listing the values of an enumerated data type in a subprogram heading is *not* allowed.

Values of an enumerated type may be compared using the relational operators = and <>, for example,

> **if** (*Day* <> *Sunday*) **and** (*Day* <> *Saturday*) **then**
>   *writeln* ('Weekday');

Since the values of an enumerated type are ordered, they may also be compared by using <, >, <=, and >=. For example, the above **if** statement can also be written as

> **if** (*Monday* <= *Day*) **and** (*Day* < *Saturday*) **then**
>   *writeln* ('Weekday');

The predefined Pascal functions *pred* and *succ* may be used to find the predecessor and successor, respectively, of a value of ordinal type. The following table gives several examples:

Function Reference	Value
pred(Monday)	*Sunday*
succ(Friday)	*Saturday*
succ(3)	4
pred(17)	16
pred('G')	'F'
succ('W')	'X'
succ(*false*)	*true*
pred(*true*)	*false*
pred(*Sunday*)	undefined
succ(*Saturday*)	undefined

Note that the function *pred* is not defined if its parameter is the first element of the ordinal type being considered, nor is *succ* if its parameter is the last element. Such references are errors.

Another predefined function used for processing ordinal data is *ord*. This function returns the **ordinal number** of an element; that is, its value is the number of the position of that element in the ordering for that type, with position numbering beginning with 0. Thus, for the data type *DaysOfWeek*,

ord(*Sunday*)

has the value 0, and

ord(*Tuesday*)

has the value 2. For the enumerated data type *FaceCard* defined by

type
    FaceCard = (*Jack, Queen, King*);

ord(*Jack*) = 0, ord(*Queen*) = 1, and ord(*King*) = 2.
For an integer n, ord(n) has the value n. Thus

ord(7) = 7

ord(−3) = −3

For boolean type, ord(*false*) has the value 0 and ord(*true*) has the value 1. For character data, the ordinal number of a character is the number of its position in the collating sequence and is thus compiler dependent. If ASCII code is used, ord('A') = 65, ord('Z') = 90, and ord('2') = 50, whereas for EBCDIC, ord('A') = 193, ord('Z') = 233, and ord('2') = 242 (see the tables of ASCII and EBCDIC codes in Appendix A).

For character data the function *chr* is the inverse of *ord*. This function has an integer parameter, and its value is the character whose ordinal number is that integer, provided that there is such a character. Thus chr(65) = 'A' and chr(50) = '2' if ASCII is used, whereas chr(193) = 'A' and chr(242) = '2' for EBCDIC. Note that for any element c of character type

chr(ord(c)) = c

and if n is the ordinal number of some character, then

ord(chr(n)) = n

One useful application of the functions *chr* and *ord* is in converting numerals to numbers and vice versa, as described in the exercises.

Because variables of an ordinal data type have values that are ordered, they may be used as control variables in **for** statements or as labels in a **case** statement. For example, if the variable *Day* is of type *DaysOfWeek*, described earlier, the statement

> **case** *Day* **of**
> > *Sunday*   : *writeln* ('Sunday');
> > *Monday*   : *writeln* ('Monday');
> > *Tuesday*   : *writeln* ('Tuesday');
> > *Wednesday* : *writeln* ('Wednesday');
> > *Thursday*   : *writeln* ('Thursday');
> > *Friday*   : *writeln* ('Friday');
> > *Saturday*   : *writeln* ('Saturday')
> **end** (∗ **case** ∗);

can be used to display the day corresponding to the value of *Day*. Such statements are necessary because values of an enumerated type cannot be read from or written to text files, including the standard system files *input* and *output*. The simple program in Figure 8.2 uses the variable *Day* of type *DaysOfWeek* in a **for** statement containing a similar **case** statement to display the names of the weekdays.

```
PROGRAM DisplayWeekdays (input, output);

(*******************************************************************

    Program illustrating use of the enumerated data type DaysOfWeek.

*******************************************************************)

TYPE
    DaysOfWeek = (Sunday, Monday, Tuesday, Wednesday,
                  Thursday, Friday, Saturday);

VAR
    Day : DaysOfWeek;

BEGIN
    FOR Day := Monday to Friday DO
        CASE Day OF
            Monday    : writeln ('Monday');
            Tuesday   : writeln ('Tuesday');
            Wednesday : writeln ('Wednesday');
            Thursday  : writeln ('Thursday');
            Friday    : writeln ('Friday')
        END (* CASE *)
END.
```

Figure 8.2

Figure 8.2   (cont.)

<u>Sample run</u>:

```
Monday
Tuesday
Wednesday
Thursday
Friday
```

A **while** statement can also be used in place of the **for** statement in this program. In this case, the function *succ* is used to "increment" the value of *Day*:

```
Day := Monday;
while Day <= Friday do
   begin
      case Day of
         Monday      : writeln ('Monday');
         Tuesday     : writeln ('Tuesday');
         Wednesday   : writeln ('Wednesday');
         Thursday    : writeln ('Thursday');
         Friday      : writeln ('Friday')
      end (* case *);
      Day := succ(Day)
   end (* while *);
```

If we attempt to print the names of all the days of the week by modifying this **while** statement as

```
Day := Sunday;
while Day <= Saturday do
   begin
      case Day of
         Sunday      : writeln ('Sunday');
         Monday      : writeln ('Monday');
         Tuesday     : writeln ('Tuesday');
         Wednesday   : writeln ('Wednesday');
         Thursday    : writeln ('Thursday');
         Friday      : writeln ('Friday');
         Saturday    : writeln ('Saturday')
      end (* case *);
      Day := succ(Day)
   end (* while *);
```

an error results. When the value of *Day* is *Saturday,* the value of *succ(Day)* is undefined.

Although values of enumerated data types cannot be read from or written to text files, it is nevertheless sometimes convenient to use them to improve program readability, by using a meaningful identifier rather than a cryptic code to represent an item. For example, using the values *Sunday, Monday, Tuesday, . . .* in place of the codes 0, 1, 2, . . . for the days of the week in a program obviously makes the program easier to read and understand. In such programs it may be necessary to use **case** statements like those described earlier to carry out the necessary conversion between the values of an enumerated data type and the numeric codes that can be input or character strings that can be displayed. The program in Figure 8.3 illustrates. It is a modification of the program in Figure 7.3 to read an employee number and an hourly rate from a permanent text file and calculate wages. During execution, the user enters the number of hours worked for each day from Sunday through Saturday. The procedure *PrintDay* is called by the procedure *GetEmployeeInfo* to display the character string corresponding to the value of *Day*.

```
PROGRAM Payroll (input, output, EmpFile);

(****************************************************************

   Program to calculate wages for several employees whose employee
   numbers and hourly rates are read from the file EmpFile and
   whose hours are entered by the user during execution.  Total
   wages for this payroll are also calculated.

****************************************************************)

VAR
    EmpFile : text;          (* the permanent employee file *)
    EmpNumber : integer;     (* employee number *)
    Hours,                   (* hours worked *)
    HourlyRate,              (* hourly pay rate *)
    Wages,                   (* total wages for employee *)
    TotalPayroll : real;     (* total wages for this payroll *)

PROCEDURE GetEmployeeInfo (VAR InFile : Text; VAR EmpNumber : integer;
                           VAR HourlyRate, WeekHours : real);

   (****************************************************************

      Procedure to read  return the employee number EmpNumber and
      HourlyRate from a text file InFile; Hours worked for each day
      are entered by the user and the total WeekHours is returned.
      The procedure PrintDay is used to print names of days.

   ****************************************************************)

   TYPE
      DaysOfWeek = (Sunday, Monday, Tuesday, Wednesday,
                    Thursday, Friday, Saturday);
```

Figure 8.3

Figure 8.3   (cont.)

```
VAR
    Day : DaysOfWeek;      (* day of the week *)
    DayHours : real;       (* hours worked each day *)



PROCEDURE PrintDay (Day : DaysOfWeek);

    (**************************************************************

        Procedure to print the name of the day corresponding to
        the value of Day of enumerated type DaysOfWeek.

    **************************************************************)

    BEGIN (* PrintDay *)
        CASE Day OF
            Sunday    : write ('Sunday:     ');
            Monday    : write ('Monday:     ');
            Tuesday   : write ('Tuesday:    ');
            Wednesday : write ('Wednesday:  ');
            Thursday  : write ('Thursday:   ');
            Friday    : write ('Friday:     ');
            Saturday  : write ('Saturday:   ')
        END (* CASE *)
    END (* PrintDay *);

BEGIN (* GetEmployeeInfo *)
    readln (EmpFile, EmpNumber, HourlyRate);
    writeln ('Hours worked for ', EmpNumber:1,' on   ');
    WeekHours := 0;
    FOR Day := Sunday TO Saturday DO
        BEGIN
            PrintDay (Day);
            readln (DayHours);
            WeekHours := WeekHours + DayHours
        END (* FOR *)
END (* GetEmployeeInfo *);



PROCEDURE CalculateWages (Hours, HourlyRate : real;
                          VAR Wages, TotalPayroll : real);

    (**************************************************************

        Procedure to calculate and return Wages for employee who has
        worked the given number of Hours at the given HourlyRate.
        Hours above HoursLimit are paid at OvertimeFactor times
        the hourly rate.  Total wages for this payroll are also
        accumlated and returned.  The function RoundCents is used
        to round wages to the nearest cent.

    **************************************************************)

CONST
    OvertimeFactor = 1.5; (* overtime multiplication factor *)
    HoursLimit = 40.0;    (* overtime hours limit *)
```

Figure 8.3   (cont.)

```
VAR
   RegWages,                 (* regular wages *)
   OverWages : real;         (* overtime pay *)

FUNCTION RoundCents (Amount : real) : real;

   (**************************************************************

           Returns Amount rounded to the nearest cent.

   **************************************************************)

   BEGIN (* RoundCents *)
      RoundCents := round(100 * Amount) / 100
   END (* RoundCents *);

   BEGIN (* CalculateWages *)
      IF Hours > HoursLimit THEN
         BEGIN (* Overtime *)
            RegWages := RoundCents(HourlyRate * HoursLimit);
            OverWages :=
               RoundCents(OvertimeFactor * HourlyRate * (Hours - HoursLimit))
         END (* Overtime *)
      ELSE
         BEGIN (* No overtime *)
            RegWages := RoundCents(HourlyRate * Hours);
            OverWages := 0
         END (* No overtime *);
      Wages := RegWages + OverWages;
      TotalPayroll := TotalPayroll + Wages
   END (* CalculateWages *);

BEGIN (* main program *)
   reset (EmpFile);
   TotalPayroll := 0;
   WHILE NOT eof (EmpFile) DO
      BEGIN
         GetEmployeeInfo (EmpFile, EmpNumber, HourlyRate, Hours);
         writeln ('Hours worked:  ', Hours:4:2);
         writeln ('Hourly rate:   $', HourlyRate:4:2);
         CalculateWages (Hours, HourlyRate, Wages, TotalPayroll);
         writeln ('Wages:  $', Wages:4:2);
         writeln
      END (* WHILE *);
   writeln;
   writeln ('Total wages = $', TotalPayroll:4:2)
END (* main program *).


Listing of EmpFile:

3123  7.50
3164  8.75
3185  9.35
3202 10.50
```

Figure 8.3   (cont.)

Sample run:

```
Hours worked by 3123 on
Sunday:      0
Monday:      8
Tuesday:     8
Wednesday:   8
Thursday:    8
Friday:      8
Saturday:    0
Hours worked:  40.00
Hourly rate:    $7.50
Wages:  $300.00

Hours worked by 3164 on
Sunday:      0
Monday:      7.5
Tuesday:     9.25
Wednesday:   8
Thursday:    8
Friday:      10
Saturday:    0
Hours worked:  42.75
Hourly rate:    $8.75
Wages:  $386.09

Hours worked by 3185 on
Sunday:      0
Monday:      8
Tuesday:     8
Wednesday:   9
Thursday:    8.5
Friday:      6
Saturday:    4
Hours worked:  43.50
Hourly rate:    $9.35
Wages:  $423.09

Hours worked by 3202 on
Sunday:      0
Monday:      0
Tuesday:     0
Wednesday:   0
Thursday:    8
Friday:      8
Saturday:    0
Hours worked:  16.00
Hourly rate:    $10.50
Wages:  $168.00


Total wages = $1277.18
```

8.3 Subrange Data Types

In the preceding section we considered the predefined ordinal data types *integer, boolean,* and *char* and enumerated types. The set of values of each of these types is an ordered set. In some cases it may be convenient to use a data type that is a **subrange** of such a set. Subrange types are defined by specifying the first and last elements in the subrange in a declaration of the form

> *first-value .. last-value*

where *first-value* and *last-value* are values of some ordinal type called the **base type** and *first-value* ≤ *last-value*. A value of this subrange type may be any value *x* of the associated base type such that

> *first-value* ≤ *x* ≤ *last-value*

Subrange definitions may be used in the variable section of a program unit to declare the type of a variable, or they may be associated with a type identifier in the type section. To illustrate, consider the following:

```
type
    DaysOfWeek = (Sunday, Monday, Tuesday, Wednesday, Thursday,
                    Friday, Saturday);
    Weekdays = Monday .. Friday;
    WholeNumber = 0 .. maxint;
    Digit = '0' .. '9';

var
    SchoolDay : Weekdays;
    n : WholeNumber;
    DaysInMonth : 28..31;
    Cents : 0..99;

function F(n : integer) : WholeNumber;
    ⋮
procedure WorkSchedule (Day : Weekdays; var Code : Digit);
    ⋮
```

Note that although the same value may not be listed in two different enumerated type definitions, it is permissible to use a value in two different subrange definitions.

A value to be assigned to a variable or function of a subrange type is checked to determine whether this value is in the specified range. If such **range checking** indicates that a value is out of range, an error message to that effect is displayed, and execution is usually terminated. Thus, in the preceding example, if the value to be assigned to *F* is negative, then this value is out of range, and an out-of-range error occurs.

The main use of subrange types is to specify index types for arrays, as described in the next chapter. They can also be used to ensure that input data values are in a certain specified range, but in this case program execution will usually be terminated if an out-of-range error occurs. Thus it is perhaps better to allow invalid data values and use an **if** statement to check to see whether they lie outside the given range; for example,

> *readln* (*Cents*);
> **if** (*Cents* < 0) **or** (*Cents* > 99) **then**
>   *writeln* ('Data value ', *Cents*:1, ' out of range — ignored')
> **else**
> $\vdots$

The rules that govern the use of an ordinal type also apply to any subrange of that type. For example, because an integer value may be assigned to a real variable, it is also permissible to assign a value of type *WholeNumber* to a real variable in the preceding example. In general, two simple data types are said to be **compatible** if they are the same type, one is a subrange of the other, or both are subranges of the same base type. If *A* and *B* are two compatible data types, then wherever *A* may be used, *B* may also be used. Thus, in the preceding example, the function reference

> *F(DaysInMonth)*

is valid, since the type 28..31 of the actual parameter *DaysInMonth* is a subrange of type *integer* and is therefore compatible with the integer formal parameter *n*. The assignment statement

> *Cents* := *F(DaysInMonth)*;

also is valid, since both the type *WholeNumber* of function *F* and the type 0..99 of *Cents* are subranges of type *integer* and hence are compatible. It must be realized, of course, that range checking is performed. Thus, if the value of *F* in this reference is 100 or larger, range checking of the value to be assigned to *Cents* will indicate an error.

Exercises

1. **(a)** Write a type section that defines the enumerated type *MonthAbbrev*, whose values are abbreviations of the months of the year and consist of the first three letters of the months' names; also, define the subrange type *MonthNumber* consisting of the integers 1, 2, 3, . . . , 12.
   (b) Write a function whose parameter is the number of a month and whose value is the corresponding value of type *MonthAbbrev*.

2. **(a)** Write a type section that defines type *Numeral* to be the subrange of character type consisting of the characters '0', '1', '2', . . . , '9' and the type *Number* to be the subrange of integers consisting of the values 0, 1, 2, . . . , 9.

(b) Write a function whose parameter is a variable of type *Numeral* and whose value is the corresponding numeric value. (*Hint:* Use the function *ord.*)

(c) Write another function whose parameter is an integer in the range 0 through 9 and whose value is the corresponding numeral. (*Hint:* Use the functions *ord* and *chr.*)

3. For the enumerated type *MonthAbbrev* of Exercise 1, find the values of the following expressions:

(a) *Jan* < *Aug*   **(b)** *Sep* <= *Sep*   **(c)** *succ(Sep)*

(d) *pred(Apr)*   **(e)** *succ(succ(Aug))*   **(f)** *pred(pred(Aug))*

(g) *succ(pred(Mar))*   **(h)** *succ(pred(Jan))*   **(i)** *ord(Jun)*

(j) *ord(Sep)* − *ord(Jan)* **(k)** *ord(succ(May))* − *ord(May)*

(l) *chr(ord(Sep)* + *ord('0'))*

4. Write a function or procedure whose parameters are a nonnegative integer *n* and a month abbreviation *Abbrev,* like that in Exercise 1, and finds the "*n*th successor" of *Abbrev*. The 0th successor of *Abbrev* is *Abbrev* itself; for *n* > 0, the *n*th successor of *Abbrev* is the *n*th month following *Abbrev*. For example, the fourth successor of *Aug* is *Dec,* and the sixth successor of *Aug* is *Feb*.

5. Repeat Exercise 4 but define the function or procedure recursively.

6. Using the enumerated type *DaysOfWeek* in the text, write a program to read a customer's account number and current balance; then for each weekday (Monday through Friday) read a series of transactions by that customer of the form D (deposit) or W (withdrawal) followed by an amount, and update the balance with this amount. Display the new balance after all transactions for the week have been processed.

7. **(a)** Write a function whose parameters are a month of type *Month-Abbrev* (see Exercise 1) and a year in the range from 1538 through 1999 and whose value is the number of days in the month. Remember that February has 28 days, except in a leap year, when it has 29. A leap year is one in which the year number is divisible by 4, except for centesimal years (those ending in 00); these centesimal years are not leap years unless the year number is divisible by 400. (Thus 1950 and 1900 are not leap years, but 1960 and 1600 are.)

   (b) Use the function of part (a) in a program to read two dates in the form *mm dd yyyy* (such as 7 4 1776 and 1 1 1990), and calculate the number of days that have elapsed between the two dates.

Programming Pointers

In this chapter we discussed user-defined ordinal types. The following are some of the major points to remember when using them:

1. *Type identifiers must be used to declare formal parameters in a sub-program and the type of a function.* One may not list the values of an ordinal type in a function or procedure heading to specify the type of a parameter or the type of a function value. For example, the heading

   function *CardValue(Card* : (*Jack, Queen, King*)) : 11..13;

   is not valid. The enumerated type (*Jack, Queen, King*) and the subrange type 11..13 must be associated with type identifiers such as

   type
      FaceCard = (*Jack, Queen, King*);
      FaceValue = 11..13;

   in a program unit that contains this function definition, and these type identifiers used in the heading:

   function *CardValue(Card* : *FaceCard*) : *FaceValue*;

2. *The scope rules given in Section 6.4 apply to type identifiers.*

3. *Values listed in an enumerated type definition must be legal identifiers and may not appear in any other enumerated type definition within that program unit.* For example, the declaration

   type
      PassengerType = (*first-class, coach, standby*);

   is not allowed because *first-class* is not a legal identifier. The declarations

   type
      Weekdays = (*Monday, Tuesday, Wednesday,*
                     Thursday, Friday);
      VacationDays = (*Friday, Saturday, Sunday, Monday*);

   are not allowed because the same identifier may not be used in both of these type definitions.

4. *The function* pred(x) *is undefined if* x *is the first value of an ordinal type;* succ(x) *is undefined if* x *is the last value.*

5. *Values of an enumerated data type cannot be input from or output to text files, including the standard files* input *and* output.

6. *If a variable or function is declared to be of some subrange type, an error will result if one attempts to assign it a value that is not in this subrange.* For example, if *x* and *y* are declared by

   var
      x, y : 1..10;

the statement

```
for x := 1 to 10 do
    begin
        y := x * x;
        writeln (y)
    end (* for *);
```

results in an error when x reaches the value 4 because the value of $x * x$ is then outside the range 1..10 and cannot be assigned to y.

Variations and Extensions

Most Pascal dialects are consistent with the standard in processing ordinal types. However, there are a few variations and extensions:

- Input/output of enumerated types may be allowed. (Macintosh)
- Special type-conversion features may be provided. (Turbo)
- Special compiler directives may be required to enable range checking. (Turbo)

Appendix G contains details of these features.

9

One-Dimensional Arrays

With silver bells, and cockle shells,
And pretty maids all in a row.

MOTHER GOOSE

The simple data types we have considered thus far represent single values. In many situations, however, it is necessary to process a collection of values that are related in some way, for example, a list of test scores, a collection of measurements resulting from some experiment, or a sales-tax table. Processing such collections using only simple data types can be extremely cumbersome, and for this reason, most high-level languages include special features for structuring such data. As we noted in Chapter 8, Pascal provides four structured data types: arrays, files, records, and sets. In this chapter we consider arrays, their implementation in Pascal, and how they can be used to process lists.

9.1 Introduction to Arrays; Indexed Variables

In many of our examples, a collection of data values was processed by reading the data items one at a time and processing each item individually, for example, reading a test score and assigning it to a variable, counting it, and adding it to a running sum. When the value was no longer needed, a new value was read for the same variable, counted and added to the running sum, and the process repeated again and again. There are many problems, however, in which the collection of data items must be processed several times. To illustrate, suppose that a program is to be developed to

1. Read a list of test scores.
2. Find their mean.

3. Print a list of scores greater than the mean.
4. Sort the list so the scores are in ascending order.

The following are two possible solutions:

Solution 1. Use one variable for each test score. Suppose, for example, that there are 100 test scores. We might use 100 different variables, *Score1*, *Score2*, . . . , *Score100*, thus creating 100 different memory locations to store the test scores:

Although this approach may be practical if we have only a few data values to process, it is obviously cumbersome and awkward for large data sets, as the following program skeleton vividly demonstrates:

program *ProcessScores* (*input, output*);

var
    Score1, Score2, Score3, Score4, Score5,
    Score6, Score7, Score8, Score9, Score10,
        ⋮
    Score96, Score97, Score98, Score99, Score100 : integer;
    Mean : real;

begin
    (∗ Read the scores ∗)
    read (Score1);
    read (Score2);
    read (Score3);
        ⋮
    read (Score100);

    (∗ Calculate the mean score ∗)
    Mean := (*Score1* + *Score2* + *Score3* + *Score4* +
           Score5 + *Score6* + *Score7* + *Score8* +
               ⋮
           Score97 + *Score98* + *Score99* + *Score100*) / 100;
    writeln ('Mean = ', *Mean*:6:2);

```
        (* Display scores above the mean *)
        if Score1 > Mean then
           writeln (Score1:5);
        if Score2 > Mean then
           writeln (Score2:5);
        if Score3 > Mean then
           writeln (Score3:5);
                 ⋮
        if Score100 > Mean then
           writeln (Score100:5);
        (* After more than 450 lines of code, sort them?
           There must be a better way! *)

   end.
```

Solution 2. Use a data file. If we do not use 100 different memory locations to store all of the test scores, then we are forced to read the scores several times. Reentering them again and again so that the required processing can be carried out is obviously not practical. In this solution we prepare a data file containing the scores and read the scores from it as described in Chapter 7, closing and reopening the file for input each time we need to read through the list of scores.

```
   program ProcessScores (input, output, ScoresFile);

   var
       Score, NumScores, i : integer;
       Sum, Mean : real;
       ScoresFile : text;

   begin
       (* Read and count the test scores *)
       reset (ScoresFile);
       NumScores := 0;
       while not eof(ScoresFile) do
          begin
              NumScores := NumScore + 1;
              readln (ScoresFile, Score)
          end (* while *);

       (* Calculate the mean score *)
       reset (ScoresFile);
       Sum := 0;
       for i := 1 to NumScores do
          begin
              readln (ScoresFile, Score);
              Sum := Sum + Score
          end (* for *);
       Mean := Sum / NumScores;
       writeln ('Mean = ', Mean:6:2);
```

```
(* Display scores above the mean *)
reset (ScoresFile);
for i := 1 to NumScores do
   begin
      readln (ScoresFile, Score);
      if Score > Mean then
         writeln (Score:5)
   end (* for *);

(* Sort them??? Hm-m-m-m *)
```

end.

Although this program is more manageable than that in Solution 1, it is not a good solution to the problem because files are usually stored in secondary memory, from which data retrieval is rather slow.

To solve this problem efficiently, we need a data structure to store and organize the entire collection of test scores, as in Solution 2. However, because of the slowness of file input/output, we need the scores stored in main memory, as in Solution 1. Also, many kinds of list processing such as sorting cannot be done efficiently if the data items can be retrieved only **sequentially**, that is, when an item can be accessed only by searching from the beginning of the list. What is needed instead is a **direct access** structure that allows a data item to be stored or retrieved directly by specifying its location in the structure, so that it takes no longer to access the item in location 100 than to access the item in location 5. And we prefer that the structure be stored in main memory so that storage and retrieval are fast. One such data structure is an **array**, in which a fixed number of data items, all of the same type, are organized in a sequence and each item can be accessed directly by specifying its position in this sequence.

If an array is to be used in a Pascal program to solve the test scores problem, the computer must first be instructed to reserve a sequence of 100 memory locations for the scores. A simple declaration that does this is

var
    Score : **array**[1..100] **of** *integer*;

This declaration instructs the compiler to establish an array with name *Score* consisting of 100 memory locations in which values of type *integer* can be stored:

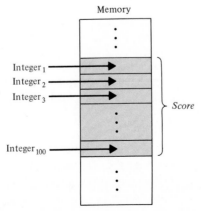

In the program we can then refer to this entire array of integers by using the *array variable Score*, but we can also access each individual element or *component* of the array by using an *indexed variable* formed by appending an *index* enclosed in brackets to the array variable. This index specifies the position of an array component. Thus *Score*[1] refers to the first component of the array *Score*, *Score*[2] to the second component, and so on. The array declaration

    var
        Score : **array**[1..100] **of** *integer*;

thus not only reserves a block of memory locations in which to store the elements of the array *Score*, but it also associates the indexed variables *Score*[1], *Score*[2], *Score*[3], . . . , *Score*[100] with these locations:

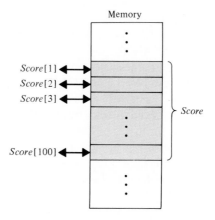

Each indexed variable names an individual memory location and hence can be used in much the same way as an ordinary variable can. For example, the assignment statement

    Score[4] := 83

stores the value 83 in the fourth location of the array *Score*, and the output statement

    writeln (*Score*[10]:5)

displays the value stored in the tenth location of *Score*.

An important feature of this indexed notation for arrays is that the index may be a variable. For example, the statement

    if *Score*[n] > 90 **then**
        writeln (*Score*[n]:3, ' = A')

retrieves the *n*th item of the array *Score*, compares it with 90, and prints it with a letter grade of A if it exceeds 90. The index may even be an expression, as in

if *Score*[*i*] > *Score*[*i* + 1] **then**
   begin
     Temp := *Score*[*i*];
     Score[*i*] := *Score*[*i* + 1];
     Score[*i* + 1] := *Temp*
   end (∗ **if** ∗);

This statement interchanges the contents of *Score*[*i*] and *Score*[*i* + 1] if the first is greater than the second.

Using an array reference in which the index is a variable or an expression within a loop that changes the value of the index on each pass through the loop is a convenient way to process each item in the array. Thus

for *n* := 1 **to** 100 **do**
   if *Score*[*n*] > 90 **then**
     writeln (*Score*[*n*]:3, ' = A')

retrieves each item of the array *Score* in sequence, beginning with *Score*[1], compares it with 90, and prints it with a letter grade of A if it exceeds 90. It is equivalent to the following sequence of **if** statements:

if *Score*[1] > 90 **then**
   writeln (*Score*[1]:3, ' = A');
if *Score*[2] > 90 **then**
   writeln (*Score*[2]:3, ' = A');
if *Score*[3] > 90 **then**
   writeln (*Score*[3]:3, ' = A');
            ⋮
if *Score*[100] > 90 **then**
   writeln (*Score*[100]:3, ' = A');

Figure 9.1 illustrates.

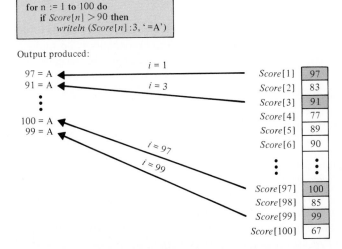

Figure 9.1. Using a variable index to access each element of array *Score*.

Arrays such as *Score* involve only a single index and are commonly called ***one-dimensional arrays***. Pascal programs, however, may process arrays of more than one dimension, in which case each element of the array is designated by attaching the appropriate number of indices to the array name. In this chapter we confine our attention to one-dimensional arrays; multidimensional arrays are considered in Chapter 11.

The name of a one-dimensional array, the type of its components, and the type of its index are declared by using an ***array declaration***, of the form shown in the following syntax diagram. (Note that an array declaration may include the specification ***packed***, which directs the compiler to store the data internally in a special compact format. Packed arrays are discussed in more detail in the next chapter.)

one-dimensional
array
declaration

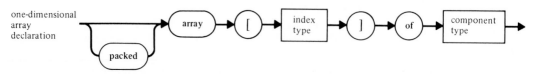

From this syntax diagram we see that an array declaration thus has the form

    array[*index-type*] **of** *component-type*

where *index-type* specifies the type of the indices and may be any ordinal type; *component-type* specifies the type of the array elements, or components, and may be any type. For example, the array declaration

    array[1..10] **of** *real*

specifies a one-dimensional array whose index may be any of the values 1, 2, 3, . . . , 10 and whose elements are of type *real*. The array declaration

    array['A'..'Z'] **of** *integer*

specifies a one-dimensional array whose index may be any of the characters A, B, . . . , Z, and each of whose 26 components is an integer.

Although array declarations may appear in the variable section of a program's declaration part to specify the type of an array, it is preferable to associate them with type identifiers, as in

    const
      NumLimit = 100;

    type
      xRange = −5..10;
      Letter = 'A'..'Z';
      RealArray = **array**[*xRange*] **of** *real*;
      ArrayOfNumbers = **array**[0..*NumLimit*] **of** 1..999;
      FrequencyArray = **array**[*Letter*] **of** *integer*;
      Line = **array**[1..80] **of** *char*;

These type identifiers can then be used to declare the types of array variables such as

var
   Coordinate : *RealArray*;
   Number : *ArrayOfNumbers*;
   CharCount : *FrequencyArray*;
   TextLine : *Line*;

They may also be used to declare the types of formal parameters, as in

procedure *Sort* (**var** *List* : *ArrayOfNumbers*);

It is important to note that the array declaration **array**[0..*NumLimit*] **of** 1..999 cannot be used to specify the type of the parameter *List*:

procedure *Sort* (**var** *List* : **array**[0..*NumLimit*] **of** 1..999);
   (***** This is not a valid procedure heading. *****)

Like all formal parameters, the type of a formal array parameter must be specified by a type identifier.

As we have noted, each component of an array is directly accessible. This direct access is accomplished by means of ***address translation***. The first word in the memory block reserved for an array is used to store the first component. Its address is called the ***base address*** of the array, and the address of any other component is calculated in terms of this base address. For example, if the base address for the array *Score* is b and each score can be stored in a single memory word, then the address of *Score*[1] is b, the address of *Score*[2] is $b + 1$, that for *Score*[3] is $b + 2$, and in general, the address of *Score*[i] is $b + i - 1$.

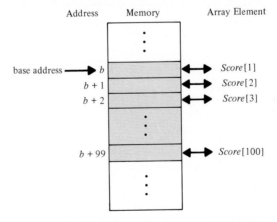

If w memory words are required for each component, then *Score*[1] would be stored in w consecutive words beginning at the word with address b, *Score*[2] in a block beginning at address $b + w$, and in general, *Score*[i] in a block of size w beginning at address $b + (i - 1) * w$. Each time an array component is accessed using an indexed variable, this address translation must be performed by the system software and/or hardware to determine the location of that component in memory.

9.2 List Processing Using One-Dimensional Arrays

Many problems involve processing lists, a list of test scores, a list of names, a list of employee records, and so on. Such processing includes displaying all the items in the list, inserting new items, deleting items, searching the list for a specified item, and sorting the list so that the items are in a certain order. Since most programming languages do not provide a predefined list type (LISP, an acronym for LISt Processing, is one exception), lists must be processed using some other structure. This is commonly done using an array to store the list, storing the ith list item in the ith position of the array.

To illustrate, suppose we wish to process a list of test scores, as in the example of the preceding section. If we declare the array *Score* by

> **const**
>   *ScoresLimit* = 100;
>
> **type**
>   *ListOfScores* = **array**[1..*ScoresLimit*] **of** *integer*;
>
> **var**
>   *Score* : *ListOfScores*;

we can read the scores into the array *Score* by using an input statement within a repetition structure. For example, we might use a **for** statement

> **for** i := 1 **to** *ScoresLimit* **do**
>   *read* (*Score*[i]);

where the type of the control variable i is compatible with the subrange type 1..*NumScores* specified for the array indices in the array declaration. A **while** statement

> i := 1;
> **while** $i <=$ *ScoresLimit* **do**
>   **begin**
>   *read* (*Score*[i]);
> i := i + 1
>   **end** (∗ **while** ∗);

or a **repeat-until** statement

> i := 1;
> **repeat**
>   *read* (*Score*[i]);
> i := i + 1
> **until** $i >$ *ScoresLimit*;

could also be used. If the number of scores to be processed is not always the same, we might declare an integer variable *NumScores* and use only part of the array:

> **var**
>   *Score* : *ListOfScores*;
>   *NumScores* : *integer*;

The statements

> *readln* (*NumScores*);
> **if** *NumScores* > *ScoresLimit* **then**
>   *writeln* ('At most ', *ScoresLimit*:1, ' scores can be processed')
> **else**
>   **for** *i* := **to** *NumScores* **do**
>   *read* (*Score*[*i*]);

might then be used to read and store the test scores in the first *NumScores* locations of the array *Score*. Note that after a value is read for *NumScores*, a check is made to ensure that this value is not too large, since *an error results if an attempt is made to use an index that is out of range.* If the value 15 is read for *NumScores*, the *read* statement is executed fifteen times, and values are assigned to the first fifteen positions *Score*[1], *Score*[2], . . . , *Score*[15] of the array. The rest of the array, *Score*[16], . . . , *Score*[100], is unchanged; these array elements are undefined unless values have previously been assigned to them.

The items in a list may be displayed by placing an output statement within a repetition structure. For example, the statement

> **for** *i* := 1 **to** *NumScores* **do**
>   *writeln* (*Score*[*i*]:3);

displays the first *NumScores* entries of the list *Score* on separate lines, one per line. The statement

> **for** *i* := 1 **to** *NumScores* **do**
>   *write* (*Score*[*i*]:3);

displays these entries on the same line. Note that subsequent output will also appear on this same line. This can be avoided by following the **for** statement with a *writeln* statement having no output list:

> **for** *i* := 1 **to** *NumScores* **do**
>   *write* (*Score*[*i*]:3);
> *writeln*;

Other kinds of list processing are also easy using repetition structures. For example, the mean of the scores in the list *Score* can be calculated by

> *Sum* := 0;
> **for** *i* := 1 **to** *NumScores* **do**
>   *Sum* := *Sum* + *Score*[*i*];
> *MeanScore* := *Sum* / *NumScores*;
> *writeln* ('Mean of the scores is: ', *MeanScore*:3:1);

To display the scores that are greater than the mean, we can use the statement

> **for** $i := 1$ **to** *NumScores* **do**
>   **if** *Score[i]* $>$ *MeanScore* **then**
>   *writeln (Score[i]:3)*

The program in Figure 9.2 uses these statements to solve the first part of the problem stated in the preceding section. It reads a list of up to 100 scores, calculates their mean, and displays a list of scores greater than the mean. The sorting part of the problem is solved in Section 9.3.

```
PROGRAM TestScores (input, output);

(******************************************************************

   Program to read a list of test scores, calculate their mean,
   and print a list of scores greater than the mean.

******************************************************************)

CONST
   ScoresLimit = 100;       (* maximum number of scores *)

TYPE
   ListOfScores = ARRAY[1..ScoresLimit] OF integer;

VAR
   Score : ListOfScores;    (* list of scores *)
   NumScores,               (* number of scores *)
   i : integer;             (* index *)
   Sum,                     (* sum of the scores *)
   MeanScore : real;        (* mean of the scores *)

BEGIN
   write ('Enter number of scores:  ');
   readln (NumScores);
   IF NumScores > ScoresLimit THEN
      writeln ('At most ', ScoresLimit:1, ' scores can be processed')
   ELSE
      BEGIN
         (* Read the scores and store them in array Score *)

         writeln ('Enter the scores, as many per line as desired.');
         FOR i := 1 TO NumScores DO
            read (Score[i]);

         (* Calculate the mean of the scores *)

         Sum := 0;
         FOR i := 1 TO NumScores DO
            Sum := Sum + Score[i];
         MeanScore := Sum / NumScores;
         writeln ('Mean of the scores is ', MeanScore:3:1);
```

Figure 9.2

Figure 9.2 (cont.)

```
        (* Print list of scores greater than the mean *)

        writeln;
        writeln ('List of scores greater than the mean:');
        FOR i := 1 TO NumScores DO
           IF Score[i] > MeanScore THEN
              writeln (Score[i]:3)
     END (* ELSE *)
END.
```

Sample run:

```
Enter number of scores:  15
Enter the scores, as many per line as desired.
88 77 56 89 100 99 55 35 78 65
69 83 71 38 95
Mean of the scores is 73.2

List of scores greater than the mean:
 88
 77
 89
100
 99
 78
 83
 95
```

In most of our examples of arrays, the indices have been positive integers, ranging from 1 up through some upper limit. This is probably the most common index type, but as noted in the preceding section, the type of the index may be any ordinal type. For example, the declarations

> **type**
>   *DaysOfWeek* = (*Sunday, Monday, Tuesday, Wednesday, Thursday,*
>   *Friday, Saturday*);
>   *DaysArray* = **array**[*DaysOfWeek*] **of** *real*;

> **var**
>   *HoursWorked* : *DaysArray*;

establish a one-dimensional array *HoursWorked* with seven locations, each of which can store a real number:

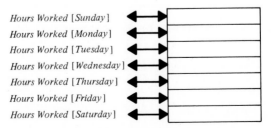

Values can be read into these seven locations by the statement

for *Day* : = *Sunday* **to** *Saturday* **do**
    read (*HoursWorked*[*Day*]);

where the index *Day* is assumed to be of type *DaysOfWeek*, and the values read into the array are of real type. In general, the type of the indices in any array reference must be compatible with that specified in the array declaration, and the type of values stored in the array must be compatible with the component type. Recall that two *types are compatible* if they are the same, one is a subrange of the other, or both are subranges of the same underlying type.

To illustrate further the use of nonnumeric indices to access array elements, consider the problem of reading a line of uppercase text and counting the number of occurrences of each of the letters A, B, . . . , Z. The program in Figure 9.3 solves this problem. It uses the array *Frequency* declared by

type
    Letter = 'A'..'Z';
    CharCountArray = **array**[*Letter*] **of** *integer*;

var
    Frequency : *CharCountArray*;

to count the occurrences of each of the letters, so that *Frequency*['A'] is the number of occurrences of A in the line of text, *Frequency*['B'] is the number of occurrences of B, and so on.

```
PROGRAM LetterCount (input, output);

(******************************************************************

    Program to count the occurrences of each of the letters A, B, ..., Z
    (or their lowercase equivalents a, b, ..., z) in several lines of
    text.  The array Frequency indexed by the subrange 'A'..'Z' is used
    for this.  If Character is any one of these 26 letters,
    Frequency[Character] is the number of occurrences of Character.

******************************************************************)

CONST
    EndOfData = '#';

TYPE
    Letter = 'A'..'Z';
    CharCountArray = ARRAY[Letter] OF integer;

VAR
    Frequency : CharCountArray;   (* frequencies of letters *)
    Character : char;             (* character from text line *)
```

Figure 9.3

Figure 9.3 (cont.)

```
FUNCTION Cap(Ch : char) : char;

    (***************************************************************

        Function returns uppercase equivalent of lowercase letter Ch
        or Ch itself if it is not a lower case letter.

        **************************************************************)

    BEGIN (* Cap *)
        IF ('a' <= Ch) AND (Ch <= 'z') THEN
            Cap := chr(ord('A') + ord(Ch) - ord('a'))
        ELSE
            Cap := Ch
    END (* Cap *);

BEGIN (* main program *)

    (* First initialize all frequencies to 0 *)

    FOR Character := 'A' TO 'Z' DO
        Frequency[Character] := 0;

    (* Read the lines of text and count occurrences of letters *)

    writeln ('Enter the lines of text.  Enter ',EndOfData, ' to stop.');
    writeln;
    read (Character);
    WHILE Character <> EndOfData DO
        BEGIN
            Character := Cap(Character);
            IF ('A' <= Character) AND (Character <= 'Z') THEN
                Frequency[Character] := Frequency[Character] + 1;
            read (Character);
        END (* WHILE *);

    (* Print the frequencies *)

    writeln;
    writeln ('In the text processed, the letters A - Z occurred with');
    writeln ('the following frequencies:');
    writeln;
    FOR Character := 'A' TO 'Z' DO
        writeln ('Frequency of ', Character, ':   ', Frequency[Character]:2)
END (* main program *).
```

Sample run:

Enter the lines of text. Enter # to stop.

Figure 9.3 (cont.)

```
These two lines of text are being used to test this program.
THE QUICK BROWN FIX JUMPED OVER THE LAZY DOGS AND RAN AWAY.
#
In the text processed, the letters A - Z occurred with
the following frequencies:

Frequency of A:    7
Frequency of B:    2
Frequency of C:    1
Frequency of D:    4
Frequency of E:   12
Frequency of F:    2
Frequency of G:    3
Frequency of H:    4
Frequency of I:    5
Frequency of J:    1
Frequency of K:    1
Frequency of L:    2
Frequency of M:    2
Frequency of N:    5
Frequency of O:    7
Frequency of P:    2
Frequency of Q:    1
Frequency of R:    6
Frequency of S:    6
Frequency of T:   10
Frequency of U:    3
Frequency of V:    1
Frequency of W:    3
Frequency of X:    2
Frequency of Y:    2
Frequency of Z:    1
```

Sometimes it is necessary to copy the elements of one array into a second array. Suppose, for example, that arrays *Alpha* and *Beta* are declared by

> **type**
>   *RealList* = **array**[1..5] **of** *real*;
>
> **var**
>   *Alpha, Beta* : *RealList*;

If values have been assigned to the array *Alpha*, they can be copied to the array *Beta* by the statement

> **for** $i := 1$ **to** 5 **do**
>   *Beta*[i] := *Alpha*[i]

This assignment of the elements of the array *Alpha* to the array *Beta* can be done more simply by the assignment statement

> *Beta* := *Alpha*

In general, one array may be assigned to another array only when they have the *same type* and the array components are not files. This means that they must be declared in the same type declaration or by the same type identifier or by *equivalent* type identifiers. Two type identifiers are equivalent if their definitions can be traced back to a common *type identifier*. For example, consider the following type definitions:

type
    Aarray = **array**[1..5] **of** *real*;
    Barray = *Aarray*;
    Carray = *Aarray*;
    Darray = *Barray*;
    Earray = **array**[1..5] **of** *real*;

Type identifiers *Barray* and *Carray* are equivalent to *Aarray* and to each other, since they are synonyms for the type identifier *Aarray*. Similarly, *Darray* is a synonym for *Barray* and is therefore equivalent to *Barray*. Type identifiers *Aarray*, *Barray*, *Carray*, and *Darray* are equivalent because their definitions can be traced back to a common type *identifier* (*Aarray*). It is important to note, however, that even though the definitions of *Aarray* and *Earray* are identical, these type identifiers are not equivalent because they are not defined using a common type *identifier*. Thus, if arrays *A*, *A1*, *B*, *C*, *D*, and *E* are declared by

var
    A, A1 : *Aarray*;
    B : *Barray*;
    C : *Carray*;
    D : *Darray*;
    E : *Earray*;

the array assignment statements

    A1 := *A*;
    B := *A*;
    B := *C*;
    B := *D*;
    C := *D*;

all are valid because arrays *A*, *A1*, *B*, *C*, and *D* all have the same type, but the assignment statement

    A := *E*;

is not valid.[1]

    Arrays may also be used as parameters for functions and procedures, but

---

[1] In some versions of Pascal, the definition of "same type" may be less restrictive; arrays *A* and *E* might be considered to have the same type.

the value of a function may not be an array. To illustrate, consider the following function:

function *Mean* (**var** *Item* : *List*; *NumItems* : *integer*) : *real*;

    (∗ Function to find the mean of a list of *NumItems*
       numbers stored in an array *Item*. ∗)

  var
    i : *integer*; (∗ index ∗)
    Sum : *real*; (∗ sum of the numbers ∗)

  begin (∗ *Mean* ∗)
    if *NumItems* = 0 **then**
      begin
        writeln ('No elements—returning mean of 0');
        Mean := 0
      end (∗ **if** ∗)
    else
      begin
        Sum := 0;
        for *i* := 1 **to** *NumItems* **do**
          Sum := *Sum* + *Item*[*i*];
        Mean := *Sum* / *NumItems*
      end (∗ **else** ∗)
  end (∗ *Mean* ∗);

Because the types of formal parameters must be specified by type identifiers, an array declaration such as **array**[1..100] **of** *integer* cannot be used to specify the type of the formal parameter *Item*.

When this function is referenced, the type of each actual parameter that is an array must be the same as the type of the corresponding formal parameter. Thus, to reference this general function in the program of Figure 9.2 with the statement

    MeanScore := *Mean*(*Score*, *NumScores*);

it would be necessary to set the type identifier *List* equal to the type identifier *ListOfScores* in the main program:

type
  ListOfScores = **array**[1..*ScoresLimit*] **of** *integer*;
  List = *ListOfScores*;

or use the same type identifier, either *ListOfScores* or *List*, both in the main program and in the heading of this function.

In this function *Mean*, the array *Item* is a variable parameter, although this is not required. If it were a value parameter, however, then a reference to this function would require copying the elements of the actual array into *Item*. This would produce two copies of the same list of values and would therefore not be an efficient use of memory. Moreover, the process of copying the elements of one array into another is time-consuming.

An array must be a variable parameter if the subprogram is to return the array to the program unit that calls it. For example, a procedure to read a list of items into an array *Item*, count the number of elements that were read, and return both this array and the count to the main program must declare both the array and the count as variable parameters:

> **procedure** *ReadList* (**var** *Item* : *List*; *ListLimit* : *integer*;
> **var** *Count* : *integer*);

> (∗ Procedure to read list elements into array *Item* that has
> at most *ListLimit* elements and count the elements
> read. Both *Item* and *Count* are returned. ∗)

> **var**
> *Response* : *char*; (∗ user response ∗)

> **begin** (∗ *ReadList* ∗)
> *writeln* ('Enter the list of items, as many per line as desired.');
> *writeln* ('Note: At most ', *ListLimit*:1, ' items can be read.');
> *writeln*;
> *Count* := 0;
> **repeat**
> *write* ('Items: ');
> **while not** *eoln* **do**
> **begin**
> *Count* := *Count* + 1;
> *read* (*Item*[*Count*])
> **end** (∗ **while** ∗);
> *readln*;
> *write* ('More (Y or N)? ');
> *readln* (*Response*)
> **until** (*Response* <> 'Y') **and** (*Response* <> 'y')
> **end** (∗ *ReadList* ∗);

The examples in this section indicate that arrays are very useful for processing lists. The array implementation of lists does have its drawbacks, however. One is that whereas a list need not have a fixed length, an array must have a fixed number of elements. This means that it is possible to declare the array to have exactly the right size only if the list is *static*, that is, its size never changes. The common approach otherwise is to estimate the maximum size of the list and declare the array to have this number of components. However, if we declare the array too small, we run the risk of an error arising from indices that are out of range, or we may lose some of the list elements because there is no room for them in the array. If we make the array too large, then we may be wasting a considerable part of the memory allocated to it.

Another weakness of the array implementation of lists is that although algorithms for the insertion and deletion operations are quite easy to write (as the exercises ask you to do), they are not very efficient. For example, inserting the new value 75 at position 6 in the list of ten integers

$$23, 34, 48, 55, 68, 80, 82, 89, 91, 97$$

would require shifting the array elements in positions 6 through 10 into positions 7 through 11 to make room for the new value:

$$23, 34, 48, 55, 68, 80, 82, 84, 91, 97$$

$$23, 34, 48, 55, 68, 75, 80, 82, 84, 91, 97$$

Similarly, deleting an item requires moving array elements; for example, to remove the second number in this last list, we must shift the array elements in positions 3 through 11 into positions 2 through 10 to "close the gap":

$$23, 34, 48, 55, 68, 75, 80, 82, 84, 91, 97$$

$$23, 48, 55, 68, 75, 80, 82, 84, 91, 97$$

If insertions and deletions are restricted to the ends of the list, then array implementations that do not require moving array elements are possible. Two important special cases are stacks and queues. A *stack* is a list in which elements may be inserted (*pushed*) and deleted (*popped*) at only one end, called the *top* of the stack. If elements may be inserted only at one end (the *rear*) and deleted only at the other (the *front*), the list is called a *queue*. Array implementations of stacks and queues are described in the exercises at the end of the next section. Array implementations of stacks are considered in detail in Section 16.1, and this implementation is used in Section 16.2 to process arithmetic expressions. This application of arrays does not require any additional background, and those who are interested may wish to consider it in addition to the applications of arrays presented in the next section.

Arrays work very well for static lists and reasonably well for lists whose maximum sizes can be estimated and for which insertions and deletions are infrequent or are restricted to the ends of the list. *Dynamic* lists whose sizes may vary greatly during processing and those in which items are frequently inserted and/or deleted anywhere in the list are better implemented using a linked structure, as described in Chapter 16.

9.3 Examples: Class Averages, Sorting, and Searching

EXAMPLE 1: Class Averages.   Consider the problem of calculating the average score received on a test by students in each of the four classes freshman, sophomore, junior, and senior. For each student, a score is to be read together with a class code of 1, 2, 3, or 4, representing the class to which the student belongs. For each class we must calculate the average score received by the students in that class.

Since there are four classes, we can use an array *Number* with four elements to record the number of students in the classes and another array *SumOfScores* to record the sum of the scores received by students in the various classes. These arrays could be indexed 1..4, but to illustrate the use of arrays indexed by an enumerated type, we will use

$$ClassName = (Freshman, Sophomore, Junior, Senior)$$

for indices. We thus will use the following arrays:

Number:	*Number[Class]* is the number of students in the class specified by the index *Class* which is of type *ClassName*.
SumOfScores:	*SumOfScores[Class]* is the sum of the test scores for all students in the class specified by the value of *Class*.

There are three main tasks to be performed in solving this problem. The first is to initialize the arrays *Number* and *SumOfScores* to 0. The second task is to read and tabulate the pairs of class codes and test scores in the arrays *Number* and *SumOfScores*. Finally, after all the data have been read, the class averages must be calculated and displayed. The following diagram summarizes the structure of the program in Figure 9.4 that solves this problem.

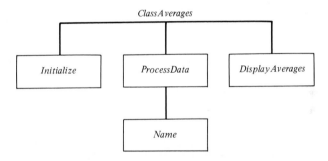

Initialization consists simply of setting each of the elements of the arrays *Number* and *SumOfScores* to 0. In the program this is done by calling the procedure *Initialize*.

An algorithm for the second task is

ProcessData

(∗ Algorithm to read pairs of class codes (1, 2, 3, 4) and test scores and tabulate these in the arrays *Number* and *SumOfScores* whose indices are of type *ClassName*. ∗)

1. Read *ClassCode* and *Score*.
2. While data values have been successfully read, do the following:
   a. If *ClassCode* is less than 1 or greater than 4
      Display an illegal class code message.
      Otherwise do the following:
         i. Convert *ClassCode* to *Class* of type *ClassName*.
        ii. Add 1 to *Number[Class]*.
       iii. Add *Score* to *SumOfScores[Class]*.
   b. Read next *ClassCode* and *Score*.

The procedure *ProcessData* in the program implements this algorithm. The conversion from *ClassCode* to *Class* whose type is the enumerated type *ClassName* is accomplished using the function *Name*.

An algorithm for the third task is straightforward:

DisplayAverages

(* Algorithm to calculate and display the class averages. *)

1. Print suitable headings for the output.
2. For *Class* ranging from *Freshman* to *Senior*, do the following:
   a. Write the class number.
   b. If *Number[Class]* is 0
        Display a message that there were no test scores for this class.
        Otherwise do the following:
        i. Calculate *Average* =
              SumOfScores[Class] / *Number[Class]*.
        ii. Display *Average*.

This algorithm is implemented by the procedure *DisplayAverages* in the program in Figure 9.4.

```
PROGRAM ClassAverages (input, output);

(*******************************************************************

    Program to calculate the average score received on a test by
    students in each of four classes:  Freshman (1), Sophomore (2),
    Junior (3) and Senior (4).

*******************************************************************)

TYPE
    ClassName = (Freshman, Sophomore, Junior, Senior);
    ClassList = ARRAY[ClassName] OF integer;

VAR
    Number,                      (* Number[Class] = # of students in Class *)
    SumOfScores : ClassList;     (* SumOfScores[Class] = sum of scores for
                                    students in Class *)
    Class : ClassName;           (* index *)

PROCEDURE Initialize (VAR Number, SumOfScores : ClassList);

    (*******************************************************************

        Procedure to initialize the arrays Number and SumOfScores
        to zero.

    *******************************************************************)

    VAR
        Class : ClassName;
```

Figure 9.4

Figure 9.4   (cont.)

```
   BEGIN (* Initialize *)
      FOR Class := Freshman TO Senior DO
         BEGIN
            Number[Class] := 0;
            SumOfScores[Class] := 0
         END (* FOR *)
   END (* Initialize *);

PROCEDURE ProcessData (VAR Number, SumOfScores : ClassList);

   (***************************************************************

      Procedure to read each pair of class codes and scores, increase
      the appropriate counter Number[Class] by 1, and add the test
      score to SumOfScores[Class], the sum  of scores for this class.

   ***************************************************************)

   TYPE
      ClassNumber = 1..4;

   VAR
      ClassCode : integer;    (* class code *)
      Class : ClassName;      (* class name corresponding to class code *)
      Score : integer;        (* student's test score *)

FUNCTION Name(ClassCode : ClassNumber) : ClassName;

   (**************************************************************

      Function to convert class code (1, 2, 3, 4) to the
      corresponding value of enumerated type ClassName.

   **************************************************************)

   BEGIN (* Name *)
      CASE ClassCode OF
         1 : Name := Freshman;
         2 : Name := Sophomore;
         3 : Name := Junior;
         4 : Name := Senior
      END (* CASE *)
   END (* Name *);

BEGIN (* ProcessData *)
   writeln ('Enter the class codes and the test scores in pairs,');
   writeln ('as many per line as desired.  Enter 0''s to signal');
   writeln ('the end of data.');
   writeln;
   read (ClassCode, Score);
   WHILE ClassCode <> 0 DO
      BEGIN
         IF (ClassCode < 1) OR (ClassCode > 4) THEN
            writeln ('** Illegal class code **')
         ELSE
            BEGIN
               Class := Name(ClassCode);
               Number[Class] := Number[Class] + 1;
               SumOfScores[Class] := SumOfScores[Class] + Score
            END (* ELSE *);
         read (ClassCode, Score)
      END (* WHILE *)
END (* ProcessData *);
```

Figure 9.4 (cont.)

```
PROCEDURE DisplayAverages (VAR Number, SumOfScores : ClassList);

   (****************************************************************

      Procedure to calculate and display the average score for each
      of the four classes.

   ****************************************************************)

   VAR
      Class : ClassName;   (* index *)

   BEGIN (* DisplayAverages *)
      writeln;
      writeln ('CLASS #  AVE. SCORE');
      writeln ('======= ==========');
      FOR Class := Freshman TO Senior DO
         BEGIN
            write (1 + ord(Class):4);
            IF Number[Class] = 0 THEN
               writeln ('    No scores')
            ELSE
               writeln (SumOfScores[Class] / Number[Class]:11:1)
         END (* FOR *)
   END (* DisplayAverages *);

BEGIN (* main program *)
   Initialize (Number, SumOfScores);
   ProcessData (Number, SumOfScores);
   DisplayAverages (Number, SumOfScores)
END (* main program *).
```

Sample run:

Enter the class codes and the test scores in pairs,
as many per line as desired. Enter 0's to signal
the end of data.

```
1 95   1 88   3 77   4 100  4 67   1 58   3 62   3 99
3 87   4 72   4 58   1 66   4 89
0 0
```

```
CLASS # AVE. SCORE
======= ==========
   1       76.8
   2       No scores
   3       81.3
   4       77.2
```

EXAMPLE 2: Sorting. A common programming problem is *sorting*, that is, arranging the items in a list so that they are in either ascending or descending order. There are many sorting methods, most of which use an array to store the items to be sorted. In this section we describe one of the simplest sorting methods known as *simple selection sort*. Although it is not an efficient sorting method for large lists, it does perform reasonably well for small lists, and it is easy to understand. More efficient sorting schemes are described in the exercises at the end of this section.

The basic idea of a selection sort of a list is to make a number of passes through the list or a part of the list, and on each pass to select one item to be correctly positioned. For example, on each pass through a sublist, the smallest item in this sublist might be found and then moved to its proper location.

As an illustration, suppose that the following list is to be sorted into ascending order:

$$67 , \quad 33 , \quad 21 , \quad 84 , \quad 49 , \quad 50 , \quad 75$$

We scan the list to locate the smallest item and find it in position 3:

$$67 , \quad 33 , \quad \boxed{21} , \quad 84 , \quad 49 , \quad 50 , \quad 75$$

We interchange this item with the first item and thus properly position the smallest item at the beginning of the list:

$$21 , \quad 33 , \quad 67 , \quad 84 , \quad 49 , \quad 50 , \quad 75$$

We now scan the sublist consisting of the items from position 2 on to find the smallest item

$$21 , \quad \boxed{33} , \quad 67 , \quad 84 , \quad 49 , \quad 50 , \quad 75$$

and exchange it with the second item (itself in this case) and thus properly position the next-to-smallest item in position 2:

$$21 , \quad 33 , \quad 67 , \quad 84 , \quad 49 , \quad 50 , \quad 75$$

We continue in this manner, locating the smallest item in the sublist of items from position 3 on and interchanging it with the third item, then properly positioning the smallest item in the sublist of items from position 4 on, and so on until we eventually do this for the sublist consisting of the last two items:

$$21 , \quad 33 , \quad \boxed{49} , \quad 84 , \quad 67 , \quad 50 , \quad 75$$

$$21 , \quad 33 , \quad 49 , \quad \boxed{50} , \quad 67 , \quad 84 , \quad 75$$

$$21 , \quad 33 , \quad 49 , \quad 50 , \quad \boxed{67} , \quad 84 , \quad 75$$

$$21 , \quad 33 , \quad 49 , \quad 50 , \quad 67 , \quad \boxed{75} , \quad 84$$

Positioning the smallest item in this last sublist obviously also positions the last item correctly and thus completes the sort.

An algorithm for this simple selection sort is

SIMPLE SELECTION SORT ALGORITHM

(* Algorithm to sort the list of items $X[1]$, $X[2]$, . . . , $X[NumItems]$ so they are in ascending order. *)

For i ranging from 1 to $NumItems - 1$, do the following:

(* On the ith pass, first find the smallest item in the sublist $X[i]$, . . . , $X[NumItems]$. *)
a. Set *SmallPos* equal to i.
b. Set *Smallest* equal to $X[SmallPos]$.
c. For j ranging from $i + 1$ to *NumItems* do the following:
   If $X[j] <$ *Smallest* then   (* smaller item found *)
       i. Set *SmallPos* equal to j.
       ii. Set *Smallest* equal to $X[SmallPos]$.

(* Now interchange this smallest item with the item at the beginning of this sublist. *)

d. Set $X[SmallPos]$ equal to $X[i]$.
e. Set $X[i]$ equal to *Smallest*.

The program in Figure 9.5 implements this algorithm as procedure *SelectionSort*. It reads a list of up to 100 items, using procedure *ReadList* given in the preceding section, sorts them using selection sort, and then displays the sorted list.

```
PROGRAM Sort (input, output);

(******************************************************************

   Program to read and count a list of items
        Item[1], Item[2], ..., Item[NumItems],
   sort them in ascending order, and then display the sorted list.

******************************************************************)

CONST
   ListLimit = 100;  (* maximum # of items in the list *)

TYPE
   ItemType = integer;
   List = ARRAY[1..ListLimit] of ItemType;

VAR
   NumItems,      (* number of items *)
   i: integer;    (* index *)
   Item : List;   (* list of items to be sorted *)
```

Figure 9.5

Figure 9.5 (cont.)

```
PROCEDURE ReadList (VAR Item : List; ListLimit : integer;
                    VAR Count : integer);

   (***************************************************************

      Procedure to read list elements into array Item which has
      at most ListLimit elements and to count the elements
      read.  Both Item and Count are returned.

    ***************************************************************)

   VAR
      Response : char;  (* user response *)

   BEGIN (* ReadList *)
      writeln ('Enter the list of items, as many per line as desired.');
      writeln ('Note:  At most ', ListLimit:1, ' items can be read.');
      writeln;
      Count := 0;
      REPEAT
         write ('Items:  ');
         WHILE NOT eoln DO
            BEGIN
               Count := Count + 1;
               read (Item[Count])
            END (* WHILE *);
         readln;
         write ('More (Y or N)?  ');
         readln (Response)
      UNTIL Response <> 'Y'
   END (* ReadList *);

PROCEDURE SelectionSort(VAR Item : List; NumItems : integer);

   (****************************************************************

      Procedure to sort Item[1], ..., Item[NumItems] into ascending
      order using the simple selection sort algorithm.  For descending
      order, change < to > in the boolean expression Item[j] < Smallest.

    ****************************************************************)

   VAR
      Smallest : ItemType;    (* smallest item in current sublist *)
      SmallPos,               (* position of Smallest *)
      i, j : integer;         (* indices *)

   BEGIN (* Selectionsort *)
      FOR i := 1 TO NumItems - 1 DO
         BEGIN

            (* find smallest item in sublist Item[i], ..., Item[NumItems] *)

            SmallPos := i;
            Smallest := Item[SmallPos];
            FOR j := i + 1 TO NumItems DO
               IF Item[j] < Smallest THEN   (* smaller item found *)
                  BEGIN
                     SmallPos := j;
                     Smallest := Item[j]
                  END (* IF *);
```

Figure 9.5 (cont.)

```
            (* interchange smallest item with Item[i] at beginning
               of sublist *)

            Item[SmallPos] := Item[i];
            Item[i] := Smallest
         END (* FOR i *)
   END (* SelectionSort *);

PROCEDURE PrintItems (VAR Item : List; NumItems : integer);

   (****************************************************************

         Procedure to print the list of items.

   ****************************************************************)

   VAR
      i : integer;      (* index *)

   BEGIN (* PrintItems *)
      writeln;
      writeln ('Sorted list of ', Numitems:1, ' items:');
      writeln;
      FOR i := 1 TO NumItems DO
         writeln (Item[i])
   END (* PrintItems *);

BEGIN (* main program *)
   ReadList (Item, ListLimit, NumItems);
   SelectionSort (Item, NumItems);
   PrintItems (Item, NumItems)
END (* main *).
```

Sample run:

```
Enter the list of items, as many per line as desired.
Note:  At most 100 items can be read.

Items:   55 88 34 85 21
More (Y or N)?  Y
Items:   99 5 83 71
More (Y or N)?  N

Sorted list of 9 items:

      5
     21
     34
     55
     71
     83
     85
     88
     99
```

EXAMPLE 3: Searching. Another important problem in data processing is *searching* a collection of data for a specified item and retrieving some information associated with that item. For example, one searches a telephone directory for a specific name in order to retrieve the phone number listed with that name. In a *linear search*, one begins with the first item in a list and searches sequentially until either the desired item is found or the end of the list is reached. The following algorithm describes this method of searching:

LINEAR SEARCH ALGORITHM

(* Algorithm to linear search a list $X[1]$, $X[2]$, . . . , $X[NumItems]$ for a
    specified *Item*. *Found* is set to true and *Location* to the position of
    Item if the search is successful; otherwise, *Found* is set to false. *)

1. Initialize *Location* to 1 and *Found* to false.
2. While *Location* $\leq$ *NumItems* and not *Found*, do the following:
    If *Item* $=$ $X[Location]$ then
        Set *Found* to true.
    Else
        Increment *Location* by 1.

Although linear search may be an adequate method for small data sets, a more efficient technique is needed for large collections. If the list to be searched has been sorted, the *binary search* algorithm may be used. With this method, we first examine the middle item in the list; if this is the desired entry, the search is successful. Otherwise, we determine whether the item being sought is in the first half or the second half of the list and then repeat this process, using the middle entry of that sublist.

To illustrate, suppose that the list to be searched is

1331
1373
1555
1824
1882
1898
1989
2002
2335
2665
3103

and that we are looking for 1989. We first examine the middle number, 1898, in the sixth position. Because 1989 is greater than 1898, we can disregard the first half of the list and concentrate on the second half:

1989
2002
2335
2665
3103

The middle number in this sublist is 2335 and the desired item 1989 is less than 2335, so we discard the second half of this sublist and concentrate on the first half:

<u>1989</u>

2002

Since there is no middle number in this half, we examine the number immediately preceding the middle position, that is, 1989. In this case, we have located the desired entry with three comparisons rather than seven, as required in a linear search.

In general, the algorithm for binary search is as follows:

BINARY SEARCH ALGORITHM

(* Algorithm to binary search a list $X[1]$, $X[2]$, . . . , $X[NumItems]$ that has been ordered so the elements are in ascending order. *Found* is set to true and *Location* to the position of the *Item* being sought if the search is successful; otherwise, *Found* is set to false. *)

1. Initialize *First* to 1 and *Last* to *NumItems*. These represent the positions of the first and last items of the list or sublist being searched.
2. Initialize *Found* to false.
3. While *First* ≤ *Last* and not *Found*, do the following:
   a. Find the middle position in the sublist by setting *Middle* equal to the integer quotient of (*First* + *Last*) divided by 2.
   b. Compare the *Item* being searched for with $X[Middle]$. There are three possibilities:
      (i) *Item* < $X[Middle]$: *Item* is in the first half of the sublist; set *Last* equal to *Middle* − 1.
      (ii) *Item* > $X[Middle]$: *Item* is in the last half of the sublist; set *First* equal to *Middle* + 1.
      (iii) *Item* = $X[Middle]$: *Item* has been found; set *Location* equal to *Middle* and *Found* to true.

Figure 9.6 is a program for information retrieval. It reads student numbers, section letters, and test scores for a group of students and stores these in three arrays:

Snumb: *Snumb*[i] is the ith student number.
Section: *Section*[i] is the section letter (A, B, . . . , Z) for the ith student number.
TestScore: *TestScore*[i] is the test score for the ith student number.

The user of the program can then enter a student's number, and the section code and test score for that student are retrieved and displayed. Since the data triples in the file are arranged so that the student numbers are in ascending order, these numbers will also be in ascending order in the array *Snumb*. Consequently, the binary search algorithm can be used to search this array for the given student's number.

The structure of this program is summarized by the following structure diagram:

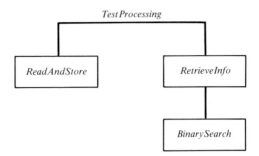

The procedure *ReadAndStore* reads the student numbers, section letters, and test scores from a file and stores them in the arrays *Snumb*, *Section*, and *TestScores*, respectively. The procedure *RetrieveInfo* then repeatedly accepts a student's number from the user and retrieves the section letter and test score for that student. It uses the procedure *BinarySearch* to search the array *Snumb*.

```
PROGRAM TestProcessing (input, output,TestFile);

(*****************************************************************

   This program reads in a list of student numbers, class codes,
   and test scores from TestFile and then sorts them so the student
   numbers are in ascending order.  A student number can then be
   input, the list searched using a binary search, and the
   corresponding class code and test score displayed.

*****************************************************************)

CONST
   ListLimit = 100;  (* maximum # of items in the list *)

TYPE
   ItemType = integer;
   List = ARRAY[1..ListLimit] OF ItemType;

VAR
   Snumb,               (* Snumb[i] = i-th student number *)
   Class,               (* Class[i] = class code for i-th student *)
   TestScore: List;     (* TestScore[i] = test score for i-th student *)
   NumScores : integer; (* number of test scores *)
   TestFile : text;     (* file from which student data is read *)
```

Figure 9.6

Figure 9.6 (cont.)

```
PROCEDURE ReadAndStore (VAR Snumb, Class, TestScore : List;
                        VAR Count : integer);

    (***************************************************************

        Procedure to read the items from TestFile and store them in
        the arrays Snumb, Class, and TestScore.

    ***************************************************************)

    BEGIN (* ReadAndStore *)
        reset (TestFile);
        Count := 0;
        WHILE NOT eof(TestFile) DO
            BEGIN
                Count := Count + 1;
                readln (TestFile, Snumb[Count], Class[Count], TestScore[Count])
            END (* WHILE *)
    END (* ReadAndStore *);

PROCEDURE RetrieveInfo (VAR Snumb, Class, TestScore : List;
                        NumItems : integer);

    (***************************************************************

        Procedure to accept a student number and then search the list
        Snumb for it.  If it is found, the class code and test score
        for that student are displayed.

    ***************************************************************)

VAR
    SnumbDesired : ItemType;   (* student # to search for *)
    Found : boolean;           (* indicates if search was successful *)
    Location : integer;        (* location of number in the list *)

PROCEDURE BinarySearch (VAR Item : List; NumItems : integer;
                        ItemSought : ItemType; VAR Found : boolean;
                        VAR Location : integer);

    (***************************************************************

        Procedure to search the list Item for ItemSought using the
        binary search algorithm.  If ItemSought is found in the list,
        a value of true is returned for Found and the Location of the
        item is returned; otherwise, false is returned for Found and
        0 for Location.

    ***************************************************************)

VAR
    First,              (* first item in sublist being searched *)
    Last,               (* last item in sublist *)
    Middle : integer;   (* middle item in sublist *)
```

Figure 9.6 (cont.)

```
    BEGIN (* BinarySearch *)
        First := 1;
        Last := NumItems;
        Found := false;
        WHILE (First <= Last) AND (NOT Found) DO
            BEGIN
                Middle := (First + Last) DIV 2;
                IF ItemSought < Item[Middle] THEN
                    Last := Middle - 1
                ELSE IF ItemSought > Item[Middle] THEN
                    First := Middle + 1
                ELSE
                    BEGIN
                        Location := Middle;
                        Found := TRUE
                    END (* ELSE *)
            END (* WHILE *)
    END (* BinarySearch *);

    BEGIN (* RetrieveInfo *)
        writeln ('To stop searching, enter student number of 0.');
        write ('Student number?  ');
        readln (SnumbDesired);
        WHILE SnumbDesired <> 0 DO
            BEGIN
                BinarySearch (Snumb, NumScores, SnumbDesired, Found, Location);
                IF Found THEN
                    BEGIN
                        writeln ('Student ', SnumbDesired:1, ' is in class ',
                                    Class[Location]:1);
                        writeln ('His/her test score was ', TestScore[Location]:1)
                    END (* IF Found *)
                ELSE
                    writeln ('Student ', SnumbDesired:1, ' not found');
                writeln;
                write ('Student number?  ');
                readln (SnumbDesired)
            END (* WHILE *)
    END (* RetrieveInfo *);

BEGIN (* main program *)
    ReadAndStore (Snumb, Class, TestScore, NumScores);
    RetrieveInfo (Snumb, Class, TestScore, NumScores)
END (* main program *).
```

Listing of TestFile:

```
1111 1  99
2222 2 100
3333 3  77
4444 1  55
5555 2  87
6666 1  63
7777 3  93
```

Figure 9.6   (cont.)

Sample run:

```
To stop searching, enter student number of 0.
Student number?  1111
Student 1111 is in class 1
His/her test score was 99

Student number?  5555
Student 5555 is in class 2
His/her test score was 87

Student number?  8888
Student 8888 not found

Student number?  3333
Student 3333 is in class 3
His/her test score was 77

Student number?  0
```

Exercises

1. Assume that the following declarations have been made:

> **type**
>   *Color* = (*red, yellow, blue, green, white, black*);
>   *ColorArray* = **array**[*Color*] **of** *real*;
>   *LittleArray* = **array**[1..10] **of** *integer*;
>   *CharCountArray* = **array**['A'..'F'] **of** *integer*;
>
> **var**
>   *Price* : *ColorArray*;
>   *Number* : *LittleArray*;
>   *LetterCount* : *CharCountArray*;
>   *i* : *integer*;
>   *Ch* : *char*;
>   *Col* : *Color*;

For each of the following, tell what value (if any) will be assigned to each array element, or explain why an error occurs:

(a) for $i :=$ 1 **to** 10 **do**
    Number[i] $:=$ i **div** 2;

(b) for $i :=$ 1 **to** 6 **do**
    Number[i] $:=$ $i * i$;
  for $i :=$ 7 **to** 10 **do**
    Number[i] $:=$ *Number*[$i - 5$];

(c) $i := 0$;
   while $i <> 10$ **do**
     begin
       if $(i \bmod 3) = 0$ **then**
         $Number[i] := 0$
       else
         $Number[i] := i$;
       $i := i + 1$
     end (* **while** *);

(d) $Number[1] := 1$;
   $i := 2$;
   repeat
     $Number[i] := 2 * Number[i - 1]$;
     $i := i + 1$
   until $i = 10$;

(e) **for** $Ch := $ 'A' **to** 'F' **do**
    if $Ch = $ 'A' **then**
      $LetterCount[Ch] := 1$
    else
      $LetterCount[Ch] := LetterCount[pred(Ch)] + 1$;

(f) **for** $Col := yellow$ **to** $white$ **do**
   $Price[Col] := 13.95$;

(g) **for** $Col := red$ **to** $black$ **do**
   case Col **of**
     $red, blue$: $Price[Col] := 19.95$;
     $yellow$: $Price[Col] := 12.75$;
     $green, black$: $Price[Col] := 14.50$;
     $white$:
   end (* **case** *);

2. For each of the following, write appropriate declarations and statements to create the specified array:

(a) An array whose indices are the integers from 0 through 5 and in which each element is the same as the index.

(b) An array whose indices are the integers from -5 through 5 and for which the elements are the indices in reverse order.

(c) An array whose indices are the uppercase letters and in which each element is the same as the index.

(d) An array whose indices are the integers from 1 through 20 and for which an array element has the value true if the corresponding index is even, and false otherwise.

(e) An array whose indices are the uppercase letters and for which each element is the letter preceding the index, except that the array element corresponding to A is Z.

(f) An array whose indices are the uppercase letters and in which each array element is the number of the position of the corresponding index in the sequence A, B, C, . . . , Z.

(g) An array whose indices are the lowercase letters and in which an array element has the value true if the index is a vowel, and false otherwise.

(h) An array whose indices are the names of the five subjects mathematics, chemistry, speech, history, and economics and in which the array elements are the letter grades received: A in mathematics and speech, B in chemistry, F in history, and C in economics.

3. Assuming that values of type *integer* and *char* are stored in one memory word and *reals* require two memory words, indicate with a diagram like that in Section 9.1 where each component of an array *A* of the following type would be stored if the base address of *A* is *b*; also, give the general address translation formula for *A*[*i*].

(a) **array**[1..5] **of** *integer*.

(b) **array**[1..5] **of** *real*.

(c) **array**[− 5..5] **of** *char*.

(d) **array**['A'..'Z'] **of** *integer*. (*Hint:* Use the *ord* function.)

4. Write a function *Max* that finds the largest value in an integer array *Number* of type *NumberArray* having *NumElements* components.

5. Write a procedure to locate and return the smallest and largest integers in an array *Number* as described in Exercise 4 and their positions in the array. It should also find and return the range of the numbers, that is, the difference between the largest number and the smallest.

6. Write a procedure to implement the linear search algorithm given in the text.

7. Write a procedure *Insert* for inserting an item at a specified position of a list implemented as an array and a procedure *Delete* for deleting an item at a specified position.

8. One possible implementation of a stack is to use an array *Stack* indexed 1..*StackLimit*, with the top of the stack at position 1 of the array.

(a) Why isn't this a good implementation?

(b) A better implementation is to let the stack grow from position 1 toward position *StackLimit* and maintain an integer variable *Top* to "point" to the current top of the stack. Write procedures for the push and pop operations in this implementation.

(c) Use the procedures of part (b) in a program that reads a command I (Insert) or D (Delete); for I, read an integer and push it onto the stack; for D, pop an integer from the stack and display it.

9. For a queue, we might imitate the array implementation of a stack in Exercise 8, using an array *Queue* indexed 1..*QueueLimit* and maintaining two "pointers," *Front* to the item at the front of the queue

and *Rear* to the item at the rear. To add an item to the queue, simply increment *Rear* by 1 and store the item in *Queue*[*Rear*]; to remove an item, simply increment *Front* by 1.

(a) Describe the inadequacies of this implementation. Consider, for example, an integer array with five elements and the following sequence of queue operations: Insert 37, Insert 82, Insert 59, Delete an item, Delete an item, Insert 66, Insert 13, Insert 48.

(b) A better implementation is to think of the array as being circular, with the first element following the last. For this, index the array beginning with 0 and increment *Front* and *Rear* using addition **mod** *QueueLimit*. Write procedures for the insertion and deletion operations, assuming this implementation. Use these procedures in a program that reads a command I (Insert) or D (Delete); for I, read an integer and add it to the queue; for D, remove an integer from the queue and display it.

10. The Cawker City Candy Company records the number of cases of candy produced each day over a four-week period. Write a program that reads these production numbers and stores them in an array. The program should then accept from the user a week number and a day number and should display the production level for that day. Assume that each week consists of five workdays.

11. The Cawker City Candy Company manufactures different kinds of candy, each identified by a product number. Write a program that reads in two arrays, *Number* and *Price*, where *Number*[1] and *Price*[1] are the product number and unit price for the first item, *Number*[2] and *Price*[2] are the product number and unit price for the second item, and so on. The program should then allow the user to select one of the following options:

(a) Retrieve and display the price of a product whose number is entered by the user. (Use the linear search procedure developed in Exercise 7 to determine the index in the array *Number* of the specified item.)

(b) Print a table displaying the product number and the price of each item.

12. The Cawker City Candy Company maintains two warehouses, one in Chicago and one in Detroit, each of which stocks at most 25 different items. Write a program that first reads the product numbers of items stored in the Chicago warehouse and stores them in an array *Chicago*, and then repeats this for the items stored in the Detroit warehouse, storing these product numbers in an array *Detroit*. The program should then find and display the *intersection* of these two lists of numbers, that is, the collection of product numbers common to both lists. The lists should not be assumed to have the same number of elements.

13. Repeat Exercise 12 but find and display the **union** of the two lists, that is, the collection of product numbers that are elements of at least one of the lists.

14. If $\bar{x}$ denotes the mean of the numbers $x_1, x_2, \ldots, x_n$, the **variance** is the average of the squares of the deviations of the numbers from the mean:

$$\text{Variance} = \frac{1}{n} \sum_{i=1}^{n} (x_i - \bar{x})^2$$

and the **standard deviation** is the square root of the variance. Write a program that reads a list of real numbers, counts them, and then calculates their mean, variance, and standard deviation. Print with appropriate labels how many numbers there are, their mean, variance, and standard deviation. Use functions or procedures to calculate the mean, variance, and standard deviation.

15. Letter grades are sometimes assigned to numeric scores by using the grading scheme commonly called "grading on the curve." In this scheme, a letter grade is assigned to a numeric score according to the following table:

x = Numeric Score	Letter Grade
$x < m - \dfrac{3}{2}\sigma$	F
$m - \dfrac{3}{2}\sigma \leq x < m - \dfrac{1}{2}\sigma$	D
$m - \dfrac{1}{2}\sigma \leq x < m + \dfrac{1}{2}\sigma$	C
$m + \dfrac{1}{2}\sigma \leq x < m + \dfrac{3}{2}\sigma$	B
$m + \dfrac{3}{2}\sigma \leq x$	A

where m is the mean score and σ is the standard deviation. Extend the program of Exercise 14 to read a list of real numbers representing numeric scores, calculate their mean and standard deviation, and display the letter grade corresponding to each numeric score.

16. **Insertion sort** is an efficient sorting method for small data sets. It begins with the first item x_1, then inserts x_2 into this one-item list in the correct position to form a sorted two-element list, then inserts x_3 into this two-element list in the correct position, and so on. For example, to sort the list 7, 1, 5, 2, 3, 4, 6, 0, the steps are as follows (the element being inserted is highlighted):

List

7
1, 7   (shift 7 one position to the right)
1, 5, 7   (shift 7 to the right again)
1, 2, 5, 7   (shift 5 and 7 to the right)
1, 2, 3, 5, 7   (shift 5 and 7 to the right)
1, 2, 3, 4, 5, 7   (shift 5 and 7 to the right)
1, 2, 3, 4, 5, 6, 7   (shift 7 to the right)
0, 1, 2, 3, 4, 5, 6, 7   (shift all of 1 through 7 to the right)

Write a program to sort a list of items, using this insertion sort method.

17. The investment company of Shyster and Shyster has been recording the trading price of a particular stock over a 15-day period. Write a program that reads these prices and sorts them into increasing order, using the insertion sort scheme described in the preceding exercise. The program should display the trading range, that is, the lowest and highest prices recorded, and also the median price.

18. Selection sort is not an efficient sorting scheme for large lists. One reason for its inefficiency is that only one item is moved into its correct position on each scan through the list. *Shell sort* (named after Donald Shell) tries to improve on this by moving several items toward their proper positions. On each scan through the list, items that are a specified distance apart are compared, and if they are out of order (a larger item precedes a smaller one), they are interchanged. When no more interchanges are made for a given distance, the distance is cut in half, and the compare-interchange scans continue. The initial distance is commonly taken to be $n/2$ for a list of n items. For example, for the list

$$6,1,5,2,3,4,0$$

the following sequence of distances and scans would be used:

Scan #	Distance	Rearranged List	Interchanges
1	3	2,1,4,0,3,5,6	(6,2), (5,4), (6,0)
2	3	0,1,4,2,3,5,6	(2,0)
3	3	0,1,4,2,3,5,6	none
4	1	0,1,2,3,4,5,6	(4,2), (4,3)
5	1	0,1,2,3,4,5,6	none

Write a program to sort a list of items, using the Shell sort method.

19. Peter the postman became bored one night, and to break the monotony of the night shift, he carried out the following experiment with a row

of mailboxes in the post office. These mailboxes were numbered 1 through 150, and beginning with mailbox 2, he opened the doors of all the even-numbered mailboxes. Next, beginning with mailbox 3, he went to every third mail box, opening its door if it was closed and closing it if it was open. Then he repeated this procedure with every fourth mailbox, then every fifth mailbox, and so on. When he finished, he was surprised at the distribution of closed mailboxes. Write a program to determine which mailboxes these were.

20. A *prime number* is an integer greater than 1 whose only positive divisors are 1 and the integer itself. One method for finding all the prime numbers in the range from 1 through n is known as the *Sieve of Eratosthenes*. Consider the list of numbers from 2 through n. Two is the first prime number, but the multiples of 2 (4, 6, 8, . . .) are not, and so they are crossed out in the list. The first number after 2 that was not crossed out is 3, the next prime. We then cross out from the list all higher multiples of 3 (6, 9, 12, . . .). The next number not crossed out is 5, the next prime, and so we cross out all higher multiples of 5 (10, 15, 20, . . .). We repeat this procedure until we reach the first number in the list that has not been crossed out and whose square is greater than n. All the numbers that remain in the list will be the primes from 2 through n. Write a program that uses this sieve method to find all the prime numbers from 2 through n. Run it for $n = 50$ and for $n = 500$.

21. Write a program to add two large integers of length up to 300 digits. One approach is to treat each number as a list, each of whose elements is a block of digits of the number. For example, the integer 179,534,672,198 might be stored with $Block[1] = 198$, $Block[2] = 672$, $Block[3] = 534$, and $Block[4] = 179$. Then add the integers (lists) element by element, carrying from one element to the next when necessary.

22. Proceeding as in Exercise 21, write a program to multiply two large integers of length up to 300 digits.

23. Write a recursive procedure to carry out the binary search method described in this section.

Programming Pointers

In this chapter we discussed one-dimensional arrays. It is quite common for beginning programmers to have some difficulty when using arrays. The following are some of the major points to remember:

1. *The types of the components of an array may be any predefined or user-defined type. The types of the indices may be any ordinal data type.*

2. *In an indexed variable the index must be compatible with the type specified in the array declaration.* The most common error is that of an index getting out of range. For example, suppose that the array *Number* is declared by

> **type**
>   *ListOfNumbers* = **array**[1..10] **of** *integer*;
>
> **var**
>   *Number* : *ListOfNumbers*;

and consider the following statements designed to read and count the elements of this array, where *i* is assumed to be of integer type, *Temp* is of integer type, and −999 is an end-of-data flag:

> *i* := 0;
> **repeat**
>   *i* := *i* + 1;
>   *read* (*Temp*);
>   **if** *Temp* <> −999 **then**
>   *Number*[*i*] := *Temp*
> **until** *Temp* = −999;

These statements correctly read values for the entries of *Number*, provided that there are no more than ten values preceding the end-of-data flag. But if there are more than ten values, an error results when the value of *i* reaches 11, because an attempt is made to read a value for *Number*[11], and an error message such as the following may be displayed:

```
*** Value 11 out of range, must be <= 10 ***
```

As this example demonstrates, it is important to check **boundary conditions** when processing the elements of arrays, that is, to check to make sure that the index is not out of range. Thus, the preceding set of statements could better be written as

> *i* := 0;
> **repeat**
>   *i* := *i* + 1;
>   *read* (*Temp*);
>   **if** *Temp* <> −999 **then**
>   *Number*[*i*] := *Temp*
> **until** (*Temp* = −999) **or** (*i* = 10);
> **if** *Temp* <> −999 **then**
>   *writeln* ('End-of-data flag not encountered');

3. *When reading the elements of an array of characters, remember that end-of-line marks are read as blanks.*

4. *Assignment of one array to another requires that the arrays have the same type.*

5. *To utilize memory efficiently, it is usually advisable to specify as variable parameters the formal parameters of functions and procedures that represent arrays (especially if they are large).* If value parameters are used for arrays, two copies of the array are stored in memory; also, the elements of the actual array must be copied to that of the subprogram, and this is quite time-consuming for large arrays.

Variations and Extensions

There are only a few variations from or extensions to the array-processing features of standard Pascal in other versions of Pascal. Two of them are

- Arrays of the same type may be compared with the relational operators = and <>. (UCSD).
- Arrays may be initialized in the declaration part of the program. (Turbo)

See Appendix G for additional details.

10

Strings

An average English word is four letters and a half. By hard, honest labor I've dug all the large words out of my vocabulary and shaved it down till the average is three and a half. . . .

MARK TWAIN

The word *compute* usually suggests arithmetic operations performed on numeric data; thus, computers are sometimes thought to be mere "number crunchers," devices whose only function is to process numeric information. We know that this is not the case, however, for in Chapter 1 we considered coding schemes used to represent character as well as boolean information, and in subsequent chapters we introduced some of the capabilities of Pascal for processing character and boolean data. We have also seen examples of problems that required processing character data. For example, the program in Figure 7.4 was designed to remove extra blanks from lines of text, and that in Figure 9.3 counted the occurrences of characters in a document. In each of these examples, the input data items were individual characters, and in this chapter we extend our study to problems in which the characters are grouped together in finite sequences called *strings*.

10.1 String Processing

A *string* is a finite sequence of characters drawn from the Pascal character set. Most text-editing and word-processing applications require string-processing operations such as determining the length of a string, concatenating (joining) two strings, determining the position of one string in another string, and copying a substring from a string. Some programming languages such as BASIC, FORTRAN 77, SNOBOL, and some versions of Pascal provide a predefined string data type together with predefined functions and procedures such as *length, concat, pos,* and *copy* to implement the basic operations (see the Variations and Extensions section at the end of this chapter). Standard Pascal, as we have seen, does provide the type *char* for processing single characters and does allow **string constants,** strings of characters enclosed in single quotes, which we have used in many of our sample programs to label output or to prompt the user to enter appropriate data. It does not, however, provide a predefined string data type, and strings must therefore be processed using some other structure. Arrays of character type are commonly used for this purpose, with each array element storing a single character of the string. For example, a one-dimensional array *Name* having five components of character type might be used to store the string SMITH; *Name*[1] would have the value S, *Name*[2] the value M, and so on.

In our discussion in Section 1.3 of the internal representation of data, we noted that the commonly used coding schemes ASCII and EBCDIC require only 8 bits (or 1 byte) to store a single character. In many computers, the length of each memory word is more than 8 bits, and thus a word can store more than one character. Some Pascal compilers, however, allocate an entire memory word for each variable, in particular for variables of character type. Because the values assigned to such variables require only 8 bits for storage, this is an inefficient use of memory. For example, in a 32-bit word machine, only 8 bits of a 32-bit word are used to store a character, and thus three fourths of each such word is wasted. Memory utilization in such machines can be improved by using **packed arrays** in which several array elements or characters are stored in a single word.

To illustrate the difference between unpacked and packed arrays, suppose that arrays *U* and *P* are declared by

```
type
    UnpackedCharArray = array[1..8] of char;
    PackedCharArray = packed array[1..8] of char;

var
    U : UnpackedCharArray;
    P : PackedCharArray;
```

For some computers, the array *U* would be allocated eight memory words:

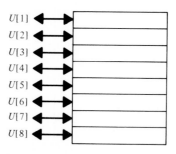

For a 32-bit machine, however, the packed array need be allocated only two memory words, since each word can store four characters:

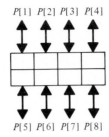

Memory is obviously used more efficiently in the second case than in the first, but the address translation that must be performed to locate an array element is more complex. Not only must the address of the memory word in which that element is stored be calculated, but the number of the byte within that word containing the component also must be determined.

The usual array operations can also be applied to packed arrays.[1] For example, packed arrays of the same type may appear in an assignment statement of the form

   $array1 := array2$

This assignment statement would not be valid, however, if either *array1* or *array2* was packed and the other was not.

Although arrays of any type may be specified as packed arrays, the most important use of packed arrays is to process strings. Thus we restrict our attention to packed arrays of characters in this chapter. (Packed arrays of other types are considered in Appendix F.)

A packed array of type *char* whose index type is a subrange of the form $1..n$ for some integer $n > 1$ will be called a **string** type.[2] For example, consider the following type definitions:

type
    A = **packed array**[1..10] **of** *char*;
    B = **array**[1..10] **of** *char*;
    C = **packed array**[0..9] **of** *char*;
    D = **packed array**[1..10] **of** 'A'..'Z';
    E = **packed array**[1..1] **of** *char*;

Only type A is a string type. B, C, D, and E are not string types because arrays of type B are not packed; the subscript type for C does not begin with 1; the component type for D is not *char*; and the index type for E does not have two or more values.

A string constant may be used to assign a value to an array of string type, provided its length (number of characters) is the same as the number of array

---

[1] One exception is that a component of a packed array may not be an actual parameter that corresponds to a variable formal parameter.
[2] Most versions of Pascal that provide a predefined string type also allow packed character arrays for processing strings. The two string types may or may not be compatible.

elements. For example, if the array *Name* is declared by

type
    NameString = **packed array**[1..10] **of** *char*;

var
    Name : *NameString*;

then the assignment statement

    Name := 'John Smith'

is valid. The string constant 'J. Doe' cannot be assigned to *Name* because it has only six characters. If four blanks are appended to this string, however, the resulting string may be assigned to *Name*:

    Name := 'J.ḃDoeḃḃḃḃ'

(where ḃ denotes a blank). Similarly, the string constant 'Johann VanderDoe' cannot be assigned to *Name* because it has more than ten characters. Thus we see one of the drawbacks of using arrays to process strings: Strings need not have a fixed length, but arrays must have a fixed number of elements. (In versions of Pascal that provide a predefined string data type, lengths of strings are allowed to vary dynamically.)

This difficulty also arises in comparing strings. Two values of string type may be compared with the relational operators $<$, $>$, $=$, $<=$, $>=$, and $<>$, *provided they have the same length.* Thus,

    'cat' $<$ 'dog'

is a valid boolean expression and is evaluated by comparing, character by character, the strings 'cat' and 'dog', using the collating sequence described in Section 4.2. Thus this boolean expression is true because 'c' precedes 'd' in the collating sequence. Similarly, the boolean expression

    'cat' $>$ 'car'

is true because 't' follows 'r' in the collating sequence. Note, however, that the strings 'apples' and 'oranges' cannot be compared because they have different lengths; that is, they do not have the same number of characters. The boolean expression

    'applesḃ' $<$ 'oranges'

is valid, however, and is true. Similarly, if each of *Name1* and *Name2* is of type *NameString,* then the following are valid boolean expressions:

    Name1 $<$ 'John Smith'

    Name2 $<>$ 'applesḃḃḃḃ'

    Name1 $>=$ *Name2*

String values may also appear in the output list of a *write* or *writeln* statement. We have already used this feature when string constants appeared in an output statement such as

writeln ('Mean of the scores is ', *MeanScore*:3:1);

The name of an array of string type may also appear in the output list. Thus if *Name* and *EmpNumber* are declared by

    const
      StringLimit = 12;

    type
      String = **packed array**[1..*StringLimit*] **of** *char*;

    var
      Name : *String*;
      EmpNumber : *integer*;

and have values JohnbDoebbbb and 13520, respectively, then the statement

writeln (*Name*, *EmpNumber*:6)

will produce the output

<u>John Doe   13520</u>

Although standard Pascal requires that string values be allowed as items in output lists of *write* and *writeln* statements, it makes no similar provision for the input of strings. Consequently, some versions of Pascal do not allow the name of a variable of string type to appear in the input list of a *read* or *readln* statement. Thus a statement such as

readln(Name)

would not be allowed. Instead, the array elements must be read individually:

    for *i* := 1 **to** 12 **do**
      read (*Name*[*i*])

If the string

<u>John Doe   </u>

is entered, then the value assigned to *Name* is the string JohnbDoebbbb. The value of *Name*[1] is the character J, the value of *Name*[2] is o, and so on.[3]

---

[3] Some compilers do not allow the elements of a packed array to be read. In this case, values can be read into an unpacked array, and these elements then must be copied into the packed array.

In this example, twelve characters must be read. Although we may prefer to enter only the name John Doe, we must also enter characters for the other four elements of the array. Thus we entered four trailing blanks to be assigned to *Name*[9], . . . , *Name*[12].

Entering blanks or some other characters to fill up the positions of a character array is rather tedious. We prefer to enter only the characters in which we are interested and have the program assign blanks to the remaining positions. If we signal the end of the string being read with an end-of-line character (generated by depressing the return key), we can use the *eoln* function as indicated in the following procedure.[4] Recall that *eoln* has the value true if the end of the current input line has been reached and is false otherwise.

procedure *ReadString* (**var** *Str* : *String*; *MaxString* : *integer*);

  (∗ Procedure to read characters into string variable *Str* until
     an end of line is encountered or the upper limit *MaxString*
     on the length of *Str* is reached. Any positions for which
     no characters are read will be filled with blanks. ∗)

var
  i : *integer*;

begin (∗ *ReadString* ∗)
  for *i* := 1 **to** *MaxString* **do**
    if not *eoln* **then**
      read (*Str*[*i*])
    else
      Str[*i*] := ' ';
  readln
end (∗ *ReadString* ∗);

Suppose, for example, that *Name* has been declared by

const
  StringLimit = 12;

type
  String = **packed array**[1..*StringLimit*] **of** *char*;

var
  Name : *String*;

and consider the procedure call

  ReadString (*Name*, *StringLimit*);

If the string

`John Doe`

---

[4] Some versions of Pascal allow a value to be read for a string variable by using the variable name in a *readln* statement such as *readln* (*Name*). In this case, the characters are read and stored in the packed array in the same way as for procedure *ReadString*; that is, characters are read and stored until either the array is full or an end-of-line character is read, which then causes blank filling to occur.

is entered, the eight characters J, o, h, n, b̷, D, o, and e are read and assigned to *Name*[1], *Name*[2], . . . , *Name*[8]. Because the end of the input line is now encountered, the value of *eoln* is true. No more characters are read, and blanks are assigned to *Name*[9], . . . , *Name*[12].

In our discussion of input in Chapter 7, we observed that values for the variables in the list of an input statement are obtained from the standard system file *input*. When this file is loaded from data lines entered by the user during execution, a data pointer is positioned at the beginning of the file and advances through the file as the values are read. When the end of an input line is reached, an **end-of-line mark** is entered into the input file. For example, the two lines of input

```
John Doe
Mary Smith
```

produce the following contents in the file *input*:

where, as before, ● denotes an end-of-line mark and ↑ represents the data pointer. When the procedure *ReadString* is executed, characters are read until the data pointer reaches the first end-of-line mark; then blank filling begins.

The *readln* statement then advances the data pointer beyond the end-of-line mark so that *eoln* becomes false. If this statement were omitted, *eoln* would remain true and subsequent calls to procedure *ReadString* would return strings consisting of all blanks.

The program in Figure 10.1 uses the techniques described in this section to implement a simple cryptographic scheme, that is, a scheme for coding a message as a scrambled sequence of characters, known as a **cryptogram**. A positive integer is added to the code for each character in the message, and the **mod** operation is used to keep the resulting value in the range of ASCII codes for printable characters, 32 through 126.

```
PROGRAM Coder (input, output);

(**************************************************************

   This program scrambles a message by converting each character of
   the message to its numeric code, adding an integer to this code,
   then converting the resulting number back to a character.

***************************************************************)
```

Figure 10.1

Figure 10.1 (cont.)

```
CONST
   StringLimit = 80;    (* limit on length of strings *)
   EndOfString = '#';   (* end-of-string mark *)

TYPE
   String = PACKED ARRAY [1..StringLimit] OF char;

VAR
   Message : String;       (* message to be scrambled *)
   NewCode,                (* new code for character *)
   Scrambler,              (* integer to be added to scramble message *)
   i : integer;            (* index *)
   MoreChars : boolean;    (* signals end of message *)

PROCEDURE ReadString (VAR Str : String; MaxString : integer);

   (**************************************************************

      Procedure to read characters into string variable Str until
      an end-of-line mark is encountered or the upper limit
      MaxString on the length of Str is reached.  Any positions
      for which no characters are read will be filled with blanks.

   **************************************************************)

   VAR
      i : integer;          (* index *)

   BEGIN (* ReadString *)
      FOR i := 1 TO MaxString DO
         IF NOT eoln THEN
               read (Str[i])
         ELSE
            Str[i] := ' '
   END (* ReadString *);

BEGIN (* main program *)
   writeln ('Enter message to be scrambled with ', EndOfString,
            ' at the end:');
   ReadString (Message, StringLimit);
   write ('Enter positive integer to use in scrambling:  ');
   readln (Scrambler);
   i := 1;
  MoreChars := true;
   WHILE MoreChars AND (Message[i] <> EndOfString) DO
      BEGIN
         NewCode := ord(Message[i]) + Scrambler;
         IF NewCode >= 127 THEN
            NewCode := 32 + NewCode MOD 127;
         Message[i] := chr(NewCode);
         i := i + 1;
         MoreChars := (i >= StringLimit)
      END (* WHILE *);
   writeln;
   writeln ('Coded message:');
   writeln (Message)
END (* main program *).
```

Figure 10.1   (cont.)

```
Sample run (assuming ASCII):

Enter message to be scrambled with # at the end:
THE REDCOATS ARE COMING.#
Enter positive integer to use in scrambling:  5

Coded message:
YMJ%WJIHTFYX%FWJ%HTRNSL3#
```

Because access to the elements of a packed array may be more time-consuming than that of an unpacked array, the method used to input the elements of the packed array *Str* in procedure *ReadString* may be inefficient and, as we have noted, may not be allowed with some compilers. This difficulty can be avoided by reading each character into a temporary character variable and then assigning it to the appropriate array element. For example, the procedure *ReadString* could be modified by declaring a local variable *TempChar* of type *char* and replacing the **if** statement with

> **if not** *eoln* **then**
> > **begin**
> > > *read* (*TempChar*);
> > > *Str*[*i*] : = *TempChar*
> > **end** (∗ **if** ∗)
> **else**
> > *Str*[*i*] : = ' '

Alternatively, we could use the predefined Pascal procedures *pack* and *unpack* to transfer elements between an unpacked array and a packed array. These procedures are described in Appendix F.

10.2   A Package of Basic String-Processing Functions and Procedures

As we noted in the preceding section, standard Pascal does not provide a predefined string type or procedures and functions that implement the basic string operations, with the exception of *write* and *writeln* for the output of strings. As users of versions of Pascal that provide these features will attest, such functions and procedures are very useful in text-processing applications, especially in text-editing and word-processing programs. In this section we describe a "package" of basic string-processing functions and procedures that can be used in those versions of Pascal that do not provide them. It assumes that strings are implemented as described in the preceding section, that is, that the type *String* is defined by a type definition of the form

> *String* = **packed array**[1..*StringLimit*] **of** *char*;

for some constant *StringLimit*.

Input/Output.   As we observed in the last section, strings may be displayed by including them in the output list of *write* and *writeln* statements. No input procedure for reading strings is provided in standard Pascal, however, and so a procedure like *ReadString* described in the preceding section must be used.

Length.   Padding strings with blanks when assigning a value to a string value or reading a string value using a procedure like *ReadString* makes it difficult to implement the length operation, because trailing blanks that are part of the string cannot be distinguished from those that are used to fill the unused array positions. If these trailing blanks are ignored, the length operation can be easily implemented by the following Pascal function:

> **function** *Length* (*Str* : *String*) : *integer*;
>
> > (∗ Function to determine the length of *Str*, assuming
> > that trailing blanks are not counted in strings. ∗)
>
> **var**
> > *i* : *integer*;
> > *EndOfString* : *boolean*;
>
> **begin** (∗ *Length* ∗)
> > *i* := *StringLimit*;
> > *EndOfString* := *false*;
> > **while** (*i* > 0) **and not** *EndOfString* **do**
> > > **if** *Str*[*i*] = ' ' **then**
> > > > *i* := *i* − 1
> > > **else**
> > > > *EndOfString* := *true*;
> > *Length* := *i*
> **end** (∗ *Length* ∗);

Concatenation.   The concatenation of a string *Str1* with a string *Str2* is obtained by appending *Str2* to *Str1*. For example, if *Str1* is the string 'list' and *Str2* is 'en', the concatenation of *Str1* with *Str2* is

> 'listen'

and the concatenation of *Str2* with *Str1* is

> 'enlist'

If the sum of the lengths of two strings does not exceed the maximum string length allowed, the strings can be concatenated by copying the characters in the first string followed by those in the second string into a third string. The following procedure implements this concatenation operation:

> **procedure** *Concat* (*Str1* : *String*; *Num1* : *integer*;
> >   *Str2* : *String*; *Num2* : *integer*; **var** *Str3* : *String*);
>
> > (∗ Procedure to concatenate *Str1* having *Num1* characters with *Str2*
> > having *Num2* characters and return the resulting string *Str3*. ∗)

```
var
    i : integer;

begin (* Concat *)
    if (Num1 + Num2) <= StringLimit then
        begin
            (* copy Str1 to Str3; blanks used to pad Str1
               are also used to pad Str3 *)
            Str3 := Str1;
            (* copy the Num2 characters of Str2 into Str3
               beginning at position Num1 + 1 *)
            for i := 1 to Num2 do
                Str3[Num1 + i] := Str2[i]
        end (* if *)
    else
        writeln ('Strings too long')
end (* Concat *);
```

Copy.   The copy or substring operation retrieves a (sub)string of a specified length from a given string beginning at some specified position. For example, if *Str* is the string 'ABCDEFG', the substring of *Str* of length 3 beginning at position 2 is

'BCD'

The copy operation should produce a copy of this substring without changing *Str* itself.

A procedure to implement the copy operation is as follows:

procedure *Copy* (*Str* : *String*; *p*, *n* : *integer*; **var** *Substr* : *String*);

(* Procedure to copy the *n* characters beginning in position *p* of *Str* into *Substr*. *)

```
var
    i, Last : integer;

begin (* Copy *)
    Last := p + n - 1; (* position of last character to copy *)
    if Last <= StringLimit then
        begin
            (* copy required characters from Str into Substr
               and pad Substr with blanks *)
            for i := 1 to n do
                Substr[i] := Str[p + i - 1];
            for i := n + 1 to StringLimit do
                Substr[i] := ' '
        end (* if *)
    else
        writeln ('Index out of range')
end (* Copy *);
```

Position. The position or **index** operation determines the starting location of the first occurrence of one string within a second string, or it gives the value 0 if the first string does not appear in the second string. As an illustration of a "brute force" implementation of this operation, suppose we wish to find the position of *Str1* = 'abcabd' in *Str2* = 'abcabcabdabba'. The search for *Str1* in *Str2* begins at the first position of each. The first five characters match, but a mismatch occurs when the sixth characters are compared:

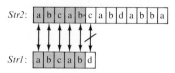

We then backtrack and start the search over again at the second character in *Str2*:

A mismatch occurs immediately, so we must backtrack again and restart the search with the third character in *Str2*:

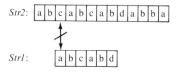

Once again, a mismatch occurs, so we backtrack again and restart at the fourth character in *Str2*:

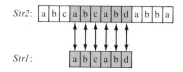

Now the six characters in *Str1* match the corresponding characters in positions 4 through 9 in *Str2*, and thus the index of *Str1* in *Str2* is 4.

The following function implements this approach:

function *Pos(Str1 : String; Num1 : integer;*
              Str2 : String; Num2 : integer) : integer;

    (* Function to determine the index of *Str1* having *Num1*
       characters in *Str2* having *Num2* characters. *)

```
var
    i, j, Index : integer;

begin (* Pos *)
    Index := 1;    (* beginning position of Str1 in Str2 *)
    i := 1;        (* index running through Str1 *)
    j := 1;        (* index running through Str2 *)
    while (i <= Num1) and (j <= Num2) do
        if Str1[i] = Str2[j] then (* continue matching *)
            begin
                i := i + 1;
                j := j + 1
            end (* if *)
        else (* backtrack and start over at next position in Str2 *)
            begin
                Index := Index + 1;
                j := Index;
                i := 1
            end (* else *);
    if i > Num1 then        (* Str1 found in Str2 *)
        Pos := Index
    else                    (* Str1 not found in Str2 *)
        Pos := 0
end (* Pos *);
```

Insert. The insert operation modifies a string by inserting another string into it at some specified position. For example, inserting $Str1 = $ 'XY' into the string $Str2 = $ 'abc' at position 3 changes $Str2$ to 'abXYc'; inserting it at position 1 changes Str to 'XYabc'. Insertion at a position greater than the length of Str is not permitted; the concatenation operation can be used to do this.

The following procedure implements this operation:

```
procedure Insert (Str1 : String; var Str2 : String; Position : integer);

    (* Procedure to insert Str1 in Str2 at the specified Position. It uses
       the function Length and procedures Copy and Concat. *)

    var
        First, Last : String; (* first and last parts of Str2 *)
        FSize, LSize,          (* size of First, Last *)
        Len : integer;         (* length of Str1 *)

    begin (* Insert *)
        if (Position > 0) and (Position <= Length(Str2) then
            begin
                FSize := Position - 1;
                LSize := Length(Str2) - FSize;
```

```
            Len := Length (Str1);
            Copy (Str2, 1, FSize, First);
            Copy (Str2, Position, LSize, Last);
            Concat (First, FSize, Str1, Len, First);
            Concat (First, FSize + Len, Last, LSize, Str2)
        end (* if *)
    else
        writeln ('Position to insert negative or too large')
end (* Insert *);
```

Delete.   The delete operation modifies a string by deleting from it a substring of some specified length at some specified position. For example, deleting the substring of length 3 at position 2 from Str = 'compute' changes Str into 'cute'. Deleting characters beyond the end of the string, that is, characters in positions greater than the length of the string, is not allowed.

The following procedure implements the delete operation:

procedure *Delete* (**var** *Str* : *String*; *Position*, *Size* : *integer*);

(* Procedure to delete a substring of the specified *Size* from string *Str* at the specified *Position*. It uses the function *Length* and procedures *Copy* and *Concat*. *)

```
var
    First, Last : String;         (* first and last parts of Str *)
    FSize, LSize,                 (* size of First, Last *)
    Len : integer;                (* length of Str *)

begin (* Delete *)
    Len := Length(Str);
    if (Position > 0) and (Size >= 0) and
       (Size <= Len − Position + 1) then
        begin
            FSize := Position − 1;
            Copy (Str, 1, FSize, First);
            Position := Position + Size;
            LSize := Len − Position + 1;
            Copy (Str, Position, LSize, Last;
            Concat (First, FSize, Last, LSize, Str)
        end (* if *)
    else
        writeln ('Starting position or size negative or substring too long')
end (* Delete *);
```

10.3 Example: Text Editing

The preparation of textual material such as letters, books, and computer programs often requires the insertion, deletion, and replacement of parts of the text. The software of most computer systems includes an ***editor*** that makes it easy to carry out these operations. To illustrate how these text-editing operations can be performed in Pascal, we consider the problem of implementing the change or replacement text-editing function. More precisely, we consider how to replace a specified substring in a given line of text with another string.

A level-one algorithm for solving this problem is

TEXT-EDITING ALGORITHM

1. Open the input file *TextFile* and a new file *NewTextFile* for the edited output.
2. While the end of *TextFile* has not been reached, do the following:
   a. Read the next line from *TextFile*.
   b. Edit the line of text and write it to *NewTextFile*.

The predefined procedures *reset* and *rewrite* can be used to open the files as required in Step 1, and the procedure *ReadString* developed in Section 10.1 can be easily modified to read a line from a file, as required in Step 2, by simply changing the *read* statement to

read (*TextFile*, *Str*[*i*])

The heart of the algorithm is the editing task in Step 2(b), and so we now develop an algorithm for it.

The form of the editing commands that the user enters is

old-string/*new-string*/

where *old-string* is the part of the current text line that is to be replaced by *new-string*. An algorithm for processing such editing commands is as follows:

Edit

1. While more editing is required, do the following:
   a. Read an edit change and extract *OldString* and *NewString*.
   b. Find the *Location* of *OldString* in the current text line.
   c. If *OldString* is not found in this line, then
        Display a message indicating this fact.
     Otherwise
        Replace the first occurrence of *OldString* in the line
        with *NewString*.
2. Write the edited line to *NewTextFile*.

The processing of edit commands required in Step 1(a) of this algorithm can be carried out using the basic string operations length, position, copy, and delete described in the preceding sections. An algorithm for this is

GetEditChange

1. Read an *EditChange* of the form *OldString*/*NewString*/.
2. Calculate the length of *OldString* by determining the position of the first slash (/) in *EditChange*.

3. Use the copy operation to copy *OldString* from *EditChange*.
4. Delete *OldString* and the first / from *EditChange*.
5. Find the length of *NewString*.
6. Use the copy operation to extract *NewString* from *EditChange*.

The string operations length, insert, delete, and concatenate can be used to carry out the replacement operation required in Step 1(c) of the editing algorithm, as follows:

Replace

1. Delete the first occurrence of *OldString* from *TextLine*.
2. If this occurrence was not at the end of *TextLine*, then
   Use the insert operation to insert *NewString* in *TextLine*.
   Otherwise
   Use the concatenate operation to append *NewString* to *TextLine*.
3. Display the edited line to the user.

The program in Figure 10.2 uses these algorithms to solve the text-editing problem. Its organization is shown in the following structure diagram:

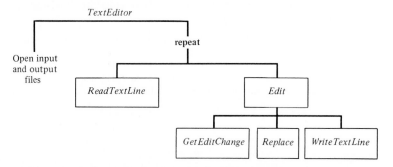

It assumes the availability of a collection of string-processing functions and procedures like those described in the preceding section. The sample run shows that in addition to string replacements, the program can be used to make insertions and deletions. For example, changing the substring

A N

in the line of text

A NATION CONCEIVED IN LIBERTY AND AND DEDICATED

to

A NEW N

yields the edited line

A NEW NATION CONCEIVED IN LIBERTY AND AND DEDICATED

Entering the edit change

AND //

changes the substring

ANDƀ

(where ƀ denotes a blank) in the line of text to an empty string containing no characters, and so the edited result is

A NEW NATION CONCEIVED IN LIBERTY AND DEDICATED

```
PROGRAM TextEditor (input, output, TextFile, NewTextFile);

(*******************************************************************

   Program to perform some basic text-editing functions on lines of
   text.  The basic operation is replacing a substring of the text
   with another string.  This replacement is accomplished by a
   command of the form
                        OldString/NewString/
   OldString specifies the substring in the text to be replaced
   with the specified string NewString; NewString may be an empty
   string; this causes the substring OldString (if found) to be
   deleted.  Neither of OldString or NewString may end with a blank.
   The text lines are read from TextFile, and after editing is
   completed, the edited lines are written to NewTextFile.  The
   program used the package of string-processing functions and
   procedures described in Section 10.2.

********************************************************************)

CONST
   StringLimit = 80;  (* maximum length of lines of text *)

TYPE
   String = PACKED ARRAY[1..StringLimit] OF char;

VAR
   TextFile,              (* file of original text *)
   NewTextFile : text;    (* file of edited text *)
   TextLine : String;     (* line of text to be edited *)

(*******************************************************************
 ********************************************************************
 ** Insert the package of string-processing functions and procedures **
 **                      ReadString                               **
 **                      Length                                   **
 **                      Concat                                   **
 **                      Copy                                     **
 **                      Pos                                      **
 **                      Insert                                   **
 **                      Delete                                   **
 ** here.                                                         **
 ********************************************************************
 ********************************************************************)
```

Figure 10.2

Figure 10.2 (cont.)

```
PROCEDURE ReadTextLine (VAR TextFile : text; VAR TextLine : String);

   (****************************************************************

      Procedure to read and echo a line of text from TextFile.

   ****************************************************************)

   VAR
      i : integer;          (* index *)

   BEGIN (* ReadTextLine *)
      FOR i := 1 TO StringLimit DO
         IF NOT eoln(TextFile) THEN
            read (TextFile, TextLine[i])
         ELSE
            TextLine[i] := ' ';
      readln (TextFile);
      writeln;
      writeln (TextLine)
   END (* ReadTextLine *);

PROCEDURE Edit (TextLine : String);

   (****************************************************************

      Procedure to carry out the editing operations on TextLine.
      After editing is completed, edited line is written to
      NewTextFile.

   ****************************************************************)

   VAR
      OldString,               (* old string in edit change *)
      NewString : String;      (* new string in edit change *)
      Location : integer;      (* location of OldString in TextLine *)
      Response : char;         (* user response *)

   PROCEDURE GetEditChange (VAR OldString, NewString : String);

      (****************************************************************

         Procedure to read the edit change of the form
                   OldString/NewString/
         It returns OldString and NewString.

      ****************************************************************)

      VAR
         SlashStr,               (* string beginning with / *)
         EditChange : String;    (* editing change *)
         i,                      (* index *)
         OldLength,              (* length of OldString *)
         NewLength : integer;    (* length of NewString *)
```

Figure 10.2 (cont.)

```
    BEGIN (* GetEditChange *)
       writeln ('Edit change:  ');
       ReadString (EditChange, StringLimit);
       SlashStr[1] := '/';
       FOR i := 2 TO StringLimit DO
          SlashStr[i] := ' ';
       OldLength := Pos(SlashStr, 1,  EditChange, Length(EditChange)) - 1;
       Copy(EditChange, 1, OldLength, OldString);
       Delete(EditChange, 1, OldLength + 1);
       NewLength := Length(EditChange) - 1;
       Copy(EditChange, 1, NewLength, NewString)
    END (* GetEditChange *);

PROCEDURE Replace (VAR TextLine: String; OldString, NewString : String;
                   Start : integer);

   (**************************************************************

      Procedure to replace a substring OldString beginning at
      position Start of TextLine with NewString.

    **************************************************************)

    VAR
       LenText,                (* length of TextLine *)
       LenOld : integer;       (* length of OldString *)

    BEGIN (* Replace *)
       LenText := Length(TextLine);
       LenOld := Length(OldString);
       Delete(TextLine, Start, LenOld);
       LenText := LenText - LenOld;
       IF Start <= LenText THEN
          Insert(NewString, TextLine, Start)
       ELSE
          Concat(TextLine, LenText, NewString, Length(NewString), TextLine);
       writeln (TextLine)
    END (* Replace *);

BEGIN (* Edit *)
   write ('Edit this line?  ');
   readln (Response);
   WHILE (Response = 'Y') OR (Response = 'y') DO
      BEGIN
         GetEditChange (OldString, NewString);
         Location := Pos(OldString, Length(OldString),
                         TextLine, Length(TextLine));
         IF Location = 0 THEN
            writeln ('Not found:  ', OldString)
         ELSE
            Replace (TextLine, OldString, NewString, Location);
         write ('More editing (Y or N)?  ');
         readln (Response)
      END (* WHILE *);
   writeln (NewTextFile, TextLine)
END (* Edit *);
```

Figure 10.2 (cont.)

```
BEGIN (* main program *)
   reset (TextFile);
   rewrite (NewTextFile);
   WHILE NOT eof(TextFile) DO
      BEGIN
         ReadTextLine (TextFile, TextLine);
         Edit (TextLine)
      END (* WHILE *)
END (* main program *).
```

Listing of TextFile:

```
FOURSCORE AND FIVE YEARS AGO, OUR MOTHERS
BROUGHT FORTH ON CONTINENT
A NATION CONCEIVED IN LIBERTY AND AND DEDICATED
TO THE PREPOSITION THAT ALL MEN
ARE CREATED EQUAL.
```

Sample run:

```
FOURSCORE AND FIVE YEARS AGO, OUR MOTHERS
Edit this line?
Y
Edit change:
FIVE/SEVEN/
FOURSCORE AND SEVEN YEARS AGO, OUR MOTHERS
More editing (Y or N)?
Y
Edit change:
MOTHER/FATHER/
FOURSCORE AND SEVEN YEARS AGO, OUR FATHERS
More editing (Y or N)?
N

BROUGHT FORTH ON CONTINENT
Edit this line?
Y
Edit change:
ON C/ON THIS C/
BROUGHT FORTH ON THIS CONTINENT
More editing (Y or N)?
N

A NATION CONCEIVED IN LIBERTY AND AND DEDICATED
Edit this line?
Y
Edit change:
A N/A NEW N/
A NEW NATION CONCEIVED IN LIBERTY AND AND DEDICATED
More editing (Y or N)?
Y
Edit change:
AND //
A NEW NATION CONCEIVED IN LIBERTY AND DEDICATED
More editing (Y or N)?
N
```

Figure 10.2 (cont.)

```
TO THE PREPOSITION THAT ALL MEN
Edit this line?
Y
Edit change:
PRE/PRO/
TO THE PROPOSITION THAT ALL MEN
More editing (Y or N)?
N

ARE CREATED EQUAL.
Edit this line?
N
```

Listing of NewTextFile:

```
FOURSCORE AND SEVEN YEARS AGO, OUR FATHERS
BROUGHT FORTH ON THIS CONTINENT
A NEW NATION CONCEIVED IN LIBERTY AND DEDICATED
TO THE PROPOSITION THAT ALL MEN
ARE CREATED EQUAL.
```

Exercises

1. Assume that the following declarations have been made:

type
  $Color$ = (*red, yellow, blue, green, white, black*);
  $ColorCodeArray$ = **packed array**[*Color*] **of** *char*;
  $ArrayOfCharacters$ = **array**[1..10] **of** *char*;
  $StringType$ = **packed array**[1..10] **of** *char*;

var
  $ColorCode$: *ColorCodeArray*;
  $CharArray$: *ArrayOfCharacters*;
  $TextLine$: *StringType*;
  Col : *Color*;
  i, j : *integer*;

Assume also that the following data are entered:

ABCDEFG
HI$

For each of the following, tell what value (if any) will be assigned to each array element, or explain why an error occurs.

(a) **for** $i := 1$ **to** 7 **do**
      read (*TextLine*[i]);
    readln;
    for $i := 8$ **to** 10 **do**
      read (*TextLine*[i]);

(b) for *Col* := *black* **downto** *red* **do**
     read (*ColorCode*[*Col*]);

(c) for *i* := 1 **to** 10 **do**
     read (*TextLine*[*i*]);

(d) for *i* := 10 **downto** 1 **do**
     read (*TextLine*[*i*]);

(e) for *Col* := *red* **to** *black* **do**
     read (*ColorCode*[*Col*]);
   for *Col* := *red* **to** *black* **do**
     TextLine[*ord*(*Col*) + 1] := *ColorCode*[*Col*];
   for *i* := 7 **to** 10 **do**
     read (*TextLine*[*i*]);

(f) for *Col* := *red* **to** *black* **do**
     read (*ColorCode*[*Col*]);
   TextLine := *ColorCode*;

(g) for *i* := 1 **to** 10 **do**
     read (*CharArray*[*i*]);
   TextLine := *CharArray*;

(h) for *i* := 1 **to** 10 **do**
     read (*CharArray*[*i*]);
   write (*CharArray*);

(i) for *i* := 1 **to** 10 **do**
     if not *eoln* **then**
       read (*TextLine*[*i*])
     else
       TextLine[*i*] := '¢';

(j) for *i* := 1 **to** 10 **do**
     if not *eoln* **then**
       read (*TextLine*[*i*])
     else
       readln;

(k) for *i* := 1 **to** 5 **do**
     if not *eoln* **then**
       read (*CharArray*[*i*], *CharArray*[*i* + 5])
     else
      begin
       CharArray[*i*] := '$';
       CharArray[*i* + 5] := '¢'
      end;

(l) $i := 0$;
　　for $j := 1$ **to** 2 **do**
　　　begin
　　　　while not *eoln* **do**
　　　　　begin
　　　　　　$i := i + 1$;
　　　　　　read (*TextLine*[i])
　　　　　end (∗ **while** ∗);
　　　　readln
　　　end (∗ **for** ∗);
(m) $i := 0$;
　　repeat
　　　while not *eoln* **do**
　　　　begin
　　　　　$i := i + 1$;
　　　　　read (*TextLine*[i])
　　　　end (∗ **while** ∗);
　　　readln
　　until *TextLine*[i] = '$';

2. Write a procedure to convert a string of lowercase and uppercase letters into all lowercase letters.

3. Write a program to count all double-letter occurrences in a given line of text.

4. The local chapter of the Know-Nothing party maintains a file of names and addresses of its contributors. Each line of the file contains the following items of information in the order indicated:

> Last name: a string of length 12
> First name: a string of length 10
> Middle initial: a character
> Street address: a string of length 15
> City and state: a string of length 20
> Zip code: an integer

Each of the strings is assumed to be padded with blanks as necessary; for example,

Doebbbbbbbbbb JohnbbbbbbbQ 123bSomeStreetbAnyTown,bAnyStatebbb12345

Write a program that reads each line of the file and produces a mailing label having the format

> John Q. Doe
> 123 SomeStreet
> AnyTown, AnyState 12345

5. Repeat Exercise 4 but assume that the strings are not padded with blanks in the file; rather, all of the items in each line are separated by

some delimiter such as #; for example,

Doe#John#Q#123 SomeStreet#AnyTown, AnyState#12345

Use the basic string operations to locate these delimiters and to split this string into its individual parts so that a mailing label of the following form can be printed:

John Q. Doe
123 SomeStreet
AnyTown, AnyState 12345

6. Write a program to print a "personalized" contest letter like those frequently received in the mail. It might have a format like that of the following sample, with the underlined locations filled in with appropriate data:

Mr. John Q. Doe
123 SomeStreet
AnyTown, AnyState 12345

Dear Mr. Doe:

How would you like to see a brand new Cadillac parked in front of 123 SomeStreet in AnyTown, AnyState? Impossible, you say? No, it isn't, Mr. Doe. Simply keep the enclosed raffle ticket and validate it by sending a $100.00 tax-deductible political contribution and 10 labels from Shyster & Sons chewing tobacco. Not only will you become eligible for the drawing to be conducted on February 29 by the independent firm of G.Y.P. Shyster, but you will also be helping to reelect Sam Shyster. That's all there is to it, John. You may be a winner!!!

7. Write a program that permits the input of a name consisting of a first name, a middle name or initial, and a last name, in that order, and then prints the last name, followed by a comma, and then the first and middle initials, each followed by a period. For example, the input John H. Doe should produce Doe, J. H.

8. The encoding scheme used in this section to produce a cryptogram consists simply of adding a specified integer to the code of each character of the message. This is a special case of the technique known as *keyword* encoding, in which a sequence of integers corresponding to the characters of a specified keyword is added in order to the codes of the message characters. To illustrate, if the keyword is ABC and the message is MEETATNOON, the codes for A, B, and C are added to the codes for M, E, and E, respectively, and then added to the codes for T, A, and T, respectively, and so forth, producing the cryptogram NGHUCWOQRO (assuming this is an ASCII machine). Write a program to implement this keyword method of encoding.

9. Another method of encoding uses substitutions, for example,

letter: A B C D E F G H I J K L M N O P Q R S T U V W X Y Z
substitute: T F H X Q J E M U P I D C K V B A O L R Z W G N S Y

Each letter of the input message is then replaced with its substitute, for example,

message: T H E R E D C O A T S A R E C O M I N G
cryptogram: R M Q O O Q X H V T R L T O Q H V C U K E

Write a program that permits the input of either a message or a cryptogram and then encodes or decodes it by using substitutions.

10. There are 3 teaspoons in a tablespoon, 4 tablespoons in a quarter of a cup, 2 cups in a pint, and 2 pints in a quart. Write a program to convert units in cooking. The program should call for the input of the amount, the units used, and the new units desired. For example, the input 0.5, CUPS, TEASPOONS asks for the conversion of one-half cup to teaspoons.

11. Frequency counts can be graphically displayed by using a *histogram*. For example, if the frequency counts of persons in three education levels, high school, college, and graduate, were 15, 8, and 12, respectively, these could be displayed by the following histogram:

High School: XXXXXXXXXXXXXXX
College: XXXXXXXX
Graduate: XXXXXXXXXXXX

Write a program to read several pairs of strings and frequencies and to plot a histogram displaying the information.

12. Write a program to convert ordinary Hindu-Arabic numerals into Roman numerals and vice versa. (I = 1, V = 5, X = 10, L = 50, C = 100, D = 500, and M = 1,000.)

13. A string is said to be a *palindrome* if it does not change when the order of characters in the string is reversed. For example,

MADAM

463364

ABLE WAS I ERE I SAW ELBA

are palindromes. Write a program to read a string and then determine whether it is a palindrome.

14. Repeat Exercise 13, but this time use a recursive procedure to determine whether a string is a palindrome.

15. Graphs of equations can also be plotted by using the computer. For example, Figure 10.3 shows computer-generated plots of

$$Y = X^2 \text{ for } -3 \leq X \leq 3$$

and

$$Y = X^3 \text{ for } -2 \leq X \leq 2$$

using an X increment of 0.25 in each case. Note that for convenience, the X axis has been printed vertically and the Y axis horizontally. Write a program to produce a similar plot of a given equation, using

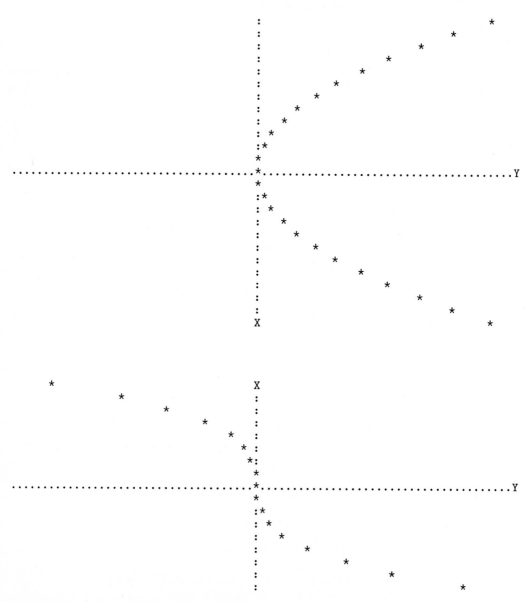

Figure 10.3. Plots of $Y = X^2$ and $Y = X^3$.

a packed character array with the number of array elements equal to the width of the page. For each X value, set all of the array elements equal to blanks, or equal to the marks comprising the Y axis if $X = 0$; then set one array element equal to the X axis mark and another equal to the plotting character; the position of this latter array element should correspond to the Y coordinate of the point on the graph for that X value.

16. Write a program to determine whether a specified string occurs in a given string, and if so, to print an asterisk (*) under the first position of each occurrence.

17. Write a program to count the occurrences of a specified string in several lines of text.

18. Write a program that accepts two strings and determines whether one string is an *anagram* of the other, that is, whether one string is a permutation of the characters in the other string. For example, "dear" is an anagram of "read," as is "dare."

Programming Pointers

1. *Values of string type may be compared with the standard relational operators, provided they have the same length. They may also be output using the* write *and* writeln *procedures.* This is not the case, however, for unpacked arrays. Also, the elements of arrays cannot usually be read by including the array name in the input list of a *read* or *readln* statement. This must be accomplished by reading the individual elements of the arrays, and in some versions of Pascal, these may not be elements of a packed array.

Variations and Extensions

By far the most useful and most common extension of standard Pascal is the inclusion of a predefined string data type and a number of predefined functions and procedures to manipulate strings. What follows are some of the string-processing features provided in those versions of Pascal that have a predefined string type:

● *String declarations.* A string declaration commonly has the form

  string[length-limit]

where *string* is a predefined identifier (Macintosh, UCSD) or a reserved word (Turbo); *length-limit* is a positive integer constant no greater than some specified value such as 80 (UCSD) or 255 (Macintosh, Turbo); it specifies the maximum length (number of characters) that a string of this type may have. Examples of variable declarations using this type are

var
    Name : *string*[20];   (* maximum length is 20 *)
    Sentence : *string*[255];   (* maximum length is 255 *)
    Initial : *string*[1];   (* string of length 1 *)

Some versions (Macintosh, UCSD) also allow string declarations of the form *string* with no specification of a length limit. In this case, a default maximum length is assumed.

- *String*[#] versus **packed array**[1 . . #] **of** *char*. The lengths of strings assigned to a variable of a predefined string type are *dynamic,* whereas strings assigned to a variable declared to be a packed character array have *constant* lengths. Because of this fundamental difference, these two types may not be compatible. For the same reason, types *string*[1] and *char* may be incompatible. The following features illustrate some of the similarities and differences between these two string types. They assume the declarations

var
    Ident : **packed array**[1..20] **of** *char*;
    Name : *string*[20];

- *Lengths of strings*. Values for *Ident* will be strings of length exactly 20, but the actual lengths of strings assigned to *Name* may vary from a minimum length of 0 (the **empty string** is a legal value) to a maximum length of 20. Thus, in the assignment statements

    Name : = 'John Doe';
    Ident : = 'John Doebbbbbbbbbbbb';

the string 'John Doe' of length 8 is assigned to *Name*; padding with twelve blanks is required in the similar assignment to *Ident*.

- *Input of strings*. A value can be read for *Name* by simply using the string variable in an input statement; for example,

    readln (*Name*);   Input: John Doe

When the end-of-line character (carriage return) is encountered, the assignment of the string 'John Doe' of length 8 to *Name* is complete; no padding with blanks occurs.

- *Output of strings*. The default field width used to display the value of *Name* is the current length (8) of this value:

    writeln (*Name*, '-11/29/38');   Output: John Doe-11/29/38

If *Name* were replaced by *Ident,* a default field width of 20 would be used, and the blanks used to pad the string would be displayed.

- *Use of indices.* The individual characters in the value of a variable of a predefined string type can be accessed in the same manner as for packed character arrays by using an index that can range from 1 up through the current length. For example, the following **if** statement can be used to display the value of *Name* if it begins with the letter J:

  if *Name* [1] = 'J' **then**
    writeln (*Name*);

- *Comparison of strings.* Values of type *string*[#] need not have the same length to be compared. For example, if *Name1* and *Name2* are of type *string*[20] and have the values 'Doe' and 'Smith', respectively, then the following is a valid boolean expression and has the value true:

  Name1 < *Name2*

- *Predefined string functions and procedures.* Four predefined functions are provided for manipulating strings, *concat, copy, length,* and *pos*. A function reference of the form

  concat(str-1, str-2, . . . , str-n)

  returns the string formed by concatenating the strings *str-1, str-2, . . . , str-n* in this order. The function reference

  copy(str, index, size)

  returns a substring of the specified *size* from the string *str,* beginning at position *index*. A reference to the *length* function

  length(str)

  returns the current length (integer) of the specified string. A function reference of the form

  pos(str-1, str-2)

  returns the position of the first character of the first occurrence of string *str-1* within the string *str-2,* or 0 if *str-1* is not found in *str-2*.
  Two predefined procedures, *delete* and *insert,* are also provided:

  delete (str, index, size)

modifies the value of string *str* by removing a substring of the specified size, starting at position *index*;

> *insert (str-1, str-2, index)*

modifies string *str-2* by inserting the string *str-1* at position *index*.

The program in Figure 10.4 is a modification of the text editor program in Figure 10.2. It uses the predefined string type and string functions and procedures of Turbo Pascal to carry out the basic text-editing operations.

```
PROGRAM TextEditor (input, output, TextFile, NewTextFile);

(*******************************************************************

   Program to perform some basic text-editing functions on lines of
   text.  The basic operation is replacing a substring of the text
   with another string.  This replacement is accomplished by a
   command of the form
                      OldString/NewString/
   OldString specifies the substring in the text to be replaced with
   the specified string NewString; NewString may be an empty
   string; this causes the substring OldString (if found) to be
   deleted.  The text lines are read from TextFile, and after editing
   is completed, the edited lines are written to NewTextFile.

********************************************************************)

CONST
   MaxString = 80;                 (* maximum length of lines in TextFile *)

TYPE
   StringType = string[MaxString];

VAR
   TextFile,                       (* file of original text *)
   NewTextFile : text;             (* file of edited text *)
   OldFileName,                    (* actual name of text file to be edited *)
   NewFileName : string[20];       (* actual name for new file to be produced *)
   TextLine : StringType;          (* line of text to be edited *)

PROCEDURE GetTextLine (VAR TextLine : StringType);

   (*******************************************************************

      Procedure to read and echo a line of text from TextFile.

   ********************************************************************)

   BEGIN (* GetTextLine *)
      readln (TextFile, TextLine);
      writeln;
      writeln (TextLine)
   END (* GetTextLine *);
```

Figure 10.4

Figure 10.4 (cont.)

```
PROCEDURE Edit (TextLine : StringType);

   (**************************************************************

      Procedure to carry out the editing operations on TextLine.
      After editing is completed, edited line is written to
      NewTextFile.

   **************************************************************)

   VAR
      OldString,                (* old string in edit change *)
      NewString : StringType;   (* new string in edit change *)
      Location : integer;       (* location of OldString in TextLine *)
      Response : char;          (* user response *)

PROCEDURE GetEditChange (VAR OldString, NewString : StringType);

   (*************************************************************

      Procedure to read the edit change of the form
                  OldString/NewString/
      It returns OldString and NewString.

   *************************************************************)

   VAR
      EditChange : StringType;  (* editing change *)
      OldLength,                (* length of OldString *)
      NewLength : integer;      (* length of NewString *)

   BEGIN (* GetEditChange *)
      writeln ('Edit change:  ');
      readln (EditChange);
      OldLength := pos('/', EditChange) - 1;
      OldString := copy(EditChange, 1, OldLength);
      delete(EditChange, 1, OldLength + 1);
      NewLength := length(EditChange) - 1;
      NewString := copy(EditChange, 1, NewLength)
   END (* GetEditChange *);

PROCEDURE Replace (VAR TextLine: StringType;
                   OldString, NewString : StringType; Start : integer);

   (*************************************************************

      Procedure to replace a substring OldString beginning at
      position Start of TextLine with NewString.

   *************************************************************)

   BEGIN (* Replace *)
      delete(TextLine, Start, length(OldString));
      IF Start < length(TextLine) THEN
         insert(NewString, TextLine, Start)
      ELSE
         TextLine := concat(TextLine, NewString);
      writeln (TextLine)
   END (* Replace *);
```

Figure 10.4   (cont.)

```
BEGIN (* Edit *)
   writeln ('Edit this line?  ');
   readln (Response);
   WHILE Response = 'Y' DO
      BEGIN
         GetEditChange (OldString, NewString);
         Location := pos (OldString, TextLine);
         IF Location = 0 THEN
            writeln (OldString, ' not found')
         ELSE
            Replace (TextLine, OldString, NewString, Location);
         writeln ('More editing (Y or N)?  ');
         readln (Response)
      END (* WHILE *);
   writeln (NewTextFile, TextLine)
END (* Edit *);

BEGIN (* main program *)
   write ('Name of file to be edited?  ');
   readln (OldFileName);
   assign (TextFile, OldFileName);
   reset (TextFile);
   write ('Name of new file to be produced?  ');
   readln (NewFileName);
   assign (NexTextFile, NewFileName);
   rewrite (NewTextFile);
   WHILE NOT eof (TextFile) DO
      BEGIN
         GetTextLine (TextLine);
         Edit (TextLine)
      END (* WHILE *);
   close (NewTextFile)
END (* main program *).
```

11

Multidimensional Arrays

Everyone knows how laborious the usual Method is of attaining to Arts and Sciences; whereas by his Contrivance, the most ignorant Person at a reasonable Charge, and with a little bodily Labour, may write Books in Philosophy, Poetry, Politicks, Law, Mathematicks, and Theology, without the least Assistance from Genius or Study. He then led me to the Frame, about the sides whereof all his Pupils stood in Ranks. It was Twenty Foot square . . . linked by slender Wires. These Bits . . . were covered on every Square with Paper pasted upon them; and on These Papers were written all the Words of their Language. . . .

The Professor then desired me to observe, for he was going to set his Engine at work. The Pupils at this Command took each of them hold of an Iron Handle, whereof there were Forty fixed round the Edges of the Frame; and giving them a sudden Turn, the whole Disposition of the Words was entirely changed. . . .

JONATHAN SWIFT, *Gulliver's Travels*

In Chapter 9 we considered one-dimensional arrays and used them to process lists. We also observed that Pascal allows arrays of more than one dimension and that two-dimensional arrays are useful when the data being processed can be arranged in rows and columns. Similarly, a three-dimensional array is appropriate when the data can be arranged in rows, columns, and ranks. When there are several characteristics associated with the data, still higher dimensions may be appropriate, with each dimension corresponding to one of these characteristics. In this chapter we consider how such multidimensional arrays are processed in Pascal programs.

11.1 Introduction to Multidimensional Arrays; Multiply Indexed Variables

There are many problems in which the data being processed can be naturally organized as a table. For example, suppose that water temperatures are recorded four times a day at each of three locations near the discharge outlet of the cooling system of a nuclear power plant. These temperature readings can be arranged in a table having four rows and three columns:

Time	Location 1	2	3
1	65.5	68.7	62.0
2	68.8	68.9	64.5
3	70.4	69.4	66.3
4	68.5	69.1	65.8

In this table, the three temperature readings at time 1 are in the first row, the three temperatures at time 2 are in the second row, and so on.

These twelve data items can be conveniently stored in a ***two-dimensional array***. The array declaration

```
const
    MaxTimes = 4;
    MaxLocations = 3;

type
    TemperatureTable = array[1..MaxTimes, 1..MaxLocations] of real;

var
    TempTab : TemperatureTable;
```

reserves 12 memory locations for these data items. The doubly indexed variable

TempTab[2, 3]

then refers to the entry in the second row and third column of the table, that is, to the temperature 64.5 recorded at time 2 at location 3. In general,

TempTab[*i*, *j*]

refers to the entry in the *i*th row and *j*th column, that is, to the temperature recorded at time *i* at location *j*.

As another example, suppose that seat reservations for a small commuter airplane are recorded by marking an "X" on a seating diagram for the airplane. The rows are numbered 1, 2, 3, . . . , 12, and in each row are seats labeled A, B, C, and D. This seating diagram can be arranged as a table having 12 rows and 4 columns in which each entry is either a blank or an X indicating an empty seat or an assigned seat, respectively.

	A	B	C	D
12	X			
11	X	X	X	X
10	X	X		
9	X		X	X
8	X	X		X
7				X
6				X
5	X	X	X	X
4	X	X		
3	X		X	X
2	X			X
1				

This table can be represented by a two-dimensional array whose components are of type *char*, whose first index is in the subrange 1..12 of type *integer*, and whose second index is in the subrange 'A'..'D' of type *char*. The following array declaration can thus be used to declare this array:

const
    MaxRows = 12;

type
    SeatingDiagram = **array**[1..*MaxRows*, 'A'..'D'] **of** *char*;

var
    Seat : *SeatingDiagram*;

A value of 'X' for the doubly indexed variable *Seat*[5, 'D'] indicates that seat 5D has been assigned.

To illustrate the use of an array with more than two dimensions, suppose that the temperatures in the first example are recorded for one week, so that seven such tables are collected:

Time	Location 1	2	3	
1	66.5	69.4	68.4	
2	68.4	71.2	69.3	Saturday
3	70.1	71.9	70.2	
4	69.5	70.0	69.4	

∴

Time	Location 1	2	3	
1	63.7	66.2	64.3	
2	64.0	66.8	64.9	Monday
			66.3	
			65.8	

Time	Location 1	2	3	
1	65.5	68.7	62.0	
2	68.8	68.9	64.5	Sunday
3	70.4	69.4	66.3	
4	68.5	69.1	65.8	

A ***three-dimensional array*** *Temp* declared by

const
    MaxTimes = 4;
    MaxLocations = 3;

type
    DaysOfWeek = (*Sunday, Monday, Tuesday, Wednesday, Thursday,*
                            Friday, Saturday);
    ThreeDimTempArray =
        array[*DaysOfWeek*, 1..*MaxTimes*, 1..*MaxLocations*]

var
    Temp : *ThreeDimTempArray*;

can be used to store these 84 temperature readings. The value of the triply
indexed variable

    Temp[*Monday*, 1, 3]

is the temperature recorded on Monday at time 1 at location 3, that is, the
value 64.3 in the second table, first row, and third column. In general,

    Temp[*Day*, *Time*, *Loc*]

is the temperature recorded on day *Day* at time *Time* at location *Loc*.

In some problems, even higher-dimensional arrays may be useful. For
example, suppose that a retailer maintains an inventory of jeans. He carries
several different brands of jeans and for each brand stocks a variety of styles,
waist sizes, and inseam lengths. A four-dimensional array can be used to record
the inventory, with each element of the array being the number of jeans of a
particular brand, style, waist size, and inseam length currently in stock. The
first index represents the brand; thus it might be of type

    BrandType = (*Levi, Wrangler, CalvinKlein, Lee, BigYank*);

The second index represents style and is of type

    StyleType = 'A'..'F';

The third and fourth indices represent waist size and inseam length, respectively. Their types might be given by

    WaistSize = 28..40;
    InseamSize = 28..36;

In a Pascal program for maintaining this inventory, the following type
section is thus appropriate:

> **type**
>   *BrandType* = (*Levi, Wrangler, CalvinKlein, Lee, BigYank*);
>   *StyleType* = 'A'..'F';
>   *WaistSize* = 28..40;
>   *InseamSize* = 28..36;
>   *JeansArray* = **array**[*BrandType, StyleType, WaistSize, InseamSize*]
>   **of** *integer*;

The four-dimensional array *JeansInStock* having indices of the types just described can then be declared by

> **var**
>   *JeansInStock* : *JeansArray*;

The value of the quadruply indexed variable

> *JeansInStock* [*Levi*, 'B', 32, 31]

is the number of Levi style-B 32 × 31 jeans in stock. The statement

> *JeansInStock*[*b, s, w, i*] := *JeansInStock*[*b, s, w, i*] − 1

records the sale of one pair of jeans of brand *b*, style *s*, waist size *w*, and inseam length *i*.

The Pascal standard places no limit on the number of dimensions of an array, but the type of each index must be declared. The general form of the declaration of an ***n-dimensional array*** is

> **array**[*index-type-1, index-type-2, . . . , index-type-n*] **of** *component-type*

where *index-type-i* specifies the type of the *i*th index and may be any ordinal type. The syntax diagram for array declarations is

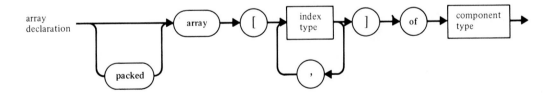

An equivalent method of declaring a multidimensional array is as an ***array of arrays***, that is, an array whose elements are other arrays. To illustrate, reconsider the seating diagram for a small airliner. The seating diagram can be thought of as a list of 12 rows; thus, from this perspective, the diagram can be viewed as a one-dimensional array with 12 elements:

Each element of this array represents a list of 4 seats and is thus an array itself. The entire seating diagram can be viewed therefore as a one-dimensional array whose components are also one-dimensional arrays.

Pascal allows array declarations to be given in a form that reflects this perspective. If we define the types *SeatRows* and *ArrayOfSeatRows* by

> **const**
>   *MaxRows* = 12;
>
> **type**
>   *SeatRows* = **array**['A'..'D'] **of** *char*;
>   *ArrayOfSeatRows* = **array**[1..*MaxRows*] **of** *SeatRows*;
>
> **var**
>   *Seat* : *ArrayOfSeatRows*;

or

> **const**
>   *MaxRows* = 12;
>
> **type**
>   *ArrayOfSeatRows* =
>   **array**[1..*MaxRows*] **of** *array*['A'..'D'] **of** *char*;
>
> **var**
>   *Seat* : *ArrayOfSeatRows*;

the singly indexed variable

> *Seat*[2]

refers to the second row of seats in this diagram:

A B C D

2 | X | | X |

The doubly indexed variable

   $Seat[2]['D']$

or, equivalently,

   $Seat[2, 'D']$

then refers to the seat labeled D in this row, and the fact that its value is 'X' indicates that this seat has been assigned. In general, if i is an integer in the range 1 through 12 and Ch is a character variable whose value is one of 'A', 'B', 'C', or 'D',

   $Seat[i][Ch]$ or $Seat[i, Ch]$

refers to the character in row i and column Ch.

   The array of temperature tables considered earlier can also be thought of as an array of arrays. In particular, since one temperature table was recorded for each day, the entire three-dimensional array can be viewed as a list of temperature tables, that is, as a one-dimensional array whose components are two-dimensional arrays. If we adopt this point of view, we are led to the array declarations

```
const
    MaxTimes = 4;
    MaxLocations = 3;

type
    DaysOfWeek = (Sunday, Monday, Tuesday, Wednesday, Thursday,
                        Friday, Saturday);
    TemperatureTables =
        array[1..MaxTimes, 1..MaxLocations] of real;

    ListOfTemperatureTables =
        array[DaysOfWeek] of TemperatureTables;

var
    Temp : ListOfTemperatureTables;
```

The singly indexed variable

   $Temp[Monday]$

then refers to the temperature table recorded on Monday; that is, $Temp[Monday]$ is a two-dimensional array.

To access the temperature 64.3 at time 1 at location 3 in this table, we could use the notation

Temp[*Monday*][1, 3]

or, equivalently,

Temp[*Monday*, 1, 3]

It might be noted that, as in the seating diagram example, each row in a temperature table can be viewed as a one-dimensional array of temperatures, and each table can be viewed therefore as a one-dimensional array of the temperature arrays. The doubly indexed variable

Temp[*Monday*][1]

then refers to the first row in the temperature table for Monday,

63.7   66.2   64.3

and

Temp[*Monday*][1][3]

denotes the third temperature in this row, as do any of the following:

Temp[*Monday*, 1, 3]
Temp[*Monday*][1, 3]
Temp[*Monday*, 1][3]

11.2 Processing Multidimensional Arrays

In the preceding section we gave several examples of multidimensional arrays and showed how such arrays are declared in a Pascal program. We also noted that any element of the array can be accessed directly by using a multiply indexed variable consisting of the array name followed by the indices that indicate that item's location in the array. In this section we consider the processing of multidimensional arrays, including the input and output of arrays or parts of arrays, copying the elements of one array into another array, and using multidimensional arrays as parameters in subprograms.

As we observed in Chapter 9, the most natural order for processing the elements of a one-dimensional array is the usual sequential order, from first item to last. For multidimensional arrays there are several different orders in which the indices may be varied when processing the array elements.

Two-dimensional arrays are often used when the data can be organized as a table consisting of rows and columns. This leads to two natural orders for processing the entries of a two-dimensional array, *rowwise* and *columnwise*. Rowwise processing means that the array elements in the first row are processed first, then those in the second row, and so on, as shown in Figure 11.1(a) for

the 3 × 4 array *A* having three rows and four columns. In columnwise processing, the entries in the first column are processed first, then those in the second
column, and so on, as illustrated in Figure 11.1(b).

In the list of array elements shown in Figure 11.1(b), we see that in the
columnwise processing of a two-dimensional array, it is the first index that
varies first and the second index second; that is, the first index must vary over
its entire set of values before the second index changes. For arrays of three or
more dimensions, the same pattern of processing is commonly used; that is,
the first index varies first, followed by the second index, and then by the third,
and so on. This is illustrated in Figure 11.2 for the 2 × 4 × 3 array *B* having
two rows, four columns, and three ranks.

The elements of a multidimensional array can be read by using nested
repetition structures; we simply place an input statement within a pair of nested
for (or **while** or **repeat-until**) loops, each of whose control variables controls
one of the indices of the array. For example, to read the twelve entries of a
3 × 4 integer array *A* in rowwise order so that it has the value

$$\begin{bmatrix} 22 & 37 & 0 & 0 \\ 0 & 1 & 17 & 32 \\ 6 & 18 & 4 & 12 \end{bmatrix}$$

we could use the nested **for** statements

> **for** *row* := 1 **to** 3 **do**
>   **for** *column* := 1 **to** 4 **do**
>   *read* (*A*[*row*, *column*]);

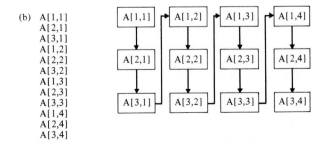

Figure 11.1   (a) Rowwise processing; (b) columnwise processing.

B[1,1,1]
B[2,1,1]
B[1,2,1]
B[2,2,1]
B[1,3,1]
B[2,3,1]
B[1,4,1]
B[2,4,1]
B[1,1,2]
B[2,1,2]
B[1,2,2]
B[2,2,2]
B[1,3,2]
B[2,3,2]
B[1,4,2]
B[2,4,2]
B[1,1,3]
B[2,1,3]
B[1,2,3]
B[2,2,3]
B[1,3,3]
B[2,3,3]
B[1,4,3]
B[2,4,3]

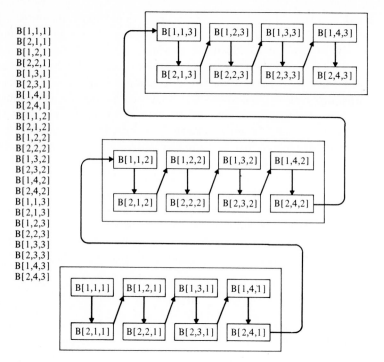

Figure 11.2

When these statements are executed, the outer for loop sets the value of the control variable *row* to 1, and the inner for loop is then executed, using 1 as the value for *row*; the effect, therefore, is the same as executing

> **for** *column* := 1 **to** 4 **do**
>   *read* (*A*[1, *column*]);

which is equivalent to the following four *read* statements:

> *read* (*A*[1, 1]);
> *read* (*A*[1, 2]);
> *read* (*A*[1, 3]);
> *read* (*A*[1, 4]);

The first pass through the outer for loop thus reads values for the first row of *A*, so that the first four values entered must be 22, 37, 0, and 0.

Now the outer for loop sets the value of the control variable *row* to 2, and the inner for loop is executed again:

> **for** *column* := 1 **to** 4 **do**
>   *read* (*A*[2, *column*]);

which is equivalent to the four *read* statements

read (A[2, 1]);
read (A[2, 2]);
read (A[2, 3]);
read (A[2, 4]);

so that the next four values entered must be those in the second row of *A*: 0, 1, 17, and 32.

Finally, the outer for loop sets the value of *row* to 3, and the inner for loop is executed again:

for *column* := 1 **to** 4 **do**
   read (A[3, *column*]);

which has the same effect as

read (A[3, 1]);
read (A[3, 2]);
read (A[3, 3]);
read (A[3, 4]);

for which the values in the third row of *A* must be entered: 6, 18, 4, and 12. The entries in this table must thus be entered in the order

22 37 0 0 0 1 17 32 6 18 4 12

for rowwise processing or, perhaps better,

22	37	0	0
0	1	17	32
6	18	4	12

to emphasize the rowwise arrangement. Note that if *readln* had been used instead of *read*, it would have been necessary to enter the values one per line, thus requiring twelve separate lines of data.

Columnwise input is also possible. We need only reverse the order of the two for loops

for *column* := 1 **to** 4 **do**
  for *row* := 1 **to** 3 **do**
    read (A[*row*, *column*]);

and enter the values in the order 22, 0, 6, 37, 1, 18, 0, 17, 4, 0, 32, 12.

Special care must be taken when reading values for a character array. For example, consider the 3 × 3 table

$$\begin{bmatrix} A & B & C \\ D & E & F \\ G & H & I \end{bmatrix}$$

To read these nine characters into the 3 × 3 character array *CharArray* in rowwise order, we could use the statement

>**for** *row* := 1 **to** 3 **do**
>   **for** *column* := 1 **to** 3 **do**
>   *read* (*CharArray*[*row*, *column*]);

and enter all the data items on one line:

>ABCDEFGHI●

(Here ● denotes the end-of-line mark generated by depressing the RETURN key.)

But the data cannot be entered on separate lines because an end-of-line character is read and stored as a blank. Thus, if the characters are entered as

>ABC●
>DEF●
>GHI●

then the table actually stored in the array *CharArray* is

$$\begin{bmatrix} A & B & C \\ b & D & E \\ F & b & G \end{bmatrix}$$

because the end-of-line character is read for both *CharArray*[2, 1] and *CharArray*[3, 2] and is stored as a blank (b) in these locations. If the preceding nested **for** statements are changed to

>**for** *row* := 1 **to** 3 **do**
>   **begin**
>   **for** *column* := 1 **to** 3 **do**
>   *read* (*CharArray*[*row*, *column*]);
>   *readln*
>   **end** (* **for** *);

the data can be entered as

>ABC●
>DEF●
>GHI●

because in this case the *readln* statement with no input list advances the data pointer past the next end-of-line mark.

The elements of an array can be displayed by using repetition structures similar to those used for input. For example, the statement

for *row* := 1 **to** 3 **do**
   begin
      for *column* := 1 **to** 4 **do**
         write (*A*[*row*, *column*]:4);
      writeln
   end (* **for** *);

where *A* is the integer array considered earlier, produces as output

```
  22   37    0    0
   0    1   17   32
   6   18    4   12
```

Note that the *write* statement displays the values in each row on the same line and that a *writeln* statement is used to terminate this line.

These same input/output techniques can be applied to higher-dimensional arrays. For example, values could be read into the $2 \times 4 \times 3$ array *B* in the order indicated in Figure 11.2 by the nested **for** statements

for *rank* := 1 **to** 3 **do**
   for *column* := 1 **to** 4 **do**
      for *row* := 1 **to** 2 **do**
         read (*B*[*row*, *column*, *rank*]);

Other types of array processing can also be carried out using nested repetition structures. To illustrate, consider the 4×3 array *TempTab* used in Section 11.1 to store the following table of temperature readings:

Time	Location 1	2	3
1	65.5	68.7	62.0
2	68.8	68.9	64.5
3	70.4	69.4	66.3
4	68.5	69.1	65.8

To calculate the average temperature at each of the four times, it is necessary to calculate the sum of the entries in each row and to divide each of these sums by 3. The following program segment can be used to carry out this computation and to display the average temperature at each time:

for *Time* := 1 **to** 4 **do**
   begin
      Sum := 0;
      for *Loc* := 1 **to** 3 **do**
         Sum := *Sum* + *TempTab*[*Time*, *Loc*];
      MeanTemp := *Sum* / 3;
      writeln ('Mean temperature at time ', *Time*:1, ' is ', *MeanTemp*:3:1)
   end (* **for** *);

Nested repetition structures can also be used to copy the entries of one array into another array. For example, if *A* and *B* are 5 × 10 arrays, the nested **for** statements

for *row* := 1 **to** 5 **do**
    for *column* := 1 **to** 10 **do**
        B[row, column] := *A[row, column]*;

will copy the entries of *A* into the corresponding locations of array *B*, assuming, of course, that the component type of *A* is compatible with the component type of *B*. If *A* and *B* have the *same types* (see Section 9.2), this can be done more simply with the array assignment statement

B := *A*;

Multidimensional arrays may also be used as parameters for functions and procedures. The rules governing the use of array₋ as parameters, which were described in detail in Section 9.2 for one-dimensional arrays, also apply to multidimensional arrays. These rules are summarized as follows:

1. The types of formal parameters in a function or procedure heading must be specified by type identifiers. Thus, for example, the array declaration *Grades* : **array**[1..25, 1..4] **of** *real* may not be used to declare the type of a formal parameter in a procedure or function heading. It may be given in the form *Grades* : *Table*, where *Table* is a type identifier associated with **array**[1..25, 1..4] **of** *real*.
2. The types of arrays used as actual parameters must be the same as the types of the corresponding arrays used as formal parameters.
3. The type of a function value may not be an array.

11.3   Examples: Automobile Sales, Matrix Multiplication, Sorting Names, Inventory Control

EXAMPLE 1: Automobile Sales. Suppose that a certain automobile dealership sells fifteen different models of automobiles and employs ten salesmen. A record of sales for each month can be represented by a table in which the first row contains the number of sales of each model by salesman 1, the second row contains the number of sales of each model by salesman 2, and so on. For example, suppose that the sales table for a certain month is the following:

0	0	2	0	5	6	3	0	10	0	3	2	5	7	5
5	1	9	0	0	2	3	2	1	1	3	1	5	3	0
0	0	0	1	0	0	0	0	0	0	2	0	8	2	3
1	1	1	0	2	2	2	1	1	0	2	0	3	0	12
5	3	2	0	0	2	5	5	7	0	0	2	0	0	2
2	2	1	0	1	1	0	0	6	8	0	0	0	2	0
3	2	5	0	1	2	0	4	8	0	0	2	2	2	1
3	0	7	1	3	5	2	4	4	3	5	1	7	2	4
0	2	6	1	0	5	2	1	4	3	0	0	4	0	5
4	0	2	0	3	2	1	0	9	0	1	4	5	4	8

A program is to be written to produce a monthly sales report, displaying the monthly sales table in the form

SALESMAN:	MODEL														
	1	2	3	4	5	6	7	8	9	10	11	12	13	14	15
1 :	0	0	2	0	5	6	3	0	10	0	3	2	5	7	5
2 :	5	1	9	0	0	2	3	2	1	1	3	1	5	3	0
3 :	0	0	0	1	0	0	0	0	0	0	2	0	8	2	3
4 :	1	1	1	0	2	2	2	1	1	0	2	0	3	0	12
5 :	5	3	2	0	0	2	5	5	7	0	0	2	0	0	2
6 :	2	2	1	0	1	1	0	0	6	8	0	0	0	2	0
7 :	3	2	5	0	1	2	0	4	8	0	0	2	2	2	1
8 :	3	0	7	1	3	5	2	4	4	3	5	1	7	2	4
9 :	0	2	6	1	0	5	2	1	4	3	0	0	4	0	5
10 :	4	0	2	0	3	2	1	0	9	0	1	4	5	4	8

and which also displays the total number of automobiles sold by each salesman and the total number of each model sold by all salesmen.

The input to the program is to be a sales table, as just described, and the output is to be a report of the indicated form. The required processing is given by the following algorithm:

ALGORITHM FOR SALES REPORT

1. Read the sales table into a 10×15 array *Sales* so that each of the ten rows contains the sales information for one of the ten salesmen, and each of the fifteen columns contains the information for one of the fifteen models.
2. Print the array *Sales* with appropriate headings.
3. Calculate and print the totals of the entries in each of the rows. These totals are the sales totals for each of the ten salesmen.
4. Calculate and print the totals of the entries in each of the columns. These totals are the total sales for each of the fifteen models.

Each of the tasks listed in this algorithm can be implemented as a separate procedure so that the structure of the program that solves this problem is

In the preceding section we considered several examples of array input/output, and these can be easily adapted to give procedures *ReadTable* and *PrintSalesTable*. We also considered the problem of calculating the averages of rows in a temperature table, and the techniques used there can be used to develop procedures *FindSalesmanTotals* and *FindModelTotals*. The program in Figure 11.3 implements the preceding algorithm, using these four procedures to perform the required tasks.

```
PROGRAM AutomobileSales (input, output, SalesFile);

(*******************************************************************

   Program to read in a sales table and calculate total sales for
   each salesman and total sales of each model of automobile.

*******************************************************************)

CONST
   RowLimit = 25;      (* limit on number of rows in table *)
   ColumnLimit = 25;   (* limit on number of columns in table *)

TYPE
   Table = ARRAY[1..RowLimit, 1..ColumnLimit] OF integer;

VAR
   Rows,                (* number of rows (salesmen) in sales table *)
   Columns : integer;   (* number of columns (models) in sales table *)
   Sales : Table;       (* sales table *)
   SalesFile : text;    (* file containing the sales data *)

PROCEDURE ReadTable (VAR Sales : Table; VAR Rows, Columns : integer);

   (****************************************************************

      Procedure to read the number of rows and columns in the sales
      table and then read the table.  The data is read from the
      text file SalesFile.

   ****************************************************************)

   VAR
      Man,               (* row index -- salesman number *)
      Model : integer;   (* column index -- model number *)

   BEGIN (* ReadTable *)
      reset (SalesFile);
      readln (SalesFile, Rows, Columns);
      FOR Man := 1 TO Rows DO
         FOR Model := 1 TO Columns DO
            read (SalesFile, Sales[Man, Model])
   END (* ReadTable *);

PROCEDURE PrintSalesTable (VAR Sales : Table; Rows, Columns : integer);

   (****************************************************************

      Procedure to print the sales table in the desired format.

   ****************************************************************)
```

Figure 11.3

Figure 11.3   (cont.)

```
  VAR
     Man,                  (* salesman number *)
     Model : integer;  (* model number *)

  BEGIN (* PrintSalesTable *)
     writeln ('MODEL' : 2*Columns + 9);
     write ('SALESMAN:');
     FOR Model := 1 TO Columns DO
        write (Model:4);
     writeln;
     FOR Model := 1 TO 4*Columns + 9 DO
        write('-');
     writeln;
     FOR Man := 1 TO Rows DO
        BEGIN
           write (Man:5, '    :');
           FOR Model := 1 TO Columns DO
              write (Sales[Man, Model]:4);
           writeln
        END (* FOR *)
  END (* PrintSalesTable *);

PROCEDURE FindSalesmanTotals (VAR Sales : Table; Rows, Columns : integer);

  (**************************************************************

     Procedure to find and display sum of each row of sales table.

  **************************************************************)

  VAR
     Man,                  (* row index -- salesman number *)
     Model,                (* column index -- model number *)
     RowTotal : integer;  (* row total *)

  BEGIN (* FindSalesmanTotals *)
     writeln;
     FOR Man := 1 TO Rows DO
        BEGIN
           RowTotal := 0;
           FOR Model := 1 TO Columns DO
              RowTotal := RowTotal + Sales[Man, Model];
           writeln ('Sales of salesman', Man:3, ':', RowTotal:4)
        END (* FOR *)
  END (* FindSalesmanTotals *);

PROCEDURE FindModelTotals (VAR Sales : Table; Rows, Columns : integer);

  (**************************************************************

     Procedure to find and display sum of each column of sales table.

  **************************************************************)

  VAR
     Man,                  (* row index -- salesman number *)
     Model,                (* column index -- model number *)
     ColTotal : integer;  (* column total *)
```

Figure 11.3 (cont.)

```
   BEGIN (* FindModelTotals *)
      writeln;
      FOR Model := 1 TO Columns DO
         BEGIN
            ColTotal := 0;
            FOR Man := 1 TO Rows DO
               ColTotal := ColTotal + Sales[Man, Model];
            writeln ('Sales of model   ', Model:3, ':', ColTotal:4)
         END (* FOR *)
   END (* FindModelTotals *);

BEGIN (* main program *)
   ReadTable (Sales, Rows, Columns);
   PrintSalesTable (Sales, Rows, Columns);
   FindSalesmanTotals (Sales, Rows, Columns);
   FindModelTotals (Sales, Rows, Columns)
END (* main program *).
```

Sample run:

```
                                    MODEL
SALESMAN:   1   2   3   4   5   6   7   8   9  10  11  12  13  14  15
-------------------------------------------------------------------
    1  :    0   0   2   0   5   6   3   0  10   0   3   2   5   7   5
    2  :    5   1   9   0   0   2   3   2   1   1   3   1   5   3   0
    3  :    0   0   0   1   0   0   0   0   0   2   0   8   2   3
    4  :    1   1   1   0   2   2   2   1   1   0   2   0   3   0  12
    5  :    5   3   2   0   0   2   5   5   7   0   0   2   0   0   2
    6  :    2   2   1   0   1   1   0   0   6   8   0   0   0   2   0
    7  :    3   2   5   0   1   2   0   4·  8   0   0   2   2   2   1
    8  :    3   0   7   1   3   5   2   4   4   3   5   1   7   2   4
    9  :    0   2   6   1   0   5   2   1   4   3   0   0   4   0   5
   10  :    4   0   2   0   3   2   1   0   9   0   1   4   5   4   8

Sales of salesman  1:   48
Sales of salesman  2:   36
Sales of salesman  3:   16
Sales of salesman  4:   28
Sales of salesman  5:   33
Sales of salesman  6:   23
Sales of salesman  7:   32
Sales of salesman  8:   51
Sales of salesman  9:   33
Sales of salesman 10:   43

Sales of model    1:   23
Sales of model    2:   11
Sales of model    3:   35
Sales of model    4:    3
Sales of model    5:   15
Sales of model    6:   27
Sales of model    7:   18
Sales of model    8:   17
Sales of model    9:   50
Sales of model   10:   15
Sales of model   11:   16
Sales of model   12:   12
Sales of model   13:   39
Sales of model   14:   22
Sales of model   15:   40
```

EXAMPLE 2: Matrix Multiplication. A two-dimensional array having m rows and n columns is called an **$m \times n$ matrix**. An important operation of matrix algebra is matrix multiplication, defined as follows: Suppose that *Mat1* is an $m \times n$ matrix and *Mat2* is an $n \times p$ matrix. The product *Prod* of *Mat1* with *Mat2* will then be an $m \times p$ matrix with the entry *Prod*[i, j], which appears in the ith row and the jth column given by

$Prod[i, j]$ = the sum of the products of the entries in row i of *Mat1*
with the entries of column j of *Mat2*
= $Mat1[i, 1] * Mat2[1, j] + Mat1[i, 2] * Mat2[2, j] + \cdots$
$+ Mat1[i, n] * Mat2[n, j]$

Note that the number of columns (n) in *Mat1* is equal to the number of rows in *Mat2*, which must be the case for the product of *Mat1* with *Mat2* to be defined.

For example, suppose that *Mat1* is the 2×3 matrix

$$\begin{bmatrix} 1 & 0 & 2 \\ 3 & 0 & 4 \end{bmatrix}$$

and that *Mat2* is the 3×4 matrix

$$\begin{bmatrix} 4 & 2 & 5 & 3 \\ 6 & 4 & 1 & 8 \\ 9 & 0 & 0 & 2 \end{bmatrix}$$

Because the number of columns (3) in *Mat1* equals the number of rows in *Mat2*, the product matrix *Prod* is defined. The entry in the first row and first column, *Prod*[1, 1], is

$$1 * 4 + 0 * 6 + 2 * 9 = 22$$

Similarly, the entry *Prod*[1, 2] in the first row and second column is

$$1 * 2 + 0 * 4 + 2 * 0 = 2$$

The complete product matrix *Prod* is the 2×4 matrix given by

$$\begin{bmatrix} 22 & 2 & 5 & 7 \\ 48 & 6 & 15 & 17 \end{bmatrix}$$

In general, the algorithm for multiplying matrices is

MATRIX MULTIPLICATION ALGORITHM

(* Algorithm for multiplying a *Rows1* $\times$ *Cols1* matrix *Mat1* with *Rows2* $\times$ *Cols2* matrix *Mat2*. *)

1. If *Cols1* $\neq$ *Rows2*, then the product *Prod* = *Mat1* $*$ *Mat2* is not defined; terminate the algorithm. Otherwise proceed with the following steps:
2. For an index i ranging from 1 to the number of rows *Rows1* of *Mat1*, do the following:

   For an index j ranging from 1 to the number of columns *Cols2* of *Mat2*, do the following:

    (i) Set *Sum* equal to 0.

    (ii) For an index *k* ranging from 1 to the number of columns *Cols1* of *Mat1* (= the number of rows *Rows2* of *Mat2*), add *Mat1*[*i*, *k*] * *Mat2*[*k*, *j*] to *Sum*.

    (iii) Set *Prod*[*i*, *j*] equal to *Sum*.

The program in Figure 11.4 reads two matrices and uses this algorithm to calculate and display their product.

```
PROGRAM MatrixMultiplication (input, output);

(*********************************************************************

   Program to read two matrices and calculate their product.

*********************************************************************)

CONST
   RowLimit = 20;    (* limit on number of rows in a matrix *)
   ColumnLimit = 20; (* limit on number of columns in a matrix *)

TYPE
   Matrix = ARRAY[1..RowLimit, 1..ColumnLimit] OF integer;

VAR
   Mat1, Mat2,              (* matrices being multiplied *)
   Prod : Matrix;           (* product of Mat1 with Mat2 *)
   Rows1, Cols1,            (* dimensions of Mat1 *)
   Rows2, Cols2 : integer;  (* dimensions of Mat2 *)
   ProductDefined : boolean; (* true if Cols1 = Rows2, else false *)

PROCEDURE ReadMatrix (VAR Mat : Matrix; VAR Rows, Columns : integer);

   (*************************************************************

      Procedure to read number of rows and columns in a matrix and
      then read a matrix of those dimensions.

   *************************************************************)

   VAR
      i, j : integer;   (* row, column indices *)

   BEGIN (* ReadMatrix *)
      write ('Enter number of rows & columns:  ');
      readln (Rows, Columns);
      writeln ('Enter the matrix rowwise:');
      FOR i := 1 TO Rows DO
         FOR j := 1 to Columns DO
            read (Mat[i,j]);
      readln
   END (* ReadMatrix *);
```

Figure 11.4

Figure 11.4 (cont.)

```
PROCEDURE PrintMatrix (VAR Mat : Matrix; Rows, Columns : integer);

    (*****************************************************************

        Procedure to display an integer Rows X Columns matrix.

    *****************************************************************)

    CONST
        FieldWidth = 5;    (* width of field used to display an entry *)

    VAR
        i, j : integer;    (* row, column indices *)

    BEGIN (* PrintMatrix *)
        writeln;
        FOR i := 1 TO Rows DO
            BEGIN
                FOR j := 1 TO Columns DO
                    write (Mat[i,j]:FieldWidth);
                writeln;
                writeln
            END (* FOR *)
    END (* PrintMatrix *);

PROCEDURE MatMultiply (VAR Mat1, Mat2, Prod : Matrix;
                       Rows1, Cols1, Rows2, Cols2 : integer;
                       VAR ProductDefined : boolean);

    (*****************************************************************

        Procedure to multiply the Rows1 X Cols1 matrix Mat1 and the
        Rows2 X Cols2 matrix Mat2; Cols1 must equal Rows2 for the
        product Prod to be defined.

    *****************************************************************)

    VAR
        i, j, k,        (* indices *)
        Sum : integer;  (* used to calculate product matrix *)

    BEGIN (* MatMultiply *)
        ProductDefined := (Cols1 = Rows2);
        IF ProductDefined THEN
            BEGIN
                FOR i := 1 TO Rows1 DO
                    FOR j := 1 to Cols2 DO
                        BEGIN
                            Sum := 0;
                            FOR k := 1 to Cols1 DO
                                Sum := Sum + Mat1[i,k] * Mat2[k,j];
                            Prod[i,j] := Sum
                        END (* FOR j *)
            END (* IF *)
    END (* MatMultiply *);
```

Figure 11.4 (cont.)

```
 BEGIN (* main program *)
   ReadMatrix (Mat1, Rows1, Cols1);
   writeln ('First Matrix:');
   PrintMatrix (Mat1, Rows1, Cols1);
   ReadMatrix (Mat2, Rows2, Cols2);
   writeln ('Second Matrix:');
   PrintMatrix (Mat2, Rows2, Cols2);
   MatMultiply (Mat1, Mat2, Prod, Rows1, Cols1, Rows2, Cols2,
                ProductDefined);
   IF ProductDefined THEN
      BEGIN
         writeln ('Product:');
         PrintMatrix (Prod, Rows1, Cols2)
      END (* IF *)
   ELSE
      BEGIN
         writeln ('Product undefined -- number of columns ', Cols1:1,
                  ' in first matrix');
         writeln (' is not equal to number of rows ', Rows2:1,
                  ' in second matrix')
      END (* ELSE *)
END (* main program *).
```

Sample run:

```
Enter number of rows & columns:  2 3
Enter the matrix rowwise:
1 2 3
4 0 1
First Matrix:

    1    2    3

    4    0    1

Enter number of rows & columns:  3 4
Enter the matrix rowwise
1 0 0 1
2 1 1 2
3 0 1 1
Second Matrix:

    1    0    0    1

    2    1    1    2

    3    0    1    1

Product:

   14    2    5    8

    7    0    1    5
```

EXAMPLE 3. Sorting Names.   Suppose that a list of names, each consisting of a first name followed by a blank followed by a last name, is to be read from a data file. The names in this list are then to be displayed in the form *last-name, first-name*, with the last names in alphabetical order.

The list of names to be read and processed can be stored in an array *Name* whose components are strings. Since a string is an array of characters, the array *Name* will in fact be an array of arrays. If the names are stored in this array in the format *last-name, first-name*, they can be sorted using the selection sort algorithm described in Section 9.3 and then displayed. This is summarized in the following algorithm:

ALGORITHM TO SORT A LIST OF NAMES

1. Repeat the following until all the names have been read or the array *Name* is filled:
   a. Read *TempName* and extract *FirstName* and *LastName* from it.
   b. Attach a comma followed by a blank to *LastName*.
   c. Concatenate *LastName* with *FirstName* and store the resulting string in the next location of array *Name*.
2. Alphabetize the array *Name* using the selection sort method.
3. Display the sorted list of names in the desired format.

The program in Figure 11.5 implements this algorithm. It assumes that the package of string-processing procedures and functions described in Section 10.2 is available. The procedure *ReadString* is used to read each name. The function *Pos* is then used to locate the blank separating the first and last names, and *Copy* is used to extract *FirstName* and *LastName* as required in Step 1a. Procedure *Concat* is used to carry out the operations described in Steps 1b and 1c.

```
PROGRAM NameSort (input, output);

(*******************************************************************

   Program to read a list of first and last names, sort them so
   the last names are in alphabetical order, and display them
   in the form:    Last-name, First-name.
   The program uses ReadString, Pos, Copy, and Concat from the package
   of basic string-processing procedures and functions described in
   Section 10.2.

*******************************************************************)

CONST
   StringLimit = 30;    (* limit on lengths of strings *)
   ListLimit = 100;     (* limit on length of list *)
```

Figure 11.5

Figure 11.5 (cont.)

```
TYPE
   String = PACKED ARRAY[1..StringLimit] of char;
   List = ARRAY[1..ListLimit] of String;
   ItemType = String;

VAR
   Name : List;          (* list of names *)
   i,                    (* index *)
   NumNames : integer;   (* number of names in list *)

(****************************************************************
 ****************************************************************
 ** From the package of string-processing functions and procedures **
 ** insert                                                          **
 **                          ReadString                            **
 **                          Concat                                **
 **                          Copy                                  **
 **                          Length                              **
 **                          Pos                                   **
 ** here.                                                          **
 ****************************************************************
 ****************************************************************)

PROCEDURE ReverseAndStoreNames (VAR Name : List; VAR Count : integer);

   (***************************************************************

      `Procedure to read and count the names, reverse them so they have
       the form
                    Last-Name, First-Name
       and store these reversed names in the array Name.

   ***************************************************************)

   VAR
      TempName,             (* temporary variable for name *)
      Blank,                (* string of blanks *)
      Comma,                (* string beginning with a comma *)
      FirstName,            (* first name *)
      LastName : String;    (* last name *)
      i,                    (* index *)
      BlankPos,             (* position of _ in name *)
      Len1,                 (* length of first name *)
      Len2 : integer;       (* length of last name *)

   BEGIN (* ReverseAndStoreNames *)
      (* Initialize the blank and comma strings *)
      FOR i := 1 TO StringLimit DO
         Blank[i] := ' ';
      Comma := Blank;
      Comma[1] := ',';
```

Figure 11.5   (cont.)

```
      (* Read names, reverse and store them *)
      writeln ('Enter the names in the form Firstname_Lastname,');
      writeln ('1 name per line.  Enter * to stop.');
      writeln;
      Count := 0;
      ReadString (TempName, StringLimit);
      WHILE TempName[1] <> '*' DO
         IF Count < ListLimit THEN
            BEGIN
               (* Form last-name, first-name and store in Name *)
               BlankPos := Pos(Blank, 1, TempName, Length(TempName));
               Len1 := BlankPos - 1;
               Copy (TempName, 1, Len1, FirstName);
               Len2 := Length(TempName) - BlankPos;
               Copy (TempName, BlankPos + 1, Len2, LastName);
               Concat (LastName, Len2, Comma, 2, LastName);
               Count := Count + 1;
               Concat (LastName, Len2 + 2, FirstName, Len1, Name[Count]);
               ReadString (TempName, StringLimit);
            END (* IF *)
         ELSE
            BEGIN
               writeln ('*** Too many names -- processing first ',
                        ListLimit:1, ' names ***');
               TempName[1] := '*'    (* force end of data *)
            END (* ELSE *)
   END (* ReverseAndStoreNames *);

PROCEDURE SelectionSort(VAR Item : List; NumItems : integer);

   (****************************************************************

      Procedure to sort Item[1], ..., Item[NumItems] into ascending
      order using the simple selection sort algorithm.  For descending
      order, change > to < in the boolean expression Item[i] > Item[i+1].

   ****************************************************************)

   VAR
      Smallest : ItemType;     (* smallest item in current sublist *)
      SmallPos,                (* position of Smallest *)
      i, j : integer;          (* indices *)

   BEGIN (* SelectionSort *)
      FOR i := 1 TO NumItems - 1 DO
         BEGIN

            (* find smallest item in sublist Item[i], ..., Item[NumItems] *)

            SmallPos := i;
            Smallest := Item[SmallPos];
            FOR j := i + 1 TO NumItems DO
               IF Item[j] < Smallest THEN   (* smaller item found *)
                  BEGIN
                     SmallPos := j;
                     Smallest := Item[j]
                  END (* IF *);

            (* interchange smallest item with Item[i] at beginning
                  of sublist *)

            Item[SmallPos] := Item[i];
            Item[i] := Smallest
         END (* FOR i *)
   END (* SelectionSort *);
```

Figure 11.5 (cont.)

```
BEGIN (* main program *)
   ReverseAndStoreNames (Name, NumNames);
   SelectionSort (Name, NumNames);
   FOR i := 1 TO NumNames DO
      writeln (Name[i])
END (* main program *).
```

Sample run:

```
Enter the names in the form Firstname_Lastname,
1 name per line.  Enter * to stop.

John Doe
Mary Smith
Fred Jones
Jesse James
Merry Christmas
*
Christmas, Merry
Doe, John
James, Jesse
Jones, Fred
Smith, Mary
```

EXAMPLE 4: Inventory Control. In Section 11.1 we noted that a four-dimensional array *JeansInStock* might be used in a program that maintains an inventory of jeans of various brands, styles, and sizes. In this example, the type of the first index for this array is an enumerated type:

$BrandType$ = (*Levi, Wrangler, CalvinKlein, Lee, BigYank*);

the type of the second index is a subrange of *char*:

$StyleType$ = 'A'..'F';

and the types of the third and fourth indices are subranges of *integer*:

$WaistSize$ = 28..40;
$InseamSize$ = 28..36;

The information about the current inventory is stored in a file, which contains 390 lines of numbers. The first 78 lines describe the current inventory of Levi jeans; the next 78 describe the current inventory of Wrangler jeans; and so on. Within each of these brand blocks of 78 lines, the first 13 lines pertain to style A, the next 13 to style B, and so on. Within each of these 13-line style blocks, the first line contains information about jeans with waist size 28; the second contains information about jeans with waist size 29; and so on. And each of these lines contains 9 numbers that represent the number of jeans in stock for inseam sizes 28, 29, . . . , 36. For example, the third line in the data file is

18 7 19 10 11 3 2 18 12

and from this we see that there are currently 11 Levi jeans of style A having waist size 30 and inseam 32.

The first task in solving this problem is to read this inventory information from the file and store it in the array *JeansInStock*. Because of the way in which this information is organized, nested for loops can be used to do this. The index of the outermost loop varies over the values of *BrandType*; the index of the second loop varies over the style type 'A'..'F'; the index of the third loop varies over waist sizes; and the index of the innermost loop varies over the inseam sizes.

The procedure *Initialize* in the program in Figure 11.6 that solves this problem uses such nested for loops to load the initial inventory information into the array *JeansInStock*. It also initializes an array *BrandName* that is used to convert between values of the enumerated type *BrandType* and strings that name these brands.

Once the array *JeansInStock* has been initialized, the program must update the inventory information stored in this array, based on sales entered by the user. The procedure *UpdateInventory* reads sales information entered by the user and does the necessary updating. It implements the following algorithm:

UpdateInventory

1. Read the brand name.
2. Convert this string to the corresponding value of type *BrandType*.
3. Read the style, waist size, and inseam.
4. Read the number *NumSold* of jeans sold.
5. Subtract *NumSold* from *JeansInStock*[*Brand*, *Style*, *Waist*, *Inseam*].

This procedure uses the procedure *Convert* to perform the conversion in Step 2. This procedure simply searches the array *BrandName* to find the index of type *BrandType* that corresponds to the brand name entered by the user.

After all the sales have been recorded, it is necessary to write the updated inventory information in array *JeansInStock* back to the data file. The procedure *WrapUp* in the program does this, using nested for loops much like those in *Initialize*.

The solution of the problem thus consists of three main procedures: *Initialize*, *UpdateInventory*, and *WrapUp*. The structure of the program in Figure 11.6 has the form

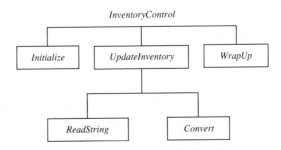

```
PROGRAM InventoryControl (input, output, InventoryFile, NewInventoryFile);

(****************************************************************

    Inventory control program that demonstrates use of a
    four-dimensional array with different types of indices.

****************************************************************)

CONST
    StringLimit = 11;                    (* lengths of strings *)
    FirstStyle = 'A'; LastStyle = 'F';   (* first, last values of StyleType *)
    SmallWaist = 28; LargeWaist = 40;    (* first, last values of WaistSize *)
    ShortInseam = 28; LongInseam = 36;   (* first, last values of InseamSize *)

TYPE
    BrandType = (Levi, Wrangler, CalvinKlein, Lee, BigYank);
    StyleType = FirstStyle..LastStyle;
    WaistSize = SmallWaist..LargeWaist;
    InseamSize = ShortInseam..LongInseam;
    JeansArray = ARRAY[BrandType, StyleType, WaistSize, InseamSize] OF integer;
    String = PACKED ARRAY[1..StringLimit] OF char;
    BrandNameArray = ARRAY[BrandType] OF String;

VAR
    JeansInStock : JeansArray;      (* array that maintains jeans inventory *)
    BrandName : BrandNameArray;     (* array of strings -- names of brands *)
    InventoryFile,                  (* original inventory file *)
    NewInventoryFile : text;        (* inventory file produces by program *)
    Response : char;                (* user response *)

PROCEDURE ReadString (VAR Str : String; MaxString : integer);

    (****************************************************************

        Procedure to read characters into string variable Str until
        an end-of-line mark is encountered or the upper limit
        MaxString on the length of Str is reached.  Any positions
        for which no characters are read will be filled with blanks.

    ****************************************************************)

    VAR
        i : integer;        (* index *)

    BEGIN (* ReadString *)
        FOR i := 1 TO MaxString DO
            IF NOT eoln THEN
                read (Str[i])
            ELSE
                Str[i] := ' ';
        readln
    END (* ReadString *);
```

Figure 11.6

Figure 11.6   (cont.)

```
PROCEDURE Initialize (VAR InventoryFile : text;
                      VAR JeansInStock : JeansArray;
                      VAR BrandName : BrandNameArray);

   (*************************************************************

      Procedure to initialize array JeansInStock from InventoryFile
      and to initialize the array BrandName of names of brands.

   *************************************************************)

   VAR
      Brand : BrandType;      (* index *)
      Style : StyleType;      (*   "   *)
      Waist : WaistSize;      (*   "   *)
      Inseam : InseamSize;    (*   "   *)

   BEGIN (* Initialize *)
      (* Read array JeansInStock from InventoryFile *)
      reset (InventoryFile);
      FOR Brand := Levi TO BigYank DO
         FOR Style := FirstStyle TO LastStyle DO
            FOR Waist := SmallWaist TO LargeWaist DO
               FOR Inseam := ShortInseam To  LongInseam DO
                  read (InventoryFile,
                        JeansInStock[Brand, Style, Waist, Inseam]);

      (* Initialize array of brand names *)
      BrandName[Levi]        := 'LEVI        ';
      BrandName[Wrangler]    := 'WRANGLER    ';
      BrandName[CalvinKlein] := 'CALVINKLEIN';
      BrandName[Lee]         := 'LEE         ';
      BrandName[BigYank]     := 'BIGYANK     '
   END (* Initialize *);

PROCEDURE UpdateInventory (VAR JeansInStock : JeansArray;
                           BrandName: BrandNameArray);

   (*************************************************************

      Procedure to read sales information and update the inventory
      information in array JeansInStock.

   *************************************************************)

   VAR
      Name : String;          (* name of brand entered by user *)
      NameFound : boolean;    (* signals if name found in array BrandName *)
      b,                      (* index *)
      Brand : BrandType;      (* index *)
      Style : StyleType;      (* index *)
      Waist : WaistSize;      (* index *)
      Inseam : InseamSize;    (* index *)
      NumSold ,               (* number sold *)
      InStock : integer;      (* number in stock *)
```

Figure 11.6   (cont.)

```
PROCEDURE Convert (Name : String; BrandName : BrandNameArray;
                   VAR NameFound : boolean;
                   VAR Brand : BrandType);

(*********************************************************************

    Searches the array BrandName to find the string Name and
    returns the corresponding index Brand of enumerated type
    BrandType.  NameFound is true or false according as the search
    is successful or not.

    ********************************************************************)

VAR
    b: BrandType;                (* index *)

BEGIN (* Convert *)
    NameFound := false;
    FOR b := Levi TO BigYank DO
        IF BrandName[b] = Name THEN
            BEGIN
                Brand := b;
                NameFound := true
            END (* IF *);
    IF NOT NameFound THEN
        writeln ('*** Not a legal brand name ***')
END (* Convert *);


BEGIN (* UpdateInventory *)
    REPEAT
        write ('BRAND (use all CAPS)?  ');
        ReadString (Name, StringLimit);
        Convert (Name, BrandName, NameFound, Brand)
    UNTIL NameFound;
    write ('Style (', FirstStyle, '-', LastStyle, ')?  ');
    readln (Style);
    write ('Waist size (', SmallWaist:1, '-', LargeWaist:1, ')?  ');
    readln (Waist);
    write ('Inseam (', ShortInseam:1, '-', LongInseam:1, ')?  ');
    readln (Inseam);
    write ('Number sold?  ');
    readln (NumSold);
    InStock := JeansInStock[Brand, Style, Waist, Inseam] - NumSold;
    IF InStock < 0 THEN
        BEGIN
            writeln ('Not enough in stock; backorder ', abs(InStock):1);
            InStock := 0
        END (* IF *);
    JeansInStock[Brand, Style, Waist, Inseam] := InStock;
END (* UpdateInventory *);
```

Figure 11.6   (cont.)

```
PROCEDURE WrapUp (VAR NewInventoryFile : text;
                  VAR JeansInStock : JeansArray);

   (**************************************************************

       Procedure to copy array JeansInStock to NewInventoryFile

    **************************************************************)

   VAR
      Brand : BrandType;      (* index *)
      Style : StyleType;      (*   "   *)
      Waist : WaistSize;      (*   "   *)
      Inseam : InseamSize;    (*   "   *)

   BEGIN (* WrapUp *)
      rewrite (NewInventoryFile);
      FOR Brand := Levi TO BigYank DO
         FOR Style := FirstStyle TO LastStyle DO
            FOR Waist := SmallWaist TO LargeWaist DO
               BEGIN
                  FOR Inseam := ShortInseam To  LongInseam DO
                     write (NewInventoryFile,
                            JeansInStock[Brand, Style, Waist, Inseam]:3);
                  writeln(NewInventoryFile)
               END (* FOR *)
   END (* WrapUp *);

BEGIN (* main program *)
   Initialize(InventoryFile, JeansInStock, BrandName);
   REPEAT
      UpdateInventory (JeansInStock, BrandName);
      writeln;
      write ('More sales (Y or N)?  ');
      readln (Response);
   UNTIL (Response <> 'Y') AND (Response <> 'y');
   WrapUp (NewInventoryfile, JeansInStock)
END (* main *).
```

InventoryFile:

```
 3  3  0 12  1 12 19 17  0
 4 15 18  2 14  2  0 14 19
18  7 19 10 11  3  2 18 12
            .
            .
            .
12 18 11 12 16 14  9 12  9
```

Sample run:

```
BRAND (use all CAPS)?   LEVI
Style (A-F)?   A
Waist size (28-40)?   28
Inseam (28-36)?   28
Number sold?   10
Not enough in stock; backorder 7
```

Figure 11.6 (cont.)

```
More sales (Y or N)?   Y
BRAND (use all CAPS)?   BIGYANK
Style (A-F)?   F
Waist size (28-40)?   40
Inseam (28-36)?   36
Number sold?   1

More sales (Y or N)?   N


NewInventoryFile:

   0   3   0  12   1  12  19  17   0
   4  15  18   2  14   2   0  14  19
  18   7  19  10  11   3   2  18  12
                   .
                   .
                   .
  12  18  11  12  16  14   9  12   8
```

Exercises

1. Consider the following type declarations:

    type
       Color = (*red, yellow, blue, green, white, black*);
       BigTable = **array**[1..50, 1..100] **of** *integer*;
       PointTable = **array**[−10..10, −10..10] **of** *real*;
       CharTable = **packed array**['A'..'Z', 'A'..'Z'] **of** *char*;
       BooleanTable = **array**[*boolean, boolean*] **of** *boolean*;
       BitArray = **array**[0..1, 0..1, 0..1, 0..1] **of** 0..1;
       Shirt = **array**[*Color*, 14..18, 32..36] **of** *integer*;
       MixedArray = **array**[*Color*, 'A'..'F', 0..10, *boolean*] **of** *real*;
       InStockArray = **array**['A'..'F'] **of array**[*Color*] **of** *boolean*;
       ShirtStock = **array**[1..5] **of** *Shirt*;

    How many elements can be stored in an array of each of the following
    types?

    (a) *BigTable*   (b) *PointTable*   (c) *CharTable*
    (d) *BooleanTable*   (e) *BitArray*   (f) *Shirt*
    (g) *MixedArray*   (h) *InStockArray*   (i) *ShirtStock*

2. Assume that the following declarations have been made:

    type
       String = **packed array**[1..6] **of** *char*;
       Array3X3 = **array**[1..3, 1..3] **of** *integer*;
       ArrayOfStrings = **array**[1..2] **of** *String*;

var
　　TextLine : ArrayOfStrings;
　　Matrix : Array3X3;
　　i, j : integer;

and that the following data are entered for those of the following
statements that involve input:

ABCD
EFGH
IJKL
MNOP
QRST
UVWX

For each of the following, tell what value (if any) is assigned to each
array element, or explain why an error results.

(a) **for** *i* := 1 **to** 3 **do**
　　　for *j* := 1 **to** 3 **do**
　　　　Matrix[*i*, *j*] := *i* + *j*;
(b) **for** *i* := 1 **to** 2 **do**
　　　begin
　　　　for *j* := 1 **to** 6 **do**
　　　　　read (*TextLine*[*i*, *j*]);
　　　　readln
　　　end (∗ **for** ∗);
(c) **for** *i* := 1 **to** 2 **do**
　　　begin
　　　　for *j* := 1 **to** 6 **do**
　　　　　read (*TextLine*[*i*][*j*]);
　　　　readln
　　　end (∗ **for** ∗);
(d) **for** *i* := 1 **to** 2 **do**
　　　for *j* := 1 **to** 6 **do**
　　　　read (*TextLine*[*i*, *j*]);
(e) **for** *j* := 1 **to** 6 **do**
　　　begin
　　　　for *i* := 1 **to** 2 **do**
　　　　　read (*TextLine*[*i*, *j*]);
　　　　readln
　　　end (∗ **for** ∗);
(f) **for** *j* := 1 **to** 6 **do**
　　　begin
　　　　for *i* := 1 **to** 2 **do**
　　　　　read (*TextLine*[*j*, *i*]);
　　　　readln
　　　end (∗ **for** ∗);

(g) **for** $i := 1$ **to** 2 **do**
     for $j := 6$ **downto** 1 **do**
         if not *eoln* **then**
             read (*TextLine*[i, j])
         else
             readln;
(h) **for** $i := 1$ **to** 3 **do**
     for $j := 3$ **downto** 1 **do**
         if $i = j$ **then**
             Matrix[i, j] $:= 0$
         else
             Matrix[i, j] $:= 1$;
(i) **for** $i := 1$ **to** 3 **do**
     for $j := 1$ **to** 3 **do**
         if $i < j$ **then**
             Matrix[i, j] $:= -1$
         else if $i = j$ **then**
             Matrix[i, j] $:= 0$
         else
             Matrix[i, j] $:= 1$;
(j) **for** $i := 1$ **to** 3 **do**
     begin
         for $j := 1$ **to** i **do**
             Matrix[i, j] $:= 0$;
         for $j := i + 1$ **to** 3 **do**
             Matrix[i, j] $:= 2$
     end (∗ **for** ∗);

3. Modify the program segment on page 393 so that it calculates and displays the average temperature at each of the three locations.

4. In procedure *Convert* of the inventory control program in Figure 11.6, a for loop is used to search the array *BrandNames* for the *Name* entered by the user. This means that the entire array is examined for each *Name*. Rewrite this program segment so the search terminates as soon as *Name* is found in the array. (*Hint*: Be careful not to "fall off the end" of the enumerated type *BrandType*. You may find it convenient to add a dummy last value in this type.)

5. Like one-dimensional arrays, multidimensional arrays are stored in a block of consecutive memory locations, and address translation formulas are used to determine the location in memory of each array element. To illustrate, consider an array A of type **array**[1..3, 1..4] **of** *integer*, and suppose that an integer can be stored in one memory word. If A is allocated memory in a rowwise manner and b is its **base address**, then the first row of A, $A[1, 1]$, $A[1, 2]$, $A[1, 3]$, $A[1, 4]$ is stored in words b, $b + 1$, $b + 2$, $b + 3$, the second row in words $b + 4$ through $b + 7$, and the third row in words $b + 8$ through $b + 11$.

Address | Memory | Array Element

	⋮	
b		$A[1,1]$
$b+1$		$A[1,2]$
$b+2$		$A[1,3]$
$b+3$		$A[1,4]$
$b+4$		$A[2,1]$
$b+5$		$A[2,2]$
$b+6$		$A[2,3]$
$b+7$		$A[2,4]$
$b+8$		$A[3,1]$
$b+9$		$A[3,2]$
$b+10$		$A[3,3]$
$b+11$		$A[3,4]$
	⋮	

In general, $A[i, j]$ is stored in word $b + 4(i - 1) + (j - 1)$.

(a) Give a similar diagram and formula for $A[i, j]$, assuming columnwise allocation.

(b) Give diagrams and formulas for both rowwise and columnwise allocation if A is of type **array**$[0..3, -1..1]$ **of** *integer*.

(c) Repeat part (b) for A of type **array**$[0..2, 4..7]$ **of** *real* where real values require two words for storage.

6. A certain company has a product line that includes five items that sell for \$100, \$75, \$120, \$150, and \$35. There are four salespersons working for this company, and the following table gives the sales report for a typical week:

Salesperson Number	Item Number				
	1	2	3	4	5
1	10	4	5	6	7
2	7	0	12	1	3
3	4	9	5	0	8
4	3	2	1	5	6

Write a program to

(a) Compute the total dollar sales for each salesperson.

(b) Compute the total commission for each salesperson if the sales commission is 10 percent.

(c) Find the total income for each salesperson for the week if each salesperson receives a fixed salary of \$200 per week in addition to commission payments.

7. Write a program to calculate and display the first ten rows of *Pascal's triangle*. The first part of the triangle has the form

```
                1
              1   1
            1   2   1
          1   3   3   1
        1   4   6   4   1
```

in which each row begins and ends with 1, and each of the other entries in a row is the sum of the two entries just above it. If this form for the output seems too challenging, you might display the triangle as

```
        1
        1   1
        1   2   1
        1   3   3   1
        1   4   6   4
```

8. A demographic study of the metropolitan area around Dogpatch divided it into three regions, urban, suburban, and exurban, and published the following table showing the annual migration from one region to another (the numbers represent percentages):

↗	Urban	Suburban	Exurban
Urban	1.1	0.3	0.7
Suburban	0.1	1.2	0.3
Exurban	0.2	0.6	1.3

For example, 0.3 percent of the urbanites (0.003 times the current population) move to the suburbs each year. The diagonal entries represent internal growth rates. Using a two-dimensional array with an enumerated type for the indices to store this table, write a program to determine the population of each region after 10, 20, 30, 40, and 50 years. Assume that the current populations of the urban, suburban, and exurban regions are 2.1, 1.4, and 0.9 million, respectively.

9. Suppose that the prices for the fifteen automobile models in the first example of Section 11.3 are as follows:

Model #	Model Price
1	$ 7,450
2	$ 9,995
3	$26,500
4	$ 5,999
5	$10,400
6	$ 8,885
7	$11,700
8	$14,440
9	$17,900
10	$ 9,550
11	$10,500
12	$ 8,050
13	$ 7,990
14	$12,300
15	$ 6,999

Write a program to read this list of prices and the sales table given in Section 11.3 and calculate the total dollar sales for each salesman and the total dollar sales for all salesmen.

10. If A and B are two $m \times n$ matrices, their **sum** is defined as follows: If A_{ij} and B_{ij} are the entries in the ith row and jth column of A and B, respectively, then $A_{ij} + B_{ij}$ is the entry in the ith row and jth column of their sum, which will also be an $m \times n$ matrix. Write a program using procedures to read two $m \times n$ matrices, display them, and calculate and display their sum.

11. The inventory control program in Example 4 of Section 11.3 simply updates the array *JeansInStock* with sales figures entered during execution. Extend the program by adding other user options such as the following:

    (a) Search the array *JeansInStock* to determine how many of a particular kind of jeans are currently in stock.
    (b) Print a reorder list of all brand names, styles, and sizes of jeans for which the number in stock is below some specified reorder point.
    (c) Do the same as in (b), but print an overstocked list of jeans for which the number in stock is above some specified overstocked point.

12. Write an inventory control program like that in Example 4 of Section 11.3 (see also the preceding exercise), but for an automobile dealership and using a five-dimensional array. The first index is the make of a car (*Chrysler, Dodge, Plymouth*), the second is style (*TwoDoor, FourDoor, StationWagon, Van*), the third is color (*blue, brown, green, red, silver, yellow*), the fourth is the year of the vehicle (a small subrange of integers), and the fifth is a sales code (A, B, C).

13. The **Morse code** is a standard encoding scheme that uses substitutions similar to those in the scheme described in Exercise 9 of Section 10.3. The substitutions used in this case are shown in the following table. Write a program to read a message either in plain text or in Morse code and then encode or decode the message.

A ·—	M ——	Y —·——
B —···	N —·	Z ——··
C —·—·	O ———	1 ·————
D —··	P ·——·	2 ··———
E ·	Q ——·—	3 ···——
F ··—·	R ·—·	4 ····—
G ——·	S ···	5 ·····
H ····	T —	6 —····
I ··	U ··—	7 ——···
J ·———	V ···—	8 ———··
K —·—	W ·——	9 ————·
L ·—··	X —··—	0 —————

14. A *magic square* is an $n \times n$ matrix in which each of the integers 1, 2, 3, . . . , n^2 appears exactly once and all column sums, row sums, and diagonal sums are equal. For example, the following is a 5×5 magic square in which all the rows, columns, and diagonals add up to 65:

17	24	1	8	15
23	5	7	14	16
4	6	13	20	22
10	12	19	21	3
11	18	25	2	9

The following is a procedure for constructing an $n \times n$ magic square for any odd integer n. Place 1 in the middle of the top row. Then after integer k has been placed, move up one row and one column to the right to place the next integer $k + 1$, unless one of the following occurs:

   (i) If a move takes you above the top row in the jth column, move to the bottom of the jth column and place the integer there.
  (ii) If a move takes you outside to the right of the square in the ith row, place the integer in the ith row at the left side.
 (iii) If a move takes you to an already filled square or if you move out of the square at the upper right-hand corner, place $k + 1$ immediately below k.

Write a program to construct an $n \times n$ magic square for any odd value of n.

15. The famous mathematician G. H. Hardy once mentioned to the brilliant young Indian mathematician Ramanujan that he had just ridden in a taxi whose number he considered to be very dull. Ramanujan promptly replied that on the contrary, the number was very interesting because it was the smallest positive integer that could be written as the sum of two cubes (that is, written in the form $x^3 + y^3$, with x and y integers) in two different ways. Write a program to find the number of Hardy's taxi.

16. A *directed graph*, or *digraph*, consists of a set of *vertices* and a set of *directed arcs* joining certain of these vertices. For example, the following diagram pictures a directed graph having five vertices numbered 1, 2, 3, 4, and 5, and seven directed arcs joining vertices 1 to 2, 1 to 4, 1 to 5, 3 to 1, 3 to itself, 4 to 3, and 5 to 1:

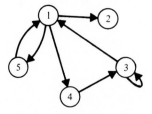

A directed graph having n vertices can be represented by its ***adjacency matrix***, which is an $n \times n$ matrix, with the entry in the ith row and jth column a 1 if vertex i is joined to vertex j, 0 otherwise. The adjacency matrix for the preceding graph is

$$\begin{bmatrix} 0 & 1 & 0 & 1 & 1 \\ 0 & 0 & 0 & 0 & 0 \\ 1 & 0 & 1 & 0 & 0 \\ 0 & 0 & 1 & 0 & 0 \\ 1 & 0 & 0 & 0 & 0 \end{bmatrix}$$

If A is the adjacency matrix for a directed graph, then the entry in the ith row and jth column of A^k gives the number of ways that vertex j can be reached from vertex i by following k edges. Write a program to read the number of vertices in a directed graph and a collection of ordered pairs of vertices representing directed arcs; construct the adjacency matrix; and then find the number of ways that each vertex can be reached from every other vertex by following k edges for some value of k.

17. The game of ***Life***, invented by the mathematician John H. Conway, is intended to model life in a society of organisms. Consider a rectangular array of cells, each of which may contain an organism. If the array is considered to extend indefinitely in both directions, then each cell has eight neighbors, the eight cells surrounding it. Births and deaths occur according to the following rules:
    (i) An organism is born in any empty cell having exactly three neighbors.
    (ii) An organism dies from isolation if it has fewer than two neighbors.
    (iii) An organism dies from overcrowding if it has more than three neighbors.
    (iv) All other organisms survive to the next generation.

    To illustrate, the following shows the first five generations of a particular configuration of organisms:

    Write a program to play the game of Life and investigate the patterns produced by various initial configurations. Some configurations die off rather rapidly; others repeat after a certain number of generations; others change shape and size and may move across the array; and still others may produce "gliders" that detach themselves from the society and sail off into space.

18. The game of Nim is played by two players. There are usually three piles of objects, and on his or her turn, each player is allowed to take

any number (at least one) of objects from one pile. The player taking the last object loses. Write a program that allows the user to play Nim against the computer. You might have the computer play a perfect game, or you might design the program to "teach" the computer. One way for the computer to "learn" is to assign a value to every possible move, based on experience gained from playing games. The value of each possible move is stored in some array; initially, each value is 0. The value of each move in a winning sequence of moves is increased by 1, and those in a losing sequence are decreased by 1. At each stage, the computer selects the best possible move (that having the highest value).

19. The game of Hangman is played by two persons. One person selects a word and the other person tries to guess the word by guessing individual letters. Design a program to play Hangman. You might store a list of words in an array or file and have the program randomly select a word for the user to guess (see Section 6.3).

20. Write a program that allows the user to play Tic-Tac-Toe against the computer.

Programming Pointers

Many of the difficulties encountered when using multidimensional arrays are similar to those for one-dimensional arrays considered in Chapter 9. The first five of the following programming pointers are simply restatements of some of the programming pointers in Chapter 9, and the reader should refer to those for an expanded discussion.

1. *The types of the components of an array may be any predefined or user-defined data type, and the type of each index may be any ordinal type.*

2. *When processing the elements of a multidimensional array, each index must be compatible with the type specified for that index in the array declaration.*

3. *When reading the elements of an array of characters, remember that end-of-line marks are read as blanks.*

4. *Assignment of one array to another requires that the arrays have the same type.*

5. *Multidimensional arrays that are parameters of procedures or functions should be variable parameters so that memory is utilized more efficiently.*

6. *The amount of memory required to store a multidimensional array may be quite large, even though each index is restricted to a small range*

of values. For example, the three-dimensional array *ThreeD* declared by

type
    ThreeDimArray = **array**[1..20, 1..20, 1..20] **of** *integer*;
var
    ThreeD : *ThreeDimArray*;

requires 20 × 20 × 20 = 8,000 memory locations.

7. *When processing the elements of a multidimensional array by using nested repetition structures, these structures must be arranged so that the indices vary in the intended order.* To illustrate, suppose that the two-dimensional array *Table* is declared by

type
    Array3X4 = **array**[1..3, 1..4] **of** *integer*;
var
    Table : *Array3X4*;

and the following data are to be read into the array:

    11   22   27   35   39   40   48   51   57   66   67   92

If these values are to be read and assigned in a rowwise manner so that the value is the matrix

$$\begin{bmatrix} 11 & 22 & 27 & 35 \\ 39 & 40 & 48 & 51 \\ 57 & 66 & 67 & 92 \end{bmatrix}$$

then the following nested **for** statements are appropriate:

    for *row* := 1 **to** 3 **do**
        for *col* := 1 **to** 4 **do**
            read (*Table*[*row*, *col*]);

If the values are to be read and assigned in a columnwise manner so that *Table* is

$$\begin{bmatrix} 11 & 35 & 48 & 66 \\ 22 & 39 & 51 & 67 \\ 27 & 40 & 57 & 92 \end{bmatrix}$$

then the statements should be

    for *col* := 1 **to** 4 **do**
        for *row* := 1 **to** 3 **do**
            read (*Table*[*row*, *col*]);

Variations and Extensions

As in the case of one-dimensional arrays, there are only a few variations from or extensions to the array-processing features of standard Pascal in other versions of Pascal. Two that we noted at the end of Chapter 9 were

- Arrays of the same type may be compared with the relational operators = and <> (UCSD).

- Arrays may be initialized in the declaration part of the program. (Turbo)

See Appendix G for additional details.

12

Records

Yea, from the table of my memory
I'll wipe away all trivial fond records.

WILLIAM SHAKESPEARE, *Hamlet*

In Chapters 9 and 11, we introduced one of Pascal's structured data types, the array, which may be used to store elements of the same type. In many situations, however, we need to process items that are related in some way but that are not all of the same type. For example, a date consists of a month name (of string type), a day (of type 1..31), and a year (of type 1900..2000 perhaps); an employee record might contain, among other items, an employee name (string), age (integer), number of dependents (integer), and an hourly pay rate (real). Such related data items of different types can be organized in a ***record***. In this chapter we consider how records are implemented and processed in Pascal.

12.1 Introduction to Records and Fields

A ***record*** is a data structure in which a collection of related data items of possibly different types may be stored. The positions in which these data items are stored are called the ***fields*** of the record. Thus, an employee record might contain a name field, an age field, a dependents field, and an hourly rate field.

Records can be implemented in Pascal by using the structured data type ***record***. A record declaration has the form

> **record**
>   *field-list*
> **end**;

where *field-list* is of the form

$$list\text{-}1 : type\text{-}1;$$
$$list\text{-}2 : type\text{-}2;$$
$$\vdots$$
$$list\text{-}m : type\text{-}m$$

Each *list-i* is a single identifier or a list of identifiers, separated by commas, that name the fields of the record, and *type-i* specifies the type of each of these fields. This is summarized in the following syntax diagrams:

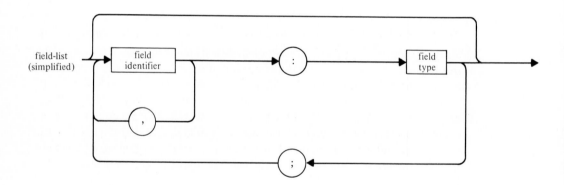

To illustrate, an employee record, as we have described it, could be declared by

record
    Name : **packed array**[1..20] **of** *char*;
    Age, Dependents : *integer*;
    HourlyRate : *real*
end;

Such declarations of records, like those of other data types, may be used in the variable section of a program's declaration part to specify the types of variables. But as with other structured types, it is preferable to assign them to type identifiers in the type section and then use these identifiers to declare record variables. For example, consider

type
  NameString = **packed array**[1..20] **of** *char*;
  NameOfMonth = **packed array**[1..8] **of** *char*;
  EmployeeRecord = **record**
                        Name : *NameString*;
                        Age, Dependents : *integer*;
                        HourlyRate : *real*
                     end;
  BirthRecord = **record**
                     Month : *NameOfMonth*;
                     Day : 1..31;
                     Year : 1900..2000
                  end;

var
  Employee : *EmployeeRecord*;
  Birth : *BirthRecord*;

The variable *Employee* may have as a value any record of type *Employee-Record*. The first field of the record is of type *NameString* and is named with the field identifier *Name*; the second and third fields are of type *integer* and have the names *Age* and *Dependents*; and the fourth field is of type *real* and is named *HourlyRate*. The variable *Birth* may have as a value any record of type *BirthRecord*. The first field of the record is of type *NameOfMonth* and is named *Month*; the second field is of subrange type 1..31 and is named *Day*; and the third field is of type 1900..2000 and is named *Year*. Typical values for *Employee* and *Birth* might be pictured as follows:

Name	*Age*	*Dependents*	*HourlyRate*
John Q. Doe	48	4	12.25

Month	*Day*	*Year*
January	15	1941

We have seen that each element of an array can be accessed directly by using an indexed variable formed by attaching an index enclosed in brackets to the array name. In a similar manner, one can access each field of a record directly by using a ***field-designated variable,*** which we abbreviate to ***fielded variable,*** of the form

  record-name.field-name

in which a period followed by the field name is attached to the record name. Thus *Employee.Name* designates the first field of the record variable *Employee*. For the record displayed here, the value of *Employee.Name* would be the string JohnƀQ.ƀDoeƀƀƀƀƀƀƀƀƀƀ (where ƀ denotes a blank). Similarly, *Employee.Age, Employee.Dependents,* and *Employee.HourlyRate* refer to the second, third, and fourth fields and would have the values 48, 4, and 12.25, respectively. If the second record is the value of the record variable *Birth,* then *Birth.Month* has the value Januaryb, *Birth.Day* has the value 15, and *Birth.Year* has the value 1941.

The scope of a field identifier is the record in which that identifier is declared. This means that the same identifier may not be used to specify two different fields within the same record, but an identifier that names a field may be used elsewhere in the program for some other purpose.

The fields that comprise a record may be of any data type; in particular, they may be other records. For example, the declarations

type
    NameString = **packed array**[1..20] **of** *char*;
    NameOfMonth = **packed array**[1..8] **of** *char*;
    Date = **record**
            Month : *NameOfMonth*;
            Day : 1..31;
            Year : 1900..2000
      end;
    PersonnelRecord = **record**
                Name : *NameString*;
                Birth : *Date*;
                Age, Dependents : *integer*;
                HourlyRate : *real*
            end;

var
    Employee : *PersonnelRecord*;

specify that variable *Employee* may have as a value any record of type *PersonnelRecord*. Such a record consists of five fields: The first field is of type *NameString* and is identified by *Name*; the second field is of type *Date* and is itself a record having three fields (*Month, Day,* and *Year*); the third and fourth fields are named *Age* and *Dependents* and are of type *integer*; and the fifth field is of type *real* and is named *HourlyRate*. A typical value for *Employee* might be pictured as follows:

	Birth					
Name	*Month*	*Day*	*Year*	*Age*	*Dependents*	*HourlyRate*
John Q. Doe	January	15	1941	48	4	12.25

The fields within such a ***nested record*** or ***hierarchical record*** may be accessed by simply affixing a second field identifier to the name of the larger record. Thus, *Employee.Birth.Month* refers to the first field in the inner record of type *Date*; for this record, its value would be the string Januaryb. Similarly, the values of *Employee.Birth.Day* and *Employee.Birth.Year* would be 15 and 1941, respectively.

All the records considered in this section consist of a fixed number of fields, each of which has a fixed type. It is also possible to declare records in which some of the fields are fixed but the number and types of other fields may vary. Thus, the number and types of fields in a variable of this record type may change during program execution. Such *variant records* are discussed in Section 12.5.

12.2 Processing Records

In the previous section we saw that records may be used to store several related data items that may be of different types and that each item or field in a record can be accessed with a fielded variable of the form

> *record-name.field-name*

In this section we discuss how values can be assigned to the fields within a record, how these values can be read and displayed, and how the value of one record variable can be copied to another.

Because both fielded variables and indexed variables serve to specify a particular item in a structure, they are used in much the same way. To illustrate, consider the record type *ClassRecord* and the record variable *Student* declared by

```
const
    NameLength = 15;
    NumScores = 5;
    MaxScore = 100;

type
    NameString = packed array[1..NameLength] of char;
    ListOfScores = array[1..NumScores] of 0..MaxScore;
    ClassRecord = record
                    Snumb : integer;
                    Name : NameString;
                    Sex : char;
                    TestScore : ListOfScores
                  end;

var
    Student : ClassRecord;
```

Because the fielded variable *Student.Snumb* is of integer type, it may be assigned an integer value in an assignment statement

> *Student.Snumb* := 12345;

or by an input statement

> *readln (Student.Snumb)*;

and its value can be displayed by using an output statement

> *writeln* ('Student number: ', *Student.Snumb*);

Similarly, because *Student.TestScore* is an array, *Student.TestScore*[1] may be used to reference the first test score for this particular student.

Input and output of an entire record to or from a text file (including *input* and *output*) must be done by reading or displaying the value of each field in the record. For example, to read a value for the record variable *Student*, the following statements might be used:

> *readln (Student.Snumb)*;
> *ReadString (Student.Name, NameLength)*;
> *readln (Student.Sex)*;
> **for** *i* := 1 **to** *NumScores* **do**
>   *read (Student.TestScore[i])*;
> *readln*;

where *ReadString* is the procedure for reading strings described in Section 10.1.

To illustrate record processing, suppose that a data file contains information about the students in a certain class as just described: student number, first name, last name, sex, and five test scores:

> 12345
> John Doe
> M
> 44 55 78 83 72
> 15651
> Mary Smith
> F
> 94 85 62 66 83
> 22001
> Pete Vandervan
> M
> 34 44 29 51 47
>   ⋮

A program is to be designed to read this information and calculate and display the average of the test scores for each student.

Since the information in this file consists of students' numbers, names, sex, and test scores, it is natural to organize this information in records of type *ClassRecord*. The processing required to solve this problem is summarized in the following algorithm:

ALGORITHM TO PROCESS STUDENT RECORDS

1. Read first student record.
2. While the end of the file has not been reached, do the following:
   a. Calculate the average score for this student.
   b. Display student's number, name, sex, and average score.
   c. Read the next student record.

The program in Figure 12.1 implements this algorithm. The procedure *ReadRecord* uses statements like those given earlier to read a value for the record variable *StudentInfo*. The function *Mean* of Section 11.2 is used to calculate the average test scores.

```pascal
PROGRAM StudentAverages1 (input, output, StudentInfoFile);

(*****************************************************************

   Program to read student records each of which includes a student's
   number, name, sex, 5 test scores; calculate the average of the
   test scores; and display this average together with the student's
   number, name, and sex.  The student records are read from the
   text file StudentInfoFile.

*****************************************************************)

CONST
   StringLimit = 15;
   NumScores = 5;
   MaxScore = 100;

TYPE
   String = PACKED ARRAY[1..StringLimit] OF char;
   ListOfScores = ARRAY[1..NumScores] OF 0..MaxScore;
   ClassRecord = RECORD
                    Snumb : integer;
                    Name : String;
                    Sex : char;
                    TestScore :  ListOfScores
                 END;

VAR
   StudentInfoFile : text;   (* file containing student records *)
   Student : ClassRecord;    (* record for current student *)
   i,                        (* index *)
   Sum : integer;            (* sum of test scores *)
   AveScore : real;          (* average test score *)

PROCEDURE ReadRecord (VAR StudentInfoFile : text;
                      VAR Student : ClassRecord);

   (*****************************************************************

      Procedure to read and return a student's record Student from
      the text file StudentInfoFile.

   *****************************************************************)

   VAR
      i : integer;   (* index *)
```

Figure 12.1

Figure 12.1   (cont.)

```
PROCEDURE ReadString (VAR TextFile : text; VAR Str : String;
                      MaxString : integer);

   (**************************************************************

      Procedure to read characters into string variable Str from
      TextFile until an end-of-line mark is encountered or the
      upper limit MaxString on the length of Str is reached.
      Any positions for which no characters are read will be
      filled with blanks.

      **************************************************************)

   VAR
      i : integer;          (* index *)

   BEGIN (* ReadString *)
      FOR i := 1 TO MaxString DO
         IF NOT eoln(TextFile) THEN
            read (TextFile, Str[i])
      ELSE
         Str[i] := ' ';
      readln (TextFile)
   END (* ReadString *);

BEGIN (* ReadRecord *)
   readln (StudentInfoFile, Student.Snumb);
   ReadString (StudentInfoFile, Student.Name, StringLimit);
   readln (StudentInfoFile, Student.Sex);
   FOR i := 1 TO NumScores DO
      read (StudentInfoFile, Student.TestScore[i]);
   readln (StudentInfoFile)
END (* ReadRecord *);

FUNCTION Mean (VAR Item : ListOfScores; NumItems : integer) : real;

(**************************************************************

   Function to find the mean of a list of NumItems numbers
   stored in the array Item.

   **************************************************************)

VAR
   i,                (* index *)
   Sum : integer;  (* sum of the numbers *)

BEGIN (* Mean *)
   IF NumItems = 0 THEN
      BEGIN
         writeln ('No elements -- returning mean of 0');
         Mean := 0
      END (* IF *)
   ELSE
      BEGIN
         Sum := 0;
         FOR i := 1 TO NumItems DO
            Sum := Sum + Item[i];
         Mean := Sum / NumItems
      END (* ELSE *)
END (* Mean *);
```

Figure 12.1 (cont.)

```
BEGIN (* main program *)
   reset (StudentInfoFile);

   (* Print headings *)

   writeln ('Student                         Test');
   writeln ('Number        Name       Sex  Average');
   writeln ('======        ====       ===  =======');

   WHILE NOT eof(StudentInfoFile) DO
      BEGIN
         ReadRecord (StudentInfoFile, Student);
         AveScore := Mean(Student.TestScore, NumScores);
         writeln (Student.Snumb:5, Student.Name:17, Student.Sex:2,
                  AveScore:8:1)
      END (* WHILE *)
END (* main program *).
```

Listing of StudentInfoFile:

```
12345
John Doe
M
44 55 78 83 72
15651
Mary Smith
F
94 85 62 66 83
22001
Pete Vandervan
M
34 44 29 51 47
```

Sample run:

Student Number	Name	Sex	Test Average
======	====	===	=======
12345	John Doe	M	66.4
15651	Mary Smith	F	78.0
22001	Pete Vandervan	M	41.0

Sometimes it is necessary to copy the fields of one record into another record. This can be done with a series of assignment statements that copy the individual fields, but it can be done more conveniently with a single assignment statement of the form

record-variable-1 := *record-variable-2*

In this case, *the two record variables must have the same type*, which means that they must be declared using the same or equivalent type identifiers (see Section 9.2).

Recall that the value of a function may not be a structured type; in particular, it may not be a record. Records may, however, be used as parameters of functions and procedures, and in this case, the corresponding records must have the same type.

To illustrate the use of records as parameters for subprograms, consider the problem of finding the length of the segment joining two points in a plane and finding the equation of the line that passes through these points. The length of the segment joining P_1 with coordinates (x_1, y_1) and point P_2 with coordinates (x_2, y_2) is given by

$$\sqrt{(x_2 - x_1)^2 + (y_2 - y_1)^2}$$

The *slope-intercept* form of the equation of the line through P_1 and P_2 is

$$y = mx + b$$

where m is the *slope* of the line and is calculated by

$$m = \frac{y_2 - y_1}{x_2 - x_1}$$

(provided that $x_1 \neq x_2$); and b is the **y-intercept** of the line; that is, $(0, b)$ is the point where the line crosses the y axis. Using the slope m, we can calculate b as

$$b = y_1 - mx_1$$

In case $x_1 = x_2$, there is no y-intercept and the slope is not defined; the line through P_1 and P_2 is the vertical line having the equation

$$x = x_1$$

The program in Figure 12.2 uses the function *Length* to calculate the length of the segment joining points *P1* and *P2* and calls the procedure *FindLine* to find the equation of the line passing through *P1* and *P2*. Points are represented as records having two fields of real type named x and y, which represent the x and y coordinates, respectively:

```
Point = record
           x, y : real
        end;
```

```
PROGRAM PointsAndLines (input, output);

(********************************************************************

   Program to read two points represented as records, calculate
   the length of the line segment joining them, and find the
   slope-intercept equation of the line passing through them.

********************************************************************)
```

Figure 12.2

Figure 12.2 (cont.)

```
TYPE
   Point = RECORD
                x, y : real
            END;

VAR
   P1, P2 : Point;   (* 2 points being processed *)
   Response : char;  (* user response *)

FUNCTION Length (P1, P2 : Point) : real;

   (****************************************************************

      Function to calculate the length of the line segment joining
      the two points P1 and P2.

   ****************************************************************)

   BEGIN (* Length *)
      Length := sqrt(sqr(P2.x - P1.x) + sqr(P2.y - P1.y))
   END (* Length *);

PROCEDURE FindLine (P1, P2 : Point);

   (****************************************************************

      Procedure to find the slope-intercept equation  y = mx + b
      of the line passing though points P1 and P2.

   ****************************************************************)

   VAR
      m,          (* slope of line *)
      b : real;   (* y intercept of line *)

   BEGIN (* FindLine *)
      IF P1.x = P2.x THEN
         writeln ('Line is vertical line  x = ', P1.x:4:2)
      ELSE
         BEGIN
            m := (P2.y - P1.y) / (P2.x - P1.x);
            b := P1.y - m * P1.x;
            writeln ('Equation of line is y = ', m:4:2, 'x + ', b:4:2)
         END (* ELSE *)
   END (* FindLine *);

BEGIN (* main program *)
   REPEAT
      write ('Enter coordinates of points P1 and P2:  ');
      readln (P1.x, P1.y, P2.x, P2.y);
      writeln ('For points (', P1.x:4:2, ',', P1.y:4:2, ') and (',
               P2.x:4:2, ',', P2.y:4:2, '):');
      writeln ('Length of segment joining P1 & P2 is ',
               Length(P1,P2):4:2);
      FindLine (P1, P2);
      writeln;
      write ('More (Y or N)?  ');
      readln (Response)
   UNTIL Response <> 'Y'
END (* main program *).
```

Figure 12.2   (cont.)

Sample run:

```
Enter coordinates of points P1 and P2:   0 0   1 1
For points (0.00,0.00) and (1.00,1.00):
Length of segment joining P1 & P2 is 1.41
Equation of line is y = 1.00x + 0.00

More (Y or N)?   Y
Enter coordinates of points P1 and P2:   1 1   1 5
For points (1.00,1.00) and (1.00,5.00):
Length of segment joining P1 & P2 is 4.00
Line is vertical line   x = 1.00

More (Y or N)?   Y
Enter coordinates of points P1 and P2:   3.1 4.2   -5.3 7.2
For points (3.10,4.20) and (-5.30,7.20):
Length of segment joining P1 & P2 is 8.92
Equation of line is y = -0.36x + 5.31

More (Y or N)?   N
```

12.3   The *with* Statement

Writing out the complete fielded variable for each of a record's fields can be quite cumbersome. For example, consider the record type *PersonnelRecord* of the preceding section:

type
  NameString = **packed array**[1..20] **of** *char*;
  NameOfMonth = **packed array**[1..8] **of** *char*;
  Date = **record**
            Month : *NameOfMonth*;
            Day : 1..31;
            Year : 1900..2000
          end;
  Personnel Record = **record**
                        Name : *NameString*;
                        Birth : *Date*;
                        Age, Dependents : *integer*;
                        HourlyRate : *real*
                      end;

var
  CompanyName : *NameString*;
  Employee : *PersonnelRecord*;
  StartingDate : *Date*;

To display the values of *StartingDate* and *Employee,* we must display the values of each of their fields:

write ('Date of first employment: ');
writeln (*StartingDate.Month, StartingDate.Day*:3, ',',
    StartingDate.Year:5);
writeln;
writeln (*Employee.Name*);
writeln ('Birthday: ', *Employee.Birth.Month*,
    Employee.Birth.Day:3, ',', *Employee.Birth.Year*:5,
    ' Age = ', *Employee.Age*:1);
writeln ('# of dependents: ', *Employee.Dependents*:1);
writeln ('Hourly pay rate: $', *Employee.HourlyRate*:4:2);

To simplify references to the fields in a record, Pascal provides an option in which it is not necessary to specify the record name each time that a field within that record is referenced. This is accomplished by using the **with** *statement* of the form

with *record-name* **do**
    statement

The record name is automatically combined with each field identifier in the specified statement to form a complete fielded variable. Thus the statement

with *StartingDate* **do**
    writeln (*Month, Day*:3, ',', *Year*:5);

attaches the record name *StartingDate* to the field identifiers *Month, Day,* and *Year* to form the fielded variables *StartingDate.Month, StartingDate.Day,* and *StartingDate.Year.* It is thus equivalent to the second statement above.

Identifiers in a **with** statement that are not field identifiers are not combined with the record name but, rather, are treated in the usual way. Thus, in the statement

with *StartingDate* **do**
    writeln (*Month, Day*:3, ',', *Year*:5, *CompanyName*:30);

the identifier *CompanyName* is not a field identifier in the record *StartingDate* and hence is not modified by the **with** statement. This statement is equivalent, therefore, to

writeln (*StartingDate.Month, StartingDate.Day*:3, ',',
    StartingDate.Year:5, *CompanyName*:30);

With statements may also be *nested*; that is, one **with** statement may appear within another **with** statement. To illustrate, the preceding statements to display the value of the record variable *Employee* could be replaced by the **with** statement

```
with Employee do
   begin
      writeln (Name);
      writeln ('Birthday: ', Birth.Month, Birth.Day:3, ',',
               Birth.Year:5, ' Age = ', Age:1);
      writeln ('# of dependents: ', Dependents:1);
      writeln ('Hourly pay rate: $', HourlyRate:4:2)
   end (* with *);
```

or nested **with** statements might be used:

```
with Employee do
   begin
      writeln (Name);
      with Birth do
         writeln ('Birthday: ', Month, Day:3, ',', Year:5,
                  ' Age = ', Age:1);
      writeln ('# of dependents: ', Dependents:1);
      writeln ('Hourly pay rate: $', HourlyRate:4:2)
   end (* with *);
```

In this case, the inner **with** statement first attaches the record name *Birth* to the field identifers *Month, Day,* and *Year* to form the fielded variables *Birth.Month, Birth.Day,* and *Birth.Year*; but it does not attach *Birth* to the identifier *Age,* because this is not a field identifier within the record *Birth.* The outer **with** statement then attaches the record name *Employee* to form the fielded variables *Employee.Name, Employee.Birth.Month, Employee.Birth.Day, Employee.Birth.Year,* and *Employee.Age.*

An extended form of the **with** statement allows several record names to be listed:

```
with record-name-1, record-name-2, . . . , record-name-n do
   statement
```

This form is equivalent to

```
with record-name-1 do
   with record-name-2 do
         ·

         ·

         ·
         with record-name-n do
            statement
```

For example, the preceding nested **with** statement could also be written as

> **with** *Employee, Birth* **do**
>   **begin**
>   *writeln* (*Name*);
>   *writeln* ('Birthday: ', *Month, Day*:3, ',', *Year*:5, ' Age = ', *Age*:1);
>   *writeln* ('# of dependents: ', *Dependents*:1);
>   *writeln* ('Hourly pay rate: $', *HourlyRate*:4:2)
>   **end** (* **with** *);

The program in Figure 12.1 to read student records and display them together with an average test score can be simplified using **with** statements. Figure 12.3 shows the resulting program.

```
PROGRAM StudentAverages2 (input, output, StudentInfoFile);

(**********************************************************************

   Program to read student records, each of which includes a student's
   number, name, sex, 5 test scores; calculate the average of the
   test scores; and display this average together with the student's
   number, name, and sex.  The student records are read from the
   text file StudentInfoFile.

**********************************************************************)

CONST
   StringLimit = 15;
   NumScores = 5;
   MaxScore = 100;

TYPE
   String = PACKED ARRAY[1..StringLimit] OF char;
   ListOfScores = ARRAY[1..NumScores] OF 0..MaxScore;
   ClassRecord = RECORD
                    Snumb : integer;
                    Name : String;
                    Sex : char;
                    TestScore :  ListOfScores
                 END;

VAR
   StudentInfoFile : text;    (* file containing student records *)
   Student : ClassRecord;     (* record for current student *)
   i,                         (* index *)
   Sum : integer;             (* sum of test scores *)
   AveScore : real;           (* average test score *)
```

Figure 12.3

Figure 12.3 (cont.)

```
PROCEDURE ReadRecord (VAR StudentInfoFile : text;
                      VAR Student : ClassRecord);

   (*****************************************************************

      Procedure to read and return a student's record Student from
      the text file StudentInfoFile.

   *****************************************************************)

   VAR
      i : integer;   (* index *)

   PROCEDURE ReadString (VAR TextFile : text; VAR Str : String;
                         MaxString : integer);

      (*****************************************************************

         Procedure to read characters into string variable Str from
         TextFile until an end-of-line mark is encountered or the
         upper limit MaxString on the length of Str is reached.
         Any positions for which no characters are read will be
         filled with blanks.

      *****************************************************************)

      VAR
         i : integer;       (* index *)

      BEGIN (* ReadString *)
         FOR i := 1 TO MaxString DO
            IF NOT eoln(TextFile) THEN
               read (TextFile, Str[i])
         ELSE
            Str[i] := ' ';
         readln (TextFile)
      END (* ReadString *);

   BEGIN (* ReadRecord *)
      WITH Student DO
         BEGIN
            readln (StudentInfoFile, Snumb);
            ReadString (StudentInfoFile, Name, StringLimit);
            readln (StudentInfoFile, Sex);
            FOR i := 1 TO NumScores DO
               read (StudentInfoFile, TestScore[i]);
            readln (StudentInfoFile)
         END (* WITH *)
   END (* ReadRecord *);

FUNCTION Mean (VAR Item : ListOfScores; NumItems : integer) : real;

   (*****************************************************************

      Function to find the mean of a list of NumItems numbers
      stored in the array Item.

   *****************************************************************)
```

Figure 12.3 (cont.)

```
    VAR
        i,                  (* index *)
        Sum : integer;  (* sum of the numbers *)

    BEGIN (* Mean *)
        IF NumItems = 0 THEN
            BEGIN
                writeln ('No elements -- returning mean of 0');
                Mean := 0
            END (* IF *)
        ELSE
            BEGIN
                Sum := 0;
                FOR i := 1 TO NumItems DO
                    Sum := Sum + Item[i];
                Mean := Sum / NumItems
            END (* ELSE *)
    END (* Mean *);

BEGIN (* main program *)
    reset (StudentInfoFile);

    (* Print headings *)

    writeln ('Student                     Test');
    writeln ('Number      Name        Sex  Average');
    writeln ('======      ====        ===  =======');

    WHILE NOT eof(StudentInfoFile) DO
        BEGIN
            ReadRecord (StudentInfoFile, Student);
            AveScore := Mean(Student.TestScore, NumScores);
            WITH Student DO
                writeln (Snumb:5, Name:17, Sex:2, AveScore:8:1)
        END (* WHILE *)
END (* main program *).
```

In some cases it may not be desirable to use **with** statements. For example, the statement

$$readln \ (P1.x, \ P1.y, \ P2.x, \ P2.y);$$

in the program of Figure 12.2 to read coordinates of points *P1* and *P2* cannot be written as

    with *P1, P2* **do**
        readln (x, y, x, y);

since this would attach the record variable *P2* to the field identifiers *x* and *y* and is thus equivalent to

$$readln \ (P2.x, \ P2.y, \ P2.x, \ P2.y);$$

which reads a value only for the record *P2* (twice). The statement could be written

    with *P1* **do**
      readln (*x*, *y*, *P2.x*, *P2.y*);

or

    with *P1* **do**
      read (*x*, *y*);
    with *P2* **do**
      readln (*x*, *y*);

but neither of these seems better than the original. Similarly, replacing the statement

    Length := *sqrt(sqr(P2.x − P1.x) + sqr(P2.y − P1.y)*

with

    with *P1*, *P2* **do**
      Length := *sqrt(sqr(x − x) + sqr(y − y))*

is obviously incorrect, since it is equivalent to the statement

    Length := *sqrt(sqr(P2.x − P2.x) + sqr(P2.y − P2.y))*

which would always assign 0 to *Length*.

12.4 Example: Grading on the Curve and Sorting an Array of Records

Consider the problem of assigning letter grades to students by using the grading scheme commonly called "grading on the curve." In this scheme, a letter grade is assigned to a numerical grade according to the following table:

x = Numeric Score	Letter Grade
$x < m - \dfrac{3}{2}\sigma$	F
$m - \dfrac{3}{2}\sigma \leq x < m - \dfrac{1}{2}\sigma$	D
$m - \dfrac{1}{2}\sigma \leq x < m + \dfrac{1}{2}\sigma$	C
$m + \dfrac{1}{2}\sigma \leq x < m + \dfrac{3}{2}\sigma$	B
$m + \dfrac{3}{2}\sigma \leq x$	A

where m is the mean numeric score and σ is the standard deviation (see Exercises 14 and 15 of Section 9.3).

For each student we have the following information: student number and name and three numeric scores, one for homework, another for tests, and the third for the final examination. The final numeric grade is a weighted average of these scores and is to be calculated by

$$.2 \times \text{(homework score)} + .5 \times \text{(tests score)} + .3 \times \text{(exam score)}$$

The output is to be a list of student numbers, final numeric scores, and final letter grades, arranged so that the scores are in descending order.

One alternative for storing this information would be to use seven **parallel arrays,** one of integer type to store the student numbers, another of string type to store the names, four arrays of real type to store the numeric scores, and an array of character type to store the letter grades. However, since the fields of a record may be of different types, it is much more convenient to use a single array whose components are records containing these items of information.

In the program in Figure 12.4, the given information, together with the calculated numeric score and letter grade for each student, is stored in a record having the following structure:

```
StudentRecord = record
                   Snumb : integer;
                   Name : NameString;
                   Scores : record
                               HomeWork, Tests, Exam : real
                            end;
                   FinalNumScore : real;
                   LetterGrade : char
                end;
```

There is one record for each student, and the array *Student* is used to store these records so that *Student*[*i*] refers to the record of the *i*th student.

The structure of the program is displayed by the following structure diagram:

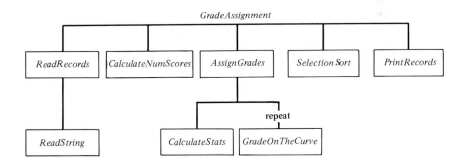

The procedure *ReadRecords* is first called to read each student's number, name, and three scores, storing these in the array *Student*. This array is then passed to the procedure *CalculateNumScore,* which calculates the final numeric score for each student and inserts it in the field *FinalNumScore* of his or her record. The array of records is then passed to the procedure *AssignGrades*, which inserts the final letter grade in the field *LetterGrade* of each record. The procedure *AssignGrades* uses the procedure *CalculateStats* to calculate the mean and standard deviation of the final scores needed by the function *GradeOn-TheCurve*, which calculates the final letter grade. Finally, the program calls the procedure *SelectionSort* to arrange the records so that final numeric grades are in descending order and then calls the procedure *PrintRecords* to display the desired information. The procedure *SelectionSort* uses the selection sort algorithm described in Section 9.3, with the modification that entire records are interchanged when necessary.

```
PROGRAM GradeAssignment (input, output, ScoresFile);

(*******************************************************************

   Program to read students' records, each of which contains a
   student's number, name, and three numeric scores, one for
   homework, another for tests, and a third for the final exam.
   It calculates the final numeric grade as a weighted average of
   these scores using the weighting constants HomeworkWeight,
   TestWeight, and ExamWeight.  A letter grade is then calculated by
   "grading on the curve."  A list of student numbers with final
   numeric and letter grades is then displayed with numeric grades
   in descending order.  The student information is read from the
   text file ScoresFile.

*******************************************************************)

CONST
   NameLength = 15;
   ListLimit = 100;

TYPE
   String = PACKED ARRAY[1..NameLength] OF char;
   StudentRecord = RECORD
      Snumb : integer;
      Name : String;
      Scores : RECORD
         Homework, Tests, Exam : real
         END;
      FinalNumScore : real;
      LetterGrade : char
   END;
   StudentRecordList = ARRAY[1..ListLimit] of StudentRecord;

VAR
   ScoresFile : text;              (* file of student scores *)
   Student : StudentRecordList;    (* list of student records *)
   NumStudents,                    (* number of students *)
   i : integer;                    (* index *)
```

Figure 12.4

Figure 12.4   (cont.)

```
PROCEDURE ReadRecords (VAR Student : StudentRecordList;
                       VAR Count : integer);

   (****************************************************************

      Procedure to read and count the list Student[1], Student[2], ...
      Student[Count] of student records.

   ****************************************************************)

   VAR
      i : integer;    (* index *)

   PROCEDURE ReadString (VAR TextFile : text; VAR Str : String;
                         MaxString : integer);

      (*************************************************************

         Procedure to read characters into string variable Str from
         TextFile until an end-of-line mark is encountered or the
         upper limit MaxString on the length of Str is reached.
         Any positions for which no characters are read will be
         filled with blanks.

      *************************************************************)

      VAR
         i : integer;          (* index *)

      BEGIN (* ReadString *)
         FOR i := 1 TO MaxString DO
            IF NOT eoln(TextFile) THEN
               read (TextFile, Str[i])
            ELSE
               Str[i] := ' ';
         readln (TextFile)
      END (* ReadString *);

   BEGIN (* ReadRecords *)
      reset (ScoresFile);
      Count := 0;
      WHILE NOT eof(ScoresFile) DO
         BEGIN
            Count := Count + 1;
            WITH Student[Count], Scores DO
               BEGIN
                  readln (ScoresFile, Snumb);
                  ReadString (ScoresFile, Name, NameLength);
                  readln (ScoresFile, Homework, Tests, Exam)
               END (* WITH *)
         END (* WHILE *)
   END (* ReadRecords *);
```

Figure 12.4 (cont.)

```
PROCEDURE CalculateNumScores (VAR Student : StudentRecordList;
                              NumStudents : integer);

   (**************************************************************

   Procedure to calculate final numeric grades for each student
   as a weighted average and insert it into his/her record.

   **************************************************************)

   CONST
     HomeWorkWeight = 0.2;
     TestWeight = 0.5;
     ExamWeight = 0.3;

   VAR
     i : integer;  (* index *)

   BEGIN (* CalculateNumScores *)
     FOR i := 1 TO NumStudents DO
        WITH Student[i], Scores DO
           FinalNumScore := HomeWorkWeight * Homework + TestWeight * Tests
                            + ExamWeight * Exam
   END (* CalculateNumScores *);

PROCEDURE AssignGrades (VAR Student : StudentRecordList;
                        NumStudents : integer);

   (**************************************************************

   Procedure to insert letter grades in the students' records.

   **************************************************************)

   VAR
     i : integer;                (* index *)
     Mean,                       (* mean of final numeric scores *)
     StandardDeviation : real;   (* standard deviation of final scores *)

   PROCEDURE CalculateStats (VAR Student : StudentRecordList;
                             NumStudents : integer;
                             VAR Mean,  StandardDeviation : real);

      (**************************************************************

      Procedure to find the mean and standard deviation of the
      students' final numeric grades.

      **************************************************************)

      VAR
        i : integer;        (* index *)
        Sum,                (* used to calculate necessary totals *)
        Variance : real;    (* variance of the scores *)
```

Figure 12.4 (cont.)

```
BEGIN (* CalculateStats *)

   (* Find the mean *)

   Sum := 0;
   FOR i := 1 TO NumStudents DO
         Sum := Sum + Student[i].FinalNumScore;
   Mean := Sum / NumStudents;

   (* Find the variance and standard deviation *)

   Sum := 0;
   FOR i := 1 TO NumStudents DO
      Sum := Sum + sqr(Student[i].FinalNumScore - Mean);
   Variance := Sum / NumStudents;
   StandardDeviation := sqrt(Variance)
END (* CalculateStats *);

FUNCTION GradeOnTheCurve (Score, Mean, StDev : real) : char;

   (**************************************************************

   Function using "grading on the curve" to assign letter grade to
   numeric Score; Mean is the mean score, StDev is the standard
   deviation.

   **************************************************************)

   BEGIN (* GradeOnTheCurve *)
      IF Score < (Mean - 1.5 * StDev) THEN
         GradeOnTheCurve := 'F'
      ELSE IF Score < (Mean - 0.5 * StDev) THEN
         GradeOnTheCurve := 'D'
      ELSE IF Score < (Mean + 0.5 * StDev) THEN
         GradeOnTheCurve := 'C'
      ELSE IF Score < (Mean + 1.5 * StDev) THEN
         GradeOnTheCurve := 'B'
      ELSE
         GradeOnTheCurve := 'A'
   END (* GradeOnTheCurve *);

BEGIN (* AssignGrades *)
   CalculateStats (Student, NumStudents, Mean, StandardDeviation);
   FOR i := 1 TO NumStudents DO
      WITH Student[i] DO
         LetterGrade :=
               GradeOnTheCurve (FinalNumScore, Mean, StandardDeviation)
END (* AssignGrades *);

PROCEDURE SelectionSort(VAR Student : StudentRecordList;
                        NumStudents : integer);

   (**************************************************************

   Procedure to sort Student[1], ..., Student[NumStudents] using
   the selection sort algorithm so that key fields FinalNumScore
   are in descending order.

   **************************************************************)
```

Figure 12.4 (cont.)

```
    VAR
        Largest : StudentRecord;     (* record with largest key *)
        LargePos,                    (* position of Largest *)
        i, j : integer;              (* indices *)

    BEGIN (* SelectionSort *)
        FOR i := 1 TO NumStudents - 1 DO
            BEGIN

                (* find record with largest key in the sublist
                    Student[i], ..., Student[NumStudents] *)

                LargePos := i;
                Largest := Student[LargePos];
                FOR j := i + 1 TO NumStudents DO
                    IF Student[j].FinalNumScore > Largest.FinalNumScore THEN
                        BEGIN    (* larger item found *)
                            LargePos := j;
                            Largest := Student[j]
                        END (* IF *);

                (* interchange record with largest key with Student[i]
                    at beginning of sublist *)

                Student[LargePos] := Student[i];
                Student[i] := Largest
            END (* FOR i *)
    END (* SelectionSort *);

PROCEDURE PrintRecords (VAR student : StudentRecordList;
                        NumStudents : integer);

    (****************************************************************

        Procedure to print the final grades for all students.

    ****************************************************************)

    VAR
        i : integer;   (* index *)

    BEGIN (* PrintRecords *)
        writeln ('Student    Final      Final');
        writeln ('Number     Score      Grade');
        writeln ('======     =====      =====');
        FOR i := 1 TO NumStudents DO
            WITH Student[i] DO
                writeln (Snumb:5, FinalNumScore:11:2, LetterGrade:8)
    END (* PrintRecords *);

BEGIN (* main program *)
    ReadRecords (Student, NumStudents);
    CalculateNumScores (Student, NumStudents);
    AssignGrades(Student, NumStudents);
    SelectionSort (Student, NumStudents);
    PrintRecords (Student, NumStudents)
END (* main *).
```

Figure 12.4 (cont.)

Listing of ScoresFile:

```
1234
John Doe
50 53 57
1441
Mary Smith
62 59 65
1531
Fred Jones
72 65 70
1554
Pete Vander
100 100 100
1638
Jane Doe
22 15 19
1734
Al Johnson
62 58 55
```

Sample run

Student Number	Final Score	Final Grade
======	=====	=====
1554	100.00	A
1531	67.90	C
1441	61.40	C
1734	57.90	C
1234	53.60	C
1638	17.60	F

12.5 Variant Records

As we noted in Section 12.2, records may have a *variant part* in addition to a *fixed part*. The number and types of the fields in the fixed part of a record variable do not change during program execution, but those in the variant part may change in number and/or in type. In this section we discuss such *variant records*.

To illustrate variant records, consider the employee record described by

EmployeeRecord1 = **record**
        Name : *NameString*;
        Age, Dependents : *integer*;
        DeptCode : *char*;
        HourlyRate : *real*
    end;

where *NameString* is a user-defined type such as **packed array**[1..20] **of** *char*. Such records are appropriate for factory employees who are paid on an hourly basis. For office employees, the records might have the following structure:

$$EmployeeRecord2 \; = \; \textbf{record}$$
$$Name : NameString;$$
$$Age, \, Dependents : integer;$$
$$Salary : real$$
$$\textbf{end};$$

and for salespersons, an appropriate record structure might be

$$EmployeeRecord3 \; = \; \textbf{record}$$
$$Name : NameString;$$
$$Age, \, Dependents : integer;$$
$$MileageAllowance : integer;$$
$$BasePay, \, CommissionRate : real$$
$$\textbf{end};$$

All of these record structures can be incorporated into a single record by using a record with a variant part:

$$EmployeeRecord \; = \; \textbf{record}$$
$$Name : NameString;$$
$$Age, \, Dependents : integer;$$
$$\textbf{case} \; EmpCode : char \; \textbf{of}$$
$$\text{'F'} : (DeptCode : char;$$
$$HourlyRate : real);$$
$$\text{'O'} : (Salary : real);$$
$$\text{'S'} : (MileageAllowance : integer;$$
$$BasePay, \, CommissionRate : real)$$
$$\textbf{end};$$

This record has a fixed part that is the same for all values of type *EmployeeRecord,* and this fixed part consists of the fields *Name, Age,* and *Dependents.* In addition to these three fields, some values have *DeptCode* and *HourlyRate* fields; others have only a *Salary* field; and still others have *MileageAllowance, BasePay,* and *CommissionRate* fields. If *EmpCode* has the value F, then the fields *DeptCode* and *HourlyRate* are in effect; if *EmpCode* has the value O, then the field *Salary* is in effect; and if the value of *EmpCode* is S, then the *MileageAllowance, BasePay,* and *CommissionRate* fields are in effect.

The field *EmpCode* is called the **tag field** in this record. The values it may have label the variant fields of the record and determine the structure of a particular value of type *EmployeeRecord.* Thus, if the value of *EmpCode* is F, which labels the variant for a factory employee, the structure of the record is the same (except for the extra tag field) as one of type *EmployeeRecord1.* If the value of *EmpCode* is O, which labels the variant for an office employee, the structure of the record is essentially that of type *EmployeeRecord2.* Finally, if the value of *EmpCode* is S, which labels the variant for a salesperson, the structure is basically the same as that of type *EmployeeRecord3.* Note that the variant part of a record follows the fixed part and that each variant field list is enclosed in parentheses.

In a variant record, several tag field values may label the same variant field list. It is also permissible for tag field values to label empty variant field lists. To illustrate, suppose that the following type declarations have been made:

```
type
    NameString = packed array[1..20] of char;
    TransactionType = (Deposit, Withdrawal, LoanPayment, Transfer,
                        Void);
    Date = record
                Month, Day, Year : integer
           end;
```

and consider the following definition of a record to store certain items of information related to banking transactions:

```
    Transaction = record
                    CustomerName : NameString;
                    Number : integer;
                    TransDate : Date;
                    case TransType : TransactionType of
                        Deposit, Withdrawal : (Amount : real);
                        LoanPayment         : (LoanNumber : integer;
                                                Payment, Interest,
                                                NewBalance : real);
                        Transfer            : (TransferAccount : integer;
                                                AmountOfTransfer : real;
                                                Code : char);
                        Void                : ()
                  end;
```

Note that the tag field *TransType* may have any of the five values specified by the enumerated type *TransactionType*. If the value of *TransType* is either *Deposit* or *Withdrawal*, the field in effect is the single real field *Amount*. If the value of *TransType* is *LoanPayment*, then four fields are in effect: one integer field *LoanNumber* and three real fields, *Payment*, *Interest*, and *NewBalance*. For the value *Transfer* of *TransType*, there are three effective fields: *TransferAccount* of integer type, *AmountOfTransfer* of real type, and *Code* of character type (which indicates whether the transfer is to or from *Transfer-Account*). Finally, the value of *TransType* may be *Void*, in which case no information is required and thus no field is in effect.

Now suppose that the following variables have been declared:

```
var
    Account : Transaction;
    TransactionCode : char;
```

To read information into the record variable *Account*, one typically first reads values for the fixed field identifiers:

```
with Account do
   begin
      for i : = 1 to 20 do
         read (CustomerName[i]);
      readln;
      readln (Number);
      with TransDate do
         readln (Month, Day, Year)
   end (* with *);
```

Next, a value is read for *TransactionCode* that indicates whether the transaction is a deposit (D), withdrawal (W), loan payment (L), transfer (T), or void (V). This value can then be used to set the corresponding value of the tag field *TransType*. These codes of type *char*, rather than the actual values of *TransType*, are read, because values of the enumerated type *TransactionType* cannot be read from the system file *input* (or from any other text file). A **case** statement within a **with** statement might be used to set the tag field and read the values for items in the corresponding field list:

```
with Account do
   case TransactionCode of
      'D' : begin
               TransType : = Deposit;
               readln (Amount)
            end;
      'W' : begin
               TransType : = Withdrawal;
               readln (Amount)
            end;
      'L' : begin
               TransType : = LoanPayment;
               readln (LoanNumber, Payment)
            end;
      'T' : begin
               TransType : = Transfer;
               readln (TransferAccount, AmountOfTransfer, Code)
            end;
      'V' : TransType : = Void
   end (* case *);
```

As this example illustrates, a record structure may be quite complex, as there may be records nested within records (e.g., *TransDate* of record type *Date* nested within *Account* of record type *Transaction*); and although our example does not illustrate it, these nested records may themselves have variant parts.

The general form of a record structure is

```
record
   field-list
end
```

where *field-list* has one of the following forms:

| *fixed-part* | *fixed-part*; | *variant-part* |
| | *variant-part* | |

Here *fixed-part* has the form described in preceding sections:

list-1 : type-1;
list-2 : type-2;
⋮
list-m : type-m

where each *list-i* is a single identifier or a list of identifiers, separated by commas, that name the fields of the record, and *type-i* specifies the type of these fields. The *variant-part* has the form

case *tag-field* : *tag-type* **of**
tag-list-1 : (variant-1);
tag-list-2 : (variant-2);
⋮
tag-list-n : (variant-n)

where each *variant-i* is a field list of the form previously described; thus, the syntax of each *variant-i* is the same as for a record, but parentheses, rather than the reserved words **record** and **end,** are used to enclose it. The type of the *tag-field* may be any ordinal type, and each of the possible values of the tag field must appear in exactly one *tag-list-i*. This general form of a record is displayed in the following syntax diagrams:

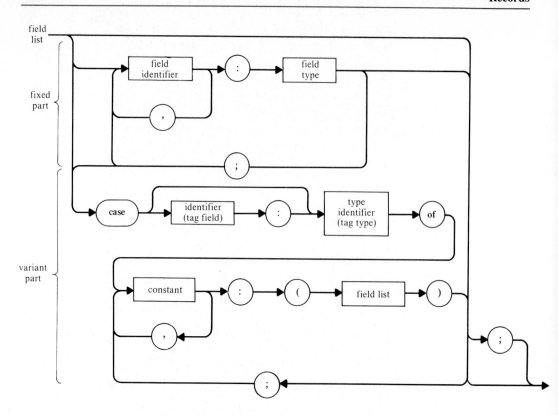

Note that a record may have both a fixed part and a variant part, only a fixed part, or only a variant part. It might also be noted that the tag field identifier, but not its type identifier, may be omitted. In this case, access to the items in a variant field list is still possible, but because no tag field identifier is used, the tag field itself cannot be accessed. Such records might be used when it is possible to determine by some other means which variant field list is in effect, for example, when the first fifty records in an array of one hundred records all use the same variant field list and the remaining fifty records involve some other variant field list. Omitting the tag field identifier, however, can easily lead to subtle errors and should normally be avoided (see Programming Pointer 8 at the end of this chapter). Finally, as the syntax diagram indicates, records may be packed to permit the compiler to minimize the amount of storage required for a record.

12.6   Example: Information Retrieval

Records are frequently used in problems that require storing and retrieving information, since in many such problems not all the items of information are of the same type. For example, consider a file of employee records as described in the preceding section. Each record contains the name, age, and number of dependents for an employee and other information determined by his or her job classification. A department code and an hourly rate are stored for factory employees; a salary for office employees; and a mileage allowance, a base pay, and a commission rate for salespersons.

The program in Figure 12.5 reads these records from the text file *EmployeeFile,* using the procedure *ReadRecords,* and stores them in the array *Employee,* whose components are variant records of type *EmployeeRecord.* We assume that the records in *EmployeeFile* have been sorted so that the employee names are in alphabetical order. Thus the array *Employee* will also be sorted so that the procedure *BinarySearch* can be used to locate the record for a given employee. If this record is found, the procedure *PrintRecords* is then called to retrieve and display the information in this record.

```
PROGRAM InfoRetrieval (input, output, EmployeeFile);

(***************************************************************

   Program to copy the information in the file EmployeeFile into an
   array of variant records and then search this array to retrieve
   information about a given employee.  The file and thus the array
   also are assumed to be sorted so employee names are in alphabetical
   order; a binary search is then used to retrieve an employee's record.

***************************************************************)

CONST
   MaxString = 20;              (* upper limit on lengths of strings *)
   ArrayLimit = 100;            (* limit on size of array *)

TYPE
   String = PACKED ARRAY[1..MaxString] OF char;
   EmployeeRecord = RECORD
                       Name : String;
                       Age, Dependents : integer;
                       CASE EmpCode : char OF
                          'F' : (DeptCode : char; HourlyRate : real);
                          'O' : (Salary : real);
                          'S' : (MileageAllowance : integer;
                                 BasePay, CommissionRate : real)
                    END;
   ArrayOfRecords = ARRAY [1..ArrayLimit] of EmployeeRecord;

VAR
   Employee : ArrayOfRecords;   (* array of employee records *)
   EmployeeFile : text;         (* file containing employee information *)
   Count,                       (* number of records *)
   Location : integer;          (* location of specified record in the array *)
   NameSought : String;         (* name of employee to be searched for *)
   Found : boolean;             (* indicates if record is found *)
```

Figure 12.5

Figure 12.5   (cont.)

```
PROCEDURE ReadRecords (VAR EmployeeFile : text;
                       VAR Employee: ArrayOfRecords; VAR Count : integer);

   (************************************************************

      Procedure to read and Count array Employee of employee records
      from the text file EmployeeFile.

      ************************************************************)

   VAR
      i : integer;     (* index *)

   BEGIN (* ReadRecords *)
      reset (EmployeeFile);
      Count := 0;
      WHILE NOT eof(EmployeeFile) DO
         BEGIN
            Count := Count + 1;
            WITH Employee[Count] DO
               BEGIN
                  FOR i := 1 TO MaxString DO
                     read (EmployeeFile, Name[i]);
                  readln (EmployeeFile, Age, Dependents);
                  read (EmployeeFile, EmpCode);
                  CASE EmpCode OF
                     'F' : readln (EmployeeFile, DeptCode, HourlyRate);
                     'O' : readln (EmployeeFile, Salary);
                     'S' : readln (EmployeeFile, MileageAllowance,
                                     BasePay, CommissionRate)
                  END (* CASE *)
               END (* WITH *)
         END (* WHILE *)
   END (* ReadRecords *);

PROCEDURE ReadString (VAR Str : String; MaxString : integer);

   (************************************************************

      Procedure to read characters into string variable Str until an
      end-of-line mark is encountered or the upper limit MaxString
      on the length of Str is reached.  Any positions for which no
      characters are read will be filled with blanks.

      ************************************************************)

   VAR
      i : integer;        (* index *)

   BEGIN (* ReadString *)
      FOR i := 1 TO MaxString DO
         IF NOT eoln THEN
            read (Str[i])
         ELSE
            Str[i] := ' ';
      readln
   END (* ReadString *);
```

Figure 12.5 (cont.)

```
PROCEDURE BinarySearch (VAR Employee : ArrayOfRecords; n : integer;
                        NameSought : String;
                        VAR Mid : integer; VAR Found : boolean);

    (***************************************************************

        Procedure to binary search the array Employee of size n for the
        record containing a specified employee name.  True is returned
        for Found if the search is successful and Mid is then the
        location of this record; else Found is set to false.

    ***************************************************************)

    VAR
        First, Last : integer;  (* first and last positions of
                                     the sublist being searched *)

    BEGIN (* BinarySearch *)
        Found := false;
        First := 1;
        Last := n;
        WHILE (First <= Last) AND NOT Found DO
            BEGIN
                Mid := (First + Last) DIV 2;
                WITH Employee[Mid] DO
                    IF NameSought < Name THEN
                        Last := Mid - 1
                    ELSE IF NameSought > Name THEN
                        First := Mid + 1
                    ELSE
                        Found := true
            END (* WHILE *)
    END (* BinarySearch *);

PROCEDURE PrintRecord (Employee : EmployeeRecord);

    (***************************************************************

        Procedure to print the record of Employee.

    ***************************************************************)

    BEGIN (* PrintRecord *)
        WITH Employee DO
            BEGIN
                writeln ('Age . . . . . . . . . .', Age:2);
                writeln ('Dependents  . . . . . .', Dependents:2);
                CASE EmpCode OF
                    'F' : BEGIN
                            writeln ('Department code . . . . ', DeptCode);
                            writeln ('Hourly rate  . . .', HourlyRate:7:2)
                          END;
                    'O' : writeln ('Salary  . . . . .', Salary:7:2);
                    'S' : BEGIN
                            writeln ('Mileage allowance . . ', MileageAllowance:3);
                            writeln ('Base pay . . . . ', BasePay:7:2);
                            writeln ('Commission rate . . ', CommissionRate:5:3)
                          END
                END (* CASE *)
            END (* WITH *)
    END (* PrintRecord *);
```

Figure 12.5   (cont.)

```
BEGIN (* main program *)
   ReadRecords (EmployeeFile, Employee, Count);
   writeln ('Enter names in the form    Last-name, First-name');
   writeln ('using all upper case letters.  Enter * for name to quit.');
   writeln;
   write ('Employee''s Name?  ');
   ReadString (NameSought, MaxString);
   WHILE NameSought[1] <> '*' DO
      BEGIN
         BinarySearch (Employee, Count, NameSought, Location, Found);
         IF Found THEN
            PrintRecord (Employee[Location])
         ELSE
            writeln ('Employee''s record not found');
         writeln;
         write ('Employee''s Name?  ');
         ReadString (NameSought, MaxString)
      END (* WHILE *)
END (* main program *).
```

Listing of EmployeeFile used in sample run:

```
DOE, JOHN              35 3
0 35000
JONES, FRED           58 4
FM 13.55
SMITH, MARY           22 0
0 31150
VANDERVAN, PETER      29 1
S 500 12000 0.15
```

Sample run:

```
Enter names in the form    Last-name, First-name
using all upper case letters.  Enter Q for name to quit.

Employee's Name?  DOE, JOHN
Age . . . . . . . . . .35
Dependents . . . . . . 3
Salary  . . . . .35000.00

Employee's Name?  VANDER, PETER
Employee's record not found

Employee's Name?  VANDERVAN, PETER
Age . . . . . . . . . .29
Dependents . . . . . . 1
Mileage allowance . . 500
Base pay . . . . 12000.00
Commission rate . . 0.150

Employee's Name?  JONES, FRED
Age . . . . . . . . . .58
Dependents . . . . . . 4
Department code . . . . M
Hourly rate  . . . 13.55

Employee's Name?   *
```

Exercises

1. For each of the following, develop an appropriate record structure for the given information, and then write type declarations for the records:

    (a) Cards in a deck of playing cards.
    (b) Time measured in hours, minutes, and seconds.
    (c) Length measured in yards, feet, and inches.
    (d) Listings in a telephone directory.
    (e) Description of an automobile (make, model, style, color, and the like).
    (f) Description of a book in a library's card catalogue (author, publisher, and the like).
    (g) Teams in a baseball league (name, won-lost record, and the like).
    (h) Position of a checker on a checker board.

2. The data files *StudentFile, InventoryFile,* and *UsersFile* are described in Appendix E. Write appropriate record declarations to describe the information in these files.

3. For each of the following, develop a record structure using variant records for the given information, and then write type declarations for the records:

    (a) Information about a person: name, birthday, age, sex, social security number, height, weight, hair color, eye color, marital status, and, if married, number of children.
    (b) Statistics about a baseball player: name, age, birthdate, position (pitcher, catcher, infielder, outfielder); for a pitcher: won-lost record, earned-run average, number of strikeouts, number of walks; if a starting pitcher, number of complete games; and if a relief pitcher, number of innings pitched and number of saves; for the other positions: batting average; slugging average; bats right, left, or is a switch hitter; fielding percentage; also, for an infielder, the positions he can play; for a catcher, whether he can catch a knuckleball.
    (c) Weather statistics: date; city and state, province, or country; time of day; temperature; barometric pressure; weather conditions (clear skies, partly cloudy, cloudy, stormy); if cloudy conditions prevail, cloud level and type of clouds; for partly cloudy, percentage of cloud cover; for stormy conditions, snow depth if it is snowing; amount of rainfall if it is rainy; size of hail if it is hailing.

4. Like the elements of an array, the fields of a record can be stored in consecutive memory locations, and address translation is required to determine the location of a particular field. To illustrate, suppose that integers are stored in one memory word, real values require two words, and strings of characters are packed two characters per word. The declaration of the record variable *Employee* in Section 12.1 instructs the compiler to reserve a block of fourteen consecutive memory words

to store such a record. As for arrays, the address of the first word in this block is called the **base address**. If the base address for *Employee* is *b*, then the field *Employee.Name* is stored in ten consecutive memory words beginning at *b*; *Employee.Age* is stored in word *b* + 10; *Employee.Dependents* in word *b* + 11; and *Employee.HourlyRate* in words *b* + 12 and *b* + 13.

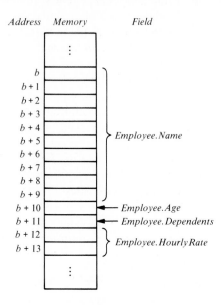

Assuming these storage requirements for integers, reals, and strings, and assuming that values of type *char* require an entire word, give a similar picture showing where each field of the following record types would be stored:

(a) *Point* in Figure 12.2.
(b) *StudentRecord* in Figure 12.4.
(c) *ClassRecord* in Figure 12.3.
(d) *Transaction* in Section 12.5. (See also Programming Pointer 8 following this set of exercises.)

5. Extend the program in Figure 12.2 to find

(a) The midpoint of the line segment joining two points.
(b) The equation of the perpendicular bisector of this line segment.

6. The **point-slope** equation of a line having slope *m* and passing through the point *P* with coordinates (x_1, y_1) is

$$y - y_1 = m(x - x_1)$$

(a) Write a record description for a line, given its slope and a point on the line.
(b) Write a program that reads the slope of a line and the coordinates of a point on the line and that then

       (i) Finds the point-slope equation of the line.

       (ii) Finds the slope-intercept equation of the line.

  (c) Write a program to read the point and slope information of two lines and determine whether they intersect or are parallel. If they intersect, find the point of intersection and also determine whether they are perpendicular.

7. Write a program that accepts a time of day in military format and finds the corresponding usual representation in hours, minutes, and A.M./P.M. or accepts the time in the usual format and finds the corresponding military representation. For example, the input 0100 should produce 1:00 A.M. as output, and the input 3:45 P.M. should give 1545. Use a record to store the time formats.

8. Write a record declaration for cards in a standard deck having fifty-two cards and two jokers. Then write a program to deal two ten-card hands from such a deck. (See Section 6.3 regarding a random number generator.) Be sure that the same card is not dealt more than once.

9. Write a declaration of a record having only a variant part for four geometric figures: circle, square, rectangle, and triangle. For a circle, the record should store its radius; for a square, the length of a side; for a rectangle, the lengths of two adjacent sides; and for a triangle, the lengths of the three sides. Then write a program that reads one of the letters C (circle), S (square), R (rectangle), T (triangle) and the appropriate numeric quantity or quantities for a figure of that type and then calculates its area. For example, the input R 7.2 3.5 represents a rectangle with length 7.2 and width 3.5; and T 3 4 6.1 represents a triangle having sides of lengths 3, 4, and 6.1. (For a triangle the area can be found by using **_Hero's formula_**:

$$\text{area} = \sqrt{s(s - a)(s - b)(s - c)},$$

where a, b, and c are the lengths of the sides and s is one half of the perimeter.

10. Write a program to read the records in *InventoryFile* (see Appendix E) and store them in an array of records, read a stock number entered by the user, and then search this array for the item having that stock number. If a match is found, the item name and number currently in stock should be displayed; otherwise, a message indicating that it was not found should be displayed.

11. Write a program to read the records in *StudentFile* and store them in an array of records, sort them so that cumulative GPAs are in descending order, and then display the student numbers, names, majors, and GPAs of the records in this sorted array.

12. A **_complex number_** has the form $a + bi$, where a and b are real numbers and $i^2 = -1$. The four basic arithmetic operations for complex numbers are defined as follows:

addition: $(a + bi) + (c + di) = (a + c) + (b + d)i$.

subtraction: $(a + bi) - (c + di) = (a - c) + (b - d)i$.

multiplication: $(a + bi) * (c + di) = (ac - bd) + (ad + bc)i$

division: $\dfrac{a + bi}{c + di} = \dfrac{ac + bd}{c^2 + d^2} + \dfrac{bc - ad}{c^2 + d^2} i$

provided $c^2 + d^2 \neq 0$.

Write a program to read two complex numbers and a symbol for one of these operations and to perform the indicated operation. Use a record to represent complex numbers, and use procedures to implement the operations.

13. A *rational number* is of the form a/b where a and b are integers with $b \neq 0$. Write a program to do rational number arithmetic, representing each rational number as a record with a numerator field and a denominator field. The program should read and display all rational numbers in the format a/b, or simply a if the denominator is 1. The following examples illustrate the menu of commands that the user should be allowed to enter:

Input	Output	Comments
3/8 + 1/6	13/24	$a/b + c/d = (ad + bc)/bd$ reduced to lowest terms.
3/8 − 1/6	5/24	$a/b - c/d = (ad - bc)/bd$ reduced to lowest terms.
3/8 * 1/6	1/16	$a/b * c/d = ac/bd$ reduced to lowest terms.
3/8 / 1/6	9/4	$a/b / c/d = ad/bc$ reduced to lowest terms.
3/8 I	8/3	Invert a/b.
8/3 M	2 + 2/3	Write a/b as a mixed fraction.
6/8 R	3/4	Reduce a/b to lowest terms.
6/8 G	2	Greatest common divisor of numerator and denominator.
1/6 L 3/8	24	Lowest common denominator of a/b and c/d.
1/6 < 3/8	true	$a/b < c/d$?
1/6 <= 3/8	true	$a/b \leq c/d$?
1/6 > 3/8	false	$a/b > c/d$?
1/6 >= 3/8	false	$a/b \geq c/d$?
3/8 = 9/24	true	$a/b = c/d$?
2/3 X + 2 = 4/5	X = −9/5	Solution of linear equation $(a/b)X + c/d = e/f$.

Programming Pointers

A record is a collection of related data items called fields that may be of different types. In some situations, such as in assignment statements and subprogram references, records may be processed as single units. In other situations it is necessary to process the fields of a record separately by using field-designated variables. The following are some of the important points to remember when using records:

1. *The reserved word* **end** *must be used to mark the end of each record declaration.*

2. *A field in a record is accessed with a field-designated variable, or fielded variable, of the form record-name.field-name.*

3. *The scope of each field identifier is the record in which it appears.* This scope rule has the following consequences:
   - *The same identifier may not be used to name two different fields within the same record.*
   - *An identifier that names a field within a record may be used for some other purpose outside that record (but see Programming Pointer 5).*

4. *Records cannot be read or written as units to or from text files; instead individual fields must be read or written.* For example, if *InfoRec* is a record of type *InformationRecord* defined by

   type
       String20 = **packed array**[1..20] **of** *char*;
       String12 = **packed array**[1..12] **of** *char*;
       AddressRecord = **record**
                       StreetAddress : *String20*;
                       City, State : *String12*;
                       ZipCode : *integer*
               end;
       InformationRecord = **record**
                       Name : *String20*;
                       Address : *AddressRecord*;
                       Age : *integer*;
                       MaritalStatus : *char*
               end;

   its fields can be displayed as follows:

   writeln (InfoRec.Name);
   writeln (InfoRec.Address.StreetAddress);
   writeln (InfoRec.Address.City, ', ', InfoRec.Address.State,
         InfoRec.Address.ZipCode);
   writeln ('Age: ', InfoRec.Age);
   writeln ('Marital Status: ', InfoRec.MaritalStatus);

5. *The* **with** *statement attaches a given record name(s) to each identifier within the statement that names a field within the specified record(s).* For example, the output statements in Programming Pointer 4 could be replaced with

> **with** *InfoRec* **do**
> **begin**
> > *writeln* (*Name*);
> > *writeln* (*Address.StreetAddress*);
> > *writeln* (*Address.City*,', ', *Address.State, Address.ZipCode*);
> > *writeln* ('Age: ', *Age*);
> > *writeln* ('Marital Status: ', *MaritalStatus*)
> **end** (∗ **with** ∗);

The **with** statement attaches a record name to *every* identifier appearing in the **with** statement that names a field within the specified record. Consequently, if one of these identifiers is used for some other purpose outside the record, the **with** statement attaches the record name to this identifier so that the field within the record is processed, and not the value of the identifier outside the record.

A **with** statement of the form

> **with** *record-name-1, record-name-2* **do**
> *statement*

is equivalent to

> **with** *record-name-1* **do**
> > **with** *record-name-2* **do**
> > *statement*

(and similarly for **with** statements with more than two record names). This means that *record-name-2* will first be attached to all identifiers that name fields within it before *record-name-1* is attached. Thus, the preceding **with** statement to display the fields within *InfoRec* could also be written as

> **with** *InfoRec, Address* **do**
> **begin**
> > *writeln* (*Name*);
> > *writeln* (*StreetAddress*);
> > *writeln* (*City*,', ', *State, ZipCode*);
> > *writeln* ('Age: ', *Age*);
> > *writeln* ('Marital Status: ', *MaritalStatus*)
> **end** (∗ **with** ∗);

One result of this order of attachment is that if an identifier names a field in *record-name-1* and a field in *record-name-2*, then *record-name-2* will be attached to this field identifier.

6. *The value of a record may be copied into another record by using an assignment statement, provided that the two records have the same*

type, which means that they must be declared by the same or equivalent type identifiers (see Section 9.2). Thus, if the type *PersonRecord* is defined by

   PersonRecord = InformationRecord;

where *InformationRecord* is as described in Programming Pointer 3, then the record variables *RecA* and *RecB* declared by

   var
      RecA : InformationRecord;
      RecB : PersonRecord;

have the same type because *InformationRecord* and *PersonRecord* are equivalent type identifiers.

7. *Records may be used as parameters in functions or procedures, but each actual parameter must have the same type as the corresponding formal parameter. The value of a function may not be a record.*

8. *When variant records are used, sufficient memory is usually allocated to store the variant that requires the most memory, and all other variants of that record are stored using this same portion of memory.* To illustrate, consider declarations of the form

   type
      EmployeeRecord = **record**
                          ⋮   (∗ fixed part of record ∗)
                          case *EmpCode : char* **of**
                              'F': (*DeptCode : char*;
                                      HourlyRate : real);
                              'O': (*Salary : real*)
                      end;

Because the first variant is the larger, sufficient memory is allocated to store it, but the same memory locations are used for the second variant:

If values such as M and 11.25 are assigned to the fields of the first variant, a subsequent reference to this same record with the second variant is improper. An error or a "garbage" value for *Salary* may result, because an attempt is made to interpret the internal representation of the character M as part of a real value for *Salary*.

9. *The tag field in a variant record must be of ordinal type; each possible value of the tag field must appear in exactly one tag value list; the tag field may not be associated with a variable formal parameter.*

Variations and Extensions

As with arrays, there are only a few variations from or extensions to the record-processing features of standard Pascal in other versions of Pascal. Two of these are

- Records of the same type may be compared with the relational operators = and <> (UCSD).

- Records may be initialized in the declaration part of the program. (Turbo)

See Appendix G for additional details.

13

Sets

No one shall expel us from the paradise which
Cantor has created for us.

DAVID HILBERT

In mathematics and computer science the term *set* denotes an unordered collection of objects called the *elements* or *members* of the set. For example, the set of digits contains the elements 0, 1, 2, 3, 4, 5, 6, 7, 8, and 9; the set of uppercase letters consists of the letters A, B, C, . . . , Z; the set of even prime numbers contains the single element 2; and the set of all females who were U.S. presidents before 1988 is the empty set, that is, the set containing no elements.

Sets differ from arrays in that the elements of an array are ordered in a certain sequence, but the elements of a set are unordered. Thus we can speak of the first, second, third, . . . elements of an array, but it does not make sense to refer to the first, second, third, . . . elements of a set. For example, the set whose elements are the even digits 0, 2, 4, 6, and 8 is the same as the set whose elements are 4, 8, 0, 2, and 6 or the set whose elements are 8, 0, 6, 4, and 2. The ordering of array elements makes it possible to access an element directly by specifying its location in the array. Because sets are unordered, no such direct access to the elements of a set is possible.

Sets differ from records in two important ways. Data items stored in a record are directly accessible and may be of different types. In Pascal, however, the elements of a set must be of the same type, and as we have noted, they are not directly accessible.

In this chapter we discuss how sets are implemented in Pascal using the predefined data type **set** and how they are processed using the operations of set assignment, union, intersection, and difference, the membership relation, and the set relations of subset and equality.

13.1   Set Declarations, Set Constants, and Set Assignments

In a problem involving sets, the elements are selected from some given set called the **universal set** for that problem. For example, if the set of vowels or the set whose elements are X, Y, and Z is being considered, the universal set might be the set of all letters. If the universal set is the set of names of months of the year, then one might use the set of summer months: June, July, August; the set of months whose names do not contain the letter r: May, June, July, August; or the set of all months having fewer than 30 days: February.

In a Pascal program, all of the elements of a set must be of the same type, called the **base type** of the set. This base type must be an ordinal type; thus sets of real elements or sets of arrays, strings, or records are not allowed. A **set declaration** has the form

set of *base-type*

For example, if the ordinal types *Digits* and *Months* are defined by

type
    Digits = 0..9;
    Months = (*January, February, March, April, May, June, July,*
             August, September, October, November, December);

then

    set of *Digits*
    set of *Months*
    set of *char*

are valid set declarations for most Pascal compilers.

Many Pascal compilers, however, impose certain restrictions on sets. The most common restriction is a limit on the number of elements that a set may have. This limit usually excludes *integer* as a base type and, for some compilers, also excludes *char*. In these cases, subranges of integers and/or subranges of characters must be used.

To illustrate set declarations, consider the following:

type
    Digits = 0..9;
    Months = (*January, February, March, April, May, June, July,*
             August, September, October, November, December);
    DigitSet = **set of** *Digits*;
    MonthSet = **set of** *Months*;
    CapLetterSet = **set of** 'A'..'Z';
    MonthArray = **array**[1..4] **of** *MonthSet*;

var
    Dig1, Dig2 : *Digits*;
    Numbers, Evens, Odds : *DigitSet*;
    Winter : *MonthSet*;
    Vowels, Consonants : *CapLetterSet*;
    Season : *MonthArray*;

The variables *Numbers, Evens,* and *Odds* may have as values any sets of elements chosen from 0, 1, 2, . . . , 9; the value of *Winter* may be any set of elements selected from *January, February,* . . . , *December*; and the variables *Vowels* and *Consonants* have values that are sets of capital letters. The array *Season* has four components, each of which is a set of months.

A *set constant* in Pascal has the form

[*element-list*]

where *element-list* is a list (possibly empty) of constants, variables, or expressions of the same type, separated by commas and enclosed in brackets [and]. Thus, for the base types just defined,

[0, 2, 4, 6, 8]

is a valid set constant that might be the value of *Evens*. This same set constant could also be denoted by

[4, 0, 8, 2, 6]

or

[8, 6, 4, 2, 0]

or by using any other arrangement of the elements. If *Dig1* has the value 0 and *Dig2* has the value 4, then

[*Dig1, Dig1* + 2, *Dig1* + 4, *Dig1* + 6, *Dig1* + 8]

is another representation of this same set constant, as is

[*Dig1, Dig2* **div** 2, *Dig2, Dig2* + 2, 2 ∗ *Dig2*]

When some or all of the elements of a set are consecutive values of the base type, it is permissible to use subrange notation to specify them. For example, the set constant

[0, 1, 2, 3, 4]

can also be expressed as

[0..4]

or

    [*Dig1*..*Dig2*]

and the set constant

    [0, 1, 2, 5, 7, 8, 9]

can be expressed in any of the following ways:

    [0..2, 5, 7..9]
    [0..2, *Dig2* + 1, 7..9]
    [*Dig1*..2, 5, (*Dig2* + 3)..(2 ∗ *Dig2* + 1)]

    To assign a value to a variable of set type, an assignment statement of the form

    set-variable := *set-value*

may be used where *set-value* may be a set constant, a set variable, or a set expression (as described in the next section). The base type of *set-value* must be compatible with the base type of *set-variable*. (Recall that two types are compatible if they are the same type, one is a subrange of the other, or both are subranges of the same type.) Thus, for the base types defined earlier, the statement

    Evens := [0, 2, 4, 6, 8];

is a valid assignment statement and assigns the set constant [0, 2, 4, 6, 8] to the set variable *Evens*. Similarly, the statements

    Winter := [*December, January..March*];
    Season[1] := [*December, January, February*];
    Consonants := *Vowels*;
    Numbers := [*Dig1*];

are valid assignment statements. The assignment statement

    Winter := ['D', 'J', 'F', 'M'];

is not valid, however, because the base type of the set constant is not compatible with the base type of *Winter*. Similarly, the assignment statement

    Season[1] := ['D', 1, *February*];

is not valid because this is not a valid set constant (the types of the elements are not the same).

The *empty set* is denoted in Pascal by the set constant

[ ]

and may be assigned to a set variable of any base type. Thus both

Number := [ ];
Winter := [ ];

are valid assignment statements, even though the set variables *Number* and *Winter* have different base types.

13.2 Set Operations and Relations

Because sets are collections of elements, it is important to be able to determine whether a particular element belongs to a given set. This test for set membership is implemented in Pascal by the relational operator **in**. Boolean expressions used to test set membership have the form

element **in** *set*

where *set* is a set constant, set variable, or set expression, and the type of *element* and the base type of *set* are compatible. For example, if set variables *Vowels, Evens, Numbers,* and *Bits* are declared by

type
    DigitSet = **set of** 0..9;
    BinarySet = **set of** 0..1;
    SetOfCharacters = **set of** *char*;

var
    Evens, Numbers : DigitSet;
    Bits : BinarySet;
    Vowels : SetOfCharacters;
    Num : integer;

and have been assigned values by

Evens := [0, 2, 4, 6, 8];
Bits := [0, 1];
Numbers := [0..2, 6..9];
Vowels := ['A', 'E', 'I', 'O', 'U'];

then

2 **in** *Evens*
3 **in** *Numbers*
'I' **in** *Vowels*

are valid boolean expressions and have the values *true, false,* and *true,* respectively. Similarly, if *Num* has the value 3,

> *Num* **in** *Evens*
> 'B' **in** [ ]
> *Num* + 3 **in** *Numbers*

are valid boolean expressions that have the values *false, false,* and *true,* respectively. The expressions

> 5 **in** *Vowels*
> 'B' **in** *Numbers*

are not valid boolean expressions because of type incompatibility.

The relational operator **in** is used to determine whether a single element is a member of a given set, but sometimes it is necessary to determine whether all of the elements of some set *set1* are also members of another set *set2*, that is, to determine whether *set1* is a **subset** of *set2*, as pictured in the following **Venn Diagram**:

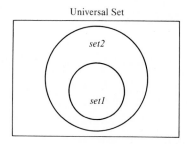

This subset relationship is indicated in Pascal by using the relational operators <= and >= to construct boolean expressions of the form

> *set1* <= *set2*   or equivalently   *set2* >= *set1*

where *set1* and *set2* are set constants, variables, or expressions with compatible base types. These expressions are true if *set1* is a subset of *set2* and are false otherwise. The following table shows some valid boolean expressions and their values, given that the variables have the values previously assigned:

Boolean Expression	Value
[0,1,4] <= [0,1,2,3,4]	*true*
[2,4] <= *Evens*	*true*
Bits >= *Evens*	*false*
Vowels <= *Vowels*	*true*
Numbers <= *Bits*	*false*
['A', 'B'] >= ['A','C']	*false*
[ ] <= *Numbers*	*true*

Two sets are said to be *equal* if they contain exactly the same elements. Set equality can be checked in Pascal with a boolean expression of the form

$set1 = set2$

where again *set1* and *set2* must have compatible base types. The relational operator $<>$ may be used to check set inequality:

$set1 <> set2$

and is equivalent to the boolean expression

not $(set1 = set2)$

For example,

$Bits = [0, 1]$
$Bits <> Evens$

are valid boolean expressions, and both have the value *true*.

In addition to the relational operators **in,** $<=$, $>=$, $=$, and $<>$, there are three binary set operations that may be used to combine two sets to form another set. These are the operations of union, intersection, and difference, which are denoted in Pascal by $+$, $*$, and $-$, respectively. The *union* of two sets *set1* and *set2* is the set of elements that are in *set1* or *set2* or both and is denoted by a set expression of the form

$set1 + set2$

This can be pictured by the following Venn Diagram:

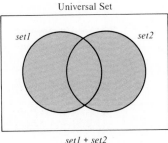

$set1 + set2$

The *intersection* of *set1* and *set2* is the set of elements that are in both sets and is denoted by

$set1 * set2$

and can be pictured as

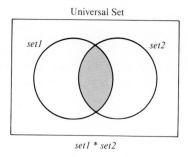

*set1 * set2*

The set *difference*

$$set1 - set2$$

is the set of elements that are in *set1* but are not in *set2*, as indicated in the following diagram:

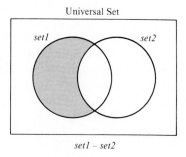

set1 - set2

For each of these set expressions, the base types of *set1* and *set2* must be compatible. The following table illustrates these set operations:

Set Expression	Value
[1,2,3] + [4,5,6]	[1,2,3,4,5,6]
[1,2,3,4] + [2,4,6]	[1,2,3,4,6]
[1,2,3] + [ ]	[1,2,3]
[1,2,3,4] * [2,4,6]	[2,4]
[1,2,3] * [4,5,6]	[ ]
[1,2,3] * [ ]	[ ]
[1,2,3,4] − [2,4]	[1,3]
[1,2,3,4] − [2,4,6]	[1,3]
[1,2,3] − [4,5,6]	[1,2,3]
[1,2,3] − [1,2,3,4]	[ ]
[1,2,3] − [ ]	[1,2,3]

When a set expression contains two or more of these operators, it is evaluated according to the following priorities:

$*$ ----------------   high priority
$+,-$ ----------------   low priority

Thus in the expression

[2,3,5] + [2,4,7] $*$ [2,4,6,8]

the intersection operation is performed first, giving the set [2,4], and

[2,3,5] + [2,4]

is then evaluated, yielding

[2,3,4,5]

Operations having the same priority are evaluated in the order in which they appear in the expression, from left to right. For example,

$$[1,2,3,4] - [1,3] + [1,2,5] = [2,4] + [1,2,5]$$
$$= [1,2,4,5]$$

and

$$[2,3,5] + [2,4,7] * [2,4,6,8] = [2,3,5] + [2,4]$$
$$= [2,3,4,5]$$

Parentheses may be used in the usual way to alter the standard order of evaluation; thus,

$$([2,3,5] + [2,4,7]) * [2,4,6,8] = [2,3,4,5,7] * [2,4,6,8]$$
$$= [2,4]$$

Compound boolean expressions that are formed using these operators and the boolean operators **not, and,** and **or** are evaluated according to the following priority levels:

Operator	Priority
not	1 (highest)
$*$, /, **div, mod, and**	2
$+$, $-$, **or**	3
$<, <=, >, >=, =, <>$, **in**	4 (lowest)

The operators $+$, $-$, and $*$ may refer to either arithmetic or set operations, and the relational operators $<, <=, >, >=, =$, and $<>$ may be used with numeric, character, ordinal, string, or set data (except that $<$ and $>$ may not be used with sets). Thus the expression

0 **in** *Evens* **and** 0 **in** *Bits*

is not a valid boolean expression because **and** has higher priority than **in**; consequently, the first operation attempted is evaluation of *Evens* **and** 0, which results in an error because *Evens* and 0 are not of boolean type. Parentheses must be used in the usual way to modify the standard order of evaluation:

(0 **in** *Evens*) **and** (0 **in** *Bits*)

Set relations and operations may be used to simplify complex boolean expressions. For example, the boolean expression

(*ch* = 'A') **or** (*ch* = 'L') **or** (*ch* = 'M') **or** (*ch* = 'N')

can be expressed more compactly as

ch **in** ['A', 'L'..'N']

The boolean expression

((*ch* $>=$ 'a') **and** (*ch* $<=$ 'z')) **or** ((*ch* $>=$ 'A') **and** (*ch* $<=$ 'Z'))

to determine whenever the value of *ch* is a lowercase or uppercase letter (assuming ASCII representation) can be expressed equivalently as

ch **in** *Lower* + *Upper*

where *Lower* and *Upper* are set variables whose values are ['a'..'z'] and ['A'..'Z'], respectively.

One situation in which such boolean expressions are useful is in checking the value of a selector in a **case** statement to ensure that it is in the correct range. For example, consider the **case** statement

```
case Num of
    5, 10, 15 : writeln ('Multiple of 5');
    7, 14     : writeln ('Multiple of 7');
    11        : writeln ('Multiple of 11')
end (* case *);
```

If the value of *Num* is not one of the integers listed as case labels, execution of the **case** statement will result in an error. The following statement avoids this error:

```
if Num in [5,7,10,11,14,15] then
    case Num of
        5, 10, 15 : writeln ('Multiple of 5');
        7, 14     : writeln ('Multiple of 7');
        11        : writeln ('Multiple of 11')
    end (* case *);
```

13.3 Processing Sets

In the preceding section we used the assignment statement to assign a value to a set variable. In this section we show how to construct a set by reading its elements, how to display the elements of a set, and how to use sets as parameters for subprograms.

To construct a set, we first initialize it to the empty set and then read each element and add it to the set, using the union operation. This process is described in the following algorithm:

ALGORITHM TO CONSTRUCT A SET

(* Algorithm to construct a set S by repeatedly reading an element x of S and adding it to S. *)

1. Initialize S to the empty set: S := [ ].
2. While there is more data, do the following:
   a. Read a value for a variable x whose type is that of the base type of S.
   b. Add x to S using the union operation: $S := S + [x]$.

To display the elements of a set, we can use the following algorithm:

ALGORITHM TO DISPLAY A SET

(* Algorithm to display a set S by repeatedly finding an element x of S, displaying it, and removing it from S. Note that the set S is destroyed, since it is reduced to the empty set. *)

1. Let x be a variable of the base type of S and initialize x to be the first element of this base type.
2. While $S <> [ ]$, do the following:
   a. While x is not in S, replace x with its successor.
   b. Display x.
   c. Remove x from S, using the difference operation: $S := S - [x]$.

If the set to be displayed with this algorithm is to be preserved, it should first be copied to some temporary set

TempSet := S;

whose elements are then displayed.

Sets may also be used as parameters of functions and procedures. Remember, however, that the type of a function must be a simple data type and hence may not be of set type. The program in Figure 13.1 illustrates the use of sets as parameters. It determines which of a set of uppercase letters appear in a given text file. The procedures *ReadSet* and *DisplaySet* implement the preceding algorithms for constructing and displaying a set, respectively.

```
PROGRAM FindLetters (output, TextFile);

(******************************************************************

    Program to determine which of a set of upper case letters
    entered by the user appear in a given text file.

******************************************************************)

TYPE
    ElementType = 'A'..'Z';
    TypeOfSet = SET OF ElementType;

VAR
    TextFile : text;        (* text file to be analyzed *)
    Symbol : char;          (* a character in text file *)
    LetterSet,              (* set of letters to be found *)
    FoundSet : TypeOfSet;   (* set of letters found in TextFile *)

PROCEDURE ReadSet (VAR S : TypeOfSet);

    (**************************************************************

        Procedure to read the elements of a set S of type TypeOfSet;
        the base type of the elements of S is ElementType which is
        char or a subrange of character or integer type.

    **************************************************************)

    VAR
        x : ElementType;

    BEGIN (* ReadSet *)
        S := [];
        WHILE NOT eoln DO
            BEGIN
                read (x);
                S := S + [x]
            END (* WHILE *)
    END (* ReadSet *);

PROCEDURE SearchFile (VAR TextFile : text;
                      VAR LetterSet, FoundSet : TypeOfSet);

    (**************************************************************

        Procedure to search TextFile for letters in LetterSet
        and add them to FoundSet

    **************************************************************)

    BEGIN (* SearchFile *)
        reset (TextFile);
        WHILE NOT eof(TextFile) DO
            BEGIN
                WHILE NOT eoln(TextFile) DO
                    BEGIN
                        read (TextFile, Symbol);
                        IF Symbol IN LetterSet THEN
                            FoundSet := FoundSet + [Symbol]
                    END (* WHILE NOT eoln *);
                readln (TextFile)
            END (* WHILE NOT eof *);
    END (* SearchFile *);
```

Figure 13.1

Figure 13.1 (cont.)

```
PROCEDURE DisplaySet (S : TypeOfSet; FirstElement : ElementType);

    (*************************************************************

        Procedure to display the elements of a set S of type TypeOfSet;
        the base type of the elements of S is ElementType which is
        char or a subrange of character or integer type. FirstElement
        is the first element in this base type.

        *************************************************************)

    VAR
        x : ElementType;

    BEGIN (* DisplaySet *)
        x := FirstElement;
        WHILE S <> [] DO
            BEGIN
                WHILE NOT (x IN S) DO
                    x := succ(x);
                writeln (x);
                S := S - [x]
            END (* WHILE *)
    END (* DisplaySet *);

BEGIN (* main program *)
    writeln ('Enter letters to search for:');
    ReadSet (LetterSet);
    FoundSet := [];
    SearchFile (TextFile, LetterSet, FoundSet);
    writeln ('Letters found:');
    DisplaySet (FoundSet, 'A')
END (* main program *).
```

Listing of TextFile:

```
    This program finds which UPPER CASE letters such as A, B, and C
appear in the file TextFile.  It uses the procedure DisplaySet to
display these letters after execution of the program is
completed.
```

Sample run:

```
Enter letters to search for:
AEIOUY
Letters found:
A
E
I
U
```

13.4 Examples: Checking Major Program Requirements; Simple Lexical Analyzer

EXAMPLE 1: Checking Major Program Requirements. Students at the University of Dispatch are required to complete a certain set of core courses as part of their major program in computer science. The secretary of the computer science department is responsible for ensuring that each major has satisfied this requirement and would like a program to assist her. A file is maintained that records the computer science courses taken each semester by each of the current majors and which is updated at the end of each semester:

```
John Doe
1 2  5 8
Mary Smith
1 2 5 6 9 10 12
Peter Van
1 2 3 4 5 7 8 9 10 11 13 14 15
   .
   .
   .
```

Each student record in this file consists of two lines: The first contains the student's name, and the second is a list of the computer science courses (encoded as positive integers) that the student has taken.

To solve this problem we must read these student records and compare the set of courses completed by each student with a set of required core courses. If the set of courses completed contains the required courses, the student has satisfied the requirements. This approach is used in the following algorithm:

ALGORITHM TO CHECK MAJOR PROGRAM REQUIREMENTS

1. Read first student record.
2. While there are more student records, do the following:
   a. If the set of courses completed contains the set of required core courses, then do the following:
      Display a message that all required courses have been taken.

      Otherwise do the following:
      i. Calculate the set of courses yet to be taken as the set difference

         {required courses} − {courses completed}

      ii. Display this set of courses yet to be taken.
   b. Read the next student record.

The program in Figure 13.2 implements this algorithm. It uses three sets, each of whose base type is an enumerated type: the set *CoreCourses*, which is the set of courses required of each major; the set *Major.Courses*, which are the courses taken by a given major; and *RemainingCourses*, which is the set *CoreCourses* − *Major.Courses* of courses yet to be taken by that major. The boolean expression *Major.Courses* <= *CoreCourses* is used to check whether or not the major has taken all of the required core courses. The procedures *ReadSet* and *PrintSet* use the algorithms of the preceding section to read and display sets of courses.

```
PROGRAM MajorRequirementChecker (input, output, MajorsFile);

(*****************************************************************

    Program that reads a file of computer science courses taken by
    majors in the computer science department and determines which of
    them have taken all of the required core courses.

*****************************************************************)

CONST
    StringLimit = 80;      (* limit on length of strings *)

TYPE
    Courses = (Programming1, Programming2, AssemblyLanguage,
               OperatingSystems, DataStructures, CompilerDesign,
               DataBase, ArtificialIntelligence, Graphics,
               TheoryOfComputation, ProgLanguages, AdvDataStructures,
               ComputerArchitecture, AlgorithmAnalysis, SoftwareDesign);
    String = PACKED ARRAY [1..StringLimit] OF CHAR;
    CourseSet = SET OF Courses;
    MajorRecord = RECORD
                      Name : String;
                      Courses : CourseSet
                  END;

VAR
    MajorsFile : text;                    (* file containing majors' records *)
    Major : MajorRecord;                  (* record for one major *)
    NumMajors : integer;                  (* number of majors *)
    CoreCourses,                          (* set of core courses *)
    RemainingCourses : CourseSet;         (* set of courses not taken *)

PROCEDURE ReadSet(VAR MajorsFile : text; VAR S : CourseSet);

    (************************************************************

        Procedure to read the numbers of courses taken by a student
        and add the corresponding enumerated constants to the set
        of courses already taken by that student.

    ************************************************************)

    VAR
        Code : integer;   (* code of a course *)
```

Figure 13.2

Figure 13.2 (cont.)

```
FUNCTION CourseName(Code : integer) : Courses;

   (*************************************************************

      Function returns the course name for the course with
      the given Code.

   *************************************************************)

   VAR
      i : integer;                (* index running through codes *)
      c : Courses;                (* index running through Courses *)

   BEGIN (* CourseName *)
      c := Programming1;
      FOR i := 2 TO Code DO
         c := succ(c);
      CourseName := c
   END (* CourseName *);

BEGIN (* ReadSet *)
   S := [];
   WHILE NOT eoln(MajorsFile) DO
      BEGIN
         read (MajorsFile, Code);
         S := S + [CourseName(Code)]
      END (* WHILE *)
END (* ReadSet *);

PROCEDURE PrintSet (S : CourseSet; FirstElement : Courses);

   (*************************************************************

      Procedure to display the numbers of the courses in set S.
      FirstElement is the first element of the base type.

   *************************************************************)

   VAR
      x : Courses;

   BEGIN(* PrintSet *)
      x:= FirstElement;
      WHILE S <> [] DO
         BEGIN
            WHILE NOT (x IN S) DO
               x := succ(x);
            write(1 + ORD(x):3);
            S := S - [x]
         END (* WHILE *)
   END (* PrintSet *);

PROCEDURE ReadARecord (VAR MajorsFile : text; VAR Major : MajorRecord);

   (*************************************************************

      Procedure to read and return a major's record from the
      textfile MajorsFile.

   *************************************************************)
```

Figure 13.2   (cont.)

```
   PROCEDURE ReadString (VAR TextFile : text; VAR Str : String;
                         MaxString : integer);

      (************************************************************

          Procedure to read characters into string variable Str from
          TextFile until an end-of-line mark is encountered or the
          upper limit MaxString on the length of Str is reached.
          Any positions for which no characters are read will be
          filled with blanks.

          ************************************************************)

      VAR
         i : integer;          (* index *)

      BEGIN (* ReadString *)
         FOR i := 1 TO MaxString DO
            IF NOT eoln(TextFile) THEN
               read (TextFile, Str[i])
            ELSE
               Str[i] := ' ';
         readln (TextFile)
      END (* ReadString *);

   BEGIN (* ReadRecord *)
      ReadString(MajorsFile, Major.Name, StringLimit);
      ReadSet(MajorsFile, Major.Courses);
      readln(MajorsFile)
   END(* ReadRecord *);

BEGIN(* main program *)
   (*Initialize set of required core courses *)
   CoreCourses := [Programming1, Programming2, AssemblyLanguage,
                   OperatingSystems, DataStructures,
                   ProgLanguages, ComputerArchitecture];

   reset(MajorsFile);
   WHILE NOT eof(MajorsFile) DO
      BEGIN
         ReadARecord(MajorsFile, Major);
         WITH Major DO
            BEGIN
               writeln (Name);
               IF CoreCourses <= Courses THEN
                  writeln ('has completed all required core courses.')
               ELSE
                  BEGIN
                     RemainingCourses := CoreCourses - Courses;
                     write ('must yet complete courses: ');
                     PrintSet(RemainingCourses, Programming1);
                     writeln
                  END (* ELSE *);
               writeLn
            END (* WITH *)
      END (* WHILE *)
END (* main program *).
```

Figure 13.2   (cont.)

Listing of input file MajorsFile used in sample run:

John Doe
1 2 5 8
Mary Smith
1 2 5 6 9 10 12
Peter Van
1 2 3 4 5 7 8 9 10 11 13 14 15
Fred Johnson
1 2 4 5 7 8 10 11 13 15
Jane Jones
1 2 3 4 5 6 7 8 9 11
Ann Van
1 2 3 4 6 7 8 10 12 13 14 15
Joe Blow
1 2 4 5
Jon Boy
1 2 3 5 6
Alice Girl
1 2 3 4 5 6 7 8 9 10 11 12 13 14 15
Gloria Bee
1 3 5 7 9
Dick Moby
2 4 6 8 10

Sample run:

John Doe
must yet complete courses: 3   4 11 13

Mary Smith
must yet complete courses: 3   4 11 13

Peter Van
has completed all required core courses.

Fred Johnson
must yet complete courses: 3

Jane Jones
must yet complete courses: 13

Ann Van
must yet complete courses: 5 11

Joe Blow
must yet complete courses: 3 11 13

Jon Boy
must yet complete courses: 4 11 13

Alice Girl
has completed all required core courses.

Gloria Bee
must yet complete courses: 2   4 11 13

Dick Moby
must yet complete courses: 1   3   5 11 13

EXAMPLE 2: Simple Lexical Analyzer.   In our discussion of system software in Chapter 1, we mentioned **compilers**, which are programs whose function is to translate a source program written in some high-level language such as Pascal into an object program in machine code. This object program is then executed by the computer.

The basic phases of the compiler are summarized in the following diagram:

Source Program

LEXICAL ANALYZER

PARSER

CODE GENERATOR

Object program

The input to a compiler is a stream of characters that comprise the source program. Before the translation can actually be carried out, this stream of characters must be broken up into meaningful groups, such as identifiers, reserved words, constants, and operators. For example, for a program segment such as

```
BEGIN
    I :=     IFI + 256;
    IF I<500 THEN
        writeln(I)
END;
```

or as a "stream" of characters

```
BEGIN•ƀƀƀIƀ:=ƀƀƀƀƀIFIƀ+ƀ256;•ƀƀƀIFƀI<500ƀTHEN•
ƀƀƀƀƀƀwriteln(I)•END;•
```

(where ƀ is a blank and • is an end-of-line mark) the lexical analyzer must identify the following units:

BEGIN	reserved word
I	identifier
:=	assignment operator
IFI	identifier
+	addition operator
256	integer constant
;	semicolon
IF	reserved word
I	identifier
<	relational operator
500	integer constant

```
THEN    --------------------reserved word
writeln --------------------identifier
(          --------------------left parenthesis
I          --------------------identifier
)          --------------------right parenthesis
END     --------------------reserved word
;          --------------------semicolon
```

These units are called **tokens,** and the part of the compiler that recognizes these tokens is called the **lexical analyzer.**

It is then the task of the **parser** to group these tokens together to form the basic **syntactic structures** of the language as determined by the syntax rules. For example, it must recognize that the three consecutive tokens

can be grouped together to form a valid (boolean) expression, that

constitute a procedure reference statement, and then that

forms a valid **if** statement. The complete **parse tree** constructed during the compilation of the preceding program segment is

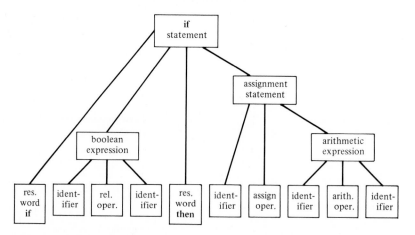

Later phases of the compiling process then generate the machine code for this **if** statement.

In designing a lexical analyzer to recognize various tokens, one can begin by representing each token by a ***finite automaton*** (also called a ***finite state machine***), which has a finite number of *states*, and there are transitions from one state to another depending on what the next input symbol is. If the machine is in certain states, called *accepting states*, after an input string is processed, then that string is said to be *recognized* or *accepted* by the automaton. For example, a finite automaton to recognize bit strings that contain 01 is

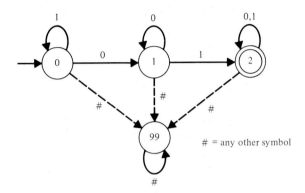

Here, the arrow pointing to State 0 indicates that this is the initial state. The automaton begins processing input symbols in this state and makes transitions from one state to another or remains in the current state as specified by the labels on the arrows.

To illustrate, consider the input string 0011. The finite automaton begins in State 0, and because the first input symbol is 0, it transfers to State 1. Since the next input symbol is a 0, the automaton remains in State 1. However, the third symbol is a 1 and this causes a transition to state 2. The final symbol is a 1 and causes no state change. The end of the input string has now been reached and because the finite automaton is in an accept state, as indicated by the double circle, it has accepted the string 0011. It is easy to see that any bit string containing 01 will be processed in a similar manner and lead to the accept state, and that only such strings will cause the automaton to terminate in State 2. For example, the string 11000 is not accepted, because the automaton will be in state 1 after processing this string, and State 1 is not an accept state. Neither is the bit string 100201 accepted since the "illegal" symbol 2 causes a transition from State 1 to State 99, which is not an accept state.

State 99 is a "reject" or "dead" state; once it is entered, it is never exited. The transitions to this state are shown as dashed lines, since the existence of such a state is usually assumed and transitions are not drawn in the diagram. For any state and any input symbol for which no transition is specified, it is assumed that the transition is to such a reject state. Thus, the finite automaton is usually drawn as

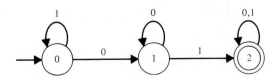

Similarly, the following finite automaton recognizes bit strings ending in 00 or 11:

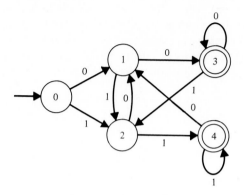

and a finite automaton to recognize Pascal identifiers is

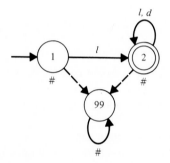

where l denotes a letter, d denotes a digit and # is any other character.

To illustrate how a finite automaton can be used to advantage in the design of lexical analyzers, we consider the problem of recognizing Pascal integer constants. A finite automaton that does this is

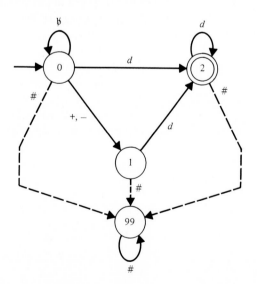

where d denotes one of the digits 0, 1, . . . , 9, b denotes a blank, and State 2 is the only accepting state. The machine begins in State 0, and if the first input symbol is a blank, it stays in State 0, "gobbling up" leading blanks; if it is + or −, it goes to State 1; if it is a digit, it goes to State 2; otherwise, the input character is not valid, and thus the string does not represent a valid integer.

Writing program statements corresponding to such a finite automaton is then straightforward. The program in Figure 13.3 illustrates this. It reads a string of characters and determines whether it represents a valid Pascal integer. The part of the program highlighted in color implements the preceding finite automaton.

```
PROGRAM LexicalAnalyzer (input, output);

(********************************************************************

   This program implements a simple lexical analyzer for Pascal
   integer constants.  A finite automaton that recognizes
   integer constants was used in designing the program.

********************************************************************)

CONST
   MaxState = 99;            (* largest state number in finite automaton *)
   DeadState = MaxState;     (* dead (reject) state *)

TYPE
   CharacterSet = SET OF char;
   StateSet = SET OF 0..MaxState;

VAR
   Digits : CharacterSet;    (* set of delimiters *)
   AcceptStates : StateSet;  (* set of accept states *)
   State : 0..MaxState;      (* current state *)
   EndOfToken : boolean;     (* signals end of token being checked *)
   Symbol,                   (* current input symbol *)
   Response : char;          (* user response *)

BEGIN
   Digits := ['0'..'9'];
   AcceptStates := [2];
   REPEAT
      (* begin in initial state *)
      State := 0;
      write ('Enter the string to be checked: ');
      WHILE NOT eoln  DO
```

Figure 13.3

Figure 13.3 (cont.)

```
            BEGIN
                read (Symbol);
                CASE State OF
                        0 : IF Symbol = ' ' THEN
                                State := 0
                            ELSE IF Symbol IN ['+', '-'] THEN
                                State := 1
                            ELSE IF Symbol IN Digits THEN
                                State := 2
                            ELSE
                                State:= DeadState;
                        1,2 : IF Symbol IN Digits THEN
                                State := 2
                            ELSE
                                State:= DeadState;
                    DeadState : (* stay in dead state *)
                END (* CASE *)
            END (* WHILE *);
        IF State IN AcceptStates THEN
            writeln ('Valid integer')
        ELSE
            writeln ('Not a valid Integer');
        readln;
        writeln;
        write ('More data (Y or N)? ');
        readln (Response)
    UNTIL NOT (Response IN ['y', 'Y'])
END.
```

Sample run:

Enter the string to be checked: 1234
Valid integer

More data (Y or N)? Y
Enter the string to be checked: −1
Valid integer

More data (Y or N)? Y
Enter the string to be checked: +9999
Valid integer

More data (Y or N)? Y
Enter the string to be checked: 123+4
Not a valid Integer

More data (Y or N)? Y
Enter the string to be checked: abccdef
Not a valid Integer

More data (Y or N)? N

Exercises

1. Given that A, B, C, and D are set variables assigned values as follows: $A := [3, 5..9, 11]$; $B := [1..5, 11, 12]$; $C := [2, 4, 6, 8]$; $D := [6..10]$; calculate the following:

(a) $A * B$	**(b)** $A + B$	**(c)** $A - B$
(d) $B - A$	**(e)** $A + D$	**(f)** $A - D$
(g) $A * D$	**(h)** $D - A$	**(i)** $C + C$
(j) $C * C$	**(k)** $C - C$	**(l)** $C - [\ ]$
(m) $A + B + C + D$	**(n)** $(A - B) - C$	**(o)** $A - (B - C)$
(p) $A * B * C * D$	**(q)** $A + B * C$	**(r)** $A * B + C$
(s) $A * B - C * D$	**(t)** $(A - (B + C)) * D$	**(u)** $A * B - (A + B)$
(v) $A - B - C - D$	**(w)** $B - B - C$	**(x)** $B - (B - C)$

2. Write appropriate declarations for the following set type identifiers:

   (a) *SmallIntegers*: set of integers from 1 through 99.
   (b) *FirstLetters*: set of letters in the first half of the alphabet.
   (c) *Days*: the set of names of days of the week.
   (d) *Suit*: set of 13 cards in a suit.

3. Write appropriate variable declarations for the following set variables, and write statements to assign to each the specified value:

   (a) *Evens*: the set of all even integers from 1 through 99; and *Odd*: the set of all odd integers in the range from 1 through 99.
   (b) *OneModThree*: the set of all numbers of the form $3k + 1$ in the range from 1 through 99 with k an integer.
   (c) *Null*: the empty set.
   (d) *LargeFactors*: the set of all numbers in the range 1 through 99 that are not divisible by 2, 3, 5, or 7.
   (e) *Divisors*: the set of all divisors of a given integer *Number*.
   (f) *Vowels*: the set of all vowels; and *Consonants*: the set of all consonants.
   (g) *WeekDays*: the set of all weekdays.
   (h) *FaceCards*: the set of all face cards in a suit; and *NumberCards*: the set of all number cards in a suit.

4. Write a procedure to print any set of characters or integers using the usual mathematical notation in which the elements are enclosed in braces { and } and are separated by commas. For example, the set of numbers 2, 5, and 7 should be displayed as {2, 5, 7}, the set whose element is 4 as {4}, and the empty set as { }.

5. Write a function to calculate the **cardinal number** of a set, that is, the number of elements in the set.

6. Sets are commonly stored in computer memory as **bit strings.** The length of these bit strings is the number of elements in the universal

set, each bit corresponding to exactly one element of the universal set. Thus sets of base type 0..9 are represented by bit strings of length 10, the first bit corresponding to 0, the second to 1, and so on. A given set S is then represented by a bit string in which the bits corresponding to the elements of S are 1 and all other bits are 0. For example, the set [1, 3, 7..9] would be represented by the bit string

$$0101000111$$

(a) Assuming this same universal set, give the bit string representations of the following sets:
   (i) the set of odd digits.
   (ii) the set of prime digits.
   (iii) the set of digits divisible by 1.
   (iv) the set of digits not divisible by 1.

(b) For the base type 'A'..'Z', describe bit strings for the following sets:
   (i) the set of vowels
   (ii) ['A'..'E', 'X', 'Y', 'Z']

7. Write a program to find the set of all vowels and the set of all consonants that appear in a given line of text.

8. Write a program to read two lines of text, and find all characters that appear in both lines.

9. Write a program to find all letters that are not present in a given line of text and display them in alphabetical order.

10. Write a program to read several lines of text, and find all words having three or more distinct vowels.

11. Write a program to deal two ten-card hands from a standard deck of fifty-two cards. Use a random number generator (see Section 6.3), and use sets to ensure that the same card is not dealt twice.

12. The Greek mathematician Eratosthenes developed an algorithm for finding all prime numbers less than or equal to a given number n, that is, all primes in the range 2 through n. This algorithm was described in Exercise 20 of Section 9.3 and can be rephrased using sets as follows:

ALGORITHM FOR THE SIEVE METHOD

1. Initialize the set *Sieve* to contain the integers from 2 through n.
2. Select the smallest element *Prime* in *Sieve*.
3. While $Prime^2 \leq n$, do the following:
   a. Remove from *Sieve* all elements of the form *Prime* * k for $k > 1$.

 b. Replace *Prime* with the smallest element in *Sieve* that is greater than *Prime*.

The elements remaining in *Sieve* when this algorithm terminates are the primes in the range 2 through *n*. Write a program to implement this algorithm.

13. Because some versions of Pascal allow only rather small sets, the Sieve Method of Eratosthenes for finding prime numbers described in Exercise 12 cannot be used to find large primes. Write a program that can. (*Hint*: Use an array *Sieve* of sets *Sieve*[0], *Sieve*[1], *Sieve*[2], . . . whose elements are integers in the range 0 through 99. Each element of *Sieve*[1] must be interpreted as 100 plus its value, each element of *Sieve*[2] as 200 plus its value, and so on.)

14. Write a program for a computer dating service similar to that in Figure 13.2. It should allow the user to enter a set of characteristics that he or she desires and that then searches a file of names and characteristics to find all persons in the file who have these traits.

15. Proceed as in Exercise 14, but search the file to find the best match(es) in case there are no persons who have all of the desired traits.

16. Write a program for a real estate firm similar to that in Figure 13.2. It should allow the user to enter a set of features that he or she is looking for in a home and that then searches a file of addresses and features of homes on the market to find all homes in the file that have these features.

17. Proceed as in Exercise 16, but search the file to find the best match(es) in case there are no homes that have all of the desired features.

18. Design a finite automaton to recognize bit strings

 (a) containing 00 or 11.
 (b) containing an even number of 1's.
 (c) containing an even number of 0's and an even number of 1's.
 (d) in which $n \bmod 3 = 1$ where n is the number of 1's.

19. A real number in Pascal has one of the forms $m.n$, $+m.n$, or $-m.n$, where m and n are nonnegative integers; or it may be expressed in exponential form xEe, $xE+e$, $xE-e$, where x is an integer or a real number not in exponential form and e is a nonnegative integer. Write a program that accepts a string of characters and then checks to see whether it represents a valid real constant.

20. Write a program for a lexical analyzer to process assignment statements of the form *identifier* := *string-constant*. Have it recognize the

following tokens: identifier, assignment operator (: =), and string constant.

21. Write a program for a lexical analyzer that processes assignment statements of the form *set-variable* : = *set-value*. Have it recognize the following tokens: identifier, set constant, set operation (+ , *, −), and assignment operator (: =).

Programming Pointers

In this chapter we considered sets and their implementation in Pascal with the set data type. Some of the key points to remember when using this structured data type are as follows:

1. *All of the elements of a set must be of the same type, called the base type for that set. This base type must be an ordinal type.*

2. *Most versions of Pascal limit the size of sets, that is, the number of elements a set may have.* In particular, the declaration

   set of *integer*

is usually not allowed, and in some versions,

   set of *char*

is also not allowed. In such cases, to use sets whose elements are integers or characters, a subrange must be specified for these elements, for example,

   set of 1..100
   set of 'A'..'Z'

3. *The only standard set operations are* + *(union),* * *(intersection), and* − *(difference).* Some versions of Pascal may also allow a unary minus to denote the complement of a set.

4. *The only standard relational operators that may be used to compare sets are* <= *(subset),* >= *(superset),* = *(equal),* <> *(not equal).* Some versions of Pascal may also allow the relational operators < (proper subset) and > (proper superset).

5. *The* **in** *relation for set membership can be used to simplify complex boolean expressions and to determine whether the value of the selector in a* **case** *statement is one of the case labels.* The examples at the end of Section 13.2 illustrate.

6. *A set value cannot be read by including the name of the set in the input list of a* read *or* readln *statement.* Instead, each element of the set must be read and added to the set. See the algorithm in Section 13.3 for constructing a set.

7. *A set value cannot be displayed by including the name of the set in the output list of a* write *or* writeln *statement.* Instead, each element must be displayed individually. The algorithm in Section 13.3 for displaying a set indicates how this can be done.

Variations and Extensions

In the various versions of Pascal, there are few variations from or extensions to the set-processing features of standard Pascal. One that we have already noted is the imposition of an upper limit on the size of sets (e.g., 255 in Turbo). Also, versions (Turbo) that allow initialization of arrays and records in the declaration part of a program also allow initialization of sets (see Appendix G for details).

14

Files

The programs that we have written up to this point have involved relatively small amounts of input/output data. In most of our examples, we have assumed that the input data was read from the standard system file *input,* which refers to an input device such as a terminal. For the most part, output has been directed to the standard system file *output,* referring to a system output device such as a terminal or printer. However, many applications involve large data sets, and these can be processed more conveniently if stored on magnetic tape or a magnetic disk or some other **secondary (auxiliary) memory.** Once data has been stored on such media, it may be used as often as desired without being reentered from a terminal. Also, several different data sets can be processed by a program, and the output produced by one program can be stored and used as input to another program.

A collection of related data items stored on some external medium is called a *file,* and the individual items are often called **components** or **records.** Usually the programmer is not concerned with the details of the actual external medium on which the data is stored because these details are handled by the operating

494

system. Instead, the programmer deals with the logical structure of the file, that is, with the relationship between the items stored in the file and with the algorithms needed to process these items.

There are two basic types of files: ***sequential*** and ***direct*** (or ***random***) ***access.*** In a sequential file, the data items must be accessed in the order in which they are stored; that is, to access any particular component, one must start at the beginning of the file and pass through all the components that precede it. In contrast, each item in a direct access file can be accessed directly by specifying its location, usually by means of a component number. Direct access files can, however, be processed sequentially when necessary, by simply accessing the components in order by component number.

Standard Pascal supports only sequential files, but many other versions support both kinds. The Variations and Extensions section at the end of this chapter describes direct access files as processed in Turbo Pascal.

Another distinction between files is based on the way in which information is represented in the file. Files in which information is stored in external character form are called ***text files,*** and those in which the information is stored in internal form are called ***binary*** or ***nontext files.*** Standard Pascal supports both kinds, and they are processed in Pascal programs by using the structured data type **file.** In this chapter we describe the file capabilities of Pascal, beginning with a review of text files considered in Chapter 7.

14.1   Review of Text Files

As a data structure, a *file* is an ordered collection of related data items, usually stored in external memory, for input to or output by a program; that is, information can be read from the file and/or written to the file. The files used in Pascal programs up to this point have been ***text files,*** whose components are characters and these characters are organized into lines. The predefined file type *text* is a standard type identifier used to declare text files. The standard system files *input* and *output* associated with the standard input and output devices are examples of text files, and in Chapter 7, we described user-defined text files. The predefined procedures *readln, writeln, eoln,* and *page* may be used only with text files.

As we noted in the introduction, Pascal also supports nontext files, whose components may be of any type, simple or structured, except that they may not be of file type. Although we restrict our attention in this section to text files, much of the discussion also applies to the other types of files considered in subsequent sections.

The principal rules governing the use of text files in standard Pascal programs as discussed in Chapter 7 may be summarized as follows:

1. *Program heading*: Pascal permits the use of ***temporary*** files and ***permanent*** files. Temporary files exist only during the execution of a program, whereas permanent files exist before and/or after program execution as well. The names of all permanent files used in a program (including the standard text files *input* and *output*) must appear in the file list of the program heading.
2. *Declaration*: All user-defined files must be declared in the declaration part

of the program. For text files, the predefined type identifier *text* can be used to specify the types of file variables.

3. *Opening files for input*: Each file from which data is to be read must be opened for input by using the predefined procedure *reset* in a statement of the form

  reset (file-variable)

Each such procedure call resets the data pointer to the beginning of the specified file. (The standard system file *input* need not be opened for input.)

4. *Opening files for output*: Each file to which data is to be written must be opened for output with the predefined procedure *rewrite,* using a statement of the form

  rewrite (file-variable)

Each such procedure call empties the specified file, so that any previous contents of the file are destroyed. (The standard system file *output* need not be opened for output.)

5. *File input*: Information can be read from a text file by using the predefined procedures *read* and *readln* in the forms

  read (file-variable, input-list)
  readln (file-variable, input-list)

If *file-variable* is omitted, values are read from the standard system file *input*.

6. *File output*: Output can be directed to a text file by using the predefined procedures *write* and *writeln* in the forms

  write (file-variable, output-list)
  writeln (file-variable, output-list)

If *file-variable* is omitted, output is directed to the standard file *output*.

7. *Copying files*: The contents of one file cannot be copied to another by using an assignment statement of the form *file-variable-1* : = *file-variable-2*. Rather, the components must be copied one at a time.

8. *Files as parameters*: Formal parameters that represent files must be variable parameters. This is a consequence of Rule 7, since value parameters require copying the values of the corresponding actual parameters.

14.2 Binary Files

The files reviewed in the preceding section are text files, that is, files whose components are of type *char* and these characters are organized into lines. As we noted, however, the components of a file may be of any predefined or user-defined data type except of file type.

The general file declaration has the form

  file of *component-type*

where *component-type* specifies the type of the components of the file. The following illustrates some file declarations:

type
    DaysOfWeek = (*Sunday, Monday, Tuesday, Wednesday,*
                  Thursday, Friday, Saturday);
    String = **packed array**[1..20] **of** *char*;
    List = **array**[1..100] **of** *integer*;
    EmployeeRecord = **record**
                  Name : *String*;
                  Number, Dependents : *integer*;
                  HourlyRate : *real*
             end;
    FileOfNumbers = **file of** *integer*;
    FileOfDays = **file of** *DaysOfWeek*;
    LongStringsFile = **file of packed array**[1..80] **of** *char*;
    FileOfLists = **file of** *List*;
    EmployeeFile = **file of** *EmployeeRecord*;

var
    CharacterSetFile : *text*;
    NumberFile : *FileOfNumbers*;
    DayFile : *FileOfDays*;
    AddressFile : *LongStringsFile*;
    ListFile : *FileOfLists*;
    EmpFile : *EmployeeFile*;

Nontext files such as *NumberFile, DayFile, AddressFile, ListFile,* and *EmpFile* can usually be created only by a program, and access to the components of such files is possible only within a program. Attempting to list the file contents by using some system command or to access them by using a system text editor usually results in "garbage" output or some error message. For example, listing the contents of the nontext file *GPAFile* produced by the program in Figure 14.1 produced the following on one system:

@Ä @|ÃÃ@hı⌐@Iôô@8ı⌐@@£◇ @æKÖæ@6ff@
p£@ææΠ?Δff?Bè[?⌐QĨ@æè\@Ä @Ä @æ @æ @@£◇ @?\)

The characters that make up a text file are stored using some coding scheme such as ASCII or EBCDIC, as described in Section 1.3, and when a text file is listed, those codes are automatically converted to the corresponding characters by the terminal, printer, or other output device and become legible to the user. On the other hand, the information in a nontext file is illegible because it is stored using the internal binary representation scheme for the particular computer being used—hence the name, binary files—and this representation usually cannot be correctly displayed in character form by the output device.

There are, however, some advantages in using binary files. The primary advantage is that the information in such files can be transferred between main memory and secondary memory more rapidly, as it is already in a form that requires no decoding or encoding. Another advantage is that data is usually stored more compactly if it is stored using its internal representation rather than its external representation in one of the standard coding schemes.

To illustrate, consider the integer 27195. If the usual binary representation described in Section 1.3 were used, this integer would be stored internally in a 16-bit word as the bit string

$$0110101000111011$$

and this would also be its representation in a file of type *integer* such as *NumFile*:

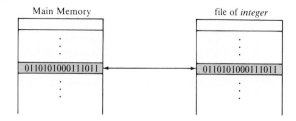

In a text file, however, it would be stored as a sequence of codes for the five characters '2', '7', '1', '9', '5':

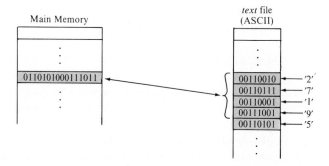

Recall that the name of each permanent file used in the program must be included in the file list of the program heading. Also, each file from which values are to be read (except *input*) must be opened by using the procedure *reset* before any of its components may be accessed. The statement

   reset (file-variable)

calls this procedure and opens the specified file for input. Because this procedure has a single argument, a separate procedure call is required for each file being opened for input. Similarly, each file to be used for output (except *output*) must be opened by using a *rewrite* procedure reference of the form

   rewrite (file-variable)

Because in most computer systems nontext files must be created by a Pascal program, we first consider the *write* and *put* procedures that are used for this purpose. Values can be written into a file by using an output statement of the form

    write (file-variable, output-list)

where *output-list* is an expression (constant, variable, or formula) or a list of expressions separated by commas, each of which must be compatible with the type of the components of *file-variable*. Note that the procedure *writeln* may *not* be used for files that are not text files.[1]

As a simple illustration, suppose that a comparison of high school and college grade point averages (GPAs) is to be made and we wish to create a data file containing pairs of such GPAs, one pair for each student. This file can be created by a program in which pairs of real values representing GPAs are entered by the user and each pair is then written into a file *GPAFile* whose components are of type

    GPARecord = **record**
                HighSchool, College : *real*
        end;

Because this file is to be a permanent file, we must list it in the program heading

    program *CreateGPAFile (input, output, GPAFile)*;

The type definitions and variable declarations required to declare the file *GPAFile* with components of type *GPARecord* are

    type
      GPARecord = **record**
                 HighSchool, College : *real*
          end;
      FileOfGPARecords = **file of** *GPARecord*;

    var
      GPAPair : *GPARecord*;
      GPAFile : *FileOfGPARecords*;

The program in Figure 14.1 creates the desired file. It first opens file *GPAFile* for output and then reads pairs of real numbers representing pairs of GPAs, writing each pair to *GPAFile*.

---

[1] As was noted in Chapter 7, file processing is quite different in some versions of Pascal. It may not be necessary or even permissible to list names of permanent files in the program heading. Modified forms of reference to procedures *reset* and *rewrite* or use of a special auxiliary procedure such as *assign* may be required to associate a file variable with the name of an actual data file in secondary memory. It may also be necessary to call a special *close* procedure to close files before program execution terminates. See Appendix G and the Variations and Extensions sections of Chapter 7 and this chapter for details.

```
PROGRAM CreateGPAFile (input, output, GPAFile);

(*********************************************************************

   Program to create the nontext file GPAFile having components
   of type GPARecord.  Pairs of grade point averages are input
   by the user during execution.

   *********************************************************************)

TYPE
    GPARecord = RECORD
                    HighSchool, College: real
                END;
    FileOfGPARecords = FILE OF GPARecord;

VAR
    GPAPair : GPARecord;          (* pair of grade point averages *)
    GPAFile : FileOfGPARecords;   (* file of GPA records created *)

BEGIN
    rewrite (GPAFile);
    writeln ('Enter negative GPA''s to stop.');
    write ('GPA pair?  ');
    readln (GPAPair.HighSchool, GPAPair.College);
    WHILE (GPAPair.HighSchool >= 0) DO
       BEGIN
           write (GPAFile, GPAPair);
           write ('GPA pair?  ');
           readln (GPAPair.HighSchool, GPAPair.College)
       END (* WHILE *);
    writeln ('Creation of GPAFile completed')
END.
```

Sample run:

```
Enter negative GPA's to stop.
GPA pair?  4.00 3.95
GPA pair?  3.64 3.15
GPA pair?  2.89 3.01
GPA pair?  3.18 2.85
GPA pair?  2.21 2.33
GPA pair?  1.55 0.76
GPA pair?  1.94 2.04
GPA pair?  4.00 4.00
GPA pair?  2.25 2.25
GPA pair?  3.01 2.99
GPA pair?  -1-1
Creation of GPAFile completed
```

Figure 14.1

Transfer of information between main memory and secondary memory is considerably slower than a transfer from one location in main memory to another. Program execution degrades unacceptably if processing must be suspended each time a data item is transferred to or from secondary memory. For this reason, special segments of main memory known as ***input/output buffers*** are used as "holding" areas to facilitate input/output.

To illustrate, consider the statement

write (GPAFile, GPAPair)

used in the program of Figure 14.1 to write the record *GPAPair* to *GPAFile*. The output to *GPAFile* actually takes place in two stages. The value of the record variable *GPAPair* is first copied into a special variable called a ***file buffer variable*** or ***file window*** that has the same type as the file components:

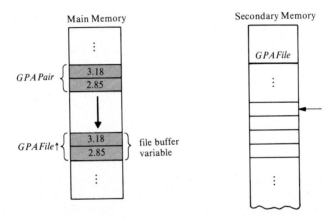

The second stage of output to *GPAFile* consists of transferring this value from the file buffer variable into the file itself. While this is being done, processing of other statements in the program can continue.

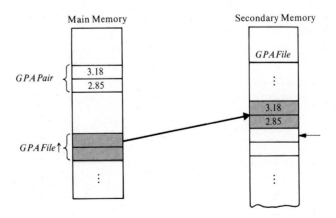

This file buffer variable is created automatically by the declaration of the file variable and is denoted by affixing an up arrow (↑) or a carat (^) to the file variable:

    file-variable↑   or   *file-variable*^

In our example, therefore, the variable

    GPAFile↑

is the buffer variable associated with the file *GPAFile*. It is of type *GPARecord*, since this is the component type of the file *GPAFile*, and it may be used in the same manner as any other variable of type *GPARecord*. For example, the assignment statement

    GPAFile↑ := *GPAPair*;

assigns the value of the record variable *GPAPair* to *GPAFile*↑. The statement

    readln (GPAFile↑.HighSchool, GPAFile↑.College);

or

    with *GPAFile*↑ **do**
       readln (HighSchool, College);

reads values for the two fields in *GPAFile*↑.

    Assignment of a value to a file buffer variable carries out only the first stage of output to a file. It does not actually write this value into the associated file; rather, it merely copies the value into the memory location assigned to this buffer variable. The second stage can then be performed using the predefined procedure *put*. This procedure is called with a statement of the form

    put (file-variable)

and transfers the value of the buffer variable *file-variable*↑ to the associated file *file-variable*. This value is actually *transferred* rather than copied, and consequently, after execution of this statement, *file-variable*↑ is undefined.

    As an illustration, the program in Figure 14.2 is a modification of the program in Figure 14.1 for creating a file of GPA pairs. Each pair of real numbers is read directly into the fields of the buffer variable with the statement

    readln (GPAFile↑.HighSchool, GPAFile↑.College);

and the statement

    put (GPAFile);

then transfers this pair from the buffer variable *GPAFile*↑ to the file. This program thus bypasses the first stage of the file output process and will therefore execute slightly faster than does that in Figure 14.1.

```
PROGRAM CreateGPAFile (input, output, GPAFile);

(*****************************************************************

    Program to create the nontext file GPAFile having components
    of type GPARecord.  Pairs of grade point averages are input
    directly into the file buffer variable by the user during execution.

******************************************************************)

TYPE
   GPARecord = RECORD
                  HighSchool, College: real
               END;
   FileOfGPARecords = FILE OF GPARecord;

VAR
   GPAFile : FileOfGPARecords;  (* file of GPA records created *)

BEGIN
   rewrite (GPAFile);
   writeln ('Enter negative GPA''s to stop.');
   write ('GPA pair?  ');
   readln (GPAFile^.HighSchool, GPAFile^.College);
   WHILE (GPAFile^.HighSchool >= 0) DO
      BEGIN
         put (GPAFile);
         write ('GPA pair?  ');
         readln (GPAFile^.HighSchool, GPAFile^.College);
      END (* WHILE *);
   writeln ('Creation of GPAFile completed')
END.
```

Figure 14.2

In general, an output statement of the form

write (file-variable, item-1, item-2, . . . , item-n)

is equivalent to the following *n* pairs of statements:

file-variable↑ := *item-1*;
put (file-variable);
file-variable↑ := *item-2*;
put (file-variable);
⋮
file-variable↑ := *item-n*;
put (file-variable)

The statements in each pair correspond to the two stages involved in producing output to a file.[2]

_____

[2] Some versions of Pascal do not allow the use of *write* with nontext files; *put* must be used. In others, *put* is not allowed and *write* must be used.

For a text file, the buffer variable is of type *char*. When a value of some other allowed type—*integer, real, boolean,* string—is written to a text file, it is converted to the appropriate string of characters, and these characters are written successively to the file using the file buffer. In the case of procedure *writeln*, this stream of characters is followed by an end-of-line character. Note that *writeln* cannot be used for nontext files because they have no line structure.

A component of a file that has been opened for input with the procedure *reset* can be read using the procedure *read* in a reference of the form

> read (*file-variable, input-list*)

where *input-list* is a single variable or a list of variables separated by commas. The type of each variable in the input list and the type of the file components must be compatible. Note that the procedure *readln* may *not* be used for files that are not text files, since such files have no line structure.

As an illustration of input from files, suppose that we wish to examine the contents of the file *GPAFile* created by the program in Figure 14.1 or Figure 14.2. This file must first be opened for input by using the statement

> reset (*GPAFile*);

Each component of the file can then be read and assigned to the variable *GPAPair* of record type *GPARecord* by using the procedure *read*:

> read (*GPAFile, GPAPair*);

and the values of the two fields of *GPAPair* can then be displayed:

> writeln (*GPAPair.HighSchool*:4:2, *GPAPair.College*:7:2)

In the program in Figure 14.3, these two statements are repeated until the end-of-file mark in *GPAFile* is encountered. This end-of-file mark is automatically placed at the end of each file created by a Pascal program.

```
PROGRAM ReadGPAFile (output, GPAFile);

(*********************************************************************

   Program to read and display the contents of the permanent file
   GPAFile created by the program of Figure 14.1 or 14.2.

*********************************************************************)

TYPE
   GPARecord = RECORD
                  HighSchool, College: real
               END;
   FileOfGPARecords = FILE OF GPARecord;
```

Figure 14.3

Figure 14.3 (cont.)

```
VAR
   GPAFile : FileOfGPARecords;    (* file of GPA records created *)
   GPAPair : GPARecord;           (* pair of grade point averages *)

BEGIN
   reset (GPAFile);
   writeln ('Contents of GPAFile:');
   WHILE NOT eof(GPAFile) DO
      BEGIN
         read (GpaFile, GPAPair);
         writeln (GPAPair.HighSchool:4:2, GPAPair.College:7:2)
      END (* WHILE *)
END.
```

<u>Sample run:</u>

```
Contents of GPAFile:
4.00    3.95
3.64    3.15
2.89    3.01
3.18    2.85
2.21    2.33
1.55    0.76
1.94    2.04
4.00    4.00
2.25    2.25
3.01    2.99
```

File input, like file output, is a two-stage process that uses the file buffer variable or file window. When a file such as *GPAFile* is opened for input with the procedure *reset*, the first file component is copied into the file buffer variable *GPAFile↑*. Later, when the statement

read (GPAFile, GPAPair);

is executed, the value of this buffer variable is copied to the record variable *GPAPair*:

Then, while execution of the program continues, the next file component is copied from the file into the file buffer variable in preparation for the next time a value must be read:

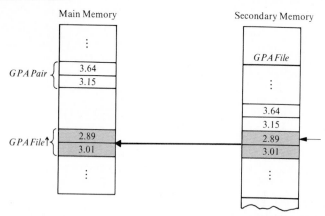

This buffer variable thus always contains a copy of the next component of the associated file, providing a "window" through which the *next* file component may be accessed. We can see what's coming without actually reading the next component.

The statement

   read (GPAFile, GPAPair);

is equivalent to the pair of statements

   GPAPair := *GPAFile*↑;
   get (GPAFile);

where *get* is a predefined procedure that copies the next file component into the associated buffer variable.[3] In general, *get* is called with a statement of the form

   get (file-variable)

and an input statement of the form

   read (file-variable, variable-1, variable-2, . . . , variable-n)

is equivalent to the *n* pairs of statements

   variable-1 := *file-variable*↑;
   get (file-variable);
   variable-2 := *file-variable*↑;
   get (file-variable);
        ⋮
   variable-n := *file-variable*↑;
   get (file-variable)

---

[3] Some versions of Pascal do not provide a file buffer variable and thus do not provide procedure *get* either. Input must then be carried out using *read*.

The program in Figure 14.4 is a modification of the program in Figure 14.3 for reading the file *GPAFile*. The statement

writeln (GPAFile↑.HighSchool:4:2, *GPAFile↑.College*:7:2);

displays each file component directly rather than first transferring it to a record variable *GPAPair* and then displaying its value. The statement

get (GPAFile)

then copies the next file component into the file buffer variable.

```
PROGRAM ReadGPAFile (output, GPAFile);

(*******************************************************************

   Program to read and display the contents of the permanent file
   GPAFile created by the program of Figure 14.1 or 14.2 by
   displaying the contents of the file buffer.

*******************************************************************)

TYPE
   GPARecord = RECORD
                   HighSchool, College: real
               END;
   FileOfGPARecords = FILE OF GPARecord;

VAR
   GPAFile : FileOfGPARecords;   (* file of GPA records created *)

BEGIN
   reset (GPAFile);
   writeln ('Contents of GPAFile:');
   WHILE NOT eof(GPAFile) DO
      BEGIN
         writeln (GPAFile^.HighSchool:4:2, GPAFile^.College:7:2);
         get (GPAFile)
      END (* WHILE *)
END.
```

Figure 14.4

In the examples in this section, we used one program to create *GPAFile* and a separate program to read the file. In the first program, *GPAFile* was opened for output by using the procedure *rewrite*. After the file was created, this same program could have opened it for input by using the procedure *reset* and then read and displayed the contents. The program in Figure 14.5 does precisely this and thus combines the functions of the programs in Figures 14.2 and 14.4 into a single program. Recall that opening a file for input and reading

its contents does not alter the contents of the file but that opening a file for
output does destroy any previous contents of the file.

```
PROGRAM CreateAndVerifyGPAFile (input, output, GPAFile);

(******************************************************************

   Program to create the nontext file GPAFile having components
   of type GPARecord.  Pairs of grade point averages are input
   directly into the file buffer variabley the user during execution.
   The contents of the file are then verified by opening it for
   input, reading the contents, and displaying each pair of GPAs.

******************************************************************)

TYPE
   GPARecord = RECORD
                    HighSchool, College: real
                 END;
   FileOfGPARecords = FILE OF GPARecord;

VAR
   GPAFile : FileOfGPARecords;   (* file of GPA records created *)

BEGIN
   (* Create GPAFile *)

   rewrite (GPAFile);
   writeln ('Enter negative GPA''s to stop.');
   write ('GPA pair?  ');
   readln (GPAFile^.HighSchool, GPAFile^.College);
   WHILE (GPAFile^.HighSchool >= 0) DO
      BEGIN
         put (GPAFile);
         write ('GPA pair?  ');
         readln (GPAFile^.HighSchool, GPAFile^.College);
      END (* WHILE *);

   (* Verify the contents of GPAFile *)

   reset (GPAFile);
   writeln;
   writeln ('Contents of GPAFile:');
   WHILE NOT eof(GPAFile) DO
      BEGIN
         writeln (GPAFile^.HighSchool:4:2, GPAFile^.College:7:2);
         get (GPAFile)
      END (* WHILE *)
END.
```

Figure 14.5

Figure 14.5 (cont.)

Sample run:

```
Enter negative GPA's to stop.
GPA pair?   4.00 3.95
GPA pair?   3.64 3.15
GPA pair?   2.89 3.01
GPA pair?   3.18 2.85
GPA pair?   2.21 2.33
GPA pair?   1.55 0.76
GPA pair?   1.94 2.04
GPA pair?   4.00 4.00
GPA pair?   2.25 2.25
GPA pair?   3.01 2.99
GPA pair?   -1 -1


Contents of GPAFile:
4.00    3.95
3.64    3.15
2.89    3.01
3.18    2.85
2.21    2.33
1.55    0.76
1.94    2.04
4.00    4.00
2.25    2.25
3.01    2.99
```

When the procedure *read* (or *readln*) is used to read an integer or a real value from a text file, the characters are transferred one at a time to the file buffer variable and are converted to their corresponding numeric values, and the numeric equivalent of the string of characters representing the number in the file is formed. Leading blanks and leading end-of-line characters are ignored, and characters are transferred and converted until some character that could not belong to a string representing an integer or a real number is encountered.

When an end-of-line character is encountered in a text file, the value of

eoln(file-variable)

becomes true (it is false otherwise), and a blank is placed in the file window. This blank is read as the next component, unless it is bypassed by using a statement of the form

get (file-variable)

A statement of the form

readln (file-variable)

may also be used to bypass an end-of-line character because it is equivalent to

while not *eoln*(*file-variable*) **do**
   get (*file-variable*);
get (*file-variable*)

In either case, the file window *file-variable*↑ will contain the first character of the next line.

The procedures *get* and *read* (and *readln* for text files) copy the next file component into the file window unless the end of the file has been reached. In this case, the value of

eof(*file-variable*)

becomes true (it is false otherwise), and the file buffer variable is undefined. Any subsequent calls to the procedures *get* and *read* result in an error, because an attempt is made to access information beyond the end of the file.

As an illustration, note the use of the *eof* function and file buffer variables in the following procedure, which copies the contents of one file into another:

procedure *CopyFile* (**var** *FromFile, ToFile : FileType*);

   (∗ Procedure to copy the contents of *FromFile* into *ToFile*. ∗)

begin (∗ *CopyFile* ∗)
  reset (*FromFile*);
  rewrite (*ToFile*);
  while not *eof*(*FromFile*) **do**
    begin
     ToFile↑ := *FromFile*↑;
     put (*ToFile*);
     get (*FromFile*)
    end (∗ **while** ∗)
end (∗ *CopyFile* ∗);

This procedure copies one component at a time from *FromFile* to *ToFile*. This is necessary because the contents of a file can be accessed only one component at a time; it is not possible to copy one file into another file by using an assignment statement of the form *file-1* := *file-2*.

One consequence is that files used as parameters, as in procedure *CopyFile*, must be variable parameters. Value parameters cannot be used, because this would require copying an entire actual file into the corresponding formal file parameter. Corresponding actual file parameters and formal file parameters must have the same type, and as for the other predefined data structures in Pascal, this requirement means that they must be declared by the same or equivalent type identifiers (see Section 9.2).

Our examples in this section have thus far dealt only with permanent files, which exist before and/or after as well as during program execution. The comments in this section regarding files also apply to temporary files, that is, to files that exist only during execution of the program. One exception, however, is that names of temporary files are not listed in the program heading.

A data-processing problem in which it is convenient to use temporary files is that of appending data to an existing permanent file. Because opening a file for output erases its previous contents, it is not possible to add the data by simply writing to the existing file. Instead, we first must copy the permanent file to a temporary work file, then add the additional data to this file, and finally copy the resulting work file back to the permanent file. Because the work file is needed only during program execution, it may be a temporary file. The program in Figure 14.6 uses the temporary file *WorkFile* to append data entered by the user to the file *GPAFile*. created earlier. Note that although *WorkFile* is not listed in the program heading, it is declared and opened in the usual manner.

```
PROGRAM AppendToGPAFile (input, output, GPAFile);

(******************************************************************

   Program to read pairs of GPA's entered by the user and add
   these pairs to the end of the previously created GPAFile.
   The contents of GPAFile are first copied into the temporary
   file WorkFile, the new pairs are appended to WorkFile, and
   the contents of WorkFile are then copied back to GPAFile.
   The contents of GPAFile are then verified by reading and
   displaying each pair in it.

******************************************************************)

TYPE
    GPARecord = RECORD
                    HighSchool, College : real
                END;
    FileOfGPARecords = FILE OF GPARecord;
    FileType = FileOfGPARecords;

VAR
    WorkFile,                       (* temporary file of GPA records *)
    GPAFile : FileOfGPARecords;     (* file of GPA records created *)

PROCEDURE CopyFile (VAR FromFile, ToFile : FileType);

   (*************************************************************

      Procedure to copy the contents of FromFile into ToFile.

   *************************************************************)

   BEGIN (* CopyFile *)
      reset (FromFile);
      rewrite (ToFile);
      WHILE NOT eof(FromFile) DO
         BEGIN
            ToFile^ := FromFile^;
            put (ToFile);
            get (FromFile)
         END (* WHILE *)
   END (* CopyFile *);
```

Figure 14.6

Figure 14.6 (cont.)

```
BEGIN (* main program *)

   (* Copy contents of GPAFile to WorkFile *)

   CopyFile (GPAFile, WorkFile);

   (* Append new records to the end of WorkFile *)

   writeln ('Enter negative GPA''s to stop.');
   write ('GPA pair?  ');
   readln (WorkFile^.HighSchool, WorkFile^.College);
   WHILE (WorkFile^.HighSchool >= 0) DO
      BEGIN
         put (WorkFile);
         write ('GPA pair?  ');
         readln (WorkFile^.HighSchool, WorkFile^.College)
      END (* WHILE *);

   (* Now copy the contents of WorkFile to GPAFile *)

   CopyFile (WorkFile, GPAFile);

   (* Finally, verify the contents of GPAFile *)

   reset (GPAFile);
   writeln;
   writeln ('Contents of GPAFile:');
   WHILE NOT eof(GPAFile) DO
      BEGIN
         writeln (GPAFile^.HighSchool:5:1, GPAFile^.College:7:1);
         get (GpaFile)
      END (* WHILE *)
END (* main program *).
```

Sample run:

```
Enter negative GPA's to stop.
GPA pair?  3.3 3.3
GPA pair?  2.9 2.4
GPA pair?  1.1 1.3
GPA pair?  -1 -1

Contents of GPAFile:
  4.0    3.9
  3.6    3.1
  2.9    3.0
  3.2    2.8
  2.2    2.3
  1.5    0.8
  1.9    2.0
  4.0    4.0
  2.3    2.3
  3.0    3.0
  3.3    3.3
  2.9    2.4
  1.1    1.3
```

14.3 Example: Updating a File

To illustrate the file-processing techniques discussed in this chapter, we consider the important problem of updating a master file with the contents of a transaction file. For example, the master file may be an inventory file that is to be updated with a transaction file containing the day's sales, or the master file may be a file of students' records and the transaction file a file containing the students' grades for the semester just concluded.

In this section we consider the problem of updating a master file containing information regarding the users of a university's computing system. Suppose that components of the master file *UsersFile* are records containing the following information about each system user: identification number, name, password, limit on resources, and resources used to date. A daily log of the system's activity is also maintained. Among the other items of information, this log contains a list of user identification numbers and resources used for each job entered into the system. This list is maintained in the transaction file *UpdateFile*. At the end of each day, the master file *UsersFile* must be updated with the contents of *UpdateFile* to incorporate the activities of that day. We assume that both *UsersFile* and *UpdateFile* have been sorted so that the identification numbers are in ascending order. An algorithm for performing the file update is as follows:

FILE UPDATE ALGORITHM

(∗ Algorithm to update records in *UsersFile* with information from
   UpdateFile to produce *NewUsersFile*. It is assumed that records in
   these files are ordered so that identification numbers are in ascending
   order and that all identification numbers in *UpdateFile* are valid. ∗)

1. Read the first record from *UsersFile* and assign it to *UserRec*.
2. Read the first record from *UpdateFile* and assign it to *UpdateRec*.
3. Set a boolean variable *EndOfUpdate* to *false*.
4. While not *EndOfUpdate*, do the following updating:
   Compare the identification number in *UserRec* with that in
   UpdateRec. If they match, do the following:
       a. Update *UserRec* by adding the value of *ResourcesUsed* from
          UpdateRec to *UsedToDate* in *UserRec*.
       b. If the end of *UpdateFile* has been reached, set *EndOfUpdate* to
          true; otherwise, read the next value for *UpdateRec* from
          UpdateFile.
   If the identification numbers do not match, do the following:
       a. Write *UserRec* to *NewUsersFile*.
       b. Read a new value for *UserRec* from *UsersFile*.
5. Because the last updated user record has not been written, write
   UserRec to *NewUsersFile*.
6. Copy any remaining records in *UsersFile* into *NewUsersFile*.

The program in Figure 14.7 implements this algorithm. Also shown are the contents of two small files used in a test run and the output file produced.

These listings were obtained by executing a program that reads each record from a nontext file and then displays each field of the record by using a program segment of the form

```
reset (NonTextFile);
while not eof(NonTextFile) do
    begin
        with NonTextFile↑ do
            writeln ( field-1, field-2, . . .);
        get (NonTextFile)
    end
```

```
PROGRAM UserFileUpdate (UsersFile, UpdateFile, NewUsersFile);

(********************************************************************

    Program to update the entries in the master file UsersFile with
    the entries in the transactions file UpdateFile.  The records
    in UsersFile contain the id-number, name, password, resource
    limit, and resources used to date for each system user;
    UpdateFile represents the log of a day's activities; each
    record contains a user's id-number and resources used for a
    job entered into the system.  Both files are sorted so that
    id-numbers are in ascending order, and all id-numbers in
    UsersFile are assumed to be valid. The updated records are
    written to the output file NewUsersFile.

********************************************************************)

CONST
    NameLength = 20;                  (* lengths of names *)
    PasswordLength = 4;               (* lengths of passwords *)

TYPE
    NameString = PACKED ARRAY[1..NameLength] OF char;
    PasswordString = PACKED ARRAY[1..PasswordLength] OF char;
    UserRecord = RECORD
                    IdNumber : integer;
                    Name : NameString;
                    Password : PasswordString;
                    ResourceLimit,
                    UsedToDate : integer
                 END;
    UserUpdateRecord = RECORD
                         UpdateNumber,
                         ResourcesUsed : integer
                       END;
    MasterFile = FILE OF UserRecord;
    TransactionFile = FILE OF UserUpdateRecord;
```

Figure 14.7

Figure 14.7 (cont.)

```
VAR
    UserRec : UserRecord;               (* record from UsersFile *)
    UpdateRec : UserUpdateRecord;       (* record from UpdateFile *)
    UsersFile,                          (* file containing user information *)
    NewUsersFile : MasterFile;          (* updated user file *)
    UpdateFile : TransactionFile;       (* file to update UsersFile *)
    EndOfUpdate : boolean;              (* signals end of UpdateFile *)

BEGIN
    reset (UsersFile);
    reset (UpdateFile);
    rewrite (NewUsersFile);

    (* Read first record from each file *)

    read (UsersFile, UserRec);
    read (UpdateFile, UpdateRec);

    (* Update records of UsersFile with records of UpdateFile *)

    EndOfUpdate := false;
    WHILE NOT EndOfUpdate DO
        BEGIN
            WITH UserRec, UpdateRec DO
                IF IdNumber = UpdateNumber THEN      (* id-numbers match *)
                    BEGIN
                        UsedToDate := UsedToDate + ResourcesUsed;
                        IF eof(UpdateFile) THEN
                            EndOfUpdate := true
                        ELSE
                            read (UpdateFile, UpdateRec)
                    END (* IF *)
                ELSE                                 (* no match *)
                    BEGIN
                        write (NewUsersFile, UserRec);
                        read (UsersFile, UserRec)
                    END (* ELSE *)
        END (* WHILE *);

    (* Write UserRec to NewUsersFile; then copy any
       remaining records from UsersFile *)

    write (NewUsersFile, UserRec);
    WHILE NOT eof (UsersFile) DO
        BEGIN
            read (UsersFile, UserRec);
            write (NewUsersFile, UserRec)
        END (* WHILE *)
END.
```

Contents of UsersFile:

```
12300JOHN DOE          GERM 200 125
12310MARY SMITH        SNOW 200  75
13320PETE VANDERVAN    RAIN 300 228
13400FRED JONES        FROM 100   0
13450JANE TARZAN       JUST 200  63
13490JACK JACKSON      DATE 300 128
14000ALBERT ALBERTS    LIST 400 255
14010JESSE JAMES       GUNS 100  38
14040DIRTY GERTIE      MESS 100  17
14100PRINCE ALBERT     CANS 300 185
```

Figure 14.7 (cont.)

Contents of UpdateFile:

```
12300 10
12300 24
12310 17
12310 3
12310 5
12310 10
13400 28
13450 25
13450 3
13450 1
13450 13
14010 22
14010 5
14010 12
14010 7
```

Contents of NewUsersFile:

```
12300JOHN DOE           GERM 200 159
12310MARY SMITH         SNOW 200 110
13320PETE VANDERVAN     RAIN 300 228
13400FRED JONES         FROM 100  28
13450JANE TARZAN        JUST 200 105
13490JACK JACKSON       DATE 300 128
14000ALBERT ALBERTS     LIST 400 255
14010JESSE JAMES        GUNS 100  84
14040DIRTY GERTIE       MESS 100  17
14100PRINCE ALBERT      CANS 300 185
```

Exercises

In these exercises, the files *UsersFile*, *InventoryFile*, *StudentFile*, *InventoryUpdate*, and *StudentUpdate* should be processed as files of records. For descriptions of these files, see Appendix E.

1. Each of the following program segments is intended to read a text file *InFile* in which each line contains an integer and to find the sum of all the integers in the file. Explain why each fails to do so.

(a) *reset (InFile)*;
   Sum := 0;
   while not *eof(InFile)* **do**
      begin
         read (InFile, Number);
         Sum := *Sum* + *Number*
      end (* **while** *)

(b) *reset (InFile)*;
   Sum := 0;
   readln (InFile, Number);
   while not *eof(InFile)* **do**
      begin
         Sum := *Sum* + *Number*;
         readln (InFile, Number)
      end (* **while** *)

    (c) *reset (InFile)*;
       Sum := 0;
      repeat
        get (InFile);
        Sum := Sum + InFile↑
      until *eof(InFile)*

2. Each of the following program segments is intended to display all nonblank characters in the text file *InFile*, with no error resulting. For each, describe a text file for which it fails.

    (a) *reset (InFile)*;
       read (InFile, Ch);
      repeat
        if *InFile↑* = ' ' **then**
         get (InFile)
        else
         begin
           writeln (InFile↑);
           get (InFile)
         end (* **else** *)
      until *eof(InFile)*

    (b) *reset (InFile)*;
       read (InFile, Ch);
      while not *eof(InFile)* **do**
        begin
          while *Ch* = ' ' **do**
           read (InFile, Ch);
          writeln (Ch);
          read (InFile, Ch)
        end (* **while** *)

    (c) *reset (InFile)*;
       read (InFile, Ch);
      while not *eof(InFile)* **do**
        begin
          if *Ch* <> ' ' **then**
           writeln (Ch);
          read (InFile, Ch);
        end (* **while** *)

3. Write a procedure to concatenate two files of identical type.

4. The file update algorithm in this section assumes that all identification numbers in *UpdateFile* are valid. Modify this algorithm and the program in Figure 14.7 so they will work correctly even if *UpdateFile* has not been previously validated.

5. Modify Exercise 6 of Section 10.3 to print "personalized" junk-mail letters in which certain blanks in a form letter are filled in with personal information obtained from a file containing that information.

6. Write a program to read *UsersFile* to find and display the password for a specified user's identification number.

7. Write a program to read *StudentFile* and produce a report for all freshmen with GPAs below 2.0. This report should include the student's first name, middle initial, last name, major, and cumulative GPA, with appropriate headings.

8. At the end of each month, a report is produced that shows the status of the account of each user in *UsersFile*. Write a program to read the current date and produce a report of the following form:

USER ACCOUNTS—09/30/89

USER NAME	USER-ID	RESOURCE LIMIT	RESOURCES USED
Joseph Miltgen	10101	$750	$381
Isaac Small	10102	$650	$599***
⋮	⋮	⋮	⋮

in which the three asterisks (***) indicate that the user has already used 90 percent or more of the resources available to him or her.

9. Write a program to update *InventoryFile* with *InventoryUpdate* to produce a new inventory file. Each record in *InventoryFile* for which there is no record in *InventoryUpdate* with a matching item number should remain unchanged. Each record with one or more corresponding records in *InventoryUpdate* should be updated with the entries in the update file. For transaction code R, the number of items returned should be added to the number in stock. For transaction code S, the number of items sold should be subtracted from the number currently in stock; if more items are sold than are in stock, display a message showing the order number, stock number, item name, and how many should be back ordered (that is, the difference between the number ordered and the number in stock), and set the number currently in stock to zero.

10. Write a program to read the files *StudentFile* and *StudentUpdate* and produce an updated grade report. This grade report should show

    (a) the current date.

    (b) the student's name and student number.

    (c) a list of the names, grade, and credits for each of the current courses under the headings COURSE, GRADE, and CREDITS.

    (d) current GPA (multiply credits by numeric grade—A = 4.0, A− = 3.7, B+ = 3.3, B = 3.0, . . . , D− = 0.7, F = 0.0—for each course to find honor points earned for that course, sum these to find total new honor points, and then divide total new honor points by total new credits to give the current GPA, rounded to two decimal places).

    (e) total credits taken (old credits from *StudentFile* plus total new credits).

    (f) new cumulative GPA (first calculate old honor points = old credits times old cumulative GPA and then new cumulative GPA = sum of old honor points and new honor points divided by updated total credits).

11. Write a simple *text-formatting* program that reads a text file and produces another text file in which no lines are longer than some given length. Put as many words as possible on the same line. You will have to break some lines of the given file, but do not break any words or put punctuation marks at the beginning of a new line.

12. Extend the text-formatting program of Exercise 11 to right-justify each line in the new text file by adding evenly distributed blanks in lines where necessary. Also, preserve all indentation of lines in the given text file that begin a new paragraph.

13. (Project) Most system text formatters also allow command lines to be placed within the unformatted text. These command lines might have forms like the following:

.P m n	Insert m blank lines before each paragraph and indent each paragraph n spaces.
.W n	Width of page (line length) is n.
.L n	Page length (number of lines per page) is n.
.I n	Indent all lines following this command line n spaces.
.U	Undent all following lines and reset to previous left margin.

Extend the program of Exercises 11 and 12 to implement command lines.

14. (Project) A *pretty-printer* is a special kind of text formatter that reads a text file containing a program and then prints it in a ''pretty'' format. For example, a pretty-printer for Pascal programs might insert blank lines between procedures and indent and align statements within other statements, such as **if** statements, compound statements, type declarations, and variable declarations to produce a format similar to that used in the sample programs of this text. Write a pretty-print program for Pascal programs to indent and align statements in a pleasing format.

15. (Project) Write a menu-driven program that uses *StudentFile* and *StudentUpdate* and allows (some of) the following options. For each option, write a separate procedure so that options and corresponding procedures can be easily added or removed.

1. Locate a student's permanent record when given his or her student number and print it in a nicer format than that in which it is stored.

2. Same as Option 1, but locate the record when given his or her name.

3. Print a list of all student names and numbers in a given class (1, 2, 3, 4, 5).

4. Same as Option 3, but for a given major.

5. Same as Option 3, but for a given range of cumulative GPAs.

6. Find the average cumulative GPAs for all
   (a) females   (b) males   (c) students with a specified major
   (d) all students. (These are suboptions of Menu Option 6.)

7. Produce updated grade reports having the following format:

GRADE REPORT—SEMESTER #1
12/23/89

DISPATCH UNIVERSITY

10103   James L. Johnson

	GRADE	CREDITS
ENGL 176	C	4
EDUC 268	B	4
EDUC 330	B+	3
P E 281	C	3
ENGR 317	D	4
Cumulative Credits:	33	
Current GPA:	2.22	
Cumulative GPA:	2.64	

(See Exercise 10 for descriptions of these last items.)

8. Same as Option 7, but instead of producing grade reports, produce a new permanent file containing the updated total credits and new cumulative GPAs.

9. Produce an updated file when a student (a) drops or (b) adds a course.

10. Produce an updated file when a student (a) transfers to or (b) withdraws from the university.

Programming Pointers

In this chapter we reviewed text files and introduced files of other types. Many of the programming pointers at the end of Chapter 7 regarding text files apply to files in general. These are summarized here; for additional details, see the Programming Pointers of Chapter 7.

1. *Each file variable that names a permanent file must appear in the file list of the program heading and must be declared to be of file type in the variable section of the program.*

2. *Before any input operation can be attempted from a file, that file must be opened for input by using the procedure* reset. *Similarly, before any output to a file is attempted, the file must be opened for output by using the procedure* rewrite.

3. *Each call of the procedure* reset *loads the file window with the first component of the file.*

4. *Each call of the procedure* rewrite *empties the file, and any previous contents the file may have had are destroyed.*

5. *After values have been obtained for each variable in the input list, the procedure* read *loads the file window with the next file component to be read unless the end of the file is encountered, in which case the file buffer variable is undefined.*

6. *Nontext files have no line structure, and thus the procedures* readln *and* writeln *and the function* eoln *cannot be used with them.*

7. *Assignment statements of the form file-variable-1* := *file-variable-2 are not allowed. The components of one file must be copied to another file individually.*

8. *File variables used as formal parameters in functions and procedures must be variable parameters.*

9. *The file window for an input file always contains the next file component, if there is one.* For text files, the file components are characters. Consequently, if *Number* is a numeric variable, an assignment statement of the form

   $Number := TextFile\uparrow$

   is an error, because it attempts to assign a character to *Number*.

10. *The procedure* get *replaces the contents of the file window with the next file component.* Thus, *get* should not be referenced before the processing of the file component currently in the file window has been completed.

11. *The procedure* put *transfers (does not copy) the component currently in the file window to the specified file.* Thus, *put* should not be called until the processing of the file component currently in the file window has been completed. After the procedure *put* has been executed, the file window is undefined.

Variations and Extensions

Text files were introduced in Chapter 7, and the file-processing features described in the Variations and Extensions section at the end of that chapter should be reviewed at this point. Here we consider *direct access* or *random access* files which, as we have noted, are provided in addition to sequential files in many versions of Pascal (e.g., Macintosh, Turbo, and UCSD). These are files in which each component can be accessed directly by specifying its location in the file, thus allowing components to be read or written anywhere in the file. Such files cannot usually be text files, but any other type of file is allowed. The following describes the common features for processing direct access files. Each version of Pascal may also provide its own special features, and some of these are described in Appendix G.

- *Program heading.* The program heading may be optional (Turbo), or a modified form may be allowed or required (Macintosh, UCSD). It is not always used to specify permanent files used in the program.
- *Opening for input/output.* In some versions of Pascal, the procedure *reset* used to open sequential files for input is also used to open direct access files for both input and output:

    reset (*file-variable, file-name*);   (* UCSD *)

or

    assign (*file-variable, file-name*);   (* Turbo *)
    reset (*file-variable*);

Some versions (Macintosh), however, require a special predefined procedure to open a direct access file, for example,

    open (*file-variable, file-name*);

- *The procedure* seek. The components in a file are assumed to be numbered, beginning with 0, and the predefined procedure *seek* is used to locate a particular component. It is called with a statement of the form

    seek (*file-variable, component-number*)

where *component-number* is an integer expression specifying the number of the component in the file to be located. The result of a call to *seek* with a component number too small (negative) or too large is system dependent. Commonly, seeking a component whose number is one more than the number of the last component sets *eof*(*file-variable*) to true and positions the data pointer just past the last component, thus making it possible to append new components to the file.

- *Writing to a file.* Once a component in a direct access file has been located, the procedure *put* can be used to replace this component with the contents of the file buffer variable (Macintosh, UCSD),

    seek (*file-variable, component-number*);
    file-variable↑ := *expression*;
    put (*file-variable*);

or the procedure *write* can be used to carry out this replacement (Macintosh, Turbo, UCSD):

> *seek* (*file-variable, component-number*);
> *write* (*file-variable, new-component*);

- *Reading from a file*. When *seek* is called, the component of the file that is located is *not* copied into the file buffer, since it is not known at that time whether the next operation will be to read from the file or to write to it. Consequently, if this component is to be read, the procedure *get* must first be called to copy this component into the file buffer (Macintosh, UCSD):

> *seek* (*file-variable, component-number*);
> *get* (*file-variable*);
> *variable* := *file-variable*↑;

Alternatively, the procedure *read* may be used to read this component (Macintosh, Turbo, UCSD):

> *seek* (*file-variable, component-number*);
> *read* (*file-variable, variable*);

- *Closing a file*. It may be necessary to invoke a special *close* procedure to close a file before program execution is completed (Macintosh, Turbo, UCSD).

The program in Figure 14.8 illustrates the use of direct access files in Turbo Pascal. It is a file update program in which component numbers correspond to part numbers in an inventory file.

```
PROGRAM InventoryUpdate (input, output, PartsFile);

(*****************************************************************

   Program to update a direct access file PartsFile in which the
   numbers of records in the file are interpreted as part numbers.
   A part number is entered by the user, the corresponding record
   is retrieved and displayed, modifications are made, and the
   updated record then rewritten to the file.

*****************************************************************)

CONST
   MaxNumRecords = 100;          (* upper limit on record numbers *)

TYPE
   InvRecord = RECORD
                  ItemName : string[20];
                  NumInStock : integer;
                  Price : real;
               END;
   InventoryFile = FILE OF InvRecord;
```

Figure 14.8

Figure 14.8 (cont.)

```
VAR
      PartsFile : InventoryFile; (* file to be updated *)
      FileName : string[20];      (* actual name of  file *)
      PartsRec : InvRecord;       (* a record from PartsFile *)
      NumSold,                    (* number sold/returned *)
      PartNum : integer;          (* part number *)

BEGIN
   (* open PartsFile *)
   write ('Name of file to be updated?  ');
   readln (FileName);
   assign (PartsFile, FileName);
   reset (PartsFile);

   (* update the file *)
   writeln ('Enter negative part number to stop.');
   writeln;
   write ('Part #?  ');
   readln (PartNum);
   WHILE (PartNum >= 0) DO
      BEGIN
         IF PartNum <= MaxNumRecords THEN
            BEGIN
               seek (PartsFile, PartNum);
               read (PartsFile, PartsRec);
               WITH PartsRec DO
                  BEGIN
                     writeln (ItemName);
                     writeln (NumInStock:1, ' in stock');
                     writeln ('Price:  $', Price:4:2);
                     write ('# sold (negative if returned)?  ');
                     readln (NumSold);
                     NumInStock := NumInStock - NumSold
                  END (* WITH *);
               seek (PartsFile, PartNum);
               write (PartsFile, PartsRec)
            END (* IF *)
         ELSE
            writeln ('Part # > ', MaxNumRecords:1, ' -- out of range');
         writeln;
         write ('Part #?  ');
         readln (PartNum)
      END (* WHILE *);
   writeln;
   writeln ('File updating completed');
   close (PartsFile)
END.
```

```
Sample run:

Name of file to be updated?  PARTSFILE
Enter negative part number to stop.

Part #?  1
V-378 FAN BELT
30 in stock
Price:  $7.95
# sold (negative if returned)?  5
```

Figure 14.8 (cont.)

```
Part #?  72
HALOGEN HEADLIGHT PR-378
82 in stock
Price:  $13.90
# sold (negative if returned)?  12

Part #?  30
FORD MUFFLER MF-3668
10 in stock
Price:  $25.95
# sold (negative if returned)?  -2

Part #?  -1

File updating completed
```

15

Pointers and Linked Lists

[Pointers] are like jumps, leaping wildly from one part of a data structure to another. Their introduction into high-level languages has been a step backward from which we may never recover.

C. A. R. HOARE

I've got a little list, I've got a little list.

GILBERT AND SULLIVAN, *The Mikado*

Variables are symbolic addresses of memory locations. This relationship between a variable and the memory location it names is a static one that is established when the program is compiled and remains fixed throughout the execution of the program. Although the contents of a memory location associated with a variable may change during execution; that is, the value of the variable may change, variables themselves can be neither created nor destroyed during execution. Consequently, these variables are called *static variables.*

In some situations, however, the memory requirements will be known only while the program is executing, so that static variables are not adequate. In such cases, a method for acquiring additional memory locations as needed during execution and for releasing them when they are no longer needed is required. Variables that are created and disposed of during execution are called *dynamic* (or *anonymous*) *variables.* At one point during execution, there may be a particular memory location associated with a dynamic variable, and at a later time, no memory location or a different one may be associated with it. Pascal provides for such dynamic memory allocation and deallocation by using *pointers* and the predefined procedures *new* and *dispose.*

Unlike *static data structures* such as arrays whose sizes and associated memory locations are fixed at compile time, *dynamic data structures* expand or contract as required during execution, and their associated memory locations change. A dynamic data structure is a collection of elements called *nodes* of

526

the structure—usually of record type—that are linked together. This linking is established by associating with each node a pointer that points to the next node in the structure. One of the simplest linked structures is a *linked list* that might be pictured as follows:

Dynamic data structures are especially useful for storing and processing data sets whose sizes change during program execution, for example, the collection of jobs that have been entered into a computer system and are awaiting execution or the collection of passenger names and seat assignments on a given airplane flight. In this chapter we consider pointers and the procedures *new* and *dispose* and how they can be used to construct and process dynamic data structures.

15.1 Pointers; The Procedures *new* and *dispose*

As noted in the introduction, construction of a dynamic data structure requires the ability to allocate memory locations as needed during program execution. Because the number of locations is not known in advance, they cannot be allocated in the usual manner using variable declarations, since such allocations are made at compile time. Instead the predefined procedure *new* is used for this purpose. When it is called, it returns the address of a memory location (possibly consisting of several memory words) in which a node of the data structure can be stored. To access this memory location so that data can be stored in it or retrieved from it, a special kind of variable called a **pointer variable** or simply **pointer** is used. The value of a pointer is thus the address of some memory location.

The nodes of a dynamic data structure may be of any type but are most often of some record type. The type of a pointer that is used to reference the memory location storing one of these nodes must be specified by

$\uparrow$*type-identifier*   or $^\wedge$*type-identifier*

where *type-identifier* specifies the type of the nodes. The pointer is said to be **bound** to this type, since it may not be used for nodes of any other type. For example, if the nodes are records defined by

type
    EmployeeRecord = **record**
                            Number : *integer*;
                            HourlyRate : *real*
                        end;

then the type of a pointer for such nodes is

$\uparrow$*EmployeeRecord*

Thus, the declarations

> **type**
>   *EmployeeRecord* = **record**
>   *Number* : *integer*;
>   *HourlyRate* : *real*
>   **end**;
>   *PointerToEmployeeRecord* = ↑*EmployeeRecord*;
>
> **var**
>   *EmpPtr* : *PointerToEmployeeRecord*;

can be used to declare a pointer *EmpPtr* for such nodes. This pointer is said to be bound to the type *EmployeeRecord* because it may be used only for nodes of this type.

The procedure *new* may then be used during program execution to acquire a memory location in which an employee record may be stored. This procedure is called with a statement of the form

> *new* (*pointer*)

which assigns the address of a memory location to *pointer* and is thus equivalent to a statement of the form

> *pointer* := *memory-address*

Thus the statement

> *new* (*EmpPtr*)

assigns to *EmpPtr* a memory address, say 1074; that is, the value of *EmpPtr* is this memory address:

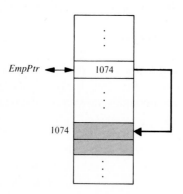

This is the address of a memory location where a value of type *EmployeeRecord* can be stored. We say that *EmpPtr* "points" to this memory location and picture this by a diagram like the following:

The contents of boxes representing fields of an employee record are shown here as question marks to indicate that these fields are initially undefined.[1]

Because this area of memory can be used to store values of type *EmployeeRecord*, it is a variable, but it has no name! Such variables are thus sometimes referred to as **anonymous variables,** and pointers are said to point to anonymous variables. Since these variables come into existence during program execution and may later cease to exist, we shall instead refer to them as **dynamic variables.**

Each call of the procedure *new* acquires a new memory location and assigns its address to the specified pointer. Thus, if *TempPtr* is also a pointer of type *PointerToEmployeeRecord,* the statement

   new (TempPtr)

acquires a new memory location pointed to by *TempPtr:*

The value of a pointer is the address of a memory location. The value stored in this memory location can be accessed by appending the **dereferencing operator** $\uparrow$ (or $^\wedge$ in some systems) to the pointer:

   pointer$\uparrow$ or   *pointer*$^\wedge$

For the pointer *EmpPtr* of type *PointerToEmployeeRecord,* the value of *EmpPtr*$\uparrow$ is therefore the employee record pointed to by *EmpPtr.* Thus, *EmpPtr*$\uparrow$ is a variable of type *EmployeeRecord* and may be used in the same manner as any other record variable of this type. For example, values can be assigned to the fields of this record by the input statements

   readln (EmpPtr$\uparrow$*.Number, EmpPtr*$\uparrow$*.HourlyRate)*

or

   with *EmpPtr*$\uparrow$ **do**
      readln (Number, HourlyRate)

If the values

   3511 7.50

---

[1] An alternative form of reference to the procedure *new* may be used for variant records, which allows the system to allocate memory locations more efficiently. This form is described in Appendix F.

are read, we then have

Because both *EmpPtr* and *TempPtr* are bound to type *EmployeeRecord*, *EmpPtr*↑ and *TempPtr*↑ are of the same type. Thus, the statement

    TempPtr↑ := *EmpPtr*↑

is a valid assignment statement. It copies the contents of the record pointed to by *EmpPtr* into the location pointed to by *TempPtr*:

Similarly, if *NewEmpRecord* is a static variable of type *EmployeeRecord*, the statement

    NewEmpRecord := *EmpPtr*↑

is valid.

Because the values of pointers are addresses of memory locations, the operations that may be performed on them are limited: Only assignment and comparison using the relational operators = and <> are allowed. If *pointer1* and *pointer2* are bound to the same type, an assignment statement of the form

    pointer1 := *pointer2*

assigns the value of *pointer2* to *pointer1* so that both point to the same memory location. The previous location (if any) pointed to by *pointer1* can no longer be accessed unless pointed to by some other pointer. The following diagrams illustrate:

Before assignment:

After assignment *pointer1* := *pointer2*:

Before assignment:

After assignment *pointer1* : = *pointer2*:

Because inaccessible nodes may be unusable by the system, the situation pictured in the first set of diagrams should be avoided.

As an illustration, suppose that *TempPtr* and *EmpPtr* are pointers of type *PointerToEmployeeRecord,* pointing to the following employee records:

	Number	Hourly Rate
EmpPtr →	3511	7.50

	Number	Hourly Rate
TempPtr →	4422	9.25

The assignment statement

    TempPtr : = *EmpPtr*

causes *TempPtr* to point to the same employee record as does *EmpPtr,* and so the second employee record can no longer be accessed (unless pointed to by some other pointer of type *PointerToEmployeeRecord*):

	Number	Hourly Rate
EmpPtr →	3511	7.50

	Number	Hourly Rate
TempPtr ↗	4422	9.25

Note that this result is very different from that produced by the assignment statement

    TempPtr↑ : = *EmpPtr*↑

which copies the employee record pointed to by *EmpPtr* into the memory location pointed to by *TempPtr*:

	Number	Hourly Rate
EmpPtr →	3511	7.50

	Number	Hourly Rate
TempPtr →	3511	7.50

The relational operators $=$ and $<>$ can be used to determine whether two pointers *bound to the same type* point to the same memory location. Thus the boolean expression

$TempPtr = EmpPtr$

is true only if *TempPtr* and *EmpPtr* point to the same memory location:

Note that this is *not* equivalent to the boolean expression

$TempPtr\uparrow = EmpPtr\uparrow$

since this is an attempt to compare the record pointed to by *TempPtr* with the record pointed to by *EmpPtr*. In this example, this is not a valid boolean expression since records cannot be compared with relational operators. Obviously, if $TempPtr = EmpPtr$ is true, the records pointed to by *TempPtr* and *EmpPtr,* that is, the values of $TempPtr\uparrow$ and $EmpPtr\uparrow$, are identical. The converse is not true, however. These two records may be identical, that is, $TempPtr\uparrow$ and $EmpPtr\uparrow$ may have the same value, but $TempPtr = EmpPtr$ may be false.

In some situations it may be necessary to assign a value to a pointer variable that indicates that it does not point to any memory location. This can be done by assigning the pointer constant **nil** in an assignment statement of the form

$pointer :=$ **nil**

This value **nil** may be assigned to a pointer of any type. We picture a nil pointer as simply a dot with no arrow emanating from it:

pointer ●

It should be noted that a pointer having the value **nil** is *not* the same as its being undefined. For example, if *TempPtr* is undefined, any attempt to use its value, as in the boolean expression

$TempPtr = EmpPtr$

is an error, as is any reference to $TempPtr\uparrow$. If *TempPtr* has the value **nil,** however, this boolean expression is valid. Any reference to $TempPtr\uparrow$ would still be an error, however, since *TempPtr* points to no memory location.

If the memory location pointed to by a pointer is no longer needed, it may be released and made available for later allocation by calling the procedure

dispose with a statement of the form

    dispose (pointer)

This procedure frees the memory location pointed to by *pointer* and leaves *pointer* undefined.[2]

    Pointers may also be used as parameters in user-defined functions and procedures. These parameters may be either value or variable parameters, but corresponding pointer parameters must be bound to the same type. The value of a function may also be a pointer.[3] Pointers are used as parameters in several examples in the next section.

15.2 Introduction to Linked Lists

Pointer variables, which we introduced in the preceding section, are not very useful by themselves. Their importance lies in the fact that they make it possible to implement dynamic data structures. As we noted in the introduction to this chapter, dynamic structures are more appropriate than are static structures for modeling a data set whose size changes during processing. In this section we consider a simple dynamic structure, a linked list, and show how it can be constructed using pointers.

    A *linked list* consists of a collection of elements called *nodes* linked together by pointers, together with a pointer to the first node in the list. The nodes contain two different kinds of information: (1) the actual data item being stored and (2) a *link* or pointer to the next node in the list. A linked list containing the integers 95, 47, and 83 with 95 as the first element might thus be pictured as follows:

In this diagram, *FirstPtr* is a pointer to the first node in the list. The *Data* field of each node stores one of the integers, and the *Next* field is a pointer to the next node; the dot in the last node having no arrow emanating from it represents a nil pointer and indicates that there is no next node.

    The nodes in a linked list are represented in Pascal as records having two kinds of fields, *data fields* and *link fields.* The data fields have types that are appropriate for storing the necessary information, and the link fields are of pointer type. For example, the nodes in the preceding linked list may be declared by

---

    [2] An alternative form of reference to the procedure *dispose* may be used for variant records; see Appendix F.

    [3] If f is a pointer-valued function, a function reference of the form $f(actual\text{-}parameters)\uparrow$ is not permitted. The value of the function must be assigned to a pointer variable, and this variable used to access the contents of the memory location to which it points.

type
    ListPointer = ↑*ListNode*;
    ListNode = **record**
                Data : *integer*;
                Next : *ListPointer*
          end;

Each node in this list is a record of type *ListNode*, consisting of two fields. The first field *Data* is of integer type and is used to store the data. The second field *Next* is a pointer of type *ListPointer* and points to the next node in the list. Note that the definition of the pointer type *ListPointer*

    ListPointer = ↑*ListNode*;

precedes the definition of the record type *ListNode*. This is the only situation in which it is permissible to use an identifier (*ListNode*) before it is defined.

In addition to the nodes of the list in which to store the data items, a pointer to the first node is needed. Thus we declare a pointer variable *FirstPtr* by

var
    FirstPtr : *ListPointer*;

To illustrate the basic steps in the construction of a linked list, suppose that the integers 83 and 47 have already been stored in a linked list

and we wish to add 95 to this list. In the construction, we use two pointers, *FirstPtr* to point to the first node in the list and *TempPtr* as a temporary pointer.

var
    FirstPtr, TempPtr : *ListPointer*;

We first acquire a new node temporarily pointed to by *TempPtr*,

    new (*TempPtr*);

and store 95 in the data field of this record:

    TempPtr↑.*Data* := 95;

This node can then be joined to the list by setting its link field so that it points to the first node:

TempPtr↑.Next := FirstPtr;

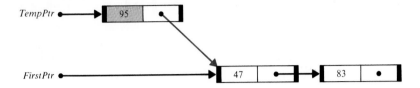

The pointer *FirstPtr* is then updated to point to this new node:

FirstPtr := TempPtr;

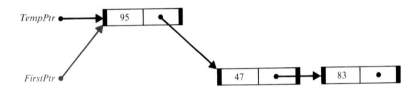

To construct the entire list, we could first initialize an empty list:

FirstPtr := **nil**;

and then repeat the preceding four statements three times, replacing 95 by 83 in the second assignment statement, then by 47, and finally using the value 95. In practice, however, such linked lists are usually constructed by reading the data values rather than assigning them by means of assignment statements. In this example, the linked list could be constructed by using the following program segment:

```
(* Initially the list is empty. *)
FirstPtr := nil;

(* Read the data values and construct the list. *)
while not eof do
  begin
    new (TempPtr);
    readln (TempPtr↑.Data);
    TempPtr↑.Next := FirstPtr;
    FirstPtr := TempPtr
  end (* while *);
```

Once a linked list has been constructed, we may want to *traverse* the list from beginning to end and display each element in it. In Chapter 9 we saw that to traverse a list stored in an array, we could easily move through the list from one element to the next by varying an array index in some repetition structure. The analog for a linked list is to move through the list by varying a pointer variable in a repetition structure.

To illustrate, suppose we wish to display the integers stored in the linked list

We begin by initializing a pointer variable *CurrPtr* to point to the first node

  CurrPtr := *FirstPtr*;

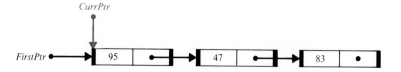

and display the integer stored in this node:

  writeln (*CurrPtr*↑.*Data*);

To move to the next node, we follow the link from the current node:

  CurrPtr := *CurrPtr*↑.*Next*;

After displaying the integer in this node, we move to the next node

  CurrPtr := *CurrPtr*↑.*Next*;

and display its data. Since we have now reached the last node, we need some way to signal this condition. But this is easy, for if we attempt to move to the next node, *CurrPtr* becomes nil:

The boolean condition *CurrPtr* <> **nil** can thus be used to control repetition in a while loop:

> *CurrPtr* := *FirstPtr*;
> **while** *CurrPtr* <> **nil do**
>   **begin**
>   *writeln* (*CurrPtr*↑.*Data*);
>   *CurrPtr* := *CurrPtr*↑.*Next*;
>   *end* (∗ **while** ∗)

Also note that this program segment correctly traverses an empty list, since in this case, *FirstPtr* is nil and the while loop is bypassed.

The program in Figure 15.1 uses these techniques for constructing and traversing a linked list to reverse the characters in a string. It reads a sequence of characters and stores them in a linked list, adding each character to the beginning of the list as it is read. When the special symbol $ is read, signaling the end of the string, the list is traversed. Since the last characters read are at the beginning of the list, they are displayed in reverse order. (The Last-In-First-Out processing suggests an alternative to the array implementation of stacks described in Exercise 8 of Section 9.3. Linked stacks and queues are considered in the next chapter.)

```
PROGRAM ReverseAString (input, output);

(********************************************************************

    Program to reverse a string by reading characters and adding them
    to the beginning of a linked list until the end-of-string mark ($)
    is read, then traversing the list and displaying the characters.

    ********************************************************************)

CONST
    EndMark = '$';                    (* marks the end of the string *)

TYPE
    DataType = char;
    ListPointer = ^ListNode;
    ListNode = RECORD
                   Data : DataType;
                   Next : ListPointer
               END;

VAR
    FirstPtr : ListPointer;           (* pointer to first node in linked list *)
    Symbol,                           (* current character from string or list *)
    Response : char;                  (* user response *)
```

Figure 15.1

Figure 15.1   (cont.)

```
PROCEDURE AddToList (VAR FirstPtr : ListPointer; Element : DataType);

   (*****************************************************************

       Procedure to add Element at beginning of linked list pointed
       to by FirstPtr.  New value of FirstPtr is returned.

   *****************************************************************)

   VAR
      TempPtr: ListPointer;  (* temporary pointer *)

   BEGIN (* AddToList *)
      new (TempPtr);
      TempPtr^.Data := Element;
      TempPtr^.Next := FirstPtr;
      FirstPtr := TempPtr
   END (* AddToList *);

PROCEDURE Traverse (FirstPtr : ListPointer);

   (*****************************************************************

       Procedure to traverse linked list pointed to by FirstPtr,
       displaying each element in the list.

   *****************************************************************)

   VAR
      CurrPtr: ListPointer;  (* temporary pointer *)

   BEGIN (* Traverse *)
      CurrPtr := FirstPtr;
      WHILE CurrPtr <> NIL DO
         BEGIN
            write (CurrPtr^.Data);
            CurrPtr := CurrPtr^.Next
         END (* WHILE *);
      writeln
   END (* Traverse *);

BEGIN (* main program *)
   REPEAT

      (* Initialize empty list *)

      FirstPtr := NIL;

      (* Read the string, adding each character at front of the list *)

      writeln ('Enter the string to be reversed:');
      read (Symbol);
      WHILE Symbol <> EndMark DO
         BEGIN
            AddToList (FirstPtr, Symbol);
            read (Symbol)
         END (* WHILE *);
      readln;
```

Figure 15.1   (cont.)

```
     (* Now traverse the list and display the characters *)

     writeln;
     writeln ('Reversed string:');
     Traverse (FirstPtr);
     writeln;
     write ('More strings (Y or N)? ');
     readln (Response);
  UNTIL NOT (Response IN ['y', 'Y'])
END (* main program *).
```

Sample run:

Enter the string to be reversed:
Kelloggs Cornflakes$

Reversed string:
sekalfnroC sggolleK

More strings (Y or N)? Y

Enter the string to be reversed:
able was I ere I saw elba$

Reversed string:
able was I ere I saw elba

More strings (N or N)? Y

15.3   Processing Unordered Linked Lists

In Chapter 9 we used arrays to store and process lists, and observed that although this was a good implementation for static lists, it was not efficient for dynamic ones. The fixed size of an array limits the size of the list, and the array may become full, so that no more insertions are possible. We also noted that inserting a new item into a list required moving array elements to make room for it, and deleting an item required shifting array elements to fill the position vacated by this item. In this section we show how these problems of size limitation and movement of list elements can be avoided by using linked lists.

The type declarations we have used to define linked lists have had the general form

```
type
    DataType = . . . ; (* type of data to be stored in list nodes *)
    ListPointer = ↑ListNode;
    ListNode = record
                   Data : DataType;
                   Next : ListPointer
               end;
```

Here *DataType* represents the type of the data items to be stored in the linked list. It might be a simple type like *integer* or *char,* as in the examples in the preceding section, but it may in fact be any type. In particular, it may be a record if several items of information are to be stored in each node. For example, to define a linked list of employee records, each containing an employee number and an hourly rate, we might use the following declarations:

```
type
    EmployeeRecord = record
                         Number : integer;
                         HourlyRate : real
                     end;
    DataType = EmployeeRecord;
    ListPointer = ↑ListNode;
    ListNode = record
                   Data : DataType;
                   Next : ListPointer
               end;
```

Suppose also that the following variables have been declared:

```
var
    FirstPtr, CurrPtr : ListPointer;
    EmpNumber : integer;
    NewRate : real;
    Found : boolean;
```

Access to this list of records is by means of the pointer *FirstPtr,* which points to the first employee record:

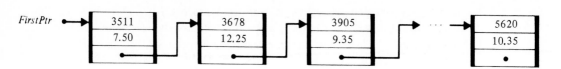

To traverse this list and display the employee records, we might use

```
CurrPtr := FirstPtr;
while CurrPtr <> nil do
    begin
        with CurrPtr↑.Data do
            writeln ('Number:', Number:6,'    Rate: $', HourlyRate:4:2);
        CurrPtr := CurrPtr↑.Next
    end (* while *)
```

Searching a linked list for a given item is done similarly. We initialize an auxiliary pointer to the first node and move through the list via the link fields until the desired node is found or we reach the end of the list. For example, to search the preceding linked list for the record of the employee whose number is *EmpNumber*, the following statements may be used:

> *Found* := *false*;
> *CurrPtr* := *FirstPtr*;
> **while** (*CurrPtr* <> **nil**) **and** (**not** *Found*) **do**
>   **if** *CurrPtr*↑.*Data.Number* = *EmpNumber* **then**
>   *Found* := *true*
>   **else**
>   *CurrPtr* := *CurrPtr*↑.*Next*;

The preceding while loop is terminated when the desired record is found, in which case *CurrPtr* points to the node containing that record or the end of the list is reached and the record is not found; in this last case, *CurrPtr* has the value **nil.** If the record is found, the information in this record can be displayed:

> **if** *Found* **then**
>   *writeln* ('Hourly rate for employee ', *EmpNumber*:1, ' is ',
>   *CurrPtr*↑.*Data.HourlyRate*:4:2)
> **else**
>   *writeln* ('Employee ', *EmpNumber*:1, ' not found')

or perhaps modified, for example, by changing the hourly rate:

> **if** *Found* **then**
>   *CurrPtr*↑.*Data.HourlyRate* := *NewRate*
> **else**
>   *writeln* ('Employee ', *EmpNumber*:1, ' not found')

The search technique we have used here is a ***linear search*** and is the only feasible searching strategy for linked lists. The more efficient binary search described in Section 9.3 for ordered lists implemented as arrays is not a real option for linked lists. Although ordered linked lists can be constructed, as we shall show in the next section, binary search is still not practical, since it requires repeatedly accessing the middle element of the part of the list being searched, and this can be done efficiently only when each list element can be accessed directly. For a linked list, however, we have direct access only to the first node; to access any other node, we must traverse the first part of the list, following the links, until we reach that node. (In the next chapter we shall describe a ***multiply linked structure*** called a ***binary search tree*** in which a binarylike search is possible.)

In general, linked lists are preferred over arrays for processing dynamic lists, whose sizes vary as items are added and deleted, because the number of nodes that a linked list may have is limited only by the available memory and because the insertion and deletion operations are easy to implement. Since we are considering unordered linked lists in this section, that is, lists in which the elements need not be arranged in a particular order, we can insert a new element at any convenient location in the list. And as we observed in the preceding section, inserting it at the beginning of the list is easy:

1. Obtain a new node and store the element in its data field.
2. Set the link field of this node to point to the first node in the list.
3. Reset the pointer *FirstPtr* to point to this new node.

The following procedure implements these steps:

procedure *Insert* (**var** *FirstPtr* : *ListPointer*; *Element* : *DataType*);

    (* Procedure to insert *Element* at the beginning of the linked list
       pointed to by *FirstPtr*. The new pointer to the linked list is
       returned. *)

var
    TempPtr : *ListPointer*; (* temporary pointer to a new node *)

begin (* *Insert* *)
    new (*TempPtr*);
    TempPtr↑.Data := *Element*;
    TempPtr↑.Next := *FirstPtr*;
    FirstPtr := *TempPtr*
end (* *Insert* *);

For deletion, there are two cases to consider: (1) deleting the first element in the list and (2) deleting an element that has a predecessor. The first case is easy and consists of the following steps, assuming that *CurrPtr* points to the node to be deleted:

1. Set *FirstPtr* to point to the second node in the list.
2. Dispose of the node pointed to by *CurrPtr*.

For the second case, suppose that the predecessor of the node to be deleted is pointed to by *PredPtr*:

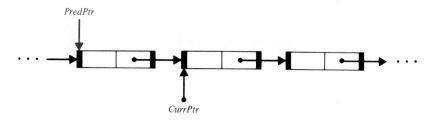

Deletion is accomplished by setting the link field of the node pointed to by *PredPtr* so that it points to the successor of the node to be deleted:

    PredPtr↑.Next := *CurrPtr↑.Next*;

MISSION COLLEGE BOOKSTORE - 988-2450

ECT YOUR INVESTMENT
AVE THIS RECEIPT ⟶

NO RECEIPT — NO RETURNS

NNING OF THE SEMESTER RETURNS POLICY

given on new or used books IF.........
YOUR CASH REGISTER RECEIPT. —————

arr or write in your Books - Return New Books in brand new,
COMPUTER SOFTWARE IS NOT RETURNABLE. ⟶

d merchandise must not be unwrapped or opened.
for fall or spring by the END OF THE THIRD WEEK from the

...ng of that respective semester.

5. You return books for SUMMER BY THE END OF THE FIRST WEEK from the
   starting of Summer School.

6. The Manager reserves the right to make the decision on the condition or
   saleability of the merchandise.

STANDARD RETURN POLICY

1. Same as above except you have ONLY 5 WORKING DAYS from the DATE ON
   YOUR RECEIPT.

2. No refunds will be given during the last five weeks of any semester.

KEEP YOUR RECEIPT

```
MISSION
BOOKSTORE
RETAIN RECEIPT
FOR REFUND

NNBK        AD   30.80
SUB              30.80

TAX1             2.23

TOTL        $33.03

ACT# 303368131
CHEK        33.03
CHNG          .00

ITEM          1
              0
B007
2322   7:20PM  6/19/90
```

SELL BACK POLICY

SELL YOUR NEW & USED BOOKS FOR CASH AT THE BOOKSTORE DURING FINALS WEEK. YOUR BOOKS MAY BE WORTH UP TO 50% OF NEW PRICE IF THE BOOKSTORE HAS RECEIVED A REQUISITION FROM THE INSTRUCTOR STATING YOUR BOOK IS BEING USED THE FOLLOWING SEMESTER AND THE BOOKSTORE IS NOT OVERSTOCKED. WHOLESALE MARKET VALUE WILL BE PAID ON CURRENT EDITIONS NOT USED OR NEEDED THE FOLLOWING SEMESTER.

RECEIPTS NOT NEEDED

THE BOOKSTORE CANNOT GUARANTEE THE BUYBACK OF ANY BOOK AT ANY TIME.

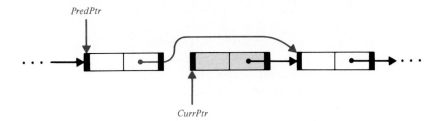

PredPtr

CurrPtr

As these diagrams illustrate, a delete procedure requires the two pointers *CurrPtr* to the node to be deleted and *PredPtr* to its predecessor, if there is one. A linear search as described earlier can be used to locate the item to be deleted and thus set *CurrPtr* to point to the node containing this item. *PredPtr* will be correctly positioned if it follows *CurrPtr* through the list, always pointing to the predecessor of the node pointed to by *CurrPtr*. Since the data part of a node is usually a record, this search must be based on one of the fields in the record such as an employee number or name. Such a field is called a **key field.**

The following procedure uses the linear search technique to position the pointers *CurrPtr* and *PredPtr*. It assumes declarations of the form

```
type
    DataType = record (* type of data part of nodes *)
                  ⋮
               Key : KeyType;
                  ⋮
               end;
    ListPointer = ↑ListNode;
    ListNode = record
                  Data : DataType;
                  Next : ListPointer
               end;

procedure Search(FirstPtr : ListPointer; KeyValue : KeyType;
                 var PredPtr, CurrPtr : ListPointer;
                 var Found : boolean);
```

(* Procedure to search a linked list having first node pointed to by *FirstPtr* for a node containing the specified *KeyValue*. If the item is not found, *Found* is returned as false; otherwise, *CurrPtr* points to the first node containing the item, and *PredPtr* points to its predecessor or is nil if there is none. *)

```
begin (* Search *)
    CurrPtr := FirstPtr;
    PredPtr := nil;
    Found := false;
    while (not Found) and (CurrPtr <> nil) do
        if CurrPtr↑.Data.Key = KeyValue then
            Found := true
```

```
                     else
                        begin
                           PredPtr := CurrPtr;
                           CurrPtr := CurrPtr↑.Next
                        end (* else *)
              end (* Search *);
```

The following procedure *Delete* calls the procedure *Search* to position the pointers *PredPtr* and *CurrPtr* and then deletes the node pointed to by *CurrPtr* using the techniques described earlier. In the case in which the first node is to be deleted, it has no predecessor, and procedure *Search* returns the value **nil** for *PredPtr*. Thus the boolean expression *PredPtr* = **nil** can be used to distinguish between the two cases of deleting the first node or deleting a node that has a predecessor.

```
procedure Delete (var FirstPtr : ListPointer; KeyValue : KeyType);

   (* Procedure to delete a node having the specified KeyValue from a
      linked list with first node pointed to by FirstPtr. *)

var
   CurrPtr,                    (* pointer to node containing KeyValue *)
   PredPtr : ListPointer;      (* pointer to its predecessor *)
   Found : boolean;            (* indicates if KeyValue found *)

begin (* Delete *)
   Search (FirstPtr, KeyValue, PredPtr, CurrPtr, Found);
   if Found then
      begin
         if PredPtr = nil then       (* first node to be deleted *)
            FirstPtr := CurrPtr↑.Next
         else                        (* node has a predecessor *)
            PredPtr↑.Next := CurrPtr↑.Next;
         dispose (CurrPtr)
      end (* if *)
   else
      writeln ('Item not found in the list')
end (* Delete *);
```

15.4 Ordered Linked Lists

One of the important programming problems we have considered on several occasions is that of sorting a list of items. In each of our examples, these items were stored in an array, since direct access to each element of the array was required to use the sorting techniques we considered. As we have seen, however, an array is not the best data structure to use for dynamic lists; for if an item is inserted into a sorted array, all the array elements following it must be moved to make room for it, and when an element is deleted, all elements following it must be moved forward, or a "hole" results. Maintaining an

ordered list whose contents change frequently because of insertions and deletions is done more efficiently by using an ordered linked list.

An ***ordered linked list*** is a linked list in which the nodes are linked in
such a way that the items stored in the nodes occur in ascending (or descending)
order as the list is traversed. If the data part of a node is a record, then one of
the fields in this record is designated as the ***key field,*** and the ordering is based
on the values that appear in this field.

To insert an element into a linked list, we first obtain a new node temporarily accessed via a pointer *TempPtr*:

new (TempPtr);

and store the element in its data field

TempPtr↑.Data := *Element*;

There are now two cases to consider: (1) inserting the element at the beginning
of the list and (2) inserting it after some specified element in the list. The first
case is simply the insert operation considered in the preceding section. For the
second case, suppose that the new node is to be inserted between the nodes
pointed to by *PredPtr* and *CurrPtr*:

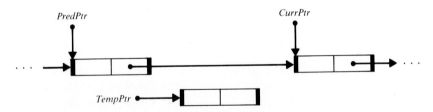

Insertion is accomplished by setting the pointer in the link field of the new
node to point to the node pointed to by *CurrPtr*

TempPtr↑.Next := *CurrPtr*;

and then resetting the pointer in the link field of the node pointed to by *PredPtr*
to point to the new node

PredPtr↑.Next := *TempPtr*;

The following diagram illustrates:

Note that once again two pointers are required, *CurrPtr,* which points to the successor of the new node, and *PredPtr,* which points to its predecessor. These two pointers can be positioned by using a modification of the linear search technique described in the preceding section. Because the list is ordered, the new item must be inserted just before the first item in the list whose key is greater than the key of the new item, or at the end of the list if the key of the new item is greater than the keys of all of the list items. Consequently, the search can be terminated as soon as the key field in *CurrPtr↑.Data* is greater than the key of the new item or when the end of the list is reached, that is, when *CurrPtr* becomes nil.

The following procedure *OrderedSearch* uses this approach to position the pointers *PredPtr* and *CurrPtr.* It assumes type declarations of the form

```
type
    DataType = record (* type of data part of nodes *)
                 ⋮
               Key : KeyType;
                 ⋮
             end;
    ListPointer = ↑ListNode;
    ListNode = record
                 Data : DataType;
                 Next : ListPointer
               end;

procedure OrderedSearch (FirstPtr : ListPointer; KeyValue : KeyType;
                         var PredPtr, CurrPtr : ListPointer;
                         var Found : boolean);
```

(* Procedure to search an ordered linked list having first node pointed to by *FirstPtr* for a node containing the specified *KeyValue* or for a position to insert a new node. *CurrPtr* points to the first node having a key >= *KeyValue* or is **nil** if *KeyValue* is greater than the keys of all nodes in the list. *PredPtr* points to its predecessor or is **nil** if *KeyValue* is smaller than the keys of all nodes in the list. *Found* is returned as true if a node containing *KeyValue* is already in the list. The procedure assumes that the keys are in ascending order; for descending order, change >= to <= in the **if** statement. *)

```
var
    DoneSearching : boolean; (* indicates when search is complete *)

begin (* OrderedSearch *)
    CurrPtr := FirstPtr;
    PredPtr := nil;
    Found := false;
    DoneSearching := false;
    while (not DoneSearching) and (CurrPtr <> nil) do
        if CurrPtr↑.Data.Key >= KeyValue then
```

```
      begin
         DoneSearching := true;
         Found := (CurrPtr↑.Data.Key = KeyValue)
      end (* if *)
   else
      begin
         PredPtr := CurrPtr;
         CurrPtr := CurrPtr↑.Next
      end (* else *)
end (* OrderedSearch *);
```

The following procedure *Insert* calls the procedure *OrderedSearch* to position the pointers *PredPtr* and *CurrPtr* and then inserts a new node containing the specified item, using the techniques described earlier. In the case where the new node is being inserted at the beginning of the list, it has no predecessor, and *OrderedSearch* returns the value **nil** for *PredPtr*. Thus the boolean expression *PredPtr* = **nil** can be used to distinguish between the two cases of inserting at the beginning of the list and inserting at some other point in the list.

```
procedure Insert (var FirstPtr : ListPointer; Item : DataType);

   (* Procedure to insert Item into an ordered linked list having first
      node pointed to by FirstPtr. This element is to be inserted between
      the nodes pointed to by PredPtr and CurrPtr. A nil value for
      PredPtr indicates insertion at the beginning of the list. A value of
      true for Found indicates that there is already a node containing
      Item.Key in its key field; no new node is then inserted into the list. *)

var
   PredPtr, CurrPtr,
   TempPtr : ListPointer; (* pointer to new node *)

begin (* Insert *)
   OrderedSearch (FirstPtr, Item.Key, PredPtr, CurrPtr, Found);
   if Found then
      writeln ('Item already in the list')
   else
      begin
         new (TempPtr);
         TempPtr↑.Data := Item;
         if PredPtr = nil then      (* insert at beginning of list *)
            begin
               TempPtr↑.Next := FirstPtr;
               FirstPtr := TempPtr
            end (* if *)
         else                        (* there is a predecessor *)
            begin
               TempPtr↑.Next := CurrPtr;
               PredPtr↑.Next := TempPtr
            end (* else *)
      end (* else *)
end (* Insert *);
```

For an ordered linked list, the deletion operation is essentially the same as for unordered lists. The procedure *Delete* of the preceding section can be used if we replace the call to procedure *Search* with a call to *OrderedSearch*.

procedure *Delete* (**var** *FirstPtr* : *ListPointer*; *KeyValue* : *KeyType*);

    (* Procedure to delete a node having the specified *KeyValue* from an ordered linked list with first node pointed to by *FirstPtr*. *)

var
    CurrPtr,   (* pointer to node containing *KeyValue* *)
    PredPtr : *ListPointer*;   (* pointer to its predecessor *)
    Found : *boolean*;   (* indicates if *KeyValue* found *)

begin (* *Delete* *)
    OrderedSearch (*FirstPtr*, *KeyValue*, *PredPtr*, *CurrPtr*, *Found*);

    if *Found* **then**
      begin
        if *PredPtr* := **nil then**   (* first node to be deleted *)
          FirstPtr := *CurrPtr*↑.*Next*
        else   (* node has a predecessor *)
          PredPtr↑.*Next* := *CurrPtr*↑.*Next*,
        dispose (*CurrPtr*)
      end (* **if** *)
    else
      writeln ('Item not found in the list')
end (* *Delete* *);

As an illustration of processing linked lists with these procedures, suppose we wish to create and maintain an ordered linked list of employee records, each of which contains an employee's number, age, number of dependents, and hourly pay rate. These records are in a file, so the first task is to create the initial ordered linked list by reading these records and inserting them into the list, beginning with an empty list. The second task is to update this list by adding new records to the list, deleting records, and modifying existing records. Finally, after all of the necessary updating, the list must be copied back to the file. A first-level algorithm for solving this problem is as follows:

ALGORITHM TO MAINTAIN A LINKED LIST OF EMPLOYEE RECORDS

1. Create the initial ordered linked list by reading records from a file and inserting them into the list, beginning with an empty list.
2. Repeat the following until *Option* = 0:
    a. Read an *Option*.
    b. If *Option* is
        1: Read an employee number and delete the record for that employee.
        2: Read a new employee record and insert it into the list.
        3: Modify an existing record.
        0: Copy the list to a file and terminate processing.

The program in Figure 15.2 implements this algorithm. It first calls the procedure *Initialize* to create the ordered linked list by reading the records from a file and repeatedly calling procedure *Insert* to insert these into the list. The user then selects from a menu of options for deleting, inserting, or modifying an employee record or for terminating processing. The delete and insert options are implemented using the procedures *Delete* and *Insert* given in this section. A record is modified by calling procedure *OrderedSearch* to locate the desired record and then allowing the user to enter new values for the fields in this record. When the last option is selected, the updated list is copied back into a file, using the list traversal techniques described in the preceding section. The structure of this program is displayed in the following structure diagram. (Recall that a shaded corner in a box indicates a procedure that is shared by two or more program units.)

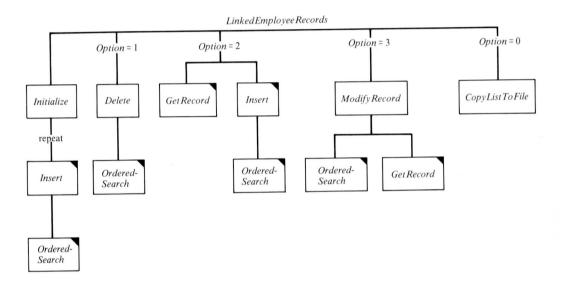

```
PROGRAM LinkedEmployeeRecords (input, output, EmpFile);

(************************************************************

    Program to process employee records.  Options are displayed
    by procedure PrintMenu.  The records are stored in an ordered
    linked list; employee names are in alphabetical order.

************************************************************)

CONST
    NumberOfOptions = 3;          (* number of options in menu *)
```

Figure 15.2

Figure 15.2   (cont.)

```
TYPE
   EmployeeRecord = RECORD
                         Key, Age, Dependents : integer;
                         HourlyRate : real
                     END;
   EmployeeFile = FILE of EmployeeRecord;
   DataType = EmployeeRecord;
   KeyType = integer;
   ListPointer = ^ListNode;
   ListNode = RECORD
                   Data : DataType;
                   Next : ListPointer
              END;

VAR
   FirstPtr : ListPointer;        (* pointer to first employee record *)
   Option : integer;              (* option selected by user *)
   EmpRecord : EmployeeRecord;    (* record for an employee *)
   EmpFile : EmployeeFile;        (* permanent file of employee records *)
   EmpNumber : integer;           (* number of an employee *)
   Response : char;               (* user response *)

PROCEDURE OrderedSearch (FirstPtr : ListPointer; KeyValue : KeyType;
                         VAR PredPtr, CurrPtr : ListPointer;
                         VAR Found : boolean);

   (****************************************************************

     Procedure to search an ordered linked list having first node
     pointed to by FirstPtr for a node containing the specified
     KeyValue or for a position to insert a new node.  CurrPtr points
     to the first node containing key value >= KeyValue or is NIL if
     KeyValue follows all keys in the list.  PredPtr points to its
     predecessor or is NIL if KeyValue precedes all keys in the list.
     Found is returned as true if a node containing KeyValue is already
     in the list.  The procedure assumes that the key fields are in
     ascending order; for descending order, change >= to <= in the
     IF statement.

   ****************************************************************)

   VAR
      DoneSearching : boolean;  (* indicates when search is complete *)

   BEGIN (* OrderedSearch *)
      CurrPtr := FirstPtr;
      PredPtr := NIL;
      Found := false;
      DoneSearching := false;
      WHILE (NOT DoneSearching) AND (CurrPtr <> NIL) DO
         IF CurrPtr^.Data.Key >= KeyValue THEN
            BEGIN
               DoneSearching := true;
               Found := CurrPtr^.Data.Key = KeyValue
            END (* If *)
         ELSE
            BEGIN
               PredPtr := CurrPtr;
               CurrPtr := CurrPtr^.Next
            END (* ELSE *)
   END (* OrderedSearch *);
```

Figure 15.2 (cont.)

```
PROCEDURE Insert (VAR FirstPtr : ListPointer; Item : DataType);

    (******************************************************************

       Procedure to insert Item into list having first node pointed
       to by FirstPtr.  This element is to be inserted between the
       nodes pointed to by PredPtr and CurrPtr.  A NIL value for
       PredPtr indicates insertion at the beginning of the list.
       A value of true for Found indicates that there is already a
       node containing Item.Key in its key field; no new node is
       then inserted into the list.

    ******************************************************************)

    VAR
       PredPtr,
       CurrPtr,
       TempPtr: ListPointer;   (* pointer to new node *)
       Found : boolean;

    BEGIN (* Insert *)
       OrderedSearch (FirstPtr, Item.Key, PredPtr, CurrPtr, Found);
       IF Found THEN
          writeln ('Item already in the list')
       ELSE
          BEGIN
             new (TempPtr);
             TempPtr^.Data := Item;
             IF PredPtr = NIL THEN  (* insert at beginning of list *)
                BEGIN
                   TempPtr^.Next := FirstPtr;
                   FirstPtr := TempPtr
                END (* IF *)
             ELSE                        (* there is a predecessor *)
                BEGIN
                   TempPtr^.Next := CurrPtr;
                   PredPtr^.Next := TempPtr
                END (* ELSE *)
          END (* ELSE *)
    END (* Insert *);

PROCEDURE Initialize (VAR EmpFile : EmployeeFile;
                      VAR FirstPtr : ListPointer);

    (******************************************************************

       Procedure to read employee records from EmpFile and construct
       linked list of these records with first record pointed to by
       FirstPtr.

    ******************************************************************)

    BEGIN (* Initialize *)
       reset (EmpFile);
       FirstPtr := NIL;
       WHILE NOT eof(EmpFile) DO
          BEGIN
             Insert (FirstPtr, EmpFile^);
             get (EmpFile)
          END (* WHILE *)
    END (* Initialize *);
```

Figure 15.2 (cont.)

```
PROCEDURE Delete (VAR FirstPtr : ListPointer; KeyValue : KeyType);

   (*****************************************************************

   Procedure to delete a node having the specified KeyValue from an
      ordered linked list with first node pointed to by FirstPtr.

   *****************************************************************)

   VAR
      CurrPtr,                   (* pointer to node containing KeyValue *)
      PredPtr : ListPointer; (* pointer to its predecessor *)
      Found : boolean;           (* indicates if KeyValue found *)

   BEGIN (* Delete *)
      OrderedSearch (FirstPtr, KeyValue, PredPtr, CurrPtr, Found);
      IF Found THEN
         BEGIN
            IF PredPtr = NIL THEN     (* first node to be deleted *)
               FirstPtr := FirstPtr^.Next
            ELSE                      (* node has a predecessor *)
               PredPtr^.Next := CurrPtr^.Next;
            dispose (CurrPtr)
         END (* IF *)
      ELSE
         writeln ('Item not found in the list')
   END (* Delete *);

PROCEDURE GetRecord (VAR EmpRecord : EmployeeRecord);

   (*****************************************************************

      Procedure to get record of an employee from the user

   *****************************************************************)

   BEGIN (* GetRecord *)
      writeln ('Enter employee''s number, age, dependents, and hourly rate:');
      WITH EmpRecord DO
         readln (Key, Age, Dependents, HourlyRate)
   END (* GetRecord *);

PROCEDURE ModifyRecord (FirstPtr : ListPointer);

   (*****************************************************************

      Procedure to modify record of a specified employee

   *****************************************************************)

   VAR
      EmpNumber : integer;        (* employee's number *)
      CurrPtr,                    (* pointer to old record *)
      PredPtr : ListPointer;      (* and its predecessor *)
      Found : boolean;            (* indicates if record was found *)
```

Figure 15.2   (cont.)

```
    BEGIN (* ModifyRecord *)
        write ('Employee''s number?  ');
        readln (EmpNumber);
        OrderedSearch (FirstPtr, EmpNumber, PredPtr, CurrPtr, Found);
        IF Found THEN
            WITH CurrPtr^.Data DO
                BEGIN
                    writeln ('Age: ', Age:1, '    Dependents: ', Dependents:1,
                             '    Hourly Rate:   $', HourlyRate:4:2);
                    write ('Enter new age, dependents, and hourly rate:  ');
                    readln (Age, Dependents, HourlyRate)
                END (* WITH *)
        ELSE
            writeln ('Employee ', EmpNumber:1, ' not found')
    END (* ModifyRecord *);

PROCEDURE CopyListToFile (FirstPtr: ListPointer;
                          VAR EmpFile : EmployeeFile);

    (*****************************************************************

    Procedure to write the list pointed to by FirstPtr to EmpFile

    *****************************************************************)

    VAR
        CurrPtr: ListPointer;    (* pointer to current node *)

    BEGIN (* CopyListToFile *)
        rewrite (EmpFile);
        CurrPtr := FirstPtr;
        WHILE CurrPtr <> NIL DO
            BEGIN
                write (EmpFile, CurrPtr^.Data);
                CurrPtr := CurrPtr^.Next
            END (* WHILE *)
    END (* CopyListToFile *);

BEGIN (* main program *)
    Initialize (EmpFile, FirstPtr);
    REPEAT
        writeln ('To delete, add, or modify an employee''s record, enter');
        write  ('      1      2   or   3      (0 to quit):  ');
        readln (Option);
        IF Option in [0..NumberOfOptions] THEN
            CASE Option OF
                0 : CopyListToFile (FirstPtr, EmpFile);
                1 : BEGIN
                        write ('Number of employee to be deleted:  ');
                        readln (EmpNumber);
                        write ('Sure (Y or N)?  ');
                        readln (Response);
                        IF Response in ['Y', 'y'] THEN
                            Delete (FirstPtr, EmpNumber);
                    END (* case 1 *);
                2 : BEGIN
                        GetRecord (EmpRecord);
                        Insert (FirstPtr, EmpRecord)
                    END (* case 2 *);
                3 : ModifyRecord (FirstPtr)
            END (* CASE *)
        ELSE
            writeln ('*** Illegal Option ***');
        writeln
    UNTIL Option = 0
END (* main program *).
```

Figure 15.2 (cont.)

Sample run:

```
To delete, add, or modify an employee's record, enter
     1     2    or    3      (0 to quit):   3
Employee's number?  1112
Employee 1112 not found

To delete, add, or modify an employee's record, enter
     1     2    or    3      (0 to quit):   3
Employee's number?  1111
Age: 39   Dependents: 3   Hourly Rate:  $10.50
Enter new age, dependents, and hourly rate:  39 3 10.75

To delete, add, or modify an employee's record, enter
     1     2    or    3      (0 to quit):   2
Enter employee's number, age, dependents, and hourly rate:
3137 44 2 11.25

To delete, add, or modify an employee's record, enter
     1     2    or    3      (0 to quit):   1
Number of employee to be deleted:   2222
Sure (Y or N)?   Y

To delete, add, or modify an employee's record, enter
     1     2    or    3      (0 to quit):   4
*** Illegal Option ***

To delete, add, or modify an employee's record, enter
     1     2    or    3      (0 to quit):   0
```

Exercises

In these exercises, the files *InventoryFile, StudentFile,* and *UsersFile* should be processed as files of records. For descriptions of these files, see Appendix E.

1. Assume the following declarations:

> **var**
> X : *integer*;
> *P1, P2* : ↑*integer*;
> *Q1, Q2* : ↑*real*;

What (if anything) is wrong with each of the following statements?

(a) *writeln (P1)*;   **(b)** *readln (P1↑)*;

(c) *P1* := *Q1*;   **(d)** *new (X)*;

(e) **if** *P1↑* = **nil then**   **(f)** **begin**
        Q1 := *Q2*;   *P1↑* := 17;
                        new (P1)
                end

2. Write type declarations needed to construct a linked list of records from

   (a) *InventoryFile*   **(b)** *StudentFile*   **(c)** *UsersFile*

3. Write a function to count the nodes in a linked list.

4. Write a boolean-valued function that determines whether the data items in a linked list are arranged in ascending order.

5. Write a function that returns a pointer to the last node in a linked list having first node pointed to by *FirstPtr*.

6. Write a procedure to reverse a linked list; that is, the last node becomes the first node, and all links between nodes are reversed.

7. Modify the procedures *Insert* and *Delete* so that they require only the pointer *PredPtr* to the predecessor of the item to be inserted or deleted rather than the two pointers *PredPtr* and *CurrPtr*. Also, write a function *Predecessor* that searches the linked list and returns this pointer.

8. The procedures *Insert* and *Delete* given in the text require checking to see whether the item to be inserted or deleted has a predecessor in the list. These procedures can be shortened if we require every linked list to have a dummy node, called a ***head node,*** at the beginning of the list so that the first node that stores the actual data has the head node as a predecessor. Modify the procedures *Insert* and *Delete* for linked lists having head nodes.

9. The method of successive division for converting a base-10 number to base *b* described in Exercise 12 of Section 1.3 produces the digits of the base-*b* representation in reverse order. Write a program implementing this algorithm to convert a base-10 integer to base *b*; use a linked list to store the digits so they can be printed in the usual left-to-right order.

10. Suppose that jobs entering a computer system are assigned a job number and a priority from 0 through 9. The numbers of jobs awaiting execution by the system are kept in a ***priority queue.*** A job entered into this queue is placed ahead of all jobs of lower priority but after all those of equal or higher priority. Write a program to read one of the letters R (remove), A (add), or L (list). For R, remove the first item in the queue; for A, read a job number and priority and then add it to the priority queue in the manner just described; for L, list all the job numbers in the queue. Maintain the priority queue as a linked list.

11. Write a program to read the records from *StudentFile* and construct five linked lists of records containing a student's name, number, and cumulative GPA, one list for each class. Each list is to be an ordered linked list in which the names are in alphabetical order. After the lists have been constructed, print each of them with appropriate headings.

12. A *polynomial of degree n* has the form

$$a_0 + a_1 x + a_2 x^2 + \cdots + a_n x^n$$

where $a_0, a_1, \ldots, a_n$ are numeric constants called the *coefficients* of the polynomial and $a_n \neq 0$. For example,

$$1 + 3x - 7x^3 + 5x^4$$

is a polynomial of degree 4 with integer coefficients.

(a) Develop an ordered linked list that can represent any such polynomial. Let each node store a nonzero coefficient and the corresponding exponent.

(b) Write a program to read the nonzero coefficients and exponents of a polynomial, construct its linked representation, and print it, using the usual mathematical format with x^n written as $x \uparrow n$ or $x^\wedge n$. The program should then read values for x and evaluate the polynomial for each of them.

13. Write a program that reads the nonzero coefficients and exponents of two polynomials, possibly of different degrees, stores them in linked lists (as described in Exercise 12), and then calculates and displays their sum and product.

14. The number of elements in an ordered list may grow so large that searching the list, always beginning with the first node, is not efficient. One way to improve efficiency is to maintain several smaller linked lists with an array of pointers to the first nodes of these lists. Write a program to read several lines of uppercase text and to produce a *text concordance*, which is a list of all distinct words in the text. Store distinct words beginning with A alphabetically ordered in one linked list, those beginning with B in another, and so on. Use an array with subscripts of type 'A'..'Z', with each array element being a pointer to the first node in the list of words that begin with the corresponding subscript. After all the text lines have been read, print a list of all these words in alphabetical order.

15. Modify the program of Exercise 14 so that the concordance also includes the frequency with which each word occurs in the text.

16. *Directed graphs* and their representations using adjacency matrices were described in Exercise 16 of Section 11.3.

(a) Imitating the construction in Exercise 14, develop a representation of a directed graph by using an array of pointers (one for each vertex) to linked lists containing the vertices that can be reached directly (following a single directed arc) from the vertex corresponding to the subscript.

(b) Draw a diagram showing the linked representation for the following directed graph:

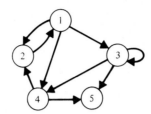

(c) Write a program to read the numbers (or names) of the vertices of a directed graph and ordered pairs of vertices representing the directed arcs, construct the linked representation for the digraph, and then use it to display the adjacency matrix.

17. In Chapter 11 we represented matrices by two-dimensional arrays. For a *sparse matrix,* that is, one with few nonzero entries, this is not an efficient representation.

(a) Imitating the construction in Exercise 14, develop a representation for a sparse matrix by using one ordered linked list for each row and an array of pointers to the first nodes in these lists. Do not store zero entries of the matrix. (*Hint*: Store a matrix entry and the number of the column in which it appears.)

(b) Write a program to read the nonzero entries of a sparse matrix and their locations in the matrix, and construct its linked representation. Then print the matrix in the usual table format with all entries (including 0's) displayed.

18. Extend the program of Exercise 17 to read two sparse matrices and calculate their sum and product (see Section 11.3).

Programming Pointers

The variables that we have considered in previous chapters have as values specific data items such as integers, real numbers, characters, strings, sets, and records. Pointer variables, however, have memory addresses as values. Consequently, the manner in which pointer variables are used is quite different from that in which other kinds of variables are processed; thus, pointers can cause special difficulties for both beginning and experienced programmers. Pointers are used to create dynamic data structures, such as linked lists, which are processed in a way quite different from that in which static data structures, such as sets and arrays, are processed. The following are some of the main features to remember when using pointer variables and dynamic structures in Pascal programs:

1. *Each pointer variable is bound to a certain type; a pointer is the address of a memory location in which only a value of that type can be stored.* For example, if *P* and *Q* are pointer variables declared by

   type
       String = **packed array**[1..20] **of** *char*;

   var
       P : ↑*integer*;
       Q : ↑*String*;

   then *P* is bound to the type *integer* and *Q* to the type *String*. Memory locations pointed to by *P* can store only integers, whereas those to which *Q* points can store only strings of length 20.

2. *Because pointers have memory addresses as values, the operations that can be performed on them are limited.* Some of these limitations are as follows:

   - *The only values that may be assigned to a pointer variable using an assignment statement are the value* **nil** *or the value of another pointer bound to the same type.* Other values are assigned to pointers by using the procedure *new*, which obtains a memory location in which a value of the type to which the pointer is bound can be stored and assigns the address of this location to the pointer.
   - *Arithmetic operations cannot be performed on pointers.* For example, the values (memory addresses) of two pointer variables cannot be added, nor can a numeric value be added to the value of a pointer variable.
   - *Pointer values cannot be compared with the relational operators* <, <=, >, *and* >=. Only the relational operators = and <> are allowed, and then only to determine whether two pointers bound to the same type point to the same memory location or to determine whether a pointer is nil.
   - *Pointer values cannot be read or displayed.*
   - *Pointers may be used as parameters in functions and procedures, but corresponding actual and formal parameters cannot be bound to different types.* Also, if pointer variable *P* of type ↑*integer* is used as a formal parameter of a function or procedure, it cannot be declared in the subprogram heading using

     . . . *P* : ↑*integer*; . . .

     because the types of formal parameters must be specified using type identifiers. A type identifier must be associated with the pointer type ↑*integer*

     type
         IntegerPointer = ↑*integer*;

and this type identifier used to specify the type of *P*:

　. . . *P* : *IntegerPointer*; . . .

Similarly, the value of a function may be a pointer, but it must also be specified by a type identifier.

3. *The value of a pointer* P *is the address of a memory location, whereas the value of* P↑ *is the data item stored in that location.* For example, suppose that the pointer variable *P* is declared by

　var
　　P : ↑*integer*;

The statement *writeln* (*P*) is not allowed, because the value (memory address) of a pointer cannot be displayed. The statement *writeln* (*P*↑) is valid, however, provided that *P* has been assigned to a memory location and a value has been stored in that location. This statement displays the integer stored in the location pointed to by *P*. Similarly, the statement *P* := *P* + 1 is not valid, but *P*↑ := *P*↑ + 1 is valid, assuming again that *P* has been assigned some memory location.

4. *An undefined pointer is not the same as a nil pointer.* A pointer becomes defined when it is assigned the address of a memory location or the value **nil.** Assigning a pointer the value **nil** is analogous to "blanking out" a character (or string) variable or "zeroing out" a numeric variable.

5. *If* P *is a pointer that is undefined or nil, then an attempt to use* P↑ *is an error.*

6. *Memory locations that were once associated with a pointer variable and that are no longer needed should be returned to the "storage pool" of available locations by using the procedure* dispose. Special care is required so that inaccessible memory locations are avoided. For example, if *P* and *Q* are pointer variables bound to the same type, the assignment statement

　P := *Q*

causes *P* to point to the same memory location as that pointed to by *Q*. Any memory location previously pointed to by *P* becomes inaccessible and cannot be disposed of properly unless it is pointed to by some other pointer. One should always use temporary pointers when necessary to maintain access, as in the following statements:

　TempPtr := *P*;
　P := *Q*;
　dispose (*TempPtr*)

7. *Processing linked structures requires attention to special cases and to the problem of losing access to nodes.* Some errors commonly made when using linked lists include the following:

- *Attempting to process data items beyond the end of a linked list.* For example, consider the following attempt to search a nonempty linked list for a given item:

  CurrPtr := *FirstPtr*;
  while *CurrPtr↑.Data* <> *ItemSought* **do**
     CurrPtr := *CurrPtr↑.Next*;

  If the item is not present in any node of the linked list, *CurrPtr* will eventually reach the last node in the list. *CurrPtr* then becomes nil, and an attempt is made to examine the *Data* field of a nonexistent node, resulting in an error message such as

  *** Attempted access via NIL pointer ***

  An attempted solution to the problem might be the following:

  CurrPtr := *FirstPtr*;
  while (*CurrPtr* <> **nil**) **and**
       (*CurrPtr↑.Data* <> *ItemSought*) **do**
     CurrPtr := *CurrPtr↑.Next*;

  In some versions of Pascal this will also result in an error if the item is not in the list. The reason is that boolean expressions may be evaluated in their entirety. Thus, when the end of the list is reached and *CurrPtr* becomes nil, the second part of the boolean expression is evaluated, and an error results when an attempt is made to access the *Data* field of a nonexistent node.

  Another attempt to avoid running past the end of a nonempty list might be the following:

  Found := *false*;
  CurrPtr := *FirstPtr*;
  while *CurrPtr↑.Next* <> **nil do**
    if *CurrPtr↑.Data* = *ItemSought* **then**
      Found := *true*
    else
      CurrPtr := *CurrPtr↑.Next*;

  Although this avoids the problem of moving beyond the end of the list, it will fail to locate the desired item (that is, set *Found* to *true*) if this item is the last one in the list. When *CurrPtr* reaches the last node, the value of *CurrPtr↑.Next* is nil, and repetition is terminated without examining the *Data* field of this last node. Another problem is that if the item is found in the list, the remaining nodes (except the last) will also be examined.

One solution is to use a boolean variable together with an end-of-list check to control the repetition:

Found := *false*;
CurrPtr := *FirstPtr*;
while (*CurrPtr* <> **nil**) **and** (**not** *Found*) **do**
    if *CurrPtr↑.Data* = *ItemSought* **then**
        Found := *true*
    else
        CurrPtr := *CurrPtr↑.Next*;

If the item is found in the list, then *Found* is set to *true* and repetition is terminated. If it is not in the list, *CurrPtr* eventually becomes nil and repetition terminates.

● *Attempting to access items in an empty list.* An example of this is the set of statements

CurrPtr := *FirstPtr*;
while *CurrPtr↑.Data* <> *ItemSought* **do**
    CurrPtr := *CurrPtr↑.Next*;

An error will result if the list is empty—that is, if *FirstPtr* is nil—because the first value of *CurrPtr* is then nil and an attempt is made to examine a field in a nonexistent node. This is also the case with the following example:

Found := *false*;
CurrPtr := *FirstPtr*;
while *CurrPtr↑.Next* <> **nil do**
    if *CurrPtr↑.Data* = *ItemSought* **then**
        Found := *true*
    else
        CurrPtr := *CurrPtr↑.Next*;

For an empty list, *CurrPtr* is initially nil, and the *Next* field of a nonexistent node cannot be examined.

● *"Burning bridges before they are crossed," more precisely, changing some link in a list before certain other links have been reset.* As an example, suppose that a node pointed to by *NewNodePtr* is to be inserted at the beginning of a list with first node pointed to by *FirstPtr*. The statements

FirstPtr := *NewNodePtr*;
NewNodePtr↑.Next := *FirstPtr*;

are not used in the correct order. As soon as *FirstPtr* is set to *NewNodePtr*, access to the remaining nodes in the list (those previously pointed to by *FirstPtr*) is lost. The second statement then simply sets the *Next* field of the node pointed to by *NewNodePtr* (and by

FirstPtr) to point to the node itself. The new node must first be linked into the list before *FirstPtr* is reset:

NewNodePtr↑.Next := *FirstPtr*;
FirstPtr := *NewNodePtr*

Variations and Extensions

Most versions of Pascal process pointer variables as described for standard Pascal in this chapter. One exception is that some versions (Turbo) do not allow the special forms of reference to procedures *new* and *dispose* mentioned in the footnotes of Section 15.1 and described in Appendix F. Some versions (UCSD) may not even provide the procedure *dispose* but, rather, require the use of other special predefined procedures for dynamic memory management.

16

Data Structures and Algorithms

Algorithms + Data Structures = Programs

NIKLAUS WIRTH

There is nothing more difficult to take in hand, more perilous to conduct, or more uncertain in its success, than to take the lead in the introduction of a new order of things.

NICCOLÒ MACHIAVELLI, *The Prince*

We have now considered all of the Pascal statements, data types, procedures, and functions, with the exception of a few seldom-used features that are described in Appendix F. The first eight chapters dealt mainly with designing algorithms to solve problems and implementing these algorithms with Pascal programs and subprograms. In later chapters we noted that in many problems it is necessary to organize the data in an appropriate data structure, and thus we undertook a study of the ***predefined data structures*** provided in Pascal: arrays, records, sets, and files. We have also seen that there are useful ***user-defined*** or ***higher-level data structures*** that are not provided in Pascal and must therefore be implemented using those structures that are available. In particular, in the preceding chapter we considered linked lists and showed how they can be implemented in Pascal using pointers and records. There are many other important user-defined data structures, and quite often there are several ways to implement them. In this chapter we describe some of the simpler ones and a few of their applications.

An important aspect of implementing a data structure is the design of algorithms for the basic operations used to process the data. Although some attention was paid to the efficiency of the algorithms in the preceding chapters, most of them were designed to show as simply as possible the various features of the Pascal language. In situations in which there are several algorithms that might be used, for example, in sorting and searching problems, some means of comparing algorithms is necessary. Thus, in this chapter we also consider more carefully the design and analysis of algorithms and introduce some techniques for measuring their efficiency more precisely.

16.1   Stacks and Queues

As we have learned, solving a problem often involves the manipulation of data, and an important part of the solution is the careful organization of the data. This requires that we identify the collection of data items and the possible relationships between them and the basic operations that must be performed on these data items. Such a collection together with the relevant operations and relations is called an ***abstract data structure*** or simply a ***data structure*** or an ***abstract data type***, commonly abbreviated as ***ADT***. The terms *abstract data structure* and *abstract data type* are often used interchangeably. However, the term *data structure* is more appropriate when data is being studied at a logical or conceptual level, independent of any programming considerations. The term *abstract data type* is appropriate when the structure is being viewed as an object to be processed in a program. We will illustrate this distinction in this chapter. In both cases, the word *abstract* refers to the fact that the data and the basic operations and relations defined on it are being studied independently of any implementation.

An ***implementation*** of a data structure consists of ***storage structures*** to store the data items and ***algorithms*** for the basic operations and relations. As we will see, there may be several different implementations, and some are better than others. The idea of ***data abstraction***, in which the definition of a data structure is separated from its implementation, is an important concept that is a natural part of a top-down approach to program development. It makes it possible to study and use the structure without being concerned about the details of its implementation.

To illustrate how the analysis of a problem leads to the organization of the data into a data structure, consider the following problems:

Problem 1. A program is to be written to simulate a certain card game. One aspect of this simulation is to maintain a discard pile. On any turn, a player may discard a single card from his hand to the top of this pile, or he may retrieve the top card from this discard pile. What data structure is needed to model this discard pile?

Problem 2. A program is to be written to model a railroad switching yard. One part of the switching network consists of a main track and a siding onto which cars may be shunted and removed at any time (see Figure 16.1). What data structure can be used to model the operation of this siding?

Problem 3. One task that must be performed by a compiler is to scan an arithmetic expression containing parentheses to determine whether these parentheses balance, that is, if each left parenthesis has exactly one matching right parenthesis that appears later in the expression. What data structure will facilitate this syntax checking?

Figure 16.1

Each of these problems involves a collection of related data items, a deck of cards in Problem 1, a set of railroad cars in Problem 2, and a collection of left and right parentheses in Problem 3. In Problem 1, the basic operations that must be performed are adding to and removing from the top of the discard pile. In Problem 2, the basic operations are pushing a car onto the siding and removing the last car placed on the siding. To solve Problem 3, we must scan the expression and temporarily store each left parenthesis until a right parenthesis is encountered. This right parenthesis matches the last left parenthesis that was stored, and thus that left parenthesis is removed from storage and the scan is continued.

In each case, we are led to a data structure in which items can be stored and retrieved in a *Last-In-First-Out (LIFO)* order; that is, the last item stored is the first item to be retrieved. Such a data structure is called a *stack* (or *push-down stack*) because it functions in the same manner as does a spring-loaded stack of plates or trays used in a cafeteria. Plates are added to the stack by pushing them onto the *top* of the stack. When a plate is removed from the top of the stack, the spring causes the next plate to pop up. For this reason, the store and retrieve operations for a stack are commonly called *push* and *pop*, respectively.

A stack can be viewed as a special kind of list in which one of the ends is designated as the top of the stack and access to the data items is restricted to this end of the list. Since we have used arrays to process lists, it should also be possible to implement this new data structure using arrays.

In an array, however, each item can be accessed directly, whereas in a stack, only the top item can be accessed. One way to make an array operate as a stack is to designate the first position in the array as the top of the stack and adopt the convention that data items will be stored in and retrieved from only this position. For example, suppose the data items are characters and the array *Stack* is declared by

> **var**
> *Stack* : **array**[1..50] **of** *char*;

The sequence of stack operations

Push 'A', Push 'B', Push 'C', Pop

might then be traced as follows:

Push 'A': $Stack[1]$ | A |
                        $Stack[2]$ | |
                        $Stack[3]$ | |
                                    ⋮
                        $Stack[50]$ | |

Push 'B': $Stack[1]$ | B |
                        $Stack[2]$ | A | Move $Stack[1]$ down to $Stack[2]$
                        $Stack[3]$ | |
                                    ⋮
                        $Stack[50]$ | |

Push 'C': $Stack[1]$ | C |
                        $Stack[2]$ | B | Move $Stack[1]$ down to $Stack[2]$ after
                        $Stack[3]$ | A | moving $Stack[2]$ down to $Stack[3]$
                                    ⋮
                        $Stack[50]$ | |

Pop: $Stack[1]$ | B | Move $Stack[2]$ up to $Stack[1]$; then
                        $Stack[2]$ | A | move $Stack[3]$ up to $Stack[2]$
                        $Stack[3]$ | |
                                    ⋮
                        $Stack[50]$ | |

One drawback with implementing a stack with an array in this manner is one that we noted for array implementations of lists in general: The array elements must be moved each time a push (insert) or pop (delete) operation is performed. This difficulty can be eliminated by letting the stack grow from position 1 toward position 50, and keeping a "pointer" Top, which is the index of the current top of the stack, and pushing and popping at this location. An empty stack is signaled by $Top = 0$ and a full stack by $Top = 50$. The preceding sequence of stack operations can then be pictured as follows:

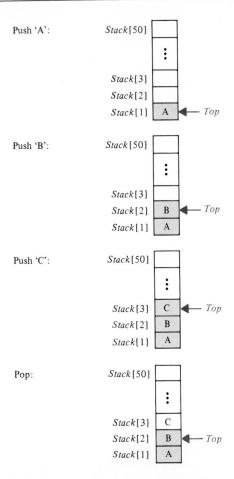

A storage structure for a stack in this improved array-based implementation thus has two parts: an array to store the stack elements and a simple variable to store the index of the current top of the stack. It is convenient to combine these two parts into a single structure, namely, a record. We are thus led to declarations of the following form:

```
const
    StackLimit = 50;        (* limit on stack size *)

type
    StackArray = array[1..StackLimit] of char;
    CharStackType = record
                        Top : 0..StackLimit;
                        Element : StackArray
                    end;
```

To complete this implementation of a stack, procedures must be written to perform the basic stack operations:

Create: To create an empty stack.
Empty: To determine if a stack is empty.

> *Pop*:   To retrieve and remove the element at the top of the stack.
> *Push*:   To insert a new element at the top of the stack.

The operation of creating an empty stack consists simply of setting *Stack.Top* to 0, and a stack will be empty when the boolean expression *Stack.Top* = 0 is true.

An algorithm for the pop operation is

Pop

(∗ Algorithm to pop *Item* from the top of *Stack*, assuming the stack is nonempty. ∗)

If *Stack* is empty, then
    Display a stack-empty message.
Otherwise do the following:
    a. Set *Item* equal to the element *Stack.Element[Top]* at the top of the stack.
    b. Decrement *Stack.Top* by 1.

And an algorithm for the push operation is

Push

(∗ Algorithm to push *Item* onto the *Stack*, assuming the array is not full. ∗)

If *Stack.Top* is equal to the array limit, then
    Display a stack-full message.
Otherwise do the following:
    a. Increment *Stack.Top* by 1.
    b. Set the element *Stack.Element[Top]* at the top of the stack equal to *Item*.

Theoretically, a stack cannot become full; but because an array has a fixed size, a stack-full condition may occur in this implementation. Thus it is necessary to determine whether the array is full before performing a push operation.

Since stacks are useful in solving many different problems, it would be convenient to have a stack data type. In some programming languages (such as Modula-2) and in some versions of Pascal (such as Turbo), one can in effect extend the language to include this abstract data type by designing a *module* or *unit* that encapsulates the declarations needed to define this type and the procedures and functions to implement its basic operations and relations. The ADT stack can then be used in a program simply by importing the necessary items from this module or unit. It can be used *abstractly*, that is, independently of its implementation details, which remain hidden in this module or unit.

Although standard Pascal makes no provision for such modules and units (as yet), it is nevertheless convenient to have available the following package of declarations for defining a stack data type and procedures and functions that implement the basic stack operations. As illustrated in Figure 16.2, we can then use this new abstract data type in a program simply by including these declarations and definitions in the program. (Some versions of Pascal even provide special compiler directives for copying a specified file into a program at compile time.)

```
const
    StackLimit = . . . ;  (* limit on stack size *)

type
    DataType = . . . ;  (* type of stack elements *)
    StackArray = array[1.. StackLimit] of DataType;
    StackType = record
                        Top : 0.. StackLimit;
                        Element : StackArray
                  end;

procedure Create (var Stack : StackType);

    (* Procedure to create an empty stack. *)

    begin (* Create *)
        Stack.Top := 0
    end (* Create *);

function Empty(Stack : StackType) : boolean;

    (* Returns true if Stack is empty, false otherwise. *)

    begin (* Empty *)
        Empty := (Stack.Top = 0)
    end (* Empty *);

procedure Pop (var Stack : StackType; var Item : DataType);

    (* Procedure to pop Item from the top of Stack, assuming the stack is
       nonempty. *)

    begin (* Pop *)
        if Empty(Stack) then
            writeln ('*** Attempt to pop from an empty stack ***')
        else
            with Stack do
                begin
                    Item := Element[Top];
                    Top := Top − 1
                end (* with *)
    end (* Pop *);

procedure Push (var Stack : StackType; Item : DataType);

    (* Procedure to push Item onto Stack, assuming the stack is not full. *)
```

```
begin (* Push *)
    if Stack.Top = StackLimit then
        writeln ('*** Attempt to push onto a full stack ***')
    else
        with Stack do
            begin
                Top := Top + 1;
                Element[Top] := Item
            end (* with *)
end (* Push *);
```

The program in Figure 16.2 illustrates the use of this ADT stack. It reads a string of characters and displays them in reverse order. It uses the declarations, procedures, and functions obtained by setting *DataType* = *char* in the preceding package. An empty stack is created, and then as each character is read, it is pushed onto this stack. After all of the characters have been read, characters are popped from the stack and displayed until the stack becomes empty. Since a stack is a LIFO structure, the characters will be displayed in the opposite order from that in which they were added to the stack, that is, in reverse order.

```
PROGRAM ReverseAString (input, output);

(***********************************************************************

    Program to display the characters in a string in reverse order.
    Characters are read and pushed onto a stack.  When all of them
    have been read, characters are popped from the stack and displayed
    until the stack becomes empty.  It uses the procedures Create,
    Pop, and Push and function Empty from the package of basic stack
    operations described in Section 16.1

    ***********************************************************************)

CONST
    StackLimit = 50;        (* limit on stack size *)

TYPE
    DataType = char;
    StackArray = ARRAY[1..StackLimit] OF DataType;
    StackType = RECORD
                    Top : 0..StackLimit;
                    Element : StackArray
                END;

VAR
    Stack : StackType;      (* stack of characters·*)
    Symbol,                 (* current character from string or list *)
    Response : char;        (* user response *)
```

Figure 16.2

Figure 16.2 (cont.)

```
(****************************************************************
 ****************************************************************
 ** Insert the following procedures and functions from the package of **
 ** basic stack operations described in Section 16.1 here:        **
 **                           Create                              **
 **                           Empty                               **
 **                           Pop                                 **
 **                           Push                                **
 ****************************************************************
 ****************************************************************)

BEGIN (* main program *)
   REPEAT
      (* Initialize an empty stack *)

      Create (Stack);

      (* Read the characters, pushing each onto the stack *)

      writeln;
      writeln ('Enter the string to be reversed:');
      WHILE NOT eoln DO
         BEGIN
            read (Symbol);
            Push (Stack, Symbol)
         END (* WHILE *);
      readln;

      (* Now pop and display the characters on the stack *)

      writeln;
      writeln ('Reversed string:');
      WHILE NOT Empty (Stack) DO
         BEGIN
            Pop (Stack, Symbol);
            write (Symbol)
         END (* WHILE *);
      writeln; writeln;
      write ('More strings (Y or N)? ');
      readln (Response)
   UNTIL NOT (Response IN ['y', 'Y'])
END (* main program *).
```

Sample run:

```
Enter the string to be reversed:
Kelloggs Cornflakes

Reversed string:
sekalfnroC sggolleK

More strings (Y or N)? Y

Enter the string to be reversed:
able was I ere I saw elba

Reversed string:
able was I ere I saw elba

More strings (Y or N)? N
```

Another important data structure is a *queue*, a list in which items may be added only at one end, called the **rear** or **back**, and removed only at the other end, called the **front** or **head**. This **First-In-First-Out (FIFO)** structure functions like a waiting line at a service facility; arriving customers enter the line at the rear, and when a customer reaches the front of the line, he or she is removed from the line and served.

Queues are also commonly used to model waiting lines that arise in the operation of computer systems. These queues are formed whenever more than one process requires a particular resource such as a printer or a disk drive or the central processing unit. As processes request a particular resource, they are placed in a queue to wait for service by that resource. For example, several personal computers may be sharing the same printer, and a **spool queue** is used to schedule output requests in a first-come–first-served manner. If a request for a print job is made and the printer is free, it is immediately assigned to this job. While this output is being printed, other jobs may need the printer. They are placed in a spool queue to wait their turns. When the output from the current job terminates, the printer is released from that job and is assigned to the first job in the spool queue.

Another important use of queues in computing systems is for **input/output buffering**. The transfer of information from an input device or to an output device is relatively slow, and if the processing of a program must be suspended while data is transferred, program execution is slowed dramatically. One common solution to this problem uses sections of main memory known as **buffers** and transfers data between the program and these buffers rather than between the program and the input/output device directly.

In particular, consider the problem in which data being processed by a program is to be read from a disk file. This information is transferred from the disk file to an input buffer in main memory while the central processing unit (CPU) is performing some other task. When data is required by the program, the next value stored in this buffer is retrieved. While this value is being processed, additional data values can be transferred from the disk file to the buffer. Clearly, the buffer must be organized as a first-in-first-out structure, that is, as a queue. A queue-empty condition indicates that the input buffer is empty, and program execution is suspended while the operating system attempts to load more data into the buffer or signals the end of input. Of course, such a buffer has a limited size, and thus a queue-full condition must also be used to signal when the buffer is full and no more data is to be transferred from the disk file to it.

Because a queue resembles a stack in many ways, we might imitate the implementation of a stack to construct an implementation of a queue. Thus we might use an array to store the elements of the queue and maintain two variables: *Front* to record the position in the array of the element that can be removed, that is, the first queue element; and *Rear* to record the position in the array at which an element can be added, that is, the position following the last queue element. An element is then removed from the queue by retrieving the array element at position *Front* and then incrementing *Front* by 1. An item is added to the queue by storing it at position *Rear* of the array, provided *Rear* does not exceed some maximum size *MaxSize* allowed for the array, and then incrementing *Rear* by 1.

The difficulty with this implementation is that elements "shift to the right" in the array, so that eventually all the array elements may have to be shifted back to the beginning positions. For example, consider a queue for which *MaxSize* = 5 and whose elements are integers. The sequence of operations *AddQ* 70, *AddQ* 80, *AddQ* 50 produces the following configuration:

Now suppose that two elements are removed:

and that 90 and 60 are then added:

Before another item can be inserted into the queue, the elements in the array must be shifted back to the beginning of the array:

This shifting of array elements can be avoided if we think of the array as *circular*, with the first element following the last. This can be done by indexing the array beginning with 0, and incrementing *Front* and *Rear* using addition modulo *MaxSize*. For the sequence of operations just considered, this implementation yields the following configurations:

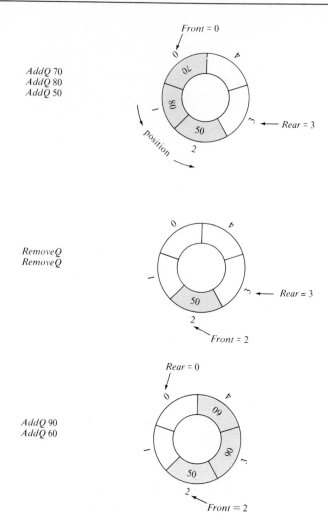

Another insertion is now possible without our having to move any array elements; we simply store the item in position $Rear = 0$.

Now consider the basic operation *EmptyQ* to determine whether a queue is empty. If the queue contains a single element, it is in position *Front* of the array, and *Rear* is the vacant position following it. If this element is deleted, *Front* is incremented by 1 so that *Front* and *Rear* have the same value. Thus, to determine if a queue is empty, we need only check the condition *Front* = *Rear*. Initially, *CreateQ* will set both *Front* and *Rear* equal to 0.

Just as the array implementation for a stack introduced the possibility of a stack-full condition, the implementation of a queue raises the possibility of a queue-full condition. To see how this condition can be detected, suppose the array is almost full, with only one empty location remaining:

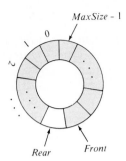

If an item is stored in this location, *Rear* would be incremented by 1 and thus would have the same value as *Front*. However, the condition *Front = Rear* indicates that the queue is empty. Thus, we would not be able to distinguish between an empty queue and a full queue if this location were used to store an element. We can avoid this difficulty if we maintain one empty position in the array; the condition indicating that a queue is full then becomes (*Rear* + 1) **mod** *MaxSize = Front*.

Development of the basic declarations and basic procedures and functions to implement queues using circular arrays as just described is left as an exercise. Declarations for a type *QueueType* are much like those for stacks, and procedures and functions *CreateQ*, *EmptyQ*, *AddQ*, and *RemoveQ* are straightforward.

Exercises

1. Using the ADT stack, write a program that reads a string, one character at a time, and determines whether the string contains balanced parentheses, that is, whether each left parenthesis (if there are any) has exactly one matching right parenthesis that appears later in the string.

2. Using the ADT stack, write a program that reads nonnegative integer values in base-10 notation and converts them to base-2 notation using the repeated division scheme described in Exercise 12 of Section 1.3. As the remainders are generated, push characters representing them onto a stack until the division process terminates. Then pop these remainders and display them.

3. Proceed as in Exercise 2, but convert from base 10 to any of the bases 2, 3, . . . , 16.

4. Proceed as in Exercise 2, but have the program convert from base 10 to base 26; use ''digits'' 'A' for 1, 'B' for 2, . . . , 'Y' for 25, and 'Z' for 0.

5. Imitating the declarations for stacks given in the text, write constant and type definitions for queues implemented using a circular array to store the queue elements, as described in this section.

6. Assuming the declarations in Exercise 5, write

(a) a procedure *CreateQ* to create an empty queue.
(b) a function *EmptyQ* to check whether a queue is empty.
(c) a procedure *AddQ* to add an item at the end of a queue.
(d) a procedure *RemoveQ* to remove the element at the front of a queue.

7. A *deque* (pronounced "deck") is a double-ended queue, that is, a list into which items may be inserted and from which items may be removed at either end.

(a) Write constant and type definitions for a deque of character strings implemented as a record having three fields, two of which are integer values providing access to the front and rear of the deque and the third a "circular" array for storing the deque elements.
(b) Write a procedure for adding a string to the deque; one of the parameters should specify at which end the item is to be added.
(c) Write a procedure for removing a string from the deque; one of the parameters should specify from which end the item is to be removed.

8. Write a program that reads a question from a file, displays it, and accepts an answer from the user. If the answer is correct, go on to the next question. If it is not correct, put the question into a queue. When the file of questions is exhausted, the questions that were missed are displayed again. Keep a count of the correct answers and display the final count. Also, display the correct answer when necessary in the second round of questioning.

16.2 Application of Stacks: Reverse Polish Notation

The task of a compiler is to generate the machine language instructions required to carry out the instructions of the source program written in a high-level language (see Section 1.3). One part of this task is to generate the machine instructions for evaluating arithmetic expressions like that in the assignment statement

$$X := A * B + C$$

The compiler must generate machine instructions to

1. Retrieve the value of A from the memory location where it is stored and load it into the accumulating register.
2. Retrieve the value of B and multiply it by the value in the accumulating register.
3. Retrieve the value of C and add it to the value in the accumulating register.
4. Store the value in the accumulating register in the memory location associated with X.

Arithmetic expressions are ordinarily written using *infix* notation like that above, in which the symbol for each binary operation is placed between the operands. In many compilers, the first step in evaluating such infix expressions is to transform them into *postfix* notation in which the operation symbol follows the operands. Machine instructions are then generated to evaluate this postfix expression. Likewise, calculators commonly evaluate arithmetic expressions using postfix notation. The reason for this is that conversion from infix to postfix is straightforward and postfix expressions are generally easier to evaluate mechanically than are infix expressions.

When infix notation is used for arithmetic expressions, parentheses are often needed to indicate the order in which the operations are to be carried out. For example, parentheses are placed in the expression 2 * (3 + 4) to indicate that the addition is to be performed before the multiplication. If the parentheses are omitted, giving 2 * 3 + 4, the standard priority rules would dictate that the multiplication is to be performed before the addition.

In the early 1950s, the Polish logician Jan Lukasiewicz observed that parentheses are not necessary in postfix notation, also called *Reverse Polish Notation (RPN)*. For example, the infix expression

$$2 * (3 + 4)$$

can be written in RPN as

$$2\ 3\ 4\ +\ *$$

To illustrate how such RPN expressions are evaluated, consider

$$1\ 5\ +\ 8\ 4\ 1\ -\ -\ *$$

which corresponds to the infix expression $(1 + 5) * (8 - (4 - 1))$. This expression is scanned from left to right until an operator is found. At that point, the last two preceding operands are combined, using this operator. For our example, the first operator encountered is +, and its operands are 1 and 5, as indicated by the underline in the following:

$$\underline{1\ 5\ +}\ 8\ 4\ 1\ -\ -\ *$$

Replacing this subexpression with its value 6 yields the reduced RPN expression

$$6\ 8\ 4\ 1\ -\ -\ *$$

Resuming the left-to-right scan, we next encounter the operator − and determine its two operands:

$$6\ 8\ \underline{4\ 1\ -}\ -\ *$$

Applying this operator then yields

$$6\ 8\ 3\ -\ *$$

The next operator encountered is another − and its two operands are 8 and 3:

$$6\ \underline{8\ 3\ -}\ *$$

Evaluating this difference gives

$$6\ 5\ *$$

The final operator is $*$,

$$\underline{6\ 5\ *}$$

and the value 30 is obtained for this expression.

This method of evaluating an RPN expression requires that the operands be stored until an operator is encountered in the left-to-right scan. At this point, the last two operands must be retrieved and combined using this operation. This suggests that a LIFO structure, that is, a stack, should be used to store the operands. Each time an operand is encountered, it is pushed onto the stack. When an operator is encountered, the top two values are popped from the stack, the operator applied to them, and the result pushed back onto the stack. The following algorithm summarizes this procedure:

ALGORITHM TO EVALUATE RPN EXPRESSIONS

1. Initialize an empty stack.
2. Repeat the following until the end of the expression is encountered:
   a. Get the next *Token* (constant, variable, arithmetic operator) in the RPN expression.
   b. If *Token* is an operand, push it onto the stack. If it is an operator, do the following:
      (i) Pop the top two values from the stack. (If the stack does not contain two items, an error due to a malformed RPN expression has occurred and evaluation is terminated.)
      (ii) Apply the operator *Token* to these two values.
      (iii) Push the resulting value back onto the stack.
3. When the end of the expression is encountered, its value is on top of the stack (and in fact must be the only value in the stack).

Figure 16.3 illustrates this algorithm for the RPN expression

$$2\ 4\ *\ 9\ 5\ +\ -$$

The up-arrow ($\uparrow$) indicates the current token.

To illustrate how a stack is also used in the conversion from infix to RPN, consider the infix expression

$$7\ +\ 2\ *\ 3$$

In a left-to-right scan of this expression, 7 is encountered and may be immediately displayed. Next, the operator $+$ is encountered, but since its right operand has not yet been displayed, it must be stored and thus is pushed onto a stack of operators:

Output	Stack
7	$\boxed{+}$

Next, the operand 2 is encountered and displayed. At this point, it must be determined whether 2 is the right operand for the preceding operator $+$ or the left operand for the next operator. This is determined by comparing the operator $+$ on the top of the stack with the next operator $*$. Since $*$ has higher priority

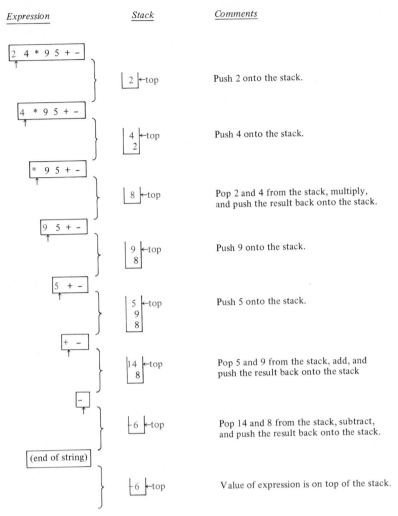

Expression   *Stack*   *Comments*

Push 2 onto the stack.

Push 4 onto the stack.

Pop 2 and 4 from the stack, multiply, and push the result back onto the stack.

Push 9 onto the stack.

Push 5 onto the stack.

Pop 5 and 9 from the stack, add, and push the result back onto the stack

Pop 14 and 8 from the stack, subtract, and push the result back onto the stack.

Value of expression is on top of the stack.

Figure 16.3 Evaluation of the RPN expression 2 4 $*$ 9 5 $+$ $-$.

than $+$, the preceding operand 2 that was displayed is the left operand for $*$; thus we push $*$ onto the stack and search for its right operand:

Output   Stack

7 2

The operand 3 is encountered next and displayed. Since the end of the expression has now been reached, the right operand for the operator $*$ on the top of the stack has been found, so $*$ can now be popped and displayed:

Output   Stack

7 2 3 $*$

The end of the expression also signals that the right operand for the remaining operator + in the stack has been found, so it too can be popped and displayed, yielding the RPN expression

$$7 \ 2 \ 3 \ast \ +$$

Parentheses within infix expressions present no real difficulties. A left parenthesis indicates the beginning of a subexpression, and when encountered, it is pushed onto the stack. When a right parenthesis is encountered, operators are popped from the stack until the matching left parenthesis rises to the top. At this point, the subexpression originally enclosed by the parentheses has been converted to RPN, so the parentheses may be discarded and conversion continues. All of this is contained in the following algorithm:

ALGORITHM TO CONVERT INFIX EXPRESSIONS TO RPN

1. Initialize an empty stack.
2. Repeat the following until the end of the infix expression is reached.
   a. Get the next input *Token* (constant, variable, arithmetic operator, left parenthesis, right parenthesis) in the infix expression.
   b. If *Token* is

(i) a left parenthesis:	Push it onto the stack.
(ii) an operand:	Display it.
(iii) an operator:	If the stack is empty or *Token* has higher priority than the top stack element, push *Token* onto the stack.
	Otherwise, pop an operator from the stack and display it; then repeat the comparison of *Token* with the new top stack item.
	Note: A left parenthesis in the stack is assumed to have a lower priority than any of the operators.
(iv) a right parenthesis:	Pop and display stack elements until a left parenthesis is on top of the stack. Pop it also, but do not display it.

3. When the end of the infix expression is reached, pop and display stack items until the stack is empty.

Figure 16.4 illustrates this algorithm for the infix expression

$$7 \ast 8 - (2 + 3)$$

An up-arrow ($\uparrow$) has been used to indicate the current input symbol and the symbol displayed by the algorithm. The program in Figure 16.5 implements this algorithm, using the ADT stack described in the preceding section.

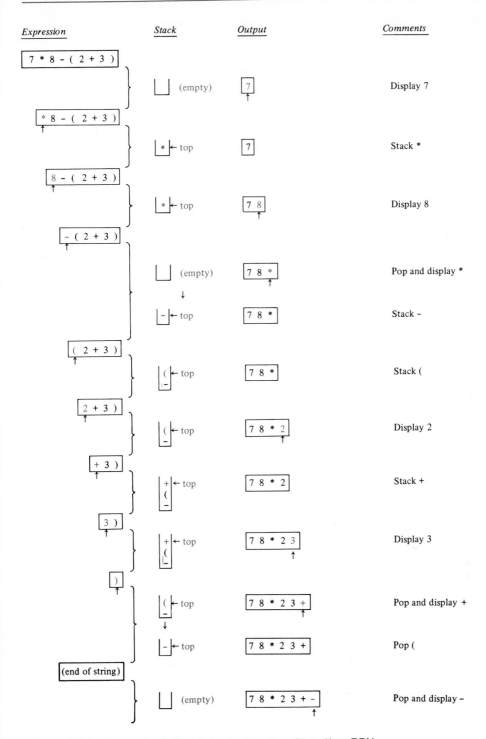

Figure 16.4 Converting infix expression 7 ∗ 8 − (2 + 3) to RPN.

```
PROGRAM InfixToRPN (input, output);

(*******************************************************************

    Program to convert an infix expression to Reverse Polish Notation.

*******************************************************************)

CONST
    MaxExpression = 80;          (* limit on expression length *)
    StackLimit = 50;             (* limit on stack size *)
    EndMark = ';';               (* marks end of infix expression *)

TYPE
    Expression = PACKED ARRAY[1..MaxExpression] OF char;
    DataType = char;
    StackType = RECORD
                    Top : 0..StackLimit;
                    Element : PACKED ARRAY[0..StackLimit] OF DataType;
                END;

VAR
    Exp : Expression;            (* infix expression *)
    i : integer;                 (* index of a token in Exp *)
    Response : char;             (* user response *)

(*******************************************************************
*******************************************************************
** Insert the following procedures and function                  **
**                          Create                               **
**                          Empty                                **
**                          Pop                                  **
**                          Push                                 **
** from the package of basic stack operations described in       **
** Section 16.1                                                  **
*******************************************************************
*******************************************************************)

PROCEDURE ConvertToRPN (Exp : Expression);

    (*******************************************************************

            Procedure to convert infix expression Exp to RPN.

    *******************************************************************)

    VAR
        Stack : StackType;       (* stack of characters *)
        i : integer;             (* index *)
        Error : boolean;         (* signals error in expression *)
        Token : char;            (* a character in the expression *)
```

Figure 16.5

Figure 16.5 (cont.)

```
FUNCTION Priority (Operator : char) : integer;

    (*************************************************************

        Function to find the priority of an arithmetic operator or (.

    *************************************************************)

    BEGIN  (* Priority *)
        CASE Operator OF
                '(' : Priority := 0;
            '+', '-' : Priority := 1;
            '*', '/' : Priority := 2
        END (* CASE *)
    END (* Priority *);

PROCEDURE ProcessRightParen (VAR Stack : StackType;
                             VAR Error : boolean);

    (*************************************************************

        Procedure to pop and display stack elements until a left
        parenthesis is on top of the stack; it too is popped but
        not displayed.  Error is returned as true if the stack
        becomes empty with no left parenthesis being found.

    *************************************************************)

    VAR
        TopToken : char;        (* token on top of stack *)

    BEGIN (* ProcessRightParen *)
        REPEAT
            IF Empty(Stack) THEN
                Error := true
            ELSE
                BEGIN
                    Pop (Stack, TopToken);
                    If TopToken <> '(' THEN
                        write (TopToken:2)
                END (* ELSE *)
        UNTIL (TopToken = '(') OR Error
    END (* ProcessRightParen *);

PROCEDURE ProcessOperator (Operator : char;
                           VAR Stack : StackType);

    (*************************************************************

        Process to process an arithmetic operator.  Operators are
        popped from the stack until the stack becomes empty or an
        operator appears on the top of the stack whose priority
        is less than or equal to that of Operator.  Operator is
        then pushed onto the stack.

    *************************************************************)
```

Figure 16.5 (cont.)

```
     VAR
         TopOperator : char;        (* operator on top of stack *)
         DonePopping : boolean;     (* signals completion of stack popping *)

     BEGIN (* ProcessOperator *)
         DonePopping := false;
         REPEAT
             IF Empty(Stack) THEN
                 DonePopping := true
             ELSE
                 BEGIN
                     Pop (Stack, TopOperator);
                     IF Priority(Operator) <= Priority(TopOperator) THEN
                         write (TopOperator:2)
                     ELSE
                         BEGIN
                             Push (Stack, TopOperator);
                             DonePopping := true
                         END (* ELSE *)
                 END (* ELSE *)
         UNTI1 DonePopping;
         Push (Stack, Operator)
     END (* ProcessOperator *);

BEGIN (* ConvertToRPN *)

    (* Initialize an empty stack *)
    Create (Stack);
    Error := false;

    (* Begin the conversion to RPN *)
    i := 1;
    Token := Exp[1];
    WHILE (Token <> EndMark) AND NOT Error DO
        BEGIN
            IF Token <> ' ' THEN                          (* skip blanks *)
                IF Token = '(' THEN                       (* left parenthesis *)
                    Push (Stack, Token)
                ELSE IF Token = ')' THEN                  (* right parenthesis *)
                    ProcessRightParen(Stack, Error)
                ELSE IF Token IN ['+','-','*','/'] THEN    (* operator *)
                    ProcessOperator (Token, Stack)
                ELSE                                      (* operand *)
                    write (Token:2);

            (* Now get next Token and process it *)
            i := i + 1;
            Token := Exp[i]
        END (* WHILE *);

    (* If no error detected, pop and display any operands on the stack *)
    IF NOT Error THEN
        BEGIN
            WHILE NOT Empty(Stack) DO
                BEGIN
                    Pop (Stack, Token);
                    write (Token:2)
                END (* WHILE *);
            writeln
        END (* IF *)
    ELSE
        writeln ('*** Error in infix expression ***')
END (* ConvertToRPN *);
```

Figure 16.5   (cont.)

```
BEGIN (* main program *)
   writeln ('*** Enter ', EndMark, ' at end of each infix expression ***');
   writeln;
   REPEAT
     (* read infix expression *)

       write ('Enter infix expression: ');
       i := 0;
       REPEAT
          i := i + 1;
          read (Exp[i])
       UNTIL Exp[i] = EndMark;
       readln;

       (* convert to RPN *)

       writeln;
       write ('RPN Expression:          ');
       ConvertToRPN (Exp);
       writeln;
       write ('More (Y or N)?  ');
       readln (Response)
   UNTIL NOT (Response IN ['y', 'Y'])
END (* main program *).
```

Sample run:

```
*** Enter ; at end of each infix expression ***

Enter infix expression: A + B;

RPN Expression:         A B +

More (Y or N)?  Y
Enter infix expression: A - B - C;

RPN Expression:         A B - C -

More (Y or N)?  Y
Enter infix expression: A - (B - C);

RPN Expression:         A B C - -

More (Y or N)?  Y
Enter infix expression: ((A + 5)/B - 2)*C;

RPN Expression:         A 5 + B / 2 - C *

More (Y or N)?  N
```

Exercises

1. Suppose that $A = 7.0$, $B = 4.0$, $C = 3.0$, and $D = -2.0$. Evaluate the following RPN expressions:

   (a) $A\ B\ +\ C\ /\ D\ *$ **(b)** $A\ B\ C\ +\ /\ D\ *$
   (c) $A\ B\ C\ D\ +\ /\ *$ **(d)** $A\ B\ +\ C\ +\ D\ +$
   (e) $A\ B\ +\ C\ D\ +\ +$ **(f)** $A\ B\ C\ +\ +\ D\ +$
   (g) $A\ B\ C\ D\ +\ +\ +$ **(h)** $A\ B\ -\ C\ -\ D\ -$
   (i) $A\ B\ -\ C\ D\ -\ -$ **(j)** $A\ B\ C\ -\ -\ D\ -$
   (k) $A\ B\ C\ D\ -\ -\ -$

2. Convert the following infix expressions to RPN:

   (a) $A * B + C - D$ **(b)** $A + B/C + D$
   (c) $(A + B)/C + D$ **(d)** $A + B/(C + D)$
   (e) $(A + B)/(C + D)$ **(f)** $(A - B) * (C - (D + E))$
   (g) $(((A - B) - C) - D) - E$ **(h)** $A - (B - (C - (D - E)))$

3. Convert the following RPN expressions to infix notation:

   (a) $A\ B\ C\ +\ -\ D\ *$ **(b)** $A\ B\ +\ C\ D\ -\ *$
   (c) $A\ B\ C\ D\ +\ -\ *$ **(d)** $A\ B\ +\ C\ -\ D\ E\ *\ /$
   (e) $A\ B\ /\ C\ /\ D\ /$ **(f)** $A\ B\ /\ C\ D\ /\ /$
   (g) $A\ B\ C\ /\ D\ /\ /$ **(h)** $A\ B\ C\ D\ /\ /\ /$

4. The symbol $-$ cannot be used for the unary minus operation in postfix notation because ambiguous expressions result. For example, $5\ 3\ -\ -$ could be interpreted as either $5 - (-3) = 8$ or $-(5 - 3) = -2$. Suppose that $\sim$ is used for unary minus.

   (a) Evaluate the following RPN expressions if $A = 7$, $B = 5$, and $C = 3$:

        (i) $A \sim B\ C\ +\ -$ **(ii)** $A\ B \sim C\ +\ -$
       (iii) $A\ B\ C \sim +\ -$ **(iv)** $A\ B\ C\ +\ \sim\ -$
         (v) $A\ B\ C\ +\ -\ \sim$ **(vi)** $A\ B\ C\ -\ -\ \sim\ \sim\ \sim$

   (b) Convert the following infix expressions to RPN:

        (i) $A * (B + \sim C)$ **(ii)** $\sim(A + B/(C - D))$
       (iii) $(\sim A) * (\sim B)$ **(iv)** $\sim(A - (\sim B * (C + \sim D)))$

5. Convert the following boolean expressions to RPN:

   (a) P **and** Q **or** R
   (b) P **and** (Q **or not** R)
   (c) **not** (P **and** Q)
   (d) (P **or** Q) **and** (R **or** (S **and not** T))
   (e) ($A = B$) **or** ($C = D$)
   (f) (($A < 3$) **and** ($A > 9$)) **or not** ($A > 0$)
   (g) (($B * B - 4 * A * C$) $>= 0$) **and** (($A > 0$) **or** ($A < 0$))

6. An alternative to postfix notation is **prefix** notation, in which the symbol for each operation precedes the operands. For example, the infix expression 2 * 3 + 4 would be written in prefix notation as + * 2 3 4 and 2 * (3 + 4) would be written as * 2 + 3 4. Convert each of the infix expressions in Exercise 2 to prefix notation.

7. Suppose that $A = 7.0$, $B = 4.0$, $C = 3.0$, and $D = -2.0$. Evaluate the following prefix expressions (see Exercise 6):

(a) * A/ + B C D   (b) * / + A B C D
(c) − A − B − C D   (d) − − A B − C D
(e) − A − − B C D   (f) − − − A B C D
(g) + A * B − C D   (h) + + * A B − C D
(i) + * − A B C D

8. Convert the following prefix expressions to infix notation (see Exercise 6):

(a) * + A B − C D   (b) + + * A B − C D
(c) − − A B − C D   (d) − − A − B C D
(e) − − − A B C D   (f) / + * A B − C D E
(g) / + * A B C − D E   (h) / + A * B C − D E

9. Write a procedure to implement the algorithm for evaluating RPN expressions that involve only one-digit integers and the binary operators +, −, and *.

10. Write a program that reads an RPN expression and determines whether it is well formed, that is, whether each binary operator has two operands and the unary operator ~ has one (see Exercise 4).

11. Write a program that converts an integer expression involving the operators +, −, *, **div**, **mod**, and integer constants from infix notation to RPN.

12. For prefix notation as described in Exercise 6, write procedures to

(a) Convert infix expressions into prefix.
(b) Evaluate prefix expressions containing only one-digit integers and the binary operators +, −, and *.

16.3 Linked Stacks and Queues

One of the weaknesses of the array-based implementation of a stack is that because of the fixed array size, the stack may become full. A stack-full condition is not inherent in the stack data structure itself, but rather is an artifact of the implementation. In some applications of stacks, a stack-full condition may be a nuisance or may even be intolerable, and we would prefer an implementation in which the stack can grow to any size. Since a linked list is a dynamic structure and a stack is a special kind of list, it should be possible to implement stacks using linked lists. In fact, it is more natural to use a linked list than an array to store the stack elements, since only the first node in a linked list may be accessed directly.

To define such a ***linked stack***, we can use type definitions similar to those in the preceding chapter:

type
$\quad$ *DataType* = . . . ; (* type of data part of nodes *)
$\quad$ *StackPointer* = $\uparrow$*StackNode*;
$\quad$ *StackNode* = **record**
$\qquad\qquad\qquad$ *Data* : *DataType*;
$\qquad\qquad\qquad$ *Next* : *StackPointer*
$\qquad\qquad$ **end**;
$\quad$ *StackType* = *StackPointer*;

and declare a pointer to the top of the stack:

var
$\quad$ *TopPtr* : *StackType*;

A linked stack of integers, for example, might then be pictured as follows:

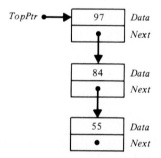

To push an item onto a linked stack, we simply insert it at the beginning of this linked list. A procedure to implement the push operation is therefore a simple modification of the procedure *Insert* described for unordered linked lists in Chapter 15:

procedure *Push* (**var** *TopPtr* : *StackType*; *Item* : *DataType*);

$\quad$ (* Procedure to push *Item* onto the stack pointed to by *TopPtr*.
$\quad$ The new pointer to the top of the stack is returned. *)

var
$\quad$ *TempPtr* : *StackType*; (* temporary pointer to a new node *)

begin (* *Push* *)
$\quad$ *new* (*TempPtr*);
$\quad$ *TempPtr*$\uparrow$.*Data* := *Item*;
$\quad$ *TempPtr*$\uparrow$.*Next* := *TopPtr*;
$\quad$ *TopPtr* := *TempPtr*
end (* *Push* *);

The following diagram illustrates the procedure reference

Push (TopPtr, 77)

for the preceding linked stack of integers:

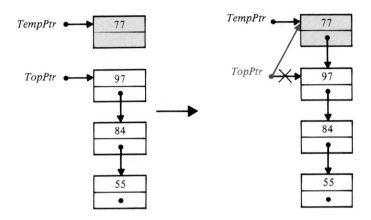

To pop an element from a linked stack, we first retrieve the data in the top node

Item := *TopPtr↑.Data*;

and then remove this node from the stack by first setting a temporary pointer to it

TempPtr := *TopPtr*;

so that it can be properly disposed of later, and then resetting *TopPtr* to point to the next node in the stack:

TopPtr := *TopPtr↑.Next*;

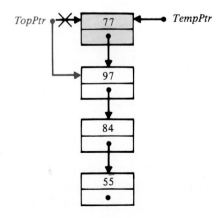

The procedure *dispose* can now be used to free this node for later allocation:

> *dispose* (*TempPtr*);

The following procedure uses these four statements to implement the pop operation:

> **procedure** *Pop* (**var** *TopPtr* : *StackType*; **var** *Item* : *DataType*);
>
> > (∗ Procedure to pop *Item* from the top of the linked stack
> > pointed to by *TopPtr*, assuming the stack is nonempty. ∗)
>
> **var**
> > *TempPtr* : *StackPointer*;
>
> **begin** (∗ *Pop* ∗)
> > **if** *Empty*(*TopPtr*) **then**
> > > *writeln* ('∗∗∗ Attempt to pop from an empty stack ∗∗∗')
> >
> > **else**
> > > **begin**
> > > > *TempPtr* := *TopPtr*;
> > > > *Item* := *TopPtr*↑.*Data*;
> > > > *TopPtr* := *TopPtr*↑.*Next*;
> > > > *dispose* (*TempPtr*)
> > >
> > > **end** (∗ **else** ∗)
> >
> **end** (∗ *Pop* ∗);

Here *Empty* is a function like the following that checks to see whether a linked stack is empty:

> **function** *Empty*(*TopPtr* : *StackType*) : *boolean*;
>
> > (∗ Returns true if stack is empty, false otherwise. ∗)
>
> **begin** (∗ *Empty* ∗)
> > *Empty* := (*TopPtr* = **nil**)
>
> **end** (∗ *Empty* ∗);

Once again, these procedures and function with the procedure

> **procedure** *Create* (**var** *TopPtr* : *StackType*);
> > (∗ Procedure to create an empty stack. ∗)
>
> **begin** (∗ *Create* ∗)
> > *TopPtr* := **nil**
>
> **end** (∗ *Create* ∗);

can be collected together in a package for processing linked stacks. The programs in Figures 16.2 and 16.5, which used the original array-based package, may also use this new one. No changes in the program are necessary except for the declarations needed for linked stacks and the substitution of this new linked stack–processing package for the array-based one.

Like a stack, a queue is a special kind of list and can be implemented as a linked list. In this case, we might use two pointers, *FrontPtr*, which points to the node at the front of the queue, and *RearPtr*, which points to the node at the rear. For example, a linked queue containing the integers 573, −29, and 616 in this order, might be pictured as

Inserting the number 127 produces the queue

A convenient structure for such linked queues is a record having two fields, *FrontPtr* and *RearPtr*:

```
type
   DataType = . . . ; (* type of data part of nodes *)
   PointerToQueueNode = ↑QueueNode;
   QueueNode = record
                    Data : DataType;
                    Next : PointerToQueueNode
               end;
   QueuePointers = record
                       FrontPtr,
                       RearPtr : PointerToQueueNode
                   end;
   QueueType = QueuePointers;
```

Procedures and functions to implement the basic queue operations using this linked implementation are left as exercises.

Exercises

1. Assuming the declarations for a linked queue given in the text, write a procedure or function to add an item to a linked queue and one to remove an item from a linked queue.

2. Using the declarations for a linked queue given in the text and the subprograms of Exercise 1, and writing a procedure or function to create an empty linked queue and one for checking to see whether a queue is empty, write a program for Exercise 8 of Section 16.1.

3. Write a program that reads a nonnegative integer value in base-10 and converts it to base-two using the repeated division scheme in Exercise 12 of Section 1.3. Use a linked stack to store the remainders as they are generated, and then pop these remainders when the division process terminates.

4. Proceed as in Exercise 3, but convert from base-10 to any of the bases 2, 3, . . . , 16.

5. Write a program that reads a character string, pushing each character onto a linked stack as it is read and simultaneously adding it to a linked queue. When the end of the string is encountered, use the basic stack and queue operations to determine whether the string is a palindrome, that is, whether it reads the same from left to right as from right to left.

6. A *priority queue* is a list of items, each of which has a certain priority, and these items are stored in such a way that those with the highest priority are near the front of the queue so that they will be removed from the queue before those of lower priority are. Write appropriate declarations for a linked priority queue and procedures and functions for the basic operations: Create an empty priority queue; check to see whether the priority queue is empty; add an item to the queue, placing it ahead of all items with lower priority and behind all items with equal or higher priority; and remove the front item of the priority queue. You may assume that each of the items is a record, one of whose fields is an integer that indicates its priority.

16.4 Evaluating Data Structures and Algorithms

Problem solving requires not only the design of an algorithm but also the selection of an appropriate data structure to organize the data of the problem. Both aspects of program development, algorithm design and data structure selection, are equally important. Indeed, Niklaus Wirth, the originator of the Pascal language, entitled one of his books

Algorithms + Data Structures = Programs

In this section we describe some of the factors that should be taken into consideration when selecting a data structure and show how the efficiency of algorithms to process the data can be measured.

Each of the data structures we have considered, both predefined and user-defined, consists of a collection of data items together with certain basic operations to be performed on these items. For a user-defined data structure, an *implementation* of that structure must be designed if it is to be used in a program. Such an implementation consists of one or more *storage structures* to store the items and *algorithms* to carry out the operations. Since these storage structures and algorithms must be implemented in some programming language, they must be designed to take advantage of the features of that language. This means that when possible, they should be based on the predefined data types, operations, functions, and procedures available in that language.

For example, in our first attempt to implement a stack, we used an array for the storage structure, with the top of the stack being the first position of the array. In this case, however, we observed that algorithms for the push and pop operations required moving the array elements each time one of these operations was performed. By storing the stack items differently in the array and using a variable *Top* to keep track of the top item, we found that the push and pop algorithms did not require shifting the array elements and thus were more efficient. Then we described yet another implementation of a stack, using a linked list in which the push algorithm, unlike the implementation using arrays, did not require checking for stack overflow. Thus we see the interdependence of storage structures and algorithms. The data structure must always be selected in conjunction with design of the algorithms, since these are inextricably linked.

When choosing an implementation of a data structure, it is important to evaluate the efficiency of the various alternatives. Efficiency is usually measured according to two criteria. The first is *space utilization*, which is the amount of memory required for the storage structure; the second is *time efficiency*, which is the amount of time required to execute the algorithms. Unfortunately, it is usually not possible to minimize both the space and time requirements for an implementation. The algorithms for those storage structures that require the least memory are often slower than are the algorithms for which the storage structures use more memory. For example, the push algorithm for a linked stack does not require checking to see whether the stack is full, whereas for an array-based implementation, it does. The linked stack does require more space, however, since in addition to the data items, a link must also be stored for each item. Thus the programmer is usually faced with a trade-off between space efficiency and time efficiency. When forced to choose which of these to optimize, the time efficiency of algorithms is usually considered to be the more important of the two. In this chapter, we concentrate on measuring time efficiency.

In addition to the space–time trade-off that often faces a programmer choosing among alternative implementations, there is also frequently a trade-off between efficiency and clarity. Ideally, algorithms should be efficient, easy to understand, and easily translated into programs. Again, these goals sometimes conflict, since the most efficient algorithms may not be the most understandable or the easiest to program. If a program is to be used only a few times or with only a small amount of input data, it is usually appropriate to select a less efficient but simpler algorithm over a more efficient but complicated one. The time saved in writing, debugging, and maintaining the program will compensate for the less efficient execution.

There are many factors that influence a program's execution time. The first of these is the size of the input. Obviously, the number of input items usually affects the time required to process them. For example, the time required to sort a list of items surely depends on how many there are. This means that the execution time T of an algorithm must be expressed as a function $T(n)$ of the size n of the input.

In many cases, T may depend not only on the size of the input but also on the arrangement of the input items. For example, it may take less time to sort a list of items that are nearly in order initially than to sort a list in which the items are in reverse order. Thus we might attempt to measure T in the **worst case** or in the **best case**, or we might attempt to compute the **average** value of T over all possible cases. The best-case performance of an algorithm is usually not very informative, and the average performance is often quite difficult to determine; thus $T(n)$ is commonly taken as a measure of the algorithm's performance in the worst case.

The kinds of instructions and the speed with which the machine can execute them also influence execution time. These factors, however, depend on the particular computer being used; consequently, we cannot expect to express the value of $T(n)$ meaningfully in real time units such as seconds. Instead, $T(n)$ will be the (approximate) number of instructions executed.

Another factor that influences computing time is the quality of the code generated by the compiler. The fact that not all compilers generate equally efficient code implies that $T(n)$ cannot be computed as the number of machine instructions executed. Thus, $T(n)$ is taken to be the number of times the instructions in the algorithm (or in the source program) are executed.

To illustrate how the computing time of an algorithm is measured, we first examine the two methods for searching a list described in Chapter 9, linear search and binary search. There we claimed that binary search is more efficient than linear search, and we now substantiate this claim.

Recall that a linear search is carried out by examining each element in a list sequentially, beginning with the first element, until either the desired item is found or the end of the list is reached. The algorithm given in Section 9.3 can be summarized as follows:

LINEAR SEARCH ALGORITHM

(∗ Algorithm to linear search a list of items $X[1], X[2], \ldots, X[n]$ for a specified *Item*. *Found* is set to true and *Location* to the position of *Item* if the search is successful; otherwise, *Found* is false. ∗)

(1) Set *Found* to false.
(2) Set *Location* equal to 1.
(3) While *Location* $\leq n$ and not *Found* do the following:
(4)   If *Item* $=$ $X[Location]$ then
(5)   Set *Found* to true.
(6)   Else
             Increment *Location* by 1.

(In this algorithm, the statements have been numbered for easy reference.)

The worst case for the linear search algorithm obviously occurs when *Item* is not in the list; thus, to measure the performance of this algorithm, we count the number of times each statement is executed in this case. Clearly, Statements 1 and 2 are executed only once. The boolean expression in Statement 3 is evaluated $n + 1$ times, once for each value of *Location* from 1 through $n + 1$. Statements 4 and 6 are executed n times, once on each pass through the while loop, and Statement 5 is never executed, since *Item* is not in the list. The following table summarizes these statement counts:

Statement	Count
1	1
2	1
3	$n + 1$
4	n
5	0
6	n
Total:	$3n + 3$

Thus the total number of statements expressed as a function of the size n of input is

$$T(n) = 3n + 3$$

For sufficiently large values of n ($n \geq 3$), we see that

$$T(n) \leq 4n$$

and so we say that $T(n)$ has **order of magnitude n** and denote this using the "big Oh" notation:

$$T(n) = O(n)$$

In general, the execution time $T(n)$ of an algorithm is said to have **order of magnitude g(n)**, denoted

$$T(n) = O(g(n))$$

if there exists some constant C so that

$$T(n) \leq C \cdot g(n)$$

for all sufficiently large values of n.

The binary search algorithm for ordered lists given in Section 9.3 can be summarized as follows:

BINARY SEARCH ALGORITHM

(∗ Algorithm to binary search a list $X[1]$, $X[2]$, . . . , $X[n]$ that has been ordered so the elements are in ascending order. *Found* is set to true and *Location* to the position of the *Item* being sought if the search is successful; otherwise, *Found* is set to false. ∗)

(1) Set *First* equal to 1.
(2) Set *Last* equal to n.
(3) Set *Found* equal to false.

(4) While *First* $\le$ *Last* and not *Found*, do the following:
(5)   a. Calculate *Location* $=$ (*First* $+$ *Last*) **div** 2.
(6)   b. If *Item* $<$ *X*[*Location*] then
(7)   Set *Last* equal to *Location* $-$ 1.
(8)   Else if *Item* $>$ *X*[*Location*] then
(9)   Set *First* equal to *Location* $+$ 1.
(10)   Else
                 Set *Found* equal to true.

In this algorithm, it is clear that Statements 1, 2, and 3 are executed exactly once, and to determine the worst-case performance, we must determine the number of times the loop composed of Statements 4 through 10 is executed when *Item* is not in the list. This is not as easy to determine as it is for linear search, and so we first consider some particular values of n.

First, consider a list containing only one element $X[1]$, and suppose that *Item* is greater than $X[1]$. After Statements 1, 2, and 3 are executed, the boolean expression in Statement 4 is evaluated and found to be true (*First* $=$ 1, *Last* $=$ 1, and *Found* $=$ false). Thus the body of the while loop is executed; Statement 5 calculates the value 1 for *Location*, and Statements 8 and 9 set *First* equal to 2. The boolean expression in Statement 4 is then evaluated again and found to be false (*First* $=$ 2, *Last* $=$ 1), causing repetition to terminate. Thus we see that for $n = 1$, one pass through the loop is made, and one additional evaluation of the boolean expression is made to terminate repetition.

Next, consider a list of size $n = 2$, $X[1]$, $X[2]$, and suppose that *Item* is greater than both elements of this list. A first pass through the loop sets *First* equal to 2 so that the sublist yet to be searched is reduced from two elements to one, $X[2]$. As we have just seen, a list of size 1 requires one pass through the loop and one more evaluation of the boolean expression in Statement 4 to terminate repetition. Thus, for $n = 2$, the loop is executed twice and Statement 4 one additional time.

Now consider a list of size $n = 4$, $X[1]$, $X[2]$, $X[3]$, $X[4]$, with *Item* greater than each list element. A first pass through the loop reduces the list to one of size 2, $X[3]$, $X[4]$. From what we have just determined for a list of two elements, we see that for a list of size 4, the loop is executed three times, and the boolean expression in Statement 4 is evaluated one additional time.

Continuing this analysis with values 8, 16, . . . for n, we obtain the following table:

n	Number of Passes Through the Loop
$1 = 2^0$	1
$2 = 2^1$	2
$4 = 2^2$	3
$8 = 2^3$	4
.	.
.	.
.	.
2^k	$k + 1$

Thus we see that a list of size 2^k requires $k + 1 = \log_2(2^k) + 1$ passes through the loop. In general, a list of size n requires no more than $\log_2 n + 1$ passes through the loop.

Since only Statements 5, 8, and 9 are executed in the worst case and Statement 4 is executed one more time than the number of loop repetitions, we obtain the following (approximate) counts for executions of the statements in the binary search algorithm:

Statement	Count
1	1
2	1
3	1
4	$\log_2 n + 2$
5	$\log_2 n + 1$
6	0
7	0
8	$\log_2 n + 1$
9	$\log_2 n + 1$
10	0
Total:	$4\log_2 n + 8$

Thus we see that in the worst case, the computing time of binary search is $T(n) = 4\log_2 n + 8$, and since

$$T(n) \leq 5\log_2 n$$

for large n ($n \geq 2^8$), we see that $T(n)$ has order of magnitude $\log_2 n$,

$$T(n) = O(\log_2 n)$$

In summary, we have the following measures of worst-case performance of the linear search and binary search algorithms (which also measure the average case performance):

Linear search: $O(n)$
Binary search: $O(\log_2 n)$

Since the function $\log_2 n$ grows less rapidly than n as the number n of inputs increases, it follows that binary search is more efficient than linear search for large lists. For small lists, however, linear search may, and in fact does, outperform binary search. Empirical studies indicate that linear search is more efficient than binary search for lists of up to 20 elements. Moreover, binary search can be used only for ordered lists; consequently, it may be necessary to sort the list before it can be used. We are thus led to consider the efficiency of sorting algorithms.

SIMPLE SELECTION SORT ALGORITHM

(* Algorithm for sorting into ascending order a list of n elements stored in an array $X[1], X[2], \ldots, X[n]$. *)

(1) For $i = 1$ to $n - 1$ do the following:

(* On the ith pass, first find the smallest element in the sublist $X[i], \ldots, X[n]$. *)

(2) a. Set *SmallPos* equal to i.
(3) b. Set *Smallest* equal to $X[SmallPos]$.

(4)   c. For $j = i + 1$ to n do the following:
(5)   If $X[j] <$ *Smallest* then (* smaller element found *)
(6)   i. Set *SmallPos* equal to j.
(7)   ii. Set *Smallest* equal to $X[SmallPos]$.
            (* Now interchange this smallest element with the element at the beginning of this sublist. *)
(8)   d. Set $X[SmallPos]$ equal to $X[i]$.
(9)   e. Set $X[i]$ equal to *Smallest*.

Statement 1 is executed n times (for i ranging from 1 through the value n, which causes termination); and Statements 2, 3, 8, and 9 each are executed $n - 1$ times, once on each pass through the outer loop. On the first pass through this loop with $i = 1$, Statement 4 is executed n times; Statement 5 is executed $n - 1$ times, and assuming a worst case when the items are in descending order, so are Statements 6 and 7. On the second pass with $i = 2$, Statement 4 is executed $n - 1$ times and Statements 5, 6, and 7 $n - 2$ times, and so on. Thus Statement 4 is executed a total of $n + (n - 1) + \cdots + 2$ times, and Statements 5, 6, and 7 each are executed a total of $(n - 1) + (n - 2) + \cdots + 1$ times. These sums are equal to $n(n + 1)/2 - 1$ and $n(n - 1)/2$, respectively; thus the total computing time is given by

$$T(n) = n + 4(n - 1) + \frac{n(n + 1)}{2} - 1 + 3\left(\frac{n(n - 1)}{2}\right)$$

which simplifies to

$$T(n) = 2n^2 + 4n - 5$$

Since $n \leq n^2$ for all $n \geq 0$, we see that

$$2n^2 + 4n - 5 \leq 2n^2 + 4n^2 = 6n^2$$

and hence that

$$T(n) \leq 6n^2 \text{ for all } n \geq 0$$

Thus,

$$T(n) = O(n^2)$$

Besides $O(\log_2 n)$, $O(n)$, and $O(n^2)$, other computing times that frequently arise in algorithm analysis are $O(\log_2(\log_2 n))$, $O(n \cdot \log_2 n)$, $O(n^3)$, and $O(2^n)$. The following table displays values of these functions for several values of n:

$\log_2(\log_2 n)$	$\log_2 n$	n	$n \cdot \log_2 n$	n^2	n^3	2^n
—	0	1	0	1	1	2
0	1	2	2	4	8	4
1	2	4	8	16	64	16
1.58	3	8	24	64	512	256
2	4	16	64	256	4096	65536
2.32	5	32	160	1024	32768	2147483648
2.6	6	64	384	4096	2.6×10^5	1.85×10^{19}
3	8	256	4.48×10^2	6.55×10^4	1.68×10^7	1.16×10^{77}
3.32	10	1024	1.02×10^4	1.05×10^6	1.07×10^9	1.8×10^{308}
4.32	20	1048576	2.1×10^7	1.1×10^{12}	1.1×10^{18}	6.0×10^{315652}

It should be clear from this table that algorithms whose computing times are exponential are practical only for solving problems in which the number of inputs is small. To demonstrate this, suppose that each instruction in some algorithm can be executed in 1 microsecond (0.000001 second). The following table shows the time required for each of the common computing times with $n = 256$ inputs:

Function	Time
$\log_2(\log_2 n)$	3 microseconds
$\log_2 n$	8 microseconds
n	0.25 millisecond (0.001 second)
$n \cdot \log_2 n$	2 milliseconds
n^2	65 milliseconds
n^3	17 seconds
2^n	3.7×10^{61} centuries

Exercises

1. Which of the orders of magnitude given in this section is the best O-notation to describe the following computing times?

   (a) $T(n) = n^3 + 100n \cdot \log_2 n + 5000$ **(b)** $T(n) = 2^n + n^{99} + 7$

   (c) $T(n) = \dfrac{n^2 - 1}{n + 1} + 8\log_2 n$ **(d)** $T(n) = 1 + 2 + 4 + \cdots + 2^{n-1}$

2. What would it mean to say that an algorithm has computing time $T(n) = O(1)$? Give an example of such an algorithm.

3. Using one of the "big Oh" computing times given in the text, give the worst-case computing time for each of the following program segments as a function of n.

   (a) (* Calculate mean *)
   ```
   Sum := 0;
   for i := 1 to n do
      begin
         readln (x);
         Sum := Sum + x
      end (* for *);
   Mean := Sum / n;
   ```

   (b) (* Matrix addition *)
   ```
   for i := 1 to n do
      for j := 1 to n do
         A[i,j] := B[i,j] + C[i,j];
   ```

   (c) (* Matrix multiplication *)
   ```
   for i := 1 to n do
      for j := 1 to n do
         begin
            A[i,j] := 0;
            for k := 1 to n do
               A[i,j] := A[i,j] + B[i,k] * C[k,j]
         end (* for *)
   ```

(d) (* Bubble sort *)
NumPairs := *n* − 1;
repeat
  Sorted := *true*;
  for *i* := 1 **to** *NumPairs* **do**
    if $X[i] > X[i + 1]$ **then**
      begin
        Temp := $X[i]$;
        $X[i] := X[i + 1]$;
        $X[i + 1]$:= *Temp*;
        Sorted := *false*
      end (* **if** *);
  NumPairs := *NumPairs* − 1
until *Sorted*;

(e) **while** $n \geq 1$ **do**
  n := *n* **div** 2;

(f) *x* := 1;
  for *i* := 1 **to** *n* − 1 **do**
    begin
      for *j* := 1 **to** *x* **do**
        writeln (*j*);
      x := 2 ∗ *x*
    end (* **for** *);

16.5 Quicksort

On several occasions we have considered the important problem of sorting a list of items. In several examples we used the selection sort algorithm, and in the preceding section we showed that it has worst-case computing time $O(n^2)$ and noted that this is also its average computing time. The **quicksort** method of sorting described in this section is more efficient. Although its worst-case computing time is $O(n^2)$, its average computing time is $O(n \cdot \log_2 n)$. It is in fact one of the fastest methods of sorting and is most often implemented by a recursive algorithm. In our description of this method, we assume, for the sake of simplicity, that the items being sorted are simple items. If they are records, sorting is carried out using a key field in the records.

    The basic idea of quicksort for sorting a list of elements into ascending order is to select one element from the list and then to rearrange the list so that this element is in its proper position; that is, all list elements that precede it are less than this item, and all those that follow it are greater than the item. This divides the original list into two sublists, each of which may then be sorted independently in the *same* way. As might be expected, this divide-and-conquer strategy leads naturally to a recursive algorithm for quicksort.

    To illustrate this splitting of a list into two sublists, consider the following list of integers:

50, 30, 20, 80, 90, 70, 95, 85, 10, 15, 75, 25

If we select the first number as the item to be properly positioned, we must rearrange the list so that 30, 20, 10, 15, and 25 are placed before 50, and 80, 90, 70, 95, 85, and 75 are placed after it. To carry out this rearrangement, we search from the right end of the list for an element less than 50 and from the left end for an item greater than 50.

This locates the two numbers 25 and 80, which we now interchange to obtain

We then resume the search from the right for a number less than 50 and from the left for a number greater than 50:

This locates the numbers 15 and 90, which are then interchanged:

A continuation of the searches locates 10 and 70:

Interchanging these gives

When we resume our search from the right for a number less than 50, we locate the value 10, which was found on the previous left-to-right search. This signals the end of the two searches, and we interchange 50 and 10, thus giving

10 , 30 , 20 , 25 , 15 , 50 , 95 , 85 , 70 , 90 , 75 , 80

The two underlined sublists now have the required properties: All elements in the first sublist are less than 50, and all those in the right sublist are greater than 50. Consequently, 50 has been properly positioned.

Both the sublist

$$10, 30, 20, 25, 15$$

consisting of the numbers in positions 1 through 5 and the sublist

$$95, 85, 70, 90, 75, 80$$

consisting of numbers in positions 7 through 12 can now be sorted independently. For this, a procedure is needed to split a list of items in the array positions given by two parameters *Low* and *High*, denoting the beginning and end positions of the sublist, respectively. If we assume declarations of the form

```
const
    ListLimit = . . . ; (* limit on length of list *)

type
    DataType = . . . ; (* type of elements in the list *)
    List = array[1..ListLimit] of DataType;
```

then the following procedure carries out the desired splitting of the (sub)list *X*[*Low*], . . . , *X*[*High*].

```
procedure Split (var X : List; Low, High : integer; var Mid : integer);

    (* Procedure to rearrange X[Low], . . . , X[High] so that one item is
       properly positioned; it returns the rearranged list and the final
       position Mid of that item. *)

    var
        Left,                   (* index for searching from the left *)
        Right : integer;        (* index for searching from the right *)
        TempItem : DataType;    (* temporary item used for interchanging *)

    begin (* Split *)
        (* Initialize indices for left and right searches *)
        Left := Low;
        Right := High;

        (* Carry out the searches *)
        while Left < Right do    (* While searches haven't met *)
            begin
                (* Search from the right *)
                while X[Right] > X[Low] do
                    Right := Right − 1;
```

```
                    (* Search from the left *)
                    while (Left < Right) and (X[Left] <= X[Low]) do
                        Left := Left + 1;

                    (* Interchange items if searches have not met *)
                    if Left < Right then
                        begin
                            TempItem := X[Left];
                            X[Left] := X[Right];
                            X[Right] := TempItem
                        end (* if *)
                end (* while *);

            (* End of searches; place selected item in proper position *)
            Mid := Right;
            TempItem := X[Mid];
            X[Mid] := X[Low];
            X[Low] := TempItem
        end (* Split *);
```

A recursive procedure to sort a list is now easy to write:

```
        procedure QuickSort (var X : List; Low, High : integer);

        (* Procedure to quicksort X[Low], . . . , X[High]. *)

        var
            Mid : integer;   (* final position of selected item *)

        begin (* QuickSort *)
(*1*)       if Low < High then   (* list has more than one item *)
                begin
(*2*)               Split (X, Low, High, Mid);   (* split into two sublists *)
(*3*)               QuickSort (X, Low, Mid - 1); (* sort first sublist *)
(*4*)               QuickSort (X, Mid + 1, High) (* sort second sublist *)
                end (* if *)
(*5*)       end (* QuickSort *);
```

(Some of the statements have been numbered for later reference.) This procedure is called with a statement of the form

        QuickSort (Item, 1, NumItems)

where *NumItems* is the number of elements in the given list *Item* to be sorted.

To demonstrate this procedure, suppose that the following list of integers is to be sorted:

$$8, 2, 13, 5, 14, 3, 7$$

We can use treelike diagrams to display the action of *QuickSort*. In each tree, a circle indicates an item placed in its proper position, with a shaded circle indicating the item being positioned at this step. Rectangles represent sublists to be sorted, and a shaded rectangle indicates the next sublist to be sorted. In the list of comments, a label such as II.3 indicates the level (II) in the tree of the sublist being processed and the statement (3) in *QuickSort* currently being executed.

Tree	Comments

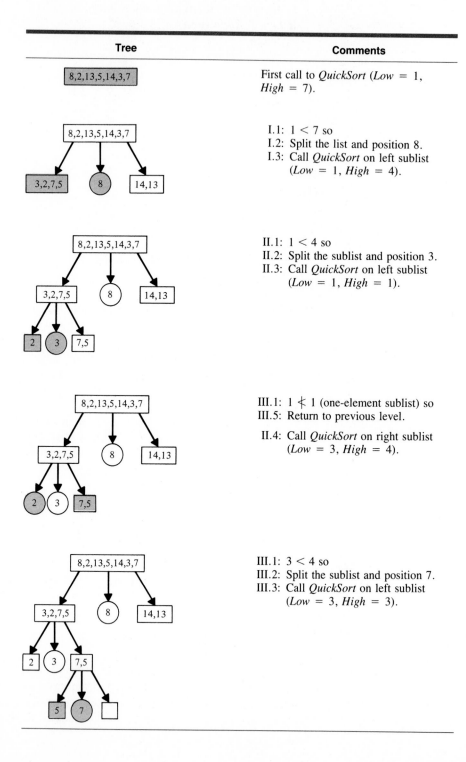

First call to *QuickSort* (*Low* = 1, *High* = 7).

I.1: 1 < 7 so
I.2: Split the list and position 8.
I.3: Call *QuickSort* on left sublist
(*Low* = 1, *High* = 4).

II.1: 1 < 4 so
II.2: Split the sublist and position 3.
II.3: Call *QuickSort* on left sublist
(*Low* = 1, *High* = 1).

III.1: 1 ≮ 1 (one-element sublist) so
III.5: Return to previous level.

II.4: Call *QuickSort* on right sublist
(*Low* = 3, *High* = 4).

III.1: 3 < 4 so
III.2: Split the sublist and position 7.
III.3: Call *QuickSort* on left sublist
(*Low* = 3, *High* = 3).

Tree	Comments
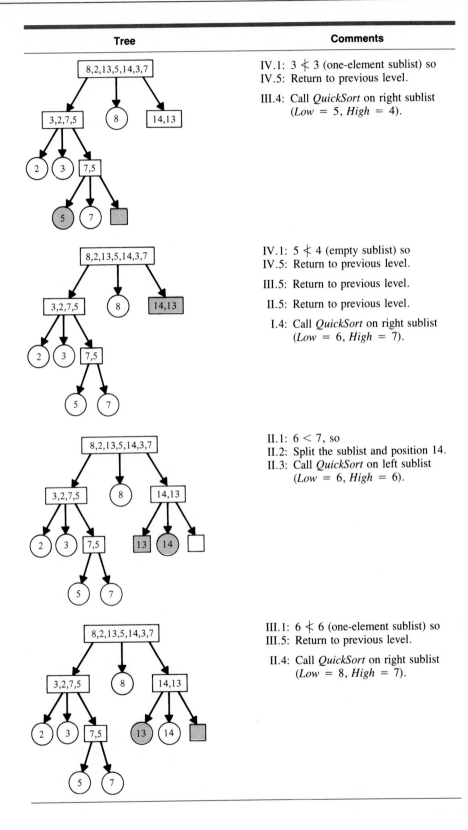	IV.1: $3 \not< 3$ (one-element sublist) so
	IV.5: Return to previous level.
	III.4: Call *QuickSort* on right sublist ($Low = 5$, $High = 4$).
	IV.1: $5 \not< 4$ (empty sublist) so
	IV.5: Return to previous level.
	III.5: Return to previous level.
	II.5: Return to previous level.
	I.4: Call *QuickSort* on right sublist ($Low = 6$, $High = 7$).
	II.1: $6 < 7$, so
	II.2: Split the sublist and position 14.
	II.3: Call *QuickSort* on left sublist ($Low = 6$, $High = 6$).
	III.1: $6 \not< 6$ (one-element sublist) so
	III.5: Return to previous level.
	II.4: Call *QuickSort* on right sublist ($Low = 8$, $High = 7$).

Tree	Comments
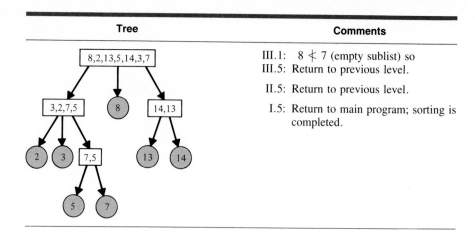	III.1: 8 ⊀ 7 (empty sublist) so III.5: Return to previous level. II.5: Return to previous level. I.5: Return to main program; sorting is completed.

The program in Figure 16.6 reads a list of numbers, calls the procedures *Split* and *QuickSort* to sort the numbers into ascending order, and then displays the sorted list.

```
PROGRAM SortWithQuickSort (input, output);

(*****************************************************************

   Program to read and count a list of items, sort them using the
   quicksort algorithm, and then display the sorted list.

*****************************************************************)

CONST
  ListLimit = 100;       (* upper limit on length of list *)
  EndDataFlag = -9999;   (* signals end of data *)

TYPE
  DataType = integer;
  List = ARRAY[1..ListLimit] OF DataType;

VAR
  Item : List;           (* list of items to be sorted *)
  Temp : DataType;       (* temporary item read *)
  NumItems,              (* number of items *)
  i : integer;           (* index *)

PROCEDURE Split (VAR X : List; Low, High : integer; VAR Mid : integer);

   (*************************************************************

      Procedure to rearrange X[Low], ..., X[High] so that one item
      (originally in position Low) is properly positioned; it returns
      rearranged list and the final position Mid of that item.

   *************************************************************)
```

Figure 16.6

Figure 16.6 (cont.)

```
VAR
    Left,                    (* index for searching from the left *)
    Right : integer;         (* index for searching from the right *)
    TempItem : DataType;     (* temporary item used for interchanging *)

BEGIN (* Split *)

    (* Initialize indices for left and right searches *)

    Left := Low;
    Right := High;

    (* Continue searches until they meet *)

    WHILE Left < Right DO
        BEGIN

            (* search from the right *)

            WHILE X[Right] > X[Low] DO
                Right := Right - 1;

             (* search from the left *)

            WHILE (Left < Right) AND (X[Left] <= X[Low]) DO
                Left := Left + 1;

            (* interchange items if searches haven't met *)

            IF Left < Right THEN
                BEGIN
                    TempItem := X[Left];
                    X[Left] := X[Right];
                    X[Right] := TempItem
                END (* IF *)
        END (* WHILE *);

    (* End of search; place selected item in proper position *)

    Mid := Right;
    TempItem := X[Mid];
    X[Mid] := X[Low];
    X[Low] := TempItem
END (* Split *);

PROCEDURE QuickSort (VAR X : List; Low, High : integer);

    (*************************************************************

            Procedure to QuickSort X[Low], ..., X[High]

    *************************************************************)

    VAR
        Mid : integer;   (* final position of selected item *)
```

Figure 16.6 (cont.)

```
    BEGIN (* QuickSort *)
        IF Low < High THEN                    (* list has more than one item *)
            BEGIN
                Split (X, Low, High, Mid);    (* split into two sublists *)
                QuickSort (X, Low, Mid - 1);  (* sort first sublist *)
                QuickSort (X, Mid + 1, High)  (* sort second sublist *)
            END (* IF *)
    END (* QuickSort *);

BEGIN (* main program *)
    NumItems := 0;
    writeln ('Enter the items (', EndDataFlag:1,
             ' to signal the end of data).');
    read (Temp);
    WHILE (Temp <> EndDataFlag) AND (NumItems < ListLimit) DO
        BEGIN
            NumItems := NumItems + 1;
            Item[NumItems] := Temp;
            read (Temp)
        END (* WHILE *);
    QuickSort (Item, 1, NumItems);
    writeln ('Sorted list:');
    FOR i := 1 TO NumItems DO
        writeln (Item[i])
END (* main program *).
```

```
Sample run:

Enter the items (-9999 to signal the end of data).
54 67 34 99 27 5 62 45 83
-9999
Sorted list:
        5
       27
       34
       45
       54
       62
       67
       83
       99
```

The worst-case computing time for quicksort is $O(n^2)$, and the average time is $O(n \cdot \log_2 n)$. Although a rigorous derivation of these computing times is quite difficult, it is possible to see intuitively why these are correct, by using tree diagrams like those we have used to describe the operation of quicksort. At each level of the tree, the split procedure is applied to several sublists whose total size is at most n; hence, each of the statements in the while loop of procedure *Split* is executed at most n times on each level. The computing time for quicksort is thus $O(n \cdot$ (number of levels in the tree)). In the worst case, one of the sublists produced by *Split* is always empty; consequently, the tree has n levels. It follows that quicksort has computing time $O(n^2)$ in this case. If, however, the two sublists produced by *Split* are of approximately equal size, the number of levels will be approximately $\log_2 n$, giving $O(n \cdot \log_2 n)$ as the computing time for quicksort.

Exercises

1. Draw a sequence of trees like those in the text to illustrate the actions of *Split* and *QuickSort* while sorting the following lists:

(a) 5, 1, 6, 4, 3, 2   (b) 1, 2, 3, 6, 5, 4
(c) 6, 5, 4, 3, 2, 1   (d) 1, 2, 3, 4, 5, 6

2. One of the lists in Exercise 1 shows why the condition *Left* < *Right* is needed to control the search from the left in procedure *Split*. Which is it? What would happen if this condition were omitted?

3. Modify the procedures *Split* and *QuickSort* to sort a list of records so that the values in a key field are in ascending order. Use these procedures in a program to read the student names, numbers, and addresses from *StudentFile* and then quicksort them so that the students' last names are in alphabetical order. (See Appendix E for a description of *StudentFile*.)

4. The procedure *QuickSort* always sorts the left sublist before the right. Its performance will improve slightly if the shorter of the two sublists is the first to be sorted. Modify *QuickSort* to sort the shorter sublist first.

5. Another improvement of the quicksort method is to use some other sorting algorithm to sort small sublists. For example, insertion sort is usually better than quicksort when the list has fewer than 20 items. Modify the quicksort scheme to use insertion sort (see Exercise 16 of Section 9.3) if the sublist has fewer than *LBound* items for some constant *LBound*, and otherwise, use quicksort.

6. The procedure *Split* always selects the first element of the sublist to position. Another common practice is to use the "median-of-three" rule in which the median of the three numbers $X[Low]$, $X[Middle]$, and $X[High]$ is selected, where *Middle* = (*Low* + *High*) **div** 2. (The median of three numbers a, b, and c, arranged in ascending order, is the middle number b.) Modify *Split* to use this median-of-three rule.

16.6 Mergesort

All of the sorting algorithms we have considered thus far are ***internal*** sorting schemes; that is, the entire collection of items to be sorted must be stored in main memory. In many problems, however, the data sets to be sorted are too large to store in main memory and so must be stored in external memory. To sort such collections of data, an ***external*** sorting algorithm is required. One popular and efficient external sorting method is the **mergesort** technique, a variation of which, called **natural mergesort**, is examined in this section.

As the name mergesort suggests, the basic operation in this sorting scheme is merging data files. The merge operation combines two files that have previously been sorted so that the resulting file is also sorted. To illustrate, suppose that *File1* has been sorted and contains the integers

$$File1 \quad : \quad 2 \quad 4 \quad 5 \quad 7 \quad 9 \quad 15 \quad 16 \quad 20$$

and *File2* contains

$$File2 \quad : \quad 1 \quad 6 \quad 8 \quad 10 \quad 12$$

To merge these files to produce *File3*, we read one element from each file, say X from *File1* and Y from *File2*.

$$File1 \quad : \quad 2 \quad 4 \quad 5 \quad 7 \quad 9 \quad 15 \quad 16 \quad 20$$
$$\uparrow$$
$$X$$
$$File2 \quad : \quad 1 \quad 6 \quad 8 \quad 10 \quad 12$$
$$\uparrow$$
$$Y$$

We write the smaller of these values, in this case Y, into *File3*:

$$File3 \quad : \quad 1$$

and then read another value for Y from *File2*:

$$File2 \quad : \quad 2 \quad 4 \quad 5 \quad 7 \quad 9 \quad 15 \quad 16 \quad 20$$
$$\uparrow$$
$$X$$
$$File2 \quad : \quad 1 \quad 6 \quad 8 \quad 10 \quad 12$$
$$\uparrow$$
$$Y$$

Now X is smaller than Y, and so it is written to *File3*, and a new value for X is read from *File1*:

$$File1 \quad : \quad 2 \quad 4 \quad 5 \quad 7 \quad 9 \quad 15 \quad 16 \quad 20$$
$$\uparrow$$
$$X$$
$$File2 \quad : \quad 1 \quad 6 \quad 8 \quad 10 \quad 12$$
$$\uparrow$$
$$Y$$
$$File3 \quad : \quad 1 \quad 2$$

Again X is less than Y, and so X is written to *File3*, and a new X value is read from *File1*:

File1 : 2 4 5 7 9 15 16 20

                  ↑

                  X

File2 : 1 6 8 10 12

            ↑

            Y

File3 : 1 2 4

Continuing in this manner, we eventually reach the value 15 for X and the value 12 for Y:

File1 : 2 4 5 7 9 15 16 20

                         ↑

                         X

File2 : 1 6 8 10 12

                      ↑

                      Y

File3 : 1 2 4 5 6 7 8 9 10

Because Y is smaller than X, we write Y to *File3*:

File3 : 1 2 4 5 6 7 8 9 10 12

Because the end of *File2* has been reached, we simply copy the remaining values in *File1* to *File3* to obtain the final sorted file *File3*:

File3 : 1 2 4 5 6 7 8 9 10 12 15 16 20

The general algorithm to merge two sorted files *File1* and *File2* is as follows:

MERGE ALGORITHM

1. Open *File1* and *File2* for input, *File3* for output.
2. Read the first element X from *File1* and the first element Y from *File2*.
3. Repeat the following until the end of either *File1* or *File2* is reached:
   If $X < Y$, then
       (i) Write X to *File3*.
       (ii) Read a new X value from *File1*.
   Otherwise
       (i) Write Y to *File3*.
       (ii) Read a new Y value from *File2*.
4. If the end of *File1* was encountered, copy any remaining elements from *File2* into *File3*. If the end of *File2* was encountered, copy the rest of *File1* into *File3*.

In this algorithm, we have assumed that the file components are simple components. If the files contain records that are sorted on the basis of some key field, the key field of X is compared with the key field of Y in Step 3.

To see how the merge operation is used in sorting a file, consider the following file F containing fifteen integers:

F : 75 55 15 20 80 30 35 10 70 40 50 25 45 60 65

Notice that several segments of F contain elements that are already in order:

F : | 75 | 55 | 15 20 80 | 30 35 | 10 70 | 40 50 | 25 45 60 65 |

These segments, enclosed by the vertical bars, are called *subfiles* or *runs* in F and subdivide F in a natural way.

We begin by reading these subfiles of F and alternately writing them to two other files, $F1$ and $F2$:

$F1$: | 75 | 15 20 80 | 10 70 | 25 45 60 65 |
$F2$: | 55 | 30 35 | 40 50 |

and then identifying the sorted subfiles in $F1$ and $F2$.

$F1$: | 75 | 15 20 80 | 10 70 | 25 45 60 65 |
$F2$: | 55 | 30 35 40 50 |

Note that although the subfiles of $F1$ are the same as those copied from F, two of the original subfiles written into $F2$ have combined to form a larger subfile.

We now merge the first subfile of $F1$ with the first subfile of $F2$, storing the elements back in F.

F : | 55 75 |

Next, the second subfile of $F1$ is merged with the second subfile of $F2$ and written to F.

F : | 55 75 | 15 20 30 35 40 50 80 |

Corresponding subfiles are merged until the end of either or both of the files $F1$ and $F2$ is reached. If either file still contains subfiles, they are simply copied into F. Thus in our example, because the end of $F2$ has been reached, the remaining subfiles of $F1$ are copied back into F.

F : | 55 75 | 15 20 30 35 40 50 80 | 10 70 | 25 45 60 65 |

Now file F is again split into files $F1$ and $F2$, by copying its subfiles alternately into $F1$ and $F2$.

$F1$: | 55 75 | 10 70 |
$F2$: | 15 20 30 35 40 50 80 | 25 45 60 65 |

Identifying the sorted subfiles in each of these files, we see that for this splitting, none of the original subfiles written into either $F1$ or $F2$ combine to form larger ones. Once again we merge corresponding subfiles of $F1$ and $F2$ back into F.

$F :$ | 15 20 30 35 40 50 55 75 80 | 10 25 45 60 65 70 |

When we now split F into $F1$ and $F2$, each of the files $F1$ and $F2$ contains a single sorted subfile, and each is therefore completely sorted.

$F1 :$ | 15 20 30 35 40 50 55 75 80 |
$F2 :$ | 10 25 45 60 65 70 |

Thus when we merge $F1$ and $F2$ back into F, F will also contain only one sorted subfile and hence will be sorted.

$F :$ | 10 15 20 25 30 35 40 45 50 55 60 65 70 75 80 |

From this example we see that the mergesort method has two steps: (1) splitting file F into two other files, $F1$ and $F2$, and (2) merging corresponding subfiles in these two files. These steps are repeated until each of the smaller files contains a single sorted subfile, and when these are merged, the resulting file is completely sorted.

The splitting operation is carried out by the following algorithm:

SPLITTING ALGORITHM

1. Open file F for input and files $F1$ and $F2$ for output.
2. While the end of F has not been reached, do the following:
   a. Copy a sorted subfile of F into $F1$ as follows: Repeatedly read an element of F and write it into $F1$ until the next element in F is smaller than this copied item or the end of F is reached.
   b. If the end of F has not been reached, copy the next sorted subfile of F into $F2$ in a similar manner.

In this algorithm we have assumed that the elements of file F are simple. If they are records, the key field on which the sorting is based is used when comparing file elements.

The following algorithm implements the merge operation illustrated in the example.

ALGORITHM TO MERGE SORTED SUBFILES

1. Open files $F1$ and $F2$ for input; open F for output.
2. While neither the end of $F1$ nor the end of $F2$ has been reached, do the following:
   a. While the end of no subfile in $F1$ or $F2$ has been reached, do the following:
      If the next element in $F1$ is less than the next element in $F2$, then copy the next element from $F1$ into F; otherwise, copy the next element from $F2$ into F.

      b. If the end of a subfile in *F1* has been reached, copy the rest of the corresponding subfile in *F2* to *F*; otherwise, copy the rest of the corresponding subfile in *F1* to *F*.

3. Copy any remaining subfiles in *F1* or *F2* to *F*.

In this algorithm, the copying of a subfile from *F1* to *F* can be done by using the technique described in the splitting algorithm if the roles of *F* and *F1* are interchanged. A similar modification can be used to copy a subfile from *F2* to *F*.

The program in Figure 16.7 implements the mergesort algorithm and has the structure shown in the following diagram:

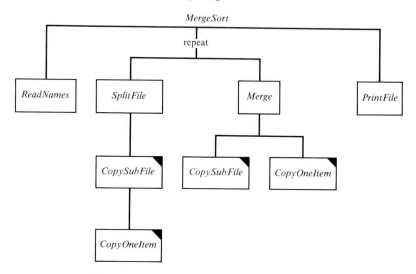

(Recall that a shaded corner in a box indicates a procedure that is shared by two or more program units.) This program reads names from *NameFile*, displaying them in their original order, and copies them into file *F*, using the procedure *ReadNames*. It then calls the procedures *SplitFile* and *Merge* to sort the file of names, using the mergesort algorithm, and finally calls *PrintFile* to display the contents of the sorted file. *SplitFile* and *Merge* use the procedures *CopyOneItem* and *CopySubFile* to copy one item or a sorted subfile, respectively, from one file to another.

```
PROGRAM MergeSort (input, output, NameFile);

(*****************************************************************

   Program to sort the external file NameFile using the natural
   mergesort algorithm.

*****************************************************************)

CONST
   MaxString = 30;            (* upper limit on lengths of strings *)
```

Figure 16.7

Figure 16.7 (cont.)

```
TYPE
   String = PACKED ARRAY[1..MaxString] OF char;
   FileType = String;
   DataFile = FILE OF FileType;

VAR
   NumSubFiles : integer;     (* number of subfiles merged at each stage *)
   F1, F2, F,                 (* files to be used in mergesort *)
   NameFile : DataFile;       (* external file to be sorted *)

PROCEDURE ReadNames (VAR F, NameFile : DataFile);

   (******************************************************************

      Procedure to read the names from NameFile and copy them
      to file F.

    ******************************************************************)

   BEGIN (* ReadNames *)
      reset (NameFile);
      rewrite (F);
      writeln ('Contents of original file:');
      writeln;
      WHILE NOT eof(NameFile) DO
         BEGIN
            read (NameFile, F^);
            writeln (F^);
            put (F)
         END (* WHILE *);
      writeln
   END (* ReadNames *);

PROCEDURE CopyOneItem (VAR FileA, FileB : DataFile;
                       VAR NextItemSmaller : boolean);

   (******************************************************************

      Procedure to copy one item from FileA to FileB and to check
      if the next item in FileA is smaller than the one just copied
      (indicating the end of a subfile in FileA).

    ******************************************************************)

   BEGIN (* CopyOneItem *)
      IF NOT eof(FileA) THEN
         BEGIN
            read (FileA, FileB^);
            IF eof(FileA) THEN
               NextItemSmaller := true
            ELSE
               NextItemSmaller := (FileA^ < FileB^);
            put (FileB)
         END (* IF *)
   END (* CopyOneItem *);
```

Figure 16.7   (cont.)

```
PROCEDURE CopySubFile (VAR FileA, FileB: DataFile;
                       VAR EndSubFile : boolean);

   (*****************************************************************

       Procedure to copy a sorted subfile from FileA to FileB.

    ****************************************************************)

   BEGIN (* CopySubFile *)
      EndSubfile := false;
      WHILE NOT EndSubfile DO
         CopyOneItem (FileA, FileB, EndSubfile)
   END (* CopySubFile *);

PROCEDURE SplitFile (VAR F, F1, F2 : DataFile);

   (*****************************************************************

       Procedure to read sorted subfiles from file F and write them
       alternately to files F1 and F2.

    ****************************************************************)

   VAR
      FileNum : 1..2;         (* # of file being written to *)
      EndSubfile : boolean;   (* indicates end of subfile *)

   BEGIN (* SplitFile *)

      (* Open the files *)

      reset (F);
      rewrite (F1);
      rewrite (F2);

      (* Split the file *)

      FileNum := 1;
      WHILE NOT eof(F) DO
         BEGIN
            CASE FileNum OF
               1 : CopySubFile (F, F1, EndSubfile);
               2 : CopySubFile (F, F2, EndSubfile)
            END (* CASE *);

            (* Switch to other file *)

            FileNum := 3 - FileNum
         END (* WHILE *)
   END (* SplitFile *);

PROCEDURE Merge (VAR F, F1, F2 : DataFile; VAR NumSubFiles : integer);

   (*****************************************************************

       Procedure to merge sorted subfiles in F1 and F2 and write these
       to file F; NumSubFiles is the number of subfiles written to F.

    ****************************************************************)
```

Figure 16.7   (cont.)

```
VAR
    FileNum : 1..2;                  (* # of file being used *)
    EndSubfile : ARRAY[1..2] OF boolean;
                                     (* indicate end of subfiles in F1 and F2 *)

BEGIN (* Merge *)

    (* Open the files *)

    reset (F1);
    reset (F2);
    rewrite (F);

    (* Now merge subfiles of F1 & F2 into F *)

    NumSubFiles := 0;
    WHILE NOT (eof(F1) OR eof(F2)) DO
        BEGIN

            (* set end-of-subfile indicators *)

            EndSubfile[1] := false;
            EndSubfile[2] := false;

            (* merge two subfiles *)

            WHILE NOT (eof(F1) OR eof(F2) OR
                       EndSubfile[1] OR EndSubfile[2]) DO
                IF F1^ < F2^ THEN
                    CopyOneItem (F1, F, EndSubfile[1])
                ELSE
                    CopyOneItem (F2, F, EndSubfile[2]);

            (* copy rest of other subfile *)

            IF EndSubfile[1] THEN
                CopySubFile (F2, F, EndSubfile[2])
            ELSE
                CopySubFile (F1, F, EndSubfile[1]);
            NumSubFiles := NumSubFiles + 1
        END (* WHILE *);

    (* Now copy any remaining subfiles in F1 or F2 to F *)

    WHILE NOT eof(F1) DO
        BEGIN
            CopySubFile (F1, F, EndSubfile[1]);
            NumSubFiles := NumSubFiles + 1
        END (* WHILE *);
    WHILE NOT eof(F2) DO
        BEGIN
            CopySubFile (F2, F, EndSubfile[2]);
            NumSubFiles := NumSubFiles + 1
        END (* WHILE *)
END (* Merge *);
```

Figure 16.7 (cont.)

```
PROCEDURE PrintFile (VAR F : DataFile);

   (****************************************************************

            Procedure to print the contents of file F.

   ****************************************************************)

   BEGIN (* PrintFile *)
      reset (F);
      WHILE NOT eof(F) DO
         BEGIN
            writeln (F^);
            get (F)
         END (* WHILE *)
   END (* PrintFile *);

BEGIN (* main program *)
   ReadNames (F, NameFile);

   (* Now split and merge subfiles until
      number of sorted subfiles is 1 *)

   REPEAT
      SplitFile (F, F1, F2);
      Merge (F, F1, F2, NumSubFiles)
   UNTIL NumSubFiles = 1;

   (* Display sorted file *)

   writeln ('Contents of sorted file:');
   writeln;
   PrintFile (F)
END (* main program *).
```

Sample run:

Contents of original file:

```
Doe, John Q.
Smith, Mary J.
Jones, Frederick N.
Vandervan, Peter F.
Adams, John Q.
Zzcyk, Stanislaw S.
Gertie, Dirty
James, Jesse
Terrific, Tom T.
Jackson, R.
```

Contents of sorted file:

```
Adams, John Q.
Doe, John Q.
Gertie, Dirty
Jackson, R.
James, Jesse
Jones, Frederick N.
Smith, Mary J.
Terrific, Tom T.
Vandervan, Peter F.
Zzcyk, Stanislaw S.
```

Mergesort can also be used as an internal sorting method for lists. The splitting and merge algorithms can easily be modified to use arrays or linked lists in place of files F, $F1$, and $F2$.

The worst case for mergesort occurs when the items are in reverse order. In this case the subfiles have sizes 1, 2, 4, 8, and so on. It follows that to sort a file or list of n items, $\log_2 n$ split and merge operations are required, and each of the n items must be examined in each of them. Hence, in the worst case, and as can be shown for the average case as well, the computing time for mergesort is $O(n \cdot \log_2 n)$.

Exercises

1. Following the example of the text, show the various splitting-merging stages of mergesort for the following lists of numbers:

   (a) 1, 5, 3, 8, 7, 2, 6, 4
   (b) 1, 8, 2, 7, 3, 6, 5, 4
   (c) 1, 2, 3, 4, 5, 6, 7, 8
   (d) 8, 7, 6, 5, 4, 3, 2, 1

2. Modify mergesort to sort a file of records so that the values in a key field are in order. Then write a program to read records from *UsersFile* (see Appendix E) and sort them so that the resources used to date are in increasing order.

3. One variation of the mergesort method is obtained by modifying the splitting operation as follows: Copy some fixed number of elements into main memory, sort them using an internal sorting method such as insertion sort (see Exercise 16 of Section 9.3), and write this sorted list to *F1*; then read the same number of elements from *F* into main memory, sort them internally, and write this sorted list to *F2*, and so on, alternating between *F1* and *F2*. Write procedures for this modified mergesort scheme, using insertion sort to sort internally the sublists containing *Size* elements for some constant *Size*.

4. Write a program that uses mergesort, appropriately modified, to sort a list stored in an array.

5. Proceed as in Exercise 4, but for a list stored in a linked list. For the merge operation, merge the two linked lists by simply changing links rather than actually copying the list elements into a third list.

16.7 Multiply Linked Structures: Trees

In Section 16.3 we analyzed the linear and binary search algorithms and showed that binary search is significantly more efficient than linear search. For each of these algorithms, however, the list was assumed to be stored in an array rather than in a linked list, as described in the preceding chapter. As we observed there, a linear search can be carried out with a linked list, but binary search is not feasible, since it requires direct access to each item in the list. In this section we describe another data structure, a ***binary search tree***, which makes a binary search possible while maintaining the flexibility of a linked structure. A binary search tree is a special kind of ***tree***, an important data structure that is commonly implemented as a ***multiply linked structure***, that is, one in which the nodes have more than one link field. In addition to their use in representing trees, such structures have many other applications, some of which are explored in the exercises.

A tree is a special case of a more general structure called a ***directed graph***. A directed graph consists of a finite set of elements called ***vertices*** or ***nodes*** and a finite set of ***directed arcs*** that connect pairs of vertices. For example, a directed graph having five vertices numbered 1, 2, 3, 4, 5 and seven directed arcs joining vertices 1 to 2, 1 to 4, 1 to 5, 2 to 3, 2 to 4, 3 to itself, 4 to 2, and 4 to 3 might be pictured as

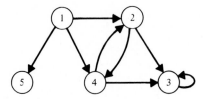

A ***tree*** is a directed graph in which one of the nodes, called the ***root***, has no incoming arcs but from which each node in the tree can be reached by exactly one path, that is, by following a unique sequence of consecutive arcs. Thus the preceding directed graph is not a tree. The only vertex having no incoming arcs is vertex 1, and hence it is the only possibility for a root. However, because there are many different paths from vertex 1 to vertex 3 ($1 \rightarrow 2 \rightarrow 3$, $1 \rightarrow 4 \rightarrow 3$, $1 \rightarrow 4 \rightarrow 2 \rightarrow 3$, $1 \rightarrow 4 \rightarrow 2 \rightarrow 4 \rightarrow 3$, $1 \rightarrow 2 \rightarrow 3 \rightarrow 3 \rightarrow 3$, and so on), this directed graph is not a tree.

Trees are so named because they have a treelike appearance, except that they are usually drawn upside down with the root at the top. For example,

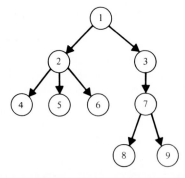

shows a tree having nine vertices in which vertex 1 is the root. Vertices having no outgoing arcs are called ***leaves***; in this example, vertices 4, 5, 6, 8, and 9 are the leaves of the tree. Nodes that can be reached directly from a given node—that is, by using only one directed arc—are called the ***children*** of that node, and a node is said to be the ***parent*** of each of its children. For example, in the tree just shown, vertex 2 is the parent of vertices 4, 5, and 6, and these vertices are the children of vertex 2.

Applications of trees are many and varied. For example, a ***genealogical tree*** such as the following is a convenient way to picture a person's descendants:

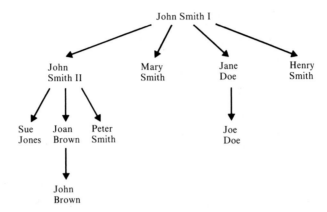

Game trees like the following, which shows the various configurations possible in the Towers of Hanoi problem with two disks (see Section 6.6), are used to analyze games and puzzles.

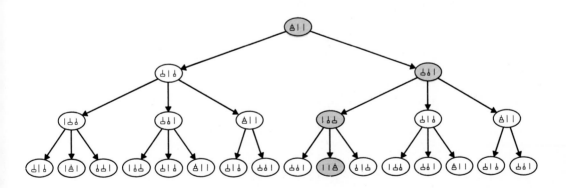

Parse trees constructed during compilation of a program are used to check the program's syntax; for example, the following parse tree might be produced for the Pascal statement

if $x < 0$ **then**
   $Flag := 1$

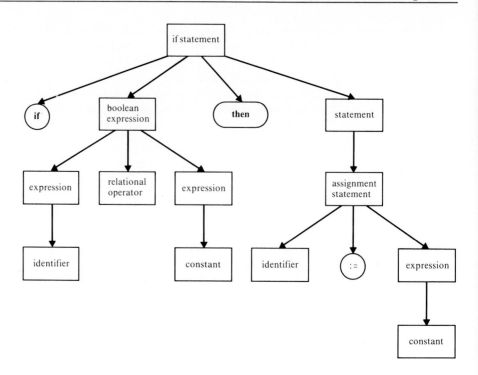

Binary trees, in which each node has at most two children, are especially useful in modeling processes in which an activity proceeds in stages and at each stage there are two possible outcomes, on or off, 0 or 1, Yes or No, · or −, and so on. For example, a binary tree can be used to decode a message transmitted in Morse code (see Exercise 13 of Section 11.3). In this case, the nodes represent the characters being encoded, and each directed arc is labeled with a dot or a dash. Thus, part of the tree for Morse code is

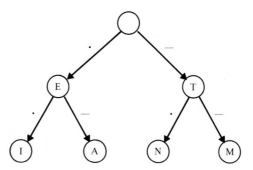

The sequence of dots and dashes labeling a path from the root to a particular node corresponds to the Morse Code for that character; for example, ·· is the code for I and −· is the code for N.

In this section we confine our attention to binary trees. This is not a serious limitation, however, because any tree can be represented by a binary tree, as described in the exercises.

Binary trees can be represented as multiply linked structures in which each node has two link fields, one being a pointer to the left child of that node and the other being a pointer to the right child. Such nodes can be represented in Pascal by records whose declarations have the form

```
type
    DataType = . . . ; (* type of data items in the nodes *)
    TreePointer = ↑TreeNode;
    TreeNode = record
                    Data : DataType;
                    LChild, RChild : TreePointer
              end;
```

The two link fields *LChild* and *RChild* are pointers to nodes representing the left and right children, respectively,

or are nil if the node does not have a left or right child. A leaf node is characterized, therefore, by having nil values for both *LChild* and *RChild*.

The binary tree

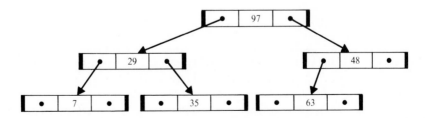

can thus be represented as the following linked tree of records:

This binary tree has directed arcs from the root node containing 97 to the nodes containing 29 and 48. Each of these nodes is itself the root of a binary *subtree*:

In the same way, there are arcs from the node containing 29 to the nodes containing 7 and 35. Each of these may be thought of as the root of a binary subtree consisting of a single node (its left and right subtrees are empty):

This leads to the following *recursive definition of a binary tree*:

A binary tree either

1. is empty or
2. consists of a node called the *root,* which has pointers to two disjoint binary (sub)trees called the *left subtree* and the *right subtree.*

This recursive definition suggests that it may be easy to develop recursive algorithms for processing binary trees.

The first operation for binary trees that we consider is *traversing* the tree, that is, visiting each node in the binary tree exactly once. There are three basic steps in traversing a binary tree recursively: (1) visiting a node, (2) traversing the left subtree of that node, and (3) traversing the right subtree of that node. These three steps can be performed in any order. If we denote these steps by

N: visit a node
L: traverse the left subtree
R: traverse the right subtree

then the six different orders are

NLR
LNR
LRN
NRL
RNL
RLN

We can reduce this list to the first three orders if we agree always to traverse the left subtree before the right subtree. The traversals that result from these three orders are given special names:

NLR: *preorder traversal*
LNR: *inorder traversal*
LRN: *postorder traversal*

To illustrate these traversals, consider the following binary tree:

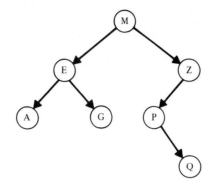

The three types of traversals visit the nodes in the following sequences:

preorder: M E A G Z P Q
inorder: A E G M P Q Z
postorder: A G E Q P Z M

The postorder traversal is obtained as follows: We begin at the root M, but before we list it, we must traverse its left and right subtrees. These subtrees are highlighted in the following diagram:

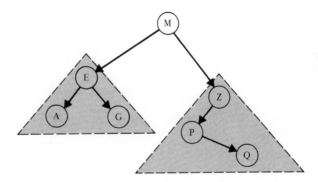

The left subtree has root E, but before listing it, we must traverse its left and right subtrees.

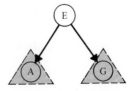

The left subtree has root A, but again we must first traverse its left and right subtrees before listing it.

Because these subtrees are empty, A may now be listed. The right subtree of
E has root G, which also has empty left and right subtrees,

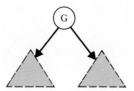

and thus G may be listed. Because both the left and right subtrees of E have
been traversed, E may now be listed. The sequence of nodes visited thus far
is

   A G E

Because the left subtree of M has been traversed, we consider its right
subtree, having root Z. Before listing Z, we must traverse its left and right
subtrees.

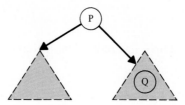

The left subtree has root P, and before listing P, we must traverse its left and
right subtrees.

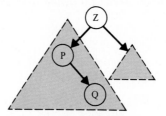

The left subtree is empty, and the right subtree has root Q.

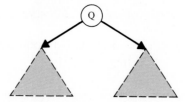

Because the left and right subtrees of Q are empty, Q may now be listed:

   A G E Q

The left and right subtrees of P have now been traversed, and so P is listed:

A G E Q P

The left subtree of Z has now been traversed, and because its right subtree is empty, Z may now be listed:

A G E Q P Z

Finally, we may list the vertex M, as both its left and right subtrees have been traversed:

A G E Q P Z M

The reader should derive the preorder and inorder traversals in a similar manner.

The names *preorder, inorder,* and *postorder* for traversals of a binary tree are appropriate because they correspond to the prefix, infix, and postfix forms for an arithmetic expression. (See Section 16.2 and Exercise 9 in that section.) To illustrate, consider the arithmetic expression

$$A - B * C + D$$

This can be represented as a binary tree by representing each operand as a child of a node that represents the corresponding operator:

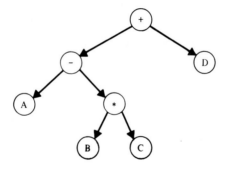

An inorder traversal of this binary tree produces the infix expression

$$A - B * C + D$$

A preorder traversal yields the prefix expression

$$+ - A * B C D$$

And a postorder traversal gives the postfix (RPN) expression

$$A B C * - D +$$

The method we have used for traversing a binary tree is a recursive one, since traversing a tree (or subtree) requires traversing each of the subtrees pointed to by its root. Thus it is natural to use recursive procedures to traverse a binary tree. For example, a recursive procedure for inorder traversal is as follows:

procedure *InOrder* (*RootPtr* : *TreePointer*);

   (∗ Procedure for inorder traversal of a binary tree. ∗)

  begin (∗ *InOrder* ∗)
    if *RootPtr* <> **nil then**   (∗ tree is not empty ∗)
      begin
        InOrder (*RootPtr*↑.*LChild*);   (∗ L operation ∗)
        Visit (*RootPtr*);   (∗ N operation ∗)
        InOrder (*RootPtr*↑.*RChild*)   (∗ R operation ∗)
      end (∗ **if** ∗)
  end (∗ *InOrder* ∗);

Here *Visit* is a procedure to process the data field *RootPtr*↑.*Data* of the node pointed to by *RootPtr*. Procedures for the preorder and postorder traversals are obtained by simply changing the order of the statements representing the L, N, and R operations and are left as exercises.

    To demonstrate how this procedure operates, suppose that the procedure *Visit* simply displays the data stored in a node, and consider the following binary tree:

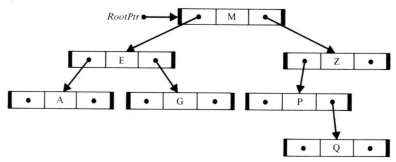

The statement

   InOrder (*RootPtr*)

calls the procedure *InOrder* to perform an inorder traversal of this tree. The action of this procedure while traversing the tree is indicated by the following table:

Contents of Current Node	Level in the Tree	Action	Output
M	1	Call *InOrder* with pointer to root (E) of the left subtree.	
E	2	Call *InOrder* with pointer to root (A) of left subtree.	

Contents of Current Node	Level in the Tree	Action	Output
A	3	Call *InOrder* with pointer (nil) to root of left subtree.	
None	4	None; return to parent node.	
A	3	Display contents of node.	A
A	3	Call *InOrder* with pointer (nil) to root of right subtree.	
None	4	None; return to parent node.	
A	3	Return to parent node.	
E	2	Display contents of node.	E
E	2	Call *InOrder* with pointer to root (G) of right subtree.	
G	3	Call *InOrder* with pointer (nil) to root of left subtree.	
None	4	None; return to parent node.	
G	3	Display contents of node.	G
G	3	Call *InOrder* with pointer (nil) to root of right subtree.	
None	4	None; return to parent node.	
G	3	Return to parent node.	
E	2	Return to parent node.	
M	1	Display contents of node.	M
M	1	Call *InOrder* with pointer to root (Z) of right subtree.	
Z	2	Call *InOrder* with pointer to root (P) of left subtree.	
P	3	Call *InOrder* with pointer (nil) to root of left subtree.	
None	4	None; return to parent node.	
P	3	Display contents of node.	P
P	3	Call *InOrder* with pointer to root (Q) of right subtree.	
Q	4	Call *InOrder* with pointer (nil) to root of left subtree.	
None	5	None; return to parent node.	
Q	4	Display contents of node.	Q
Q	4	Call *InOrder* with pointer (nil) to root of right subtree.	
None	5	None; return to parent node.	
Q	4	Return to parent node.	
P	3	Return to parent node.	

Contents of Current Node	Level in the Tree	Action	Output
Z	2	Display contents of node.	Z
Z	2	Call *InOrder* with pointer (nil) to root of right subtree.	
None	3	None; return to parent node.	
Z	2	Return to parent node.	
M	1	Terminate procedure; traversal complete.	

In the preceding example, the output produced by *InOrder* was

A E G M P Q Z

Note that the letters are in alphabetical order. This is because this binary tree has the special property that the items in the left subtree of each node are less than the item in that node, which in turn is less than all items in the right subtree. A binary tree having this property is called a ***binary search tree (BST)*** because it can be searched using an algorithm, much like the binary search algorithm for arrays.

To illustrate, suppose we wish to search the following BST for 41:

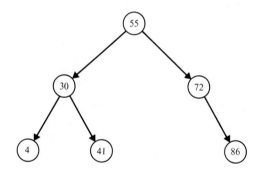

We begin at the root, and since 41 is less than the value 55 in the root, we know that the desired value is located in the left subtree of the root:

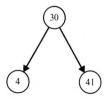

Now we continue the search by comparing the desired value with the value in the root of this subtree. Since $41 > 30$, we know that the right subtree should be searched:

Examining the value in the root of this one-node subtree locates the desired value.

Similarly, in searching for the value 64, we are led to the right subtree after comparing 64 with the value 55 in the root:

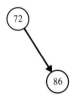

Now, because $64 < 72$, if the desired value is in the tree, it will be in the left subtree of the node containing 72; however, since this left subtree is empty, we conclude that the value 64 is not in the tree.

The following procedure *BSTSearch* for searching a binary search tree incorporates these techniques. The pointer *CurrPtr* begins at the root of the BST and then is repeatedly replaced by its left or right link, depending on whether the item for which we are searching is less than or greater than the value stored in the current node. This continues until either the desired item is found or *CurrPtr* becomes nil, indicating an empty subtree, in which case the item is not in the tree.

```
procedure BSTSearch (RootPtr : TreePointer; Item : DataType;
                     var CurrPtr : TreePointer;
                     var Found : boolean);

(* Procedure to search the BST with root pointed to by RootPtr
   for a specified Item. Found is returned as true and CurrPtr
   points to a node containing Item if the search is successful;
   otherwise, Found is returned as false. *)

begin (* BSTSearch *)
   CurrPtr := RootPtr;                          (* begin at the root *)
   Found := false;
   while not Found and (CurrPtr <> nil) do
      with CurrPtr↑ do
         if Item < Data then                    (* search left subtree *)
            CurrPtr := LChild
         else if Item > Data then               (* search right subtree *)
            CurrPtr := RChild
         else                                    (* Item found *)
            Found := true
   end (* BSTSearch *);
```

Because each time we move down to a subtree we search it in the same manner as the preceding (sub)tree, we could have written this procedure recursively (as the exercises ask you to do). This recursive procedure, however, is no shorter or easier to understand than is the nonrecursive one given here.

For *balanced* binary search trees like that in this example, in which the left and right subtrees of each node contain approximately the same number of nodes, the elements are searched in a manner much like that of binary search for arrays of elements. At each stage, the number of elements in the subtree still to be searched is approximately one-half that of the current subtree. Binary search trees need not, however, have such a balanced structure. For example, the following is a BST containing the same values:

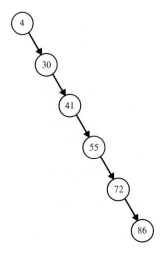

For such unbalanced BSTs, search times increase, since the search procedure degenerates into a linear search.

A binary search tree can be constructed by repeatedly calling the following procedure to insert elements into a BST that is initially empty (*RootPtr* = **nil**). The method used to determine where an element is to be inserted is similar to that used in *BSTSearch*. We move down to a left or right subtree of a node, beginning at the root, depending on whether the element is less than or greater than the value in that node. (For elements that are records, a key field in these records is the basis for comparison.) If the element is not already in the tree, we will eventually reach an empty subtree in which the item is to be inserted. As in the case of the search procedure, an insert procedure can be written either recursively or nonrecursively; in this case, the recursive formulation is considerably shorter and easier to understand.

procedure *RecBSTInsert* (**var** *RootPtr* : *TreePointer*;
                                              Element : *DataType*);

(∗ Recursive procedure to insert *Element* into the BST with root
   pointed to by *RootPtr*. ∗)

```
begin (* RecBSTInsert *)
    if RootPtr = nil then                    (* insert in empty tree *)
      begin
        new (RootPtr);
        with RootPtr↑ do
          begin
            Data := Element;
            LChild := nil;
            RChild := nil
          end (* with *)
      end (* if *)
    else
      with RootPtr↑ do
        if Element < Data then               (* insert in left subtree *)
          RecBSTInsert (LChild, Element)
        else if Element > Data then          (* insert in right subtree *)
          RecBSTInsert (RChild, Element)
        else                                 (* Element already in tree *)
          writeln ('Item already in the tree')
end (* RecBSTInsert *);
```

The order in which items are inserted into a BST determines the shape of the tree. For example, inserting the letters C, A, B, L, and E into a BST of characters in this order gives

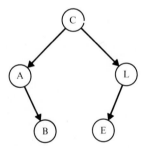

but inserting them in the order A, B, C, E, L yields

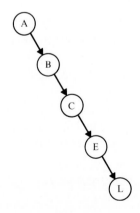

As we noted earlier, search time increases for such unbalanced trees. Insertion algorithms that avoid construction of such unbalanced trees are known, but are beyond the level of this introductory text.

If we combine this method of constructing a binary search tree with that for performing an inorder traversal, we obtain a new scheme for sorting a list of elements. We simply insert the list items into a BST that is initially empty and then use an inorder traversal to copy them back into the list. The following algorithm uses this technique to sort a list stored in an array:

TREESORT ALGORITHM

(∗ Algorithm that uses a BST to sort a list of n items stored in an array X so that they are in ascending order. ∗)

1. Initialize an empty BST.
2. For i ranging from 1 to n:
   Insert $X[i]$ into the BST.
3. Initialize an index i to 0.
4. Perform an inorder traversal of the BST, in which visiting a node consists of the following two steps:
   a. Increment i by 1.
   b. Set $X[i]$ equal to the data item in the current node.

Deleting a leaf node in a binary search tree is easy to do, but deleting an interior node (one having at least one child) is more complicated. The exercises explore the deletion operation in more detail.

Exercises

1. For each of the following lists of letters

   (a) Draw the binary search tree that is constructed when the letters are inserted in the order given.
   (b) Perform inorder, preorder, and postorder traversals of the tree and show the sequence of letters that results in each case.

       (i) M, I, T, E, R   **(ii)** T, I, M, E, R
     (iii) R, E, M, I, T   **(iv)** C, O, R, N, F, L, A, K, E, S

2. For the trees in Exercise 1, traverse each tree, using the following orders:

   (a) NRL   **(b)** RNL   **(c)** RLN

3. For each of the following arithmetic expressions, draw a binary tree that represents the expression, and then use tree traversals to find the equivalent prefix and postfix (RPN) expressions:

   (a) $A + B + C/D$
   (b) $(A + B)/C - D$

(c) $(A + B) * ((C + D)/(E + F))$
(d) $A - (B - (C - (D - E)))$

4. Write procedures for preorder and postorder traversals of a binary tree.

5. (a) Preorder traversal of a certain binary tree produced

A D F G H K L P Q R W Z

and inorder traversal produced

G F H K D L A W R Q P Z

Draw the binary tree.

(b) Postorder traversal of a certain binary tree produced

F G H D A L P Q R Z W K

and inorder traversal gave the same result as in part (a). Draw the binary tree.

(c) Show by example that knowing the results of a preorder traversal and a postorder traversal does not uniquely determine the binary tree. That is, give an example of two different binary trees for which a preorder traversal of each gives the same result, and so does a postorder traversal.

6. As noted in the text, every tree can be represented by a binary tree. This can be done by letting node x be a left child of node y in the binary tree if x is the leftmost child of y in the given tree, and by letting x be the right child of y if x and y are siblings (have the same parent) in the original tree. For example, the tree

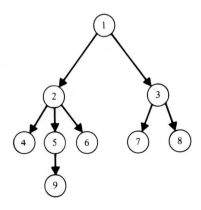

can be represented by the binary tree

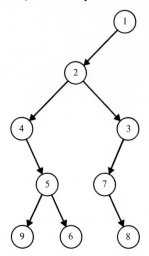

Represent each of the following by binary trees:

(a)

(b)

(c)

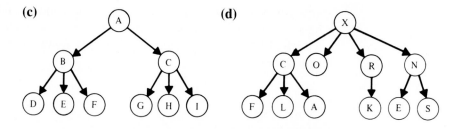

(d)

7. Write a recursive version of the procedure *BSTSearch*.

8. Write a recursive function to count the leaves in a binary tree. (*Hint*: How is the number of leaves in the entire tree related to the number of leaves in the left and right subtrees of the root?)

9. Write a recursive function to find the depth of a binary tree. The depth of an empty tree is 0, and for a nonempty tree it is one more than the larger of the depths of the left and right subtrees of the root.

10. Write a recursive function to find the level in a BST at which a given item is located. The root is at level 0, and its children are at level 1.

11. Repeat Exercise 10, but do not assume that the binary tree is a BST.

12. Write a program to process a BST whose nodes contain characters. Allow the user to select from the following menu of options:

   I followed by a character: To insert a character
   S followed by a character: To search for a character
   TI: For inorder traversal
   TP: For preorder traversal
   TR: For postorder traversal
   QU: To quit

13. Write a procedure *TreeSort* that implements the treesort algorithm for sorting a list of items stored in (a) an array and (b) a linked list. You may assume that the procedures *InOrder* and *BSTInsert* have been previously defined.

14. Write a program that reads a collection of records consisting of student numbers and names and then uses the procedure *TreeSort* of Exercise 13 to sort them so that the student numbers are in ascending order.

15. Complete the binary tree begun in this section for decoding messages in Morse code for the table of characters and codes in Exercise 13 of Section 11.3.

16. Write a program that uses a binary tree as described in Exercise 15 to decode messages in Morse code.

17. To delete a node *x* from a BST, three cases must be considered: (1) *x* is a leaf; (2) *x* has only one subtree; and (3) *x* has two subtrees. Case 1 is handled easily. For Case 2, simply replace *x* with the root of its subtree by linking the parent of *x* to this root. For Case 3, *x* must be replaced with its inorder successor (or predecessor). The following diagram illustrates this case:

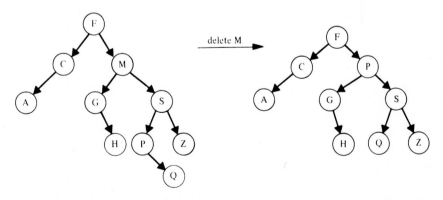

Write a procedure to delete an item from a BST. A procedure like *BSTSearch* can be used to locate the item and its parent in the tree.

18. (Project) For a certain company, the method by which the pay for each employee is computed depends on whether that employee is classified as an *Office* employee, a *Factory* employee, or a *Salesman*. Suppose that a file of employee records is maintained in which each record is a variant record containing the following information for each employee:

> Name (20 characters).
> Social security number (integer).
> Age (integer).
> Number of dependents (integer).
> Employee code (character O, F, S representing *Office*, *Factory*, and *Salesman*, respectively).
> Hourly rate if employee is *Factory*.
> Annual salary if employee is *Office*.
> A base pay (real) and a commission percentage (real) if employee is *Salesman*.

Write a menu-driven program that allows at least the following options to be selected by the user of the program:

GET: Get the records from the employee file and store them in a binary search tree, sorted so that the names are in alphabetical order.

INS: Insert the record for a new employee into the BST.

UPD: Update the record of an employee already in the tree.

RET: Retrieve and display the record for a specified employee.

LIS: List the records (or perhaps selected items in the records) in order. This option should allow suboptions

> ALL—to list for all employees
> OFF—to list for only *Office* employees
> FAC—to list for only *Factory* employees
> SAL—to list for only *Salesman* employees

SAV: Copy the records from the BST into a permanent file.

DEL: Delete the record of an employee from the BST.

19. An alternative storage structure for a BST is an array. We simply number each of the possible positions in the BST from top to bottom, numbering from left to right on each level

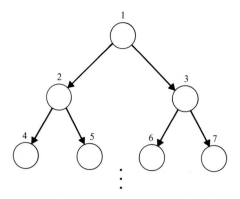

and then store an item in the *i*th position of the BST in the *i*th location of an array *B*.

(a) Show what each element of array *B* would be for the BSTs in Exercise 1.

(b) In general, why is this an inefficient way to store BSTs? For what kinds of BSTs is this a good storage structure to use?

20. Assume that array *B* is used to store a BST containing positive integers, as described in Exercise 19. Write a procedure to perform *BSTSearch* for this implementation.

21. In a *doubly* or *symmetrically linked list*, each node has two link fields, one containing a pointer to the predecessor of that node and the other containing a pointer to its successor. It might be pictured as follows

and is especially useful when it is necessary to traverse a linked list or a part of it in either direction.

(a) Write the necessary type declarations for such a doubly linked list.

(b) Write a procedure for traversing the list from left to right.

(c) Write a procedure for traversing the list from right to left.

(d) Write a procedure for inserting an item (1) after or (2) before some other given element in a doubly linked list.

(e) Write a procedure to delete an item from a doubly linked list.

22. A *doubly linked ring* or *doubly linked circular list* is a doubly linked list in which the nil right pointer in the last node is replaced with a pointer to the first node, and the nil left pointer in the first node is replaced with a pointer to the last node.

Assuming that *FirstPtr* points to the first node, write procedures to

(a) Traverse the list from left to right.

(b) Traverse the list from right to left.

(c) Insert an item (1) after or (2) before a given element in the list.

(d) Delete an item from the list.

23. Another application of multiply linked lists is to maintain a list sorted in two or more different ways. For example, consider the following multiply linked list having two links per node:

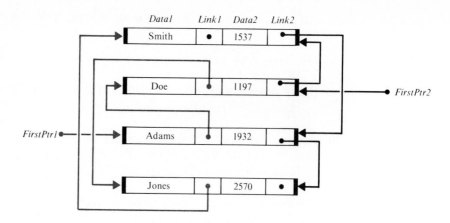

If this list is traversed and the data fields displayed by using *FirstPtr1* to point to the first node and following the pointers in the field *Link1*, the names will be in alphabetical order:

Adams	1932
Doe	1197
Jones	2570
Smith	1537

A traversal using *FirstPtr2* to point to the first node and following pointers in the field *Link2* gives the identification numbers in ascending order:

Doe	1197
Smith	1537
Adams	1932
Jones	2570

This list is logically ordered, therefore, in two different ways. Write a program to read the first ten records from *UsersFile* (see Appendix E), and store them in a multiply linked list that is logically sorted so that the user identification numbers are in ascending order and the resources used to date are in descending order. Traverse the list and display the records so that the identification numbers are in ascending order. Then traverse the list and display the records so that the resources used to date are in descending order.

24. In Exercise 12 of Section 15.4, a linked list representation for a polynomial in x

$$P(x) = a_0 + a_1 x + a_2 x^2 + \cdots + a_n x^n$$

was described. A *polynomial in two variables* x and y can be viewed as a polynomial in one variable y, with coefficients that are polynomials in x; that is, it has the form

$$P(x, y) = A_0(x) + A_1(x)y + \cdots + A_{m-1}(x)y^{m-1} + A_m(x)y^m$$

where each $A_i(x)$ is a polynomial in x. For example,

$$6 + 8x^4 + y^2 - 3xy^2 + 4x^5y^2 + 5x^2y^3 + 7x^5y^3$$

can be rewritten as

$$(6 + 8x^4) + (1 - 3x + 4x^5)y^2 + (5x^2 + 7x^5)y^3$$

A multiply linked representation for such polynomials is obtained by representing each term of the form $A_k(x)y^k$ by a node that stores the exponent of y and two links, one containing a pointer to a linked list representing the polynomial $A_k(x)$ and the other a pointer to the next term. For example, the first term in the preceding example can be represented as

(a) Draw a multiply linked representation for

$$P(x, y) = 1 + 4x + x^2 + 9y + 2xy + xy^4$$
$$+ 6x^2y^4 - 7xy^5 + 5x^7y^5 + 3x^9y^5$$

(b) Write a program to read triples of the form

(coefficient, x-exponent, y-exponent)

for a polynomial in x and y and construct its linked representation. Then read values for x and y and evaluate the polynomial.

(c) Modify the program in part (b) so that the exponents of x and the exponents of y need not be read in increasing order.

A

ASCII and EBCDIC

ASCII and EBCDIC codes of printable characters

Decimal	Binary	Octal	Hexadecimal	ASCII	EBCDIC
32	00100000	040	20	SP (Space)	
33	00100001	041	21	!	
34	00100010	042	22	"	
35	00100011	043	23	#	
36	00100100	044	24	$	
37	00100101	045	25	%	
38	00100110	046	26	&	
39	00100111	047	27	' (Single quote)	
40	00101000	050	28	(	
41	00101001	051	29	)	
42	00101010	052	2A	*	
43	00101011	053	2B	+	
44	00101100	054	2C	, (Comma)	
45	00101101	055	2D	- (Hyphen)	
46	00101110	056	2E	. (Period)	
47	00101111	057	2F	/	
48	00110000	060	30	0	
49	00110001	061	31	1	
50	00110010	062	32	2	
51	00110011	063	33	3	
52	00110100	064	34	4	
53	00110101	065	35	5	
54	00110110	066	36	6	
55	00110111	067	37	7	
56	00111000	070	38	8	
57	00111001	071	39	9	
58	00111010	072	3A	:	
59	00111011	073	3B	;	
60	00111100	074	3C	<	
61	00111101	075	3D	=	
62	00111110	076	3E	>	
63	00111111	077	3F	?	
64	01000000	100	40	@	SP (Space)
65	01000001	101	41	A	
66	01000010	102	42	B	

Decimal	Binary	Octal	Hexadecimal	ASCII	EBCDIC
67	01000011	103	43	C	
68	01000100	104	44	D	
69	01000101	105	45	E	
70	01000110	106	46	F	
71	01000111	107	47	G	
72	01001000	110	48	H	
73	01001001	111	49	I	
74	01001010	112	4A	J	¢
75	01001011	113	4B	K	. (Period)
76	01001100	114	4C	L	<
77	01001101	115	4D	M	(
78	01001110	116	4E	N	+
79	01001111	117	4F	O		
80	01010000	120	50	P	&
81	01010001	121	51	Q	
82	01010010	122	52	R	
83	01010011	123	53	S	
84	01010100	124	54	T	
85	01010101	125	55	U	
86	01010110	126	56	V	
87	01010111	127	57	W	
88	01011000	130	58	X	
89	01011001	131	59	Y	
90	01011010	132	5A	Z	!
91	01011011	133	5B	[	$
92	01011100	134	5C	\	*
93	01011101	135	5D	]	)
94	01011110	136	5E	∧	;
95	01011111	137	5F	_ (Underscore)	¬ (Negation)
96	01100000	140	60	`	- (Hyphen)
97	01100001	141	61	a	/
98	01100010	142	62	b	
99	01100011	143	63	c	
100	01100100	144	64	d	
101	01100101	145	65	e	
102	01100110	146	66	f	
103	01100111	147	67	g	
104	01101000	150	68	h	
105	01101001	151	69	i	
106	01101010	152	6A	j		
107	01101011	153	6B	k	, (Comma)
108	01101100	154	6C	l	%
109	01101101	155	6D	m	_ (Underscore)
110	01101110	156	6E	n	>
111	01101111	157	6F	o	?
112	01110000	160	70	p	
113	01110001	161	71	q	
114	01110010	162	72	r	
115	01110011	163	73	s	
116	01110100	164	74	t	
117	01110101	165	75	u	
118	01110110	166	76	v	
119	01110111	167	77	w	
120	01111000	170	78	x	

Decimal	Binary	Octal	Hexadecimal	ASCII	EBCDIC
121	01111001	171	79	y	
122	01111010	172	7A	z	:
123	01111011	173	7B	{	#
124	01111100	174	7C			@
125	01111101	175	7D	}	' (Single quote)
126	01111110	176	7E	~	=
127	01111111	177	7F		"
128	10000000	200	80		
129	10000001	201	81		a
130	10000010	202	82		b
131	10000011	203	83		c
132	10000100	204	84		d
133	10000101	205	85		e
134	10000110	206	86		f
135	10000111	207	87		g
136	10001000	210	88		h
137	10001001	211	89		i
.	.	.	.		.
.	.	.	.		.
.	.	.	.		.
145	10010001	221	91		j
146	10010010	222	92		k
147	10010011	223	93		l
148	10010100	224	94		m
149	10010101	225	95		n
150	10010110	226	96		o
151	10010111	227	97		p
152	10011000	230	98		q
153	10011001	231	99		r
.	.	.	.		.
.	.	.	.		.
.	.	.	.		.
162	10100010	242	A2		s
163	10100011	243	A3		t
164	10100100	244	A4		u
165	10100101	245	A5		v
166	10100110	246	A6		w
167	10100111	247	A7		x
168	10101000	250	A8		y
169	10101001	251	A9		z
.	.	.	.		.
.	.	.	.		.
.	.	.	.		.
192	11000000	300	C0		}
193	11000001	301	C1		A
194	11000010	302	C2		B
195	11000011	303	C3		C
196	11000100	304	C4		D
197	11000101	305	C5		E
198	11000110	306	C6		F
199	11000111	307	C7		G
200	11001000	310	C8		H
201	11001001	311	C9		I

Decimal	Binary	Octal	Hexadecimal	ASCII	EBCDIC
.	.	.	.		.
.	.	.	.		.
.	.	.	.		.
208	11010000	320	D0		}
209	11010001	321	D1		J
210	11010010	322	D2		K
211	11010011	323	D3		L
212	11010100	324	D4		M
213	11010101	325	D5		N
214	11010110	326	D6		O
215	11010111	327	D7		P
216	11011000	330	D8		Q
217	11011001	331	D9		R
.	.	.	.		.
.	.	.	.		.
.	.	.	.		.
224	11100000	340	E0		\
225	11100001	341	E1		
226	11100010	342	E2		S
227	11100011	343	E3		T
228	11100100	344	E4		U
229	11100101	345	E5		V
230	11100110	346	E6		W
231	11100111	347	E7		X
232	11101000	350	E8		Y
233	11101001	351	E9		Z
.	.	.	.		.
.	.	.	.		.
.	.	.	.		.
240	11110000	360	F0		0
241	11110001	361	F1		1
242	11110010	362	F2		2
243	11110011	363	F3		3
244	11110100	364	F4		4
245	11110101	365	F5		5
246	11110110	366	F6		6
247	11110111	367	F7		7
248	11111000	370	F8		8
249	11111001	371	F9		9
.	.	.	.		
.	.	.	.		
.	.	.	.		
255	11111111	377	FF		

ASCII codes of control characters

Decimal	Binary	Octal	Hexadecimal	Character
0	00000000	000	00	NUL (Null)
1	00000001	001	01	SOH (Start of heading)
2	00000010	002	02	STX (End of heading and start of text)
3	00000011	003	03	ETX (End of text)
4	00000100	004	04	EOT (End of transmission)
5	00000101	005	05	ENQ (Enquiry—to request identification)
6	00000110	006	06	ACK (Acknowledge)
7	00000111	007	07	BEL (Ring bell)
8	00001000	010	08	BS (Backspace)
9	00001001	011	09	HT (Horizontal tab)
10	00001010	012	0A	LF (Line feed)
11	00001011	013	0B	VT (Vertical tab)
12	00001100	014	0C	FF (Form feed)
13	00001101	015	0D	CR (Carriage return)
14	00001110	016	0E	SO (Shift out—begin non-ASCII bit string)
15	00001111	017	0F	SI (Shift in—end non-ASCII bit string)
16	00010000	020	10	DLE (Data link escape—controls data transmission)
17	00010001	021	11	DC1 (Device control 1)
18	00010010	022	12	DC2 (Device control 2)
19	00010011	023	13	DC3 (Device control 3)
20	00010100	024	14	DC4 (Device control 4)
21	00010101	025	15	NAK (Negative acknowledge)
22	00010110	026	16	SYN (Synchronous idle)
23	00010111	027	17	ETB (End of transmission block)
24	00011000	030	18	CAN (Cancel—ignore previous transmission)
25	00011001	031	19	EM (End of medium)
26	00011010	032	1A	SUB (Substitute a character for another)
27	00011011	033	1B	ESC (Escape)
28	00011100	034	1C	FS (File separator)
29	00011101	035	1D	GS (Group separator)
30	00011110	036	1E	RS (Record separator)
31	00011111	037	1F	US (Unit separator)

EBCDIC codes of control characters

Decimal	Binary	Octal	Hexadecimal	Character
0	00000000	000	00	NUL (Null)
1	00000001	001	01	SOH (Start of heading)
2	00000010	002	02	STX (End of heading and start of text)
3	00000011	003	03	ETX (End of text)
4	00000100	004	04	PF (Punch off)
5	00000101	005	05	HT (Horizontal tab)
6	00000110	006	06	LC (Lowercase)
7	00000111	007	07	DEL (Delete)
10	00001010	012	0A	SMM (Repeat)
11	00001011	013	0B	VT (Vertical tab)
12	00001100	014	0C	FF (Form feed)
13	00001101	015	0D	CR (Carriage return)
14	00001110	016	0E	SO (Shift out—begin non-ASCII bit string)
15	00001111	017	0F	SI (Shift in—end non-ASCII bit string)
16	00010000	020	10	DLE (Data link escape—controls data transmission)
17	00010001	021	11	DC1 (Device control 1)
18	00010010	022	12	DC2 (Device control 2)
19	00010011	023	13	DC3 (Device control 3)
20	00010100	024	14	RES (Restore)
21	00010101	025	15	NL (New line)
22	00010110	026	16	BS (Backspace)
23	00010111	027	17	IL (Idle)
24	00011000	030	18	CAN (Cancel—ignore previous transmission)
25	00011001	031	19	EM (End of medium)
26	00011010	032	1A	CC (Unit backspace)
28	00011100	034	1C	IFS (Interchange file separator)
29	00011101	035	1D	IGS (Interchange group separator)
30	00011110	036	1E	IRS (Interchange record separator)
31	00011111	037	1F	IUS (Interchange unit separator)
32	00100000	040	20	DS (Digit select)
33	00100001	041	21	SOS (Start of significance)
34	00100010	042	22	FS (File separator)
36	00100100	044	24	BYP (Bypass)
37	00100101	045	25	LF (Line feed)
38	00100110	046	26	ETB (End of transmission block)
39	00100111	047	27	ESC (Escape)
42	00101010	052	2A	SM (Start message)
45	00101101	055	2D	ENQ (Enquiry—to request identification)
46	00101110	056	2E	ACK (Acknowledge)
47	00101111	057	2F	BEL (Ring bell)
50	00110010	062	32	SYN (Synchronous idle)
52	00110100	064	34	PN (Punch on)
53	00110101	065	35	RS (Record separator)
54	00110110	066	36	UC (Uppercase)
55	00110111	067	37	EOT (End of transmission)
60	00111100	074	3C	DC4 (Device control 4)
61	00111101	075	3D	NAK (Negative acknowledge)
63	00111111	077	3F	SUB (Substitute a character for another)

B

Reserved Words, Standard Identifiers, and Operators

Reserved Words

and	end	mod	repeat
array	file	nil	set
begin	for	not	then
case	forward	of	to
const	function	or	type
div	goto	packed	until
do	if	procedure	var
downto	in	program	while
else	label	record	with

Standard Identifiers

Predefined Constants

false   *true*   *maxint*

Predefined Types

boolean   *char*   *integer*   *real*   *text*

Predefined Files

input   *output*

Predefined Functions

abs	*exp*	*sin*
arctan	*ln*	*sqr*
chr	*odd*	*sqrt*
cos	*ord*	*succ*
eof	*pred*	*trunc*
eoln	*round*	

Predefined Procedures

dispose	*put*	*unpack*
get	*read*	*write*
new	*readln*	*writeln*
pack	*reset*	
page	*rewrite*	

Operators

Unary Arithmetic Operators

Operator	Operation	Type of Operand	Type of Result
+	unary plus	integer	integer
		real	real
−	unary minus	integer	integer
		real	real

Binary Arithmetic Operators

Operator	Operation	Type of Operands	Type of Result
+	addition	integer or real	integer if both operands are integer, otherwise real
−	subtraction	integer or real	integer if both operands are integer, otherwise real
*	multiplication	integer or real	integer if both operands are integer, otherwise real
/	division	integer or real	real
div	integer division	integer	integer
mod	modulo	integer	integer

Relational Operators

Operator	Operation	Type of Operands	Type of Result
=	equality	simple, string, set, or pointer	boolean
<>	inequality	simple, string, set, or pointer	boolean
<	less than	simple or string	boolean
>	greater than	simple or string	boolean
<=	less than or equal to, or subset	simple, string, or set	boolean
>=	greater than or equal to, or superset	simple, string, or set	boolean
in	set membership	first operand: ordinal type second operand: set type	boolean

Boolean Operators

Operator	Operation	Type of Operands	Type of Result
and	conjunction	boolean	boolean
not	negation	boolean	boolean
or	disjunction	boolean	boolean

Set Operators

Operator	Operation	Type of Operands	Type of Result
+	set union	set type	same as operands
−	set difference	set type	same as operands
*	set intersection	set type	same as operands

Assignment Operator

Operator	Operation	Type of Operands
:=	assignment	any type except file types

C

Syntax Diagrams

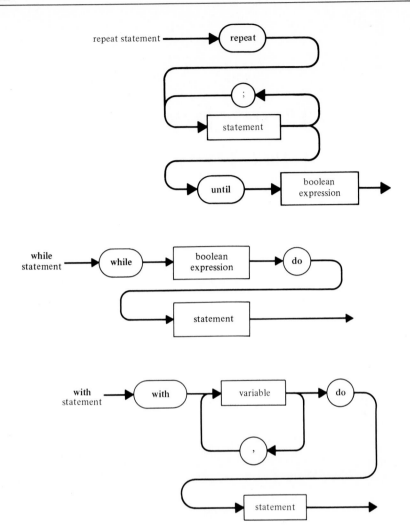

D

Predefined Functions and Procedures

Predefined functions

Function	Description	Type of Argument	Type of Value
abs(*x*)	absolute value of *x*	integer or real	same as arguments
arctan(*x*)	inverse tangent of *x* (value in radians)	integer or real	real
chr(*x*)	character whose ordinal number is *x*	integer	character
cos(*x*)	cosine of *x* (in radians)	integer or real	real
eof(*f*)	end-of-file function	file	boolean
eoln(*f*)	end-of-line function	text	boolean
exp(*x*)	exponential function e^x	integer or real	real
ln(*x*)	natural logarithm of *x*	integer or real	real
odd(*x*)	true if *x* is odd, false otherwise	integer	boolean
ord(*x*)	ordinal number of *x*	ordinal	integer
pred(*x*)	predecessor of *x*	ordinal	ordinal
round(*x*)	*x* rounded to nearest integer	real	integer
sin(*x*)	sine of *x* (in radians)	integer or real	real
sqr(*x*)	x^2	integer or real	same as argument
sqrt(*x*)	square root of *x*	integer or real	real
succ(*x*)	successor of *x*	ordinal	ordinal
trunc(*x*)	*x* truncated to its integer part	real	integer

Predefined procedures

Procedure	Description
dispose (P) *dispose (P, tag-value-list)*	Releases the memory location pointed to by pointer variable *P*, leaving *P* undefined. The second form may be used for variant records.
get (F)	Advances the data pointer in file *F* to the next component and assigns this component to the file buffer variable *F↑*.
new (P) *new (P, tag-value-list)*	Acquires a memory location and assigns its address to pointer variable *P*. The second form may be used for variant records.
pack (U, First, P)	Copies the elements of the unpacked array *U* beginning at position *First* to the packed array *P*.
page (F)	Causes a system-dependent effect on the text file *F* such that subsequent text written to *F* will be on a new page if *F* is printed on a suitable output device.
put (F)	Transfers the contents of the buffer variable *F↑* to the file *F*.
read (F, input-list)	Reads values from the file *F* and assigns these to the variables in the input list. If *F* is not specified, the standard file *input* is assumed.
readln (F, input-list)	Reads values from the text file *F*, assigns these to the variables in the input list, and then advances the data pointer in *F* past the next end-of-line mark. If *F* is not specified, the standard file *input* is assumed.
reset (F)	Opens the file *F* for input, positions the data pointer in *F* at the first file component, and assigns this component to the file buffer variable *F↑*.
rewrite (F)	Creates the empty file *F* and opens it for output. Any previous contents of *F* are destroyed.
unpack (P, U, First)	Copies the elements of the packed array *P* beginning at position *First* to the unpacked array *U*.
write (F, output-list)	Writes the values of the items in the output list to file *F*. If *F* is not specified, the standard file *output* is assumed.
writeln (F, output-list)	Writes the values of the items in the output list to text file *F* followed by an end-of-line mark. If *F* is not specified, the standard file *output* is assumed.

E

Sample Data Files

Several exercises in the text use the files *InventoryFile, InventoryUpdate, Least-SquaresFile, StudentFile, StudentUpdate,* and *UsersFile.* This appendix describes the contents of these files and gives a sample listing for each.

InventoryFile
Item number: an integer
Number currently in stock: an integer in the range 0 through 999
Unit price: a real value
Minimum inventory level: an integer in the range 0 through 999
Item name: a 25-character string

File is sorted so that item numbers are in increasing order.

Sample InventoryFile:

```
1011   20   54.95   15  TELEPHOTO POCKET CAMERA
1012   12   24.95   15  MINI POCKET CAMERA
1021   20   49.95   10  POL. ONE-STEP CAMERA
1022   13  189.95   12  SONAR 1-STEP CAMERA
1023   15   74.95    5  PRONTO CAMERA
1031    9  279.99   10  8MM ZOOM MOVIE CAMERA
1032   15  310.55   10  SOUND/ZOOM 8MM CAMERA
1041   10  389.00   12  35MM SLR XG-7 MINO. CAM.
1042   11  349.95   12  35MM SLR AE-1 PENT. CAM.
1043   20  319.90   12  35MM SLR ME CAN. CAM.
1044   13  119.95   12  35MM HI-MATIC CAMERA
1045   20   89.99   12  35MM COMPACT CAMERA
1511    7  129.95    5  ZOOM MOVIE PROJECTOR
1512    9  239.99    5  ZOOM-SOUND PROJECTOR
1521   10  219.99    5  AUTO CAROUSEL PROJECTOR
1522    4  114.95    5  CAR. SLIDE PROJECTOR
2011    4   14.95    5  POCKET STROBE
2012   12   48.55   10  STROBE SX-10
2013   10   28.99   15  ELEC.FLASH SX-10
3011   13   32.99   15  TELE CONVERTER
3012   14   97.99   15  28MM WIDE-ANGLE LENS
3013   13   87.95   15  135MM TELEPHOTO LENS
3014    8  267.95    5  35-105 MM ZOOM LENS
3015    7  257.95    5  80-200 MM ZOOM LENS
3111    4   67.50    5  HEAVY-DUTY TRIPOD
3112   10   19.95    5  LIGHTWEIGHT TRIPOD
3511   10  159.99    5  35MM ENLARGER KIT
4011    4   35.98    5  40X40 DELUXE SCREEN
4012   10   44.98    5  50X50 DELUXE SCREEN
5011   17    4.29   25  120-SLIDE TRAY
5012   33    2.95   25  100-SLIDE TRAY
5021   12    6.25   15  SLIDE VIEWER
5031   12   55.95   10  MOVIE EDITOR
6011   10   59.95    5  CONDENSER MICROPHONE
6111   80    0.89  100  AA ALKALINE BATTERY
7011   19   19.79   20  GADGET BAG
8011   45    1.49   50  135-24 COLOR FILM
8021   60    0.99   50  110-12 COLOR FILM
8022   42    1.45   50  110-24 COLOR FILM
8023   37    0.59   25  110-12 B/W FILM
8024   43    0.95   25  110-24 B/W FILM
8031   44    0.89   50  126-12 COLOR FILM
8032   27    0.59   25  126-12 B/W FILM
8041   39    6.89   50  8MM FILM CASSETTE
8042   25   11.89   20  16MM FILM CASSETTE
9111   10  959.99   12  COMBINATION CAMERA KIT
```

InventoryUpdate
Order number: three letters followed by four digits
Item number: an integer (same as those in *InventoryFile*)
Transaction code: a character (S = sold, R = returned)
Number of items sold or returned: an integer in the range 0 through 999

File is sorted so that item numbers are in increasing order. (Some items in *InventoryFile* may not have update records; others may have more than one.)

Sample InventoryUpdate:

CCI7543	1012S	2		BTP5396	3013S	1
LTB3429	1012S	7		GFL4913	3013S	8
DJS6762	1021S	9		EHQ7510	3013S	7
NQT1850	1022S	1		QQL6472	3013S	5
WYP6425	1023S	4		SVC6511	3014S	4
YOK2210	1023R	2		XJQ9391	3014S	4
QGM3144	1023S	1		ONO5251	3111S	3
NPQ8685	1031S	5		CXC7780	3111S	1
MAP8102	1031S	13		VGT8169	3112S	8
JRJ6335	1031S	1		IMK5861	3511S	2
UWR9386	1032S	3		QHR1944	3511S	1
TJY1913	1032S	11		ZPK6211	4011S	2
YHA9464	1041S	5		VDZ2970	4012S	6
SYT7493	1041S	3		BOJ9069	5011S	6
FHJ1657	1042S	7		MNL7029	5011S	9
OJQ1221	1043S	8		MRG8703	5021S	10
UOX7714	1043S	2		DEM9289	5021S	1
ERZ2147	1043S	7		BXL1651	5031S	2
MYW2540	1044S	1		VAF8733	6111S	65
UKS3587	1045S	2		UYI0368	7011S	2
AAN3759	1045S	2		VIZ6879	8011S	16
WZT4171	1045S	12		GXX9093	8011S	19
TYR9475	1511S	1		HHO5605	8021S	41
FRQ4184	1511S	1		BOL2324	8021S	49
TAV3604	1512S	2		PAG9289	8023S	15
DCW9363	1522S	1		MDF5557	8023S	17
EXN3964	1522R	1		IQK3388	8024S	12
OIN5524	1522S	1		OTB1341	8024S	28
EOJ8218	1522S	1		SVF5674	8031S	24
YFK0683	2011S	2		ZDP9484	8031S	15
PPX4743	2012S	4		OSY8177	8032S	15
DBR1709	2013S	4		GJQ0185	8032S	8
JOM5408	2013S	3		VHW0189	8041S	20
PKN0671	2013S	1		WEU9225	8041S	6
LBD8391	3011S	9		YJO3755	8041S	8
DNL6326	3012S	9				

LeastSquaresFile

This is a text file in which each line contains a pair of real numbers representing the *x* coordinate and the *y* coordinate of a point.

Sample LeastSquaresFile

2.18	1.06	5.63	8.58
7.46	12.04	8.94	15.27
5.75	8.68	7.34	11.48
3.62	4.18	6.55	9.92
3.59	3.87	4.89	7.07
7.5	12.32	9.59	15.82
7.49	11.74	1.81	0.45
7.62	12.07	0.99	−0.71
7.39	12.17	4.82	6.91
1.88	0.58	9.68	16.24
6.31	10.09	1.21	−0.22
2.53	2.04	4.54	5.64
5.44	8.25	1.48	0.3
1.21	−0.76	6.58	9.8
9.07	15.5	3.05	3.56
3.95	5.0	6.19	9.62
9.63	17.01	6.47	9.83
9.75	16.91	8.13	10.75
9.99	16.67	7.31	11.73
3.61	4.69	0.33	−1.93
9.06	15.0	5.12	7.41
5.03	6.62	5.23	7.73
4.45	6.12	7.14	11.02
4.54	5.89	1.27	−0.21
0.92	−1.02	2.51	1.59
0.82	−1.5	5.26	7.86
2.62	2.1	4.74	6.19
5.66	8.53	2.1	2.12
8.05	13.05	5.27	7.73
8.99	14.85	2.85	2.63
5.12	7.03	1.99	1.09
3.85	4.43	8.91	15.03
6.08	9.21	2.19	1.21
1.42	0	1.6	−0.05
2.58	2.38	8.93	15.12
5.99	9.42	3.19	3.56
0.63	−1.63	3.37	3.64
9.98	17.25		

StudentFile
Student number: an integer
Student's last name: a 15-character string
Student's first name: a 10-character string
Student's middle initial: a character
Hometown: 25-character string
Phone number: a seven-character string
Sex: a character (M or F)
Class level: a one-digit integer (1, 2, 3, 4, or 5 for special)
Major: a four-character string

Total credits earned to date: an integer
Cumulative GPA: a real value

File is arranged so that student numbers are in increasing order.

Sample StudentFile

```
10103JOHNSON         JAMES     L
WAUPUN, WISCONSIN            7345229M1ENGR 15 3.15
10104ANDREWS         PETER     J
GRAND RAPIDS, MICHIGAN  9493301M2CPSC 42 2.78
10110PETERS          ANDREW    J
LYNDEN, WASHINGTON          3239550M5ART  63 2.05
10113VANDENVANDER   VANNESSA  V
FREMONT, MICHIGAN           5509237F4HIST110 3.74
10126ARISTOTLE       ALICE     A
CHINO, CALIFORNIA           3330861F3PHIL 78 3.10
10144LUCKY           LUCY      L
GRANDVILLE, MICHIGAN    7745424F5HIST 66 2.29
10179EULER           LENNIE    L
THREE RIVERS, MICHIGAN  6290017M1MATH 15 3.83
10191NAKAMURA        TOKY      O
CHICAGO, ILLINOIS           4249665F1SOCI 12 1.95
10226FREUD           FRED      E
LYNDEN, WASHINGTON          8340115M1PSYC 15 1.85
10272SPEARSHAKE      WILLIAM   W
GRAND RAPIDS, MICHIGAN  2410744M5ENGL102 2.95
10274TCHAIKOVSKY     WOLFGANG  A
BYRON CENTER, MICHIGAN  8845115M3MUSC 79 2.75
10284ORANGE          DUTCH     V
GRAAFSCHAAP, MICHIGAN   3141660M2ENGR 42 2.98
10297CAESAR          JULIE     S
DENVER, COLORADO            4470338F4HIST117 3.25
10298PSYCHO          PRUNELLA  E
DE MOTTE, INDIANA           5384609F4PSYC120 2.99
10301BULL            SITTING   U
GALLUP, NEW MEXICO          6632997M1EDUC 14 1.95
10302CUSTER          GENERAL   G
BADLANDS, SOUTH DAKOTA  5552992M3HIST 40 1.95
10303FAHRENHEIT      FELICIA   O
SHEBOYGAN, WISCONSIN    5154997F2CHEM 40 3.85
10304DEUTSCH         SPRECHEN  Z
SPARTA, MICHIGAN            8861201F5GERM 14 3.05
10307MENDELSSOHN     MOZART    W
PEORIA, ILLINOIS            2410744M3MUSC 76 2.87
10310AUGUSTA         ADA       B
LAKEWOOD, CALIFORNIA    7172339F2CPSC 46 3.83
10319GAUSS           CARL      F
YORKTOWN, PENNSYLVANIA  3385494M2MATH 41 4.00
10323KRONECKER      LEO        P
TRAVERSE CITY, MICHIGAN 6763991M3MATH 77 2.75
10330ISSACSON        JACOB     A
SILVER SPRINGS, MD          4847932M5RELI 25 2.99
10331ISSACSON        ESAU      B
SILVER SPRINGS, MD          4847932M5RELI 25 2.98
10339DEWEY           JOHANNA   A
SALT LAKE CITY, UTAH        6841129F2EDUC 41 3.83
```

(cont.)

```
10348VIRUS            VERA    W
SAGINAW, MICHIGAN         6634401F4CPSC115 3.25
10355ZYLSTRA          ZELDA   A
DOWNS, KANSAS             7514008F1ENGL 16 1.95
10377PORGY            BESS    N
COLUMBUS, OHIO           4841771F2MUSC 44 2.78
10389NEWMANN          ALFRED  E
CHEYENNE, WYOMING        7712399M4EDUC115 0.99
10395MEDES            ARCHIE  L
WHITINSVILLE, MA         9294401M3ENGR 80 3.10
10406MACDONALD        RONALD  B
SEATTLE, WASHINGTON      5582911M1CPSC 15 2.99
10415AARDVARK         ANTHONY A
GRANDVILLE, MICHIGAN     5325912M2ENGR 43 2.79
10422GESTALT          GLORIA  G
WHEATON, ILLINOIS        6631212F2PSYC 42 2.48
10431GOTODIJKSTRA     EDGAR   G
CAWKER CITY, KANSAS      6349971M1CPSC 15 4.00
10448REMBRANDT        ROBERTA E
SIOUX CENTER, IOWA       2408113F1ART  77 2.20
10458SHOEMAKER        IMELDA  M
HONOLULU, HAWAII         9193001F1POLS 15 3.15
10467MARX             KARL    Z
HAWTHORNE, NEW JERSEY    5513915M3ECON 78 2.75
10470SCROOGE          EBENEZER T
TROY, MICHIGAN           8134001M4SOCI118 3.25
10482NIGHTINGALE      FLORENCE K
ROCHESTER, NEW YORK      7175118F1NURS 15 3.15
10490GAZELLE          GWENDOLYN D
CHINO, CALIFORNIA        3132446F2P E  43 2.78
10501PASTEUR          LOUISE  A
WINDOW ROCK, ARIZONA     4245170F1BIOL 16 3.10
10519ELBA             ABLE    M
BOZEMAN, MONTANA         8183226M3SPEE 77 3.40
10511LEWIS            CLARK   N
NEW ERA, MICHIGAN        6461125M4GEOG114 3.37
10515MOUSE            MICHAEL E
BOISE, IDAHO             5132771M5EDUC 87 1.99
10523PAVLOV           TIFFANY T
FARMINGTON, MICHIGAN     9421753F1BIOL 13 1.77
10530CHICITA          JUANITA A
OKLAHOMA CITY, OK        3714377F5ENGL 95 2.66
10538BUSCH            ARCH    E
ST LOUIS, MISSOURI       8354112M3ENGR 74 2.75
10547FAULT            PAIGE   D
PETOSKEY, MICHIGAN       4543116F5CPSC 55 2.95
10553SANTAMARIA       NINA    P
PLYMOUTH, MASSACHUSETTS  2351881F1HIST 15 1.77
10560SHYSTER          SAMUEL  D
EVERGLADES, FLORIDA      4421885M1SOCI 13 1.95
10582YEWLISS          CAL     C
RUDYARD, MICHIGAN        3451220M3MATH 76 2.99
10590ATANASOFF        ENIAC   C
SPRINGFIELD, ILLINOIS    6142449F1CPSC 14 1.88
10597ROCKNE           ROCKY   K
PORTLAND, OREGON         4631744M4P E 116 1.98
10610ROOSEVELT        ROSE    Y
SPRING LAKE, MICHIGAN    9491221F5E SC135 2.95
10623XERXES           ART     I
CINCINATTI, OHIO         3701228M4GREE119 3.25
```

(cont.)

```
10629LEIBNIZ          GOTTFRIED W
BOULDER, COLORADO           5140228M1MATH 13 1.95
10633VESPUCCI         VERA      D
RIPON, CALIFORNIA           4341883F5GEOG 89 2.29
10648PRINCIPAL        PAMELA    P
ALBANY, NEW YORK            7145513F1EDUC 14 1.75
10652CICERO           MARSHA    M
RAPID CITY, SD              3335910F3LATI 77 2.87
10657WEERD            DEWEY     L
DETROIT, MICHIGAN           4841962M4PHIL115 2.99
10663HOCHSCHULE       HORTENSE  C
LINCOLN, NEBRASKA           7120111F5EDUC100 2.70
10668EINSTEIN         ALFRED    M
NEWARK, NEW JERSEY          3710225M2ENGR 41 2.78
10675FIBONACCI        LEONARD   O
NASHVILLE, TENNESSEE        4921107M4MATH115 3.25
10682ANGELO           MIKE      L
AUSTIN, TEXAS               5132201M4ART 117 3.74
10688PASCAL           BLAZE     R
BROOKLYN, NEW YORK `         7412993M1CPSC 15 1.98
```

StudentUpDate
Student number: an integer (same as those used in *StudentFile*)
For each of five courses:
    Course name: a seven-character string (e.g., CPSC131)
    Letter grade: a two-character string (e.g., A−, B+, Cb)
    Course credit: an integer

File is sorted so that student numbers are in increasing order. There is one
update record for each student in *StudentFile*.

Sample StudentUpdate:

```
10103ENGL176C 4EDUC268B 4EDUC330B+3P E 281C 3ENGR317D 4
10104CPSC271D+4E SC208D-3PHIL340B+2CPSC146D+4ENGL432D+4
10110ART 520D 3E SC259F 1ENGL151D+4MUSC257B 4PSYC486C 4
10113HIST498F 3P E 317C+4MUSC139B-3PHIL165D 3GEOG222C 3
10126PHIL367C-4EDUC420C-3EDUC473C 3EDUC224D-3GERM257F 4
10144HIST559C+3MATH357D 3CPSC323C-2P E 246D-4MUSC379D+4
10179MATH169C-4CHEM163C+4MUSC436A-3MATH366D-2BIOL213A-4
10191SOCI177F 4POLS106A 4EDUC495A-3ENGR418B+2ENGR355A 4
10226PSYC116B 3GERM323B-4ART 350A 4HIST269B+4EDUC214C+3
10272ENGL558A-4EDUC169D+3PSYC483B+4ENGR335B+2BIOL228B 4
10274MUSC351B 4PSYC209C-4ENGR400F 1E SC392A 4SOCI394B-3
10284ENGR292D 4PSYC172C 4EDUC140B 4MATH274F 4MUSC101D+4
10297HIST464F 1HIST205F 1ENGR444F 1MATH269F 1EDUC163F 1
10298PSYC452B 3MATH170C+4EDUC344C-2GREE138C-2SPEE303A-3
10301EDUC197A 4P E 372B 3ENGR218D 4MATH309C 4E SC405C-4
10302CHEM283F 1P E 440A 2MATH399A-3HIST455C-4MATH387C-3
10303HIST111D-3ART151 C+3ENGL100C-3PSYC151D+3PE104  A-1
```

(cont.)

```
10304GERM526C-2CHEM243C 4POLS331B-4EDUC398A 3ENGR479D+4
10307MUSC323B+3MATH485C 4HIST232B+4EDUC180A 3ENGL130B+4
10310CPSC264B 2POLS227D+3ENGR467D-3MATH494D-4ART 420C+4
10319MATH276B 2E SC434A 3HIST197B-4GERM489B-2ART 137C-3
10323MATH377D-4EDUC210D 4MATH385D-4ENGR433C 2HIST338A-4
10330HIST546C+3E SC440B+3GREE472C+3BIOL186B 4GEOG434C+2
10331HIST546C 3E SC440B+3GREE472C 3BIOL186B+4GEOG434C+2
10339EDUC283B 3CPSC150B 3ENGR120D 4CPSC122F 4ART 216B 4
10348CPSC411C-3HIST480C+4PSYC459B 4BIOL299B+4ECON276B+3
10355ENGL130C-3CPSC282C+4CPSC181A-4CPSC146C-4SOCI113F 1
10377SOCI213D+3PSYC158D 4MUSC188C 3PSYC281D-4ENGR339B+4
10389EDUC414D+4PSYC115C-2PSYC152D-4ART 366D-3ENGR366F 4
10395ENGR396B 4HIST102F 3ENGL111A 4PSYC210D-2GREE128A 4
10406CPSC160C+4CPSC233C 1LATI494C+3ENGL115C-3MATH181A 3
10415ENGR287C 4EDUC166B-4EDUC106A-3P E 190F 3MATH171B-3
10422PSYC275A-4MATH497A 4EDUC340F 1GERM403C-4MATH245D+4
10431CPSC187D-4CPSC426F 4ENGR476B-4BIOL148B+3CPSC220F 3
10448ART 171D+3CPSC239C-3SOCI499B-4HIST113D+3PSYC116C 4
10458POLS171F 1CPSC187C+4CHEM150B 2PHIL438D-4PHIL254D 4
10467ECON335D-3E SC471B+4MATH457C+3MATH207C 2BIOL429D 4
10470MUSC415C+3POLS177C 3CPSC480A 4PSYC437B 3SOCI276D 4
10482ENGL158D-4EDUC475B 3HIST172B-2P E 316F 4ENGR294A-3
10490P E 239F 4ENGL348F 3LATI246F 4CPSC350F 4MATH114F 1
10501BIOL125F 4CPSC412F 3E SC279F 4ENGR153F 2ART 293F 1
10519SPEE386B+4HIST479C 4PSYC249B-2GREE204B-4P E 421A 1
10511E SC416B 3MATH316D-4MATH287C 2MATH499A-4E SC288D 3
10515EDUC563D+3PHIL373D-3ART 318B 4HIST451F 1ART 476C+3
10523BIOL183D-2HIST296D+4HIST380B+4ENGR216C 4MATH412B-2
10530ENGL559F 1EDUC457D+4CPSC306A 3ENGR171B+1CPSC380A 4
10538ENGR328A-4ENGR336C 3EDUC418D+3PHIL437B+4CPSC475D 4
10547CPSC537A-4ART 386D 4HIST292D-4ENGR467A-4P E 464B+4
10553HIST170A-4SOCI496D-3PHIL136B+4CPSC371D-4CPSC160A-1
10560SOCI153D+3MATH438D+4CPSC378C 4BIOL266F 3EDUC278D+3
10582MATH388A-3P E 311B 3ECON143D 4MATH304C+3P E 428C+4
10590CPSC134B-3E SC114B+3CPSC492C 4ENGL121C 4ENGR403A-4
10597P E 423A-3BIOL189D+3PHIL122D-4ENGL194C-4SOCI113D+3
10610E SC594C-3PHIL344F 4CPSC189B+2ENGR411D-3MATH241A 4
10623GREE412B-4ENGL415D-3ENGL234D-4MATH275F 1SOCI124B+3
10629MATH137D 2MATH481F 3E SC445F 1MATH339D 4ART 219B+4
10633GEOG573B 4ENGL149C+4EDUC113B+4ENGR458C-2HIST446D+4
10648EDUC132D+4MUSC103D-4ENGL263C 4ENGL134B+4E SC392A 3
10652LATI363F 3BIOL425F 1CPSC267C 4EDUC127C+3MATH338B 4
10657PHIL429F 1ART 412D-4MUSC473B-4SOCI447C-4MATH237D+2
10663EDUC580B-4ENGR351B+4SOCI283D 4ART 340C 4PSYC133D+3
10668ENGR274B+4SOCI438C 1P E 327C 4BIOL158A 4EDUC457A-4
10675MATH457A 4ENGR114C 4CPSC218C 3E SC433C-3PSYC243C+1
10682ART 483D+3GERM432C 3ENGL103B+4MUSC169C-3SOCI381C-2
10688CPSC182F 1HIST371C+4PSYC408F 1MUSC214B+4MATH151C 3
```

UsersFile
Identification number: an integer
User's name: A 30-character string in the form Last Name, First Name
Password: a 5-character string

Resource limit (in dollars): an integer of up to four digits
Resources used to date: a real value

File is arranged so that identification numbers are in increasing order.

Sample UsersFile:

```
10101MILTGEN, JOSEPH                       MOE
 750 380.81
10102SMALL, ISAAC                          LARGE
 650 598.84
10103SNYDER, SAMUEL                        R2-D2
 250 193.74
10104EDMUNDSEN, EDMUND                     ABCDE
 250 177.93
10105BRAUNSCHNEIDER, CHRISTOPHER           BROWN
 850 191.91
10106PIZZULA, NORMA                        PIZZA
 350 223.95
10107VANDERVAN, HENRY                      VAN
 750 168.59
10108FREELOADER, FREDDIE                   RED
 450  76.61
10109ALEXANDER, ALVIN                      GREAT
 650 405.04
10110MOUSE, MICHAEL                        EARS
  50  42.57
10111LUKASEWICZ, ZZZYK                     RPN
 350  73.50
10112CHRISTMAS, MARY                       NOEL
 850  33.28
10113SINKEY, CJ                            TRAIN
 750 327.53
10114NIJHOFF, LARAN                        KKID
 550 382.03
10115LIESTMA, STAN                         SAAB
 650  38.36
10116ZWIER, APOLLOS                        PJ
 350 249.48
10117JAEGER, TIM                           BIKE
 250 246.73
10118VANZWALBERG, JORGE                    EGYPT
 850 466.95
10119JESTER, COURTNEY                      JOKER
 450 281.16
10120MCDONALD, RONALD                      FRIES
 250  35.00
10121NEDERLANDER, BENAUT                   DUTCH
 550  28.82
10122HAYBAILER, HOMER                      FARM
 850  37.32
10123SPEAR, WILLIAM                        SHAKE
 450 337.01
10124ROMEO, JULIET                         XOXOX
 150 100.19
10125GREEK, JIMMY                          WAGER
 250   0.03
```

(cont.)

10126VIRUS, VERA	WORM	
750 67.35		
10127BEECH, ROCKY	BOAT	
950 256.18		
10128ENGEL, ANGEL	WINGS	
150 16.39		
10129ABNER, LIL	DAISY	
950 89.57		
10130TRACY, DICK	CRIME	
550 392.00		
10131MCGEE, FIBBER	MOLLY	
750 332.12		
10132BELL ,ALEXANDER	PHONE	
850 337.43		
20101COBB, TYRUS	TIGER	
50 32.81		
20102GEORGE, RUTH	BABE	
350 269.93		
20103DESCARTES, RONALD	HORSE	
250 109.34		
20104EUCLID, IAN	GREEK	
350 63.63		
20105DANIELS, EZEKIEL	LIONS	
350 128.69		
20106TARZAN, JANE	APES	
150 100.31		
20107HABBAKUK, JONAH	WHALE	
950 183.93		
20108COLUMBUS, CHRIS	PINTA	
850 202.24		
20109BYRD, RICHARD	NORTH	
550 168.49		
20110BUNYAN, PAUL	BABE	
550 333.47		
20111CHAUCER, JEFF	POEM	
950 37.02		
20112STOTLE, ARI	LOGIC	
750 337.74		
20113HARRISON, BEN	PRES	
550 262.97		
20114JAMES, JESSE	GUNS	
250 58.81		
20115SCOTT, FRANCINE	FLAG	
350 168.11		
20116PHILLIPS, PHYLLIS	GAS66	
650 322.22		
20117DOLL, BARBARA	KEN	
350 26.34		
20118FINN, HUCK	TOM	
350 22.86		
20119SAWYER, TOM	HUCK	
950 460.30		
20120NEWMANN, ALFRED	MAD	
450 116.00		
20121SIMPLE, SIMON	SAYS	
550 486.05		
20122SCHMIDT, MESSER	PLANE	
250 35.31		
20124LUTHER, CALVIN	REF	
777 666.66		
20125YALE, HARVARD	IVY	
150 127.70		

F

Miscellany

In the main part of this text we mentioned some special features of Pascal that were not described in detail because they are not usually covered in an introductory programming course. For completeness they are briefly described in this appendix.

Random Number Generation

As we noted in Section 6.3, a random number generator is not a predefined function/procedure in standard Pascal. Consequently, some versions of Pascal may not provide a function like *Random* assumed in the text. In such cases, the following function may be used to generate random numbers. Details of this and other techniques for generating random numbers can be found in *The Art of Computer Programming: Seminumerical Algorithms,* vol. 2, by Donald Knuth (Reading, Mass.: Addison-Wesley, 1981).

function *Random* : *real*;

(* This function generates a random real number in the interval from 0 to 1. It uses the global variable *Seed,* which is initialized by the user and should be an odd positive integer; thereafter, it is the random integer generated on the preceding reference to *Random.*
Note: The constant 65536 used in this function is appropriate for a machine having 32-bit words. For a machine having M-bit words, it should be replaced by the value of 2 to the power $M/2$. *)

const
    Modulus = 65536;
    Multiplier = 25173;
    Increment = 13849;

begin (* *Random* *)
    Seed := (*Multiplier* * *Seed* + *Increment*) **mod** *Modulus*;
    Random := *Seed* / *Modulus*
end (* *Random* *);

Indirect Recursion

The examples of recursion given in the main part of the text have illustrated *direct recursion* in which the functions and procedures reference themselves directly. *Indirect recursion* occurs when a subprogram references other sub-programs, and some chain of subprogram references eventually results in a reference to the first subprogram again. For example, function A may reference function B, which references procedure C, which references A again. Since Pascal requires that a subprogram be defined before it is referenced, B would have to be defined before A, since A references B, and C must be defined before B, since B references C. However, since C references A, A would have to be defined before C. Thus it would seem that indirect recursion is not possible in Pascal programs.

To allow indirect recursion without violating Scope Rule 4 in Section 6.4, Pascal allows *dummy definitions* of functions and procedures in addition to actual definitions. A dummy definition consists only of the subprogram heading followed by the reserved word **forward** that is a *directive* to the compiler that the actual definition appears later in the subprogram section of the program. It thus has the form

    function *name* (*formal-parameter-list*) : *result-type*; **forward**;

or

    procedure *name* (*formal-parameter-list*); **forward**;

In the heading of the corresponding actual definition of the subprogram, the formal parameter list and the result type for a function are omitted so that it has the form

    function *name*;

or

    procedure *name*;

Now consider again the situation of function A referencing function B referencing procedure C, which references A again. The following arrangement of dummy and actual subprogram definitions makes this indirect recursion possible without violating Scope Rule 4:

> **function** A (*formal-parameter-list*) : *result-type*; **forward**;
> (∗ Dummy definition of A ∗)

procedure C (*formal-parameter-list*); **forward**;
.
.
.
(∗ Actual definition of C ∗)
.
.
.

function B (*formal-parameter-list*) : *result-type*;
.
.
.
(∗ Actual definition of B ∗)
.
.
.

function A;
.
.
.
(∗ Actual definition of A ∗)
.
.
.

A can reference B (in its actual definition), since B has already been defined. Similarly, B can reference C, since C has been defined earlier. And C can reference A, since A is defined before C (albeit in a dummy fashion).

The directive **forward** is the only compiler directive in standard Pascal, but many versions of Pascal also provide others. Another common directive is **external**, which specifies that the actual definition of a subprogram is external to the program.

Statement Labels and the *goto* Statement

In Section 5.3 we saw that a repeat loop is a posttest loop in which the termination test is made at the bottom of the loop. This is in contrast to the while loop discussed in Section 4.4, which is a pretest loop in which the termination test is at the top of the loop. More general repetition structures can be implemented in Pascal. In these structures there may be several termination tests and they may be placed anywhere within the body of the loop, or there may be no termination test at all, in which case the loop is an ***infinite loop.***

A ***repeat-forever loop*** is an example of an infinite loop. It can be constructed in Pascal as a while loop,

while *true* **do**
    body of the loop

or as a repeat loop:

> **repeat**
> body of the loop
> **until** *false*

When these statements are executed, the body of the loop is executed repeatedly. Since the termination test is never false in the first case and is never true in the second, these loops will never terminate. Such infinite loops may be useful in some special applications. For example, control programs in an operating system are meant to run forever. Similarly, a program might use a non-terminating loop to continually collect data from a device monitoring some process such as the operation of a nuclear reactor.

Most programs, however, are not intended to execute forever and consequently, most loops must contain some mechanism for terminating repetition. To illustrate, consider a program for which the input data may contain errors and provision must be made to detect these errors. When an error is found, control might be passed to some other part of the program for error handling and/or execution of the program terminated. For example, if all of the data values processed by a program are no greater than 100, the following while loop might be used:

> **while** *true* **do**
> **begin**
> *read* (*Data*);
> **if** *Data* > 100 **then goto** 50;
> (∗ else process *Data* ∗)
> .
> .
> .
> **end** (∗ **while** ∗)
> 50: *writeln* ('∗∗∗ Bad data value ∗∗∗', *Data*);
> .
> .
> .

In this example, 50 is a ***statement label.*** Such labels must be declared in the label section in the declaration part of the program. This section has the form

> **label**
> *label-1, label-2, . . . label-n*;

and must be the first section in the declaration part. Each *label-i* must be a positive integer of up to four digits and can be used to label only one statement. Control can then be transferred to that statement by using a **goto** statement of the form

> **goto** *label-i*

In the preceding example, if a data value greater than 100 is read, control is transferred to the statement with label 50. A label section such as the following must therefore be used to define this statement label:

label 50;

The statement label 50 followed by a colon (:) can then be attached as a prefix to any statement in the program unit in which this label section appears. In our example, it is attached to an output statement that displays an error message.

A statement of the form

if *boolean-expression* **then goto** *statement-label*

can be placed anywhere within a loop to cause an exit from it. For example,

```
while true do
    begin
        statement-sequence-1;
        if boolean-expression then goto ##;
        statement-sequence-2
    end (* while *);
##: next-statement
```

If *statement-sequence-1* is omitted, this loop is a pretest loop; if *statement-sequence-2* is omitted, it is a posttest loop; if both *statement-sequence-1* and *statement-sequence-2* are present, it is a ***test-in-the-middle loop.*** The loop might also contain multiple exits

```
while true do
    begin
        statement-sequence-1;
        if boolean-expression-1 then goto ##;
        statement-sequence-2;
        if boolean-expression-2 then goto ##;
            .
            .
            .
        statement-sequence-k;
        if boolean-expression-k then goto ##;
        statement-sequence-k + 1
    end (* while *);
##: next-statement
```

In most applications, however, while and repeat-until loops are preferred because the logical flow in such single-exit loops is easier to follow than it is in loops that allow multiple exits. Moreover, loops having the termination test at the top or at the bottom of the loop are easier to read and understand than are those that allow exits in the middle.

The scope rules considered in Section 6.4 dealt only with identifiers and did not mention statement labels. The scope rules for labels may be obtained by simply replacing the word ''identifier'' with ''statement label'' in the fundamental scope principle and in the first three scope rules. Thus the ***fundamental scope principle for labels*** is

> The scope of a statement label is the program unit in which it is declared.

and the three ***scope rules for labels*** are

1. A statement label declared in a program unit is not accessible outside that unit.
2. A global statement label is accessible in any subprogram in which that label is not declared locally.
3. Statement labels declared in a subprogram can be accessed by any subprogram defined within it, provided that the label is not declared locally in the internal subprogram.

The Procedure *page*

The procedure *page* is designed to insert page breaks into the output produced by a program. This procedure is called with a statement of the form

> *page (file-name)*

or

> *page*

In the second form, the standard file *output* is assumed. The effect of a call to procedure *page* is system dependent, and the details must be determined by consulting the system reference manuals. The Pascal standard states only that

> *Page (f)* shall cause an implementation-defined effect on the textfile *f*, such that subsequent output to *f* will be on a new page if the textfile is printed on a suitable device and shall perform an implicit *writeln*. . . .

Alternate Forms of Procedures *new* and *dispose*

Alternate forms of reference to the procedures *new* and *dispose* may be used for variant records. The procedure *new* may be called with a statement of the form

> *new (pointer, tag-value-1, tag-value-2, . . . , tag-value-n)*

Here *tag-value-1, tag-value-2, . . . , tag-value-n* represent values of tag fields in increasingly nested variant parts of the record; that is, this procedure reference may be used to allocate a memory location for a record having the structure

```
record
    fixed-part-1;
    case tag-field-1 : tag-type-1 of
                        .
                        .
                        .
        tag-value-1 : (fixed-part-2;
                        case tag-field-2 : tag-type-2 of
                                            .
                                            .
                                            .
                            tag-value-2 : (fixed-part-3;
                                            case tag-field-3 : tag-type-3 of
                                                                .
                                                                .
                                                                .
                                                tag-value-3 : (. . .
                                .
                                .
                                .

end;
```

When a memory location is allocated for a variant record with a procedure call of the form

   new (*pointer*)

it is sufficiently large to store the largest variant in that record. If it is known that a record with a particular variant is being processed, the alternative form of the procedure call may be used. This allows the system to allocate a location whose size is appropriate for that variant. To illustrate, consider the following declarations:

```
type
    NameString = packed array[1..20] of char;
    EmployeeRecord = record
                        Name : NameString;
                        Age, Dependents : integer;
                        case EmpCode : char of
                            'F' : (* Factory employee *)
                                    (DeptCode : char;
                                    HourlyRate : real);
                            'O' : (* Office employee *)
                                    (Salary : real);
                            'S' : (* Salesperson *)
                                    (MileageAllowance : integer;
                                    BasePay, CommissionRate : real)
                    end;
```

If it is known that a location is needed to store the record of an office employee (*EmpCode* is O) and *P* is to point to this location, the procedure reference

new (P, 'O')

may be used.

When a memory location is allocated in this manner, however, it may then be used only for a record with this particular structure, that is, to store a record for an office employee. Also, to dispose of this memory location, an alternate form of reference to the procedure *dispose* is required. For this example, it would be

dispose (P, 'O')

The form for *dispose* that corresponds to the general form of the procedure reference for *new* is

dispose (pointer, tag-value-1, tag-value-2, . . . , tag-value-n)

The alternate forms of procedure references to *new* and *dispose* allow the system (but do not require it) to allocate memory more efficiently for variant records. When each of the variant parts is about the same size, however, there is no real advantage in using these alternate forms.

The Procedures *pack* and *unpack*

The procedures *pack* and *unpack* transfer elements between unpacked arrays and packed arrays. The procedure *pack* is called with a statement of the form

pack (unpackedarray, first, packedarray)

where *unpackedarray* is the unpacked array and *first* is the position of the first element of *unpackedarray* to be transferred to the packed array *packedarray*. To illustrate, the technique used in procedure *ReadString* of Section 10.1 for reading a string into a packed array could be modified to declare an unpacked array *Buffer*,

Buffer : **array**[1..*StringLimit*] **of** *char*;

read characters into *Buffer*,

```
for i := 1 to StringLimit do
    if not eoln then
        read (Buffer[i])
    else
        Buffer[i]) := ' ';
readln;
```

and then transfer these to the string variable *Str* of type **packed array**[1 . . *StringLimit*] **of** *char*;

    pack (*Buffer*, 1, *Str*);

The procedure *unpack* transfers the elements from a packed array to an unpacked array. This procedure is called with a statement of the form

    unpack (*packedarray*, *unpackedarray*, *first*)

where *packedarray* is the packed array whose elements are to be transferred to the unpacked array *unpackedarray; first* denotes the position in *unpackedarray* where the first element of *packedarray* is to be placed.

For both of the procedures *pack* and *unpack,* the component type of the two arrays must be the same, but the indices may be of different ordinal types. The number of array elements transferred is the number of elements in the packed array. Consequently, the segment of the unpacked array to which or from which values are being transferred must be at least as large as the number of elements in the packed array.

Arrays of any type may be packed. In particular, packing may be useful in processing boolean arrays, since the boolean constants *false* and *true* are normally represented internally as 0 and 1, each of which can be stored in a single bit. A 32-bit memory word can, therefore, store 32 boolean constants. The declaration

    type
        Barray = **packed array**[1..100] **of** *boolean*;

therefore allows memory to be allocated more efficiently than

    type
        Barray = **array**[1..100] **of** *boolean*;

The beginning programmer should not be overly concerned with the details of how data is stored internally but instead should expect the computer to utilize the memory as efficiently as possible. Consequently, the procedures *pack* and *unpack* and the packed array specification are seldom used except for character arrays.

G

Other Versions of Pascal

As we have noted, there are several popular versions of Pascal that vary some-what from the ANSI/IEEE standard version of Pascal described in this text. In this appendix we summarize the major variations and extensions in three such dialects of Pascal.

Turbo Pascal

Turbo Pascal is a popular version of Pascal for microcomputers. It was developed and marketed by Borland International. The following is a summary of the major Turbo variations and extensions, organized by chapters for easy reference.

Chapter 3

- *Additional data types*. In addition to type *integer*, the integer types *byte, shortint, word,* and *longint* are provided. Their ranges of values are given by

Type	Range
byte	0 through 255
shortint	-128 through 127
integer	-32768 through 32767
word	0 through 65535
longint	-2147483647 through 2147483648

For processing reals, the types *real, single, double,* and *extended* are provided as is *comp* for processing integers stored in a real format. (The special compiler directive for numeric processing({$N}) must be turned on when using types *single, double, extended,* and *comp.* This is all that is required if your machine has an 8087 chip. If it does not, a special emulation directive ({$E}) can be turned on to provide 8087 emulation in software.) For these types the ranges and number of significant digits are given by

Type	Range	Significant Digits
real	2.9E–39 through 1.7E + 38	11–12
single	1.5E–45 through 3.4E + 38	7–8
double	5.0E–324 through 1.7E + 308	15–16
extended	3.4E–4932 through 1.1E + 4932	19–20
comp	1 − 2E + 63 through 2E + 63 − 1	19–20

Turbo Pascal also provides the type **string** for processing strings of characters. Strings are limited to 255 characters.

● *Alternative representations of numbers.* Integers may be expressed in hexadecimal notation obtained by placing a dollar sign ($) in front of its hexadecimal representation.

● *Predefined constants. Maxint* has the value 32767 and *MaxLongInt* has the value 2147483647.

● *Reserved words.* The following are additional reserved words in Turbo Pascal: **absolute, external, implementation, inline, interface, interrupt, shl, shr, string, unit, uses,** and **xor**.

● *Identifiers.* An identifier consists of a letter followed by any number of additional letters, digits, or underscores (__); only the first 63 characters are used.

● *Arithmetic operators.* The value of i **mod** j is the remainder that results when i is divided by j. Also, i **div** j is defined for all nonzero integers i and j. The shift operators **shl** and **shr** shift the bits in the binary representation of an integer a specified number of positions to the left or right, respectively. For example, 4 **shl** 6 = 256 and 256 **shr** 6 = 4. **Shl** and **shr** have the same priorities as the multiplication and division operators. The boolean operators **not, and, or,** and **xor** may also be used to perform bitwise boolean operations on integer values (see the Turbo Pascal notes for Chapter 4).

● *Arithmetic functions. Frac, int* and *pi* are predefined arithmetic functions; $frac(x)$ returns the fractional part of the real or integer parameter x and $int(x)$ returns the integer part; pi returns the value of π.

● *Program heading.* In Turbo Pascal, the program heading is optional.

● **Uses** *clause.* A Turbo Pascal program may contain a **uses** clause of the form

    uses *unit-name*

which precedes the declaration part of the program. This clause makes available all of the constants, types, variables, procedures, and functions that are defined in the specified unit (see the Turbo notes for Chapter 6).

- *Declaration part.* The sections of the declaration part may appear any number of times and in any order.
- *Typed constants.* Turbo Pascal allows typed constants. These are not true constants but are, in fact, variables whose initial values are specified in a modified form of the usual constant declaration. For example,

    const
       Sum : integer = 0;
       Radius : real = 2.5;
       Code : char = 'A';

declares the integer variable *Sum* and initializes it to 0, the real variable *Radius* and initializes it to 2.5, and the character variable *Code*, initializing it to 'A'.

- *Increment and decrement operations.* Turbo Pascal provides two special procedures that can be used to increment or decrement integer variables. These procedures have the forms

    Inc (variable, step)
    Dec (variable, step)

where *variable* is an integer variable whose value is to be incremented by *step*, where *step* is an integer-valued expression. For example, the assignment statement

    Sum := Sum + Counter

can also be written

    Inc (Sum, Counter)

If the step size is omitted in these statements, it is taken to be 1. For example,

    Dec (Counter)

is an alternative to the assignment statement

    Counter := Counter − 1

Chapter 4

- *Boolean operators.* In addition to **not, and,** and **or,** the exclusive-or operator **xor** is provided; P **xor** Q is true if exactly one of P or Q is true and is false otherwise. Also, these four boolean operators may be applied bitwise to integer values (0 = false, 1 = true). For example,

$$14 \textbf{ and } 23 = 0000000000001110_2 \textbf{ and } 0000000000010111_2$$
$$= 0000000000000110_2 = 6$$

Similarly, 14 **or** 23 = 31 and 14 **xor** 23 = 25.

Chapter 5

- **case** *statement*.   Ranges of values may be specified in the form

    first-value .. last-value

    in label lists of a **case** statement. Also, a **case** statement may have an **else** clause; for example,

    case *Class* **of**
          1 : *writeln* ('Freshman');
       2..4 : *writeln* ('Upperclassman')
        else
                 writeln ('Special')
    end (* **case** *)

    If the value of the selector is not in any of the label lists, the statement in the **else** clause is executed; if no **else** clause is present, execution "falls through" the **case** statement and continues with the next statement. This example also illustrates that subrange notation may be used in label lists to indicate a range of consecutive values.
- **for** *statement*.   When execution of a **for** statement is completed, the control variable retains its last value.

Chapter 6

In addition to the standard predefined Pascal procedures and functions, Turbo Pascal provides a number of others. These include the function *Random* and the procedure *Randomize* for generating random numbers:

- *Random, Random (Num)*. This function generates random numbers. The first form returns a random real number in the interval [0, 1), and the second returns a random integer value in the interval [0, *Num*).
- *Randomize*. This procedure initializes the random number generator with a random value.

The string functions *concat, copy, length,* and *pos* and the string procedures *delete* and *insert* described in the Variations and Extensions section at the end of Chapter 10 are also provided. In addition, there are a number of special graphics subprograms.

- *Function and procedure parameters*. The declarations of function and procedure parameters differ from those in standard Pascal. For example, in Turbo Pascal, the function *ApproxArea* in Section 6.7 would be written

    function *ApproxArea*(*f* : *RealFunction*; *a*, *b* : *real*; *n* : *integer*) : *real*;

    (* Returns the approximate area under the graph of function *f* from $x = a$ to $x = b$ using the rectangle method with altitudes chosen at the midpoints of the *n* subintervals. *)

The type identifier *RealFunction* must be defined in a type section in the declaration part of the program. In this example, the type section might have the form

type
    RealFunction = **function**(*x* : *real*) : *real*;

The type identifier *RealFunction* can then be used to specify that the value of a formal parameter (or variable or other identifier) is a function having one parameter of type *real* and whose value is of type *real*. (Whenever a function or procedure is used as a parameter, the compiler directive {$F+} must be included in the program, or alternatively, the Force Far Calls option in the Compiler submenu of the main menu Options must be turned on.)

- *Units*. A unit has three parts, a heading that names the unit, an interface part that describes the processing done by this unit, and an implementation part that specifies how this processing is carried out:

    unit heading
    interface part
    implementation part

The ***unit heading*** consists of the reserved word **unit** followed by a name for the unit:

    unit name;

The ***interface part*** begins with the reserved word **interface** and this is followed by an optional uses clause and a modified form of the declaration part of a program:

    interface
    uses clause (optional)
    declaration part (modified)

The **uses** clause has the same form as in a program and specifies other units that contain special items to be used in this unit; these items are also available to any programs or other units that use this unit. In the declaration part, constant, variable, and type (and label) sections have the usual forms, but subprogram sections contain only headings of the procedures and functions defined in this unit.

The ***implementation part*** of a unit consists of the reserved word **implementation** followed by an optional **uses** clause, a declaration part, and an initialization part:

    implementation
    uses clause (optional)
    declaration part
    initialization part.

The **uses** clause has the usual form and specifies other units that contain special items to be used in this unit. However, unlike the case where the **uses** clause appears in the interface part, these items are *not* available to programs or other units that use this unit. The various sections of the declaration part have the usual forms. One of the subprogram sections must contain the complete procedure and function definitions for those procedures and functions whose headings where given in the interface part. The headings in these definitions must of course be the same as those in the interface part. The *initialization part* may be trivial, consisting simply of the reserved word **end,** or it may have the same form as the statement part of a program. In the second case, the statements in this statement part are executed before those in any program or other unit in which this unit is used. In either case a period follows the initialization part to mark the end of the unit.

The following is an example of a unit that might be used in developing financial and accounting programs. It contains procedures *ProcessCredit* and *ProcessDebit,* which are renamed versions of *ProcessDeposit* and *ProcessCheck* from Section 4.7:

```
unit TransProcessing:
```
> (∗ Unit contains procedures *ProcessDeposit* and *ProcessDebit* to use in financial and accounting programs. ∗)

interface

procedure *ProcessCredit* (**var** *Balance, TotalCredits* : *real*;
                                    var *NumberOfCredits* : *integer*);

> (∗ Procedure to process a credit. Returns updated values of *Balance, TotalCredits*, and *NumberOfCredits*. ∗)

procedure *ProcessDebit* (**var** *Balance, TotalDebits,*
                                    TotalServiceCharges : *real*;
                                var *NumberOfDebits* : *integer*);

> (∗ Procedure to process a debit. Returns updated values of *Balance, TotalDebits, TotalServiceCharges,* and *NumberOfDebits*. ∗)

implementation

procedure *ProcessCredit* (**var** *Balance, TotalCredits* : *real*;
                                    var *NumberOfCredits* : *integer*);

> **var**
>   *Credit* : *real*;   (∗ amount of credit ∗)
>
> **begin** (∗ *ProcessCredit* ∗)
>   *write* ('Enter credit: $');
>   *readln* (*Credit*);
>   *Balance* := *Balance* + *Credit*;
>   *TotalCredits* := *TotalCredits* + *Credit*;
>   *NumberOfCredits* := *NumberOfCredits* + 1
> **end** (∗ *ProcessCredit* ∗);

```
procedure ProcessDebit (var Balance, TotalDebits,
                            TotalServiceCharges : real;
                        var NumberOfDebits : integer);

  const
    ServiceCharge = 0.20;
  var
    Debit : real;        (* amount of debit *)

  begin (* ProcessDebit *)
    write ('Enter debit: $');
    readln (Debit);
    Balance := Balance − Debit;
    TotalDebits := TotalDebits + Debit;
    TotalServiceCharges := TotalServiceCharges + ServiceCharge;
    NumberOfDebits := NumberOfDebits + 1
  end (* ProcessDebit *)

end (* TransProcessing *).
```

Once a unit has been compiled, a program (or another unit) can use items from it simply by specifying the unit's name in a **uses** clause. Thus, if the **uses** clause

uses *TransProcessing*;

were inserted after the program heading in the program of Figure 4.13, the procedures *ProcessDeposit* and *ProcessCheck* could be removed and the procedures *ProcessDebit* and *ProcessCredit* called in the main program to carry out the necessary processing.

Chapter 7

- *Opening a file.* Before a permanent file can be opened with the procedures *reset* or *rewrite*, a name must be assigned to it with the procedure *assign*. This procedure is called with a statement of the form

  assign (file-variable, file-name)

  where *file-name* is the actual name of the data file stored in secondary memory to be associated with *file-variable*.
- *Closing a file.* When output to a file is completed, the file should be closed by calling the procedure *close* with a statement of the form

  close (file-variable)

  Failure to do so may cause some values to be left in the output buffer and not transferred to the file.

Chapter 8

- *Type conversion.* Any ordinal type identifier *OrdType* may be used as a function to convert a value of any other ordinal type to the value of type *OrdType* having the same ordinal number. For example, for the declarations

type
    DaysOfWeek = (*Sunday, Monday, Tuesday, Wednesday,*
                  Thursday, Friday, Saturday);
    FaceCard = (*Jack, Queen, King*);
    CardRange = 1..13;

integer (*Queen*) = *CardRange* (*Queen*) = 1, *DaysOfWeek*(2) = *Tuesday*, and *FaceCard* (*Sunday*) = *Jack*.

- *Range-checking.* The range-checking compiler option must be enabled (or equivalently, the compiler directive {$R +} included in the program) for range checking to be performed.
- Inc *and* Dec. The procedures *Inc* and *Dec* may be used with any ordinal types (see the Turbo Pascal notes for Chapter 3).

Chapter 9

In Turbo Pascal, there are only a few variations from and extensions to the array-processing features of standard Pascal:

- *Range-checking.* The range-checking compiler option must be enabled (or equivalently, the compiler directive {$R +} included in the program) for range checking to be performed.
- *Array constants.* An array variable may be initialized as a typed constant by using a declaration of the form

const
    array-name : array-type = (*list-of-array-elements*);

For example, the declarations

type
    DigitType = 0..9;
    NumeralType = '0'..'9';
    NumeralArray = **array**[*DigitType*] **of** *NumeralType*;
const
    Numeral : NumeralArray = ('0', '1', '2', '3', '4',
                  '5', '6', '7', '8', '9');

initialize the array *Numeral* with *Numeral*[0] = '0', *Numeral*[1] = '1', ..., *Numeral*[9] = '9'. An alternative form of constant section could also have been used:

const
    Numeral : NumeralArray = '0123456789';

Similar declarations can be used to initialize multidimensional arrays. In this case, nested parentheses enclose the array elements in each dimension with the innermost constants corresponding to the rightmost dimensions. For example, to initialize a two-dimensional array A so that

$$A = \begin{bmatrix} 1 & 2 & 3 \\ 2 & 4 & 6 \\ 3 & 6 & 9 \end{bmatrix}$$

we could use

> **const**
>   *RowLimit* = 3;
>   *ColumnLimit* = 3;
>
> **type**
>   *Matrix* = **array** [1..*RowLimit*, 1..*ColumnLimit*] **of** *integer*;
>
> **const**
>   *Mat* : *Matrix* = ((1, 2, 3), (2, 4, 6), (3, 6, 9));

- *Packed Arrays.* Although the reserved word **packed** is allowed, it has no effect, since packing of arrays is done automatically whenever possible. Consequently, the procedures *pack* and *unpack* are not provided in Turbo Pascal.

Chapter 10

As noted in the text, many versions of Pascal include a predefined string type and a number of predefined string functions and procedures. In particular, this is true of Turbo Pascal, which also has the following variations and extensions.

- *String type.* String declarations using the predefined type *string* have the form *string[n]*, where *n* is an integer constant in the range 1 through 255 indicating the maximum length of strings of this type. This maximum length must always be specified; no default value is provided. Strings are implemented as character arrays having index type 0..*n*. The individual characters are stored in positions 1 through *n*, and position 0 stores *chr(length)*, where *length* is the current length of the string. Thus, if *Str* is a string variable, *length(Str)* is equivalent to *ord(Str[0])*.
- *Strings and characters.* Characters and strings of length 1 are compatible, and character arrays may be viewed as strings of constant length. When a character array appears in a string expression, it is converted to a string with length equal to the (fixed) size of the array. As in standard Pascal, a string constant may be assigned to a character array, provided they have the same length, but string variables and computed values of string expressions may not be.
- *String functions.* In addition to the string functions *concat, copy, length*, and *pos* and the string procedures *delete* and *insert* described in the Variations and Extensions section of Chapter 10, Turbo Pascal provides the following:
  - + *operator.* Concatenation may also be accomplished by using the + operator. For example, 'John' + ' Henry' + 'Doe' yields the string 'John Henry Doe'.

- *val procedure*. The procedure call *val(numeral, number, error)* converts the value of the string expression *numeral* representing an integer or real numeral into the corresponding numeric value *number*. For example, val('123', *Number, Error*) assigns the integer value 123 to *Number*. *Error* is an integer variable for which a value of 0 is returned if there is no conversion error; if an error occurs, *number* is undefined and the value of *error* is the position of the first erroneous character in *numeral*.
- *str procedure*. The procedure call *str(number, numeral)* converts the integer or real value *number* into the string of characters representing the corresponding *numeral*. For example, *str*(123, *Numeral*) assigns the string '123' to string variable *Numeral*.

Chapter 11

See the Turbo Pascal notes for Chapter 9.

Chapter 12

- *Record constants*. A record variable may be initialized as a typed constant by using a declaration of the form

  const
      record-name : *record-type* = *(list-of-field-constants)*;

  where each field constant has the form *field-name* : *field-value*. For example, the declarations

  type
    Point = **record**
                X, Y : *real*
          end;
  const
      Origin : *Point* = (*X* : 0.0, *Y* : 0.0);

  initializes the record variable *Origin* with both *Origin.X* and *Origin.Y* equal to 0.0.

Chapter 13

- *Restrictions on sets*. The maximum number of elements in a set is 256. The ordinal values of the base type must be in the range 0..255.
- *Set constants*. A set variable may be initialized as a typed constant by using a declaration of the form

  const
      set-name : *set-type* = *set constant*;

for example,

type
    LetterSet = **set of** 'a'..'z';

const
    Vowels : *LetterSet* = ['a', 'e', 'i', 'o', 'u'];

Chapter 14

- *Opening/closing files.* As described in the Turbo Pascal notes for Chapter 7, a file must be assigned a name with the procedure *assign* before it is opened with *reset* or *rewrite*, and a file should be closed with the procedure *close* when output to it has been completed.
- *get* and *put*. The standard predefined procedures *get* and *put* are not provided. Instead, all file i/o is done using *read* and *write*. Consequently, file buffer variables are not used in Turbo Pascal.
- *Direct access files.* Direct access files are opened in the usual manner using the *assign*, *reset*, and *rewrite* procedures. The procedure *seek* is used to position the file pointer as described in the Variations and Extensions section of Chapter 14.
- *Additional procedures and functions.* There are a number of other predefined procedures for processing files. These include:
  - ***erase.*** *erase* (*file-variable*) erases the specified file. The file should be closed before it is erased.
  - ***flush.*** *flush* (*file-variable*) empties the buffer associated with the specified file.
  - ***rename.*** *rename* (*file-variable, str*) renames the specified file with the string *str*.

  Two additional predefined functions, ***filepos*** and ***filesize***, are also provided:
  - *filepos*(*file-variable*) is the current position of the file pointer in the specified file.
  - *filesize*(*file-variable*) is the number of components in the specified file. Since components are numbered beginning with zero, the value of this function is one more than the number of the last component in the file.

Chapters 15 and 16

Pointer variables can be processed as in standard Pascal except that the alternative forms of reference to procedures *new* and *dispose* for variant records as described in Appendix F are not allowed.

Miscellany

- *Procedure page.* This procedure is not provided in Turbo Pascal.
- *Procedures new and dispose.* The alternative forms of reference to procedures *new* and *dispose* for variant records described in Appendix F are not allowed.

Macintosh Pascal

Macintosh Pascal is that version of Pascal distributed by Apple Computer, Inc., for use with its Macintosh personal computers. It conforms very closely to standard Pascal with the following variations and extensions.

Chapter 3

- *Additional data types.* The predefined types *longint* (long integer), *double extended*, and *computational* (fixed point decimal) are provided. The range of *integer* values is $-2^{15} = 32768$ through $2^{15} - 1 = 32767$; the range of values of type *longint* is $-2^{31} = -2147483648$ through $2^{31} - 1 = 2147483647$, and these may be used wherever integers are used, provided they fall in the smaller range. In integer expressions that involve both types, all operands are converted to *longint* before any integer arithmetic is performed, and the result is always of type *longint*. The range of positive *real* values is $1.5E-45$ through $3.4E+38$ with 7–8 significant decimal digits. The range of positive values of type *double* is $5.0E-324$ through $1.7E+308$ with 15–16 significant decimal digits. The range of positive values of type *extended* is $1.9E-4951$ through $1.1E+4932$ with 19–20 significant decimal digits. In mixed mode expressions, all *integer* and *real* operands are converted to *extended* before any real arithmetic is performed and the result is always *extended*. An extended value may be used wherever *real, double*, or *computational* values are used, provided it falls within the range of permissible values.
- *Alternative representations of numbers.* Integers may be expressed in hexadecimal notation consisting of a dollar sign ($) followed by up to four hexadecimal digits for type *integer*, eight for type *longint*.
- *Predefined constants. Maxint* has the value 32767. *MaxLongInt* is a predefined *longint* constant with the value 2147483647.
- *Reserved words.* The following are additional reserved words in Macintosh Pascal: **otherwise, string,** and **uses.**
- *Identifiers.* An identifier consists of a letter followed by up to 255 additional letters, digits, or underscores (_), all of which are significant.
- *Program heading.* Only *input* and *output* may appear in the file list of the program heading.

Chapter 4

The control structures described in this chapter are the same as in standard Pascal.

Chapter 5

- *case statement.* A **case** statement may have an **otherwise** clause; for example,

case *Class* **of**
      1 : *writeln* ('Freshman');
      2,3,4 : *writeln* ('Upperclassman')
otherwise
          writeln ('Special')
end (* **case** *)

If the value of the selector is not in any of the label lists, the statement in the **otherwise** clause is executed.

Chapter 6

In addition to the standard predefined Pascal procedures and functions, Macintosh Pascal provides a large number of others. Some of the more useful functions are:

- *Random.* This function generates random integers in the range -32768 through 32767. (Another random number generator is available in the SANE library.)
- *BitNot(Long1)*, *BitAnd(Long1, Long2)*, *BitOr(Long1, Long2)*, *BitXor (Long1, Long2)*. These functions perform bitwise **not, and, or,** and exclusive-or operations on the *longint* values *Long1* and *Long2*; the result is of type *longint*. For example, $BitAnd(14, 23) = 6$, $BitOr(14, 23) = 31$, $BitXor(14, 23) = 25$ (see notes on Chapter 4 for Turbo Pascal).
- *BitShift(Long, Number).* This function shifts the bits in the binary representation of the *longint* value *Long* the specified number of bits to the left or right according to whether *Number* is positive or negative; the result is of type *longint*. For example, $BitShift(4, 6) = 256$ and $BitShift(256,6) = 4$.

The string functions and procedures described in the Variations and Extensions section at the end of Chapter 10 are provided in Macintosh Pascal. Two additional functions are *omit* and *include*; these are described in the Macintosh Pascal notes for Chapter 10. A large number of other predefined functions and procedures are provided for memory management, event management, screen management, sound generation, graphics, and advanced numerical applications. Some of these are in the special libraries *QuickDraw1*, *QuickDraw2*, and *SANE*, and attaching a clause of the form **uses** *library-name* to the program heading makes them accessible in a program.

Chapter 7

- *Program heading.* Only *input* and *output* may appear in the file list of the program heading.
- *reset* and *rewrite*. These procedures for opening files may be referenced in the standard manner with a single parameter or with the alternative forms

    reset (*file-variable, file-name*)
    rewrite (*file-variable, file-name*)

where *file-name* is an expression with a string value. These extended forms with two parameters associate the file variable used in the program with the name of an actual data file stored in secondary memory and are needed for permanent files. The standard one-parameter forms are used for temporary (''anonymous'') files.

- *Closing a file.* When input from or output to a permanent file is completed, the file should be closed by calling the procedure *close* in a statement of the form

     close (file-variable)

  Failure to do so many result in loss of data in the file, inability to access it, or some other misfortune.

Chapter 8

- *Input of enumerated types.* Values of an enumerated type can be read from text files. The longest string of characters that form an identifier of that type (ignoring the case of the letters) is read and the corresponding identifier assigned.
- *Output of enumerated types.* Values of an enumerated type can be written to text files. If a format descriptor of the form :*w* is used to specify the field width, the field will be extended if necessary.
- *ord* function. The *ord* function returns a value of type *longint*.

Chapter 9

Array processing is the same as in standard Pascal.

Chapter 10

As noted in the text, many versions of Pascal include a predefined string type and a number of predefined string functions and procedures. In particular, this is true of Macintosh Pascal.

- *String type.* String declarations have the form

     string or *string[#]*

  where # is an integer constant in the range 1 through 255 indicating the maximum length of strings of this type; in the first form, the default maximum length 255 is used.
- *Strings and characters.* Characters and strings of length 1 are assignment-compatible. Also, a packed array of type *char* with index type 1..# may be assigned to a variable of type *string* provided its length does not exceed the maximum length specified for that string variable. Conversely, a string value may be assigned to such a packed character array, provided they have the same length.
- *String functions.* In addition to the string functions *concat, copy, length,*

and *pos* and the string procedures *delete* and *insert*, Macintosh Pascal provides the following string functions:

- *Omit(str, index, size).* This function returns the string formed by deleting a substring of the specified *size*, starting at position *index*, from the string *str*. Unlike procedure *delete, omit* leaves *str* unchanged.
- *Include(str-1, str-2, index).* This function returns the string formed by inserting the string *str-1* into the string *str-2* at position *index*. Unlike procedure *insert, include* leaves *str-2* unchanged.

Chapters 11, 12, and 13

Array, record and set processing are the same as in standard Pascal.

Chapter 14

- *Program heading.* Permanent files are not listed.
- *Opening/Closing files.* As described earlier, alternative forms of reference to procedures *reset* and *rewrite* are necessary to associate names with permanent files. Also, permanent files should be closed with the procedure *close* when input from or output to them has been completed.
- *Direct access files.* Direct access files are opened using the procedure *open*:

    open (*file-variable, file-name*)

  The procedure *seek* is used to position the file pointer as described in the Variations and Extensions section of Chapter 14.
- The *filepos* function. *filepos(file-variable)* is the component number of the position of the file pointer in the specified file.

Chapters 15 and 16

Pointer variables can be processed as in standard Pascal.

UCSD Pascal

UCSD Pascal was developed at the University of California at San Diego. Its variations and extensions of standard Pascal have been incorporated into many of the popular dialects of Pascal.

Chapter 3

- *Maxint.* The value of *maxint* is usually 32767.
- *Identifiers.* Identifiers consist of a letter followed by any number of letters and digits, but only the first eight characters are significant.

- *Arithmetic Functions.* Two additional predefined arithmetic functions are:
  - **log:** *log* (*x*) returns the base-10 logarithm of the integer or real parameter *x*.
  - **pwroften:** *pwroften*(*n*) returns the real value of 10 raised to the integer power *n*.
- *Program heading.* The file list is not required in the program heading; if present, it is ignored.
- *Output of boolean values.* Boolean values cannot be displayed.

Chapter 4

The control structures described in this chapter are the same as in standard Pascal.

Chapter 5

- *case statement.* If the value of the selector is not in any of the label lists, execution "falls through" to the next statement.

Chapter 6

- *Additional functions.* In addition to the standard predefined Pascal functions, UCSD Pascal provides the arithmetic functions *log* and *pwroften* (see the notes on Chapter 3 for UCSD Pascal). It also provides the string functions described in the Variations and Extensions section of Chapter 10.
- *Functions and procedures as parameters.*
- *Units.* Units are provided (see the Turbo Pascal notes for Chapter 6.)

Chapter 7

- *Output of boolean values.* Boolean values cannot be written to text files.
- *Program heading.* The file list is not required in the program heading; if present, it is ignored.
- *Input from the keyboard.* The *read* and *readln* procedures may be called with statements of the form

    read (keyboard, input-list)

or

    readln (keyboard, input-list)

to read values from the keyboard without echoing them on the screen.
- *Interactive files.* The difficulty caused by the look-ahead property of the data pointer described in Programming Pointer 4 in Chapter 7 does not arise because the file *input* is a special file type called *interactive* and is not a text file. When an interactive file is opened with the *reset* proce-

dure, the functions *eoln* and *eof* are intialized to false, and they remain false until the end-of-line character (carriage return) or a special end-of-file character is entered.

● *Procedures reset and rewrite.* Files are opened with the modified references to procedures *reset* and *rewrite*

  reset (*file-variable, file-name*)
  rewrite (*file-variable, file-name*)

(See the Macintosh Pascal notes for Chapter 7.)

● *Closing files.* Any file to which output has been directed must be closed after output is completed with a statement of the form

  close (*file-variable,* **lock**)

if the file is to be retained after execution or

  close (*file-variable,* **purge**)

if it is to be deleted.

Chapter 8

UCSD Pascal is consistent with standard Pascal in the use of ordinal types.

Chapter 9

● *Comparison of arrays.* Arrays of the same type may be compared with the relational operators = and <>.
● ***Pack and unpack.*** Procedures *pack* and *unpack* are not provided; packing of arrays is done automatically when necessary.

Chapter 10

● *String type and string functions.* String declarations have the form

  string or *string*[#]

where # is an integer constant in the range 1 through 255 indicating the maximum length of strings of this type; in the first form, the default maximum length 255 is used. Also, UCSD Pascal provides the string functions *concat, copy, length,* and *pos* together with procedures *delete* and *insert* as described in the Variations and Extensions at the end of Chapter 10.

Chapters 11, 12, and 13

Arrays, records and sets of the same type may be compared with = and <>.

Chapter 14

In addition to the variations and extensions for file processing described in the notes for Chapter 7, UCSD also provides the following:

- *Interactive files.* For a file of type *interactive*, a statement of the form

    read (file-variable, character)

  is equivalent to

    get (file-variable);
    character : = *file-variable*↑;

  which is the reverse of the order for ordinary text files.
- *Direct access files.* UCSD Pascal supports direct access files as described in the Variations and Extensions section of Chapter 14.

Chapters 15 and 16

- **dispose** *procedure.* The *dispose* procedure may not be provided.

Miscellany

- **goto** *statement.* The **goto** statement may not transfer control outside the program unit in which the statement appears.
- **exit** *procedure.* UCSD Pascal provides the predefined procedure *exit* for this purpose to provide a ''clean'' exit from a program unit. It is called with a statement of the form *exit (name)* where *name* is the name of the function or subprogram to be exited.

H

Answers to
Selected Exercises

Section 1.3 (P. 21)

5. (a) 9   (c) 64   (e) 1.5

6. (a) 83   (c) 4096   (e) 7.25

7. (a) 18   (c) 2748   (e) 8.75

8. (a) 1010011   (c) 1000000000000   (e) 111.01

9. (a) 10010   (c) 101010111100   (e) 1000.11

10. (a) 11   (c) 100   (e) 1.4

11. (a) 9   (c) 40   (e) 1.8

12. (a) (i) $(11011)_2$ (ii) $(33)_8$ (iii) $(1B)_{16}$
    (c) (i) $(100111010)_2$ (ii) $(472)_8$ (iii) $(13A)_{16}$

13. (a) (i) $(0.1)_2$ (ii) $(0.4)_8$ (iii) $(0.8)_{16}$
    (d) (i) $(10000.0001)_2$ (ii) $(20.04)_8$ (iii) $(10.1)_{16}$

14. (a) (i) $(0.0\overline{1001})_2$ (ii) $(0.2\overline{3146})_8$ (iii) $(0.4\overline{C})_{16}$
    (c) (i) $(0.00\overline{0011})_2$ (ii) $(0.0\overline{3146})_8$ (iii) $(0.0\overline{C})_{16}$

15. (a) 64   (c) -65 (e) -256

16. (a) 0000000011111111
    (c) 1111111100000001
    (e) 1100011010001001

18. (a) (i) 0110000000011111   (ii) Same as (i)

    (c) (i) 0101000000011100   (ii) Same as (i)

    (e) (i) 0110011001111101   (ii) Same as (i)

19. (a) (i)

0	1	0	1	0	1	0	0	0	1	0	0	1	1	1	1

           T   O

    (ii)

1	1	1	0	0	0	1	1	1	1	0	1	0	1	1	0

           T   O

    (d) (i)

0	1	0	0	0	1	0	1	0	1	0	1	0	1	0	0

        E   T

0	1	0	0	0	1	0	0	0	0	1	0	1	1	1	0

        C   .

    (ii)

1	1	0	0	0	1	0	1	1	1	1	0	0	0	1	1

        E   T

1	1	0	0	0	0	1	1	0	1	0	0	1	0	1	1

        C   .

Section 2.5 (P. 43)

2. Given information: Two temperature scales. Celsius and Fahrenheit, with 0° Celsius corresponding to 32° Fahrenheit, 100° Celsius corresponding to 212° Fahrenheit, and that a linear relationship of the form $F = aC + b$ holds in general. Also given some temperature C on the Celsius scale.

To find: The corresponding number F of degrees on the Fahrenheit scale.

We first must find the specific linear relationship between the two scales. In general, $C°$ Celsius corresponds to $F°$ Fahrenheit, where $F = aC + b$ for some constants a and b. Because 0° Celsius corresponds to 32° Fahrenheit, we must have

$$32 = a \cdot 0 + b$$

so that $b = 32$. This means, then, that

$$F = aC + 32$$

Because 100° Celsius corresponds to 212° Fahrenheit, we must have

$$212 = a \cdot 100 + 32$$

which gives $a = 9/5$, so that our equation becomes

$$F = \frac{9}{5} C + 32$$

The algorithm for solving the problem is now straightforward;

(* This algorithm converts a temperature of *DegreesC* on the Celsius scale
   to the corresponding *DegreeF* on the Fahrenheit scale. *)
1. Enter *DegreesC*.
2. Calculate
     DegreesF = (9 * *DegreesC*)/5 + 32.
3. Display *DegreesF*.

7. Given information: A list of scores in the range 50 through 100 and a
   method for assigning letter grades: A if score $\geq$ 90, B if 75 $\leq$ score
   < 90, and C if 50 $\leq$ score < 75.

   To find: The corresponding letter grades for the scores in the list.

   An algorithm for solving this problem is the following:

   (* Algorithm to assign letter grades to numeric scores. A negative score
      is used to signal the end of data. *)
   1. Initialize *ALine*, *BLine*, and *CLine* to 90, 75, and 50, respectively.
   2. Enter first value for *Score*.
   3. While *Score* $\geq$ 0, do the following:
      a. If *Score* $\geq$ *ALine*, display 'A'; else if *Score* $\geq$ *BLine*, display
         'B'; else if *Score* $\geq$ *CLine*, display 'C'; else display 'Erroneous
         score'.
      b. Enter next value for *Score*.

14. **program** *CelsiusToFahrenheit* (*input, output*);

    (* Program to convert a temperature on the Celsius scale to the
       corresponding temperature on the Fahrenheit scale. *)

    var
        DegreesC,   (* degrees Celsius *)
        DegreesF : *real*;   (* degrees Fahrenheit *)

    begin
        write ('Enter temperature in degrees Celsius: ');
        readln (*DegreesC*);
        DegreesF := (9 * *DegreesC*) / 5 + 32;
        writeln ('Corresponding temperature in degrees Fahrenheit is ',
               DegreesF:8:2)
    end.

Section 3.2 (P. 53)

2. (a) 12 is an integer constant.

   (b) 12. is not a valid constant (real constants may not end in a period).

   (c) 12.0 is a real constant.

3. (a) 'X' is legal.

   (c) IS' is not legal (missing first quote)

   (e) 'DO''ESNT' is legal.

4. (c) **var**
   Mileage : real;
   Cost, Distance : integer;

5. (c) **const**
   Year = 1776;
   Female = 'F';
   Blank = ' ';

Section 3.3 (P. 58)

1. (a) 1

   (d) Not a valid expression. 9 / 2 is a real value, and **div** requires integer operands.

   (g) 2

   (j) 2

   (m) 0

   (p) 18.0

   (s) 3.25

   (v) 4.0

2. (a) 8.0   (c) $2.\overline{6}$ (e) 5.1   (g) 6.25

3. (a) $10 + 5 * B - 4 * A * C$

   (c) $sqrt(a + 3 * sqr(b))$

Section 3.4 (P. 63)

1. (a) Valid

   (d) Valid

   (g) Not valid; variable must be to the left of an assignment operator.

   (j) Valid

   (m) Not valid; string constant may not be assigned to a boolean variable.

2. (a) 15.0

   (d) 6

   (g) Not valid; an integer value may not be assigned to a character variable.

(**j**) Not valid; a real value may not be assigned to a character variable.

(**m**) Not valid; a character value may not be assigned to a real variable.

(**p**) 2

3. (**a**) *Number* := *Number* + 77

   (**d**) *Number* := *Number* + *Number* **mod** 10

4. (**a**) *Distance* := *Rate* * *Time*

   (**d**) *Area* := (*b* * *h*) / 2

5. (**a**) For $a = 2$, $b = 4$, $c = 8$, $a * (b$ **div** $c) = 0$, $a * b$ **div** $c = 1$.

Section 3.5 (P. 76)

1. (**d**) $\underline{\;\;436\;\;872}$ (**e**) $\underline{\;\;-567.4\;\;436\;\;\;\;\;\;}$.

        $\underline{\;\;\;0.00040}$ $\underline{Tolerance:\;\;0.00040}$

2. (**a**) $\underline{\;\;New\;balance\;=\;2559.50}$

        $\underline{\;\;\;\;C\;\;\;\;\;8.02\;\;\;\;\;\;\;\;\;\;}$

3. (**a**) *writeln* (*R1*:9:4, *C*:4, *N1*:5);
      writeln (*N2*:5, 'PDQ', *R2*:8:5)

4. (**a**) $A \leftarrow 1$, $B \leftarrow 2$, $C \leftarrow 3$, $X \leftarrow 4.0$, $Y \leftarrow 5.5$, $Z \leftarrow 6.6$

   (**e**) Same as (a).

Section 3.8 (P. 85)

7. **program** *RightTriangle* (*input, output*);

   (* Program to read the lengths of two legs of a right triangle and calculate the area of the triangle and the length of the hypotenuse. *)

var
   Leg1, Leg2,
   Area,
   Hypotenuse : *real*;

begin
   write ('Enter the lengths of the two legs of right triangle: ');
   readln (*Leg1, Leg2*);
   Area := (*Leg1* * *Leg2*)/2;
   Hypotenuse := *sqrt*(*sqr*(*Leg1*) + *sqr*(*Leg2*));
   writeln ('Area = ', *Area*:4:2);
   writeln ('Hypotenuse = ', *Hypotenuse*:4:2)
end.

Section 4.2 (P. 103)

1. (a)

a	b	a or not b
true	true	true
true	false	true
false	true	false
false	false	true

(d)

a	true	(1 + 2 = 4)	a and true or (1 + 2 = 4)
true	true	false	true
false	true	false	false

2. (a) $x > 3$

(d) $(Alpha > 0)$ **and** $(Beta > 0)$

(g) $(a < 6)$ **or** $(a > 10)$

3. (a) a **and** b **and not** c

5. (a) (i) $Sum1 := (A$ **or** $B)$ **and not** $(A$ **and** $B)$
$Carry1 := A$ **and** B

(ii) $Sum := (Sum1$ **or** $CIn)$ **and not** $(Sum1$ **and** $CIn)$
$Carry := Carry1$ **or** $(Sum1$ **and** $CIn)$

Section 4.3 (P. 116)

1. (b) **if** $Code = 1$ **then**
    begin
        $readln (X, Y)$;
        $Sum := X + Y$;
        $writeln$ ('X = ', X, 'Y = ', Y, 'Sum = ', Sum)
    end (∗ **if** ∗)

(e) **if** $(Distance >= 0)$ **and** $(Distance <= 100)$ **then**
    $Cost := 5.00$
    else if $Distance <= 500$ **then**
    $Cost := 8.00$
    else if $Distance < 1000$ **then**
    $Cost := 10.00$
    else
    $Cost := 12.00$

Section 4.5 (P. 129)

1. **(a)** 4
   5
   6

2. **(a)** **while** $x > 0$ **do**
   begin
   writeln ('x = ', x);
   $x := x - 0.5$
   end (* **while** *)

   (c) *Number* := 1;
   while *Number* $<= 100$ **do**
   begin
   writeln (*sqr(Number)*);
   Number := *Number* + 1
   end (* **while** *)

Section 4.7 (P. 150)

1. **(a)** Can be used.

   (d) Cannot be used; a constant ('M') cannot be passed to a variable parameter.

4. **procedure** *Switch* (**var** *VarA, VarB* : *integer*);

   (* Procedure to interchange the values of *VarA* and *VarB*. *)

   var
   TempVar : *integer*;

   begin (* *Switch* *)
   TempVar := *VarA*;
   VarA := *VarB*;
   VarB := *TempVar*
   end (* *Switch* *);

Section 5.1 (P. 166)

1. **(a)** **case** *TransCode* **of**
   'D' : *Balance* := *Balance* + *Amount*;
   'W' : *Balance* := *Balance* − *Amount*;
   'P' : *writeln* (*Balance*)
   end (* **case** *)

Section 5.4 (P. 183)

1. (a)
```
-2 squared = 4
-1 squared = 1
 0 squared = 0
 1 squared = 1
 2 squared = 4
 3 squared = 9
```

(d)
```
111
121
122
131
132
133
222
232
233
333
```

Section 6.3 (P. 209)

1. (a) Can be used.

(d) Cannot be used; illegal function reference. (f is a function, not a procedure.)

(g) Can be used.

(j) Cannot be used; invalid boolean expression since there is no value associated with a procedure.

(m) Can be used.

4. function *IsADigit*(*Character* : *char*) : *boolean*;

    (∗ Function to determine if *Character* is a digit. ∗)

    begin (∗ *IsADigit* ∗)
      IsADigit := (*Character* >= '0') **and** (*Character* <= '9')
    end (∗ *IsADigit* ∗);

8. function *NumberOfBacteria* (*N, k, t* : *real*) : *real*;

    (∗ Function to calculate the number of bacteria present at time *t* for initial population *N* and rate constant *k* ∗)

    begin (∗ *NumberOfBacteria* ∗)
      NumberOfBacteria := *N* ∗ *exp*(−*k* ∗ *t*)
    end (∗ *NumberOfBacteria* ∗);

Section 6.4 (P. 222)

1. (a) true   **(d)** true   **(g)** true   **(j)** false

2. _____6_____7_____
_____14_____24_____

Section 6.6 (P. 249)

3. (a) function *Fib*(*n* : *integer*) : *integer*;
(∗ Recursive function to calculate the *n*th Fibonacci number ∗)

begin (∗ *Fib* ∗)
  if $n <= 2$ **then**   (∗ anchor ∗)
    Fib := 1
  else
    Fib := *Fib*(*n* − 1) + *Fib*(*n* − 2)   (∗ inductive step ∗)
end (∗ *Fib* ∗);

Section 7.1 (P. 266)

1. (a) The values assigned to *Num1*, *Num2*, *Num3*, and *Num4* will be 1, − 2, 3, and 4, respectively.

(d) The values assigned to *Num1*, *Num2*, *Num3*, and *Num4* will be 1, −2, 4, and −5, respectively.

2. (a) *N1* ← 123   **(d)** *C1* ← X
  R1 ← 45.6   *N1* ← 78
  C1 ← X   *C2* ← ♭ (blank)
  N2 ← 78   *R1* ← − 909.8
  R2 ← − 909.8   *R2* ← 7.0
  C2 ← −   *N2* ← −65
  N3 ← 65   *C3* ← $
  C3 ← $ *R3* ← 432.10

(g) 123 is read and assigned to *N1*; 45.6 is read and assigned to *R1*; the end-of-line mark is read, and a blank is assigned to *C1*; then an error occurs because X is nonnumeric and thus cannot be read for *N2*.

3. (a) *N1* ← 54
  N2 ← 32
  C1 ← E
  C2 ← 1
  R1 ← −6.78
  C3 ← $
  N3 ← 90

(d) Same as (a).

(g) $R1 \leftarrow 54.0$
$R2 \leftarrow 32E1$
$C1 \leftarrow -$
$N1 \leftarrow 6$
$C2 \leftarrow .$
$N2 \leftarrow 78$
$C3 \leftarrow \$$
$N3 \leftarrow 90$

5	4		3	2	E	1	●	-	6	.	7	8	\$	9	0	●	●		1	●

Section 7.2 (P. 281)

1. **(a)** I think that I shall never see
A poem lovely as a tree.

−JOYCE KILMER (1914)

Section 8.3 (P. 304)

1. **(a)** **type**
    MonthAbbrev = (*Jan, Feb, Mar, Apr, May, Jun, Jul, Aug,*
                Sep, Oct, Nov, Dec);
    MonthNumber = 1..12;

3. **(a)** *true*   **(d)** *Mar*   **(g)** *Mar*   **(j)** 8

Section 9.3 (P. 340)

1. **(a)** *Number*[1] ← 0   **(d)** *Number*[1] ← 1
    Number[2] ← 1   *Number*[2] ← 2
    Number[3] ← 1   *Number*[3] ← 4
    Number[4] ← 2   *Number*[4] ← 8
    Number[5] ← 2   *Number*[5] ← 16
    Number[6] ← 3   *Number*[6] ← 32
    Number[7] ← 3   *Number*[7] ← 64
    Number[8] ← 4   *Number*[8] ← 128
    Number[9] ← 4   *Number*[9] ← 256
    Number[10] ← 5   *Number*[10] no value assigned

(g) *Price*[*red*] ← 19.95
    Price[*yellow*] ← 12.75
    Price[*blue*] ← 19.95
    Price[*green*] ← 14.50
    Price[*white*] no value assigned
    Price[*black*] ← 14.50

2. **(a)** Declarations:

> **type**
> *SmallNumberArray* = **array**[0..5] **of** 0..5;
>
> **var**
> *Number* : *SmallNumberArray*;
> *i* : *integer*;

Statement:

> **for** *i* := 0 **to** 5 **do**
> *Number*[*i*] := *i*;

(d) Declarations:

> **type**
> *BooleanArray* = **array**[1..20] **of** *boolean*;
>
> **var**
> *TFQuestion* : *BooleanArray*;
> *Num* : *integer*;

Statement:

> **for** *Num* := 1 **to** 20 **do**
> *TFQuestion*[*Num*] := **not** *odd*(*Num*);

3. **(b)**

A[*i*] is stored in two consecutive words beginning at $b + 2(i - 1)$

4. **function** *Max* (**var** *Number* : *NumberArray*; *NumElements* : *integer*) :
   integer;

> (∗ Returns the largest element in the integer array *Number* which has
> *NumElements* elements ∗)

> **var**
> *i*,   (∗ index ∗)
> *Largest* : *integer*;   (∗ Largest element found so far ∗)

```
begin (* Max *)
  if NumElements = 0 then
    writeln ('Empty array')
  else
    begin
      Largest := Number[1];
      for i := 2 to NumElements do
        if Number[i] > Largest then
          Largest := Number[i];
      Max := Largest
    end (* else *)
end (* Max *);
```

Section 10.3 (P. 369)

1. **(a)** *TextLine*[1] ← A   **(d)** *TextLine*[1] ← I
        TextLine[2] ← B   *TextLine*[2] ← H
        TextLine[3] ← C   *TextLine*[3] ← ♭
        TextLine[4] ← D   *TextLine*[4] ← G
        TextLine[5] ← E   *TextLine*[5] ← F
        TextLine[6] ← F   *TextLine*[6] ← E
        TextLine[7] ← G   *TextLine*[7] ← D
        TextLine[8] ← H   *TextLine*[8] ← C
        TextLine[9] ← I   *TextLine*[9] ← B
        TextLine[10] ← $ *TextLine*[10] ← A

   (g) *CharArray*[1] ← A
        CharArray[2] ← B
        CharArray[3] ← C
        CharArray[4] ← D
        CharArray[5] ← E
        CharArray[6] ← F
        CharArray[7] ← G
        CharArray[8] ← ♭
        CharArray[9] ← H
        CharArray[10] ← I

Error occurs when the assignment statement

   TextLine := *CharArray*

is encountered since an unpacked array may not be assigned to a packed array.

   (j) Same as (a).   **(m)** Same as (a).

Section 11.3 (P. 412)

1. **(a)** 5000   **(d)** 4   **(g)** 792

2. (a) $\begin{bmatrix} 2\ 3\ 4 \\ 3\ 4\ 5 \\ 4\ 5\ 6 \end{bmatrix}$ **(d)** $\begin{bmatrix} A\ B\ C\ D\ \flat\ E \\ F\ G\ H\ \flat\ I\ J \end{bmatrix}$

(g) $\begin{bmatrix} E\ ?\ D\ C\ B\ A \\ J\ I\ ?\ H\ G\ F \end{bmatrix}$ (? = undefined)   **(j)** $\begin{bmatrix} 0\ 2\ 2 \\ 0\ 0\ 2 \\ 0\ 0\ 0 \end{bmatrix}$

5.

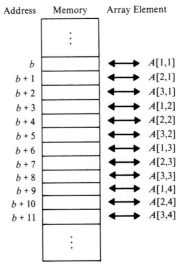

$A[i, j]$ is stored in the word with address $b + 3(j - 1) + (i - 1)$

Section 12.6 (P. 457)

1. (a) type
```
        CardSuit = (Hearts, Diamonds, Spades, Clubs);
        PlayingCard = record
                        Suit : CardSuit;
                        CardValue : 1..13
                      end;
```

(d) type
```
        String7 = packed array[1..7] of char;
        String20 = packed array[1..20] of char;
        Listing = record
                    Name, Address : String20;
                    PhoneNumber : String7
                  end;
```

3. **(a)** **type**
    NameString = **packed array** [1..20] **of** *char*;
    NumberString = **packed array**[1..11] **of** *char*;
    Color = (*blue, brown, green, other*);
    MaritalStatus = (*Married, Single*);
    Date = **record**
        Month : 1..12;
        Day : 1..31;
        Year : 1900..2000
    end;

    PersonalInfo = **record**
        Name : *NameString*;
        BirthDay : *Date*;
        Age : *integer*;
        Sex : *char*;
        SocSecNumber : *NumberString*;
        Height, Weight : *integer*;
        EyeColor : *Color*;
        case *MarStat* : *MaritalStatus* **of**
         Married : (*NumChildren* : *integer*);
         Single : ()
    end;

4. **(a)** Address Memory Record Field

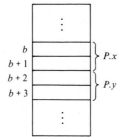

Here *P* is a record of type *Point*.

Section 13.4 (P. 489)

1. **(a)** [3, 5, 11]   **(d)** [1, 2, 4, 12]   **(g)** [6..9]
  (j) [2, 4, 6, 8]   **(m)** [1..12]   **(p)** [ ]
  (s) [3, 5, 11]   **(v)** [ ]

2. **(a)** **type**
   SmallIntegers = **set of** 1..99;

  (c) **type**
   DaysOfWeek = (*Sunday, Monday, Tuesday, Wednesday,*
         Thursday, Friday, Saturday);
   Days = **set of** *DaysOfWeek*;

3. **(a)** Declarations:

> **type**
> $SetOfNumbers$ = **set of** 1..99;
>
> **var**
> $Even, Odd$: $SetOfNumbers$;
> $Number$: $integer$;

Statements:

> $Even$:= [ ];
> **for** $Number$:= 1 **to** 49 **do**
> $Even$:= $Even$ + [2 * $Number$];
> Odd := [1..99] − $Even$;

(f) Declarations:

> **type**
> $LetterSet$ = **set of** $char$;
>
> **var**
> $Vowels, Consonants$: $LetterSet$;

Statements:

> $Vowels$:= ['A', 'E', 'I', 'O', 'U', 'a', 'e', 'i', 'o', 'u'];
> $Consonants$:= ['A'..'Z', 'a'..'z'] − $Vowels$;

(g) Declarations:

> **type**
> $DaysOfWeek$ = ($Sunday, Monday, Tuesday,$
> $Wednesday, Thursday, Friday,$
> $Saturday$);
>
> $SetOfDays$ = **set of** $DaysOfWeek$;
>
> **var**
> $WeekDays$: $SetOfDays$;

Statements:

> $WeekDays$:= [$Monday..Friday$];

6. **(a)** (i) 0101010101

 (b) (i) 100010001000001000001000000

18. (b)

Section 14.3 (P. 516)

1. **(a)** Attempts to read beyond the end of the file when the data pointer is positioned at the last end-of-line mark.

2. **(a)** Fails for all text files whose first character is not a blank.

Section 15.4 (P. 554)

1. **(a)** Values of pointer variables cannot be displayed.

    (d) The procedure *new* is used only to assign a value to a pointer variable.

3. **function** *CountNodes(FirstPtr : ListPointer)* : *integer*;

    (* Function to count the nodes in a linked list with first node pointed to by *FirstPtr*. *)

    var
        TempPtr : ListPointer;
        Count : integer;

    begin (* *CountNodes* *)
        Count := 0;
        TempPtr := *FirstPtr*;
        while *TempPtr* <> **nil do**
            begin
                Count := *Count* + 1;
                TempPtr := *TempPtr*↑.*Next*
            end (* **while** *);
        CountNodes := *Count*
    end (* *CountNodes* *);

Section 16.1 (P. 575)

5. **const**
        MaxIndex = . . . ;
        QueueLimit = . . . ;   (* *MaxIndex* − 1 *)

    type
        DataType = . . . ;   (* type of queue elements *)
        QueueArray = **array**[0..*MaxIndex*] **of** *DataType*;
        QueueType = **record**
                        Front, Rear : 0..*QueueLimit*;
                        Element : *QueueArray*
                    end;

    var
        Queue : *QueueType*;

6. **(c)** **procedure** *AddQ* (**var** *Queue* : *QueueType*; *Item* : *DataType*);

   (∗ Procedure to add *Item* to *Queue* ∗)

   var
       NewRear : 0..*QueueLimit*;

   begin (∗ *AddQ* ∗)
       NewRear := (*Rear* + 1) **mod** *MaxIndex*;
       with *Queue* **do**
         if *Front* = *NewRear* **then**
           writeln ('Queue full—cannot insert')
         else
           begin
             Element[*Rear*] := *Item*;
             Rear := *NewRear*
           end (∗ **else** ∗)
       end (∗ *AddQ* ∗);

Section 16.2 (P. 586)

1. **(a)** $-7.\overline{3}$ **(d)** 12.0   **(g)** 12.0   **(j)** 8.0

2. **(a)** $A\ B\ *\ C\ +\ D\ -$ **(d)** $A\ B\ C\ D\ +\ /\ +$
   (g) $A\ B\ -\ C\ -\ D\ -\ E\ -$

3. **(a)** $(A\ -\ (B\ +\ C))\ *\ D$ **(d)** $((A\ +\ B)\ -\ C)\ /\ (D\ *\ E)$
   (g) $A\ /\ ((B\ /\ C)\ /\ D)$

4. **(a)** **(i)** -15 **(iv)** 15
   (b) **(i)** $A\ B\ C\ \sim\ +\ *$ **(iii)** $A\ \sim\ B\ \sim\ *$

5. **(a)** $A\ B$ **and** C **or**   **(e)** $A\ B\ =\ C\ D\ =$ **or**

6. **(a)** $-\ +\ *\ A\ B\ C\ D$ **(d)** $+\ A\ /\ B\ +\ C\ D$
   (g) $-\ -\ -\ -\ A\ B\ C\ D\ E$

7. **(a)** -24.5 **(d)** -2.0 **(g)** 55.0

8. **(a)** $(A\ +\ B)\ *\ (C\ -\ D)$ **(d)** $A\ -\ (B\ -\ C)\ -\ D$
   (g) $(A\ *\ B\ +\ C)\ /\ (D\ -\ E)$

Section 16.3 (P. 591)

1. **procedure** *AddQ* (**var** *Queue* : *QueueType*; *Item* : *DataType*);

    (∗ Procedure to add *Item* to the linked *Queue* ∗)

    var
      TempPtr : *PointerToQueueNode*;

    begin (∗ *AddQ* ∗)
      new (*TempPtr*);
      TempPtr↑.Data := *Item*;
      TempPtr↑.Next := **nil**;
      if *EmptyQ(Queue)* **then**
        begin
          Queue.FrontPtr := *TempPtr*;
          Queue.RearPtr := *TempPtr*
        end (∗ **if** ∗)
      else
        Queue.RearPtr↑.Next := *TempPtr*
    end (∗ *AddQ* ∗);

Section 16.4 (P. 599)

1.   (a) $O(n^3)$

    (c) $O(n)$

3.   (a) $O(n)$

    (d) $O(n^2)$

Section 16.5 (P. 609)

1.   (a) | 5, 1, 6, 4, 3, 2 | First call to *QuickSort*
                                     (*Low* = 1, *High* = 6)

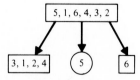

                                       I.1: 1 < 6 so
                                       I.2: Split the list and position 5.
                                       I.3: Call *QuickSort* on left sublist
                                              (*Low* = 1, *High* = 4).

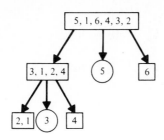

II.1: $1 < 4$ so
II.2: Split sublist and position 3.
II.3: Call *QuickSort* on left sublist
($Low = 1$, $High = 2$).

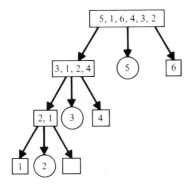

III.1: $1 < 2$ so
III.2: Split sublist and position 2.
III.3: Call *QuickSort* on left sublist
($Low = 1$, $High = 1$).

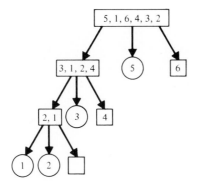

IV.1: $1 \not< 1$ (one-element sublist) so
IV.5: Return to previous level.

III.4: Call *QuickSort* on right sublist
($Low = 4$, $High = 3$).

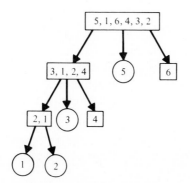

IV.1: $4 \not< 3$ (empty sublist) so
IV.5: Return to previous level.

III.5: Return to previous level.

II.4: Call *QuickSort* on right sublist
($Low = 4$, $High = 4$).

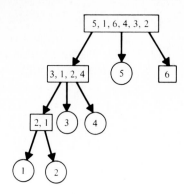

III.1: $4 \not< 4$ (one-element sublist) so
III.5: Return to previous level.

II.5: Return to previous level.

I.4: Call *QuickSort* on right sublist
($Low = 6$, $High = 6$).

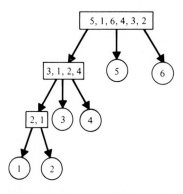

II.1: $6 \not< 6$ (one-element sublist) so
II.5: Return to previous level.

I.5: Return to main program;
sorting is completed.

Section 16.6 (P. 619)

1. (a) F: |1   5 | 3   8 | 7 | 2   6 | 4 |

   F1: |1   5   7 | 4 |
   F2: |3   8 | 2   6 |

   F: |1   3   5   7   8 | 2   4   6 |

   F1: |1   3   5   7   8 |
   F2: |2   4   6 |

   F: |1   2   3   4   5   6   7   8|

Section 16.7 (P. 634)

1. (a) (i)

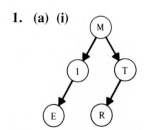

(b) (i) Inorder: E I M R T
Preorder: M I E T R
PostOrder: E I R T M

2. (a) (i) M T R I E

    (b) (i) T R M I E

    (c) (i) R T E I M

3. (a)

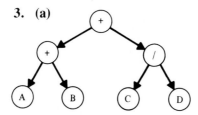

Prefix: + + A B / C D
Postfix: A B + C D / +

6. (a)

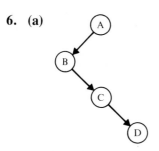

8. **function** *LeafCount*(*RootPtr* : *TreePointer*) : *integer*;

   (∗ Function to count the leaves in a binary tree with root note pointed
   to by *RootPtr*. ∗)

   begin (∗ *LeafCount* ∗)
      if *RootPtr* = **nil then**
        LeafCount := 0
      else if (*RootPtr*↑.*Left* = **nil**) **and**
           (*RootPtr*↑.*Right* = **nil**) **then**
        LeafCount := 1
      else
        LeafCount := *LeafCount*(*RootPtr*↑.*Left*)
            + *LeafCount*(*RootPtr*↑.*Right*)
   end (∗ *LeafCount* ∗);

19. (a) (i) $B[1] \leftarrow$ 'M'
           $B[2] \leftarrow$ 'I'
           $B[3] \leftarrow$ 'T'
           $B[4] \leftarrow$ 'E'
           $B[5] \leftarrow$?
           $B[6] \leftarrow$ 'R'
           $B[7] \leftarrow$?
          (All other array elements are undefined; also, ? = undefined.)

Glossary

abstract data type   See *data structure*

actual parameter   A parameter that appears in a procedure/function reference and is associated with the corresponding formal parameter in the procedure/function heading.

address   A label associated with a memory location. Each word in memory has a unique address that makes it possible to access its contents.

address translation   A computation that must be performed to determine the address of the location in memory where a particular item in a structured data type is stored.

algorithm   A sequence of clearly stated simple steps for solving a problem in a finite amount of time.

ALU   See *arithmetic logic unit*

anchor   A part of a recursive definition in which values of a function or actions of a procedure are specified for one or more values of the parameters.

anonymous variable   A variable that has no name. It is usually created by a call to *new* and is referenced through a pointer variable. (See also *dynamic variable*.)

arithmetic-logic unit (ALU)   That part of the central processing unit that performs basic arithmetic and logical operations.

array   A data structure consisting of a fixed number of data items, all of the same type, organized in a sequence, and accessed directly by specifying their locations in this sequence.

ASCII   American Standard Code for Information Interchange. One of the standard coding schemes for characters.

assembler   System software that translates programs written in assembly language into machine language.

assembly language   A language that is closely related to machine language but that uses instruction mnemonics (names) in place of numeric opcodes and symbolic addresses (variables) in place of numeric addresses.

assignment operator An operator denoted in Pascal by := that assigns a value to a variable or to a function identifier.

assignment statement A Pascal statement that uses an assignment operator to assign a value to a variable or to a function identifier.

auxiliary memory See *secondary memory*.

base address The address of the first memory word in a block of consecutive words used to store the elements of an array or record.

base of a number system In a positional number system, the digits in a numeral are coefficients of powers of the base of that number system. For example, in the *decimal* or *base-10* number system, each digit in a numeral is a coefficient of a power of 10; thus $234 = 2 \times 10^2 + 3 \times 10^1 + 4 \times 10^0$.

base type An ordinal type used in defining subrange and set types. For a subrange type it specifies the larger collection of values containing the subrange. For a set type it specifies the type of elements in the universal set.

batch processing A mode of processing in which a file containing a program, data, and certain command lines is submitted to the system, and execution proceeds without any user interaction.

big Oh notation See *order of magnitude*.

binary digit A digit, 0 or 1, in the binary number system.

binary number system A number system, using only the binary digits 0 and 1, that is commonly used for internal computer representation.

binary search A scheme for searching an ordered list by repeatedly examining the middle item in the (sub)list to determine which half of the (sub)list contains the desired item, and then continuing the search with that sublist.

binary search tree A binary tree in which the data item stored in each node is greater than the data item in its left child but less than the data item in its right child.

binary tree A tree in which each node has at most two children.

bit See *binary digit*.

boolean A predefined Pascal data type in which the only possible values are *true* and *false*.

buffer Portion of main memory used for temporary storage of data values being transferred between main memory and secondary memory. Buffers are used to reduce the effects of differences in operating speeds of various devices.

bug A progam error.

byte A group of bits, usually eight.

call A reference to a procedure or function.

case **statement** A Pascal statement implementing a multialternative selection structure in which the selection is based on the value of a selector variable or expression. Cases specifying the alternative courses of action are labeled with lists of possible values of this selector.

central processing unit (CPU) Controls the operation of the entire computer system, performs arithmetic/logic operations, stores and retrieves instructions and data.

char A predefined Pascal data type in which the values are single characters.

character   Any symbol in the Pascal character set including letters, both upper-case and lower-case, digits, and various special symbols.

character constant   A constant of type *char*. In Pascal, this character must be enclosed within single quotes (apostrophes).

children of a node   Nodes in a tree pointed to by a given node called their *parent*.

coding   Writing a program or subprogram in a high-level language.

collating sequence   A sequence used in a particular computer to establish an ordering of the character set.

comments   Used to provide documentation within a Pascal program and enclosed between the comment delimiters (* and *) or { and }.

compatible types   Two simple data types are said to be compatible if they are the same type, one is a subrange of the other, or both are subranges of the same type.

compile-time error   See *syntax error*.

compiler   System software used to translate source programs written in a high-level language into object programs in machine or assembly language.

component   An element of a data structure such as an array or file.

compound statement   A Pascal statement formed by combining several statements into a block by enclosing them between the reserved words **begin** and **end** and separating them by semicolons.

concatenation   A string operation that appends one string to another.

constant   A quantity that does not change during program execution.

constant section   That section of the declaration part of a Pascal program in which named constants are defined.

control structure   Structures that control the logical flow in an algorithm or program. Structured algorithms and programs use only the control structures: *sequence, repetition,* and *selection*.

control unit   That part of the central processing unit that fetches instructions from memory, decodes them, and directs the system to execute the operations indicated by the instructions.

control variable   A variable used to control repetition in a for loop.

CPU   See central processing unit.

data structure   A collection of related data items together with basic operations defined on this collection. They may be *predefined* data structures such as arrays and records, or they may be *user-defined* structures such as linked lists and trees.

debug   To locate and correct errors (bugs) in a program.

declaration part   That part of a Pascal program in which variables are declared and constants, types, functions, procedures, and labels are defined.

deque   Double-ended queue.

dereferencing operator (↑)   Provides access to the memory location pointed to by a pointer variable.

desk-checking   Tracing the execution of a program segment by hand to locate logical errors. The values of all or certain key variables are recorded in a trace table as the program segment is traced step by step.

digraph   See *directed graph*.

direct access   (also called *random access*) Accessing a given component in a data structure by specifying its position in the structure without examining other components, as in sequential access.

direct access file A file in which each component can be accessed directly.

direct recursion Recursion in which a function or procedure references itself directly.

directed graph A structure consisting of a finite set of vertices (nodes) together with a finite set of directed arcs that connect pairs of vertices.

disk See *magnetic disk*.

divide-and-conquer An algorithm design strategy in which problems are repeatedly divided into simpler subproblems until a solution to each subproblem is straightforward.

documentation Information that explains what a program does, how it works, what variables it uses, any special algorithms it implements, and so on.

dummy definition A definition of a function or procedure that consists of only a heading together with the **forward** directive that indicates that the actual definition of the subprogram appears later.

dynamic data structure A data structure whose size changes during processing.

dynamic variables Variables that are created and disposed of during program execution. Dynamic variables are accessed by means of a pointer rather than by a variable name; they are created by using the procedure *new* and are disposed of with the procedure *dispose*.

EBCDIC Extended Binary Coded Decimal Interchange Code. One of the standard coding schemes for characters.

editor System software used to create and modify files.

empty statement A Pascal statement used to indicate that no action is required.

end-of-data flag An artificial data value used to mark the end of a collection of input data.

end-of-file-mark A special control character used to indicate the end of a file.

end-of-line-mark A special control character used to indicate the end of a line of text.

enumerated type A user-defined ordinal data type. The definition consists of listing the values of this data type, separated by commas, and enclosed within parentheses.

equivalent type identifiers Type identifiers whose definitions can be traced back to a common type identifier.

external file See *permanent file*.

external memory See *secondary memory*.

external sorting A sorting scheme appropriate for sorting large files stored in secondary memory.

field (of a record) An element of a record.

field-designated variable A variable used to access the value stored in a field within a record. It has the form *record-name. field name*.

fielded variable See *field-designated variable*.

FIFO structure See *queue*.

file A collection of data items, usually stored in secondary memory, that are input to or output by a program.

file buffer   A buffer associated with a given file.

file buffer variable   A variable of the form *file-variable*↑ used to access the file buffer.

file window   Synonym for *file buffer variable*.

finite automaton, finite state machine   A model of a computer consisting of a finite set of states in which transitions from one state to another are determined by the next input symbol.

fixed part (of a record).   The (first) part of a record whose fields are fixed, both in number and in type.

floating point number   Synonym for *real number*.

floating point representation   See *scientific representation*.

for loop   A repetition structure in which the body of the loop is executed for each value in some specified range of values.

for **statement**   A Pascal statement that implements a for loop.

formal parameter   A parameter used in a subprogram heading to transfer information to or from the subprogram.

format descriptor   An expression used in an output statement to specify the format in which values are to be displayed.

forward **directive**   See *dummy definition*.

function   A subprogram that (ordinarily) returns a single value via the function name.

function heading   A function definition begins with a function heading of the form: **function** *function-name* (*formal-parameter-list*) : *result-type*;

function parameter   A parameter that is a function.

Fundamental Scope Principle   *The scope of an identifier is the program unit in which it is declared.*

global variable   A variable declared in the main program and therefore accessible in the main program and in all subprograms in which the same identifier is not declared locally.

goto **statement**   A seldom-used statement that transfers control to a statement with a specified label.

hardware   The actual physical components of a computer system such as disk drives, printers, central processing unit, memory, and so on.

heading   See *function heading, procedure heading,* and *program heading*.

hexadecimal number system   A base-16 number system.

hierarchical records   See *nested*.

high-level language   A language such as Pascal that is similar to natural language and that is intended to facilitate program development. Programs written in such languages must be converted into machine language using a compiler (or interpreter) before they can be executed.

identifier   Names given to programs, constants, variables, functions, procedures, and other entities in a program.

if **statement**   A Pascal statement that implements a selection structure in which selection is controlled by a boolean expression.

if-else if **construct**   A compound form of an **if** statement that implements a multialternative selection struction.

implementation of a data structure   Selection of storage structures to store the data items and the design of algorithms to carry out the basic operations.

in parameter   See *value parameter*.

in-out parameter   See *variable parameter*.

index   An expression that indicates the position in an array of a particular component.

indexed variable   A variable of the form *array-name*[*index*] used to access a particular component of an array.

indirect recursion   Recursion in which a subprogram references other subprograms and in which some chain of subprogram references eventually results in a reference to the first subprogram again.

inductive step   Part of a recursive definition of a function or procedure that specifies the value of a function or the action of a procedure for the current value(s) of the parameter(s) in terms of previously defined values or actions.

infinite loop   A loop that does not terminate.

infix notation   Notation for arithmetic expressions in which the symbol for each binary operation is placed between its operands.

inorder traversal   Traversal of a binary tree in which the left subtree of a node is visited, then the node itself, and then the right subtree of that node.

input   Data obtained by a program from an external source during execution.

input **file**   A standard default input file in Pascal. It is a text file and usually refers to an external device such as a terminal.

integer   A predefined Pascal data value in which the values are all of the integers in the range −*maxint* through *maxint* where the value of *maxint* is machine dependent.

interactive processing   A mode of processing in which the user communicates with a program during execution.

internal memory   See *memory unit*.

internal sorting   A sorting scheme appropriate for lists stored in main memory.

interpreter   System software that translates each statement in a source program into one or more machine language instructions. These instructions are executed before the next statement is translated.

key field   A field in a record on which sorting or searching is based.

label section   That section of the declaration part of a program in which statement labels are declared.

leaf node   A tree node that has no children.

lexical analyzer   The part of a compiler that groups characters in a source program into logical units such as identifiers, reserved words, operators, and so on.

LIFO structure   See *stack*.

linear search   A strategy for searching a list by examining the items sequentially, beginning with the first item.

link   A field in a node of a linked structure that points to another node.

linked list   A data structure consisting of nodes linked together by pointers, together with a pointer to the first node in the list. Each node contains two kinds of information: the actual data item being stored and a link (pointer) to the next node in the list.

local variable   A variable whose scope is a subprogram.

logical error   An error in the logical structure of a program (or algorithm).

These errors usually do not prevent the program from executing, but incorrect results are produced.

loop   See *repetition structure*.

machine language   The language used directly by a particular computer for all calculations and processing.

magnetic disk   A secondary mass storage medium that stores information on rotating disks coated with a substance that can be magnetized.

magnetic tape   A secondary mass storage medium that stores information on plastic tape coated with a substance that can be magnetized.

main memory   See *memory unit*.

maxint   A predefined identifier representing a machine-dependent integer constant that is the largest integer value that can be stored in a particular computer's memory.

memory unit   That part of the computer hardware in which the instructions and data of the currently executing program are stored.

mergesort   A sorting scheme based on the operations of creating and merging sorted subfiles.

modular programming   A programming strategy in which major tasks to be performed are identified and individual procedures/functions (called *modules*) for these tasks are designed and tested.

multialternative selection structure   A control structure in which one of several (usually more than two) actions is selected for execution.

multidimensional array   An array with two or more dimensions.

multiply indexed variable   A variable used to access a component of a multidimensional array. It is formed by attaching the appropriate number of indices enclosed within brackets to the array's name.

multiply linked structure   A linked structure in which each node has two or more link fields.

n-dimensional array   An array having n dimensions.

named constant   A constant that has been named in the constant section of a Pascal program.

nested   A term describing the placement of one structure with another, e.g., nested **if** statements and nested records.

nil   A predefined pointer constant. Assigning this value to a pointer variable indicates that it does not point to any memory location.

nil pointer   A pointer to which the value **nil** has been assigned.

node   A component of a linked structure.

object program   A machine language program produced by a compiler.

octal number system   A base-8 number system.

one-dimensional array   Often used as a synonym for *array*.

opcode   A numeric code for a machine language instruction.

operating system   System software that controls the overall operation of the computer system.

order of magnitude   An approximate measure of the computing time of an algorithm. $T(n)$ is said to have order of magnitude $g(n)$, denoted $T(n) = O(g(n))$, if there exists a constant C such that $T(n) \leq g(n)$ for all sufficiently large values of n.

ordinal number   The number of the position of a value of ordinal type in the ordering for that type.

ordinal type   A simple data type in which the values of that type are ordered so that each one except the first has an immediate predecessor and each one except the last has an immediate successor.

output   Information produced by a program.

output **file**   A standard default output file in Pascal. It is a text file and usually refers to an external device such as a terminal or printer.

overflow   A condition that results when a value is generated that is too large to be stored in the computer being used.

packed array   An array in which more than one array component is stored in a single memory word.

parameter   A variable used to pass information between program units.

parent of a node   See *children of a node.*

parser   The part of a compiler that groups tokens together according to the syntax rules of the language.

peripheral devices   Hardware devices such as terminals, printers, disk drives, and tape drives that are not part of the central processing unit.

permanent file   A file usually stored in secondary memory that exists not only during execution of a program but also before and/or after execution.

pointer, pointer variable   A variable whose value is a memory address.

pop   The deletion operation for a stack.

postfix notation   Notation for arithmetic expressions in which the symbol for each binary operation is placed after its operands.

postorder traversal   Traversal of a binary tree in which the left subtree of a node is visited, then the right subtree, and then the node itself.

prefix notation   Notation for arithmetic expressions in which the symbol for each binary operation is placed before its operands.

preorder traversal   Traversal of a binary tree in which a node is visited, then its left subtree, and then its right subtree.

primary memory   See *memory unit.*

priority rules   Rules that specify the order in which the operators in an expression are to be performed.

procedure   A subprogram that performs a particular task. Information is passed between a procedure and other program units by means of parameters.

procedure heading   A procedure definition begins with a procedure heading of the form: **procedure** *procedure-name* (*formal-parameter-list*);

procedure parameter   A parameter that is a procedure.

procedure reference statement   A Pascal statement of the form: *procedure-name* (*actual-argument-list*) that is used to call a procedure.

program heading   Every Pascal program begins with a program heading of the form: **program** *program-name* (*file-list*);

program stub   Incomplete subprograms used temporarily in designing a program in a top-down manner.

pseudocode   A loosely defined language that resembles a programming language and is used to describe algorithms.

pseudorandom numbers   A sequence of numbers that are generated by an algorithm but that appear to be random, i.e., they appear to be uniformly distributed over some range.

push   The insertion operation for a stack.

queue   A list in which items may be added only at one end, called the *back* or *rear,* and removed only at the other end, called the *front* or *head.* A queue is a *First-In-First-Out (FIFO)* structure.

quicksort   A recursive sorting scheme based on correctly positioning one element of a (sub)list so that all list items that precede it are less than this item and all those that follow it are greater than this item. The two sublists that result are then sorted independently in the same way.

random access file   See *direct access file.*

random number generator   A subprogram that generates pseudorandom numbers.

real   A predefined Pascal data type used for values that are real numbers. They may be represented either in decimal form or in scientific notation.

record   A data structure in which a collection of related data items of possibly different types may be stored. The positions in which these data items are stored are called the *fields* of the record.

recursion, recursive   The property of a function or procedure referencing itself.

relational operators   The operators $=$, $<$, $>$, $<>$, $<=$, $>=$, and **in**. They are used to form simple boolean expressions.

repeat-until loop   A posttest loop, i.e., a repetition structure in which the boolean expression that controls repetition is tested after the body of the loop is executed.

***repeat-until* statement**   A Pascal statement that implements a repeat-until loop.

repetition structure   A control structure in which one or more statements are repeatedly executed. Repetition must be controlled so that these statements are executed only a finite number of times.

reserved words   Keywords such as **begin, end,** and **var** that have a special meaning in Pascal and may be used only in the special ways required by the syntax of the language.

Reverse Polish Notation (RPN)   See *postfix notation.*

root node   See *tree.*

roundoff error   The error that results in storing a real number because of the limited number of bits used to store its fractional part.

run-time error   An error such as division by zero that occurs during execution of a program.

same type   Two types are the *same* if they are declared by the same type identifier or by equivalent type identifiers.

scientific representation   Representation of a real number (also called *floating point representation*) that consists of an integer or a real constant in decimal form followed by the letter *E* (or *e*) followed by an integer constant that is intepreted as an exponent on the base 10.

scope (of an identifier)   That part of a program in which an identifier is accessible.

secondary memory   Storage devices such as magnetic disks and magnetic tapes that provide relatively inexpensive long-term storage for large collections of information.

selection structure   A control structure in which one of a number of alternative actions is selected.

semantics   The interpretation or meaning of the statements in a language.

sequential access   A method of access in which an item can be accessed only by examining all those items that precede it.

sequential file   A file in which the components must be accessed sequentially.

sequential structure   A control structure in which the statements comprising the structure are executed in the order in which they appear.

set   A predefined structured data type used to process unordered collections of items that are all of the same type.

simple data type   A data type in which each datum is atomic, i.e., it consists of a single entity that cannot be subdivided.

simulation   Modeling a dynamic process and using this model to study the behavior of the process.

software   Computer programs.

sorting   Arranging a list of items so that they are in either ascending or descending order.

source program   A program written in a high-level language such as Pascal.

stack (push-down stack)   A list in which elements may be inserted (*pushed*) and deleted (*popped*) at only one end, called the *top* of the stack. A stack is a *Last-In-First-Out (LIFO)* structure.

statement part   The part of a Pascal program that contains the statements that actually carry out the steps of an algorithm.

static data structure   A data structure whose size remains fixed during program execution.

static variable   A variable to which memory locations are allocated at compile time. This association does not change during program execution. (See also *dynamic variables*.)

string   A finite sequence of characters.

string constant   In Pascal, a string enclosed within single quotes (apostrophes).

string type   In Pascal, a packed array of type *char* whose index type is a subrange of the form $1..n$ for some integer $n > 1$.

structure diagram   A diagram that displays the structure of an algorithm by displaying the major tasks that must be performed and the relationship between them.

structured algorithm (program)   An algorithm (program) that is designed using only the three basic control structures: sequential, selection, and repetition.

structured data type   A data type in which a datum consists of a collection of items.

subprogram   A function or procedure.

subprogram section   That section of the declaration part of a Pascal program in which functions and procedures are defined.

subrange type   An ordinal type that is defined by specifying the first and last elements in the range of values for a datum of this type.

successive refinement   See *divide-and-conquer*.

syntax   The grammar of a language, i.e., the set of rules for forming words and statements in that language.

syntax diagram   A diagram used to display the syntax of a particular statement or construct in a language.

syntax error   A violation of the syntax of the language that is detected during compilation of the program.

system software   A collection of programs such as editors, compilers, interpreters, debuggers, etc. supplied as part of the computer system.

tag field   A field within a variant record whose value determines which variant is in effect.

tape   See *magnetic tape*.

temporary file   A file that exists only during execution of a program.

text file   A file of characters that is organized into lines.

top-down design   See *divide-and-conquer*.

trace table   See *desk-checking*.

tree   A directed graph with a root node that has no incoming arcs but from which each node in the tree can be reached by exactly one path, i.e., by following a unique sequence of consecutive arcs.

type   A formal specification of the set of values that a variable may have.

type section   That section of the declaration part of a Pascal program in which data types are defined.

value parameter   A formal parameter of a subprogram that is used to pass information to the subprogram but not to return information from it.

variable   An identifier associated with a particular memory location. The value stored in this location is the value of the variable, and this value may be changed during program execution.

variable parameter   A formal parameter of a subprogram that is used both to pass information to and to return information from the subprogram. In Pascal, variable parameters must be indicated as such by preceding them with the reserved word **var**.

variant part   The (last) part of a variant record in which the number and types of fields may vary.

variable section   That section of the declaration part of a program in which variables are declared.

variant record   A record that may contain a variant part in addition to the usual fixed part. The number and types of the fields in the fixed part do not change during program execution, but those in the variant part may change in number and/or type.

walking through the code   See *desk-checking*.

while loop   A pretest loop, i.e., a repetition structure in which the boolean expression that controls repetition is tested before the body of the loop is executed.

***while* statement**   A Pascal statement that implements a while loop.

window   See *file window*.

***with* statement**   A Pascal statement used to attach a record name to identifiers of fields within that record to form fielded variables.

word   A basic storage unit consisting of a machine-dependent number of bits (commonly 16 or 32) whose contents are directly accessible by means of its address.

Index of Examples
and Exercises

Examples

Exercises

Index

Pascal Reference Chart (cont.)

Statements	Example
Assignment (59–63, 82, 322–323, 431, 462, 468, 510, 530, 532)	*Count* := 0; *Wages* := *RoundCents(Hours * Rate)*; *DeptCode* := 'A'; *OverTime* := (*Hours* > 40); *ProductName* := 'Ford-Carburetor'; *Letters* := ['A'..'F', 'P', 'S']; *EmpRec* := *InFile*↑; *EmpRec.Number* := 12345; *TempPtr* := **nil**; *FirstPtr*↑.*Data* := *ProductName*;

Sequential (94–95)
  Compound (95)

```
begin
    Wages := RoundCents(Hours * Rate);
    OverTime := false
end;
```

Selection (105–117, 162–168)
  if (105–117)

```
if Hours <= 40 then
    Wages := RoundCents(Hours * Rate)
else
    begin
        OverTime := true;
        Wages := RoundCents(HoursLimit * Rate +
            OTMult * Rate * (Hours − HoursLimit))
    end (* else *);
```

case (162–168)

```
case DeptCode of
    'o', 'O' : Dept := Office;
    'f', 'F' : Dept := Factory;
    's', 'S' : Dept := Sales
end (* case *);
```